Emerging Markets and E-Commerce in Developing Economies

Kamel Rouibah
Kuwait University, Kuwait

Omar Khalil
Kuwait University, Kuwait

Aboul Ella Hassanien
Cairo University, Egypt

INFORMATION SCIENCE REFERENCE

Hershey · New York

Director of Editorial Content:	Kristin Klinger
Director of Production:	Jennifer Neidig
Managing Editor:	Jamie Snavely
Assistant Managing Editor:	Carole Coulson
Typesetter:	Amanda Appicello
Cover Design:	Lisa Tosheff
Printed at:	Yurchak Printing Inc.

Published in the United States of America by
Information Science Reference (an imprint of IGI Global)
701 E. Chocolate Avenue, Suite 200
Hershey PA 17033
Tel: 717-533-8845
Fax: 717-533-8661
E-mail: cust@igi-global.com
Web site: http://www.igi-global.com

and in the United Kingdom by
Information Science Reference (an imprint of IGI Global)
3 Henrietta Street
Covent Garden
London WC2E 8LU
Tel: 44 20 7240 0856
Fax: 44 20 7379 0609
Web site: http://www.eurospanbookstore.com

Copyright © 2009 by IGI Global. All rights reserved. No part of this publication may be reproduced, stored or distributed in any form or by any means, electronic or mechanical, including photocopying, without written permission from the publisher.

Product or company names used in this set are for identification purposes only. Inclusion of the names of the products or companies does not indicate a claim of ownership by IGI Global of the trademark or registered trademark.

Library of Congress Cataloging-in-Publication Data

Emerging markets and e-commerce in developing economies / Kamel Rouibah, Omar Khalil and Aboul Ella Hassanien, editors.

p. cm.

Includes bibliographical references and index.

Summary: "This book provides researchers readers with a synthesis of current research on developing countries experience with e-commerce"--Provided by publisher.

ISBN 978-1-60566-100-1 (hbk.) -- ISBN 978-1-60566-101-8 (ebook)

1. Electronic commerce--Developing countries. 2. Information technology--Developing countries. I. Rouibah, Kamel. II. Khalil, Omar. III. Hassanien, Aboul Ella.

HF5548.325.D44E58 2009

381'.142091724--dc22

2008013113

British Cataloguing in Publication Data
A Cataloguing in Publication record for this book is available from the British Library.

All work contributed to this book set is original material. The views expressed in this book are those of the authors, but not necessarily of the publisher.

If a library purchased a print copy of this publication, please go to http://www.igi-global.com/agreement for information on activating the library's complimentary electronic access to this publication.

List of Reviewers

Hassan Abbas
Kuwait University, Kuwait

Frederic Adam
University of College Cork, Ireland

Fahim Akhter
Zayed University, United Arab Emirates

Aboul Ella Hassanien
Cairo University, Egypt

Vanessa Chang
School of Information Systems, Australia

Reinhold Decker
Bielefeld University, Germany

Alev M. Efendioglu
University of San Francisco, USA

Aryya Gangopadhyay
UMBC, USA

Sherif Kamel
The American University in Cairo, Egypt

Omar Khalil
Kuwait University, Kuwait

Frank Kroll
Bielefeld University, Germany

Mohammed Quaddus
Curtin University of Technology, Australia

Reda Reda
CEO, Innovation Communication Technologies, Austria

Kamel Rouibah
Kuwait University, Kuwait

Ali Salehnia
South Dakota State University, USA

Juergen Seitz
University of Cooperative Education Heidenheim, Germany

Sushil Sharma
Ball State University, USA

Timothy Shea
University of Massachusetts N. Dartmouth, USA

Troy Strader
Drake University, USA

Bob Travica
University of Manitoba, Canada

Emilija Vuksanovic
University of Kragujevac, Serbia

Charles Watkins
Villa Julie College, USA

Yi-Minn (Minnie) Yen
University of Alaska, Anchorage, USA

Table of Contents

Foreword xvi

Preface xvii

Acknowledgment xxiii

Section I
E-Commerce in DCs: An Overview

Chapter I
E-Commerce in Developing Economies: A Review of Theoretical Frameworks and Approaches 1
Richard Boateng, University of Manchester, UK
Alemayehu Molla, RMIT University, Australia
Richard Heeks, University of Manchester, UK

Chapter II
Significance and Success Factors of E-Commerce in China and Russia: An Empirical View 57
Reinholder Decker, Bielefeld University, Germany
Frank Kroll, Bielefeld University, Germany

Section II
Challenges to E-Commerce Adoption in DCs

Chapter III
Identifying Factors for Lack of E-Commerce in Developing Countries 70
Sushil K. Sharma, Ball State University, USA
Jatinder N. D. Gupta, University of Alabama in Huntsville, USA

Detailed Table of Contents

Section I
E-Commerce in DCs: An Overview

This chapter provides a synthesis of the current research on e-commerce in DCs and serves as a road map providing future directions for both academics and practitioners. Authors undertook a meta-analysis of the published literature on e-commerce in DCs. The analysis covered 245 articles published between 1993 and 2006 in seventy-six different journals on electronic commerce, information systems, global information technology, development and developing countries. In taking stock of this literature, the chapter identifies enduring research themes, classifies the existing research based on such themes, and reviews the theoretical and conceptual approaches used by researchers. The findings suggest that e-commerce research to date has mainly focused on outlining e-commerce potential and assessing adoption and implementation issues in DCs. The authors call for future research to focus more on measuring the benefits of e-commerce for DCs and on strategic understanding of how to achieve and sustain these benefits.

This chapter delineates and discusses empirical findings and conceptual ideas concerning the current and future prospects of e-commerce in emerging markets, with a special focus on China and Russia. Besides their own empirical evidence drawn from two online-surveys covering business companies from different industries as well as management consultancies in these countries, authors report the findings from a meta-analysis of a number of recent relevant studies. The resulting managerial implications are primarily based on those factors, which determine the success of e-commerce activities and the corresponding value creation.

Section II
Challenges to E-Commerce Adoption in DCs

Chapter III
Identifying Factors for Lack of E-Commerce in Developing Countries 70
Sushil K. Sharma, Ball State University, USA
Jatinder N. D. Gupta, University of Alabama in Huntsville, USA

This chapter emphasizes the fact that the past few years have seen a rise in the number of companies embracing e-commerce technologies in developing countries. However, as compared to developed nations, DCs still lag behind in e-commerce. Sharma and Gupta identify some of the reasons that may be responsible for lack of e-commerce in developing countries. For the scope of their study, they limited developing countries to China, India, Indonesia, Philippines and Sri Lanka. Their study identifies factors at the macro level to understand why the adoption of e-commerce in developing countries has not taken off as expected.

Chapter IV
E-Commerce Development in China: An Exploration of Perceptions and Attitudes 89
Antonis C. Stylianou, University of North Carolina at Charlotte, USA
Stephanie S. Robbins, University of North Carolina at Charlotte, USA
Pamela Jackson, Fayetteville State University, USA

This chapter posit that, with over 1.3 billion people and double-digit economic growth, China could potentially emerge as the largest Internet and telecommunications market in the world, if certain economic, environmental, and organizational barriers are effectively addressed. They developed and used a profile to describe the Chinese business managers' awareness of the technological infrastructure as well as their perceptions and attitudes regarding e-commerce. Their findings on the managers' views on a variety of environmental, organizational, and personal factors provide insight into the future of e-commerce in China. Chinese firms that are interested in engaging in e-commerce will likely find a knowledgeable and supportive business climate. However, e-commerce initiatives may be hindered by constraints imposed by the existing technological infrastructure and political environment.

This chapter presents a framework, proposed by Kapurubandara and Lawson, for e-commerce adoption by small and midsized enterprises (SMEs) in Sri Lanka. The framework has been developed based on an initial exploratory study of seventeen SMEs, followed by a regional survey of 625 SMEs from various industry sectors, along with interviews with the SME intermediary organizations. The framework helps an SME to identify its ICT and e-commerce sophistication maturity stages using five-stage variables, the barriers it faces in the adoption of e-commerce, and the support necessary to overcome the identified barriers. The authors argue that their framework is a preliminary framework to e-transform SMEs in DCs.

This chapter speculates that different characteristics (e.g., infrastructure and socio-economic) of the local environment create significant levels of variation in the acceptance and growth of e-commerce in different regions of the world. The findings of his research on e-commerce development in China provide insights into some of the impediments for the development and use of e-commerce. Efendioglu then discusses the impediments and proposes a number of strategies for a successful development of e-commerce in developing countries.

This chapter posits that e-government, which operates at the crossroads between information and communication technology (ICT) and government processes, can be divided into three overlapping domains: e-administration, e-services and e-society. To succeed, e-governance must be firmly embedded in the existing government processes, be supported politically and technically by the governments, and provide users with reasons to use these on-line domains. The authors used these three e-governance criteria to evaluate the achievements of the DistrictNet e-governance program in Uganda which started in 2002. The program aimed at providing transparency at the local government level and improving the provision of public information using information and communication technology (ICT). Based on the evaluation, the authors present a number of lessons that can be used to guide smaller programs at the local government level in other DCs.

This chapter illustrates the impact of e-government on e-commerce development and implementation in the DCs. Rabaiah, and Vandijck argue that since e-government is about enhancing efficiency and transparency of government operations, research efforts should explore new perspectives on how and where e-commerce can prevail in this shift in government operation paradigm. There are new opportunities for DCs to utilize new ICT offerings to achieve growth, efficiency, and cost reduction. The authors then discuss a number of these opportunities and draw a connection between e-government and e-commerce in such a way that helps decision makers in DCs to understand the potential of e-government for a better implementation of e-commerce.

This chapter presents one of a few studies that is aimed at testing the possible influence of cultural values on the acceptance of e-commerce in the two developing countries which exhibit two distinct national cultures (Malaysia and Algeria). Based on a synthesis of the technology acceptance models and cultural theories, Belkhamza and Wafa incorporated cultural values into a TAM model. The model testing results indicate that the four cultural values of individualism/collectivism, power distance, uncertainty avoidance, and masculinity/femininity identified by Hofstede are posited to explain the e-commerce acceptance in the context of these two developing countries. The role of cultural differences was found to be a noteworthy moderator in the proposed e-commerce acceptance model, emphasizing the role of cultural aspects in multi-national e-commerce research. The authors therefore suggest to look more into the social influence on the behavioral intention, which calls for attention in understanding benefits of e-commerce adoption based on cultural, rather than cognitive and norms criteria. The authors also suggest that e-commerce companies attempting to penetrate and assist the Algerian e-commerce companies should focus on creating and fostering a secure e-commerce image, and investigate the attitude of those organizations. The Malaysian culture, similar to that of Algeria, exhibits a strong relationship between usefulness and usage intention. It should be important therefore to make it a business priority to establish a strong local identity and presence in the local country.

Chapter X
Cultural Differences, Information Technology Infrastructure, and E-Commerce Behavior:
Implications for Developing Countries.. 210
Ahu Genis-Gruber, TOBB University of Economics and Technology Ankara, Turkey
Bedri Kamil Onur Tas, TOBB University of Economics and Technology Ankara, Turkey

This chapter presents a study by Genis-Gruber and Tas that was designed to investigate the role of cultural differences and information technology infrastructure on e-commerce usage in developed and developing countries. They used Hofstede's national culture taxonomy to classify the investigated countries according to both Hofstede's cultural indices and their technological and economic development. Their research design controlled for the possible impact of information infrastructure and education level on e-commerce usage. The authors found culture to play an incremental role in e-commerce usage and in the relationship between infrastructure and e-commerce.

Chapter XI
Mobile-Commerce Intention to Use via SMS: The Case of Kuwait 230
Kamel Rouibah, Kuwait University, Kuwait
Samia Ould-Ali, Kuwait University, Kuwait

This chapter presents a study that Rouibah and Ould-Ali conducted in order to test a number of models-namely, the theory of reasoned action, the theory of planned behavior, the technology acceptance model (TAM), the decomposed theory of planed behavior, Nyvseen's et al., (2005) model, as well as a revised version of TAM proposed by the authors—in explaining the intention to use short messaging systems (SMS) on banking transactions in Kuwait. A convenient sample of 171 users was used. The results suggest that the decomposed theory of planned behavior has the largest explanatory power, followed by the author's revised version of TAM. On the other hand, TAM and the theory of reasoned action have had the least explanatory power. In addition, results indicate the absence of a dominant factor (i.e. a variable that exerts the strongest effect on behavioral intention to use SMS) across the six models, which may reveal a unique characteristic of the local culture. Such a result calls for caution when applying different technology adoption models across different cultures and regions.

Section V
Strategies for Successful E-Commerce Development in DCs

Chapter XII
An Economic Framework for the Assessment of E-Commerce in Developing Countries................. 255
Ayoub Yousefi, King's University College at the University of Western Ontario, Canada

This chapter presents a theoretically-based model for economic analysis of e-commerce in DCs. The Porter diamond model is adopted in order to economically examine the factors that affect e-commerce.

The model does not only capture factors that are considered the driving forces for e-commerce, but it also facilitates the assessment of e-commerce and the identification of the global competitive advantages of the firms. Therefore, the model can be used as a framework that guides policy making and predicts the changes in the rapidly expanding e-commerce in DCs.

This chapter proposes a "tool" for managing the critical success factors (CSFs) in B2B development. The tool has been developed based on an existing framework and experiences drawn from B2B developments in the well developed countries. It includes a set of concrete and detailed guidelines that directs the actions needed during the preparation stage of B2B projects. The guidelines are further discussed considering the problems and conditions that are relevant to DCs.

This chapter emphasizes the importance of having well-designed Web sites as a requisite for successful e-commerce practices. Xanthidis, Nicholas, and Argyrides propose a template aiming at standardizing Web site evaluation. The template has been developed based on a thorough review of the relevant literature, which is rich in ideas and opinions of different professionals involved in Web site design. The template consists of fifty-three items that the design strategies of the Web sites can be checked against. The results of testing the template on 232 Websites of Greek companies suggest its appropriateness in measuring Web site quality. The authors believe that the proposed template is a step forward towards the standardization of the Web site evaluation process, which could be useful for companies in DCs.

This chapter profiles e-commerce practices and challenges in Tunisia. The profile focuses on two distinct e-commerce experiences: e-commerce transactions via the Tunisian Post Office (known as the ONP), and e-commerce operations via the Banking Association (known as the SMT). The authors explore the problems facing e-commerce in Tunisia and propose solutions that help e-commerce expansion.

Chapter XVI
Electronic Commerce in China: Can We Wake Up the Giant? 331
Hongxiu Li, Turku School of Economics, Finland
Reima Suomi, Turku School of Economics, Finland

This chapter introduces four sets of prerequisites for successful e-commerce development, including national factors, related and supporting industries, firm strategy, structure and rivalry factors, and demand conditions. Li and Suomi further discuss the status of e-commerce development in China, along with the four sets of success prerequisites, with the purpose of identifying the influential factors which impede e-commerce development in China.

Chapter XVII
Evolution of Electronic Procurement in Egypt: Case of Speedsend.com 349
Sherif Kamel, The American University in Cairo, Egypt

This chapter presents a case of an Internet startup that capitalizes on the opportunities presented by the information economy in Egypt. Since its inception in 2001, the B2B platform of speedsend.com has pioneered the electronic procurement industry in Egypt through a customized Web-based platform. The case focuses on the models deployed by the company demonstrating the internal and external challenges faced and lessons learnt. The author, Kamel, stresses that the Internet company's success is attributed to its capability to transform the classical emerging markets challenges into opportunities, including technology infrastructure deployment, community awareness, information availability, and cultural adaptation of the online business, amongst others.

Chapter XVIII
The State and Development of E-Commerce in Serbia 372
Borislav Jošanov, Higher School of Professional Business Studies, Novi Sad, Serbia
Marijana Vidas-Bubanja, Belgrade Business School, Serbia
Emilija Vuksanović, University of Kragujevac, Serbia
Ejub Kajan, High School of Applied Studies, Serbia
Bob Travica, University of Manitoba, Canada

This chapter introduces a multidimensional model for the assessment of e-commerce diffusion in a country. Jošanov and his colleagues used the model to evaluation the state of e-commerce diffusion in *Serbia.* After the breakdown of Yugoslavia and 10 years of conflicts and stagnation, Serbia started an economic reform program, and was pronounced the leading reformer in 2005 by The World Bank. The

authors found that, in general, some progress was made in e-commerce diffusion in Serbia; however, progress varied along the different dimensions of the model with problems about the need for new laws and lack of e-payment system. The chapter further discusses a B2B strategy that puts together the facilitating conditions that enable Serbia to engage in the global electronic economy.

Foreword

The world economy's center of gravity has been shifting steadily towards emerging economies and developing countries. In 2006, the *Economist* reported that according to their estimates, emerging economies produced over 50% of the world's output in 2005 for the first time, and they also accounted for over 50% of the increase in global GDP. In 2008, the *Economist* reported that in the last 20 years, the foreign direct investment in emerging economies had increased by seven times relative to GDP. As we near the start of the second decade of the 21st century, emerging markets and developing economies are becoming the high growth darlings of the global economy. No longer are they viewed by the global community as catch-up economies that need aid, but rather as attractive investment opportunities for high growth.

As emerging economies and developing countries ramp-up for large scale growth, information and communication technology infrastructures become critical enablers, and the adoption of e-commerce becomes key for accelerating economic development within a global framework. In such a rapid growth environment, the leveraging of information and communication technologies is not a luxury – it is an absolute necessity for scaling up high growth. It is thus imperative to better understand the drivers and challenges of deploying e-commerce in such developing environments.

There is much hype and hand-waving in the popular press around the exciting topic of information technology, e-commerce, and globalization. However, there are very few books that present in-depth examination and studies to help better understand the underlying drivers that enable emerging economies to take advantage of information technologies in the context of e-commerce. This timely book fills that gap and is a guide book for both practitioners and researchers who want a better understanding of e-commerce and its adoption drivers in emerging markets. It brings together in 18 chapters the diverse expertise of over 35 accomplished authors. It provides rich insights that will help guide future research on e-commerce, and will guide decisions and policies for the more effective implementation of e-commerce in developing economies.

The digital divide between the developed and emerging economies is shifting rapidly. China is expected to overtake the USA in 2008 as the country with the world's largest number of internet users. We expect to see information technology intensity and e-commerce dependence to increase from Dubai to Mumbai, and from Indonesia to Tunisia. That is why we need specific understanding of the challenges and opportunities of e-commerce adoption in these contexts. This immensely useful book sets us on the right path.

Professor Omar A. El Sawy

Preface

Countries with low-to-middle per capita income are considered emerging, or developing, market economies. Emerging markets include countries in Asia (e.g., China, and India), South and Central America (e.g. Brazil), the Eastern Bloc (e.g. Russia), Middle East (e.g. Egypt, Kuwait), and African countries (e.g. Tunisia and Uganda). Although they vary from very big to very small, these countries are emerging markets because of their developments and reforms. They constitute approximately 80% of the global population and represent about 20% of the world's economies [1].

The emerging market countries, also called developing countries (hereafter DCs), often embark on aggressive, fast economic and social reform programs. Throughout this transformational process, these countries have to weigh diverse local political, economical, and social factors as they attempts to open up their economies to the world; and leverage the opportunities made available by the advancing information and communication technologies (ICT) in searching for solutions to the emerging issues and accelerating the transformation process.

ICT and the Internet play a pivotal role in transforming the economies of DCs. This role takes different forms, including new and revamped information systems, Internet-based applications, and new forms of executing transaction, communication, and service (e.g., e-business, e-commerce, e-government, e-procurement e-payment, etc.). The adoption of these emerging technology-based applications should assist DCs to lower transaction and agency costs, enhance flexibility, and improve resources management.

The Internet World Statistics report of February 2008 illustrates that the number of Internet users worldwide exceeds 1.32 billion, of which approximately 712 millions (54%) live in DCs [2]. In addition, the numbers of Internet users in DCs continue to experience steep growth. For instance, China and India, the largest among DCs, have respectively experienced growth rates of 833% and 1100% between 2000 and 2007, with a total of 210 and 60 million of Internet users in 2007. Moreover, today, DCs account for more than half of the world's total telecommunication connections, and this will grow to 69 percent by 2010 [3].

Although young, e-commerce is rapidly growing in DCs, as a part of the transformation processes that are taking place in these countries. E-commerce is broadly defined to include not only transacting electronically over a network, mostly the Internet, but also to include electronic communication, collaboration, and coordination among participants. While e-commerce literature is relatively rich in information on e-commerce experience in developed countries, little is available on the ecommerce experience in DCs, although this represents a multitude of opportunities and risks.

This book is intended to help reduce such a disparity in the existing e-commerce literature. It compiles a collection of eighteen high quality chapters covering e-commerce development and practice in a number of DCs such as Algeria, China, Egypt, Kuwait, Malaysia, Russia, Serbia, Sri Lanka, Uganda, Tunisia, India, Indonesia, and Philippines.

This book provides researchers, professionals, managers, and policy makers with a synthesis of current research on DCs' experience with e-commerce. It accentuates e-commerce impediments, opportunities, and strategies; underlines future research directions; and underscores valuable lessons for future e-commerce initiatives. The eighteen chapters of the book are grouped into six parts, which are briefly highlighted below.

Section I, E-Commerce in DCs: An Overview, sets the stage for the rest of the book and presents an overview of the e-commerce status in DCs, as portrayed in the relevant literature. A review and synthesis of the literature on e-commerce development and practice in DCs, although is currently inadequate, is beneficial to e-commerce researchers and practitioners.

Section I includes two chapters. Chapter I, *"E-Commerce in Developing Economies: A Review of Theoretical Frameworks and Approaches,"* provides a synthesis of the current research on e-commerce in DCs and serves as a road map providing future directions for both academics and practitioners. Boateng, Molla, and Heeks undertook a meta-analysis of the published literature on e-commerce in DCs. The analysis covered 245 articles published between 1993 and 2006 in seventy-six different journals on electronic commerce, information systems, global information technology, development and developing countries. In taking stock of this literature, the chapter identifies enduring research themes, classifies the existing research based on such themes, and reviews the theoretical and conceptual approaches used by researchers. The findings suggest that e-commerce research to date has mainly focused on outlining e-commerce potential and assessing adoption and implementation issues in DCs. The authors call for future research to focus more on measuring the benefits of e-commerce for DCs and on strategic understanding of how to achieve and sustain these benefits.

Similarly, Chapter II, "*Significance and Success Factors of E-Commerce in China and Russia: An Empirical View,*" delineates and discusses empirical findings and conceptual ideas concerning the current and future prospects of e-commerce in emerging markets, with a special focus on China and Russia. Besides their own empirical evidence drawn from two online-surveys covering business companies from different industries as well as management consultancies in these countries, Decker and Kroll report the findings from a meta-analysis of a number of recent relevant studies. The resulting managerial implications are primarily based on those factors, which determine the success of e-commerce activities and the corresponding value creation.

Section II, Challenges to E-Commerce Adoption in DCs, stresses the challenges that DCs must overcome in order to successfully undertake e-commerce initiatives. While developed countries have shown impressive performance in their respective economies, many developing countries still lag behind in the e-commerce race. This lag could be due to several reasons including, but not limited to, language, education, technology and technical infrastructure.

Section II consists of three chapters. Chapter III, *"Identifying Factors for lack of E-Commerce in Developing Countries,"* emphasizes the fact that the past few years have seen a rise in the number of companies embracing e-commerce technologies in developing countries. However, as compared to developed nations, DCs still lag behind in e-commerce. Sharma and Gupta identify some of the reasons that may be responsible for lack of e-commerce in developing countries. For the scope of their study, they limited developing countries to China, India, Indonesia, Philippines and Sri Lanka. Their study identifies factors at the macro level to understand why the adoption of e-commerce in developing countries has not taken off as expected

In Chapter IV, "*E-Commerce Development in China: An Exploration of Perceptions and Attitudes,"* Stylianou, Robbins, and Jackson posit that, with over 1.3 billion people and double-digit economic growth, China could potentially emerge as the largest Internet and telecommunications market in the world, if certain economic, environmental, and organizational barriers are effectively addressed. They developed and used a profile to describe the Chinese business managers' awareness of the technological infrastructure as well as their perceptions and attitudes regarding e-commerce. Their findings on the managers' views on a variety of environmental, organizational, and personal factors provide insight into the future of e-commerce in China. Chinese firms that are interested in engaging in e-commerce will likely find a knowledgeable and supportive business climate. However, e-commerce initiatives may be hindered by constraints imposed by the existing technological infrastructure and political environment.

Chapter V, "*E-Commerce Adoption and Appropriation by SMEs in Sri Lanka,"* presents a framework, proposed by Kapurubandara and Lawson, for e-commerce adoption by small and midsized enterprises (SMEs) in Sri Lanka. The framework has been developed based on an initial exploratory study of seventeen SMEs, followed by a regional survey of 625 SMEs from various industry sectors, along with interviews with the SME intermediary organizations. The framework helps an SME to identify its ICT and e-commerce sophistication maturity stages using five-stage variables, the barriers it faces in the adoption of e-commerce, and the support necessary to overcome the identified barriers. The authors argue that their framework is a preliminary framework to e-transform SMEs in DCs.

In last chapter, Chapter VI, of Section II, " *E-Commerce in Developing Countries: Impediments & Opportunities*," Efendioglu speculates that different characteristics (e.g., infrastructure and socio-economic) of the local environment create significant levels of variation in the acceptance and growth of e-commerce in different regions of the world. The findings of his research on e-commerce development in China provide insights into some of the impediments for the development and use of e-commerce. Efendioglu then discusses the impediments and proposes a number of strategies for a successful development of e-commerce in developing countries.

Section III, E-Government in DCs, introduces examples of e-government experience in DCs. E-government is a powerful tool for bringing about changes to government processes in DCs. In order for e-government initiatives to succeed, they are expected to provide users with compelling reasons/benefits to adopt them as well as having the requisite critical success factors in terms of technological and political support to sustain them.

There are two chapters in this section. In Chapter VII, "*E-Governance in Uganda: Experiences and Lessons Learned from the DistrictNet Program*," van Reijswoud and de Jager posit that e-government, which operates at the crossroads between information and communication technology (ICT) and government processes, can be divided into three overlapping domains: e-administration, e-services and e-society. To succeed, e-governance must be firmly embedded in the existing government processes, be supported politically and technically by the governments, and provide users with reasons to use these on-line domains. The authors used these three e-governance criteria to evaluate the achievements of the DistrictNet e-governance program in Uganda which started in 2002. The program aimed at providing transparency at the local government level and improving the provision of public information using information and communication technology (ICT). Based on the evaluation, the authors present a number of lessons that can be used to guide smaller programs at the local government level in other DCs.

On the other hand, Chapter VIII, "*E-Government and its Impact on E-Commerce in LDCs*," illustrates the impact of e-government on e-commerce development and implementation in the DCs. Rabaiah, and Vandijck argue that since e-government is about enhancing efficiency and transparency of government operations, research efforts should explore new perspectives on how and where e-commerce can prevail in this shift in government operation paradigm. There are new opportunities for DCs to utilize new ICT offerings to achieve growth, efficiency, and cost reduction. The authors then discuss a number of these opportunities and draw a connection between e-government and e-commerce in such a way that helps decision makers in DCs to understand the potential of e-government for a better implementation of e-commerce.

Section IV, National Culture and E-Commerce Adoption in DCs, marks the significance of national culture on e-commerce development and behavior in DCs. Global deployment of ICT and e-commerce applications require a thorough understanding of the impediments that cultural differences may create. Cultural differences are expected to play a major role on e-commerce behavior in developing economies. However, since most of the empirical support for the technology acceptance models was mainly obtained from Western and well developed countries, these models are not necessarily applicable to all cultures. Little research has been done on technology diffusion, including e-commerce, in DCs which exhibit vast and distinctive cultural differences from developed countries.

Section IV comprises three chapters that deal with e-commerce adoption and the effect of culture. Chapter IX, "*Cultural Interpretation of E-Commerce Acceptance in Developing Countries: Empirical Evidence from Malaysia and Algeria*," presents one of a few studies that is aimed at testing the possible influence of cultural values on the acceptance of e-commerce in the two developing countries which exhibit two distinct national cultures (Malaysia and Algeria). Based on a synthesis of the technology acceptance models and cultural theories, Belkhamza and Wafa incorporated cultural values into a TAM model. The model testing results indicate that the four cultural values of individualism/collectivism, power distance, uncertainty avoidance, and masculinity/femininity identified by Hofstede are posited to explain the e-commerce acceptance in the context of these two developing countries. The role of cultural differences was found to be a noteworthy moderator in the proposed e-commerce acceptance model, emphasizing the role of cultural aspects in multi-national e-commerce research. The authors therefore suggest to look more into the social influence on the behavioral intention, which calls for attention in understanding benefits of e-commerce adoption based on cultural, rather than cognitive and norms criteria. The authors also suggest that e-commerce companies attempting to penetrate and assist the Algerian e-commerce companies should focus on creating and fostering a secure e-commerce image, and investigate the attitude of those organizations. The Malaysian culture, similar to that of Algeria, exhibits a strong relationship between usefulness and usage intention. It should be important therefore to make it a business priority to establish a strong local identity and presence in the local country.

On the other hand, Chapter X, "*Cultural Differences, Information Technology Infrastructure and E-Commerce Behavior: Implications for Developing Countries*," presents a study by Genis-Gruber and Tas that was designed to investigate the role of cultural differences and information technology infrastructure on e-commerce usage in developed and developing countries. They used Hofstede's national culture taxonomy to classify the investigated countries according to both Hofstede's cultural indices and their technological and economic development. Their research design controlled for the possible impact of information infrastructure and education level on e-commerce usage. The authors found culture to play an incremental role in e-commerce usage and in the relationship between infrastructure and e-commerce.

The last chapter in this part, Chapter XI, *"Mobile-Commerce Intention to use via SMS: The Case of Kuwait*," presents a study that Rouibah and Ould-Ali conducted in order to test a number of models-namely, the theory of reasoned action, the theory of planned behavior, the technology acceptance model (TAM), the decomposed theory of planed behavior, Nyvseen's et al., (2005) model, as well as a revised version of TAM proposed by the authors—in explaining the intention to use short messaging systems (SMS) on banking transactions in Kuwait. A convenient sample of 171 users was used. The results suggest that the decomposed theory of planned behavior has the largest explanatory power, followed by the author's revised version of TAM. On the other hand, TAM and the theory of reasoned action have had the least explanatory power. In addition, results indicate the absence of a dominant factor (i.e. a variable that exerts the strongest effect on behavioral intention to use SMS) across the six models, which may reveal a unique characteristic of the local culture. Such a result calls for caution when applying different technology adoption models across different cultures and regions.

Section V, Strategies for Successful E-Commerce Development in DCs, introduces a number of guiding principles that may increase the likelihood of e-commerce success in DCs. Compared to developed countries, e-commerce adoption in DCs has been slower and more recent. Given their tight resources, including time, developing countries seem to seldom have the luxury of affording to make mistakes and fail in their e-commerce development initiatives. Nevertheless, e-commerce developers in DCs have the opportunity to learn from the experience of, and the mistakes made by, their counterparts in the developing countries.

This section has three chapters. In Chapter XII, "*An Economic Framework for the Assessment of E-Commerce in Developing Countries*," Yousefi presents a theoretically-based model for economic analysis of e-commerce in DCs. The Porter diamond model is adopted in order to economically examine the factors that affect e-commerce. The model does not only capture factors that are considered the driving forces for e-commerce, but it also facilitates the assessment of e-commerce and the identification of the global competitive advantages of the firms. Therefore, the model can be used as a framework that guides policy making and predicts the changes in the rapidly expanding e-commerce in DCs.

In Chapter XIII, "*Guidelines for Preparing Organizations in Developing Countries for Standards-based B2B*," Aggestam and Söderström also propose a "tool" for managing the critical success factors (CSFs) in B2B development. The tool has been developed based on an existing framework and experiences drawn from B2B developments in the well developed countries. It includes a set of concrete and detailed guidelines that directs the actions needed during the preparation stage of B2B projects. The guidelines are further discussed considering the problems and conditions that are relevant to DCs.

The last chapter of this section, Chapter XIV, "*A Proposed Template for the Evaluation of Web Design Strategies*," emphasizes the importance of having well-designed Web sites as a requisite for successful e-commerce practices. Xanthidis, Nicholas, and Argyrides propose a template aiming at standardizing Web site evaluation. The template has been developed based on a thorough review of the relevant literature, which is rich in ideas and opinions of different professionals involved in Web site design. The template consists of fifty-three items that the design strategies of the Web sites can be checked against. The results of testing the template on 232 Websites of Greek companies suggest its appropriateness in measuring Web site quality. The authors believe that the proposed template is a step forward towards the standardization of the Web site evaluation process, which could be useful for companies in DCs.

Section VI, Case Studies on E-Commerce in DCs, provides in-depth examples of e-commerce experience in certain DCs. Although classified together and characterized by common characteristics, DCs have had different experiences with e-commerce development and practice. Country-specific investigations produce meticulous information on the e-commerce development, drivers, problems, successes, and failures. Understanding e-commerce development experiences in certain developing countries should be valuable to policy formulation and decision making in the other DCs that have similar conditions in their e-commerce development.

Section VI incorporates three chapters. In Chapter XV, "*Electronic Commerce Reality in Tunisia*," Ziadi and Ben Sala profile e-commerce practices and challenges in Tunisia. The profile focuses on two distinct e-commerce experiences: e-commerce transactions via the Tunisian Post Office (known as the ONP), and e-commerce operations via the Banking Association (known as the SMT). The authors explore the problems facing e-commerce in Tunisia and propose solutions that help e-commerce expansion.

Chapter XVI, "*Electronic Commerce in China: Can We wake up the Giant?*" on the other hand, introduces four sets of prerequisites for successful e-commerce development, including national factors, related and supporting industries, firm strategy, structure and rivalry factors, and demand conditions. Li and Suomi further discuss the status of e-commerce development in China, along with the four sets of success prerequisites, with the purpose of identifying the influential factors which impede e-commerce development in China.

Chapter XVII, "*Evolution of Electronic Procurement in Egypt Case of Speedsend.com*," however, presents a case of an Internet startup that capitalizes on the opportunities presented by the information economy in Egypt. Since its inception in 2001, the B2B platform of speedsend.com has pioneered the electronic procurement industry in Egypt through a customized Web-based platform. The case focuses on the models deployed by the company demonstrating the internal and external challenges faced and lessons learnt. The author, Kamel, stresses that the Internet company's success is attributed to its capability to transform the classical emerging markets challenges into opportunities, including technology infrastructure deployment, community awareness, information availability, and cultural adaptation of the online business, amongst others.

The final chapter, Chapter XVIII, "*The State and Development of E-Commerce in Serbia*," introduces a multidimensional model for the assessment of e-commerce diffusion in a country. Jošanov and his colleagues used the model to evaluation the state of e-commerce diffusion in *Serbia.* After the breakdown of Yugoslavia and 10 years of conflicts and stagnation, Serbia started an economic reform program, and was pronounced the leading reformer in 2005 by The World Bank. The authors found that, in general, some progress was made in e-commerce diffusion in Serbia; however, progress varied along the different dimensions of the model with problems about the need for new laws and lack of e-payment system. The chapter further discusses a B2B strategy that puts together the facilitating conditions that enable Serbia to engage in the global electronic economy.

REFERENCES

[1] http://www.investopedia.com/articles/03/073003.asp), (http://www.cme.com/files/EMProduct_brochure.pdf)

[2] (www.internetworldstats.com)

[3] (http://www.gartner.com/it/page.jsp?id=499110).

Acknowledgment

The editors would like to thank all people involved in the development and review process of the book: especially, Professor Juergen Seitz from the University of Cooperative Education Heidenheim in Germany, Dr. Troy Strader from the Drake University (USA), Dr. Adam Frederic from the University of College Cork (Ireland), and Dr. Ali Salehnia from South Dakota State University (USA). Many of the authors of the chapters included in this book also served as referees for chapters written by other authors. Thanks go to all those who provided constructive and comprehensive reviews.

We would also like to thank all the authors for their contributions. Special thanks go to Jessica Thompson and Julia Mosemann at IGI Global for their great support. Special thanks also go to the publishing team at IGI Global, whose contributions throughout the whole process from the inception of the initial idea to final publication have been invaluable. In particular, special thanks goes to Jessica Thompson and Julia Mosemann, who continuously prodded us via e-mail to keep the project on schedule and to Jessica Thompson, whose enthusiasm motivated us to initially accept her invitation for taking on this project.

Section I

E-Commerce in DCs:
An Overview

Chapter I
E-Commerce in Developing Economies:
A Review of Theoretical Frameworks and Approaches

Richard Boateng
University of Manchester, UK

Alemayehu Molla
RMIT University, Australia

Richard Heeks
University of Manchester, UK

ABSTRACT

This chapter undertakes a meta-analysis of the published literature on e-commerce in developing economies (DEs). The aim is to take stock of the literature, identify enduring research themes, classify the existing work based on such themes and review the theoretical and conceptual approaches used. The analysis covers 245 articles published between 1993 and 2006 in 76 different journals on electronic commerce, information systems, global information technology, development and developing countries. The findings indicate that the research area is rapidly growing and relatively well-spread across the assessment of e-commerce potential and its adoption and implementation issues in DEs. We make a case for future research to focus on developing a broad development perspective of e-commerce benefits and a strategic understanding of how to achieve and sustain these benefits. The chapter thus serves both as a synthesis of current research, and as a road map providing future directions for both academics and practitioners.

Copyright © 2009, IGI Global, distributing in print or electronic forms without written permission of IGI Global is prohibited.

INTRODUCTION

Electronic commerce (e-commerce) has been widely discussed in academic and practitioner literature. Extant research on e-commerce has largely focused on developed economies (Pani & Agrahari, 2004; Bajaj & Leonard, 2004). However, there has been a growing academic interest in e-commerce in developing economies (DEs). These studies on e-commerce in DEs are a mix of empirical and non-empirical work. They have employed several theoretical frameworks from various disciplines such as information systems (IS), management, and social sciences. A variety of research methods has also been used. Core research contributions include conceptual and evaluation frameworks that examine both the relative potential of e-commerce in DEs and the means to achieve that potential.

This chapter therefore reviews previous research on e-commerce in DEs to provide a meta-analysis of the published literature and examine the theoretical frameworks and conceptual approaches underlying e-commerce in DEs research. The objective is to identify the current knowledge gaps in relation to the application of these frameworks and use those gaps to define an agenda for future research. The value of such a review for advancing e-business knowledge and practice has been established in a previous study (Ngai & Wat, 2002). However, that earlier study had limitations related to context, coverage, and content that motivated our current work and the contribution we intend to make through this chapter.

First, in terms of context, Ngai and Wat's (2002) study focused on e-commerce research in developed economies and gave no specific attention to e-commerce in DEs. While there are some similarities and communality of issues, e-commerce in DEs has its own idiosyncratic characteristics and challenges worth investigating (Molla & Licker, 2005a). Second, in terms of coverage, this previous study reviewed e-commerce research between 1993 and 1999. This period covers the early stage of e-commerce development as a phenomenon even in the developed countries (Petrazzini & Kibati, 1999; Rodriguez & Wilson, 2000). Evidence suggests that the diffusion and use of ICTs (information and communication technologies) including the Internet in DEs increased substantially post-2000 (ITU, 2006). Further, e-commerce has gained more academic attention with the introduction of new journals such as: Journal of Electronic Commerce Research in 2000, Electronic Commerce Research in 2001, Journal of Electronic Commerce in Organizations in 2003, and other information systems journals which give priority to DEs. Third, in terms of content, the Ngai and Wat (2002) study focused on a quantitative analysis of issues addressed by e-commerce researchers without a thorough exposition of the theoretical frameworks and conceptual approaches used.

A knowledge gap therefore exists in reviewing literature by researchers and practitioners on e-commerce research in DEs. As more firms and governments in DEs seek to adopt and institutionalize this innovation, the need for such a review grows given that it can provide an evaluatory overview of the problems addressed, the theoretical and practical solutions suggested, and methods used to reach those solutions. Furthermore, the dynamic nature of the phenomena emphasizes the need for researchers and practitioners to regularly review – and if necessary – redefine the focus and approach to research, especially in relation to the context of DEs.

This chapter, in response, undertakes a review of literature on e-commerce in DEs published in 76 journals between 1993 and 2006. The review is divided into four parts. The first part presents our conceptualization of e-commerce, explaining the classification scheme adopted for this study. The second part focuses on the methodology of this study, explaining how the literature review was carried out. The third part presents findings and reviews the theoretical frameworks and conceptual approaches applied in extant research. It also identifies knowledge gaps for future research. The last part summarizes the findings in this chapter and establishes the justification, originality and direction for future research.

CLASSIFICATION FRAMEWORK

Regardless of the "e" and "commerce" built into it, the term "e-commerce" has been conceptualized in so many different ways that it is now difficult to use it in a neutral way (Ngai & Wat, 2002). Researchers, guided by their conceptualization of e-commerce, have been investigating various issues. For example, at a special session of the 1998 International Electronic Commerce Conference in Bled, Slovenia, a group of 56 business and government leaders generated 174 research issues for e-commerce, ranging from highly technical to management-oriented topics (Bauer & Glasson, 1999). In a similar fashion, a survey of the IS World community at the beginning of 2000 by Benbasat, Ives, Piccoli and Weber (2000) identified 140 research questions, which were grouped into nine emerging e-commerce research areas spanning technological, individual, organizational, societal and economic issues. In order to understand the development and direction of e-commerce research in DEs, it is essential to have a robust classificatory and analytical framework that helps in the "sense making and subsequent analysis" (Zwass, 1998).

In this chapter, we define e-commerce as the sharing of business information, maintaining of business relationships, and conducting of business transactions by means of telecommunications networks (Zwass, 1996). This includes electronically supported commercial transactions involving both organizations and individuals (Akel & Phillips, 2001).

Moving on from this definition, we can give a brief overview of research themes in the literature on e-commerce in DEs:

- Much of that literature – especially the earlier literature in the period under review - is characterized by prognoses of the potential of e-commerce in DEs and descriptions of the constraints that DEs have to overcome to realize e-commerce's potential. Subsequently, a number of works have focused on issues of e-readiness assessment (Mann, 2000; UNCTAD, 2002; Pare, 2003). Hence, we argue that works on *e-commerce's potential and constraints* represent one of the enduring themes of e-commerce in DEs research.
- A second enduring theme is that of *e-commerce adoption and diffusion*. Within this theme, research has focused on a number of issues spanning the five domains of adoption, i.e., technological, managerial, organizational, environmental, and contextual – and their interaction (Xu, Zhu & Gibbs, 2004; Molla & Licker, 2005b).
- The success of e-commerce adoption depends on a range of implementation issues such as strategy, consumer e-readiness, and support from e-commerce developers and public policy (Ngai & Wat, 2002). Hence, *support and implementation* can be considered as a third enduring theme of e-commerce research in DEs.

On the basis of the above discussion and with reference to previous works (Wigand, 1997; Ngai & Wat, 2002), the classification framework shown in Figure 1 is developed to guide the analysis in this chapter. In investigating each of the themes in Figure 1 and the issues identified under them, previous works have also relied on a number of theories and research methods. For each of the issues, we would identify and discuss the dominant theoretical or conceptual approaches that have been used in analyzing e-commerce.

First, we would briefly explain each one of the research themes and related issues identified.

Figure 1. Classification framework

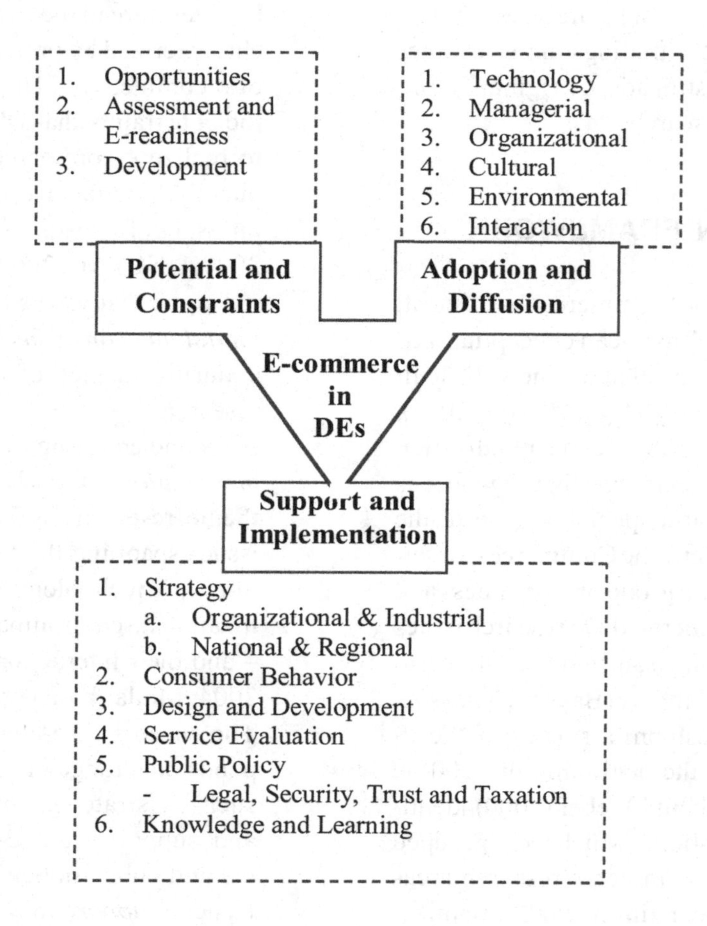

Potential Benefits and Constraints

a. ***Opportunities***: literature that argues for the potential benefits of e-commerce in DEs, which is considered as the optimistic view of e-commerce (Moodley & Morris, 2004). Benefits include reduction of transaction costs and the increased opportunity to participate in international trade and to access new markets.

b. ***Assessment***: literature that assesses the constraints to e-commerce implementation in DEs. This is considered as the pessimistic view which, while not being entirely against the notion of the potential benefits of e-commerce in DEs, tends to question the conceptual and empirical evidence for propositions of the optimistic view (Pare, 2003). It also includes publications that specifically address e-readiness of DEs at the national level.

c. ***Development:*** literature that specifically covers the impact of e-commerce on socio-economic development in DEs. This may be considered as the higher-order effect of achieving the potential benefits of e-commerce.

Adoption and Diffusion

a. ***Technology:*** literature that addresses the technological determinants of e-commerce adoption and diffusion. These include compatibility with existing infrastructure, complexity, ease of use, and usefulness of e-commerce technologies.
b. ***Managerial:*** literature that addresses the managerial determinants of e-commerce adoption and diffusion. These include the innovativeness of managers, strategic vision and decision-making, and top management knowledgeability and commitment.
c. ***Organizational:*** literature that addresses the determinants of e-commerce adoption and diffusion that lies in the internal context of the organization. These include organizational innovativeness, readiness, functional differentiation, and risk taking propensity (Molla & Licker, 2005b).
d. ***Cultural:*** literature that addresses the cultural determinants of e-commerce adoption and diffusion. These include language, values, and attributes from Hofstede's cultural dimensions: power distance, individualism, collectivism, context (high and low), uncertainty avoidance, long-term orientation and masculinity (Bin, Chen & Sun, 2003).
e. ***Environmental:*** literature that addresses the environmental determinants of e-commerce adoption and diffusion. These are external to the organization including readiness of institutional foundations and external pressure from competitors, business partners and industry.
f. ***Interaction:*** literature that addresses the interrelated determinants of e-commerce adoption and diffusion which lie in the internal and external context of the organization. These consist of a combination of the determinants listed above.

Support and Implementation

This category consists of publications that cover support and implementation issues which influence the institutionalization of e-commerce after adoption. This is divided into six sub-categories of pertinent issues addressed by these publications:

a. ***Strategy:*** literature on the strategies employed by organizations, industries and nations in order to address the challenges of e-commerce and achieve the potential benefits of e-commerce. At the organizational level, these publications discuss and evaluate strategies that go beyond e-commerce adoption to determine the means of institutionalizing and embedding e-commerce into organizational processes to achieve its potential benefits. At the national level, these publications discuss and evaluate strategies that enable a developing country to build a comprehensive e-commerce infrastructure to support organizational strategies and potentially impact on development in the nation.
b. ***Consumer Behavior:*** literature on issues related to consumer behavior in the use of e-commerce. These include online shopping behavior and attitudes of customers and consumers.
c. ***Design and Development:*** literature on technical design and development issues in relation to the implementation of e-commerce. These include the functionality/features provided and the technical development

tools and components used in developing Websites and e-commerce portals.

d. ***Service Evaluation:*** literature that evaluates the services provided by organizations through e-commerce. These include service quality evaluation of Internet banking and customer satisfaction of services of Websites.

e. ***Public Policy:*** literature covering taxation, legal, and trust and security issues related to the use of e-commerce. Trust, property rights and trade policies and agreements have to be developed to meet international standards while resonating with domestic interests and supporting the export market and services (Singh & Gilchrist, 2002, pp. 35-39). Additionally, within many DEs, specific e-commerce polices are necessary to facilitate e-commerce especially in relation to legality of electronic documents, electronic signature and electronic transactions.

f. ***Knowledge and Learning:*** literature on the relationship between knowledge management and e-commerce in DEs. This also covers literature on e-commerce education, teaching, learning and curriculum, which influence the institutionalization of e-commerce after adoption.

METHODOLOGY

This study was based on a survey of journals from a diversity of disciplines related to e-commerce research in DEs. Conference papers, masters and doctoral dissertations, textbooks, unpublished working papers, and commentaries and reviews of books were excluded. The data were sourced based on two methods. First, eight top e-commerce journals and six IS journals focused on global information technology (IT) issues, development and DEs (Bharati & Tarasewich, 2002; Lowry, Romans & Curtis, 2004) were selected and individually searched year by year (see list below). Second, relevant articles were also solicited by searching nine databases, namely *ABI-Inform (ProQuest), ACM Digital Library, EBSCO Business Source Premier, Emerald Fulltext, Google Scholar, IEEE Explore, M-Lit Online bibliographical database, ScienceDirect, and SwetsWise.*

To decide whether or not to include an article in our analysis, we searched the *abstract/citation with four keywords - [electronic commerce, e-commerce, or ecommerce and Internet commerce], and the full text with two keywords – [developing countries, or less developing countries]. Full text articles were also reviewed to eliminate those which were not related to e-commerce in DEs. From this search, 245 articles on e-commerce in DEs from 76 journals were identified and analyzed based on the classificatory framework described above.*

Appendix Two shows the distributions of articles by journals.

PRESENTATION OF FINDINGS

Descriptive Results

Table 1 shows the number and percentage of total articles published only in the top eight e-commerce/IS journals and in the six IS journals with global focus. The fourteen selected journals contribute almost 50% of the total number of journal articles – 120 from the total of 245 reviewed. On the other hand, we may also see that the majority of e-commerce in DE research (i.e. 75%) is published outside the top e-commerce/IS journals. This could reflect the immaturity of research on e-commerce in DEs – for example, a lack of quality and rigor, or it could be a normal pattern of publication and size constraints within top journals. Conversely, the presence of more than 60 articles on this topic within eight top journals can be taken as a sign of its recognized importance.

Perhaps reflecting the general recognition of the topic among top journals, one can see that – contrary to our initial expectations – there is no obvious skew towards the six "global IS" journals. Overall, then, authors are spreading their research dissemination relatively evenly between e-commerce and global IS journals. The analysis thus indicates that the top five preferred journals to publish e-commerce in DEs research are *Electronic Markets, EJISDC, Journal of Global Information Management, Journal of Global Information Technology Management* and the *Electronic Commerce Research.* Together these five journals constitute 33% of the publications. One may also take this as a guide to future publication in relation to level of interest and acceptance of e-commerce in DEs research articles.

Figure 2 shows the distribution of articles by year from 1993 to 2006. It reinforces our earlier assertion that the diffusion and use of ICTs in DEs is largely a post 2000 phenomenon.

The overall trend is that of strong growth from the late 1990s, particularly strong during the 21st century; no doubt as research follows the actual diffusion of technology in developing economies. The apparently uneven nature of publication in the latest years is explained by the publication of a set of special issues that had a particular inclusion of e-commerce in DE articles - such as *Electronic Markets* (Volume 14, issue 1), *Electronic Commerce Research* (Volume 4 Issue 3), *Journal of Global Information Management* (Volume 12 Issue 1*), Journal of Electronic Commerce in Organizations* (Volume 2 Issue 2). As a guide

Table 1. Selection of articles for review

Top E-commerce Journals	Number of Articles	IS Journals focused on Global IT Issues, DEs and Development	Number of Articles
Electronic Markets	23 (9.4%)	Electronic Journal of Information Systems in Developing Countries	18 (7.3%)
Electronic Commerce Research	11 (4.5%)	Journal of Global Information Management	14 (5.7%)
Journal of Electronic Commerce Research	9 (3.7%)	Journal of Global Information Technology Management	14 (5.7%)
International Journal of Electronic Commerce	8 (3.3%)	Information Technology for Development	7 (2.9%)
Communication of AIS	6 (2.4%)	Information Technology & People	3 (1.2%)
Journal of Management Information Systems	2 (0.8%)	Information Technologies & International Development	3 (1.2%)
Information Systems Research	2 (0.8%)		
MIS Quarterly	0 (0.0%)		
Total	61 (24.9 %)	Total	59 (24.1 %)
Other Journals	184 (75.1%)	Other Journals	186 (75.9%)
Total of All Journals	**245 (100.0%)**	**Total of All Journals**	**245 (100.0%)**

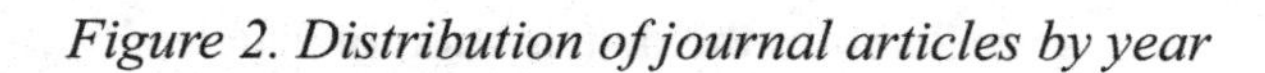

Figure 2. Distribution of journal articles by year

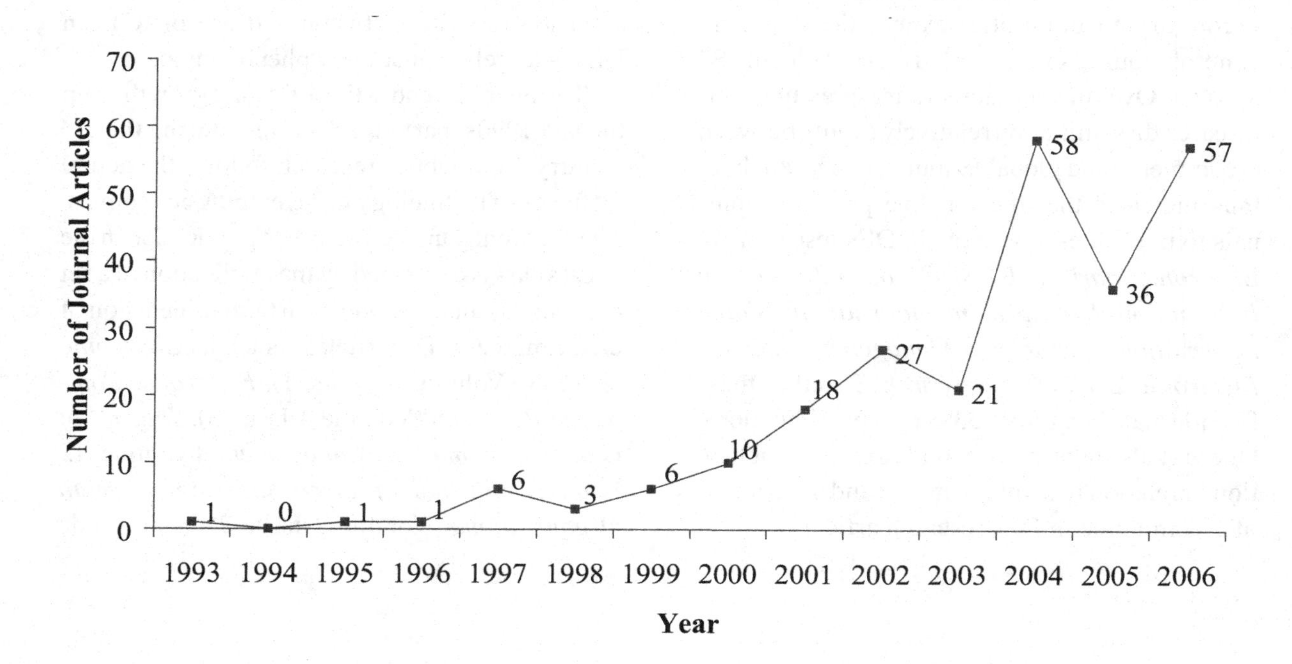

Table 2. Distributions of articles by research methods

Research Method	Number of Articles
Survey	93 (38.0%)
Case Study	57 (23.3%)
Content Analysis	2 (0.8%)
Archival Data Analysis	1 (0.4%)
Attribute Analysis	3 (1.2%)
Simulation/Experimental Study	4 (1.6%)
Mixed Methods	19 (7.8%)
Other	66 (26.9%)
Total	**245 (100%)**

to future publication, this suggests that authors may particularly seek out special issues with a focus on e-commerce in DEs, development, or globalization as much as they seek to publish in regular issues.

In terms of the research method (Table 2), survey and case study are by far the most widely used methods (61%) by e-commerce in DEs researchers. The dominance of survey reflects the entrenchment of the positivist research tradition in e-commerce in DEs research – a tendency that dominates IS research in general.

Analytical Classification

Figure 3 shows the distribution of articles by research theme. It demonstrates that extant research has particularly relatively well-spread across the three identified research themes.

Summary by E-Commerce Research Themes

In this section, further details will be provided on each of the three research themes, including identification of some of the key articles, their "sub-themes", and the theoretical/conceptual frameworks that they utilize. This will provide a greater understanding of the focus to date of e-commerce in DEs research, and also a guide to typical conceptualization.

Theme 1: Potential and Constraints

Table 3 shows theoretical frameworks used in studying issues relating to assessment of e-commerce opportunities and evaluation of e-commerce benefits after implementation. The main focus has been on benefits of e-commerce to DEs

Figure 3. Distributions of articles by research themes

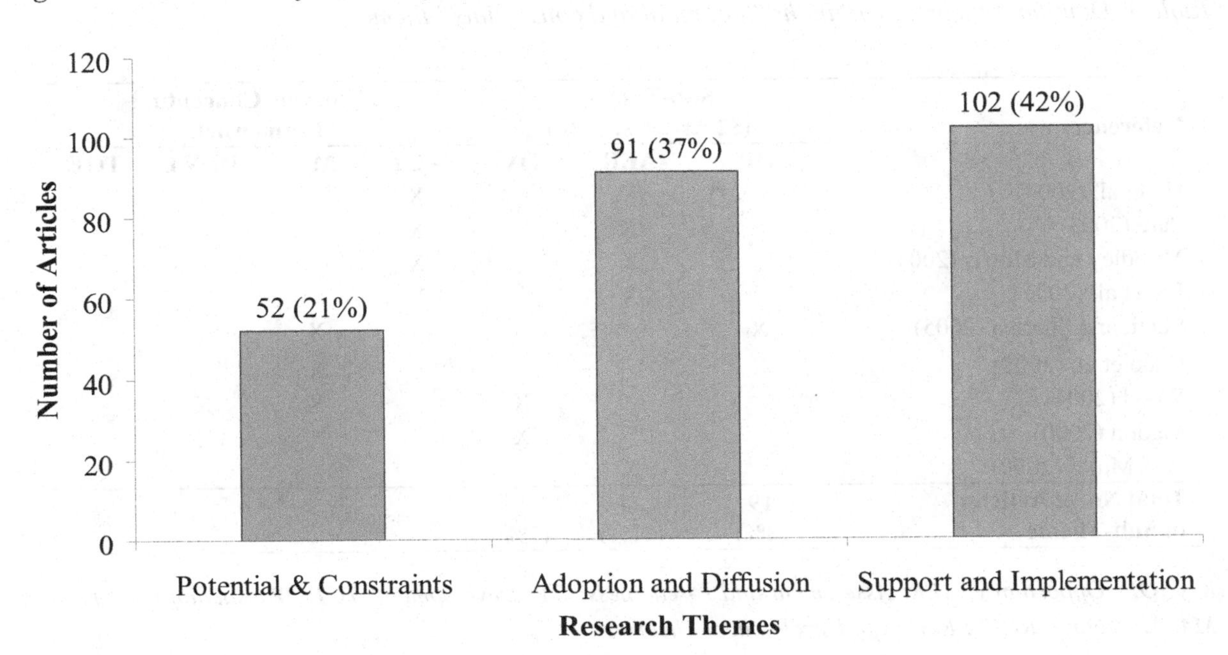

at the firm-level, particularly in reducing transaction costs and the increasing opportunity for firms in DEs to participate in international trade and access new markets. There has been relatively little work so far drawing these potential benefits out to a higher level, to understand how e-commerce may impact on the broader processes of socio-economic development. The theoretical and conceptual frameworks which have underpinned this work are transaction cost theory and the conceptual understanding of marketing (Pare 2003; Moodley & Morris, 2004). The studies (Wood, 2004; Madon, 2000) focusing on e-commerce and development have reviewed development theories, ideologies and approaches to propose a conceptual understanding of how development may be achieved.

Theme 2: Adoption and Diffusion

Table 4 shows sub-themes and theoretical frameworks used in studying issues relating to adoption and diffusion of e-commerce. At the sub-theme level, more work has so far been done on technological and interactional issues. Relatively less work has so far been done on the broader issues at a specifically managerial, organizational and wider level. Two major frameworks - the technology acceptance model (TAM), and diffusion of innovation theory – have been particularly used to provide the underpinning to this work. To a somewhat lesser extent, cultural frameworks and the theory of planned behavior/reasoned action have been used (though the latter feed the TAM). There are also more general frameworks such as

Table 3. Dominant theories within the "potential and constraints" theme

Reference	Sub-Theme (52 Articles, 21%)			Theory or Conceptual Framework			
	OP	AER	DV	TCT	MA	RDVT	TOE
Hu et al. (2004)		X		X			
Pare (2003)		X		X			
Moodley and Morris (2004)		X		X			
Lai et al. (2001)		X		X			
Sheth and Sharma (2005)	X				X		
Chao et al. (2003)	X				X		
Wood (2004)			X		X	X	
Madon (2000)			X			X	
Abd.Mukti (2000)		X					X
Total No. of Articles in Sub-Theme	19 (8%)	28 (11%)	5 (2%)				

Key: OP: Opportunity; AER: Assessment and E-readiness; DV: Development; TCT: Transaction Cost Theory; MA: Marketing; RDVT: Review of Development Theories

Table 4. Dominant theories within the "adoption and diffusion" theme

Reference	Sub-Theme (91 Articles, 37%)						Theory or Conceptual Framework					
	TC	MG	OG	CL	EV	IN	TAM	DOI	TOE	HOF	TPB	TRA
Al Sukkar and Hasan (2005)	X						X					
Al-Sabbagh and Molla (2004)	X						X					
Bolongkikit (2006)	X						X					
Brown and Molla (2005)	X						X					
Chan and Lu (2004)	X						X				X	
Cloete et al. (2002)			X				X					
Grandon and Pearson (2003)		X					X					
Kamel and Hassan (2003)	X						X					
Shang et al. (2005)	X						X					X
Shih (2004)	X						X					
Stylianou et al. (2003)						X	X					
Wu and Wang (2005)	X						X					
He et al. (2006)	X							X				
Hong and Tam (2006)	X							X				
Hung et al. (2003)	X							X				
Kamel and Hussein (2004)		X						X				
Looi (2005)	X							X				
Sia et al. (2001)	X							X				
Van Slyke et al. (2005)	X							X		X		
Ure (2002)	X							X				
Yu (2006)	X							X				
Gibbs and Kraemer (2004)						X			X			
Kuan and Chau (2001)						X			X			
Lertwongsatien and Wongpinunwatana (2003)						X			X			

Table 4. Dominant theories within the "adoption and diffusion" theme (continued)

Reference	Sub-Theme (91 Articles, 37%)						Theory or Conceptual Framework					
	TC	**MG**	**OG**	**CL**	**EV**	**IN**	**TAM**	**DOI**	**TOE**	**HOF**	**TPB**	**TRA**
Rotchanak-itumnuai and Speece (2003)						X			X			
Seyal et al. (2004)						X			X			
Xu et al. (2004)						X			X			
Zhu et al. (2004)						X			X			
Harris et al. (2005)				X						X		
Pavlou and Chai (2002)				X						X	X	
Singh et al. (2003)				X						X		
Thatcher et al. (2006)						X				X		
Yap et al. (2006)				X						X		
Brown et al. (2004)					X						X	
Grandon and Mykytyn (2004)	X										X	
Total No. of Articles in Sub-Themes	33 (13%)	11 (4%)		10 (4%)	10 (4%)	27 (11%)						

Key: TC: Technology; MG: Managerial; OG: Organizational; CL: Contextual; EV: Environmental; IN: Interactional: TAM: Technology Acceptance Model; DOI: Diffusion of Innovation Theory; TOE: Technology-Organizational-Environment Framework; HOF: Hofstede's Cultural Framework; TPB: Theory of Planned Behavior; TRA: Theory of Reasoned Action

"layered" models of technology-organization-environment. We may interpret this to say that, e-commerce in DEs research around adoption/diffusion has generally been fairly well conceptualized – work on the other two sub-themes would more often be rather a-conceptual. But this conceptualization has tended to follow the same conceptual "cow paths" as IS and e-commerce research more generally. There are few, if any, signs of the unique context and issues faced by e-commerce in DEs generating innovative conceptual ideas.

Theme 3: Support and Implementation

Table 5 analyses some key articles and overall distribution of sub-themes and theoretical frameworks used in studying operational issues – the

Table 5. Dominant theories within the "support and implementation" theme

Reference	Sub-Theme (102 Articles, 42%)						Theory or Conceptual Framework									
	STR	CB	DD	SEV	PP	KL	RBT	INT	AES	PNC	PFC	HOF	TAM	SEQ	TOE	N/A
Chiu et al. (2005)		X											X			
Gray and Sanzogni (2004)	X											X				
Grace-Farfaglia et al. (2006)			X									X				
Lim et al. (2006)					X											
Ganesh (2004)	X								X							
Jaw and Chen (2006)	X							X								
Chen and Ning (2002)	X									X						
Chen et al. (2004)	X										X					
Cui et al. (2006)	X						X									
Garcia-Murillo (2004)	X						X									
Montealegre (2002)	X						X									
Zhu and Kraemer (2005)	X						X								X	
Moeti et al. (2006)				X										X		
Jih et al. (2005)						X										X
Total No. of Articles in Sub-Themes	34 (24%)	8 (3%)	8 (3%)	11 (4%)	11 (4%)	5 (2%)										

Key: STR: Strategy; CB: Consumer Behavior; DD: Design and Development; SEV: Service Evaluation; PP: Public Policy; KL: Knowledge and Learning; RBT: Resource-Based Theory; INT: Internationalization Theories; AES: Adaptation-Evolution Strategies of Firms; PNC: Porter's National Diamond of Competitive Advantage; PFC: Porter's Five Forces Model; TAM: Technology Acceptance Model; TOE: Technology-Organizational-Environment Framework; HOF: Hofstede's Cultural Framework; N/A: None or Not Available support and implementation of e-commerce in DEs. The general pattern of the table results shows this to be a much more fragmented area of work than that in the previous two themes. A whole variety of issues has been covered, with a sense of critical mass only really being generated around e-commerce strategy. This is perhaps expected given the perceived importance of strategy in achieving, sustaining and institutionalizing e-commerce benefits; and given the dominant notion of strategy as a pre-hoc (i.e. early) managerial activity in e-commerce diffusion.

The more limited coverage of research sub-themes like consumer behavior, service evaluation, and knowledge and learning may perhaps be a reflection of the maturity of e-commerce in DEs, strategic orientation of the firms in DEs (their needs) and/or the scarcity of skills to develop and manage related e-commerce applications.

The dominant theoretical framework by far is resource-based theory (RBT) of the firm. As with other themes, this conceptualization picks up from the broader referent domains from which e-commerce research draws; particularly strategic management of information systems. It does not reflect the disciplinary interests that the particular developing economy context might impose.

DISCUSSION

In this section, we review research to-date on e-commerce in developing economies (DEs), drawing together some of the main research content and findings under the three themes identified.

Potential and Constraints

E-commerce, as a bundle of various ICTs, has been considered as one of the contributing answers to the apparent quest of developing economies for economic growth and development (UNCTAD, 2001; 2002). Academics and practitioners have debated several potential benefits of e-commerce in DEs. More often than not, reduction of transaction costs tends to be the emphasized benefit and also forms the basis of other interrelated potential benefits of e-commerce. The debate on e-commerce in DEs has therefore sought to explain, explore and give evidence for and/or against the potential of e-commerce in reducing the costs associated with transactions in the marketplace. As a result, transaction cost theory is the most commonly-used theory used in studying issues relating to assessment of e-commerce opportunities and evaluation of e-commerce benefits after implementation.

Transaction costs, described as "the costs of running a system" (Williamson, 1985, p. 19), consist of two types of costs: coordination costs and actor motivation costs (Garicano & Kaplan, 2001; Milgrom & Roberts, 1992 as cited in Pare, 2003). Coordination entails cost of searching for products, services, sellers, and buyers; negotiating and ensuring contract compliance and post contractual agreements; thus all the information and communication related costs before, during and after the transaction (Benjamin & Wigand, 1995; Wigand, Picot, & Reichwald, 1997, p. 19). Coordination costs can be categorized as (Wigand et al., 1997; Wigand, 1997): "(1) searching for products, services, sellers, and buyers; (2) negotiating and fulfilling a contract; (3) ensuring contract terms are met, and (4) adapting to contract changes during tenure of contract" (Pare, 2003, p. 124). Actor motivation costs are those deriving from incomplete or asymmetrical information and imperfect commitment, which affect decision-making, monitoring of performance, enforcement of compliance mechanisms, and thus lead to the loss of contracts and contractual disputes (Milgrom & Roberts, 1992; Pare, 2003).

Proponents of the perceived benefits of e-commerce to developing countries – who may be termed 'e-commerce optimists' (Moodley & Morris, 2004) – argue that firms seek to engage in transactions that economize on co-ordination costs (Williamson, 1981; Malone, Yates, & Benjamin, 1987). They assume that all DE firms have a potential choice of doing business electronically by integrating ICTs into their business processes. They argue that adoption and implementation of e-commerce can streamline and closely integrate transactional processes, and enable firms to potentially reduce the costs associated with pre- and post-contractual agreements (Malone et al., 1987, p. 484). E-commerce is argued to create a platform for more efficient inter-firm commercial transactions in which the constraints of transaction intermediaries and distance between buyers and sellers are relatively eliminated (Moodley, 2002a, p. 5). The aggregation of trading participants such as buyers, suppliers, sellers, manufacturers, and consumers in open marketplace-based trade and/or direct trade offer benefits of a diversity of products and services and possibly narrower price margins. This also contributes to lowering transaction costs in searching, intermediation and communication (Bakos, 1991; UNCTAD, 2001, pp. 111-113). In the view of e-commerce optimists (Goldstein & O' Connor, 2000; Mann 2000; UNCTAD, 2001; 2002; World Bank, 2001; WTO, 1998), firms in DEs gain the opportunity to participate in international trade and to access new and larger global markets. These benefits include improved access to more complete and timely information such as potential demand, customs regulations and import restrictions (WTO, 1998; Moodley & Morris, 2004).

On the other hand, some extant studies and empirical research in developing countries, (Chircu & Kaufman, 1999; Kraut, Steinfield, Chan, Butler & Hoag, 1999; Steinfield, Kraut & Plummer, 1995; Steinfield, Kraut & Chan, 2000; Pare, 2003) question the reality of benefits accrued from e-commerce. Though not entirely against the notion of the potential benefits of e-commerce in DEs, this set of views or propositions from 'e-commerce pessimists' (Moodley & Morris, 2004) question the conceptual and empirical evidence for propositions of the optimistic view. They argue that the perceived benefits stem from a technological deterministic view of ICTs (Genus & Nor, 2005). Such views – argue the pessimists – consider e-commerce as a set of 'technical entities' or even 'artifacts or simple appliances' (Sein and Harindranath, 2004) – the means to achieve something – and failing to recognize the complexity of their technological attributes in relation to their usage; particularly their usage in developing countries (Kling, 1999; Pare, 2000). The pessimists also argue that techno-centric conceptions of e-commerce fail to appreciate the "importance of the procedures and processes as well as the dynamics involved in transacting" (Pare, 2003, p. 125). E-commerce optimists are thus seen to have a relatively narrow view of transaction costs; failing to recognize the embeddedness of e-commerce in "a system of inter-related arenas (social, economic, cultural and technological arenas)" which impact on each other (Heeks & Wilson, 2000, p. 408) and, which in practice, may therefore constrain the benefits to be accrued from e-commerce within a development context.

First, consider transaction cost theory. As explained earlier, it consists of two types of costs: coordination and actor motivation costs. Optimistic accounts typically focus on reduction of co-ordination costs and therefore fail to expose the potential challenges which may arise from actor motivation costs in the contexts of DEs. More generally, DEs face technological, economic, legislative and cultural challenges which constrain the adoption of e-commerce and the delivery of e-commerce benefits (Mbarika & Okoli, 2003; Bajaj & Leonard, 2004). For example:

- Mbarika and Okoli (2003) in assessing e-commerce challenges in Sub-Saharan Africa, note the underdeveloped state of electronic payment systems and consumer preference for operating with cash rather than cheques and credit cards; a marketplace culture of bargaining and seeing products before purchase; and the existence of corruption and nepotism at all levels of society

which impact both ICT infrastructure and the costs and processes of transactions.
- Todaro and Smith (2003) draw attention to the absence or relative weakness of the legal system that enforces contracts and rules of loan repayment. The poor legal system increases the risk and reduces the confidence and commitment in electronic transactions and trading relationships.
- Frempong and Stark (2005) identify the lack of requisite telecommunication infrastructure and services which can facilitate Internet access and affordability beyond the urban areas to the rural areas in developing economies; thus limiting e-commerce roll-out.
- Institutional constraints make the coordination process complex and costly; hence information asymmetry is created, suppliers/sellers have narrow market reach, and buyers have a limited choice of products and services (Le, 2002, p. 114). With e-commerce embedded in any institutional context in which it is implemented, such constraints will in turn impact on the achievement e-commerce benefits.
- E-commerce is fundamentally about information, but developing economies suffer informational constraints. Thus, Milgrom and Roberts (1992, p. 32) note that the lack of complete and relevant information and its timely availability and accessibility negatively impacts on the overall decision-making and commitment in negotiating and fulfilling contracts.

Apart from these internal constraints, engaging in international trade brings on other challenges for DE firms. These include the inelasticities of supply and demand within the world commodity markets, meeting diverse export and product standards of export destinations, the unfair trading practices from the subsidization of products in some developed economies, and the likely increase in accessibility to local markets in DEs by firms in developed economies brought on by e-commerce (Todaro & Smith, 2003, p. 575; Molla & Taylor, 2006). All these issues make it much harder for DE firms to achieve benefits from e-commerce; in particular because they face challenges that lie well beyond their own individual sphere of action.

There is no contention against the potential of e-commerce to reduce the costs of searching for buyers, sellers and suppliers. However, to reduce other types of transaction costs, e-commerce has to be accompanied with services to improve marketplace information, to qualify and verify market participants (buyers, sellers, suppliers and consumers), to ensure contract compliance, and streamline offline activities such as transportation and delivery. Extant studies have emphasized that the relative reduction of transactional costs remains unattainable without the establishment of services including "payment/settlement mechanisms, insurance, logistic systems, inspection, certification of quality and customs clearance" alongside e-commerce (Pare, 2003, p. 125). The institutional constraints of DEs make the provision of these requisite services a major challenge and thereby stifle e-commerce benefits. They block DE firms from effective engagement with e-commerce and/or they force those firms into – often unequal – partnerships with established players.

Second, a single focus on the transactional approach makes DE firms lose sight of the potential strategic benefits they stand to gain through improved access to information. Extant studies in e-commerce show the predominant e-commerce applications used by firms in DEs were e-mail, for maintaining contacts with buyers and to accept product orders; and the Web, for obtaining general information about inputs and product markets. These applications contributed to an increase in revenues and profits by reducing communication – telephone – costs (ITC, 2001; McCormick & Kinyanjui, 2002; Moodley & Morris, 2004). A survey of garment exporters in Bangladesh, the Philippines, and Sri Lanka by the International Trade Center (ITC, 2001) revealed that e-mail was the only application used by these DE enterprises and most had never used the Internet to search for new suppliers. These firms tend to realize more operational benefits – operational synergy, timeliness, and reduction of operation costs – which translate into informational benefits – improved communication and relationships – and relatively strategic benefits including loyalty and retention of trading partners and improved revenue. These potential informational and strategic benefits could become a major incentive for DEs firms to adopt e-commerce other than just a single focus on transactional costs reduction and increased market access.

In effect, these and other similar studies appear to contradict the key propositions propounded by e-commerce optimists and rather give insights on other potential benefits that DE firms could and do seek from e-commerce. While there tends to be a mismatch between e-commerce rhetoric and the actual ICT capabilities of DE firms, the use of e-mail for inter-firm communication, information processing and to manage and support business and bilateral relationships between existing trading and channel partners, emphasize the potential strategic benefits that can be accrued (Moodley & Morris, 2004, p. 171). Additionally, this characteristic use of e-mail to enhance relationships with trading partners demonstrates the value DE firms tend to give to social relationships and networks in trade (Rauch, 2001). Previous studies have emphasized that 'physical' interpersonal relationships tend to influence the quality of electronic exchanges and transactions – in some situations the electronic transactions have been confined to only pre-existing 'physical' business relationships (Kraut et al., 1999). By considering the important role of social relationships within the economic exchanges in trade, DE firms seem to be adopting the appropriate ICT application solutions like e-mail to create such value by establishing interpersonal linkages and trust with trade partners. This further contributes to the strategic benefits DE firms may stand to obtain from e-commerce.

Transaction cost theory may provide an understanding of the potential benefits of e-commerce or doing business electronically in DEs. It also offers insight into some prerequisites such as supporting services like payment systems, legal systems and logistics necessary for creating these benefits, but what it actually fails to do is to prescribe solutions for DE firms to deal with their institutional constraints or even strategies to navigate around them and achieve e-commerce benefits. A knowledge gap exists between an understanding of benefits of e-commerce to DEs and the necessary strategies and solutions applicable by DE firms to navigate around the institutional constraints and challenges in their contexts. The knowledge being sought is not a bundle of conceptual frameworks defining what DEs firms should do, but more of a theoretically grounded and practically oriented understanding of e-commerce in DEs and how it can be achieved.

Third, we build on the earlier note that research on e-commerce in DEs have so far said little about the benefits e-commerce can contribute to broader socio-economic development (Heeks, 2000; Akel & Phillips, 2001; Wood, 2004). The link between e-commerce and development has been more focused on the benefits developing country firms can draw from e-commerce. However, the increasing number of developing country firms implementing various e-commerce solutions amidst national constraints (Montealegre, 2002; Wresch, 2003; Garica-Murillo, 2004) emphasizes the need for research to establish the macro-contribution of such initiatives in developing countries - at community, sectoral and national level. This becomes all the more important given the wider "ICTs for Development" (ICT4D) movement and investment, that specifically demands to understand the role of the new technologies in international development.

In summary, two particular knowledge gaps emerge from analysis of current literature. First, the need to develop a wider perspective on the potential benefits of e-commerce. This requires moving beyond the transaction costs perspective to determine the other strategic and informational benefits of e-commerce that firms in DEs can achieve; and moving beyond the firm level to second-order impacts. The second gap focuses on the need to develop a theoretically grounded and practically oriented understanding of how DE firms can address or navigate around the institutional constraints and challenges in their contexts to achieve the e-commerce benefits identified.

Adoption and Diffusion

Studies focused on this research theme have sought to understand the diffusion of e-commerce as an innovation by identifying factors which discriminate e-commerce adopters from non-adopters either at firm level, sector/industry level, or country level. Diffusion is "the social process by which an innovation is communicated through certain channels over time among members of a social system" (Rogers, 1995). Research to date on this theme has mainly been in the form of case studies on the diffusion of e-commerce in specific countries (Chen & Ning, 2002; Travica, 2002) or has taken a particular focus on e-commerce adoption at the firm, sector or industry level (Kamel & Hassan, 2003; Gunasekaran & Ngai, 2005; Molla & Licker, 2005b).

Within all these studies, several theoretical and conceptual frameworks have been used to examine the diffusion of e-commerce into DE context. Three major theories - diffusion of innovation, theory of planned behavior, and theory of reasoned action – tend to underpin this work, including work using the technology acceptance model (Ure, 2002; Al Sukkar & Hasan, 2005). These frameworks plus those at a broader managerial, organizational and environmental level will now be reviewed to determine means by which firms in DEs can overcome constraints and benefit from e-commerce.

Technology Adoption Frameworks

Technology adoption frameworks are those that address the technological related determinants of e-commerce adoption and diffusion at individual levels. They include the Technology Adoption Model (TAM) and Diffusion of Innovation theory (DOI). TAM has been used by both academics and practitioners as a means of predicting the measure of a system's success, whether or not that system is used (Morris & Dillion, 1997). The theory was formulated by Davis (1985) from the Theory of Reasoned Action (TRA) (Ajzen & Fishbein, 1980), as a "concise, complete reliable and valid model for predicting user acceptance" (Kamel & Hassan, 2003, p. 5). According to the TAM, the acceptance level of any technology is fundamentally affected by the user perception of ease of use and usefulness. Based on empirical evidence, TAM argues that increasing the perceived ease of use (PEOU) of a technology will increase its perceived usefulness (PU) and translate into an increased behavior intention (BI), thereby resulting in higher technology acceptance (Kamel and Hassan, 2003). Thus, PU is relatively not enough for adoption or usage - the adopter or user must also have a positive attitude toward it (Cloete, Courtney & Fintz, 2002; Shang, Chen & Shen, 2004).

However, other research (Davis, Bagozzi & Warshaw, 1989; Chau, 1996) also assert that the "influences of PEOU on PU diminish over time, as users become proficient with the target system" (Kamel & Hassan, 2003, p. 5). These researchers therefore argue that the concept is relevant in explaining some issues of user attitude and intention toward technology usage especially at the initial stages of deployment of the technology, but rather tends to be silent on the contextual influences such as culture.

In a study of the diffusion of electronic banking in Egypt, Kamel and Hassan (2003) employed the Technology Acceptance Model to study the level of customer acceptance of this e-commerce technology. The authors introduced an external attribute, trust, which with respect to e-banking payments and delivery channels and the cultural context of Egypt, had a potential influence on customer acceptance. The study showed that while it was necessary to provide customers with a convincing value proposition to obtain their target objectives, the banks also had to provide "easy-to-use trustful technology tools and delivery channels" and adapt such technologies to local values and culture of the society (Kamel & Hassan, 2003, p. 18). This supports the point just made that TAM offers an understanding on the importance of PEOU and PU as fundamental determinants of technology adoption, but it does not seem to sufficiently explain all the diverse contextual influences which can stem from issues like trust, values and culture within the different contexts of adoption.

In another study, Kamel and Hussein (2004) used diffusion of innovation (DOI) theory alongside TAM to evaluate the introduction of the Internet as a platform for commerce and business development in the King Hotel in Egypt. According to DOI (Rogers, 1983), the key influences on user acceptance behavior are relative advantage, complexity, compatibility, trialability, and observability (He, Duan, Fu & Li, 2006). The study showed that the lack of adequate infrastructure in the banking sector to handle online payments limited online reservations to e-mail reservations. As incentives, like 10% discount per reservation, were incorporated to promote e-mail reservations, occupancy rates increased appreciably despite the associated risk of unfulfilled reservations. On the other hand, the introduction of online reservations stirred some resistance among the employees; for example, the loss of some commission on the part of the sales manager was enough to create opposition to online reservations. There was also a lack of requisite human resource competencies in English, in understanding of the reservation system, and in basic computer literacy. The top management had to resort to implementing the online reservation system alongside the manual reservation system, the assistant manager taking charge of online reservations, and paying commissions to the sales manager, even for online reservations, for the first six months (Kamel & Hussein, 2004). Though these issues had to deal with poor understanding of the benefits of integrating the Internet with the Hotel's business processes, it brings to light that opposition to adoption that can occur when negative perceptions or unaddressed concerns of organizational members and top management exist.

The application of DOI showed that a single focus on PEOU and PU was not enough in dealing with issues arising from the complexity and compatibility of e-commerce with preferred work practices and existing technology in this DE setting. These technology adoption frameworks offer a technology-oriented understanding that attributes such as PEOU, PU, and compatibility of e-commerce are key drivers to adoption. But they tend to be particularly focused on the innovation and fail to address the other managerial behavior, organizational and environmental influences that facilitate or impede adoption. There is therefore a need to consider the attributes as suggested here alongside other influences that can facilitate initial adoption of e-commerce in developing countries.

Managerial and Organizational Adoption Frameworks

These frameworks address the managerial and other determinants of e-commerce adoption that lie in the internal context of the organization. The King Hotel case highlights an example of e-commerce adoption being partly facilitated by the IT knowledge and skills of top management, their innovativeness, and their perceived strategic value of e-commerce. These attributes underpin the explanation of innovation adoption as argued by managerial and organizational frameworks. Grandon and Mykytyn (2004) used Azjen's Theory of Planned Behavior (TPB) to develop a theory-based instrument for measuring the intention to adopt e-commerce among SMEs (in Chile). The theory, which is well-established and proven in the IS literature to explain and predict managers' behavioral intentions (Mykytyn & Harrison, 1993) is an extension of the Theory of Reason Action which hypothesizes that "behavior is influenced by an individual's intention to perform to the behavior in question" (Grandon & Mykytyn, 2004, p. 45). Thus, the behavior of adopting e-commerce (including possible institutionalization), is influenced by the intention to utilize e-commerce.

Previously, Azjen (1991) in explaining TPB posits that, "Intentions are assumed to capture the motivational factors that influence behavior" (p. 181). The factors that determine intention are the individual's attitude toward the behavior (A), the subjective norm (SN) and perceived behavior control (PBC). Attitude towards a behavior refers to "the degree to which a person has favorable or unfavorable evaluation of the behavior of the question" (Grandon & Mykytyn, 2004, p. 45):

- Attitude relates to the individual's perceptions of the behavior, the strategic value of e-commerce and its adoption. Cloete et al. (2002)'s study on e-commerce adoption among small businesses in the Western Province of South Africa emphasizes this motivational factor, in arguing that adoption of e-commerce was "heavily reliant on the acceptance of e-commerce by the business owner" (p. 4). This acceptance was also dependent on the owner's level of computer literacy and extent of knowledge about the application of technology in business processes.
- Subjective norm refers to "the perceived social pressure to perform or not to perform the behavior" (Grandon & Mykytyn, 2004, p. 45). In e-commerce one may consider this as pressure from competitors (directly or indirectly), social referents within the firm such as sales or IT departments and top management, and social referents outside the firm like peers within the sector, or government and e-commerce rhetoric and debates from academics, practitioners and the media.
- PBC refers to the individual's perceptions about the fact that there exist "personal and situational impediments to the performance of the behavior" (Grandon & Mykytyn, 2004, p. 45). Organizational attributes which may influence e-commerce adoption may include innovativeness, risk taking propensity, formalization, functional differentiation, and specialization (Damanpour, 1991). Rotchanakitumnuai and Speece (2003)'s study on the barriers to Internet banking adoption among corporate customers in Thailand identified that organizational barriers among non-adopters included the lack of technological and financial resources, the negative attitude of management (lack of their support and less risk taking propensity), and the lack of knowledge. The perception of managers about their internal organizational readiness to adopt e-commerce reflects their PBC.

The application of TPB offers a theoretical basis for the consideration of managerial and organizational attributes in e-commerce adoption. Other studies such as Cloete et al. (2002) and Khalfan and Alshawaf (2004) share similar conclusions even though the TPB was not used in the research. Cloete et al. (2002)'s study on e-commerce adoption among small businesses in the Western Province of South Africa notes that most SMEs are extremely cautious and hesitant in adopting e-commerce since they perceive benefits to be irrelevant or not appropriate to their organization and, moreover, because of the pressure (subjective norm) to show the return on investment (Iacovou, Benbasat, & Dexter, 1995; Akkeren & Cavaye, 1999). The study identified organizational characteristics as preferred organizational work practices and level of existing technology, and pressure from business competitors; and contextual characteristics as regard to the readiness of institutional foundations, and readiness of technology, legal, economic, political, and sociocultural foundations to support e-commerce. In effect, a manager's intention to adopt e-commerce would therefore be stronger if there was a more favorable attitude (perceived strategic value) and subjective norm (external pressure) with respect to the behavior, and a greater perceived behavioral control (organizational readiness) (Azjen, 1991). What is necessary is to determine measures that increase the internal readiness of the organization and equip them with strategic insight to address the influences in the environment.

However, though TPB manages to consider other essential perspectives of e-commerce adoption, it fails to provide the strategic means to effectively institutionalize e-commerce and exploit its benefits. We therefore continue to seek for such knowledge.

Environmental and Cultural Frameworks

These frameworks address the environmental and cultural determinants of e-commerce adoption and diffusion. Several environmental or external (to the organization) influences have been mentioned in the discussion above including the readiness of the organization or readiness of the institutional foundations, pressure from competitors and social referents like 'e-commerce optimists and pessimists', sector, industry and/or government policies, and related trade policies and regulations with regard to international trade. Singh and Gilchrist (2002) suggest a three-layer framework of e-commerce challenges in both developed and developing countries as consisting of the availability of infrastructure, availability of commercial services (similar to logistics and supporting services discussed under transaction cost theory), and trust. Governments of DEs have to work in partnership with firms in the country to address in these challenges. In terms of infrastructure, there is a need to provide basic telecommunication services and increase Internet access and affordability. With commercial services, the development and expansion of logistics and infrastructure is necessary, export procedures have to be streamlined and the requisite human resource has to be developed. With trust, property rights and trade policies and agreements have to be developed to meet international standards while matching domestic interests and supporting the export market and services (Singh & Gilchrist, 2002, p. 35-39).

Mbarika and Okoli (2003) address similar issues in a framework they developed to assess e-commerce in Sub-Saharan Africa. They argue that Sub-Saharan Africa is one of the least researched parts of the world with regard to ICT and IS-related research. The conceptual framework developed from the works of Zwass (1996), Wolcott, Press, McHenry, Goodman and Foster (2001) and Travica (2002) assess e-commerce diffusion in three main areas: sophistication of Internet use, telecommunication/Internet environments, and the traditional commercial infrastructure. A major contribution made by the framework in comparison with other frameworks discussed previously is the consideration of cultural and political issues that influence e-commerce adoption in Sub-Saharan Africa, including the underdeveloped state of electronic payment systems, and the existence of corruption and nepotism. These issues, as earlier explained, present diverse challenges in e-commerce adoption within countries in Sub-Saharan Africa. They also – unlike much of the work analyzed – bring us closer to a specific consideration of the 'DE' component of e-commerce-in-DEs research.

Based on related themes of the challenges within Sub-Saharan Africa, Bajaj and Leonard (2004) evaluated issues and possible solutions of culture, policy and technology (CPT) in promoting e-commerce readiness:

- With culture, the challenges in DEs as mentioned earlier are the trust between parties in a transaction and the trust of the parties in the institutions of the economy which may govern a transaction, corruption (including nepotism) within micro transactions (bribes) and within institutions (kickbacks and illegal payoffs), and preferences for patterns of communication in terms of face to face interaction (which facilitates more social interaction) vs. the more limited social interaction offered by e-commerce.
- Policy challenges relate to both general trade and commerce policy and to policies specific to e-commerce. Within many DEs specific e-commerce polices are necessary especially in relation to legality of electronic documents, electronic signature and electronic transactions.
- Technology challenges consider the level of technological infrastructure and human resources of requisite skill and expertise.

Bajaj and Leonard (2004) argue that it is important to realize the interrelationships between these dimensions of e-commerce challenges in order to define the practical solutions for them. For example, policy can influence culture as consumer protection laws are passed and strictly enforced to increase trust and reduce concerns about security of online transactions. Policy and technology can interrelate to influence culture when legislation is established for all e-commerce merchants to utilize safe technologies such as Secure Socket Layer (SSL) or escrow payments like PayPal for transactions. The enforcement of this regulation with severe punishments can help reduce corruption and increase the level of trust. Understanding these interrelationships tends to be critical in formulating solutions for e-commerce challenges (Bajaj & Leonard, 2004).

With a further emphasis on culture, previous studies using Hofstede's National Cultural Dimensions (Hofstede, 1985, 1991) argue that cultures with greater power distance - greater hierarchy amongst members – will face greater difficulty when transacting on the Internet (Van Slyke; Bélanger, & Sridhar, 2005; Bajaj & Leonard, 2004). These include Arab countries, Mexico, and West Africa. For the effective implementation of an e-commerce initiative, higher-level members of the hierarchy must understand or be committed to the initiative. Prior IT-business knowledge and understanding of top management or leadership of an institution would therefore be a critical resource to the adoption and institutionalization process. Additionally, countries with a low degree of individualism or with rich interpersonal communication culture like India and West Africa consider face to face interaction to be essential part of communication. In such contexts, interpersonal or social relationships are more likely to influence electronic transactions. For example in India, some merchants incorporated product review functionalities on their Websites where customer comments were published. This offered potential buyers the assurance that they are not alone and that they belong to a family of buyers (Van Slyke et al., 2005). Hence, forming bridges between virtual and physical relationships, or developing e-commerce applications around social relationships becomes a necessary consideration.

In effect, cultural and environmental challenges bring to focus the external issues that an organization has to contend with in adopting and possibly institutionalizing e-commerce. But what happens if all the constraints of these challenges are removed or reduced and the organization still lacks the technical knowledge, expertise, innovativeness and strategic insight to adopt e-commerce? The above perspectives - technological, managerial, organizational and environmental - though discussed separately, do interrelate in facilitating or inhibiting e-commerce adoption within organizations in DEs. Any model capable of addressing all these interrelated perspectives or challenges has to be holistic, addressing internal readiness of the organization and external readiness of the context. However, the objective is not to just determine or obtain an all-encompassing framework, but also to determine a framework that offers a strategic insight in enabling the DE firms to address the challenges or navigate around the constraints to achieve e-commerce benefits.

Interactionism Frameworks

Interactionism frameworks are theoretical frameworks and conceptual models that consider all the different perspectives or imperatives in determining the attributes of e-commerce adoption. They bring into focus the interrelationships between all the perspectives into one dynamic framework (Molla & Licker, 2005b), and therefore seek to explain the interrelationships between internal influences in the organizations and external influences in the context and the differences in performance of firms operating in identical contextual situations (Jarvernpaa & Leidner, 1998; Montealegre, 1999).

One well-established framework within this perspective is Technology-Organization-Environment framework (TOE), developed by Tornatzky and Fleischer (1990) as a comprehensive framework for identifying the factors of innovation adoption. The framework posits that the three contexts; technological, organizational and environmental contexts determine the discriminating factors of the adoption of a technological innovation. The technological context refers to the internal and external technologies that are relevant to an organization in facilitating its business processes and creating value. This includes those that are internally available to the firm by a form of ownership, and those that are externally available in the market by a form of acquisition, purchase or lease. Organizational context refers to similar attributes as described under the organizational imperative including formalization and complexity of management structure, availability of requisite human resources, and the slack resources available to the firm internally. In a similar relation to the environmental imperative, the environmental context refers to the external context in which the firm operates. Influences from this context include pressure from competitors and social referents, accessibility and readiness of resources provided by the institutional foundations including regulatory policies, economic and technological infrastructure. The interrelationships between these contexts determine factors which discriminate adopters from non-adopters (Tornatzky & Fleischer, 1990, pp. 152-154).

A review of studies on the TOE framework by Zhu, Kraemer and Xu (2003) showed that the framework is empirically well established in researching information system innovations. Within e-commerce, it has been used as a theoretical framework for empirical studies on EDI adoption (Iacovou et al. 1995; Chwelos, Benbasat, & Dexter, 2001; Kuan & Chau, 2001) and e-business (Xu et al., 2004). It thus has a proven "solid theoretical basis and consistent empirical support" (Xu et al., 2004, p. 14). In the studies on developing economies, the framework either focused on investigating factors of innovation adoption in different firms in a particular context or different firms in different contexts. Kuan and Chau (2001) adopted the TOE framework in investigating the factors influencing EDI adoption among small business in Hong Kong. For the technology factor, they considered the perceived direct and indirect benefits of EDI; the organization factor focused on perceived financial costs and perceived technical competence, which reflects the readiness of the organization; and the environment factor considered the industry and perceived government pressure. The study showed that EDI adoption was influenced by the three factors with organizational readiness and external (environmental) pressure being the most important (Kuan & Chau, 2001; Grandon & Pearson, 2004).

Xu et al. (2004) cross-country study on e-business adoption by companies in the United States and China yielded comparable findings to that of Kuan and Chau (2001). In this study, the technology context focused on technology competence including the use of e-business technologies and availability of IT professionals; the organizational context considered firm size (a mix of resource advantages and structural inertia), global scope, and enterprise integration; and the environmental context focused on competition intensity and the regulatory environment. The study showed that as "firms moved into the deeper stages of e-business transformation, the key determinants shift from technology infrastructure to organizational capabilities" (Xu et al., 2004, p. 21). Organizational capabilities become more critical as the organization moved from adoption into institutionalization or *deeper integration* of e-commerce.

This reinforces the findings from the King Hotel case study and related earlier discussions in this chapter. Depending on the economic environment certain structural variables like firm size could also influence the readiness of the organization and the complexity of adoption which could also affect the potential benefits of e-business. For example, within the study it was realized that large firms in DEs tend to have a potential advantage in adopting and institutionalizing e-commerce over small firms in the same context. This is because, unlike small firms of DEs, the negative effect of the structural inertia possessed by large firms in DEs tends to be neutralized by their associated resource advantages. Therefore, depending on the availability of requisite resources (including human resource) for e-commerce, the large size of firms did not relatively impede e-commerce adoption. Though small firms may be relatively more likely to engage in initial efforts to adopt e-commerce (Wresch, 2003), the institutionalization of the innovation in these firms depends on their resource profile. These findings relate to those of Riquelme (2002), whose empirical study compared business use of the Internet among small, medium and large businesses in China.

However, though TOE seems to comprehensively bring together most of the perspectives of e-commerce adoption in one dynamic framework; managerial attributes are addressed within the organizational factor which makes it a lesser consideration as it *competes* with the major attributes of the organization which influence e-commerce. Other studies have therefore built upon the basic concepts of the TOE framework and added managerial attributes to study e-commerce adoption (Grandon & Pearson, 2004) and in some cases, address both e-readiness and e-commerce adoption (Molla & Licker, 2005b).

Grandon and Pearson (2004) studied and ranked factors that differentiate adopters and non-adopters of e-commerce among small and medium sized enterprises in different industries pursuing e-commerce initiatives in Chile. Among the eight factors (including TOE) studied, the significant discriminating factors were ranked as organizational readiness, managerial productivity, external pressure, decision aids, compatibility and perceived usefulness. To measure organizational readiness they used availability of financial and technological resources, as used previously by Iacovou et al. (1995) to study the adoption of EDI. Variables used to study managerial productivity included improved information access, improved time management and improved communication. To measure external pressure, they considered direct or indirect pressure from competitors, social referents including government and industry. The study suggested that Chilean managers who were most likely to adopt e-commerce:

- possessed necessary financial and technological resources,

- perceived e-commerce as improving managerial productivity and supporting strategic decision-making,
- were externally pressured by competition, social referents and industry but insignificantly by the government, and
- perceived e-commerce as compatible with preferred work practices and existing technology infrastructure.

Perceived usefulness was the least significant discriminating factor with only two out of six variables - perception that e-commerce enhanced job effectiveness and made work easier - being significant variables. The study concluded that availability of financial and technological resources still remains a major challenge for SMEs in DEs and educating managers was critical since changing their beliefs was a prerequisite to changing their behaviors towards e-commerce.

Molla and Licker (2005b) developed the Perceived E-Readiness Model (PERM) as a "multi-perspective audit of managerial, internal organization, and external contextual issues" which provides *meaningful predictors* of e-commerce adoption (p. 879). The model consists of two constructs – Perceived Organizational E-Readiness (POER) and Perceived External E-Readiness (PEER). POER consist of technological imperative attributes (organization's perception, comprehension and projection of e-commerce and its potential benefits); managerial imperative attributes (managerial commitment); and key organizational imperative attributes (organizational resources, processes and business infrastructure). PEER refers to environmental imperative factors: the organization's assessment and evaluation of its external environment factors (Molla and Licker, 2005b, p. 879). The authors argue that the constructs are to be used in predicting and explaining discriminating factors of e-commerce adoption.

In applying this model as an instrument in a survey of South African businesses, Molla and Licker (2005b) defined variables in measuring these constructs as follows. They considered POER as the degree to which managers believed that their organization had the awareness, resources, commitment, and governance to adopt e-commerce. PEER was defined as the degree to which managers believed that market forces, government and support industries were ready to support e-commerce adoption in the organization. E-commerce adoption was measured as the extent of adoption which was considered in relation to two stages: initial adoption – the organization having *achieved* an interactive e-commerce status; and institutionalization – the organization having *attained* (extent of utilization) an interactive, transactive or integrated e-commerce status. The study concluded that, for the initial adoption stage of e-commerce, organizational attributes especially human, business and technological resources and awareness are more influential factors, and "as organizations adopt e-commerce practices, the advantages from resources become less important" and environmental factors, together with commitment from managers and the governance model that organizations implement affect institutionalization (Molla & Licker, 2005b, p. 887). Organizations that are able to move into adoption and institutionalization and exploit e-commerce to achieve benefits are those that refuse to accept the limitations of their environment (external) context or wait for it to become e-ready. However, these firms with "dynamic capabilities, committed leaders and business resources" manage to strategically develop and deploy e-commerce models which work within the constraints of their environment (Molla & Licker, 2005b, p. 888). This may be a particularly significant approach to e-commerce in DEs research, since it offers an insight beyond the simple equation of DE implementation with higher levels of constraints than found in developed country environments.

The combination of these constructs in evaluating the extent of e-commerce adoption makes the PERM model one among a very few interactionism models that manage to consider all the attributes of e-commerce adoption including internal organizational and managerial readiness. The conclusions of Molla and Licker (2005b) are similar to those of Kuan and Chau (2001), Grandon and Pearson (2004) and Xu et al. (2004). They emphasize the importance of organizational resources in initial stages of e-commerce adoption, and the essence of the commitment of managers and their strategic insight in developing and deploying dynamic capabilities to institutionalize e-commerce and exploit its benefits amidst the constraints of their environmental context. As these models and their application in e-commerce in DEs research continue to make a case for the availability of organization resources, managerial commitment and strategic insight, and dynamic capabilities, the principal question is how to create these within the organization and utilize them to achieve e-commerce benefits.

Is there a model or framework that provides organizations with the strategic insight of developing, deploying and managing organizational resources and capabilities, and that enables them navigate around the constraints of their context and achieve e-commerce benefits? The above frameworks tend to lack such orientation. They are effective in helping organizations to identify the discriminators (attributes) of e-commerce adoption among adopters and non-adopters, but they fail to give any strategic insight or guidance on how to develop, manage and deploy these attributes to realize e-commerce benefits.

Support and Implementation

After gaining an understanding of the diverse contextual challenges which firms in DEs face in their attempt to adopt e-commerce and obtain its benefits, the objective is to now move to strategy, and to review theoretical frameworks which offer strategic guidance to DE firms on exploiting the benefits of e-commerce amidst their diverse contextual influences.

As compared to literature on the potential benefits, constraints and diffusion/adoption of e-commerce in developing countries, there has been relatively little offering strategic guidance. In pure numbers, the research and literature addressing strategy at the firm-level forms about 14 percent (34 articles) of the articles reviewed. This is a limited number but still enough to be considered some type of critical mass. However, in reviewing the literature in more details – both more conceptual (Wresch, 2003) and more empirical (Gunasekaran & Ngai, 2005) – we find it more oriented to investigating discriminating factors between initial adopters and non-adopters. The research thus offers some generic critical success factors but it fails to give clear strategic guidance on how to develop and deploy these factors in order to achieve e-commerce success.

Chen, Lin, Li and Chen (2004) used Porter's five competitive forces model in a case study of a Chinese company, Haier. Though the study offers some insight on how e-business contributes to competitive advantage it seems to be more of an analysis of the company's business and market chain management model. In another related study on the same company, Li and Chang (2004) developed a holistic, dynamic and dialectical conceptual framework for e-business strategy. The study focused on the adoption and use of network application solutions like customer relationship management, supply chain management, and enterprise resource planning. Though this made the developed framework more orientated towards e-business, the case study analysis generated some critical lessons applicable to the generic paradigm of e-commerce in DEs. The study showed that DE firms adapting business models from developed countries have to adapt those models to their local conditions. Strategic alliance with foreign partners is considered a necessary imperative for the effective implementation of e-business strategies and it is also essential for them to build in-house information systems capabilities before initiating e-business programs (Li & Chang, 2004). The lessons contributed by Li and Chang (2004)'s study thus relate to the concept *organizational readiness* (in-house IS capabilities) and to *strategic insight of managers* (adaptation of business models and strategic alliance), both of which were already identified from the earlier review of adoption and diffusion literature.

Resource-Based Frameworks

As concluded from earlier discussions, the way forward for a significant contribution to e-commerce research in DEs is to define how organizations can exploit resources to achieve the relative benefits of e-commerce. However, from the above reviews and other numerous studies on e-commerce in developed countries (Zwass, 1996; Wigand, 1997; Vadapalli & Ramamurthy, 1998; Ngai & Wat, 2002), there is comparatively little research conducted on how organizations develop, deploy and manage, resources and capabilities to realize e-commerce benefits (Montealegre, 2002). A prevailing paradigm for understanding how and why firms develop the capability to gain and sustain competitive advantage and, moreover, adapt and even capitalize on rapidly changing technological environments is *Resource-Based Theory* (RBT) or the *Resource-Based View of the firm* (RBV) (Mahone & Pandian, 1992; Schendel, 1994) and its later extension, the dynamic capabilities approach (Teece, Pisano & Shuen, 1997).

Studies on e-commerce in DEs (Montealegre, 2002; Garcia-Murillo, 2004; Zhu and Kramer, 2005; Cui, Zhang, Zhang & Huang, 2006) have utilized this conceptual foundation to investigate the strategic development of organizational resources and dynamic capabilities to aid e-commerce adoption and the achievement of e-commerce benefits. Garcia-Murillo (2004) used the theory in studying institutions and e-commerce adoption in Mexico. Montealegre (2002) used RBT in studying e-commerce strategy (adoption and implementation of e-commerce) in a stock exchange company in Ecuador. Zhu and Kramer (2005) used RBT alongside TOE in assessing diffusion and post-adoption variation in the usage and value of e-business by organizations across ten countries including Mexico, Taiwan, and Brazil. Cui et al. (2006), used RBT alongside the process-oriented model (Soh & Markus, 1995) to investigate the impact of environmental resources – government regulation policies and e-government actions – on Shanghai firms' IT usage and e-business practices.

We consider resources as the "assets and capabilities that are available and useful in detecting and responding to market opportunities" (Wade & Hulland, 2004, p. 109). Assets are anything tangible or intangible which a firm uses in "its processes for creating, producing, and/or offering its products (goods or services) to a market, whereas capabilities are repeatable patterns of actions in the use of assets to create, produce, and/or offer products to a market" (Sanchez, Heene & Thomas, 1996 as cited in Wade and Hulland, 2004, p. 109). Resources are controlled by the firm and enable the firm to conceive and implement strategies which improve its efficiency and effectiveness (Barney, 1991). Assets can be classified as tangible, intangible and personnel-based resources (Grant, 1991). Tangible assets include the financial capital and the physical assets of the firm such as plant, equipment, and stocks of raw materials. Intangible assets comprise of assets such as reputation, brand image, and product quality; and personnel-based (or organizational) assets include technical know-how, managerial commitment knowledge and skills, organizational culture, employee training, and loyalty (Bharadwaj, 2000). Assets are assembled, integrated and deployed within business processes to form the capabilities which an organizations uses to improve its efficiency and effectiveness (Grant, 1991; Makadok, 2001).

Capabilities can be classified as being operational or dynamic. Operational capabilities, also known as ordinary or 'zero-level' capabilities are "those that permit a firm to 'make a living' in the short-term", while dynamic capabilities are those that "operate to extend, modify or create ordinary capabilities" (Winter, 2003, p. 991). The distinction between the forms of capabilities stems from the fact that the traditional resource-based view was limited to relatively stable environments (Leonard-Barton, 1992). Hence, Barney (1997) warned that, "if a firm's threats and opportunities change in a rapid and unpredictable manner, the firm will often be unable to maintain a sustained competitive advantage" (p. 171). This stirred up researchers to focus on the specifics of how organizations can develop capabilities and renew them to respond to shifts in the business environment. Dynamic capabilities, from the dynamic capabilities approach (Teece et al., 1997), was therefore "an extension of the resource-based view of the firm that was introduced to explain how firms can develop their capability to adapt and even capitalize on rapidly changing technological environments" (Montealegre, 2002, p. 516). They are developed through the appropriate adaptation, integration, and reconfiguration of internal and external organizational assets, capabilities and business processes to respond to the dynamic business environment (Teece et al., 1997).

From a strategic management viewpoint, resource-based theory posits that by possessing assets and capabilities that are valuable, rare, imitable, and not-strategically substitutable, an organization can create and sustain a competitive advantage or achieve a performance beyond that of its competitors in the marketplace (Barney, 1991; Teece et al., 1997). Being rare and valuable is not enough, an organization has to be able to build its assets and dynamically orient its capabilities to become imitable and not-strategically substitutable. For an asset or capability to become imitable and not-strategically substitutable, three conditions must be fulfilled; firstly, availability of the functionality or capability to the organization should be due to its unique historical conditions – because of a specific occurrence or situation in the history of organization; secondly, the link between resources and the firm's sustained competitive advantage or sustained performance is causally ambiguous; and lastly, resources themselves are socially complex in nature (Barney, 1991; Teece et al., 1997).

The notion of resources and dynamic capabilities as proposed by RBV is similar to that proposed by findings from the review of innovation diffusion, e-readiness, and strategy related literature on e-commerce in DEs. The use of RBV in the e-commerce paradigm relates to creating a sustained performance for DE firms and not particularly focused entirely on competitive advantage. Garcia-Murillo's (2004) research drew upon institutional economics as a theoretical framework for understanding the reasons why individuals and societies can or cannot change their behavior to accommodate new technologies. However, the theory was weak in providing suggestions to overcome the obstacles or exploit existing resources to obtain benefit from these technologies. Hence, RBV was introduced to provide a better framework for helping explain the strategies that Mexican firms were adopting in their efforts to implement e-commerce technologies. Within this perspective, Garcia-Murillo (2004) explores Porter's (1990) recommendations on strategies to make firms more competitive including engaging in innovation; seeking out capable competitors as motivators; forming domestic industrial clusters; tapping selective advantages in other countries; and using alliances only selectively (p. 205). The author criticizes some of these recommendations for assuming that a company is already well-established and has the resources to engage in the creation of *strong industrial clusters* or that they have *strategic capital to offer to potential allies*. The study concludes with recommendations including generating demand, educating potential clients, generating income from alternative businesses, and taking advantage of resources abroad. Example of initiatives being employed included Mexican firms taking advantage of hosting services in the United States in the absence of a reliable ICT infrastructure, a retail software store complementing its physical presence with a Website, and a company promoting ICT diffusion into homes and businesses by providing consumers with a computer and an Internet connection. In effect, these firms – by trying to address their internal resource poverty - had an attendant effect on the resource poverty in their context or country.

Only the last – taking advantage of resources abroad – mirrors what Porter recommends. The gap between these emerging or new strategies and Porter's recommendations suggests that as organizational business practices evolve with their changing business environments, more research is needed to redefine existing knowledge to be more consistent and applicable with the dynamic nature of the environment. It also indicates that, compared to firms in developed countries, firms in DEs tend to operate in more uncertain environments where assumptions and recommendations of business models of developed countries tend to be a mismatch or less applicable to DE realities (Bajaj & Leonard, 2004).

Montealegre (2002) makes an argument for the development of more process-oriented models when utilizing RBT, specifically with regards to e-commerce research. Previous studies have followed a factor-oriented model (Garcia-Murillo, 2004) or variance theory approach (McGrath, Tsai, Venkataraman & MacMillan, 1996; Miyazaki, 1995; Oliver, 1997). Montealegre's (2002) study developed a process model of capability development consisting of the *capability to strategies*, *capability to be flexible*, *capability to integrate*, and *capability to engender trust*. The model notes that dynamic capability development is a cumulative and expansive process where path dependency matters, and thus needs to be strategically planned. These strategic steps thus offer the strategic guidance on how to develop organizational assets and capabilities and dynamically orient them to implement e-commerce and relatively exploit its benefits. This can be related to the attributes of the Mexican firms described in Garcia-Murillo (2004)'s study. However, since capability development is a path-dependent process and no universal sources of advantage exist (Barney, 1997), additional study is required to understand fully the dynamics of resource development and the extent to which the findings of Garcia-Murillo (2004) and Montealegre (2002) can be generalized for firms in DEs.

In another RBT related study, Zhu and Kramer (2005) moved beyond the usual focus on discriminating factors of adoption to address the knowledge gap about how value is created after adoption. The study employed the TOE and RBT frameworks to investigate the contextual influences on e-business use and value creation among firms in developed and developing economies. Using the TOE framework, the study concludes that though e-business was a globally adoptable innovation, "its use is moderated by local environments" – thus emphasizing the relatively significant influence of TOE contexts on e-commerce institutionalization, and also confirming findings of Molla and Licker (2005b)'s study. The RBT framework demonstrated that "while both front-end and back-end capabilities contribute to e-business value, back-end integration has a much stronger impact" (Zhu and Kramer, 2005, p. 61). Front-end capabilities are e-business functionalities that "provide product information to consumers on the Internet, facilitate transaction processing, and enable customization and personalization"; and back-end integration refers to e-business functionalities that "link Web applications with back-office databases and facilities information sharing along the value chain" (Zhu and Kraemer, 2005, p. 66). These findings demonstrate the use of RBT in differentiating the value creation abilities of different organizational capabilities and they offer strategic direction on what may be critical to an organization. The researchers argue that the integration of the two models is an initial step towards understanding the complex relationships among technology, environments and organizational performance and thus necessitates further research to refine application of both theories in this interrelationship.

We may summarize that both TOE and RBT are critical frameworks that have potential value in contributing a theoretically-grounded and practical-oriented understanding to research on e-commerce adoption, institutionalization and value creation in DEs. RBT tends to give the strategic guidance required for the effective and efficient development and utilization of resources to achieve e-commerce benefits. This notion of the strategic importance of organizational resources is also emphasized by other studies (Riquelme, 2002; Wresch, 2003) in which RBT was not the underpinning framework. This, then, can be one of the major or perhaps the major developing theme in e-commerce in DEs research – one which *shifts focus from the benefits of e-commerce to the resources* that individual organizations (small, medium or large) have to achieve and exploit those benefits. However, there exist some gaps of knowledge in RBT-related literature which new research can fill by adopting RBT as its underpinning framework. Within information systems research, RBT has enjoyed very little discussion as compared to vigorous debates on the theory in strategic management and other management disciplines. In a review of RBT in IS, Wade and Hulland (2004) made eight propositions to guide future research using a resource-based view of IS.

Of notable concern to this present research review, is the question of whether IS resources (like IS infrastructure and technical skills), which have gained much focus IS literature, must interact with other constructs – non-IS resources (like firm reputation, and brand) to create e-commerce benefits. We have made arguments in our earlier discussions about the way that social and interpersonal relationships influence electronic transactions and the diffusion of e-commerce innovations. Future research exploring how such non-IS resources interact with IS resources to create e-commerce benefits will be a welcome contribution to knowledge.

Another concern which has been emphasized in strategic management literature is that previous research has blurred distinctions between resources that help firms *attain* and those that help firms *sustain* competitive advantage (or performance). Empirical research is thus considered as being critical to provide an understanding of "how firms get to be good, how they sometimes stay that way, why and how they improve and why they sometimes decline" (Teece et al., 1997). Moreover, little research has been done with the theory in respect of e-commerce in DEs – just four studies (Montealegre, 2002; Garcia-Murillo, 2004; Zhu and Kraemer, 2005; Cui et al., 2006). Hence, claims cannot be made very strongly as yet about resources or dynamic capability development for firms in DEs until further research has been done. Capability development is a lengthy, complex process influenced by multiple organizational dimensions which can make a definite path of development difficult to define (Montealegre, 2002). An understanding is thus being sought on a generalizable path of dynamic capability development defined by steps which consist of factors which are firm-specific. These gaps in the literature thus make the expected knowledge contribution of such research critical to both firms in developing and developed economies.

CONCLUSION

This chapter carried out a review of research on e-commerce in DEs to ascertain the current state of research and indicate the gaps of knowledge yet to be explored and addressed. Amidst the ongoing discourse on e-commerce's potential, the diversity of research issues and theoretical frameworks employed give evidence of the efforts of DE firms to circumvent the constraints in their context and exploit the potential of e-commerce. However, what tends to be lacking in research is, first, a wider perspective of potential benefits of e-commerce and relative e-commerce applications that can help achieve that. Literature on e-commerce potential and constraints in DEs has particularly focused on the potential firm-level opportunities and benefits, as compared to the contribution of e-commerce to development and means by which this may be achieved. A focus on how e-commerce can impact on development could also open more opportunities for firms to develop context-specific (and *relevant*) solutions and influence the resource poverty in their countries. There is also the need to explore other interrelated strategic and informational benefits which these firms can achieve from e-commerce.

The second gap focuses on the need to develop a theoretically grounded and practically oriented understanding of how DE firms can address or navigate around the institutional constraints and challenges in their contexts to achieve e-commerce benefits. As noted by this review, most literature on e-commerce in DEs tend to have been rather silent in addressing the issue of offering strategic guidance to DE firms to handle their institutional constraints and move beyond adoption to institutionalize e-commerce into organizational routine and processes. Xu et al. (2004) argue, "… such a restrictive view does not completely capture the reach and richness of the use of IT innovations" (p. 14). There is therefore the "…need to better understand how organizations facilitate and promote innovation and creativity in the use and application of IT to achieve strategic success as well as operational excellence" (Ritu Agarwal as cited in Lee, 2001, p. xiv). This requires moving beyond e-commerce adoption and diffusion, and investigating e-commerce institutionalization (Molla & Licker, 2004), or the extent of e-commerce adoption (Xu et al., 2004), in order to determine the strategic measures or paths through which DE firms achieve e-commerce benefits.

Consequently, reflecting on this study and the rapid real-world growth of e-commerce in DEs, we make a case that, first, e-commerce in DEs research seems to be a highly active area of research and one that is growing very quickly. Second, while there is undoubtedly research work published that lacks quality and rigor, we note that research on e-commerce in DEs is being published in top e-commerce and IS journals. Consequently, we see this as a research area with a vibrant future, both from an academic and from a practitioner-engagement perspective.

Third, while there is work that lacks conceptualization, a significant number of articles reviewed were grounded in conceptual and theoretical frameworks. This broadens the contribution each research item can make; increases its academic relevance and likelihood of citation; and most-likely increases the chances of publication. Having said this, the conceptual foundations are very much the "usual suspects" for those familiar with the IS domain. There is little innovation shown in selection of these foundations; and particularly – given that e-commerce in DEs research can be seen to sit at the confluence of the information systems and development studies domain, there is very little use of development studies ideas, or language, let alone theory.

This relates to our fourth point – the lack of a broad development perspective on benefits of e-commerce. This is a concern for at least two reasons. First, because strategists in government and in international development agencies will attend most to research linking e-commerce to national development goals. The absence of such research helps explain, to some extent, the relative lack of progress on contextual e-readiness. Second, because it then tends to exclude e-commerce from the broader ICT for development research and practice community. This will, for example, hamper the diffusion of e-commerce within micro-enterprise, and within enterprises in poor communities, since both of those have been the natural domain of interest and action by the ICT for development community.

In terms of "most-valued" conceptual foundations, there appears to be two. In relation to understanding adoption/diffusion, interactionism frameworks – such as PERM (Molla & Licker, 2005b) – appear to have helped to integrate the findings of more narrowly-focused research. We would therefore recommend further application and development of such frameworks for e-commerce-in-DE research. In relation to understanding strategic priorities for organizations, there seems to be mileage in using RBT. In particular, researching e-commerce in the DE context may offer a unique insight and development of RBT – an understanding of the way in which organizations and entrepreneurs in resource-poor environments can act to overcome that resource poverty. Put another way, development of this theme of research may offer insights into one of Porter's key findings – the way in which resource poverty may be a constraint for some organizations, but a spur to innovation for some other organizations.

Though not exhaustive, the attempt by this review to identify theoretical frameworks and approaches of e-commerce in DEs research has yielded several important implications and reasonable insights that can guide researchers in future research.

LIMITATIONS

This study was based on a survey of 76 journals from a diversity of disciplines related to information systems research and research in DEs. Conference papers, masters and doctoral dissertations, textbooks, unpublished working papers and commentaries and reviews of books were excluded in the search of journal databases to collect data. Future related reviews may go beyond nine academic databases and 76 journals to exhaustively cover the different disciplinary perspectives used to study e-commerce in developing economies. Extending themes or adopting other e-commerce/e-business conceptualizations and classifications to include the different business models, infrastructure and research methodologies employed in literature and research in e-commerce in DEs may contribute more knowledge and further understanding.

REFERENCES

Abd.Mukti, N. (2000). Barriers to Putting Business on the Internet in Malaysia. *Electronic Journal on Information Systems in Developing Countries, 2*(6), 1-6.

Abernathy, W. J. & Clark, K. B. (1978). Patterns of Industrial Innovation. *Technology Review, 80*(7), 40-47.

Abhilash, C. M. (2002). E-Commerce Law in Developing Countries: An Indian Perspective. *Information and Communication Technology Law, 11*(3), 269-281.

Agboola, A.A.A. (2006). Electronic Payment Systems and Tele-banking Services in Nigeria, *Journal of Internet Banking and Commerce, 11*(3).

Ainin, S., Lim, C. H. & Wee, A. (2005). Prospects and Challenges of E-banking in Malaysia. *Electronic Journal on Information Systems in Developing Countries*, *22*(1), 1-11.

Akel, M. & Phillips, R. (2001). The Internet Advantage: A Process For Integrating Electronic Commerce Into Economic Development Strategy. *Economic Development Review, 17*(3), 13-19.

Akkeren, J. & Cavaye, A. (1999). *Factors Affecting the Adoption of E-commerce Technologies by Small Business in Australia – An Empirical Study*, Australian Computer Society. Retrieved

November 30, 2005, from http://www.acs.org.au/act/events/io1999/akkern.html.

Al Sukkar, A. & Hasan, H. (2005). Toward a Model for the Acceptance of Internet Banking in Developing Countries. *Information Technology for Development, 11*(4), 381-398.

Al-Sabbagh, I. & Molla, A. (2004). Adoption and Use of Internet Banking in the Sultanate of Oman: An Exploratory Study. *Journal of Internet Banking and Commerce, 9*(2).

Aladwani, A. M. (2003). Key Internet Characteristics and E-commerce Issues in Arab Countries. *Information Technology and People, 16*(1), 9-20.

Aljifri, H. A., Pons, A. & Collins, D. (2003). Global E-commerce: A Framework for Understanding and Overcoming the Trust Barrier. *Information Management and Computer Security, 11*(2/3), 130-1358.

Ang, C., Tahar, R. M. & Murat, R. (2003). An Empirical Study on Electronic Commerce Diffusion in Malaysian Shipping Industry. *Electronic Journal on Information Systems in Developing Countries, 14*(1), 1-9.

Arunachalam, S. (1999). Information and Knowledge in the Age of Electronic Communication: A Developing Country Perspective. *Journal of Information Science, 25*(6), 465-476.

Asuncion, R. M. (1997). Potentials of Electronic Markets in the Philippines. *Electronic Markets, 7*(2), 34-37.

Au, K. F. & Ho, D. C. K. (2002). Electronic Commerce and Supply Management: Value Adding Service for Clothing Manufacturing. *Integrated Manufacturing Systems, 13*(4), 247-254.

Ayadi, A. (2006). Technological and organizational preconditions to Internet Banking implementation: Case of a Tunisian bank, *Journal of Internet Banking and Commerce, 11*(1).

Ayo, C.K. (2006). The Prospects of E-Commerce Implementation in Nigeria. *Journal of Internet Banking and Commerce, 11*(3).

Ayo, C.K. & Babajide, D.O. (2006). Designing a Reliable E-payment System: Nigeria a Case Study, *Journal of Internet Banking and Commerce, 11*(2).

Azjen, I. (1991). The Theory of Planned Behavior. *Organizational Behavior, and Human Decision Processes, 50*(2), 179-211.

Azjen, I. & Fishbein, M. (1980). *Understanding Attitudes and Predicting Social Behavior.* Englewood Cliffs, NJ: Prentice Hall.

Bajaj, A. & Leonard, L. N. K. (2004). The CPT Framework: Understanding the Roles of Culture, Policy and Technology in Promoting E-commerce Readiness. *Problems and Perspectives in Management,* 3, pp. 242-252.

Bakos, J.Y. (1991). A Strategic Analysis of Electronic Marketplaces, *MIS Quarterly, 15*(3), 295–310.

Barney, J. (1991). Firm Resources and Sustained Competitive Advantage. *Journal of Management, 17*(1), 99-120.

Barney, J. B. (1997). *Gaining and Sustaining Competitive Advantage*, Reading, MA: Addison-Wesley.

Barrientos, S. (1998). How To Do Literature Study. In A., Thomas, J. Chatway and M., Wuyts (Eds.) *Finding Out Fast.* London: Sage.

Bauer, C. & Glasson, B. (1999) A Classification Framework for Electronic Commerce Research. In A. Bytheway (Ed.), *Proceedings of BitWorld 99 Conference*, June 30th-July 2nd, Cape Town, South Africa [CD-ROM].

Benjamin, R. & Wigand, R. (1995). Electronic Markets and Virtual Value Chains on the Information Superhighway. *Sloan Management Review 36*(2), 62-72.

Bekele, D. (2000). EthioGift: A Unique Experience in Electronic Commerce in Ethiopia. *Electronic Markets, 10* (2), 146.

Benbasat, I., Ives, B., Piccoli, G., & Weber, R. (2000) E-commerce Top Questions. ISWorld. Retrieved November 20 2007 from http://www.isworld.org/isworldarchives/research.asp#.

Berril, A, Goode S. & Hart D. (2004). Managerial Expectations of Internet Commerce Adoption after the "Tech Wreck. *Journal of Global Information Technology Management, 7*(3), 45-63.

Bettman, J. R., Luce, M. F. & Payne, J. W. (1998). Constructive Consumer Choice Processes. *Journal of Consumer Research, 25*(3), 187-217.

Bharadwaj, A.S. (2000) A Resource-Based Perspective On Information Technology Capability and Firm Performance: An Empirical Investigation, *MIS Quarterly, 24*(1), 169-196.

Bharati, P. & Tarasewich, P. (2002). Global Perceptions of Journals Publishing E-Commerce Research. *Communications of the ACM, 45*(5), 21-26.

Bhatnagar, P. (1999a). Telecom Reforms in Developing Countries and the Outlook for Electronic Commerce. *Journal of World Trade, 33*(4), 143-155.

Bhatnagar, P. (1999b). Telecom Reforms in Developing Countries and the Outlook for Electronic Commerce. *Journal of International Economic Law, 2* (4), 695-712.

Bhatnagar, S. (1997). Electronic Commerce in India - The Untapped Potential. *Electronic Markets, 7*(2), 22-24.

Bin, Q., Chen, S. & Sun, S. Q. (2003). Cultural differences in E-commerce: A Comparison Between the U.S and China. *Journal of Global Information Management, 11*(2), 48-55.

Boateng, R. & Molla, A. (2006). Developing E-banking Capabilities in a Ghanaian Bank: Preliminary Lessons. *Journal of Internet Banking and Commerce, 11*(2).

Bolongkikit, J., Obit, J.H., Asing, J.G. & Geoffrey, H. (2006). An Exploratory Research of the Usage Level of E-Commerce among SMEs in the West Coast of Sabah, Malaysia, *Journal of Internet Banking and Commerce, 11*(2).

Brown, I., Hope, R., Mugera, P., Newman, P. & Stander, A. (2004). The Impact of National Environment on the Adoption of Internet Banking: Comparing Singapore and South Africa. *Journal of Global Information Management, 12*(2), 1-26.

Brown, I. & Molla, A. (2005). Determinants of Internet and Cell Phone Banking Adoption in South Africa. *Journal of Internet Banking and Commerce, 10*(1).

Bui, T., Le, T., & Jones, W. (2006). An exploratory case study of hotel e-marketing in Ho Chi Minh City. *Thunderbird International Business Review, 48*(3), 369-388.

Burgess, L. & Cooper, J. (2000). *Extending the Viability of Model of Internet Commerce Adoption (MICA) as a Metric for Explaining the Process of Business Adoption of Internet Commerce.* Paper presented at 3rd International Conference on Telecommunications and Electronic Commerce, Dallas, TX.

Chan, S. & Lu, M. (2004). Understanding Internet Banking Adoption and Use Behavior: A Hong Kong Perspective. *Journal of Global Information Management, 12*(3), 21-43.

Chao, P., Samiee, S. & Yip, L. S. (2003). International Marketing and the Asia-Pacific Region – Developments, Opportunities and Research Issues. *International Marketing Review, 20*(5), 480-492.

Chau, P. Y. K. (1996). An Empirical Assessment of a Modified Technology Acceptance Model.

Journal of Management Information Systems, 13(2), 185-204.

Chau, P. Y. K. (2001). Inhibitors to EDI Adoption in Small Business. *Journal of Electronic Commerce Research, 2*(2), 78-88.

Chen, J. C. H. & Ching, R. K. H. (2004). An Empirical Study of the Relationship of IT Intensity and Organizational Absorptive Capacity on CRM Performance. *Journal of Global Information Management, 12*(1), 1-17.

Chen, J. C., Lin, H., B., Li, L. & Chen, P. S. (2004). Logistics Management in China: A Case Study of Haier. *Human Systems Management, 23* 15-27.

Chen, C., Wu, C., Wu, C.R. (2006) e-Service enhancement priority matrix: The case of an IC foundry company, *Information & Management, 43*(5)572-586.

Chen, S. & Ning, J. (2002). Constraints on E-commerce in Less Developed Countries: The Case of China. *Electronic Commerce Research, 2*(1-2), 31-42.

Cheng, H., Fang, M., Guan, L. & Hong, Z. (2004). Design and Implementation of an E-Commerce Platform-SIMEC. *Journal of Electronic Commerce in Organizations, 2*(2), 44-54.

Chen, Y.N., Chen, H.M., Huang, W., & Ching, R.K. (2006). E-Government Strategies in Developed and Developing Countries: An Implementation Framework and Case Study, *Journal of Global Information* Management, *14*(1), 23-46.

Chwelos, P., Benbasat, I. & Dexter, A. (2001). Research Report: Empirical Test Of An EDI Adoption Model. *Information Systems Research, 12*(3), 304-321.

Chiemeke, S. C., Evwiekpaefe, A. E., & Chete, F. O. (2006). The Adoption of Internet Banking in Nigeria: An Empirical Investigation. *Journal of Internet Banking and Commerce, 11*(3).

Chircu, A. M. & Kauffman, R.J. (1999). Strategies for Internet Middlemen in the Intermediation/Disintermediation/Reintermediation Cycle, *Electronic Markets, 9*(1-2), 109-117.

Chiu, Y., Lin, C. & Tang, L. (2005). Gender Differs: Assessing A Model of Online Purchase Intentions in E-tail Service. *International Journal of Service Industry Management, 16*(5), 416-435.

Chwelos, P., Benbasat, I. & Dexter, A. (2001) Research Report: Empirical Test of an EDI Adoption Model, *Information Systems Research, 12*(3), 304-321.

Cloete, E., Courtney, S. & Fintz, J. (2002). Small Businesses Acceptance and Adoption of E-commerce in the Western Province of South Africa. *Electronic Journal on Information Systems in Developing Countries, 10*(4), 1-13.

Coase, R. H. (1937). The Nature of the Firm. *Economica, 4*, pp. 386-405.

Cui, L, Zhang, C., Zhang, C. & Huang, L. (2006). Exploring E-Government Impact on Shanghai Firms' Informatization Process. *Electronic Markets, 16*(4), 312 – 328.

Dada, D. (2006a) The failure of e-government in developing countries: A literature review, *Electronic Journal on Information Systems in Developing Countries, 26*(7), 1-10.

Dada, D. (2006b) E-readiness in developing countries: Moving focus from the environment to the users, *Electronic Journal on Information Systems in Developing Countries, 27*(6), 1-14.

Damanpour, F. (1991) Organizational Innovation: A Meta-Analysis of Effects of Determinants and Moderators. *Academy of Management Journal, 34*(3), 555–591.

Damsgaard, J. (1998). Electronic Markets in Hong Kong's Air Cargo Community: Thanks, But No Thanks. *Electronic Markets, 8*(3), 46-49.

Damsgaard, J. & Farhoomand, A. (1999). Electronic Commerce in Hong Kong A Special Administrative Region of the People's of Republic of China. *Electronic Markets, 9*(1/2), 73-80.

Darley, W. (2001). The Internet and Emerging E-commerce: Challenges and Implications for Management in Sub-Saharan Africa. *Journal of Global Information Technology Management, 4*(4), 4-18.

Darley, W. (2003). Public Policy Challenges and Implications of the Internet and the Emerging E-commerce for Sub-Saharan Africa: A Business Perspective. *Information Technology for Development, 10*(1), 1-12.

Dasgupta, P. & Sengupta, K. (2002). E-Commerce in the Indian Insurance Industry: Prospects and Future. *Electronic Commerce Research, 2*(1-2), 43-60.

Davenport, T. H. & Markus, L. M. (1999). Rigor vs. Relevance Revisited: Response to Benbasat and Zmud. *MIS Quarterly, 23*(1), 19-24.

Davis, C. H. (1999). The Rapid Emergence Of Electronic Commerce In A Developing Region: The Case Of Spanish-Speaking Latin America. *Journal of Global Information Technology Management, 2*(3).

Davis, F. D. (1985*). A Technology Acceptance Model for Empirically Testing New End-User Information Systems: Theory and Results*. Doctoral Dissertation. Cambridge, MA: MIT Sloan School of Management.

Davis, F.D., Bagozzi, R.P. & Warshaw, P.R. (1989). User acceptance of computer technology: a comparison of two theoretical models. *Management Science, 35*(8), 982-1003.

Davison, R. M., Vogel, D. R. & Harris, R. W. (2005). The E-Transformation of Western China. *Communications of the ACM, 48*(4), 62-67.

Debreceny, R. Putterill, M., Tung, L., & Gilbert, A.L. (2002). New tools for the determination of e-commerce inhibitors, *Decision Support Systems, 34*(2), 177-195.

DeGouvea, R. & Kassicieh, S. K. (2002). Brazil.com. *Thunderbird International Business Review, 44*(1), 105-115.

Dempsey, J. X. (2004). Creating the Legal Framework for Information and Communications Technology Development: The Example of E-Signature Legislation in Emerging Market Economies. *Information Technologies and International Development, 1*(2), 39-52.

Doern, D.R. & Fey, C.F. (2006). E-commerce developments and strategies for value creation: The case of Russia. *Journal of World Business, 41*(4), 315-327.

Duncombe, R., & Molla, A. (2006). E-commerce development in developing countries: profiling change-agents for SMEs. *International Journal of Entrepreneurship and Innovation, 7*(3), 185.

Dutta, A. (1997). The Physical Infrastructure for Electronic Commerce in Developing Nations: Historical Trends and the Impact of Privatization. *International Journal of Electronic Commerce, 2*(1), 61.

Efendioglu, A.M. & Yip, V. F (2004). Chinese culture and e-commerce: an exploratory study. *Interacting with Computers, 16*(1), 45-62.

Ezehoha, A. E. (2005). Regulating Internet Banking In Nigeria: Problems and Challenges – Part 1. *Journal of Internet Banking and Commerce, 10*(3).

Ezehoha, A. E. (2006).Regulating Internet Banking In Nigeria: Some Success Prescriptions – Part 2. *Journal of Internet Banking and Commerce, 11*(1).

Fay, B. (1987). Critical Social Science: Liberation and its Limits. Ithaca, NY: Cornell University Press.

Fjermestad, J., Passerini, K., Patten, K., Bartolacci, M. & Ullman, D. (2006). Moving Towards Mobile Third Generation Telecommunications Standards: The Good, and the Bad of the 'Anytime/Anywhere Solutions'. *Communications of AIS, 17*(3), 2-33.

Fraser, S. & Wresch, W. (2005). National Competitive Advantage in E-Commerce Efforts: A Report from Five Caribbean Nations. *Perspectives on Global Development and Technology, 4*(1), 27-44.

Frempong, G. and Stark, C. (2005). Ghana. In A. Gillwald, (Ed.), *Towards an African e-Index: Household and individual ICT Access and Usage across 10 African Countries.* Research ICT Africa, Retrieved March 22 2007 from http://www.researchictafrica.net/modules.php?op=modload&name=News&file=article&sid=504.

Ganesh, J., Madanmohan, T. R., Jose, P. D. & Seshadri, S. (2004). Adaptive Strategies of Firms in High-Velocity Environments: The Case of B2B Electronic Marketplaces. *Journal of Global Information Management, 12*(1), 41-59.

Garau, C. (2005). ICT Strategies for Development: Implementing Multichannel Banking in Romania. *Information Technology for Development, 11*(4), 343-362.

Garcia-Murillo, M. (2004). Institutions and the Adoption of Electronic Commerce in Mexico. *Electronic Commerce Research, 4*(3), 201-219.

Garicano, L. and Kaplan, S. (2001). *The Effects of Business-to-Business E-commerce on Transaction Costs,* Social Science Research Network (SSRN Resources). Retrieved May 01 2007, from http://ssrn.com/abstract=252210.

Genus, A. & Nor, M. A. M. (2005). Socializing the Digital Divide: Implications for ICTs and E-Business Development. *Journal of Electronic Commerce in Organizations, 3*(2), 82-94.

Gibbs, J. & Kraemer, K. (2004). A Cross Country Investigation of the Determinants of Scope of E-commerce Use: An Institutional Approach. *Electronic Markets, 14*(2), 124-137.

Goi, C.L. (2006). Factors Influence Development of E-Banking in Malaysia. *Journal of Internet Banking and Commerce, 11*(2).

Goldstein, A. and D. O'Connor (2000). *E-Commerce for Development: Prospects and Policy Issues*, Technical Paper No. 164, Paris: OECD Development Centre.

Goodman, S. (1994). Computing in South Africa: An end to 'apartness'? *Communications of the ACM, 37*(2), 19–24.

Gong, W. (2004). A Conceptual Solution to E-business Models in Developing Countries: Post-Crisis Domestic Procurement Network to Facilitate Humanitarian Assistance. *Electronic Journal on Information Systems in Developing Countries, 18*(4), 1-8.

Grace-Farfaglia, P., Dekkers, A., Sundararajan, B., Peters, L. & Park, S. (2006). Multinational Web uses and gratifications: Measuring the social impact of online community participation across national boundaries. *Electronic Commerce Research, 6*(1), 75-101.

Grandon, E. & Mykytyn, P. P. (2004). Theory-based Instrumentation to Measure the Intention to Use Electronic Commerce in Small and Medium Sized Businesses. *The Journal of Computer Information Systems, 44*(3), 44-57.

Grandon, E. & Pearson, J. M. (2003). Strategic Value and Adoption of Electronic Commerce: An Empirical Study of Chilean Small and Medium

Businesses. *Journal of Global Information Technology Management, 6*(3), 22-43.

Grandon, E. & Pearson, J. M. (2004). E-commerce Adoption: Perception of Managers/Owners of Small and Medium Sized Firms in Chile. *Communications of the Association for Information Systems, 13* 81-102.

Grant, R. M. (1991). The Resource-Based Theory of Competitive Advantage: Implications for Strategy Formulation. *California Management, Review, 33*(1), 114-135.

Gray, H. & Sanzogni, L. (2004). Technology Leapfrogging in Thailand: Issues for the Support of E-commerce Infrastructure. *Electronic Journal on Information Systems in Developing Countries, 16*(3), 1-26.

Gupta, O., Priyadarshini, K., Massoud, S. & Agrawal, S. K. (2004). Enterprise Resource Planning: A Case of a Blood Bank. *Industrial Management and Data Systems, 104*(7), 589-603.

Gunasekaran, A. & Ngai, E.W.T (2005). E-commerce in Hong Kong: An Empirical Perspective And Analysis, *Internet Research, 15*(2), 141-159

Guru, B. K., Shanmugam, B., Alam, N. & Perera, C. J. (2003). An Evaluation of Internet Banking Sites in Islamic Countries. *Journal of Internet Banking and Commerce, 8*(2).

Harris, P., Rettie, R. & Kwan, C. C. (2005). Adoption and Usage of M-Commerce: A Cross-Cultural Comparison. Journal of Electronic Commerce Research, 6 (3), 210-224.

Hawk, S. (2002). The Development of Russian E-commerce: The Case Ozon. *Management Decision, 40*(7), 702-709.

Hawk, S. (2004). A Comparison of B2C E-Commerce in Developing Countries. *Electronic Commerce Research, 4*(3), 181-199.

He, Q., Duan, Y., Fu, Z. & Li, D. (2006). An Innovation Adoption Study of Online E-Payment in Chinese Companies. *Journal of Electronic Commerce in Organizations, 4*(1), 48-69.

Heeks, R. (1999). *Information and Communication Technologies, Poverty and Development.* Development Informatics Working Papers Series No. 5. Manchester: IDPM, University of Manchester.

Heeks, R. (2000). Analyzing E-Commerce for Development, Information Technology in Developing Countries, *Information Processing (IFIP) Working Group 9.4*, 10(3).

Heeks, R. & Wilson, G. (2000). *Technology, Poverty and Development: into the 21st Century*, In T. Allen & A. Thomas (2000) Poverty and Development into the 21st Century, 2nd Edition, pp. 23-48. Oxford: Open University, Oxford University Press.

Hinson R. (2006). The Internet for Academics: Towards A Holistic Adoption Model. *Online Information Review, 30*(5).

Ho, C., Chi, Y. & Tai, Y. (2005). A Structural Approach to Measuring Uncertainty in Supply Chains. *International Journal of Electronic Commerce, 9*(3), 91-114.

Hofstede, G. (1980). *Culture's Consequences: International Differences in Work-related Values.* Newbury Park, CA: Sage.

Hofstede, G, (1985). The interaction between national and organizational value systems. *Journal of Management Studies, 22*(4), 347–357.

Hofstede, G. (1991). *Cultures and Organizations.* Berkshire: McGraw-Hill Book Company Europe.

Hong, S. & Tam, K.Y. (2006). Understanding the Adoption of Multipurpose Information Appliances: The Case of Mobile Data Services, *Information Systems Research, 17*(2), 162-179.

Hu, Q., Wu, X. & Wang, C. K. (2004). Lessons From Alibaba.com: Government's Role in Electronic Contracting. *INFO, 6* (5), 298-307.

Huang, L. (2006). Building up a B2B e-commerce strategic alliance model under an uncertain environment for Taiwan's travel agencies. *Tourism Management, 27*(6), 1308–1320.

Huang, J. H., Zhao, C. J. & Huang, H. (2004). An E-readiness Assessment Framework And Two Field Studies. *Communications of the Association for Information Systems, 14*(19), 364-386.

Huang, Z. & Palvia, P. (2001). ERP Implementation Issues in Advanced and Developing Countries. *Business Process Management Journal, 7*(3), 276-284.

Hung, S., Ku, C. & Chang, C. (2003). Critical Factors of WAP Services Adoption: An Empirical Study. *Electronic Commerce Research and Applications, 2*(1), 42-60.

Hwang, W., Jung, H.-S. & Salvendy, G. (2006). Internationalization of e-commerce: a comparison of online shopping preferences among Korean, Turkish and US populations. *Behavior and Information Technology, 25*(1) 3-18.

Iacovou, A., Benbasat L., I. & Dexter, A. (1995). Electronic Data Interchange And Small Organizations: Adoption And Impact Of Technology. *MIS Quarterly, 19*(4), 465-48.

Ismail, M. M. & El-Nawawy, M. A. (2000). The Imminent Challenge of Click and Mortar Commerce in Egypt, Africa and Middle East. *Electronic Markets, 10*(2), 73-79.

International Telecommunications Union (ITU) (2006). *ICT Statistics. World Telecommunications Indicators Database 9th Edition*. International Telecommunication Union (ITU). Retrieved March 12, 2006, from http://www.itu.int/ITU-D/ict/statistics/ict/index.html.

International Trade Centre (ITC) (2001). Are Developing Countries Ready? Three ITC Surveys, Close Up, *International Trade Forum*, 1, p.19.

Janejira, S. (2006). E-Commerce Adoption: Perceptions of Managers/Owners of Small- and Medium-Sized Enterprises (SMEs) in Thailand. *Journal of Internet Commerce, 5*(3), 53-82

Jantan, M., Ndubisi, N. O. & Yean, O. B. (2003). Viability of E-commerce As An Alternative Distribution Channel. *Logistics Information Management, 16*(6), 427-439.

Jarvenpaa, S. L. & Leidner, D. E. (1998). An Information Company In Mexico: Extending The Resource-Based View Of The Firm To A Developing Country Context. *Information Systems Research, 9*(4), 342-361.

Jaruwachirathanakul, B. & Fink, D. (2005). Internet Banking Adoption Strategies for a Developing Country: The Case of Thailand. *Internet Research, 15*(3), 295-311.

Javalgi, R., Wickramasinghe, N., Scherer, R. F. & Sharma, S. (2005). An Assessment and Strategic Guidelines for Developing E-Commerce in the Asia-Pacific Region. *International Journal of Management, 22*(4), 523-531.

Javalgi, R. G., Martin, C. L. & Todd, P. R. (2004). The Export of E-services in the Age of Technology Transformation: Challenges and Implications for International Service Providers. *Journal of Services Marketing, 18*(7), 560-573.

Jaw, Y.L. & Chen, C.L. (2006). The influence of the Internet in the internationalization of SMEs in Taiwan. *Human Systems Management, 25*(3), 167–183.

Jeffcoate, J., Chapell, C. & Feindt, S. (2000). Attitudes Towards Process Improvement Among SMEs Involved in E-commerce. *Knowledge and Process Management, 7*(3), 187-195.

Jennex, M. E. & Amoroso, D. (2002). E-business and Technology Issues for Developing Economies: A Ukraine Case Study. *Electronic Journal on Information Systems in Developing Countries, 10*(5), 1-14.

Jennex, M. E., Amoroso, D. & Adelakun, O. (2004). E-Commerce Infrastructure Success Factors for Small Companies in Developing Economies. *Electronic Commerce Research, 4*(3), 263-286.

Jih, W. K., Helms, M. M. & Mayo, D. T. (2005). Effects of Knowledge Management on Electronic Commerce: An Exploratory Study in Taiwan. *Journal of Global Information Management, 13*(4), 1-24.

Joia, L. A. & Sanz, P. S. (2006). The Financial Potential of Sporadic Customers in E-Retailing: Evidence from the Brazilian Home Appliance Sector. *Journal of Electronic Commerce in Organizations, 4*(1), 18-32.

Joia, L.A. & Sanz, P.S.(2006). The Financial Potential of Sporadic Customers in E-Retailing: Evidence from the Brazilian Home Appliance Sector. *Journal of Electronic Commerce in Organizations, 4*(1), 18-32.

Joia, L. A. & Zamot, F. (2002). Internet-Based Reverse Auctions by Brazilian Government. *Electronic Journal on Information Systems in Developing Countries, 9*(6), 1-12.

Jones, M. C., Ku, Y. & Berry, R. L. (2000). Electronic Data Interchange: A Cross-Cultural Comparison Of Key Usage Aspects Between U.S. And Taiwanese Firms. *Journal of Global Information Technology Management, 3* (4).

Jones, R. & Basu, S. (2002). Taxation of Electronic Commerce: A Developing Problem. *International Review of Law, Computers and Technology, 16*(1), 35-52.

Joseph, G. T. J. (2004). Electronic Commerce and the United Nations Double Taxation Convention. *International Tax Review, 32*(8/9), 387-401.

Juhua, C., Yong, H. & Wei, W. (2004). E-commerce Education in China. *Journal of Electronic Commerce in Organizations, 2*(2), 65-77.

Kamel, S. & Hassan, A. (2003). Assessing the introduction of electronic banking in Egypt using the technology acceptance model. In M. Khosrow-Pour (Ed.) *Annals of Cases on information Technology* (1-25). Hershey PA: IGI Publishing.

Kamel, S. & Hussein, M. (2001). The Development of E-commerce: The Emerging Virtual Context within Egypt. *Logistics Information Management, 14*(1/2), 119.

Kamel, S. & Hussein, M. (2002). The Emergence of E-commerce in a Developing Nation. *Benchmarking, 9*(2), 146-153.

Kamel, S. & Hussein, M. (2004). King Hotel Goes Online: The Case of a Medium Enterprise in Using E-commerce. *Journal of Electronic Commerce in Organizations, 2*(4), 101-115.

Kannabiran, G. & Narayan, P. C. (2005). Deploying Internet Banking and e-Commerce—Case Study of a Private-Sector Bank in India. *Information Technology for Development, 11*(4), 363-379.

Kao, D. & Decou, J. (2003). A Strategy-Based Model for E-Commerce Planning. *Industrial Management and Data Systems, 103*(4), 238-252.

Karanasios, S. & Burgess, S. (2006). Exploring the Internet use of small tourism enterprises: evidence from a developing country, *Electronic Journal on Information Systems in Developing Countries, 27*(3), 1-21.

Kardaras, D. & Karakostas, B. (2001). An empirical investigation of the management practices and the development of electronic commerce in Mauritius. *International Journal of Information Management, 21*(6), 441-455.

Kaynak, F., Tatoglu, E. & Kula, V. (2005). An Analysis of the Factors Affecting the Adoption of Electronic Commerce by SMEs. *International Marketing Review, 22*(6), 623-640.

Khalfan, A. M. & Alshawaf, A. (2004). Adoption and Implementation Problems of E-Banking: A Study of the Managerial Perspective of the Banking Industry in Oman. *Journal of Global Information Technology Management, 7*(1), 47-64.

Kini, R.B. & Thanarithiporn, S. (2004). Mobile commerce and electronic commerce in Thailand: a value space analysis, *International Journal of Mobile Communications, 2*(1), 22-37.

Kirkman, G. & Sachs, J. (2001). Subtract the Divide. *World Link, 14*(1), 60-63.

Klein, H. K. & Myers, M. D. (1999). A Set of Principles for Conducting and Evaluating Interpretive Field in Information Systems. *MIS Quarterly, 23*(1), 67-93.

Kling, R. (1999). Can the "Next-Generation Internet" Effectively Support "Ordinary Citizens", *The Information Society 15*(1), 57-63.

Kraut, R., Steinfield, C., Chan, A. P., Butler, B. & Hoag, A. (1999). Coordination and Virtualization: The Role of Electronic Networks and Personal, Relationships, *Organization Science, 10*(6), 722-740.

Kuan, K. K. Y. & Chau, P. Y. K. (2001). A Perception-based Model for EDI Adoption in Small Businesses Using A Technology-Organization-Environment Framework. *Information and Management, 38*(8), 507-521.

Kumar, R. & Best, M. L. (2006). Impact and Sustainability of E-Government Services in Developing Countries: Lessons Learned from Tamil Nadu, India. *Information Society, 22*(1), 1-12.

Lai, M. K., Humphreys, P. K. & Sculli, D. (2001). The Implications of Western Electronic Commerce for Chinese Business Networks. *Industrial Management and Data Systems, 101*(6), 281-289.

Lane, M. S., Van Der Vyer, G., Delpachitra, S. & Howard, S. (2004). An Electronic Commerce Initiative in Regional Sri Lanka: The Vision for the Central Province Electronic Commerce Portal. *Electronic Journal on Information Systems in Developing Countries, 16*(1), 1-18.

Lau, A., Yen, J. & Chau, P. Y. K. (2001). Adoption of Online Trading in the Hong Kong Financial Market. *Journal of Electronic Commerce Research, 2*(2), 58-62.

Le, T. (2002). Pathways to Leadership for Business-to-Business Electronic Marketplaces, *Electronic Markets, 12*(2), 12–119.

Le, T. T. & Koh, A. C. (2002). A Managerial Perspective on Electronic Commerce Development in Malaysia. *Electronic Commerce Research, 2*(1-2), 7-29.

Lee, A. S. (2001). Editor's comments: Research in Information Systems: What We haven't Learned. *MIS Quarterly, 25*(4), V-XV.

Lee, T., Chun, J., Shim, J. & Lee, S. (2006). An Ontology-Based Product Recommender System for B2B Marketplaces. *International Journal of Electronic Commerce, 11*(2), 125-155.

Lefebvre. L.A. & Lefebvre, E. (2002). E-commerce and virtual enterprises: issues and challenges for transition economies, *Technovation, 22*(5), 313-323.

Leonard-Barton, D. (1992). Core capabilities and core rigidities: A paradox in managing new product development. *Strategic Management Journal, 13*, pp. 111-125.

Lertwongsatien, C. & Wongpinunwatana, N. (2003). E-commerce Adoption in Thailand: An

Empirical Study of Small and Medium Enterprises. *Journal of Global Information Technology Management, 6*(3), 67-83.

Lewis, C. (2005). Negotiating the Net: The Internet in South Africa (1990–2003). *Information Technologies and International Development, 2*(3), 1-28.

Li, L. & Buhalis, D. (2006). E-Commerce in China: The case of travel. *International Journal of Information Management, 26*(2), 153-166.

Li, P. P. & Chang, S. T. (2004). A Holistic Framework of E-Business Strategy: The Case of Haier in China. *Journal of Global Information Management, 12*(2), 44-62.

Liao, C., To, P. & Shih, M. (2006) Website practices: A comparison between the top 1000 companies in the US and Taiwan. *International Journal of Information Management, 26*(3), 196-211.

Lim, K.H., Sia, C.L., Lee, M.K.O. & Benbasat, I. (2006). Do I Trust You Online, and If So, Will I Buy? An Empirical Study of Two Trust-Building Strategies. *Journal of Management Information Systems, 23*(2), 233-266.

Lima, M. I. & Alcoforado, I. (1999). Electronic Commerce: Aspects of the Brazilian Experience. *Electronic Markets 9*(1/2), 132-135.

Lin, H., & Wang, Y. (2006). An examination of the determinants of customer loyalty in mobile commerce contexts. *Information & Management, 43*(3), 271-282.

Liu, C., Marchewka, J. T. & Ku, C. (2004). American and Taiwanese Perceptions Concerning Privacy, Trust, and Behavioral Intentions in Electronic Commerce. *Journal of Global Information Management, 12*(1), 18-40.

Lohse, G. L. & Wu, D. J. (2001). Eye Movements Patterns on Chinese Yellow Pages Advertising. *Electronic Markets, 11*(2), 87-96.

Looi, H.C. (2005). E-Commerce Adoption in Brunei Darussalam: A Quantitative Analysis of Factors Influencing Its Adoption. *Communications of the Association for Information Systems, 15*(1), 61-81.

Lowry, P. B., Romans, D. & Curtis, A. (2004). Global Journal Prestige and Supporting Disciplines: A Scientometric Study of Information Systems Journals. *Journal of Association of Information Systems, 5*(2), 29-77.

Lu, J. & Lu, Z. (2004). Development, Distribution and Evaluation of Online Tourism Services in China. *Electronic Commerce Research, 4*(3), 221-239.

Lund, M. F. & McGuire, S. (2005). Institutions and Development: Electronic Commerce and Economic Growth. *Organization Studies, 26*(12), 1743-1763.

Madon, S. (2000). The Internet and Socio-Economic Development: Exploring the Interaction. *Information Technology and People, 13*(2), 85-101.

Mahmood, M. A., Bagchi, K. & Ford, T. C. (2004). On-line Shopping Behavior: Cross-Country Empirical Research. *International Journal of Electronic Commerce, 9*(1), 9-30.

Mahone, J. T. & Pandian, J. R. (1992). The Resource-Based View Within The Conversation Of Strategic Management. *Strategic Management Journal, 13*(5), 363-380.

Makadok, R. (2001). Toward a Synthesis of the Resource-Based and Dynamic-Capability Views of Rent Creation. *Strategic Management Journal, 22*(5), 387-401.

Malone, T.W., Yates, J. & Benjamin, R. (1987). Electronic markets and electronic hierarchies, *Communications of the ACM, 30* (6), 484-497.

Mann, C.L. (2000). *Electronic Commerce In Developing Countries: Issues For Domestic*

Policy And WTO Negotiations (Working Paper 00-3). Washington, DC: Institute for International Economics.

Mansell, R. (2001). Digital Opportunities and The Missing Link for Developing Countries. *Oxford Review of Economic Policy, 17*(2), 282-295.

Martinsons, M. G. (2002). Electronic Commerce in China: Emerging Success Stories. *Information and Management, 39*(7), 571-579.

Maugis, V., Choucri, N., Madnick, S. T., Siegel, M. D., Gillett, S. E., Haghseta, F., Zhu, H. & Best, M. L. (2005). Global e-Readiness—for What? Readiness for e-Banking. *Information Technology for Development, 11*(4), 313-342.

Mbarika, V. A. & Okoli, C. (2003). A Framework for Assessing E-commerce in Sub-Saharan Africa. *Journal of Global Information Technology Management, 6*(3), 44-66.

McCormick, D. & Kinkajou, M.N. (2002). *E-Commerce In The Garment Industry In Kenya, Usage, Obstacles and Policies*. Sussex: Institute For Development Studies. Retrieved November 24, 2004, from http://www.gapresearch.org/production/B2BKenyagarmentsfinal.pdf.

McConnell, S. (2000). A Champion in Our Midst: Lessons Learned from the Impacts of NGOs' Use of the Internet. *Electronic Journal on Information Systems in Developing Countries, 2*(5), 1-15.

McCubbrey, D. J. & Gricar, J. (1995). The EDI Project in Slovenia: A Case Study and Model for Developing Countries, *Information Technology and People, 8*(2), 6-16.

McGrath, R. G., Tsai, M. H., Venkataraman, S. & MacMillan, I. C. (1996). Innovation, competitive advantage, and rent: A model and test. *Management Science, 42*(3), 389-403.

McHenry, W. & Borisov, A. (2006a). Measuring e-government: a case study using Russia. *Communications of AIS, 17*(42), 905-940.

McHenry, W. & Borisov, A. (2006b). E-Government and Democracy in Russia. *Communications of AIS, 17*(48), 1064-1123.

Mhlanga, B. (2006). Information and communication technologies (ICTs) Policy for change and the mask for development: A critical analysis of Zimbabwe e-readiness survey report. *Electronic Journal of Information Systems in Developing Countries, 28*(1), 1-16.

Milgrom, P. & Roberts, J. (1992). *Economics, Organization, and Management*, Englewood, NJ: Prentice Hall.

Mitchell, A. D. (2001). Towards Compatibility: The Future of Electronic Commerce within the Global Trading System. *Journal of International Economic Law, 4*(4), 683-723.

Miyazaki, K. (1995). *Building Competences in the Firm: Lessons from Japanese and European Optoelectronics*. New York: St. Martin's Press.

Moeti, N., Mburu, P. & Kealisitse, B. (2006). Smart Card Perception Gaps: Encumbrance on E-Tailing in Botswana. *Problems and Perspectives in Management, 4*(4), 95-104.

Molla, A. & Licker, P. S. (2001). E-commerce Systems Success: An Attempt to Extend and Respecify the Delone and Maclean Model of IS Success. *Journal of Electronic Commerce Research, 2*(4), 131-141.

Molla, A. & Licker, P. S. (2004). Maturation Stage of e-commerce in Developing Countries: A Survey of South African Companies. *Information Technologies and International Development, 2*(1), 89-98.

Molla, A. & Licker, P. S. (2005a). E-commerce Adoption in Developing Countries: A Model and Instrument. *Information and Management, 42*(6), 877-899.

Molla, A. & Licker, P. S. (2005b). Perceived E-Readiness Factors in E-Commerce Adoption: An

Empirical Investigation in a Developing Country. *International Journal of Electronic Commerce, 10*(1), 83-110.

Molla, A., Taylor, R. & Licker, P.S. (2006). E-commerce Diffusion in Small Island Countries: The Influence of Institutions in Barbados, *Electronic Journal on Information Systems in Developing Countries, 28*(2), 1-15.

Montagna, J.M. (2005). A framework for the assessment and analysis of electronic government proposals. *Electronic Commerce Research and Applications, 4*(2), 204-219.

Montealegre, R. (1996). Implications of Electronic Commerce for Managers in Less-Developed Countries. *Information Technology for Development, 7*(3), 145-152.

Montealegre, R. (1999). A Case For More Case Study Research In The Implementation Of IT, *Information Technology For Development, 8*(4), 199-207.

Montealegre, R. (2001). Four Visions of E-Commerce in Latin America in the Year 2010. *Thunderbird International Business Review, 43*(6), 717-735.

Montealegre, R. (2002). A Process Model of Capability Development: Lessons from the Electronic Commerce. *Organization Science, 13*(5), 514-531.

Montealegre, R. & Keil, M. (2000). De-escalating Information Technology Projects: Lessons from the Denver International Airport. *MIS Quarterly, 24*(3), 417-447.

Moodley, S. (2002a). *E-Commerce & the Export Market Connectivity of South African Garment Producers: Disentangling Myth from Reality.* Cape Town, South Africa: Human Sciences Research Council, Knowledge Management Programme. Mimeo. Retrieved November 20, 2004, from http://www.irfd.org/events/wf2003/vc/papers/papers_africa/R34.pdf.

Moodley, S. (2002b). Global Market Access in the Internet Era: South Africa's Wood Furniture Industry. *Internet Research, 12*(1), 31-42.

Moodley, S. (2003). Whither Business-to-business Electronic Commerce in Developing Economies? The Case of the South African Manufacturing Sector. *Information Technology for Development, 10*(1), 25-40.

Moodley, S. & Morris, M. (2004). Does E-commerce Fulfill its Promise for Developing Country (South African) Garment Export Producers? *Oxford Development Studies, 32*(2), 155-178.

Morris, M.G. & Dillon, A. (1997). How User Perceptions Influence Software Use. *IEEE Software, 14*(4), 58-65.

Mukti, N. (2000) Barriers to Putting Business on the Internet in Malaysia. *Electronic Journal on Information Systems in Developing Countries, 2*(6), 1-6.

Muthitacharoen, A. & Palvia, P. (2002). B2C Internet Commerce: A Tale of Two Nations. *Journal of Electronic Commerce Research, 3*(4), 201-212.

Mutula, S. M. (2002). Current Developments in the Internet Industry in Botswana. *The Electronic Library, 20*(6), 504-511.

Myers, M. D. & Avison, D. (2002). An Introduction to Qualitative Research in Information Systems In M. D., Myers & D., Avison (Eds.) *Qualitative Research in Information Systems, A Reader.* London: Sage Publications.

Mykytyn, P.P. & Harrison, D.A. (1993) The Application of Theory of Reasoned Action to Senior Management and Strategic Information Systems. *Information Resources Management Journal, 6*(2), 15-26.

Ngai, E. W. T. (2004). Teaching and Learning of E-Commerce at the Hong Kong Polytechnic University: From A Business Education Perspective.

Journal of Electronic Commerce in Organizations, 2(2), 17-27.

Ngai, E. W. T. & Gunasekaran, A. (2004). Implementation of EDI in Hong Kong: An Empirical Analysis. *Industrial Management and Data Systems, 104*(1), 88-100.

Ngai, E. W. T. & Wat, F. K. T. (2002). A Literature Review and Classification of Electronic Commerce Research. *Information and Management, 39*(5), 415-429.

Ngudup, P., Chen, J. C. H. & Lin, B. (2005). E-commerce in Nepal: A Case Study of An

Underdeveloped Country. *International Journal of Management and Enterprise Development, 2*(3/4), 1-1.

Nolan, R. L. (1973). Managing the Computer Resource: A Stage Hypothesis. *Communications of The ACM, 16*(7), 399-405.

Nord, J. H. & Nord, G. D. (1995). MIS Research: Journal Status and Analysis. *Information and Management, 29*(1), 29-42.

Odedra, M., Lawrie, M., Bennett, M., Goodman, S. & (2003). *Information Technology in Sub-Saharan Africa, International Perspective.* Pennsylvania: CACM, University Of Pennsylvania - African Studies Center. Retrieved on November 20, 2005, from: http://www.africa.upenn.edu/Comp_Articles/Information_Technology_117.html.

Oliver, C. (1997). Sustainable competitive advantage: Combining institutional and resource-based views. *Strategic Management Journal, 18*(9), 697-713.

Orlikowski, W. J. & Baroudi, J. J. (1991). Studying Information Technology in Organizations: Research Approaches And Assumptions. *Accounting, Management And Information Technologies, 1*(1), 9-42.

Palmer, J. J. (2000). Internet Access in Bahrain: Business Patterns and Problems. *Technovation, 20*(8), 451-458.

Pani, A. K. & Agrahari, A. (2004). E-Markets in Emerging Economy: A Case Study from Indian Steel Industry. *Journal of Electronic Commerce in Organizations, 2*(4), 116-126.

Pare, D. J. (2003). Does This Site Deliver? B2B E-commerce Services for Developing Countries. *The Information Society, 19*(2), 123-134.

Parikh, D. (2006). Profiling Internet Shoppers: A Study of Expected Adoption of Online Shopping in India, *IIMB Management Review, 18*(3), 221-231.

Park, C. & Kim, Y. (2006).The Effect of Information Satisfaction and Relational Benefit on Consumers' Online Shopping Site Commitments. *Journal of Electronic Commerce in Organizations, 4*(1), 70-90.

Pavlou, P. A. & Chai, L. (2002). What Drives Electronic Commerce Across Cultures? A Cross-Cultural Empirical Investigation of the Theory of Planned Behavior. *Journal of Electronic Commerce Research, 3*(4), 240-253.

Peng, Y., Trappey, C. V. & Liu, N. Y. (2005). Internet and E-commerce Adoption by the Taiwan Semiconductor Industry. *Industrial Management and Data Systems, 105*(4), 476-490.

Petrazzini, B. & Kibati, M. (1999). The Internet in Developing Countries. *Communications of the ACM, 42*(6), 31-36.

Plouffe, C., Hulland, J. & M., V. (2001). Richness Versus Parsimony in Modeling Technology Adoption Decisions - Understanding Merchant Adoption of a Smart card-based Payment System. *Information Systems Research, 12*(2), 208-222.

Pons, A. (2004). E-Government for Arab Countries. *Journal of Global Information Technology Management, 7*(1), 30-46.

Poon, S. & Chau, P. Y. K. (2001). Octopus: The Growing E-payment System in Hong Kong. *Electronic Markets, 11*(2), 97-106.

Poon, S. & Huang, X. (2002). Success at E-Governing: A Case Study ESDLife in Hong Kong. *Electronic Markets, 12*(4), 270-280.

Porter, M.E. (1990). *The Competitive Advantage of Nations*. London: Macmillan.

Porter, M. E. (1998). *The Competitive Advantage of Nations*. Basingstoke: Macmillan.

Porter, M. E. & Millar, V. E. (1985). How Information Gives You Competitive Advantage. *Harvard Business Review, 63*(4)149-160.

Purcell, F. & Toland, J. (2004) Electronic Commerce for the South Pacific: A Review of E-Readiness. *Electronic Commerce Research, 4*(3), 241-262.

Rao, M. (1998). AD Convention: Indian Advertising Agencies Urged to Harness Internet Technologies. *Electronic Markets, 8*(1), 48-49.

Rao, S. S. (2000). E-commerce: The Medium is the Mart. *New Library World, 101*(1154), 53-59.

Ramayah, T., Taib, F. & Ling, K.P. (2006). Classifying Users and Non-Users of Internet Banking in Northern Malaysia. *Journal of Internet Banking and Commerce, 11*(2).

Rauch, J.E. (2001). Business and Social Networks in International Trade, *Journal of Economic Literature, 39*, pp.1177-1203.

Reimers, K., Li, M. & Chen, G. (2004). A Multi-Level Approach for Devising Effective B2B E-Commerce Development Strategies with an Application to the Case of China. *Electronic Commerce Research, 4*(3), 287-305.

Riquelme, H. (2002). Commercial Internet adoption in China: comparing the experience of small, medium and large businesses. *Internet Research: Electronic Networking Applications and Policy, 12*(3), 276-286.

Rodriguez, F. & Wilson, I. E. J. (2000). *Are Poor Countries Losing the Information Revolution?* InfoDEV Working Paper Series. Washington, DC: The World Bank.

Rodriguez, G. R. (2005). Information and Communication Technology and Non-Governmental Organizations: Lessons Learnt From Networking in Mexico. *Electronic Journal on Information Systems in Developing Countries, 25*(3), 1-29.

Rogers, E. M. (1983). *Diffusions of Innovation*. New York: Free Press.

Rogers, E.M. (1995). *Diffusions of Innovation, 4th Edition*. New York: Free Press.

Rohm, A., Kashyap, V., Thomas, G. B. & Milne, G. R. (2004). The Use of Online Marketplaces for Competitive Advantage: A Latin American Perspective. *Journal of Business and Industrial Marketing, 19*(6), 372-385.

Rotchanakitumnuai, S. & Speece, M. (2003). Barriers to Internet Banking Adoption: A Qualitative Study Among Customers in Thailand. *International Journal of Bank Marketing, 21*(6/7), 312-323.

Rotchanakitumnuai, S. & Speece, M. (2004). Corporate Customer Perspectives on Business Value of Thai Internet Banking. *Journal of Electronic Commerce Research, 5*(4), 270-286.

Sadowsky, G. (1993). Networking Connectivity for Developing Countries. *Communications of the ACM, 36*(8), 42-47.

Salleh, N.A.M., Rhode, F. & Green, P. (2006). The Effect of Enacted Capabilities on Adoption of a Government Electronic Procurement System by Malaysian SMEs, *Electronic Markets, 16*(4), 292–311.

Salman, A. (2004). Elusive Challenges of E-change Management in Developing Countries. *Business Process Management Journal, 10*(2), 140-156.

Sanchez, R., Heene, A. & Thomas, H. (1996). *Introduction: Towards the Theory and Practice of Competence-Based Competition*, Oxford: Pergamon Press.

Sarantakos, S. (1998). *Social Research, Second Edition.* Basingstoke, Hampshire: Palgrave.

Schendel, D. (1994). Introduction to Competitive Organizational Behavior: Toward An Organizationally Based Theory Of Competitive Advantage, *Strategic Management Journal, 15*, pp. 1-4.

Seyal, A., Awais, M. M., Shamail, S. & Abbas, A. (2004). Determinants of Electronic Commerce in Pakistan: Preliminary Evidence from Small and Medium Enterprises. *Electronic Markets, 14*(2), 372-387.

Seyal, A.H. & Rahim, M. (2006). A preliminary investigation of electronic data interchange adoption in Bruneian small business organizations. *Electronic Journal on Information Systems in Developing Countries, 24*(4), 1-21.

Shang, R., Chen, Y. & Shen, L. (2005). Extrinsic Versus Intrinsic Motivations for Consumers to Shop On-line. *Information and Management, 42*(3), 401-413.

Sharma, S. & Gupta, J. N. D. (2003). Socio-economic Influences of E-commerce Adoption. *Journal of Global Information Technology Management, 6*(3), 3-21.

Sheth, N. & Sharma, A. (2005). International E-marketing: Opportunities and Issues. *International Marketing Review, 22*(6), 611-622.

Shih, H. (2004). Extended Technology Acceptance Model of Internet Utilization Behavior. *Information and Management, 41*(6), 719-729.

Sia, C., Lee, M. K. O., Teo, H. & Wei, K. (2001). Information Instruments for Creating Awareness in IT Innovations: An Exploratory Study of Organizational Adoption Intentions of ValuNet. *Electronic Markets, 11*(3), 206-215.

Simon, S. J. (2004). Critical Success Factors for Electronic Services: Challenges for Developing Countries. *Journal of Global Information Technology Management, 7*(2), 31-53.

Simpson, J. (2002). The impact of the Internet in banking: observations and evidence from developed and emerging markets, *Telematics and Informatics, 19*(4), 315-330.

Singh, B. & Malhotra, P. (2004). Adoption of Internet Banking: An Empirical Investigation of Indian Banking Sector. *Journal of Internet Banking and Commerce, 9*(2).

Singh, J. P. & Gilchrist, S. M. (2002). Three Layers of the Electronic Commerce Network: Challenges for Developed and Developing Worlds. *INFO, 4*(2), 31-41.

Singh, N., Xhao, H. & Hu, X. (2003). Cultural Adaptation on the Web: A Study of American Companies Domestic and Chinese Websites. *Journal of Global Information Management, 11*(3), 63-80.

Siyal, M.Y., Chowdhry, B.S. & Rajput, A.Q. (2006) Socio-economic factors and their influence on the adoption of e-commerce by consumers in Singapore, *International Journal of Information Technology & Decision Making, 5*(2), 317–329.

Soh, C., and Markus, M.L. (1995). How IT Creates Business Value: A Process Theory Synthesis. In G. Ariav, et al. (Eds.), *Proceedings of the Sixteenth International Conference on Information Systems,* December 10-13. (29-41). Amsterdam, The Netherlands.

Sorensen, O. J. & Buatsi, S. (2002). Internet and Exporting: The Case of Ghana. *Journal of Business and Industrial Marketing, 17*(6), 481-500.

Sprano, E. & Zakak, A. (2000). E-commerce Capable: Competitive Advantage For Countries in the New World Economy. *Competitive Review, 10*(2), 114-122.

Sridhar, V. (2006) Modeling the growth of Mobile telephony services in India, *VISION - The Journal of Business Perspective, 10*(3).

Stafford, T.F., Turan, A.H. & Khasawneh, A.M. (2006). MIDDLE-EAST.COM: Diffusion of the Internet and Online Shopping in Jordan and Turkey. *Journal of Global Information Technology Management, 9*(3), 43-61.

Steinfield, C., Kraut, R. & Plummer, A. (1995). The Impact of Interorganizational Networks on Buyer-Seller Relationships, *Journal of Computer Mediated Communication, 1*(3).

Steinfield, C., Kraut, R., & Chan, A. (2000). Computer Mediated Markets: An Introduction and Preliminary Test of Market Structure Impacts, *Journal of Computer Mediated Communication, 5*(3).

Stylianou, A. C., Robbins, S. & Jackson, P. (2003). Perceptions and Attitudes About E-Commerce Development in China: An Exploratory Study. *Journal of Global Information Management, 11*(2), 31-47.

Suganthi, B. & Balachandran (2001). Internet Banking Patronage: An Empirical Investigation of Malaysia. *Journal of Internet Banking and Commerce, 6*(1).

Sulaiman, A., Jaafar, N. I. & Kiat, T. C. (2005). Internet Activities among Malaysian Insurance Companies. *Journal of Internet Banking and Commerce, 10*(1).

Talh, M. & Salim, A. S. A. (2005). Incorporating Electronic Business Initiatives in Health Services and Health Tourism: A Case Study of Malaysia. *Journal of Internet Banking and Commerce, 10*(1).

Tan, Z. & Ouyang, W. (2004). Diffusion and Impacts of the Internet and E-commerce in China. *Electronic Markets, 14*(1), 25-35.

Tarafdar, M. & Vaidya, S. D. (2004). Adoption of Electronic Commerce by Organizations in India: Strategic and Environmental Imperatives. *Electronic Journal on Information Systems in Developing Countries, 17*(2), 1-25.

Taylor, S. & Todd, P. (1995). Decomposition and Crossover Effects in the Theory of Planned Behavior: A Study of Consumer Adoption Intentions. *International Journal of Research in Marketing, 12*(2), 137-156.

Teece, D. J., Pisano, G. & Shuen, A. (1997). Dynamic Capabilities and Strategic Management. *Strategic Management Journal, 18*(7), 509-533.

Teltscher, S. (2002). Electronic Commerce and Development: Fiscal Implications of Digitized Goods Trading. *World Development, 30* (7), 1137-1158.

Thatcher, S. M. B., Foster, W. & Zhu, L. (2006). B2B E-commerce Adoption Decisions in Taiwan: The Interaction of Cultural and Other Institutional Factors. *Electronic Commerce Research and Applications*, 5(2), 92-104.

Tigre, P. B. & Dedrick, J. (2004). E-commerce in Brazil: Local Adaptation of a Global Technology. *Electronic Markets, 14*(1), 36-47.

Todaro, M. & Smith, S. C. (2003). *Economic Development, 8th edition.* Essex, UK: Pearson Education Ltd.

Tornatzky, L. G. & Fleischer, M. (1990). *The Processes of Technological Innovation.* Lexington, MA: Lexington Books.

Travica, B. (2002). Diffusion of Electronic Commerce in Developing Countries: The Case of Costa Rica. *Journal of Global Information Technology Management, 5*(1), 4-24.

Tsai, Y. (2006). Effect of Social Capital and Absorptive Capability on Innovation in Internet Marketing. *International Journal of Management, 23*(1), 157-166.

Tsang, M. M., Ho, S. & Liang, T. (2004). Consumer Attitudes Toward Mobile Advertising: An Empirical Study. *International Journal of Electronic Commerce, 8*(3), 65-78.

Turel, O., Serenko, A., Detlor, B., Collan, M., Nam, I. & Puhakainen, J. (2006). Investigating the Determinants of Satisfaction and Usage of Mobile IT Services in Four Countries. *Journal of Global Information Technology Management, 9*(4), 6-27.

UNCTAD (2001). *E-Commerce And Development Report, Internet Edition, Trends and Executive Summary*, United Nations Conference On Trade And Development, United Nations, New York. Retrieved 22 May 2004, from http://www.unctad.org/en/docs/ecdr01ove.en.pdf.

UNCTAD (2002) *E-Commerce And Development Report 2002.* United Nations Conference on Trade and Development, New York. Retrieved July 9, 2001, from http://r0.unctad.org/ecommerce/ecommerce_en/edr02_en.htm.

UNCTAD (2006). *UNCTAD ICT and E-business Branch Publications and Documents. E-commerce and Development Report 2001-2004.* United Nations Conference on Trade and Development. Retrieved March 12, 2006, from http://r0.unctad.org/ecommerce/ecommerce_en/docs_en.htm

Ure, J. (2002). Modeling Critical Mass for E-Commerce: the Case of Hong Kong. *Electronic Commerce Research, 2*(1-2), 87-111.

Vadapalli, A., and Ramamurthy, K. (1998). Business Use Of The Internet: An Analytical Framework And Exploratory Case Study. *International Journal of Electronic Commerce, 2*(9) 2, 71-94.

Van Rooyen, J. & Willem, R. (2004). The Future Effect of E-business on Treasury and Risk Management Systems and Treasury Management in South Africa. *Development Southern Africa, 21*(2), 399-414.

Van Slyke, C., Belanger, F. & Sridhar, V. (2005). A Comparison of American and Indian Consumers Perceptions of Electronic Commerce. *Information Resources Management Journal, 18*(2), 24-40.

Vijayan, P. & Shanmugam, B. (2003). Service Quality Evaluation Of Internet Banking In Malaysia. *Journal of Internet Banking and Commerce, 8*(1).

Vivekanandan, K. & Rajendran, R. (2006). Export marketing and the World Wide Web: perceptions of export barriers among Tirupur knitwear apparel exporters - an empirical analysis. *Journal of Electronic Commerce Research, 7*(1), 27-40.

Viswanathan, N. K. & Pick, J. B. (2005). Comparison of E-commerce in India and Mexico: An Example of Technology Diffusion in Developing Nations. *International Journal of Technology Management, 31*(1/2), 2-19.

Wade, M. & Hulland, J. (2004). Review: The Resource-Based View and Information Systems Research: Review, Extension and Suggestions For Future Research, *MIS Quarterly, 28*(1), 107-142.

Wang, S. & Cheung, W. (2004). E-Business Adoption by Travel Agencies: Prime Candidates for Mobile e-Business. *International Journal of Electronic Commerce, 8*(3), 43-63.

Wang, Y., Tang, T. & Tang, J. E. (2001). An Instrument for Measuring Customer Satisfaction toward Websites that Market Digital Products and Services. *Journal of Electronic Commerce Research, 2*(3), 89-102.

Wang, Y. C. W., Chang, C. & Heng, M. S. H. (2004). The Levels of Information Technology

Adoption, Business, Network, and A Strategic Position Model For Evaluating Supply Chain Integration. *Journal of Electronic Commerce Research, 5*(2), 85-98.

Webster, J. & Waston, R. T. (2002). Analyzing The Past To Prepare For The Future: Writing A Literature Review. *MIS Quarterly, 26*(2), 13-23.

Westland, C., Kwok, M., Shu, J., Kwok, T. & Ho, H. (1997). Electronic Cash in Hong Kong. *Electronic Markets, 7*(2), 3-6.

Westland, C., Kwok, M., Shu, J., Kwok, T. & Ho, H. (1998). Customer and Merchant Acceptance of Electronic Cash: Evidence from Mondex in Hong Kong. *International Journal of Electronic Commerce, 2*(4), 5.

Westland, C. & Ming, S. S. (1997). Automation of China's Securities Markets. *Electronic Markets, 7*(2), 25-29.

Wigand, R. Picot, A. & Reichwald, R. (1997). *Information, Organization and Management: Expanding Markets and Corporate Boundaries*. Chester, England: John Wiley and Sons.

Wigand R.T. (1995) Electronic Commerce And Reduced Transaction Costs: Firms' Migration Into Highly Interconnected Electronic Markets, *Electronic Markets, 16/17*, 1-5.

Wigand, R. T. (1997). Electronic Commerce: Definition, Theory, And Context. *The Information Society, 13*(1), 1-16.

Williamson, O. (1981). The Economics of Organization: The Transaction Cost Approach, *American Journal of Sociology, 87*(3), 548-577.

Williamson, O E. (1985). *The Economic Institutions of Capitalism: Firms, Markets, Relational Contracting*. New York: Free Press.

Wilson, E. (2000). Wiring the African Economy. *Electronic Markets, 10*(2), 80-86.

Winter, S.G. (2003). Understanding Dynamic Capabilities, *Strategic Management Journal, 24*(10), 991-995.

Wolcott, P., Press, L., McHenry, W., Goodman, S.E. & Foster, W. (2001) A Framework for Assessing the Global Diffusion of the Internet. *Journal of the Association for Information Systems, 2*(6), 1-50.

Wood, C. M. (2004). Marketing and E-commerce as Tools of Development in the Asia-Pacific Region: A Dual Path. *International Marketing Review, 21*(3), 301-320.

World Bank (2001) *Global Economic Prospects and Developing Countries 2001*, The World Bank, Washington DC. Retrieved May 09 2004, from http://www.worldbank.org/prospects/gep2001/full.htm.

World Trade Organization (WTO) (1998) *Electronic Commerce and the Role of the WTO*, World Trade Organization, Geneva.

Wresch, W. (2003). Initial E-commerce Efforts in Nine Least Developed Countries. *Journal of Global Information Management, 11*(2), 67-78.

Wu, C., Cheng, F. & Lin, H. (2004). Web site Usability Evaluation of Internet Banking in Taiwan. *Journal of Internet Banking and Commerce, 9*(1).

Wu, J. & Wang, S. (2005). What Drives Mobile Commerce? An Empirical Evaluation of the Revised Technology Acceptance Model. *Information and Management, 42*(5) 719-729.

Wynne, C., Bethon, P., Pitt, L., Ewing, M. & Napoli, J. (2001). The Impact of the Internet on the Distribution Value Chain. *International Marketing Review, 18*(4), 420-431.

Xu, S., Zhu, K. & Gibbs, J. (2004). Global Technology, Local Adoption: A Cross Country Investigation of Internet Adoption by Companies in the United States and China. *Electronic Markets, 14*(1), 13-24.

Yang, Z., Shaohan, C., Zhou, Z. & Zhou, N. (2005). Development and validation of an instrument to measure user perceived service quality of information presenting Web portals. *Information and Management*, *42*(4), 575-589.

Yap, A., Das, J., Burbridge, J., & Cort, K. (2006). A Composite-Model for E-Commerce Diffusion: Integrating Cultural and Socio-Economic Dimensions to the Dynamics of Diffusion. *Journal of Global Information Management, 14*(3), 17-34,38.

Yen, B. P. C. & Su, C. J. (1997). Information Technology Infrastructure for Textile and Apparel Industry in Hong Kong. *Electronic Markets, 7*(2), 9-12.

Yu, C. (2006). Influences on Taiwanese SME E-Marketplace Adoption Decisions. *Journal of Global Information Technology Management, 9*(2), 5-21

Yu, J. (2006). B2C Barriers and Strategies: A Case Study of Top B2C Companies in China. *Journal of Internet Commerce, 5*(3), 27-51.

Zhang, Q. B. & Chau, P. Y. K. (2002). Creating E-commerce Courses with Regional Intent. *Communications of the ACM, 45*(2), 35-37.

Zhang, X., Li, Q. & Lin, Z. (2005). E-Commerce Education in China: Driving Forces, Status, and Strategies. *Journal of Electronic Commerce in Organizations, 3*(3), 1-17.

Zhu, K. & Kraemer, K. (2005). Post-Adoption Variations in Usage and Value of E-Business by Organizations: Cross-Country Evidence from the Retail Industry. *Information Systems Research, 16*(1), 61-84.

Zhu, K., Kraemer, K.L. & Xu, S. (2003) E-business Adoption by European Firms: A Cross-country Assessment of the Facilitators and Inhibitors, *European Journal of Information Systems, 12*(4), 251-268.

Zhu, K., Kraemer, K.L., & Xu, S. (2006) The Process of Innovation Assimilation by Firms in Different Countries: A Technology Diffusion Perspective on E-Business, *Management Science, 52*(10), 1557-1576.

Zhu, K., Kraemer, K., Xu, S. & Dedrick, J. (2004). Information Technology Payoff in E-Business Environments: An International Perspective on Value Creation of E-Business in the Financial Services Industry. *Journal of Management Information Systems, 21*(1), 17-54.

Zwass, V. (1996). Electronic Commerce: Structure And Issues. *International Journal of Electronic Commerce, 1*(1), 3-23.

Zwass, V. (1998). Structure And Micro-Level Impacts Of Electronic Commerce: From Technological Infrastructure To Electronic Market Places. In E. K. Kenneth (Ed.), *Emerging Information Technologies*. (pp. 1-32) Thousand Oaks, CA: Sage Publications.

APPENDIX ONE

List of Acronyms and Abbreviations

A Attitude (as used in Theory of Planned Behavior)
AER Assessment and E-readiness
AES Adaptation-Evolution Strategies of Firms
B2B Business to Business
B2C Business to Consumer
BI Behavior Intention
CB Consumer Behavior;
CL Contextual
CPT Culture, Policy and Technology Framework
DE Developing Economy
DEs Developing Economies
DD Design and Development;
DOI Diffusion of Innovation Theory
DV Development
E-business Electronic Business
E-commerce Electronic Commerce
eGovernement Electronic Government
EV Environmental
HOF Hofstede's Cultural Framework
IT Information Technology
IN Interactional
IS Information Systems
IEEE Institute of Electrical and Electronics Engineers, Inc.
ICT Information and Communication Technology
ICTs Information and Communication Technologies
ICT4D ICTs for Development
INT Internationalization Theories
ITC International Trade Center
ITU International Telecommunications Union
KL Knowledge and Learning
MA Marketing
M-Lit Mobile Literature
N/A None or Not Available
MG Managerial
OG Organizational
OP Opportunity
PBC Perceived Behavior Control
PEER Perceived External E-Readiness
PEOR Perceived Organizational E-Readiness
PERM Perceived E-Readiness Model
PFC Porter's Five Forces Model
PNC Porter's National Diamond of Competitive Advantage
PP Public Policy
PEOU Perceived Ease of Use
PU Perceived Usefulness
RBV Resource-Based Value of the Firm
RBT Resource-Based Theory;
RDVT Review of Development Theories
SEV Service Evaluation
SMEs Small and Medium Enterprises
SN Subjective Norm
STR Strategy
TAM Technology Acceptance Model
TC Technology
TCT Transaction Cost Theory
TOE Technology-Organizational-Environment Framework
TPB Theory of Planned Behavior
TRA Theory of Reasoned Action
UNCTAD United Nations Conference On Trade And Development
WTO World Trade Organization

APPENDIX TWO

Distributions of Articles by Journals

Table 6. Distributions of articles by journals (1993-2006)

Name of Journal	Frequency of Articles by Year (Descending)															
	93	94	95	96	97	98	99	00	01	02	03	04	05	06	Total	
																%
EM					5	2	2	3	3	1		5		2	23	9.4
JIBC									1		2	3	4	10	20	8.2
EJISDC								2		3	1	4	2	6	18	7.3
JGIM											4	6	1	3	14	5.7
JGITM							1	1	1	1	4	3		3	14	5.7
ECR										4		6		1	11	4.5
JECO												5	2	3	10	4.1
I&M									1	1		1	4	2	9	3.7
JECR									3	2		2	1	1	9	3.7
IJEC					1	1						3	2	1	8	3.3
IT4D				1							2		4		7	2.9
CAIS												2	1	3	6	2.4
IMR									1		1	1	2		5	2.0
IMDS									1			2	1		4	1.6
ACM	1									1			1		3	1.2
ECRA											1		1	1	3	1.2
IJM									1					2	3	1.2
ITID												2	1		3	1.2
ITP			1					1			1				3	1.2
TIBR									1	1				1	3	1.2
BPMJ									1			1			2	0.8
HSM									1					1	2	0.8
IJM													1	1	2	0.8
INFO										1		1			2	0.8

Table 6. Distributions of articles by journals (1993-2006) (continued)

Name of Journal	Frequency of Articles by Year (Descending)														Total	
	93	94	95	96	97	98	99	00	01	02	03	04	05	06		%
IR										1			1		2	0.8
ISR													1	1	2	0.8
JBIM										1		1			2	0.8
JIC														2	2	0.8
JIEL							1		1						2	0.8
JMIS												1		1	2	0.8
LIM											1	1			2	0.8
PPM												1		1	2	0.8
TECNO								1		1					2	0.8
TIS											1			1	2	0.8
ACIT											1				1	0.4
APJML														1	1	0.4
IJSM													1		1	0.4
IJTM													1		1	0.4
IMCS											1				1	0.4
IMS										1					1	0.4
IRLCT										1					1	0.4
IRMJ													1		1	0.4
ITR												1			1	0.4
IWC												1			1	0.4
JBP														1	1	0.4
JCIS												1			1	0.4
JIS							1								1	0.4
JSM												1			1	0.4
JWB														1	1	0.4
JWT							1								1	0.4
MD										1					1	0.4
MS														1	1	0.4
NLW								1							1	0.4
OG SCI										1					1	0.4
OG STU													1		1	0.4
OXDS												1			1	0.4
OXREP									1						1	0.4
PGDT													1		1	0.4
T&I										1					1	0.4
TEL										1					1	0.4

Table 6. Distributions of articles by journals (1993-2006) (continued)

Name of Journal	Frequency of Articles by Year (Descending)														Total	
	93	94	95	96	97	98	99	00	01	02	03	04	05	06		%
TM														1	1	0.4
WD										1					1	0.4
WL									1						1	0.4
MISQ															0	0.0
Total															245	100

List of Journals Reviewed

ACIT Annals of Cases on Information Technology
APJML Asia Pacific Journal of Marketing and Logistics
BIT Behavior and Information Technology
BMARK Benchmarking
BPMJ Business Process Management Journal
ACM Communications of the ACM
CAIS Communications of the Association for Information Systems
CR Competitive Review
DSS Decision Support Systems
DSA Development Southern Africa
ECR Electronic Commerce Research
ECRA Electronic Commerce Research and Applications
EJISDC Electronic Journal on Information Systems in Developing Countries
EM Electronic Markets
HSM Human Systems Management
IIMB IIMB Management Review
IMDS Industrial Management & Data Systems
INFO INFO
ICTL Information & Communication Technology Law
I&M Information & Management
IMCS Information Management & Computer Security
IRMJ Information Resources Management Journal
ISR Information Systems Research
ITID Information Technologies and International Development
ITP Information Technology and People
IT4D Information Technology for Development
IMS Integrated Manufacturing Systems
IWC Interacting With Computers
IJBM International Journal of Banking Management
IJEC International Journal of Electronic Commerce
IJEI International Journal of Entrepreneurship and Innovation
IJM International Journal of Information Management
IJITDM International Journal of Information Technology & Decision Making
IJM International Journal of Management

IJMED International Journal of Management & Enterprise Development
IJMC International Journal of Mobile Communications
IJSM International Journal of Service Industry Management
IJTM International Journal of Technology Management
IMR International Marketing Review
IRLCT International Review of Law, Computers & Technology
IR Internet Research
ITR INTERTAX
JBIM Journal of Business and Industrial Marketing
JBP VISION-The Journal of Business Perspective
JCIS Journal of Computer Information Systems
JECO Journal of Electronic Commerce in Organizations
JECR Journal of Electronic Commerce Research
JGIM Journal of Global Information Management
JGITM Journal of Global Information Technology Management
JIS Journal of Information Science
JIEL Journal of International Economic Law
JIBC Journal of Internet Banking and Commerce
JIC Journal of Internet Commerce
JMIS Journal of Management Information Systems
JSM Journal of Services Marketing
JWB Journal of World Business
JWT Journal of World Trade
LIM Logistics Information Management.
MD Management Decision
MS Management Science
MISQ MIS Quarterly
NLW New Library World
OG SCI Organizational Science
OG STU Organizational Studies
OXDS Oxford Development Studies
OXREP Oxford Review of Economic Policy
PGDT Perspectives on Global Development and Technology
PPM Problems and Perspectives in Management
TECNO Technovation
T&I Telematics and Informatics
TEL The Electronic Library
TIS The Information Society
TIBR Thunderbird International Business Review,
TM Tourism Management
WD World Development
WL World Link

Chapter II
Significance and Success Factors of E-Commerce in China and Russia: An Empirical View

Reinhold Decker
Bielefeld University, Germany

Frank Kroll
Bielefeld University, Germany

ABSTRACT

This chapter outlines and discusses current empirical findings and conceptual ideas concerning the status quo and future prospects of e-commerce in emerging markets, with a special focus on China and Russia. Besides two own online-surveys covering business companies from different industries as well as management consultancies acting in these countries, we also refer to the results of recent studies dealing with the topic of interest in a meta-analytical sense. The resulting managerial implications are primarily based on those factors which determine the success of e-commerce activities and on the corresponding value creation.

INTRODUCTION

The significant relevance of **e-commerce** has initiated comprehensive research and numerous empirical studies referring to industrial countries such as Germany and USA. In recent years, e-commerce has also gained increasing importance in **emerging markets** like **China** and **Russia**. This far-reaching development finds its expression in a respectable number of studies that investigate the status quo and future prospects of e-commerce in such markets. However, the existing ones are

Copyright © 2009, IGI Global, distributing in print or electronic forms without written permission of IGI Global is prohibited.

mostly restricted to partial aspects of e-commerce or industries. Hawk (2004), for example, provides a comparison of B2C e-commerce in developing countries, whereas Huang et al. (2007) present an empirical study on the success factors of e-commerce in the Chinese publishing industry. Decker et al. (2005) emphasize the necessity of cross national comparisons, particularly when discussing the developments in emerging markets, if generalizations of the empirical findings are a matter of interest. In doing so, several parallels as well as interesting differences between China and Russia can be detected that suggest specific e-commerce strategies.

China and Russia are particularly interesting from an economic point of view, since both the evolution of China towards a future economic power and the relevance of Russia for the East-European market expansion is largely indisputable. In 2006, China's gross domestic product (GDP) growth rate was 10.7 per cent, the highest value for years. Over the last nine years China had a GDP growth rate of 9.2 per cent on average. Russia, on the other hand, featured a GPD growth rate of 6.7 per cent in 2006 and an average growth rate of 6.8 per cent when considering the last seven years. In comparison to this, Germany and the USA currently have an average GDP growth rate of 1.6 and 2.9 per cent (Bundesagentur fuer Aussenwirtschaft, 2007). According to its purchasing power parity, China is the second strongest nation, behind the USA. Russia ranks ninth in this context (The World Factbook, 2007). The potential future demand resulting from these markets is an important attractor for foreign companies. In 2006, China attracted over 69.5 billion US$ in foreign direct investments, i.e. 3.2 times more than Germany and 5 times more than Russia. China is covering about 9.6 million square kilometers and Russia, the largest country at all, even 17 million. Due to the enormous geographical size of these countries, the application of Internet-based e-commerce solutions, as an additional alternative to conventional market development approaches, recommends itself. According to the China Internet Network Information Center (CNNIC) about 162 million Chinese internet users are online today. The current number of internet users in Russia amounts to 28.7 million (The Public Opinion Foundation, 2007).

A review of the relevant empirical literature reveals the considerable heterogeneity of the respective studies regarding the covered topics. Xiang and Kim (2007), e.g., show that international papers more often deal with technological issues, while Chinese papers put a stronger focus on the support systems and security, one of the main aspects of e-commerce success in China. The general conditions of e-commerce in Asia, and in particular in China, are the subject of discussions in various up-to-date studies. Tan and Wu (2006), for instance, consider e-commerce in China in more detail. Among other things, they argue that there are still obstacles which hinder the widespread adoption of e-commerce in China. Nevertheless, China is moving into a stage of sustainable growth in e-commerce, despite these obstacles. Wong et al. (2004) concentrate on factors that have a significant effect on e-commerce in China. They point out that e-commerce development will be influenced in a significant way by user behavior and local economic development. The goal of a paper by Tan and Wu (2004) is to investigate the diffusion and impacts of the Internet and e-commerce in China. They state that Chinese companies have started to systematically build up an e-commerce infrastructure and an Internet presence. But the companies often fail in accomplishing transactions because of barriers in business practices, legislation, and culture. Lu et al. (2007) empirically examine how tourism and travel e-commerce has boomed in China, how the tourism value chain has changed in the new environment, and what the current status of China's tourism and travel e-commerce is. Their results suggest that most Websites primarily provide general information, but more and more also offer search, online reservation, and payment services. Furthermore, they discuss the factors affecting consumers' decision-making process in tourism and travel e-commerce and the future of this e-commerce application in China.

In contrast to China, the number of freely available e-commerce studies for Russia is still small. The contributions of Fey and Doern (2002) and Doern and Fey (2006) respectively can be mentioned here as remarkable examples. Current empirical studies comparing e-commerce in China and Russia do not yet exist to our knowledge.

Therfore, the main issues of this chapter are:

1. The interest and involvement of Chinese and Russian companies in e-commerce, as well as possible reasons of non-involvement, if so.
2. The presumptive implementation of e-commerce applications in China and Russia in the near future.
3. The key drivers of e-commerce value creation in China and Russia and resulting practical implications.

The first and the second issue will be addressed particularly by referring to the results of a comprehensive study conducted by the authors themselves. This study, among other things, aimed at verifying hypotheses that had been concluded from the relevant literature, e.g.: "By means of e-commerce the companies can enhance the efficiency of their business processes and thus increase their competitiveness.", "Including the Internet in business processes increases the level of national and international awareness and thus generates competitive advantages.", or "The companies in China and Russia are increasingly involved in e-commerce.". The data analysis methods which we used in our study are explorative factor analysis (with varimax rotation), analysis of variance, chi-square testing as well as descriptive statistics. The third issue will be addressed by reporting the results of a content analysis of recently published studies. As a matter of course, country-specific differences and conditions are focused in each case.

E-COMMERCE IN CHINA AND RUSSIA: CONDITIONS AND BACKGROUND

China and Russia are characterized by some common features that appear to be relevant for e-commerce activities. Both countries rank among the largest countries in the world with huge populations including different ethnic groups. In both countries the average income is comparatively low, which has a negative influence on the success of Internet-based B2C activities. However, the current economic developments in these countries result in a gain of income by more than 12 per cent per year in Russia (The World Factbook, 2007) and 17.6 per cent (urban residents) respectively 13.3 per cent (rural residents) in China (National Bureau of Statistics of China, 2007). According to eMarketer (2007) the B2C e-commerce sales in China will achieve 18 billion US$ in 2010, seven times more than in 2006.

An essential prerequisite of e-commerce is a well-functioning telecommunications infrastructure (cf. Hollensen, 2007). This, together with broadly available personal computers or mobile phones with internet access, enables extensive provision of e-commerce offers. Unfortunately, according to existing studies, none of these prerequisites is given to a really satisfactory degree in China or Russia at the moment. But both countries show impressive growth rates regarding the availability of private computers and the use of the Internet for private and commercial purposes. Special programs like "Electronic Russia 2002-2010", which supports the computerization of companies and private households, and the Chinese

"Enterprise Online Project", which tries to get companies online, are supporting and promoting the observable positive trends. According to the 19th Public Opinion Foundation (POF) Report 2007 the share of Internet users in Russia increased from 8 per cent in summer 2002 to 25 per cent in spring 2007. However, in both countries a strong regional discrepancy concerning the availability and the use of the Internet exists. In Russia the Internet is used mainly in large cities, especially Moscow, and in the western part of the country. About 76.3 per cent of the Russian Internet users are residing in the western regions (POF, 2007). An east-west slope can also be observed in China. Here, we have a concentration of Internet usage in the eastern areas. Overall 57.9 per cent of the Chinese Internet users reside in eastern provinces and cities of China (CNNIC, 2007). Current e-commerce efforts aiming at the whole population of the countries have to take into account the existing geographical distributions, at least for a certain period of time.

Another crucial prerequisite for successful e-commerce activities is the existence of a comprehensive legal framework. In both countries the lack of jurisdiction for e-commerce affairs was a major handicap for a long time. In the meantime, the governments have ratified various new laws to establish such a legal framework and in both countries law firms and attorneys specialized in e-commerce are increasingly offering their services.

While in Russia an operative logistics system is available in most of the relevant regions, this only partially applies to China. In view of the Olympic Games in 2008 substantial improvements of the existing logistics system have been decided by the Chinese government. Actually, the Games have induced people to deal with the Internet: 90 per cent of the ticket applications were made online. Thus, the Internet has been the dominating distribution channel for the ticket sale (CNNIC, 2007).

INTEREST AND INVOLVEMENT OF CHINESE AND RUSSIAN COMPANIES IN E-COMMERCE

To provide a more detailed picture selected results of two own **Internet-based surveys** comparing Chinese and Russian companies as well as subsidiaries of German companies on-site are reported in the following. Furthermore, we refer to the assessments of management consultants which have also been collected in these surveys. In case of Russia, complete datasets for 93 companies are available (48 Russian companies, 20 subsidiaries, and 25 Russian consultants). The sample includes commercial, industrial, and service enterprises, as well as "others" at a ratio of 41:33:18:1. Analogously, 91 datasets are available for China. Here, 37 respondents stem from Chinese companies, 30 from Chinese subsidiaries of German companies, and 19 responses came from Chinese consultants. Five respondents did not provide the respective information. The distribution of the covered branches is as follows: commercial enterprises make up 6 per cent, industrial enterprises 60 per cent and service enterprises 25 per cent. For the remaining respondents the respective categorization is missing.

In order to check whether the answers of the companies and the consultants can be pooled for each sample, chi-square tests of homogeneity have been carried out. As a result the assumption of homogenous sub-samples could not be rejected at significance level 0.05 in both cases. For a more detailed description of the data and the conducted analyses see Decker et al. (2005).

A main issue of our investigation concerned the general interest and individual involvement of the surveyed companies in e-commerce. For this purpose we asked questions on the status quo and the intended implementation of different e-commerce applications. In both China and Russia, the Internet is already intensively used for information search and online marketing activities with a special focus on online advertising. Furthermore, most of the companies already have got their own Website. However, differences occur with respect to Websites including order functions. This seems to be more relevant for Russian companies. In contrast to this the use of the intranet was much more popular in China at the time of data collection. In addition, Tan and Wu (2006) point out, that after-sales customer service is another application of the Internet which is often used by Chinese companies.

By means of chi-square testing, we checked which of the e-commerce applications could be assumed to increase significantly within the 12 months following the date of data collection. For Russia such an increase could only be stated for the use of electronic customer relationship management. In China significant changes could be assumed for the survey items "homepage with order function", "shop system", "electronic customer relationship management", "electronic supply chain management", and "eMarketplace". Obviously, both countries are increasingly involved in e-commerce activities, but the developments in China show greater dynamics which is probably caused by the better-developed IT-infrastructure. According to the Networked Readiness Index 2006-2007 (World Economic Forum, 2007) Russia ranks 70th, while China ranks 13th. Thus, China seems to be more developed concerning the Internet and can concentrate on more complex applications to exploit it in an economic respect.

Further questions were devoted to the effects of e-commerce and the Internet as a whole on the business processes and the creation of competitive advantages. Furthermore, the impact of e-commerce activities on a company's value chain and the impact of the Internet on a company's general popularity were of interest. The corresponding hypotheses read as follows:

1. "By means of e-commerce the companies can enhance the efficiency of their business processes and thus increase their competitiveness."
2. "Including the Internet in business processes increases the level of national and international awareness and thus generates competitive advantages."

Both countries are characterized by an extensive and largely identical perception of the presumptive competitive advantages. Altogether 69 per cent of the Russian and 95 per cent of the Chinese companies agreed that e-commerce induces an increase in efficiency regarding the internal processes; 61 and 92 per cent respectively also agreed about the potential increase of personal productivity. E-commerce solutions were considered to affect the company's popularity and reputation as well as the sustainability of customer orientation and the acquisition of new customers in a positive way. Russian companies indicated that e-commerce has a stronger effect on the acquisition of new domestic customers (70 per cent agreement) than on the acquisition of foreign ones (49 per cent agreement). In the Chinese sample these differences are significantly smaller, namely 78 per cent agreement for the domestic and 83 per cent for the foreign markets. The consultants also largely agreed about this issue. Concerning the realization of competitive advantages in terms of cost reduction and time saving the latter tend to show a higher level of approval. Altogether, we could identify a great enthusiasm for e-commerce in China. This, potentially, may be a customer-driven effect. According to Tan and Wu (2006) the customers of Chinese companies usually demand e-commerce more often compared to the average of a set of 10 economies including USA, Germany, France, and Mexico. Both the Chinese companies and the consultants were judging the economic advantages resulting from e-commerce more positive than the Russian respondents.

In order to obtain deeper insights in the managerial and economic effects of internet usage

Table 1. Results of the factor analysis for the Russian sample

Characteristics	**Factor loadings**
Factor 1: *Growth orientation*	
Increase of popularity in the market	0.72
Acquisition of new domestic customers	0.72
Better communication with customers/suppliers	0.61
Factor 2: *Efficiency*	
Reduction of the business process time	0.80
Increasing efficiency of the internal processes	0.73
Factor 3: *Continuance*	
Acquisition of new foreign customers	0.78
Standardization of business processes	0.77
Factor 4: *Cost savings*	
Reduction of the procurement costs	0.87
Reduction of the stock	0.75
Factor 5: *Additional benefits*	
Availability of an additional supply channel	0.86
Temporal competitive advantages	0.58

Table 2. Results of the factor analysis for the Chinese sample

Characteristics	**Factor loadings**
Factor 1: *Growth orientation*	
Reduction of the business process time	0.86
Acquisition of new foreign customers	0.82
Improved competitive position and effectivity	0.79
Factor 2: *Efficiency*	
Reduction of the procurement time	0.90
Reduction of the procurement costs	0.86
Reduction of the stock	0.74
Increase of popularity in the market	0.70
Factor 3: *Marketing advantages*	
Reduction of sales costs	0.75
Acquisition of new domestic customers	0.66
Factor 4: *Capitalization*	
Faster capitalization	0.87
Increase of sales	0.73

and e-commerce activities an explorative factor analysis was carried out. The relevant survey items significantly correlate with the latent factors depicted in Table 1 and 2. Both Tables show the items with the highest factor loadings.

In both samples the first factor can be labeled "growth orientation" and explains about 35 per cent of the total variance. In the Russian sample this factor loads high on the "increase of popularity in the market" and the "acquisition of new domestic customers". In contrast to this, the first factor of the Chinese sample shows the highest loadings on the "reduction of the business process time" and the "acquisition of new foreign customers". Already this factor foreshadows the differences in the individual strategies. According to the available data Russia more strongly concentrates on the domestic market while China puts the main focus on international markets. The representation of the economic sectors in the sample (see above) might be one explanation for this pattern. The second factor is labeled "efficiency" in both samples. It explains 12 per cent of the total variance in the Russian and 32 per cent in the Chinese sample. Apparently, efficiency plays a major role in China. Here, an increase of efficiency in business processes seems to be achievable, among other things, by optimizing the procurement processes. In Russia this primarily applies to the reduction of the business process time. The remaining three, respectively two, factors can be interpreted analogously and explain 24 and 33 per cent of the total variance.

Considering the different factors and factor loadings the conclusion that e-commerce is differently used and assessed in China and Russia is obvious. While it seems to become an essential component of business processes in China, it is primarily used as an additional but promising marketing channel in Russia. The estimates are plausible against the sample structure. In both countries e-commerce promises to play an essential role in the future with regard to the growth of the companies and the efficiency of the internal business processes. By means of analysis of variance it can be shown that those aspects (items) which significantly effect e-commerce are mainly assigned to factor 2 ("efficiency") and factor 3 ("continuance") in the Russian sample and to factor 1 ("growth orientation") and factor 2 ("efficiency") in the Chinese sample.

A further topic of interest corresponds with the question whether B2B will dominate B2C in the future, as partly supposed. The respective hypothesis ("Those companies which are involved in e-commerce are mainly active in B2B domains.") could be confirmed by means of chi-square testing at significance level 0.05 by using the answers about the companies' business environment. In Russia 60 per cent of the surveyed companies were active in B2B and 37.5 per cent in B2C (note: a company can be active in both fields). In China the discrepancy is even more obvious (B2B: 66.3 per cent, B2C: 15 per cent).

The development of e-commerce in B2B is strongly related to the availability of adequate eMarketplaces. While the available data do not suggest significant dynamics regarding the introduction of new eMarketplaces in Russia in the near future, the usage of this marketing instrument seemingly gains increasing importance in China. Research and Markets (April 2006) recently supported this rating but also mentioned that the Chinese market is mainly dominated by a few service providers.

In the final part of the questionnaires the respondents were asked to evaluate selected external and internal aspects that can be assumed to influence e-commerce commitment. Some of the collected opinions of the companies concerning these aspects are depicted in Figure 1. In both countries the legal protection of online businesses was rated rather bad, whereas significant differences occur with regard to the evaluation of the online payment systems. In contrast to Russia, we could detect an explicit negative rating of this important aspect of e-commerce in China. Even though the acceptance of online payment was growing in China during the last years, there are still reservations regarding customer protection and security. Therefore, in March 2006 the "Chinese Enterprise E-commerce Credibility Basic Regulation" was passed. However, the outstanding role of personal contacts in the sales process, in both countries, might slow down the developments in e-commerce, especially in the B2C sector.

A closer look at the answers of the consultants reveals their criticism regarding the inadequacy of the logistics system and the lack of confidence between business partners in China. The stated importance of personal contacts in selling processes further supports this impression. While the opinions of the consultants and the companies strongly differ with respect to the degree of automation of business processes in Russia, there is a basic agreement regarding this point in China. A different picture also results for the qualification of staff. While this point was rated positively by both the companies and the consultants in China, the Russian consultants criticized the existing lack of qualified staff.

KEY DRIVERS OF E-COMMERCE VALUE CREATION IN CHINA AND RUSSIA

Doern and Fey (2006) identified eight key drivers of **e-commerce value creation** in Russia, namely novelty, complementarity, efficiency, lock-in, accessibility, ease of use, ease of search, and trust. The individual drivers can be characterized as follows:

The first driver, *novelty*, refers to the introduction of new products or services. In the present context this can be an innovative offer or payment system. *Complementarity* occurs when the benefit of providing several products (i.e. goods or services) jointly is greater than the benefit that accrues when each product is provided separately. The geographical size of Russia and the corresponding logistical problems can affect the occurrence of complementarity. Business activities which increase transaction *efficiency* or decrease transaction costs normally create additional value. Therefore, the business processes can be optimized regarding synergy effects, cost reduction

Figure 1. Selection of crucial dimensions of an e-commerce commitment

and efficiency, e.g. by looking for alternatives to the Russian postal service as a distribution provider. According to our study, nearly 50 per cent of the Russian companies believe that the use of e-commerce results in a reduction of the duration of business processes and an increase of revenue. *Lock-in* refers to the process of repeating transactions with the same company, which can be achieved by appropriate loyalty programs, e.g. bonus point systems. Lock-in can be initiated by offering a broad and well-structured assortment which explicitly accounts for potential complementarities. Due to the geographical dimensions of Russia, the omnipresent availability of products is a topical subject. Against this background, *accessibility* determinates the extent to which customers have access to goods and services as well as the extent to which firms have access to buyers and sellers. In our study about 70 per cent of the Russian companies were of the opinion that e-commerce can help to acquire new domestic customers. With respect to the acquisition of foreign customers the level of agreement approached 50 per cent. In Chinese companies the agreement regarding the value of e-commerce for customer acquisition activities turned out to be even higher. Here, at the time of data collection, more than 80 per cent of the respondents were supposing that e-commerce can help to acquire new foreign customers (compared to 78 per cent in case of domestic ones). Moreover, 66 per cent of the respondents were considering e-commerce as a new distribution channel making goods and services accessible to a broader community of customers. Analogously, the *ease of use* refers to the easiness of acquiring the products offered by a company. Because of the partly low performance and expensiveness of internet connections in Russia optimizations regarding the loading and navigation of a Website seems to be an appropriate way to generate value for the users. The faster a customer finds the things s/he is looking for, the higher her/his satisfaction will be. Therefore, the *ease of search* can create value by reducing the time it takes to find the products of interest. "Slow" and complex Websites can cause the customer to leave without making a purchase. Finally, *trust* can be build up, e.g., by a professional design of the Website and the explicit promotion of the provided/guaranteed security, especially in connection with the payment process. Therefore, trust increases the value by making the customers feel confident when buying online. The importance of trust is also expressed in the demand of personal contact during the sales process (see Figure 1). Therefore, personalizing a commercial Website or rather the respective marketing message can improve its overall success.

To discuss e-commerce strategies for the Chinese market, we refer to three recently published papers. The first one, by Yu (2006), discusses possible strategies for B2C companies. The main ideas are summarized in the following:

Since face-to-face transaction is the traditional and predominant shopping format in China, Chinese customers are cautious when buying online. This is in line with Figure 1 which tells us that, in our sample, 93 per cent of the Chinese companies accentuated that the selling of products requires personal contact. Therefore, companies should prudently select the products they offer in an online shop. The most frequently purchased products have a high level of standardization, e.g. books or computers. Furthermore, a systematic education of the consumers about the benefits of online shopping is necessary. Usually those benefits are communicated with terms like "convenient", "shopping anytime anywhere" and "low-priced". According to Yu (2006) the most common value resulting from online shopping is to save money. This can also be supported by the own study, where efficiency proved to be one of the key factors causing Chinese companies to invest in e-commerce. Therefore, companies have to convince the customers that online purchasing can be more favorable to them than conventional shopping. However, the delivered benefit must be desired by the Chinese customer at all. Another

Figure 2. Model of e-commerce value creation in Russia (Doern & Fey, 2006)

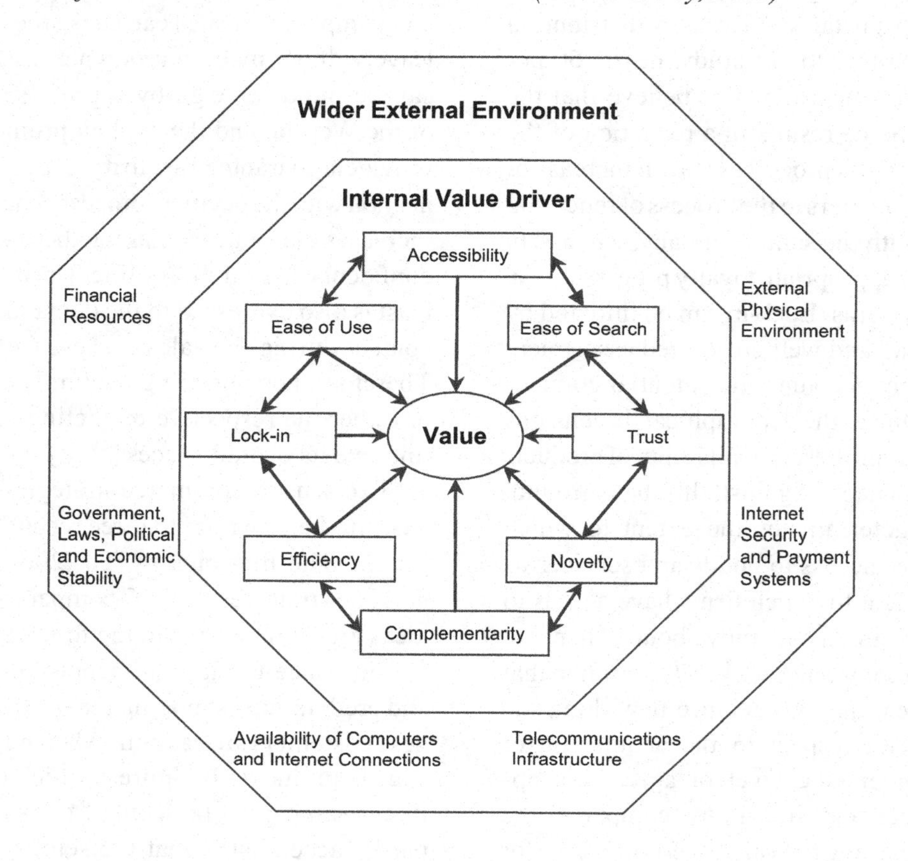

challenge results from the growing concerns about product quality. Therefore, companies should heavily promote their competence in this respect.

Since the transportation infrastructure is better developed in urban regions and since the number of internet users is significantly higher there compared to the rural areas, the companies' focus should be on the major urban markets. To be more independent from the China Postal Service, which is rated costly and slow but disposes of the only nation-wide delivery network, multiple distribution channels, e.g. direct delivery or third-party delivery, should be taken into consideration.

The majority of Chinese customers do not dispose of a credit card, although more and more young Chinese customers demand and use this means of payment. To deal with this situation different payment methods can be approached, i.e. online payment, offline payment and club membership. But all these options must be perceived as secure, which is a sound claim, if we remind that about 80 per cent of the Chinese companies were classifying online payment systems to be not or less secure (see also Figure 1). Therefore, and similar to Russia, the companies should heavily promote transaction security regarding the payment method they offer to their customers. Recently, Alipay, a company of the largest Chinese e-commerce portal Alibaba, reported to have more than 56 million registered users and to account for more than 50 per cent of the online payment market in China. In this context it seems to be worth mentioning that Alipay has been voted the "Most Trusted Online Payment System" in 2006.

A paper by Huang et al. (2007) provides some hypotheses concerning the **success factors of e-commerce** activities of traditional companies in China. The hypotheses are verified by means of an empirical study focusing on the publishing industry. The authors point out that the internal company factors "e-commerce strategy", "IT infrastructure" and "customers" are crucial for e-commerce success. Self-evidently, the cited results only apply to the publishing industry, but other studies like the one by Zhu et al. (2003) conclude with similar results. In our study only 38 per cent of the Chinese companies stated that their business partners are not online, whereas 20 per cent indicated that the systems of the business partners are not compatible with their own ones.

In a recent study Maeurer (2006) was analyzing the perception of Websites of western companies by Chinese users. A main result is that most of these Websites are rated as "conservative" because Chinese users usually have a stronger preference for colorful Web pages and a high information density than western users. Therefore, simple translations of western Websites into Chinese would not be adequate in most cases. Instead, depending on the products to be offered, significant adjustments of both the content and the layout are required.

CONCLUSION AND GENERAL IMPLICATIONS

The importance of e-commerce is largely undisputed today, also, and particularly, in countries like China and Russia. In both markets, continuously increasing e-commerce activities can be observed, despite the still not optimal telecommunications and internet infrastructure. Most of these activities are focusing on B2B, where the companies expect to realize significant efficiency and competitive advantages. Since neither in China nor in Russia the external conditions are fully satisfying at the moment the respective governments have initiated measures to improve the legal and the infrastructural environment of e-commerce. So, e-commerce activities should be concentrated on urban regions, at least when entering these markets for the first time. Nevertheless, the differences between Western Europe and the USA on the one side and China and Russia on the other side will presumptively continue to exist for some time, we suppose. Therefore, the existing and broadly consolidated e-commerce strategies of western companies cannot be applied to these markets without appropriate adjustment. Particularly for foreign companies, which want to enter the considered markets or intent to enhance their sales activities there, the findings presented in this chapter suggest to follow the popular slogan "think global and act local".

Moreover, a successful market entry requires serious consideration of country specificities. In Russia, this, e.g., concerns the current state of the IT-infrastructure and the comparatively low penetration of personal computers in the private sector, particularly outside the large metropolises. In China, the still existing mistrust in online payment systems can hamper e-commerce activities for some time. Additionally, product quality and product piracy are crucial topics at present when discussing business policies of Chinese companies. So, Chinese companies intending to acquire new customers on domestic or western markets should appropriately communicate and traceably prove the quality and uniqueness of their products.

REFERENCES

Bundesagentur fuer Aussenwirtschaft (2007). Retrieved July 31, 2007, from http://www.bfai.de/DE/Navigation/Datenbank-Recherche/datenbank-recherche-node.html.

China Internet Network Information Center (2007). Retrieved July 31, 2007, from http://www.cnnic.net.cn/en/index/0O/index.htm.

Decker, R., Hermelbracht, A., & Kroll, F. (2005). The Importance of E-Commerce in China and Russia – An Empirical Comparison. In D. Baier, R. Decker, & L. Schmidt-Thieme (Eds.), *Data Analysis and Decision Support* (pp. 212-221), Springer, Berlin.

Doern, R., & Fey, C. F. (2006). E-Commerce Developments and Strategies for Value Creation: The Case of Russia. *Journal of World Business, 41*, 315-327.

Fey, C. F., & Doern, R. (2002). *The Role of External and Internal Factors in Creating Value Using e-commerce: The Case of Russia* (Tech. Rep. No. 02-102). St. Petersburg, Russia: Stockholm School of Economics Russia.

Hawk, S. (2004). A Comparison of B2C E-Commerce in Developing Countries. *Electronic Commerce Research, 4*, 181-199.

Hollensen, S. (2007). *Global Marketing – A Decision-Oriented Approach*. Harlow, Prentice Hall.

Huang, J., Zhao, C., & Li, J. (2007). An Empirical Study on Critical Success Factors for Electronic Commerce in the Chinese Publishing Industry. *Frontiers of Business Research in China, 1*(1), 50-66.

Lu, Y., Deng, Z., & Wang, B. (2007). Tourism and Travel Electronic Commerce in China, *Electronic Markets, 17*(2), 101-112.

Maeurer, T. (2006). *The Language of the Net (in German). Asia Bridge, 10*, 36-37.

National Bureau of Statistics of China (2007). Retrieved July, 31, 2007, from http://www.stats.gov.cn/english.

Tan, Z., & Wu, O. (2004). Diffusion and Impacts of the Internet and E-Commerce in China. *Electronic Markets, 14*(1), 25-35.

Tan, Z., & Wu, O. (2006). China: Overcoming Institutional Barriers to E-Commerce. In K. L. Kraemer, J. Dedrick, N. P. Melville, & K. Zhu (Eds.), *Global e-Commerce* (pp. 209-246). Cambridge, MA: Cambridge University Press.

The World Factbook (2007). Retrieved July 31, 2007, from https://www.cia.gov/library/publications/the-world-factbook/index.html.

The Public Opinion Foundation (2007). Project "The Internet in Russia/Russia on the Internet" - 19th Release. Retrieved July 31, 2007, from http://bd.english.fom.ru/report/map/projects/ocherk/eint0702.

Wong, X., Yen, D. C., & Fang, X. (2004). E-Commerce Development in China and its Implication for Business. *Asia Pacific Journal of Marketing and Logistics, 16*(3), 68-83.

World Economic Forum (2007). The Global Information Technology Report 2006-2007. Retrieved July 31, 2007, from http://www.weforum.org/pdf/gitr/rankings2007.pdf.

Xiang, J. Y., & Kim, J. K. (2007). A Comparative Analysis of International, Korean and Chinese E-Commerce Research, *International Journal of Electronic Business, 5*(1), 65-106.

Yu, J. (2006). B2C Barriers and Strategies: A Case Study of Top B2C Companies in China, *Journal of Internet Commerce, 5*(3), 27-51.

Zhu, K., Xu, S., & Dedrick, J. (2003). Assessing Drivers of E-business Value: Results of a Cross-country Study, In: *Proceedings of the 24th International Conference on Information Systems* (pp. 181-193). Seattle: Washington State University.

Section II
Challenges to E-Commerce Adoption in DCs

Chapter III
Identifying Factors for Lack of E-Commerce in Developing Countries

Sushil K. Sharma
Ball State University, USA

Jatinder N. D. Gupta
University of Alabama in Huntsville, USA

ABSTRACT

The past few years have seen a rise in the number of companies' embracing e-commerce technologies in developing countries and the volume of e-commerce has been growing. However, as compared to developed nations, developing countries still have been lacking in e-commerce. This chapter identifies some of the reasons that may be responsible for lack of e-commerce in developing countries. For the scope of the study, we have limited developing countries to China, India, Indonesia, Philippines and Sri Lanka. The study identifies factors at the macro level to understand why the adoption of e-commerce in developing countries has been not taking off as expected.

INTRODUCTION

The use of the Internet as a vehicle for electronic commerce (e-commerce) has become a standard operating practice in many corporations throughout the world (Ah-Wong et al., 2001; Rosenbaum, 2000). The world is rapidly moving towards Internet based economic structures and information societies, which comprise networks of individuals, firms, and countries linked electronically in interdependent and interactive relationships (Heeks, 2002). The wide use of information and communication technologies (ICTs) has accelerated the growth of e-commerce in last few years in many parts of the world. These technologies have revolutionized business, economic prosperity

Copyright © 2009, IGI Global, distributing in print or electronic forms without written permission of IGI Global is prohibited.

and the way the world and its citizens communicate (Davison et. al., 2000). However, developing countries still lag behind the developed countries in technology absorption. Roche and Blaine (1997) point out that most of the developing world suffers from an "MIPS gap ratio" in the order of something like 1:26 with the developed world. The reasons for low participation level of many developing countries in the global information society for e-commerce include perceived incompatibilities between cultures and technologies, an idealistic preference for self-reliance, and simple lack of economic or human resources to acquire and utilize technology (Davison et. al., 2000).

Developing countries, while representing around 80 percent of the world's population, account for only 2 percent of the total global expenditure on informatics (Davison et al., 2000). This may create marginalization for developing countries from the mainstream economic growth of the world.

E-commerce technologies have the potential to help solve many problems faced by developing countries; from providing remote health care to education (Schech, 2002, Sprano, 2000). However, developing countries may miss major benefits of the e-commerce revolution for the next few years because of inherent problems they face in the implementation and use of e-commerce solutions. This chapter examines the state of e-commerce in developing countries and discusses issues that developing countries must address to harness the benefits of e-commerce. Our discussion includes the progress made in handling these issues and outlines the challenges facing developing nations in successfully implementing e-commerce in their economies. We also endeavor to describe approaches that can be taken to resolve some major issues and challenges related to e-commerce in developing countries. The rest of the paper is organized as follows. We first briefly describe our framework and how we derived this framework. The next six sections discuss the issues and challenges in each category identified in our framework. In these sections, each category is further divided into several sub-categories so that progress made to handle the issues and the remaining challenges can be easily illustrated.

A FRAMEWORK FOR E-COMMERCE INFRASTRUCTURE

The emergence of electronic commerce over the past decade has radically transformed the economic landscape. There has been an increasing amount of literature on the factors that affect development of the Internet and e-commerce in developing countries. On one hand, it is helping nations increase their economic growth and thereby provide more opportunities for the businesses to grow, but on the other hand it raises many technological, economic, and social challenges. While developed countries that have been offering e-commerce have shown impressive performance in their respective economies, many developing countries still lag behind in the e-business race. This could be due to several reasons including but not limited to language, education, technology and technical infrastructure.

In developing countries, internet use and its economic potential are growing exponentially. Developing countries have the advantage of learning and benefiting from the diverse experiences of industrialized countries and leapfrogging into an e-commerce revolution. However, there are still many unresolved issues that hinder the growth of e-commerce in developing countries. Many businesses and consumers in developing countries are still wary of pursuing e-commerce because of the lack of a supporting legal environment, particularly for international trade transactions. Concerns such as the enforcement of contracts, liability, intellectual property protection, privacy, and security are still unresolved to the satisfaction of those involved (Bhatnagar, 2001, Ah-Wong, 2001, Davison et. al., 2000 and E-commerce report 2001). Developing countries have a difficult task to create an e-commerce environment because of many reasons such as poor and limited access to telecommunications infrastructure and services, market restrictions, lack of capital to create infrastructure and acquire technology, and instability in economic, legal, and political environments (E-Commerce Report 2001, Ah-Wong, 2001, Sprano and Zakak, 2000, Dutta, 1997, Roche and Blaine, 1997, and Petrazzine, 1999). In 1998, Esprit listed several issues concerning e-commerce including globalization, contractual and financial issues, ownership, privacy and security, interconnectivity and interoperability and deployment (Kimbrough, & Lee, 1997). Clinton & Jr. categorized possible barriers to the expansion of e-commerce into three main subgroups: technical and financial issues, legal issues and market access issues (Mukti, 2000). There have been a large amount of different research streams on e-commerce frameworks, ICT diffusion, and ICTs in developing countries. To understand various e-commerce related issues, we conceptualized our framework from three major unique e-commerce frameworks documented in literature.

The authors conceptualized a framework from existing three major unique e-commerce frameworks documented in literature. These three frameworks are; the Zwass' (1996) generic framework for electronic commerce that assesses the different dimensions of e-commerce in general. The Wolcott's framework for assessing the global diffusion of the Internet produced by the Global Diffusion of the Internet (GDI) Project (Wolcott, Press, McHenry, Goodman, & Foster, 2001) and finally, the Travica (2002) framework, which directly examines the factors necessary for

Figure 1. A framework used for analyzing e-commerce related issues and challenges

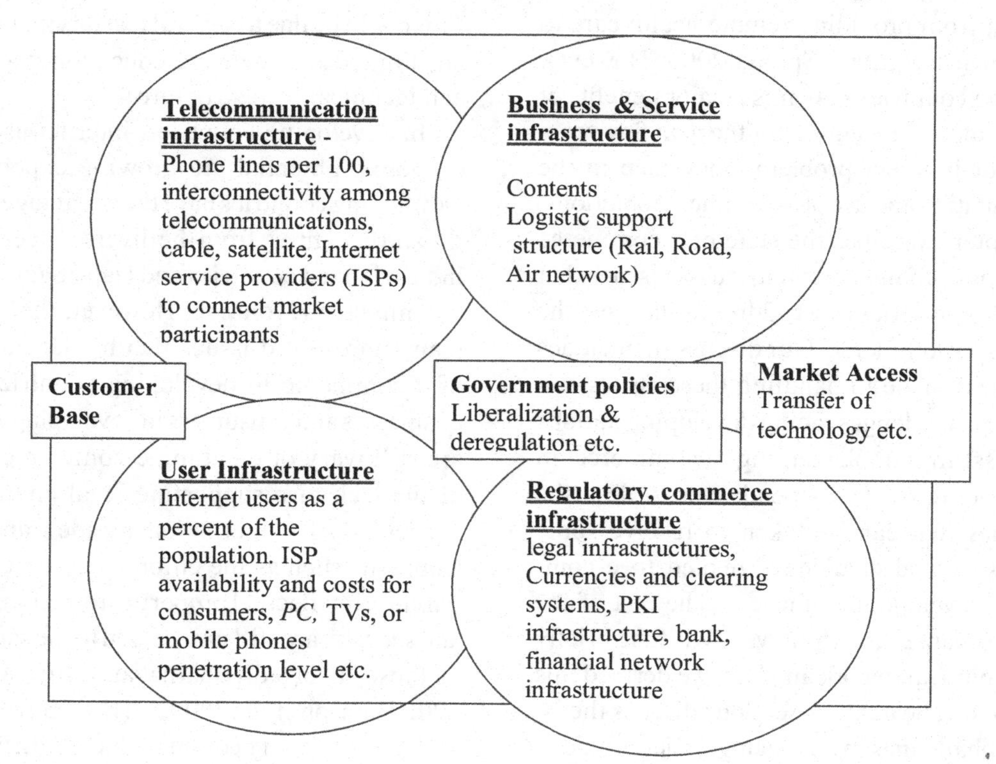

the commercial application of the Internet in the context of developing countries. Drawing various indicators from these frameworks, authors conceptualized the framework to identify some of the reasons that may be responsible for lack of e-commerce in developing countries. For the scope of the study, we have limited developing countries to China, India, Indonesia, Philippines and Sri Lanka. The study identifies factors at the macro level to understand why the adoption of e-commerce in developing countries has been not taking off as expected.

Drawing various indicators from these frameworks, we conceptualized our framework which is shown in Figure 1.

There has been an increasing amount of literature on the factors that affect development of the Internet and e-commerce in developing countries (Mbarika et. al., 2001; Mbarika, Byrd, & Raymond, 2002; Montealegre, 1996, 1998, 2001; Travica, 2002; Wolcott et al., 2001, Heeks, 2002; Schech, 2002). To understand the contextual settings of the developing countries, Travica's framework was quite helpful to conceptualize the framework (Travica, 2002). The Travica (2002) work goes beyond both Zwass' (1996) and the Wolcott's framework to specifically address the diffusion of e-commerce in developing countries. The Travica's framework helped to identify the various aspects of physical, cultural, economic and legal infrastructure that are necessary to support successful diffusion. In his study of e-commerce diffusion in Costa Rica, Travica (2002) developed a framework based on six layers of infrastructure required to support e-commerce in a developing country; transportation for delivering physical goods and documents; a reliable delivery system such as effective postal services; internet-enabling telecommunications, including both physical and legal infrastructure to facilitate the efficient operation of the Internet; a functional software industry to develop and support the necessary Internet applications; e-payment infrastructure, which includes a widespread and effective credit card system, as well as secure and efficient banking; and a cultural layer, which refers to the various cultural aspects of consumer behavior that will incline individuals to use the Internet for commercial activity.

From our e-commerce framework as shown in Figure 1, it is evident that electronic commerce requires at least four types of infrastructure to be in place before online solutions are offered. These are telecommunication infrastructure, business and services infrastructure, user infrastructure and regulatory and commerce infrastructure. Technological infrastructure is needed (e.g., interconnectivity among telecommunications, cable, satellite, or other Internet 'backbone;' Internet service providers (ISPs) to connect market participants to that backbone) to create an Internet marketplace.

User infrastructure or end-user access devices such as such as PCs, TVs, or mobile telephones are needed to access the Internet. A business and service infrastructure in the form of content, distribution and delivery systems are essential for developing e-commerce. Regulatory and commerce infrastructure is needed to make payment over the Internet possible (through credit, debit, or Smart cards, or through online currencies). E-commerce is not possible without laws, and regulations to check the legality and modality of digital transactions, signatures, certification, and encryption; and disclosure, privacy, and content regulations. In government policies and market access for promotion and growth of e-commerce, specific customer bases must be considered. Thus, keeping these important components of e-commerce in consideration, the authors used the derived framework to analyze the e-commerce-related issues in developing countries. This is in contrast to previous research studies that have focused on the technological, social, economic, and cultural aspects that hinder the growth and implementation of e-commerce in developing countries ((Ngai, & Wat, 2002, Panagariya, 2000, Yavwa and Kritzinger, 2001, Bhatnagar, 2001,

Abeyesekera et al, 1999, Domeisen). Data used for analysis is taken from developing countries such as; China, India, Indonesia, Philippines and Sri Lanka. While the findings are generalized within context, many variations were noticed within these countries for the scale of growth and implementation of e-commerce activities. The methodology adopted for the study used data collection from secondary sources. Available data for e-commerce activities within selected countries came from different time periods and it was difficult to extrapolate the data based on previous patterns.

TELECOMMUNICATION INFRASTRUCTURES

Telecommunication networks are the most important part of an organization's business strategies to compete globally. With the explosion of the Internet and the advent of e-commerce, global telecommunication networks need to be accessible, reliable, and fast in order to effectively participate in the global business environment. Telecommunications is a vital infrastructure for Internet access and hence for e-commerce. Telecommunications and Internet connectivity have now been universally recognized as key to economic development, social progress and a good investment (Schech, 2002). Communication infrastructure not only plays a key role in economic growth, but also impinges on and can impact virtually all global issues: health, education, advancement of women, cross-border and cross-cultural understanding, and tolerance. The lack of communication facilities in developing countries is a constraint to social, political and economic empowerment of the people. The major problem impeding the installation of telecommunication infrastructure in these regions is that most service providers are unable to justify the cost of investment because of the low economic activities leading to low return on investment (Yavwa and Kritzinger, 2001, Darley, 2001, Dutta, 1997, Heeks, 2002, Kibati, & Krairit, 1999).

In almost all of the developing countries, the low tele-densities are a consequence of deliberate political decisions supporting government-owned monopoly telecommunication agencies. Recently, a few of the developing countries have opened the telecommunications market to competition and foreign investment (ITU Report, 2002). Changes in regulatory environments and market conditions will have a pronounced impact on the future implementation of telecommunications infrastructure for basic telephony and Internet access (Yavwa, and Kritzinger, 2001, E-commerce Development Report 2001, 2002, 2003, Mbarika et. Al., 2002). To access the Internet, developing countries pay, on average, three times more than developed country users (Woodall, 2000). Lack of communication technologies has been the main cause of inadequate economic and social development and widening the gap between developed and developing countries. The new economy's self perpetuating cycle, where investment generates efficiency that frees more capital for investment, is not taking root in the developing world as quickly as many would like, and the rapid growth of wealth in the West is exaggerating the differences (Brandman, 2000).

Most of the developing countries rely on Public Switched Telephone Networks (PSTN) for residential users to connect to the Internet. Although, of late, a few countries have started using other media (such as cable TV network, limited ISDN, and radio links), wired infrastructure is woefully inadequate to meet the demand of basic connectivity (ITU Report, 2002). Moreover, inadequate maintenance of the access loop, low quality of cables, and high rates of accidental damage to cables lead to transmission impairments (Mbarika, et al., 2002, Simms, 2000, Sridhar, 1998). Despite initiatives taken by many developing countries to invest heavily on building up IT infrastructure, the growth of e-commerce does not commensurate with the investment. In a democratic country like India, where 40% of the people are still living below the poverty line, mobilization of the huge investment required for the implementation and growth of E-commerce is not easy (Nair and Prasad, 2002, World Bank Report, 2002). Developing countries need large scale promotion of the IT industry through domestic and foreign investment, a higher level of PC penetration and internet access. While voice-over-Internet, known as "IP Telephony," is allowed in certain developed countries, it is still illegal in many developing countries. However, if IP telephony becomes legal in those countries, how will the revenues be generated to maintain the large communication infrastructure? Developing countries that have recently invested in circuit technologies are still waiting to receive returns on their investment (Lynch, 2001).

Opportunity for Wireless Technologies

New communication technologies can even allow developing economies to leapfrog old technologies such as copper wire and analog telephones. Now they have the option to switch to new wireless technologies that are more cost effective. Also, wireless technologies can reach remote terrain where a wired infrastructure is difficult to place. These technologies, if used to connect the population, can increase the tele-density ratio and ultimately set a platform for global e-commerce. Developing countries can use these technologies effectively for health, education, and other purposes. The World Bank already uses satellites to broadcast televised courses to students in 15 African countries who communicate with teachers by e-mail, fax, and telephone (Woodall, 2000).

Lack of Electricity

Developing countries often lack electricity that is the main necessity for promoting e-commerce. Electricity, a good telecommunication infrastructure, and affordability of computer hardware, software, and servers are the three basic requirements for electronic commerce. These are all lacking in many developing countries. Governments control most of these ingredients of e-commerce, such as telecommunication infrastructure and electricity. Foreign direct investment (FDI) is currently not permitted. In order to encourage e-commerce, countries need to make a change in their financial liberalization and foreign investment policies. Present communication infrastructures in developing countries are more concentrated in urban cities rather than normally distributed in all regions. Strategically, these countries can create smart cities and set up software technology parks in those places from where they can do offshore projects for export intensive industries. However, it is equally important to create an e-commerce center of public services to improve the quality of life for all citizens. One of the strategies that developing countries can take is to rely on external financial aid from developed countries and create infrastructure. For e-commerce, one requires supportive logistics to cut the costs and speed delivery. Most of the developing countries lack logistics support and good delivery systems. While this may be desirable, it may take time. Another strategy that could be adopted is to ask foreign companies to invest in local markets and help create infrastructure.

Digital Divide

A major global concern is the so-called "digital divide" or "telecommunication gap" between countries with high telecommunication infrastructures and those without. The digital divide is one of the greatest impediments to development, and it is growing exponentially. Presently, the Internet penetration rates in these developing regions range from less than 1% to 3%, which is far below the 25% to 50% penetration rates seen in many wealthy, developed nations (Rombel, 2000). Many US companies such as IBM, Microsoft, and

America Online have recently taken initiatives to aid the developing countries. They have provided Internet-enabled computers and digital cameras to aid existing education, health, and community development work in third world countries (Rombel, 2000). If the digital divide gap can be closed by transferring technology from the rich countries to the developing world, it will foster the growth of sustainable new local businesses that will promote prosperity and reduce poverty (O'Kane, 2000). The International Telecommunications Union (ITU) and World Bank have taken the initiatives to address this problem. With the initiatives of the ITU, developing countries have gained approximately $40 billion in voice rate subsidies from the developed world in the latter half of the 1990s (Rombel, 2000). But as the dependence on communication infrastructure grows even more rapidly, these subsidies are not enough (Lynch, 2001).

USER INFRASTRUCTURE

One of the major bottlenecks to the expansion of e-commerce to the developing world is the lack of telecommunications and Internet connectivity and access to the necessary hardware and software. The tele-density, reach and geographic coverage of telephone services, its bandwidth, the cost of telephone services, the national policies governing the telecommunications sector and the number of computers are major obstacles for the growth of e-commerce in developing countries.

Internet Access Infrastructure

High Internet access rates and low penetration of computers are primary obstacles to the growth of electronic commerce in developing countries (Petrazzini and Kibati, 1999). Internet access is one of the main components of e-commerce, and Internet access is still very expensive in most developing countries, especially in Asia (Odedra, et al., 1993, Peha,, 1999, Petrazzini, & Kibati, 1999). The majority of the population in developing countries still cannot afford a personal computer (PC). For consumers, the biggest barriers are the limited diffusion of PCs, high cost of Internet access, and lack of easy payment mechanisms (Dedrick and Kraemer, 2001). The high cost of Internet access, and the low bandwidth available to most users, is a serious problem. The lack of basic telecommunications infrastructure is a severe hindrance to the growth of the Internet in any country. One of the reasons to explain the high Internet access costs is inefficiency of telephone services and low levels of tele-density.

Developing countries lag far behind developed markets in the availability of technical pre-requisites for conducting electronic commerce. In addition, telecommunication services in developing countries are unreliable and/or costly. There are also enormous differences in access to telecommunications, both between and within developing countries. For instance, while the majority of the population in developing countries lives in rural areas, over 80 percent of the main telephone lines are located in urban areas. Although the Internet revolution is growing by leaps and bounds in developing countries, intensity wise, it still lags behind the developed countries. This can have profound implications on an individual country's ability to participate in the global electronic market place.

Computer Lines and Equipment

The cost of a computer itself is so high in proportion to the average income in developing countries, that not more than 2% of the people have computers to access the Internet (Abeyesekera et. Al., 1999). The Internet subscription costs are also not affordable. When the majority of people do not have computers and Internet access, e-commerce becomes difficult. Further, the cost of local and long-distance telephone calls, giving access to the Internet, are significantly higher in developing countries.

The World Trade Organization (WTO) can take a lead in lowering the prices of information technology (IT) equipment and telephone services through the Information Technology Agreement (ITA) and the Negotiations on Basic Telecommunication Services under the General Agreement on Trade in Services (GATS) (Bhatnagar, 1999). Cheaper equipment costs and cheaper telephone services would increase the likelihood of success in e-commerce.

BUSINESS AND SERVICE INFRASTRUCTURE

Developed countries have very strong communication infrastructures, and thus they have the advantage to set up business infrastructure in form of services on the servers that can be accessed at high bandwidths. Whereas, due to lack of technology and telecommunication infrastructures, developing countries have to host all of their applications and services on the servers that would be far beyond their national boundaries in developed countries.

Business Infrastructure

Owing to the lack of infrastructure, one component of e-commerce, known as Web content, is also missing. Web content is hosted at servers that are connected at high bandwidths, typically located in developed countries. Even among these connected countries and regions in the developed and developing countries, its usage remains largely with the "haves", that is, those who can afford the hardware, software, and cost of connectivity. The International Telecommunications Union (ITU) and several other international bodies are taking various initiatives to help developing countries to prepare themselves for e-commerce, but business infrastructure in developing regions is still nonexistant.

The impact of e-commerce on the business sector has been widely accepted: it reduces transaction costs, allocates resources better, increases economies of scale and improves the competitiveness of businesses in general (E-commerce and Development Report 2001). In addition to these common problems that face all businesses, most enterprises have to deal with equally serious internal shortcomings. First is the lack of the necessary information systems and infrastructure to support e-commerce. Most firms do not have enterprise applications linking sales, production, finance, service and other functions, and many lack even more basic applications in each of those areas. Without such systems, it is difficult to conduct transactions electronically, and what is called e-commerce is actually limited to e-mail and an informational Web site ((Montealegre, 1996, 1998, 2001).

Service Infrastructure: Distribution and Delivery Systems

Service infrastructure in the form of distribution and delivery systems is very important for developing e-commerce. Speed is one of the most important manifestations of electronic commerce. Unless products are delivered faster at lesser cost, the benefits of e-commerce will not be realized. Most of the developing countries have inefficient distribution and inadequate transportation and delivery network. These countries lack nationwide delivery companies such as FedEx and UPS, and transportation infrastructure (road, rail, air) is poor in many areas (E-commerce and Development Report, 2001).

REGULATORY AND COMMERCE INFRASTRUCTURE

E-commerce depends on rapid authorization, payments, and settlement of accounts through the "financial plumbing" of the economy. Authorization for transactions between online businesses and payment institutions such as credit card companies or banks needs to be in real time. Many developing countries do not have financial institutions or financial bank network that can support e-commerce based transactions as commerce infrastructure. The lack of payment mechanisms prevents transactions from being completed online. Majority of people often prefer to pay by bank draft or cash-on-delivery. A proper regulatory framework must be in place for e-commerce to prosper. Existing laws and regulations might not be applicable as some of the online services do not exist in the physical world and boundaries between services as well as industries have become blurred. Electronic payments must be secure and legal, with liability clearly identified. In developed countries where more than eighty percent of population uses credit cards, debit, and smart cards for realizing e-commerce transactions, but the majority of the population believe in cash transactions in developing countries.

Financial Infrastructure Issues

E-commerce necessitates electronic payment systems for goods and services over the Internet. It requires a financial network that links existing electronic banking and payment systems, including credit and debit card networks, with new retail interfaces via the Internet. Electronic payment systems require support from governments to set up policy and regulation framework to support electronic transactions. E-commerce requires payments to be transmitted electronically. Changing the way financial services are used in international trade, electronic commerce will force standardization, add speed, and reduce costs. These changes can help developing countries improve their international trade competitiveness. Companies can submit loan requests, credit insurance, letter of credit confirmations and other documents in electronic form (Cattani, (2000).

Banks and Financial Network Restructuring

Payment over the Internet is an important link for developing e-commerce and is viewed as a bottleneck in developing countries. Most developing countries do not have banks that offer online electronic payment systems. It would require a massive effort to sensitize banks toward building an e-commerce infrastructure since many would likely be resistant towards this new mode. A few countries have created some form of infrastructure to support online payments, but that is still not adequate.

E-commerce involves transactions conducted using credit facilities over the Internet. In many developing countries, credit cards are rare, and consumers use upfront cash payments in a face-to-face environment. Since the Internet is not available in local languages, only a few elite could make use of the Internet for commerce. Fewer than 6% of Internet users currently reside in developing countries, which account for 84% of the world's population (Domeisen, 1999). The United Nations Development Program is trying to create cyber cafes in villages, bringing Internet and fax services to rural areas to reduce the gaps between "haves and have nots".

Banks and financial institutions, such as credit card companies must integrate their activities so that transactions can be completed online. Developing countries need to create an electronic network (between financial institutions) and the legal framework for online transactions. Banking laws and regulations thus need to be adjusted to the new formats and requirements. Converting currencies is another complex issue to be resolved. Besides banking and investment services, insurance, brokerage, credit worthiness and guaranteeing services, underwriting, and a host of other financial services require restructuring. To restructure these sectors, developing countries may need financial reforms for liberalization of financial sectors. Governments in control will find it difficult to make major reforms in these financial sectors.

Finances through Venture Capitalists (VC)

Several developing countries have skilled manpower in abundance and they have the opportunity to utilize them to develop new products and services of e-commerce. These countries, however, do not have venture capitalists to finance the ideas for innovations. Traditionally, in developing countries, financing has come from either banks or stock market listings, neither of which is suitable for young, high-risk Internet companies that have yet to launch commercial operations.

Regulatory and Tax Issues

E-Commerce does not distinguish between goods and services if they are in an electronic form. This creates difficulty to fix tariff and tax on these. Usually, goods are charged differently than services, but in e-commerce, since the entire transaction is in electronic form, it is difficult to differentiate it for tariff purposes. For example, if a CD is bought online and if music CDs or software CDs are delivered across border, one may fix a tariff for this transaction since it is a physical good being delivered, but what happens if CD contents are downloaded electronically across borders?

Another major task would be how to monitor the tax and tariff collection. Due to availability of skilled manpower, developing countries like India, China, Singapore, and Malaysia extensively export electronic goods and services. Exports may be out of tax structures because of the promotion of export revenue. However, at the same time, software and consultancy services, which are sought by these countries, deserve to have taxes or tariffs, but are not taxed because they happen in electronic mode and are too difficult to monitor. Many would argue that since digital transactions cannot be monitored, duties cannot and should not be levied.

Differentiation of Goods and Services

One of the main concerns for e-commerce, therefore, is how to classify items (goods, services and currency) that are bought and sold across the borders for tax. It is extremely difficult to regulate international commerce, which involves trade in goods, services, currencies, information or ideas, and the impact of these developments on national sovereignty, political institutions, administration, financial and trade policy, and the way of life. This may be a common concern for all countries, but developing countries will be especially hard hit because they will have less to say in devising policies and negotiations.

Developed countries had suggested a zero-duty regime for all electronic transactions where goods and services are digital. The basic problem for such an argument is how to classify digital goods wherein financial data transfer and consultancies may take place electronically. It is essential to create a policy and regulatory environment that favors the development of e-commerce and harmonizes national approaches in diverse areas including telecommunications, trade, competition, intellectual property, privacy and security.

Taxes and Regulation Restructuring

Tax planning for an e-business differs from tax planning for a traditional bricks-and-mortar company. Historically, the generation of income depended on the physical presence of assets and activities. This physical presence, or permanent establishment, generally determined which jurisdiction had the primary right to tax the income generated. Because of the growth of electronic commerce, new e-business models (including digital marketplaces, on-line catalogs, virtual communities, subscription-based information services, on-line auctions, and portals) have emerged. Each allows taxpayers to conduct business and generate income in a country with little or no physical presence in that country. The separation of assets and activities from the source of the income represents a significant departure from historic business models. This change creates new tax planning challenges and opportunities (Olin, 2001). Issues related to tariffs, intellectual property rights, electronic payment, and technological standards require international coordination. Other impediments include obstacles to Web access and e-banking, along with inadequate supply and delivery systems, as well as security concerns. The global e-commerce market for international trade has many obstacles including a lack of coordination among players, payment systems, multiple competing currencies, and technology limitations.

Regulatory and tax structures for e-commerce are not in place. Developing countries have been paying the price of expensive connectivity and lack of access to technology. Once these issues of regulatory and tax structures are resolved, international trade through e-commerce would increase. Nevertheless, many nations are looking for new sources of revenue, and may seek to levy tariffs in global electronic commerce. The World Trade Organization (WTO), OECD, and other appropriate international forums are working to see if global e-commerce can be treated as a tariff-free environment for online products or services.

Legal Framework Issues

E-commerce allows the customers and sellers to interact for any transaction nearly anywhere, crossing borders, cultures, and legal jurisdictions. It may be good news for many since it brings a number of opportunities, but many governments worry that it can lead to many other issues including access to pornography, fraud, libel, gambling, consumer protection, defense of intellectual-property rights, and taxation. Policy makers in these countries have to think about how to tackle some of these problems. Internationally, the United Nations Commission on International Trade Law (UNCITRAL) and other appropriate international bodies like the bar associations must come forward to determine an appropriate framework for encouraging governmental recognition, acceptance, and facilitation of electronic communications (i.e., contracts, notarized documents, etc.) for international contracts in electronic commerce.

Absence of Cyber-Laws

Many countries, including developed nations, are also still grappling with cyber laws. The Cyber Law Bill is getting passed in a few developing countries like India, Singapore, Malaysia, and China. For most developing countries, cyber laws do not exist. While lack of a legal framework under which Internet transactions take place is a real impediment, it is not going to stall e-commerce. However, to gain full benefits of e-commerce solutions, developing countries need to develop cyber laws that define a legal framework for Internet transactions. Further, it would be helpful if these cyber laws are consistent among different countries.

Security Problems Associated with Net Transactions

Security is seen as another impediment for e-commerce. While it is true that there are vulnerabilities with online transactions, experience shows that it is not a major concern for the users. Since developing countries do not have a strong infrastructure to back electronic payment systems, there is little security concern. The culture of credit cards, ATM cards, or purchasing on the Net has just begun in a few urban pockets and it is quite encouraging that the young generation is keen to go for electronic transactions. Culturally, by their mindset, users still do not believe in electronic transactions because people prefer face-to-face transactions to online transactions. As the people change their mindset and start believing in online transactions, security issues are brought to surface.

Intellectual Property Rights (IPR) Issues

The electronic commerce revolution, wherein information is available on a free basis and where much of the information exchange takes place across the borders, raises the issue of how to protect intellectual property rights (IPR). In addition, IPR play an important role in technology transfer and the development of the communications infrastructure in developing countries in the form of foreign direct investment, joint ventures, and licensing. Much of the exchange of information involves intellectual property rights protection. Already, there have been cases of IPR disputes. There have been conflicts of similar trademarks and domain names owned by different parties in different countries. While e-commerce provides more opportunities for free information on the net, it should be able to protect the IPR of the authors and producers. Developing countries need more awareness on these issues since, historically; these issues have not been a matter of concern.

Adequate and effective legal frameworks, therefore, are needed to protect the IPR of sellers and consumers. Sellers should be ensured that their intellectual property will not be stolen and buyers should be ensured that they are obtaining authentic products and services. The World Intellectual Property Organization (WIPO) and other appropriate forums have to work out treaties with different nations to agree on a common guideline (laws and regulations) to protect interest of copyright, patent and IPR. Bodies like WIPO should come forward to ensure that the needed technology transfer to the developing countries takes place in such a way that IPR concerns are addressed.

MARKET ACCESS AND CAPACITY BUILDING ISSUES

Access to open international markets is essential to realize benefits from electronic commerce. Therefore, once the developing countries start offering e-commerce solutions, marketing the products and services would be a challenging task. E-commerce is still perceived either as a mere direct-selling device or simply as a new form of communication. In fact, it should be seen as one of several media to conduct international marketing. Developing countries need to develop and implement effective marketing strategies. Without a critical mass of buyers and sellers, e-commerce would not see the light of day in developing countries (Abeyesekera et al, 1999).

Transfer of Technology

The doctrine of opening markets to developing countries could provide many benefits to developed countries, but developing countries may have to pay disproportional high prices for the needed technologies, products, and services. Although forums like the WTO protect the interests of the nations, developing countries find it difficult to cope up with the aggressive push of those technologies that may change procedures, regulations, cultures, and the role of the governments (Schech, 2002, Sprano, 2000). To ensure the growth of global electronic commerce over the Internet, standards are needed to assure reliability, interoperability, ease of use, and scalability in areas such as: electronic payments, security, public key infrastructure, electronic copyright and patent measures, and data interchange. Numerous organizations have been working to develop standards for the above-mentioned technologies. For the success of electronic commerce, an effective partnership between the governments and private sectors would be helpful.

Presently, developing countries have to rely on technology controlled by developed countries.

Once e-commerce becomes quite common in developing countries, the process of technology transfer will begin automatically. Technology transfer is a slow process and involves several questions related to investment, expertise, government policies, and market access. There may be much give and take between developed countries and developing countries. Developed countries need access to large markets and developing countries need technology. Since both blocks need each other, the technology transfer process will begin. In the beginning, developing countries may attract foreign investments. As time passes, real transfer of technology may take place.

E-commerce technology is maturing and so have the encryption standards that are needed for conducting e-commerce. However, developing countries have to create public key infrastructure (PKI) and Trust and Authentication Services to support e-commerce. Countries, like India, which have already passed the electronic bill to promote e-commerce, have started to set-up government-controlled PKI infrastructures to support e-commerce. Other countries may follow the model since historically all the developing countries have government interventions for developing trust among the users.

Widespread Illiteracy

The chances of success of e-commerce revolution depend upon whether the developing countries have enough intellectual capital to develop and utilize e-commerce products and services. Several countries may have intellectual capital in abundance, but those countries lack infrastructure and financial resources. Once the countries decide to create good communication infrastructure with the aid of developed blocks, it becomes mandatory to build a capacity of intellectual human capital.

E-commerce demands that people should have a good knowledge of English. Since English is predominantly used as a medium for Web sites, a working knowledge of English is required. In addition, good technical skills are needed to create content for e-commerce. All these required skills might not be easily available in developing countries. Capacity building for e-commerce skills is therefore crucial. Many researchers predict that future economies will be driven by strong intellectual capital of the countries. The development of electronic commerce, therefore, puts a premium on the development of education and training policies to ensure that the training curricula meet the needs of industry. In turn, the Internet and electronic commerce itself can contribute to the educational process, through distance learning and educational links between universities, specialized private companies offering HRD training, and between developing countries themselves.

This is a special and serious problem for many developing countries. Most of the developing countries continue to suffer from large-scale illiteracy. In many developing countries, these people also suffer from poverty. These two problems are a cause for slow progress of e-commerce. Therefore, developing countries need to find a way to expand their educational programs to reach people who cannot afford education. Since the majority of the people needing such education reside in rural areas, developing countries can effectively use the emerging distance education systems. The open university concept that combines the audio, video, text, and tutoring system used in India for example may provide a mechanism to decrease the level of illiteracy in developing countries and hence benefit e-commerce solutions.

International Forum for Coordinating E-Commerce Related Activities

Developing countries need the help of international bodies such as OECD, WTO, WIPO and UNCITRAL to prepare an e-commerce, legal custom, and taxation framework which favors not only the "haves" but also supports the "have nots."

Developing countries have a huge potential for e-commerce and they have large markets to offer to the developed countries. Market access is another issue that requires attention of international bodies to resolve. All these issues, including electronic payments, legal commercial code, intellectual property, copyright and trademark, privacy and security, and market access need resolution and developing countries should get favor of "haves". The taxation of electronic commerce, in "virtual goods," such as information, services, and physical goods is a complex issue. Trade and tariffs for goods and services delivered through electronic commerce channels may be differentiated from physical goods purchased through the Internet and delivered by traditional methods.

Many developing countries have the advantage of skilled manpower that is currently not utilized well. However, this strength, if used strategically can provide leverage in the age of knowledge driven businesses. In addition, developing countries have to protect their small and medium-sized enterprises (SMEs) because the entry of foreign companies into local markets may eat away not only the local markets but may also be a threat for the existence of SMEs. Several UN and inter-governmental agencies are presently addressing the above issues related to e-commerce. Developing countries can use these inter-governmental agencies to seek help solve their problems and thus enhance the benefits of e-commerce solutions.

GOVERNMENT POLICIES, LIBERALIZATION AND DE-REGULATION

Developing countries need domestic reforms to create infrastructure that is owned by private parties. So far many of the countries have infrastructure owned by government that has its own limitation for the growth of e-commerce and international trade. The liberalization and de-regulation initiatives taken by the governments should be aimed at supporting growth and integration with the global economy. The reforms may reduce licensing requirements; make access to foreign technology and investment easier and removed restrictions on investment. While there are currently no explicit trade barriers on electronic commerce, the infrastructures that make electronic commerce possible are still burdened by a myriad of trade and investment barriers. The growth of electronic commerce depends on continued liberalization of these infrastructures, many of which are already part of WTO commitments. E-commerce growth would also depend the political stability in that country. Political stability is the key to foreign direct investments for building e-commerce infrastructure particularly in those countries where infrastructure is weak and there are not enough funds to develop. Many countries such as China, India, Philippines are still in the transition from a planned to a market economy.

Developing countries should encourage private sector investment by privatizing government-controlled telecommunication companies. They should create competition by inviting foreign investment to government-controlled telecommunication set-ups, and by ensuring telecom connectivity at affordable low prices. They should create a regulatory framework that is pro-competitive and matches state-of-the-art technology. Governments, with the help of bodies like WTO and ISO, should be able to take proactive steps to influence Internet pricing, service delivery options, and technical standards.

Governmental Control & Policies

Legal and taxation issues are very important because they involve governments when formulating economic and financial policy. Each country would like to devise these policies in order to utilize them for competitive advantage. If developed countries drive these issues, then the very role of government would be questioned. These countries need to set up a fiscal and legal framework to promote e-commerce through several initiatives ranging from EDI for improving trade logistics, to education and training, setting up portals, cyber Cafes, software technology parks, and smart cities. Most of the developing countries have a long history of strong government-controlled markets so it is a much tougher task to convince the bureaucracy to release control to private parties.

Developing countries have special challenges and responsibilities to create a policy environment that on the one hand allows for the development of e-commerce and on the other ensures the social objective of providing access and benefits for those who cannot afford it. Electronic governance, public Internet terminals, rural access at subsidized cost, and e-awareness are some of the initiatives that must be considered and promoted.

The government of these countries must face many challenges to promote e-commerce. Economic liberalization is a painful exercise because it destabilizes many conventional structures and practices (Mann, 2000). Governments find it difficult to sustain the transition of the economy. E-commerce would certainly help to develop more trade. It may also indirectly help to raise education and health standards. E-commerce has an inherent strength to bring customers and sellers together. This provides opportunities for more choices and more markets even to those citizens who live in rural areas and are isolated in road and rail connectivity. Once people start accessing this medium, it provides a greater opportunity for people to have dialogue with their government on a regular basis thus improving the democratic process itself. E-commerce also offers opportunities to entrepreneurs to participate in creation of knowledge-based economies. To realize the benefits of e-commerce solutions, the government of a developing country needs to take the following steps.

- Prepare appropriate transparent regulatory frameworks for promoting technologies, foreign investments, and trust.
- Formulate transparent and competitive telecommunications policies.
- Safeguard the interest of local trade and industry and create an atmosphere of competition.
- Reduce controls and regulations.

Governments should ensure and assess whether e-commerce has resulted in better information and delivered better goods and services to consumers.

Business Practices Issues

Each country has its own business culture (trust, ethics, practices) and business practices that are used to deal with customers and suppliers within the country (Hofstede, 1980, Straub, et al., 2002). In e-commerce, borders and boundaries are meaningless. Therefore, the managers have to prepare themselves differently to handle issues of access, trust, security, digital contracts, and guarantees. On the one hand, there may be opportunities for new alliances but on the other hand, there may be dangers for breaking existing alliances and practices. There are predictions that major volumes of businesses will come from the B2B (Business-to-Business) model of e-commerce that may provide opportunities for alliances to SMEs. But SMEs that lack technology standards and quality would find themselves out of business. Business communities may again look towards the government to set up standards, laws, and policies that may conflict with international trade policies. Developing countries have to go for capacity-building infrastructure to support e-commerce. Trust plays an important factor to promote e-commerce. Since the entire transaction is done electronically, many customers may be concerned about quality of products and services that they will receive from e-commerce solutions. Questions are raised about what happens if products received are not as expected? Will the sellers replace the faulty products? Will customers trust sellers and vice versa? Presently, developing countries do not have national certifying authorities to break the trust barrier.

CUSTOMER BASE

E-commerce, for its viability, requires a critical mass of customers and suppliers. Due to the lack of infrastructure and affordability, a very small population has access to the Internet. The computer penetration and Internet penetration, as well as credit card and online payment facilities, are lacking in many developing countries. Also, there are very few consumers within the countries as consumers come mostly from developed countries with modern ICT and financial infrastructures (E-commerce and Development Report 2001). According to Michael Porter, one of the key factors to a country's strength in an industry is strong customer base (Porter, 1985). However, in the case of developing countries, the domestic market overall is fairly weak and the countries do not have a strong customer base. In addition, the absence of a strong domestic market hinders to the growth of competition that lacks innovation and competitive pricing.

RECOMMENDATIONS AND CONCLUSIONS

E-commerce has indeed been an impetus to globalization. One great attraction to globalization through e-commerce is the high speed and low cost of achieving a global presence. Many countries are taking initiatives for e-commerce and replacing the old systems with new ones. These transaction systems and the emerging extranets for purchasing and accounting integrate better with the new e-commerce systems to deal more efficiently with a firm's partners, customers and suppliers. This is helping the developing countries to make quicker and better business decisions for improving their economy. There is no simple way to create a global IT system or global business practice, because every country has its own rules and cultural practices. Although, every country has initiated the process of e-commerce, developing countries still lag far behind.

E-commerce, in developing countries, is still not considered a significant market driving force. Firms, in developing countries, have Internet-related constraints. Among them are telecommunications infrastructure gaps, the need to develop more local sites, translation (English is still the dominant language on the Internet) challenges to adapt existing laws to this new medium, and higher costs for installation and access. E-commerce applications are underway in developing countries, but telecommunications and banking infrastructures remain key challenges to meeting the potential of this medium. Logistics, trust, and marketing strategies are other concerns which developing countries need to resolve. Also, people are grappling with basic needs of food, water, clothing, housing and health. The prevailing notion in these countries is that e-commerce is for wealthy people and not for everyone. The general population remains, by and large, unaware and unaffected by it. The reality of limited and undependable connectivity, of course, seriously hampers its growth. Based on our discussions in this chapter and identification of the opportunities and challenges facing the developing countries preparing to offer e-commerce solutions, we recommend the following actions.

- Increase telephone density and widen telephone coverage nationwide - expand the telecommunications infrastructure across all urban and rural areas.
- Increase IT awareness - introduce computer courses in schools, colleges and universities. Train the manpower - create an IT labor force and make every citizen an IT literate.

- Create a good back bone telecommunication infrastructure to support e-commerce - satellite, fiber optics, wireless, and digital technologies network
- Market liberalization- deregulation of government ownership, provision and direct operation of telecommunications infrastructure and services.
- Create a legal framework to permit and promote more electronic-based transactions.
- Allow certain extent of foreign direct investments.
- Modify export and import formalities and customs clearance procedures to remove the regulatory impediments to physical delivery of goods ordered online.
- Develop financial network and banking to support on line payments.
- Recognize legally digital signatures for electronic transactions. Change laws to support on line transactions.
- Create a legal framework for protecting IPR, copyrights, and patents.

To make e-commerce the mainstream for business and social development is a mammoth task facing the developing countries. Future research should focus on developing easy solutions to the emerging issues and challenges and the actions items listed above so that developing countries can reap the benefits of e-commerce.

REFERENCES

Abeyesekera, A., Criscuolo, C., Barreto, E. and Gallagher P. (1999) Partners speak out: Views on e-commerce, *International Trade Forum*, (2), 23-25.

Ah-Wong, J., Gandhi, P., Patel, H., Shah, U (2001) E-commerce Progress: Enablers, Inhibitors and the Short-term Future, *European Business Journal*, vol. 13, No. 2, pp. 98-107, 2001.

Bhatnagar, S. (2001) Social Implications of Information and Communication Technology in Developing Countries: Lessons from Asian Success Stories, *The Electronic Journal on Information Systems in Developing Countries,* vol. 1, No. 4, pp. 1-10

Brandman, J. (2000) Bridging the emerging markets Internet divide, *Global Finance*, 14 (4), 34.

Cattani, C.F., (2000) Electronic finance: A cornerstone to trade and compete internationally, *International Trade Forum*, (3), 13-14.

Darley, W. K. (2001). The Internet and emerging e-commerce: Challenges and implications for management in Sub-Saharan Africa. *Journal of Global Information Technology Management, 4*(4), 4-18.

Davison, R., Vogel, D., Harris, R., and Jones, N. (2000) Technology Leapfrogging in Developing Countries - An Inevitable Luxury?, *The Electronic Journal on Information Systems in Developing Countries,* vol. 1, No. 5, pp. 1-10, 2000.

Dedrick, J. and Kraemer, K.L. (2001) China IT report, *The Electronic Journal on Information Systems in Developing Countries,* vol. 6, Issue 2, pp. 1-10, 2001.

Domeisen, N., (1999) Exporters and importers in developing countries: Investing in the Internet, *International Trade Forum*, (1), 12-13.

Dutta, A. (1997) The physical infrastructure for electronic commerce in developing nations: Historical trends and the impact of privatization. *International Journal of Electronic Commerce, 2*(1), 61-83.

E-commerce and Development Report (2001) prepared by UNCTAD Secretariat

E-commerce and Development Report (2002) prepared by UNCTAD Secretariat

E-commerce and Development Report (2003) prepared by UNCTAD Secretariat

Heeks, R. (2002) i-Development not e-development: Understanding and implementing ICTs and development, *Journal of International Development, 14*(1).

Hofstede, G. (1980) *Culture's consequences: International differences in work-related values*. Beverly Hills: Sage.

ITU Report (2002) Telecommunications Indicators, Geneva: International Telecommunication Union. http://www.itu.org

Kibati, M., & Krairit, D. (1999) The wireless local loop in developing regions. *Communications of the ACM, 42*(6), 60-66.

Kimbrough, S. O., & Lee, R. M. (1997) Formal aspects of electronic commerce: Research issues and challenges. *International Journal of Electronic Commerce, 1*(4), 11-30.

Lynch, G. (2001) The world vs. America, *America's Network,* 105 (1), 34-38.

Mann, C.L. (2000) Electronic Commerce in Developing Countries: Issues For Domestic Policy And WTO Negotiations, Institute For International Economics, March 2000

Mbarika, V. W. A., Byrd, T. A., Raymond, J., & McMullen, P. (2001) Investments in telecommunications infrastructure are not the panacea for least developed countries leapfrogging growth of tele-density, *International Journal on Media Management, 2*(1), 133-142.

Mbarika, V., Musa, P., Byrd, T.A., and McMullen, P. (2002) Tele-density Growth Constraints and Strategies for Africa's LDCs: 'Viagra' Prescriptions or Sustainable Development Strategy?, *Journal of Global Information Technology Management*, vol. 5, No.1, pp.25-42.

Montealegre, R. (1996) Implications of electronic commerce for managers in less-developed countries, *Information Technology for Development, 7*(3), 145-152.

Montealegre, R. (1998) Managing information technology in modernizing "against the odds": Lessons from an organization in a less-developed country, *Information & Management, 34*, 103-116.

Montealegre, R. (2001) Four visions of e-commerce in Latin America in the year 2010, *Thunderbird International Business Review, 43*(6), 717-735.

Nair, K.G.K. and Prasad, P.N. (2002) Development through Information Technology in Developing Countries: Experiences from an Indian State, *The Electronic Journal on Information Systems in Developing Countries,* vol. 8, Issue 2, pp. 1-13.

Ngai, E. W. T., & Wat, F. K. T. (2002) A literature review and classification of electronic commerce research, *Information & Management, 39*(5), 415-429.

O'Kane, G., (2000) World Bank to boost Internet in Africa, *African Business*, (252), 30.

Olin, J., (2001) Reducing international e-commerce taxes, *World Trade*; Troy, 14 (3), 64-67.

Odedra, M., Lawrie, M., Bennet, M., & Goodman, S. E. (1993) Sub-Saharan Africa: A technological desert, *Communications of the ACM, 36*(2), 25-29.

Panagariya, A., (2000) E-commerce, WTO and developing countries, *The World Economy*, 23 (8), 959-978.

Parker, E.B. (1992) Developing Third World Telecommunications Markets, *The Information Society*, vol. 8, No. 3, pp. 147-167.

Peha, J. M. (1999) Lessons from Haiti's Internet development, *Communications of the ACM, 42*(6), 67-72.

Petrazzini, B., & Kibati, M. (1999) The Internet in developing countries, *Communications of the ACM, 42*(6), 31-36.

Porter, M. (1985) Competitive advantage: Creating and sustaining superior performance, Free Press, USA

Roche, E. and Blaine, M.J. (1997) Research Note: The MIPS Gap, *Information Technology in Developing Countries*, vol. 7, No. 4, pp.12-13, 1997.

Rombel, A., (2000) The global digital divide, *Global Finance,* 14 (12), 47.

Rosenbaum, H. (2000) The Information Environment of Electronic Commerce: Information Imperatives for the Firm," *Journal of Information Science*, vol. 26, No. 3, pp. 161-171, 2000.

Simms, C., (2000) The third-world Web world, *LIMRA's marketFacts*, 19 (4), 54-55.

Schech, S. (2002) Wired for change: The links between ICTs and development discourses, *Journal of International Development, 14*(1), 13-23.

Sprano, E. (2000) E-commerce capable: Competitive advantage for countries in the new world e-conomy, *Competitiveness Review, 10*(2), 114.

Straub, D. W., Loch, K. D., Evaristo, R., Karahanna, E., & Srite, M. (2002) Toward a Theory Based Definition of Culture, *Journal of Global Information Management, 10*(1), 13-23.

Sprano, E. and Zakak, A., (2000) E-commerce capable: Competitive advantage for countries in the new world e-conomy , *Competitiveness Review,* 10 (2), 114-131.

Sridhar, V. (1998) Analysis of Telecommunications Infrastructure in Developing Countries. *Proceedings of the Association for Information Systems 1998 Americas Conference*, Baltimore, August 14-16, 1998.

Travica, B. (2002). Diffusion of electronic commerce in developing countries: The case of Costa Rica. *Journal of Global Information Technology Management, 5*(1), 4-24.

UNCTAD (2002) *Building Confidence. Electronic Commerce and Development.* United Nations publication, sales no. E.00.II.D.16, New York and Geneva.

Wolcott, P., Press, L., McHenry, W., Goodman, S. E., & Foster, W. (2001) A framework for assessing the global diffusion of the Internet, *Journal of the Association for Information Systems, 2*(6)

Woodall, P., 2000. Survey: The new economy: Falling through the net?, *The Economist,* 356 (8189), S34-S39.

World Bank Report (2002) *World development indicators*, Washington, D.C.: World Bank.

WTO (1998) *Electronic Commerce and the Role of the WTO.* Geneva.

Yavwa, Y. and Kritzinger, P.S. (2001) Enabling Communication In Developing Regions," *The Electronic Journal on Information Systems in Developing Countries,* vol. 6, No.1, pp. 1-15, 2001

Zwass, V. (1996). Electronic commerce: Structure and issues. *International Journal of Electronic Commerce, 1*(1), 3-23.

Chapter IV
E-Commerce Development in China:
An Exploration of Perceptions and Attitudes

Antonis C. Stylianou
University of North Carolina at Charlotte, USA

Stephanie S. Robbins
University of North Carolina at Charlotte, USA

Pamela Jackson
Fayetteville State University, USA

ABSTRACT

It is widely recognized that e-commerce represents a critical resource for most business organizations. With over 1.3 billion people and double-digit economic growth, China could potentially emerge as the largest Internet and telecommunications market in the world if certain economic, environmental, and organizational barriers are effectively addressed. This chapter develops a descriptive profile of Chinese business managers with respect to their awareness of the technological infrastructure as well as their perceptions and attitudes regarding e-commerce. Management's viewpoint on a variety of environmental, organizational, and personal factors provides insight into the future of e-commerce in China within the framework of organizational commitment to e-commerce driven innovation. Findings indicate that firms interested in engaging in e-commerce in China will find a knowledgeable and supportive business climate; however, e-commerce initiatives may be hindered by constraints imposed by the current infrastructure as well as the political environment.

Copyright © 2009, IGI Global, distributing in print or electronic forms without written permission of IGI Global is prohibited.

INTRODUCTION

The business potential of e-commerce technologies is seemingly irrefutable given the more than 1.1 billion Internet users worldwide (Internet World Stats, 2007). Of these 1.1 billion users, the largest share, almost 400 million or 36 percent, reside in Asia. Although growth in North America has been steady since the inception of the Internet and it now accounts for 21% of the total, the U.S. share of this global market has been gradually declining (211 million; 19%). In contrast, China, with the second largest Internet user population (139 million; 12.5%), is expected to continue gaining market share (572% growth between 2000 and 2007) (China Internet Network Information Center, 2007). These developments are in line with the rate of adoption theory, which describes the IT diffusion process as initially proceeding through a slow, gradual growth period, followed by dramatic and rapid growth, then gradual stabilization, and finally a decline (Rogers, 1995). With over 1.3 billion people and double-digit economic growth, China could potentially emerge as the largest Internet and telecommunications market in the world if certain economic, environmental, and organizational barriers are addressed effectively. Revenues generated through e-commerce transactions have soared to $127.5 billion in 2006, an increase of 50% from the previous year and "with an estimated 50 million Chinese engaged in e-commerce, growth is extremely promising" (Rein, 2007). However, Internet-based transactions remain a mere fraction of the total traditional business revenue. In spite of this paucity of earnings, the Internet provides the Chinese with easy access to the outside world and many are eager to embrace this new technology.

Five pivotal environmental or structural conditions adversely affect the development of a viable e-commerce market in China. First, Internet purchases are generally credit card transactions—a payment system that represents a direct contrast to China's cash-based consumer culture (Rein, 2007; Markus and Soh, 2002; Steinert-Threlkeld, 2000). Credit card penetration continues to be low (only 50 million cards in circulation compared to 1.1 billion debit cards) and "many analysts argue that Chinese consumers are conservative spenders and not willing to buy on credit" (Rein, 2007). However, the trend is showing a dramatic increase in the adoption of credit cards (500% increase between 2004 and 2007) and surveys are showing that the younger generation (18 to 28) is much more willing to purchase items on credit. A second yet related condition stems from the fact that the use of credit cards to make online purchases requires an infrastructure capable of handling electronic payments. China's substandard IT/electronic payment infrastructure (Markus and Soh, 2002; Steinert-Threlkeld, 2000) creates a somewhat formidable obstacle. According to Li and Suomi (2006), China does not have a nationwide credit card network and there is no centralized settlement system. Third, in the last 10 years, the Chinese government has enacted several pieces of legislation related to various aspects of e-commerce. These include legislation on electronic signatures, taxation, electronic contracts and others (Yan, 2005). At the same time, the government has continued to use and add restrictive/bureaucratic policies such as content regulations and user registration requirements. Current governmental restrictions continue to hamper the development of a vibrant e-commerce market in China (Li and Suomi, 2006; Markus and Soh, 2002; Rosen, 1999). Fourth, China's logistics and distribution system is inefficient and unreliable (CMIC, 2007). The final structural impediment stems from China's substandard telecommunication system (Markus and Soh, 2002). Collectively, these structural deficiencies may provide some basis for the fact that very few of the e-commerce initiatives in China have been successful (Martinsons, 2002).

A variety of environmental, organizational, and personal factors are not only instrumental in advancing IT diffusion, but also have a marked impact on management's perceptions and attitudes regarding e-commerce. Environmental factors, such as business-friendly government regulations and infrastructure improvements, are critical if e-commerce is to live up to its potential in China. Organizational factors highlight management's role in advocating the use of e-commerce within the firm. In general, a manager's perception of e-commerce will influence attitudes and managers must be cognizant of the potential of e-commerce if they are to remain competitive and capable of positioning their companies to meet the standards of the globally wired business community. Personal factors pertain to an individual's level of knowledge in IT and e-commerce domains.

Clearly, structural conditions have impeded the diffusion of IT in China. Of commensurate importance, however, is the need to examine whether management's perceptions and attitudes present yet another obstacle to the widespread diffusion of e-commerce in China. This research is designed to develop a descriptive profile of Chinese business managers' with respect to their awareness of structural conditions as well as their perceptions and attitudes regarding e-commerce. Management's viewpoint on a variety of environmental, organizational, and personal factors should provide some insight into the future of e-commerce in China within the framework of organizational commitment to e-commerce driven innovation. The sections that follow present an overview of the literature (Section 2), the research design, sampling procedure, data collection procedures, and data analysis (Section 3), findings (Section 4), and conclusions (Section 5).

LITERATURE REVIEW

Collectively, the literature suggests that a variety of external factors significantly influence the extent of IT innovation and diffusion. The IT diffusion of innovation (DOI) process may be viewed within the context of Innovation Decision Process theory (Rogers, 1995) which posits that potential adopters of a technology must learn about the innovation (knowledge); become persuaded of the value of the innovation (persuasion); decide to adopt it (decision); implement the innovation (implementation); and finally reaffirm or reject the innovation (confirmation). Researchers often employ Davis' (1986) Technology Acceptance Model (TAM) as a theoretical framework to examine external variables, conceivably because of its goal to "provide an explanation of the determinants of computer acceptance that is general, capable of examining user behavior across a broad range of end-user computing technologies and user populations" (Davis et al., 1989). The model, grounded in social psychology, reflects Fishbein and Ajzen's Theory of Reasoned Action (TRA), which theorizes that behavior is determined by intentions that are in part influenced by attitude (Fishbein and Ajzen, 1975). Attitude, or the "predisposition to respond favorably or unfavorably to a computer system, application, system staff member, or a process related to the use of that system or application" (Melone, 1990, pp.81), has a strong theoretical background and previous research has conclusively proven that attitude is an accurate predictor of use. TAM postulates that actual behavior is influenced by attitudes that are shaped by external variables as well as perceptions regarding the usefulness and ease of use of the technology under study. In fact, a key premise in TAM is that a user's attitude toward using information technology is a major determinant of whether the person actually uses the technology. Several extensions or modifications to the TAM have incorporated theoretical perspectives or constructs that reflect the salience of beliefs and attitudes, social or normative influences, and end-user characteristics on acceptance and adoption. Other research augments the TAM with individual, organizational, and system characteristics; many of which have received empirical support as moderators of IT acceptance (Igbaria et al., 1997; Mathieson et al.,

2001; Jackson et al.; 1997, Agarwal and Prasad, 1999; Davis, 1993).

The research model for this chapter examines environmental, organizational, and personal factors as antecedents to perceptions of e-commerce. Bharadwaj et al.'s (1999) multi-stage research framework, which was developed to conceptualize factors that govern a firm's IT capability, provides some justification for focusing on these external variables. With the assistance of Delphi panels and focus groups, the researchers identified 30 IT capabilities that were distributed among the following six categories: IT business partnerships, external IT linkages, business IT strategic thinking, IT business process integration, IT management, and IT infrastructure. The authors concluded that an enterprise-wide IT capability embodies both organizational and technological capabilities which, in turn, reflect the firm's ability to sustain IT innovation and respond to changing market conditions.

Several researchers (Devaraj et al., 2002; Gefen and Straub, 2000; Jiang et al., 2000; Moon and Young-Gul, 2001; Lederer et al., 2000) have employed the TAM to examine a variety of external variables related to e-commerce. Collectively, the findings suggest that TAM is a suitable theoretical framework for e-commerce-based studies. In studying user acceptance of digital libraries, Hong et al. (2002) employed the TAM to examine individual differences (self efficacy and knowledge of search domain) and system characteristics (relevance, terminology, and screen design) within the context of user acceptance of digital libraries. The researchers concluded that results strongly supported the utilization of TAM in predicting users' intention to adopt digital libraries. Venkatesh and Davis' (2000) TAM2 examined user acceptance through social influence (subjective norm, voluntariness, and image) and cognitive instrumental processes (job relevance, output quality, result demonstrability, and perceived ease of use) while Mathieson et al. (2001) augmented the TAM with a perceived resources construct as a means to examine the influence of organizational infrastructure on use. In each case, TAM proved to be a parsimonious model for predicting user acceptance.

The role of perceptions in predicting acceptance and usage decisions has also received considerable attention (Moore and Benbasat, 1991; Davis, 1993; Gefen and Straub, 1997; Morris and Dillon, 1997; Venkatesh, 1999; Agarwal, 2000; Mathieson et al., 2001). Notably, both Agarwal (2000) and Moore and Benbasat (1991) examined the influence of perceptions on IT acceptance and adoption while Mathieson et al. (2001) emphasized the need to more fully explore perceptions of real world artifacts such as technology. Possibly in response to TAM and DOI's effectiveness in explaining the propensity to use an IT, Agarwal and Prasad (1997) merged the two theories. After examining the diffusion constructs within the context of Internet usage, the researchers concluded that visibility, compatibility, and trialability influenced current levels of usage while perceived usefulness and result demonstrability influenced continued use decisions.

Chin and Marcolin (2001) emphasized the continued need to develop "deep usage" models as well as "conceptualizations of usage as they lead to individual and performance outcomes." Clearly, then, a review of the literature establishes a precedent for developing models that are derived from the constructs originally presented by Davis.

The purpose of this study is to develop a descriptive profile of Chinese business managers' perceptions and attitudes regarding e-commerce. As such, this study should not be construed as an attempt to offer yet another extension of TAM nor to validate previous findings. Instead, the research model incorporates key TAM constructs in an effort to present a comprehensive profile that represents the triangulation of external variables, perceptions, and attitudes. The theoretical foundation for the model is derived from human behavior theory, which posits that behavior is largely a function of attitudes; attitudes are formed from individual perceptions; and individual perceptions are influenced by external variables.

RESEARCH METHODOLOGY

Research Model

The model, shown in Figure 1, adopts the view that a variety of environmental, organizational and personal factors serve as antecedents to perceptions and attitudes regarding e-commerce. Environmental factors are defined within the context of structural conditions that exhibit a strong influence on e-commerce development including electronic payment systems, government regulations, legal issues, and telecommunications. Organizational factors, namely, managerial leadership, commitment, and support, influence the level of technology adoption as well as the behavior of employees in the organization (Agarwal, 2000). Innovation and diffusion of technology requires active leadership and vision by top corporate leaders who are willing to commit scarce resources (Agarwal, 2000). Of equal importance is the influence of executive support and leadership in advocating the use and acceptance of e-commerce. Personal factors pertain to an individual's knowledge of IT and e-commerce as well as information received through communication with colleagues.

The core of the model examines perceptions about e-commerce, which are measured through the following variables:

- Usefulness—The degree to which a person believes that using a particular system would enhance his or her job performance (Davis, 1989)
- Ease of use—The degree to which a person believes that using a particular system would be free of effort (Davis, 1989)
- Importance—The perception of the degree to which e-commerce will aid or improve business functions
- Security—An individual's expectations or trust in using e-commerce

The model postulates that environmental, organizational and personal factors serve as antecedents to perceptions of e-commerce, which in turn, moderate an individual's attitude regard-

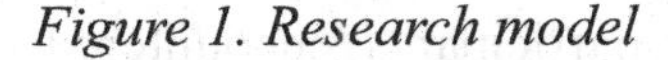

Figure 1. Research model

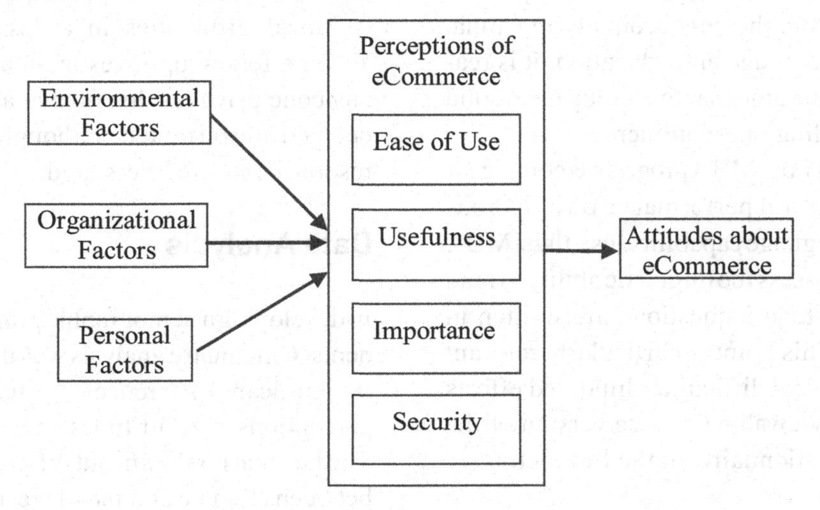

ing the implementation and use of e-commerce applications.

Research Design and Sampling Procedure

The study, which targeted MBA students in China, entailed administering an Internet-based questionnaire. Managerial experience is generally a pre-requisite for enrollment in Chinese MBA programs; thus, MBA students possess sufficient familiarity with environmental, organizational, and technological factors to provide an accurate profile of Chinese business managers' perceptions and attitudes regarding e-commerce. Other factors contributing to the decision to target this population include:

- Reports indicating that 95 percent of Chinese MBA students are enrolled part time and hold a managerial position in a corporation (http://www.mba.org.cn, 2000)
- The status accorded to an MBA degree coupled with the required managerial experience implies that respondents can reasonably be expected to have some impact on the future of e-commerce in China
- MBA students are part of generation X, or those born between 1961-1981 (Generation X: Definitions, 2002), and as such represent key players in the new economy in China. Based on their age and education, it is reasonable to assume that this group has a solid understanding of e-commerce
- Enrollment in an MBA program is contingent upon successful performance on a rigorous English language capability test; thus, MBA students possess the linguistic ability to read and understand a questionnaire written in English. This point is particularly relevant since technical difficulties hindered efforts to place a viewable Chinese version of the survey questionnaire on the Internet.

Data Collection Procedures

Lickert-based rating scales were developed to measure the variables identified in the research model. A small pilot test was conducted to assess the readability of the survey instrument. The instrument was then distributed to five business managers in China. Based on their feedback, slight modifications were made to the terminology. A final version of the Internet survey questionnaire was then designed and published.

A mailing list was prepared by collecting e-mail addresses from MBA Web sites in China. The first mailing list included about 530 addresses. An e-mail message was prepared inviting individuals to participate in the study. After nearly 50 percent of the e-mail addresses were returned because of delivery problems, a second mailing list was prepared using e-mail addresses from the most active MBA Web sites in China. The second mailing list, which contained approximately 350 addresses, resulted in a 70 percent delivery rate. In total, about 500 e-mails were successfully delivered for this survey. Sixty-six usable questionnaires were received for a response rate of 13 percent, an acceptable rate given this type of on-line survey. Notably, the low response rate may be attributed to the length of the survey, language barriers, and/or the fact that Web server logs indicated some participants encountered technical difficulties in accessing the survey. When a follow-up investigation did not provide any conclusive results, further adjustments were deemed unwarranted, although we believe the response rate is understated.

Data Analysis

In developing a demographic profile of the respondents, Chi-square analysis was used to determine if significant differences existed with regard to perceptions and attitudes toward e-commerce. The fact that no significant differences were found between (1) male and female respondents, (2) age categories, (3) years of experience as an IS user, or (4) hours using the Internet a week indicates respondents represent a fairly homogeneous group. The aggregated results provide a comprehensive profile of e-commerce use in China by upwardly mobile, well-educated individuals. Demographic information is found in Table 1.

To operationalize managerial perceptions and attitudes, descriptions were developed for each of the constructs included in the research model. These descriptions are found in Tables 2 – 11. Pearson product/moment correlation analysis was employed to assess the relationship between the research constructs (external, organizational, and personal factors, the perception variables, and attitude) and was derived by calculating the mean of the individual components for each variable. Table 12 contains the results of the correlation analysis, which is limited to those factors that were correlated at a significant level. The Cronbach's alpha for the constructs included in the correlation analysis was 0.7417.

FINDINGS

Demographic Data

Typically, respondents were male, between the ages of 25 and 34, active Internet users, and employed by a small manufacturing or service company. Table 1 presents a demographic profile of the respondents.

Environmental Factors

The literature suggests that China's development in the area of e-commerce is hampered by structural conditions or environmental factors such as a poor electronic payment infrastructure, strict

Table 1. Demographics (in %)

Organizational Level	
President/Director	7.8
Employee under supervision - Level 1	60.9
Employee under supervision - Level 2	31.3
Management Experience (in years)	
More than 10	4.8
6 - 10	20.6
3 - 5	38.1
1 - 3	34.9
Less than 1	1.6
Type of Organization	
Manufacturing	40.9
Service	36.5
Commercial – Wholesale	14.3
Commercial – Retail	1.6
Government	4.8
Firm's # of Employees	
>10,000	7.8
5,000 – 9,999	4.7
1,000 - 4,999	12.5
500 - 999	7.8
100 - 499	34.4
< 100	32.8
Sex	
Male	75.4
Female	24.6

Age	
18 – 24	10.3
25 – 34	82.5
> 34	7.2
MBA Concentration	
General Management	24.1
Marketing, Sales, Advertising	24.1
Finance, Accounting,	8.6
Information Technology	25.9
Other	17.2
Years Experience as IS User	
> 10	4.8
6 – 10	20.6
3 - 5	38.1
1 - 3	34.9
< 1	1.6
Internet Usage – Hours Per Week	
0 – 1	1.6
2 – 4	9.4
5 – 6	1.6
7 – 9	17.2
10 – 20	34.4
21 – 40	18.8
> 40	17.2

government regulations, legal issues, and poor telecommunications. The questionnaire queried respondents on their view regarding these factors (see Table 2) and findings provide empirical support for this observation, particularly in the area of on-line payment systems.

Organizational Factors

Organizational factors are defined within the context of two variables: (1) executive support/ leadership and (2) use of e-commerce in the firm (See Table 3). With respect to executive support and leadership, most respondents (54 percent) rated their CEOs vision for e-commerce along the lower end of the rating continuum while a comparable percentage indicated that their CEO occasionally endorsed major e-commerce investments. Ratings pertaining to the firm's use of e-commerce indicated an effective use of the Web although most respondents reported an inadequate or non-existent e-commerce R&D budget. In addition to the findings reported in Table 3, 54 percent of the respondents believe that their CEO considers e-commerce as one of the most vital parts of the firm's competitive strategy while 57 percent indicated that their CEOs think that funds spent on e-commerce represent a strategic investment.

Personal Factors

Tables 4 through 6 depict three personal factors; namely, IT knowledge, e-commerce knowledge, and e-commerce communication. With regard to IT knowledge, the majority of the respondents possess fundamental IT skills including a solid understanding of how to use software packages and the ability to access data as needed. However, most lack skills in high-level areas such as computer programming and database design and implementation.

Table 5 addresses e-commerce knowledge and indicates that the majority of the respondents recognize the potential of e-commerce within the organization and understand how it can be used to achieve a competitive advantage. Respondents are less clear about policies and plans within the organization for the adoption of e-commerce, how e-commerce policies and plans fit with the overall goals and objectives of the organization, and the existing e-commerce applications within the organization; possibly a consequence of the inadequacy of funds invested in e-commerce and/ or the failure of top-level executives to adequately communicate their technological vision.

Table 6 examines e-commerce communication as it relates to information received through communication with colleagues and business

Table 2. Environmental factors (in %)

	1	2	3	4	5	MEAN
The on-line payment system is:	2	5	20	36	38	4.03
Government Internet policies are:	9	27	30	23	11	3.00
The legal framework is:	2	13	31	33	22	3.61
The telecomm. environment is:	2	22	27	23	27	3.52

Note: *1=Extremely Encouraging; ...; 5=Extremely Discouraging*

Table 3. Organizational factors (in %)

Executive Support/leadership:	
Does your CEO endorse major e-commerce investments that have not been endorsed by traditional justification criteria and procedures?	
1. Frequently	
2. Occasionally	27
3. Rarely	52
	21
What is your CEO's vision for e-commerce?	
1. Strong vision	23
2. —	23
3. —	29
4. No stated vision	25
Use of e-commerce in the Firm:	
How would you describe your firm's use of information technology	
1. Industry leader	
2. Close follower	19
3. Middle of the pack	28
4. Somewhat behind	23
5. Laggard	22
	9
The organization I work for uses the Web effectively	
1. Strongly agree	
2. Somewhat agree	38
3. Neither agree nor disagree	45
4. Somewhat disagree	5
5. Strongly disagree	7
	5
Is there a research and development (R&D) budget for investments in e-commerce?	
1. Industry leader in discretionary funding for emerging e-commerce	
2. Modest budget for investments in new technology piloting	0
3. Inadequate for our needs	
4. There is no budget	23
	31
	47

associations. Respondents gave higher ratings to information related to global e-commerce than information pertaining to e-commerce in China.

Perceptions about E-Commerce

The framework for perceptions of e-commerce is comprised of four variables: usefulness, ease of use, importance, and security (Tables 7 - 10). The majority of the respondents strongly agreed that e-commerce would have a positive impact on career performance and therefore e-commerce was perceived to be very useful. Respondents also perceived that using e-commerce applications fit within the context of their work style thereby making it easy to use. Most expressed support for the perception that e-commerce technologies provide strategic and competitive advantages and perceived themselves as having the skills, resources, knowledge, and control to effectively use e-commerce applications. Finally, security issues influenced the decision to conduct business on-line with most respondents reporting a high level of concern when making purchases or banking over the Internet.

Table 4. Personal factors: IT knowledge (in %)

Level of ability to...	1	2	3	4	5	MEAN
program (e.g., in C, C++, Visual Basic, Java, etc.).	5	12	20	35	28	3.69
use software packages (e.g., Lotus 1-2-3, MS Office, etc.).	26	32	32	9	0	2.25
build models (e.g., formulate and solve complex simulation models).	9	26	9	31	25	3.35
recognize which management science model is appropriate for a particular problem.	6	35	24	27	8	2.95
access data (e.g., data retrieval, queries, etc.).	22	28	23	23	5	2.62
develop (design and implement) databases using generalized database management systems.	11	22	25	28	14	3.13

Note: 1=Extremely High; ...; 5=Extremely Low

Table 5. Personal factors: E-commerce knowledge (in %)

Knowledge about the...	1	2	3	4	5	MEAN
e-commerce policies and plans within the organization.	9	20	32	17	22	3.22
fit between e-commerce policies and plans and the overall goals and objectives of the organization.	6	25	28	25	17	3.22
existing e-commerce applications within the organization	9	25	27	20	19	3.14
potential for e-commerce technology within the organization	13	42	16	23	6	2.69
potential use of e-commerce technology to achieve competitive advantage	16	42	27	11	5	2.47

Note: 1=Extremely High; ...; 5=Extremely Low

Table 6. Personal factors: E-commerce communication (in %)

How would you describe the information you have received from colleagues, business associations, etc. about...	1	2	3	4	5	MEAN
global e-commerce	29	31	29	11	0	2.23
e-commerce in China	20	34	31	12	3	2.45

Note: 1=Very Positive; ...; 5=Very Negative

Table 7. Perception of e-commerce: Usefulness (in %)

	1	2	3	4	5	6	7	MEAN
E-commerce will be of benefit to me personally.	50	16	9	6	9	5	5	2.42
Using e-commerce applications will improve my performance.	48	16	11	9	3	2	11	2.52
The advantages of e-commerce to me will outweigh the disadvantages.	42	25	14	5	5	0	9	2.42
Overall, using e-commerce will be advantageous to me.	52	22	8	5	3	2	9	2.28

Note: 1=Strongly Agree; ...; 7=Strongly Disagree

Table 8. Perception of e-commerce: Ease of use (in %)

	1	2	3	4	5	6	7	MEAN
I have the skills, capability and knowledge necessary to use e-commerce applications.	42	24	13	11	2	3	5	2.35
Using e-commerce applications is entirely within my control.	14	33	21	14	5	6	6	3.06
Using e-commerce will fit well with the way I work.	41	23	20	11	2	0	3	2.22
Using e-commerce will fit into my work style.	38	23	20	13	3	0	3	2.33
The setup of e-commerce will be compatible with the way I work.	32	24	22	14	3	2	3	2.51

Note: 1=Strongly Agree; ...; 7=Strongly Disagree

Table 9. Perception of e-commerce: Importance (in %)

Importance in terms of ...	1	2	3	4	5	6	7	MEAN
creating new business processes.	39	33	14	5	3	3	3	2.22
improving business relationships.	30	39	16	9	0	3	3	2.33
creating new distribution channels.	33	43	8	10	0	2	5	2.24
increasing sales.	21	31	31	8	7	0	3	2.61
improving customer satisfaction.	32	22	29	8	5	2	3	2.49
creating new products.	13	22	31	17	8	8	2	3.16
enhancing the global presence of the company.	42	23	27	5	2	0	2	2.08

Note: 1=Extremely Important; ...; 7=Extremely Unimportant

Table 10. Perception of e-commerce: Security (in %)

How concerned are you about...	1	2	3	4	MEAN
Security in relation to making purchases or banking over the Internet	9	5	16	70	3.47
Security features when choosing whether or not to do business with an Internet-based company	2	20	55	23	3.00

Note: 1=Not at all Concerned; ...; 4=Very Concerned

Table 11. Attitudes toward e-commerce (in %)

	1	2	3	4	5	6	7	MEAN
Implementing e-commerce is a good and wise idea	56	25	11	5	0	0	3	1.80
I like the idea of implementing e-commerce	52	30	10	5	0	0	3	1.83
Using e-commerce applications would be a pleasant experience	43	30	18	5	0	3	2	2.05

Note: 1=Strongly Agree; ...; 7=Strongly Disagree

Attitudes toward E-Commerce

Table 11 clearly indicates that the majority of respondents have a strong positive attitude toward implementing and using e-commerce applications.

Correlation Analysis

Pearson product/moment correlation analysis was employed to assess the relationship between the environmental, organizational and personal factors, perception, and attitudes. The results of the analysis can be found in Table 12, which is limited to those factors that were correlated at a significant level.

As Table 12 illustrates, environmental factors relating to e-commerce (ECE) are positively correlated to e-commerce knowledge (ECK), which suggests that respondents who are familiar with e-commerce are aware of the issues associated with China's structural conditions. Variables related to organizational factors include both executive support/leadership (ESL) and the firm's use of e-commerce (FUEC). As one would expect, a positive correlation exists between these variables. Further, both executive support/leadership and the firm's use of e-commerce are positively correlated with e-commerce knowledge (ECK). This suggests that the greater the executive's e-commerce knowledge, the greater the influence in shaping opinion, providing leadership, and creating a technology-infused organizational environment. Analogously, executive support/leadership is positively correlated with personal IT knowledge (ITK), which is perhaps an indication that IT savvy managers are more positive about executive leadership and support.

Variables that model personal factors include IT knowledge (ITK) and e-commerce knowledge

Table 12. Pearson correlations

	ECE	ESL	FUEC	ITK	ECK	COMM	PU	PEOU	PIO	PS	ATT
ECE					.3*						
ESL			.46**	.32*	.5**						
FUEC		.46**			.59**						
ITK		.32*			.59**	.33**		.33**			
ECK	.3*	.51**	.59**	.59**		.35**	.31*	.27*			
COMM				.33**	.35**		.28*				
PU					.31*	.28*		.44**	.66**		.58**
PEOU				.33**	.27*		.44**		.67**		.68**
PIO							.66**	.67**			.76**
PS											
ATT							.579**	.677**	.759**		

**** Correlation is significant at the 0.01 level (2-tailed).**

** Correlation is significant at the 0.05 level (2-tailed).*

(ECK) and communication (COMM) about e-commerce. Again, findings indicate a positive correlation among these variables. IT and e-commerce knowledge are both positively correlated with the perception of ease of use (PEOU) while e-commerce knowledge and communication are positively correlated with perceptions of personal usefulness (PU).

The perception of e-commerce is manifested in the perception of personal e-commerce usefulness (PU), the perception of ease of use (PEOU), and e-commerce importance to the organization (PIO) variables. These variables exhibit a positive intercorrelation as well as a moderating influence on attitude about e-commerce.

While the model's variables exhibit a positive intergroup correlation, findings indicate that environmental and organizational factors do not play a role in shaping perceptions or attitudes. This suggests that Chinese manager's perceptions and attitudes toward e-commerce are independent of current environmental and organizational conditions. One implication is that this new generation of managers may be expected to continue technological pursuits in spite of the environmental shortcomings. Personal factors are partially correlated to usefulness and ease of use but not to perceptions of importance and security. With the exception of security, all of the perception variables demonstrated a positive correlation with attitude while other factors influence perception. Perhaps because all respondents are enrolled in the university system, their educational experiences may have shaped and/or influenced their perceptions and thus attitudes toward e-commerce.

CONCLUSIONS AND IMPLICATIONS

It is widely recognized that e-commerce represents a critical resource for most business organizations, whether in a role of supporting business operations and managerial decision-making or, increasingly, as a means of gaining a strategic competitive advantage. The majority of the participants in this study are cognizant of current structural deficiencies particularly with regard to payment systems, government regulations, and telecommunications. Yet in spite of these deficiencies, most reported a positive attitude toward implementing e-commerce, agreeing that it is a "good and wise idea." Respondents indicate that enhancing the global presence of the firm, creating new business processes and distribution channels, and enhancing customer satisfaction and business relationships are of key importance. One implication is that current structural conditions should not seriously impede efforts to implement e-commerce initiatives since the current focus targets relationship and process enhancements that do not require radical changes to the current infrastructure. Findings indicate that a better understanding of the organizational plans and policies regarding IT and specific e-commerce technologies is correlated with more positive perceptions about its usefulness, ease of use, and importance. A higher level of knowledge is also correlated with stronger managerial leadership. By juxtaposing executive support and leadership with vision and investment, inferences may be made with respect to organizational commitment to the implementation of e-commerce initiatives. The occasional investments in e-commerce coupled with the absence of a stated vision hampers dramatic technological innovations in the near future. However, this younger generation of Chinese managers seems to not only recognize the potential benefits of e-commerce but to also embrace the opportunities presented by e-commerce activities. One implication is that firms interested in engaging in e-commerce in China will find a knowledgeable and supportive business climate; however, e-commerce initiatives may be hindered by constraints imposed by the current infrastructure. Certainly, increased funding of R&D initiatives will allow organizations to implement e-commerce strategies that suit Chinese business practices while enhancing the ability to meet current and future e-commerce initiatives.

While this study provides a succinct profile of the perceptions and attitudes of young Chinese MBA students employed in a variety of fields, future research would benefit from expanding the sample to include a broader audience base. By doing so, additional validation tests and factor analysis can be performed. In addition, Internet-based surveys tend to have low response rates, particularly when they are not written in the native language of the population being surveyed. Therefore, a more traditional approach to survey distribution may be warranted. Finally, additional external variables must be identified to facilitate a clearer understanding of the antecedents to e-commerce perceptions.

REFERENCES

Agarwal, R. (2000). Individual Acceptance of Information Technologies. *Framing the Domains of IT Management: Projecting the Future through the Past.* Edited by Zmund, R., & Price, M. Pinnaflex Educational Resources, Inc. Cincinnati, OH., 85-104.

Agarwal, R., & Prasad, J. (1999). Are Individual Differences Germane to the Acceptance of New Information Technologies? *Decision Sciences*, 30(2), 361-391.

Agarwal, R., & Prasad, J. (1997). The Role of Innovation Characteristics and Perceived Voluntariness in the Acceptance of Information Technologies. *Decision Sciences*, 28(3), 557-582.

Bharadwaj, A., Sambamurthy, V., Zmud, M. (1999). IT Capabilities: Theoretical Perspectives and Empirical Operationalization. *ICIS Proceedings*.

Chin, W., & Marcolin, B. (2001). The Future of Diffusion Research. *The Data Base for Advances in Information Systems,* 32(3), 8–12.

China Internet Network Information Center. (2007) Statistical Survey Report on the Internet Development in China. http://www.cnnic.net.cn/uploadfiles/pdf/2007/2/14/200607.pdf

China Market Information Center. (2007) 2006-2007 Annual report on China's E-Commerce Market. http://chinamarket.ccidnet.com/pub/en-report/show_18116.html

Davis, F.D. (1986). Technology Acceptance Model for Empirically Testing New End-User Information Systems: Theory and Results. *Unpublished doctoral dissertation, Massachusetts Institute of Technology.*

Davis, F.D. (1989). Perceived Usefulness, Perceived Ease of Use and User Acceptance of Information Technology. *MIS Quarterly,* 13(3), 319-340.

Davis, F.D. (1993). User Acceptance of Information Technology: System Characteristics, User Perceptions and Behavioral Impacts. *International Journal of Man-Machine Studies,* 38(3), 475-487.

Davis, F.D., Bagozzi, R.P., & Warshaw, P.R. (1989). User Acceptance of Computer Technology: A Comparison of Two Theoretical Models. *Management Science,* 35, 982-1003.

Devaraj, S, Fan, M., Kohli,R. (2002). Antecedents of b2C channel satisfaction and preference: Validation e-Commerce metrics. *Information Systems Research*, 13(3), 316-333.

Fishbein, M., & Ajzen, I. (1975). *Belief, Attitude, Intention and Behavior: An Introduction to Theory and Research.* Reading, MA: Addison-Wesley.

Gefen, D., & Straub, D.W. (2000). The Relative Importance of Perceived Ease-of-Use in IS Adoption: A Study of E-Commerce Adoption. *Journal of the Association for Information Systems,* 1(8), 1-27.

Gefen, D., & Straub, D.W. (1997). Gender Differences in the Perception and Use of E-Mail: An Extension to the Technology Acceptance Model. *MIS Quarterly, 21(4),* 389-400.

Generation X: Definitions. (2002). http://www.coloradocollege.edu/Dept/EC/generationx96/genx/genx10.html.

http://www.mba.org.cn, April 17, 2000.

Hong, W., Thong, J.Y.L., Wong, W., & Tam, K.Y. (2002). Determinants of User Acceptance of Digital Libraries: An Empirical Examination of Individual Differences and System Characteristics. *Journal of Management Information Systems,* 18(3), 2002.

Igbaria, M., Zinatelli, N., Cragg, P., & Cavaye, A.L.M. (1997) "Personal Computing Acceptance Factors in Small Firms: A Structural Equation Model," *MIS Quarterly* 21(3), 279-305.

Internet World Stats, March 19, 2007. http://www.internetworldstats.com/stats.htm

Jackson, C.M., Chow, S., & Leitch, R.A. (1997). Towards an Understanding of the Behavioral Intention to Use an Information System. *Decision Sciences.* 28(2), 357-389.

Jiang, J., Hsu, M.K., Klein, G., Lin, B. (2000). E-Commerce User Behavior Model: An Empirical Study. *Human Systems Management,* 19(4), 265-277.

Lederer, A., Maupin, D., Sena, & M. Zhuang, Y. (2000). The Technology Acceptance Model and the World Wide Web. *Decision Support Systems,* 29(3), 269-282.

Li, H., & Suomi, R. (2006). E-Commerce Development in China: Opportunities and Challenges. *IADIS International Conference on e-Commerce,* December 9-11, Barcelona, Spain, 413-417

Markus, L., & Soh, C. (2002). Structural Influence on Global E-Commerce Activity. *Journal of Global Information Management,* 10(1), 5-12.

Martinsons, M.G. (2002). Electronic Commerce in China: Emerging Success Stories. *Information & Management*, 39(7), 571-579.

Mathieson, K, Peacock, E., & Chinn, W.C. (2001). Extending the Technology Acceptance Model: The Influence of Perceived User Resources. *The Data Base for Advances in Information Systems,* 32 (3), 86-112.

Melone, N. P. (1990). A Theoretical Assessment of the User-Satisfaction Construct in Information Systems Research. *Management Science*, 36 (1), 76-91.

Moon, J., & Young-Gul, K. (2001). Extending the TAM for a World-Wide-Web Context. *Information and Management,* 38, 217 – 230.

Moore, G.C., & Benbasat, I. (1991). Development of an Instrument to Measure the Perceptions of Adopting an Information Technology Innovation. *Information Systems Research,* 2(1), 192-222.

Morris, M.G., & Dillon, A. (1997). How User Perceptions Influence Software Use. *IEEE Software.* 14 (4), 58-65.

Rein, S. (2007) Yearning for E-Commerce in China. *e-commerce News*. February 10. http://www.e-commercetimes.com/story/55680.html

Rogers, E.M. (1995). *The Diffusion of Innovations, 4th ed.*, New York: Free Press.

Rosen, D. H. (1999). Hype Versus Hope for e-commerce in China. *The China Business Review,* July/August, 38-41.

Venkatesh, V. (1999). Creation of Favorable User Perceptions: Exploring the Role of Intrinsic Motivation. *MIS Quarterly,* 23(2), 239-260.

Venkatesh, V., & Davis, F.D. (2000). A Theoretical Extension of the Technology Acceptance Model: Four Longitudinal Studies. *Management Science*, 46(2), 186-204.

Yan, W. (2005). The Electronic Signatures Law: China's First National E-Commerce Legislation. *Intellectual Property & Technology Law Journal,* 17(6), 6.

Chapter V
E-Commerce Adoption and Appropriation by SMEs in Sri Lanka

Mahesha Kapurubandara
University of Western Sydney, Australia

Robyn Lawson
University of Western Sydney, Australia

ABSTRACT

Acceptance of the Internet has paved the way towards the development of virtual communities that keep increasing in the current information society making it imperative for business, especially the small and medium enterprises (SMEs) which form the backbone of any economy, to keep abreast with e-commerce and remain competitive. To stimulate and facilitate SME participation in business activities through the Internet, it is necessary, therefore, to provide clear guidance and direction with suitable models and frameworks specifically tailored for the purpose. This chapter highlights an attempt to develop a suitable framework for the e-transformation of SMEs in Sri Lanka. In the belief that new models and frameworks can help SMEs to equip themselves to better understand their current stage and identify the main barriers at each stage of the adoption process, this attempt starts with an initial exploratory study of 17 SMEs, followed by a regional survey involving 625 SMEs from various industry sectors, along with interviews with the SME intermediary organizations. The proposed model facilitates establishing the current stage of an SME with regard ICT and e-commerce sophistication using five stage variables. It also assists to determine current position with regard to barriers towards the adoption of e-commerce and helps determine the support necessary to overcome such identified barriers. The research detailed in this chapter establishes that barriers show variance when SMEs proceed to more advanced stages in the adoption process. Likewise, the necessary support required indicates a similar trend. Going further, the chapter proposes a model for adoption of e-commerce for SMEs in Sri Lanka and identifies the essential need for support while acknowledging available support. Finally, it proposes an initial framework to e-transform SMEs in developing countries.

Copyright © 2009, IGI Global, distributing in print or electronic forms without written permission of IGI Global is prohibited.

INTRODUCTION

The prominent role that information and communication technologies (ICT) plays in the field of commerce and trade nowadays is undisputed. While the developed world forges ahead with e-transformation of businesses, the developing world struggles to keep pace with emerging technologies. In a challenging global society, effective use of e-commerce technologies is critical to the success of business economic growth and increased productivity. This is particularly true for small and medium enterprises (SMEs). Consequently, new technologies are the key to enabling SMEs to establish contacts and participate in the world economy (Rayport & Jawaorski, 2003).

E-commerce technologies contribute significantly towards re-invigorating corporate management, and growing of the national economy (UNDP, 2004). It is also a factor in facilitating organizations to improve their business processes and communications, within the organization and with external trading partners (Chong and Pervan, 2007). E-transformation will also facilitate provision of a more level-playing field, by enabling a growing market share, and providing new opportunities for competitive advantage. Envisaging a shift to a knowledge-based economy, e-transformation is seen as an increasingly important tool for SMEs, necessary to ensure their viability and growth into the future (UNDP, 2004).

Although large organizations accept ICT advances including e-commerce technologies, the same level of adoption is not evident among SMEs (Bode & Burn, 2002; Knol & Stroeken, 2001, Marshall, Sor & McKay, 2000). This is particularly the case of SMEs in developing countries, where they face significant and unique challenges in adopting e-commerce. The reality is that many SMEs have not been successful in exploiting these potential opportunities, despite efforts by governments and donor organizations. Research indicates e-commerce offers viable and practical solutions for organizations to meet challenges of a predominantly changing environment. However, the few available studies related to SMEs in developing countries reveal a delay or a failure on the part of SMEs in adopting e-commerce technologies. In this connection, research also reveals a number of failed e-commerce ventures in developing countries without viable business models for their regions, despite high potential growth (Laosethakul & Boultan, 2007).

Where governments believe that e-commerce can foster economic development it is necessary to identify the inherent differences in developing countries with diverse economic, political, social and cultural backgrounds to understand the process of technology adoption (Mehrtens, Cragg & Mills, 2001). Governments need to address the problems that impede SMEs from adopting and using e-commerce as indicated in SME studies of e-commerce issues in developed countries with unique and very different issues (Lawson, Alcock, Cooper & Burgress, 2003; Huff & Young, 2000; OECD, 1998; Corbitt, Behrendorf & Brown-Parker, 1997). When moving towards this attempt it is crucial to identify the key determinants (facilitators and barriers for adoption) before launching effective strategies for expanding e-commerce for SMEs (Jean, Han & Lee, 2006). Currently available research has not had enough focus on adoption of e-commerce for SMEs in developing countries, where adoption has now become a necessity. Unfortunately, the absence of sufficient research allows for gaps in our understanding. It also limits the awareness of the barriers and the interplay with the circumstances unique to SMEs in developing countries that have different social, cultural, political, and infrastructure conditions. Hence, it is crucial to investigate relevant issues and examine supporting activities necessary for SMEs to become worthy business partners. Of course, when forging ahead SMEs need to accept the challenges, including the barriers as they strive for successful adoption of the available technologies. Concurrently, they also need to raise their awareness of accessible support activities while preserving limited available resources to avoid severe repercussions from costly mistakes.

Studies carried out in developed countries to investigate the factors inhibiting adoption of e-commerce have looked at organizational perspectives, owner/manager perspectives and environmental perspectives (for example, Lawson et al, 2003; Beatty, Shim & Jone , 2001; Mehrtens et al, 2001; Han & Noh, 1999). Among the few research studies carried out in developing countries are studies that investigate the facilitators/inhibitors affecting adoption (Travica, 2003; Mukti, 2000; Enns & Huff, 1999). Predominantly these studies investigate the technological, organizational, physical, and socio-economical environmental factors that hinder the adoption of e-commerce.

The differences between developed and developing countries (such as available infrastructure, social and cultural issues) do not support generalizing the findings for developed countries to developing countries. SMEs in developing countries are faced with barriers that are very specific, some more pronounced than would be in the case for SMEs in developed countries. To understand the lack, or slow uptake of e-commerce technologies, it is appropriate to examine the environment in which they operate. Due to the many constraints inherent to developing countries they are faced with many barriers within the organization and outside the organization. To gain a better understanding and assist them in overcoming the barriers, it is imperative to examine these barriers in depth.

In this regard, methodologies / frameworks for e-commerce from developed countries might not work well in the developing countries due to the differences in business environments, IT infrastructure, and cultural factors (Laosethakul & Boultan, 2007). While developed countries take advantage of well-developed infrastructure, legal and regulatory framework, and copious Internet users, developing countries have to find ways of overcoming not only, the many challenges found within the organization, but also from outside the organization. The fact that the best practices among the developing countries are limited and are not widely publicized for others in the same region to follow is also a disadvantage for SMEs (Laosethakul & Boultan, 2007). It is imperative that new methodologies / frameworks be formulated for SMEs in developing countries to address inherent differences and overcome barriers facing them. Failure to do so could lead to a loss of valuable opportunities for SMEs to stay competitive.

The overall aim of this research is to develop a model for adoption of e-commerce for SMEs in Sri Lanka. Specifically, it investigates barriers to SME adoption of e-commerce with objectives to understand and determine the importance of : (1) internal and external barriers, (2) internal and external support required to overcome the barriers. It also investigates the suitability of a proposed stage model for the adoption of e-commerce for SMEs in developing countries.

Empirical research in this area being limited, an exploratory investigation utilising qualitative and quantitative evidence was considered most suitable. The research centred on SMEs in the Colombo District in Sri Lanka (in the context of a developing country) with the highest density of companies using e-commerce. The Colombo district was the base for investigations with SME selection necessitating employee strength of 10-25 employees: not very immature but somewhat versatile in the use of e-commerce.

THEORETICAL FRAMEWORK

Barriers to E-Commerce Adoption in SMEs

This section outlines recent literature on the barriers/inhibitors for adopting e-commerce by SMEs. Many studies carried out in developed countries investigate the factors affecting the adoption of e-commerce technologies such as Internet, e-commerce, e-mail and electronic data interchange (EDI). As research on this subject in developing countries is relatively limited, the literature on developed countries can serve as a preliminary guideline to identify barriers in developing countries.

Investigations into the barriers that affect SMEs' adoption of e-commerce have identified a variety of factors, which can be grouped into several categories. A number of authors (Lawson et al, 2003; Chau & Turner, 2001; Mehrtens et al, 2001) identify factors relating to three major categories: owner/manager characteristics; firm characteristics; and costs and return on investment.

Owner/managers play an important role in decision making in SME organizations. Hence it can be concluded that a number of factors that affect adoption of e-commerce have to do with owner/manger characteristics. The knowledge of new technologies and e-commerce does affect the degree of use of e-commerce (Rashid & Al-Qirim 2001). Iacovou Benbasat & Dexter (1995) found that the owner's lack of awareness of the technology and perceived benefits is a major barrier to a take up of e-commerce. The lack of knowledge of how to use the technology and low computer literacy are other contributory factors for not adopting e-commerce (Lawson et al, 2003; Kirby & Turner, 1993). Julien and Raymond (1994) report that the owner's level of assertiveness in decision-making affects the adoption of e-commerce. If the owner is subjective and refers to the opinions of experienced people who recommend adoption of e-commerce into the organization, then the owner is more likely to accept their opinions (Harrison, Mykytyn & Riemenschneider, 1997). Concern about return on investments make them reluctant to make substantial investments when short-term returns are not guaranteed. Taken together with lack of time, these two other factors affect decisions to adopt e-commerce (Akkeren & Cavaye, 1999). Related industry experience of owners is also critical to their e-commerce success (Mahajan, Siriniwasan &Wind, 2002).

Among the barriers related to the characteristics of the organization, which affect adoption of e-commerce is the current level of technology usage within the organization (Iacovou et. al,1995). As summarised by Courtney and Fintz, (2001); low use of e-commerce by customers and suppliers, concerns about security aspects, concerns about legal and liability aspects, high costs of the development of computer and networking technologies when moving towards e-commerce, limited knowledge of e-commerce models and methodologies, and the perception of the lack of any accrued benefits to the company make many SMEs remain unconvinced about adoption of e-commerce. In addition, SMEs have limited resources (financial, time, personnel). This "resource poverty" has an effect on the adoption of e-commerce. They cannot afford to experiment with these technologies and make expensive mistakes (EBPG, 2002).

A study of Hong Kong SMEs (Chau & Jim, 2002) revealed that perceived benefits, perceived costs, IT knowledge, trading partner's influence, and government incentives are influencing factors for EDI adoption. Support from the government has been identified as a crucial factor affecting adoption of e-commerce (Rashid & Qirim, 2001; Ling, 2001).

A study in US revealed that organizational, external, technical, and financial factors inhibit the SMEs from adopting EDI (Jun & Cai, 2003). The infrastructure of the country affects the adoption to a great degree (Ling, 2001). Adoption is more prevalent in countries with good technological support and sound infrastructure (Tan & Teo, 2000).

In another study by OECD (1998), it has identified lack of awareness, uncertainty about the benefits of electronic commerce, concerns about lack of human resources and skills, set-up costs and pricing issues, concerns about security, as the most significant barriers of e-commerce for SMEs in OECD countries. SMEs' adoption of e-commerce depends mainly on their perceptions of the opportunities afforded by it and the relevance of those opportunities to their business (OECD, 1998).

Barriers to E-Commerce Adoption in Developing Countries

Much less, attention to SME e-commerce research is evident for developing countries with different economic, political, and cultural circumstances. Identifying the differences is an initial step to understanding of the process of technology adoption. This is particularly important if governments believe that electronic commerce can foster economic development (Garcia-Murillo, 2004). While e-commerce in developed countries takes advantage of the well-developed infrastructure, regulatory environment, and abundant Internet buyers, developing countries have to discover ways to overcome the many challenges found in the environment.

A study in Thailand revealed that shortage of IT infrastructure, lack of confidence in the electronic legal framework and payments systems act as inhibiting factors to engage aggressively in e-commerce (Laosethakul & Boultan, 2007). A study carried out in Vietnam has broadly categorised the inhibiting factors as internal and external with sub-categories relating to owner/manger characteristics, organizational characteristics, environmental characteristics, and characteristics of innovation (Huy & Filiatrault, 2006).

Cultural barriers in some countries may also exist to reject the acceptance of e-commerce as a way of doing business (Bingi et al, 2000). For instance, in countries like Sri Lanka and India, shopping is a social activity, and personal face-to-face contact with sellers is an important part of the shopping experience. Distrust of what businesses do with personal and credit card information is an e-commerce issue in any country, but, in countries where there may be good justification for such distrust, it could become a serious obstacle to e-commerce growth (Anigan, 1999). Lack of developed legal and regulatory systems also inhibit the development of e-commerce in developing countries.

Cloete et al (2002) in their study of SME adoption of e-commerce in South Africa found that adoption is heavily influenced by factors within the organization. Factors such as: lack of access to computers hardware and software; lack of telecommunications at a reasonable cost; low e-commerce use by competitors and supply chain partners; concerns with security and legal issues; low knowledge level of management and employees; and unclear benefits from e-commerce, were found to be the major barriers that inhibit adoption.

Dedrick and Kraemer (2001) in their study of e-commerce in China found that there are many significant barriers to adoption of e-commerce. Limited diffusion of computers, high cost of Internet access, and a lack of online payment processes were found to directly inhibit e-commerce. Inadequate transportation and delivery networks, limited availability of banking services, and uncertain taxation rules indirectly inhibit e-commerce.

El-Nawawy and Ismail (1999) in their study of electronic commerce adoption by SMEs in Egypt found that the main factors contributing to the non-adoption of e-commerce in Egypt are: awareness and education, market size, e-commerce infrastructure, telecommunication infrastructure, financial infrastructure, legal system, government role, pricing structure, and social and psychological factors.

Schmid, Stanoevska, and Tschammer (2001) suggest that the main e-commerce issues facing SMEs in Argentina are awareness, access to hardware, infrastructure, organizational culture, and financial issues. A comparison of the two studies in Argentina and Egypt, (both developing countries) suggests that the key factors of e-commerce

Table 1. Summary of e-commerce adoption barriers in developing countries

Category	Barrier	Source
Internal	Owner's lack of awareness of the technology	Schmid et al (2001), El-Nawawy & Ismail (1999), OECD (1998), Iacovou et al (1995), SLBDC (2002)
	Owner's lack of awareness perceived benefits	Cloete et al (2002), Courtney & Frintz (2001), OECD (1998), Jacovou et al (1995)
	Low computer literacy	Kirby & Turner(1993), Cloete, Courtney & Fintz (2002)
	Lack of assertiveness	Julien & Raymond (1994)
	Low level of computer usage	Iacovou et al (1995)
	Lack of resources and skills	OECD (1998), EBPG(2002), Schmid et al (2001), SLBDC (2002)
	Lack of e-commerce models	Courtney & Fintz (2001)
	Lack of qualified staff to develop and support e-commerce sites	Panagariya(2000), Bingi et al (2000), Anigan(1999)
	Lack of access to computers, software, hardware	Cloete, Courtney & Fintz (2002)
	Organizational culture	Schmid et al(2001)
	Not considered a serious business concept	SLBDC (2002)
External	Legal and liability aspects	Laosethakul & Boulton (2007), Courtney & Fintz (2001), El-Nawawy & Ismail (1999), Schmid et al (2001
	Less use by customers and suppliers	Courtney & Fintz (2001)
	Lack of national telecommunications infrastructure	Laosethakul & Boultan (2007), Panagariya(2000), El-Nawawy & Ismail (1999)
	Lack of skills among consumers needed in order to use the Internet	Panagariya(2000), Bingi et al (2000), Anigan(1999)
	Inadequate transportation and delivery network, Financial infrastructure	Dedrick & Kraemer (2001), Panagariya (2000), Bingi et al (2000), Anigan(1999),El-Nawawy & Ismail (1999)
	Low bank account and credit card penetration	Panagariya (2000), Bingi et al (2000), Anigan(1999), Dedrick & Kraemer (2001)
	Low income	Panagariya (2000), Bingi et al (2000), Anigan(1999)
	Low computer and Internet penetration	Panagariya (2000), Bingi et al (2000), Anigan(1999), Dedrick & Kraemer (2001)
	Lack of fixed telephone lines	Panagariya(2000), Bingi et al (2000), Anigan(1999)
	Underdeveloped state of the ISP	Panagariya(2000), Bingi et al (2000), Anigan(1999)
	Poor Internet connectivity	Panagariya(2000), Bingi et. al (2000), Anigan(1999)
	Cultural barriers	Bingi et al (2000)
	Telecommunications at a reasonable cost	Cloete, Courtney, & Fintz (2002), Dedrick & Kraemer (2001)
	Low e-commerce use by competitors and supply chain partners	Cloete, Courtney, & Fintz (2002)
	Concerns with security	Laosethakul & Boulton (2007), Cloete, Courtney, & Fintz (2002) Courtney & Fintz (2001), OECD (1998) Elkin (2001), Anigan(1999)
	Lack of online payment processes	Laosethakul & Boulton (2007), Dedrick & Kraemer (2001)
	Uncertain taxation rules	Dedrick & Kraemer (2001)
	Government not taking a leading role	El-Nawawy & Ismail (1999)
	Inappropriate pricing structure	Courtney & Fintz (2001),El-Nawawy & Ismail (1999), , OECD (1998)
	Limited use of Internet banking and Web portals	SLBDC (2002)

adoption in developing countries are: awareness, telecommunication infrastructure, and cost. It also suggests that SMEs in developing countries share similar issues. The Internet and e-commerce issues of SMEs in Samoa are consistent with the studies conducted in other developing countries (Schmid et al, 2001; El-Nawawy & Ismail, 1999).

In a study of Sri Lankan SME capability to adopt e-commerce conducted by the Sri Lankan Business Development Centre (2002), key factors inhibiting the adoption of e-commerce by SMEs were identified as: lack of knowledge and awareness about the benefits of e-commerce, current unpreparedness on the part of SMEs to adopt e-commerce as a serious business concept, lack of exposure to IT products and services, language barrier, and lack of staff with IT capability. Web-based selling is not seen as practical, and there is limited use of Internet banking and Web portals. In addition, there is inadequate telecommunications infrastructure.

The barriers relating to developing countries discussed above are summarised in Table 1 above.

The above literature survey reveals that the barriers to adoption of e-commerce in SMEs can be grouped to several distinct categories. The categories can be used to develop a framework for investigations. The barriers to adoption of e-commerce in developing countries for SMEs can be broadly categorised into Internal and External barriers, each having sub-categories.

Some of these barriers could be addressed by SMEs working together. The SMEs can get together irrespective of the industry sector to form clusters to share expenses, resources, and facilities. Similarly, SMEs from the same industry sector can work together to share projects. To address certain other barriers governmental intervention will be required.

Models for Adoption

E-commerce, along with IS (Information Systems) and MIS (Management Information Systems), share use of IT, providing for EDI. Therefore, e-commerce can be considered inter-organizational (Chong, 2006). In these circumstances, factors that influence adoption and implementation of technology or application, in general, proves worthy of consideration as a likely explanatory variable with regard to e-commerce (Chong, 2006). Several approaches have been published for the adoption of e-commerce in SMEs. Currently available literature on the topic reveals the existence of a number of overlapping divergent models to explain the adoption decision reached at after examining various factors.

Studies also illustrate the need for governmental support with infrastructure projects, adoption schemes and initiatives towards a positive impact on the technology uptake especially in SMEs (Wagner, Fillis & Johanson, 2003). A further study concentrates on industry competition, governmental support, and the firm's globalization orientation as the most important sub-factors in the category of environmental characteristics for SMEs in emerging economies

Based on the above literature, this study adopts the following three groups of categories as affecting adoption of e-commerce.

- Internal Barriers with the three sub categories: owner/manager, firm, and cost/ ROI providing the context within which SMEs initiated and adopted e-commerce.
- External Barriers with the four sub categories: political, infrastructure, social and cultural and legal and regulatory providing the context of the barriers within which the SMEs have to operate.
- Support Factors reflecting the organizational, industry and national support geared towards helping remove the barriers and influence adoption.

Based on the previous literature and the pilot studies carried out in Sri Lanka on adoption of e-commerce, a one stage normative model was developed which provides the basis for the research objectives. This model is depicted in Figure 1.

The Stages of Adoption: Stage Models

This chapter presents the different stages of growth models and road maps an SME could be on, in its journey towards e-transformation.

Chong (2006) argues that in an organization e-commerce is always in one of the large number of possible "states of adoption". These states vary from less advanced to more advanced. It is believed that stages of growth models or models of maturity generally reflect on the maturing nature of the use of IS in organizations and models of maturity are considered a popular approach to explain adoption while making use for descriptive or prescriptive purposes (Nolan, 1973, Galliers and Sutherland, 1994; McKay et al, 2000) making room for the need to recognize the current stage of maturity as vital without allowing for subsequent strategic steps and guidelines to become impractical to follow (Benbasat, et al, 1984).

According to available literature, there are a variety of models concerning business maturity of e-commerce where some deal with the internal processes of the business while others do not (Grant, 1999; Burgess and Cooper, 1999). Some of them are the Ecommerce Maturity Model (KPMG, 1997), the Commitment-Implementation Matrix Model (Stroud, 1998), the E-Commerce Levels (O'Connor & Galvin, 1998), the E-Business Lifecycle Model (Berryman, 1999), and the Internet Commerce Maturity Model (Poon, 1999). Reflecting on the traditional stages of growth models discussed in the previous section, they assume that organizations pass through increasingly mature stages with respect to the way they use and manage IT to involve themselves in a variety of e-commerce activities (McKay et al, 2000).

However, these models display a drawback. They do not consider the integration of the traditional IS/IT systems or "back office" of organizations with the Internet Commerce systems or "front office" in spite of the necessity to integrate and which happens to be a key aspect of EB maturity (Mackay et al, 2000). The SOGe model (Mackay et al, 2000) and the eTransformation Roadmap (Ginige et al, 2000) both depict integration, the drawback of the SOGe model being

Figure 1. Model for adoption

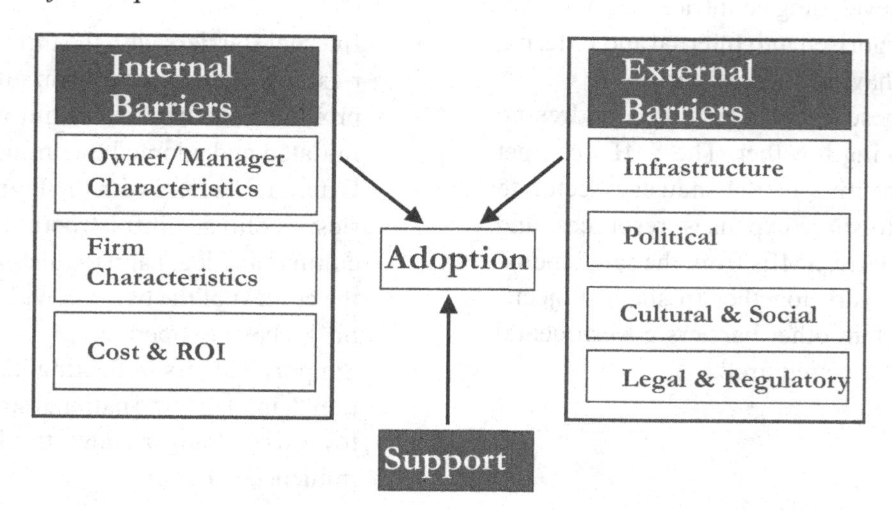

its neglect of the "people" factor. Employees and processes need to be ready for an organization to advance in the use of technology.

The e-Transformation Roadmap (Ginige et al, 2000) allows a SME company to understand how e-commerce is being used in the organization. It gives a more comprehensive picture of the e-commerce maturity of the organization as it looks into the sophistication of interaction of people, processes and technology (Ginige et al, 2000). This measurement will place an organization at a position on both internal process arm and external process arm.

However, it is observed that these models have not been specifically developed for SMEs in developing countries. Therefore, they show a lack of consideration towards issues peculiar to and predominant in developing countries with differences in infrastructure, political and cultural issues. Furthermore, issues which might seem insignificant in developed countries may play an important role in e-commerce adoption in developing countries (Tan, Tyler & Manica, 2007). Hence, generalising the available models may not prove to be adequate for developing countries. New models are needed for SMEs in developing countries to better understand the barriers as different stages of adoption.

RESEARCH METHODOLOGY

This section highlights the methodology and the approach taken with this study.

Research Approach

The study was conducted in two phases: (1) preliminary pilot interviews, and (2) a survey and interviews with SME intermediary support organizations. According to Mingers (2000), the use of such multiple methods is widely accepted as providing increased richness and validity to

Figure 2. E-transformation road map for SMEs (© Ginge 2001. Used with permission)

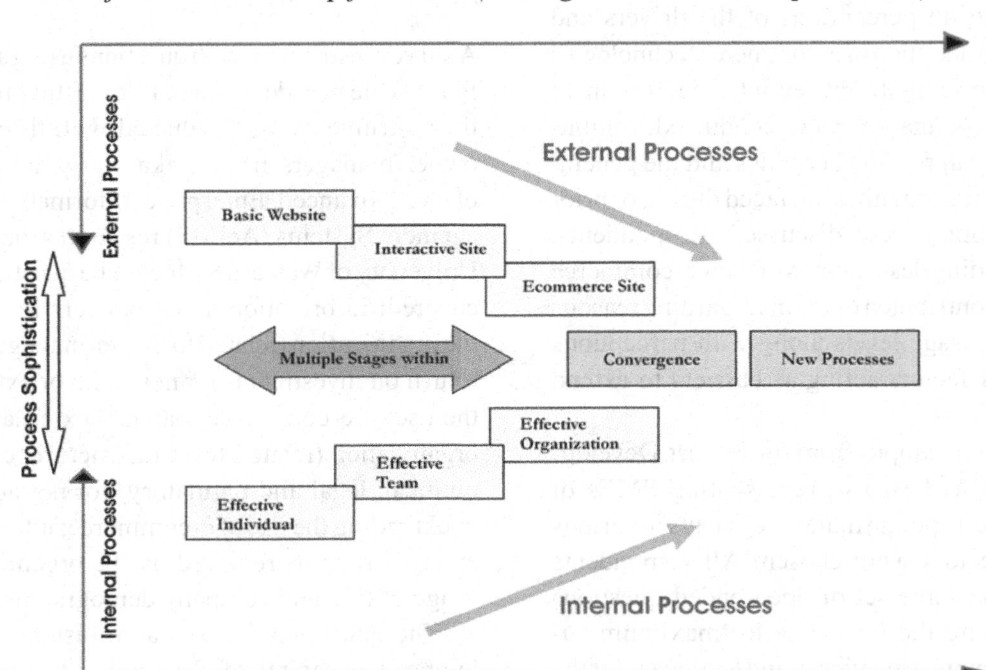

research results, and better reflects the multidimensional nature of complex real-world problems. Besides, a multi-method approach allows for the combination of benefits of both qualitative and quantitative methods, and permits empirical observations to guide and improve the survey stage of the research (Gallivan, 1997).

Phase 1: Pilot Exploratory Study with SMEs

The preliminary pilot interviews in phase 1were drawn up to highlight the barriers imperative to SMEs with the model (Figure 1) and provide data for the development of the survey instrument. Outcomes from the interviews and observations were supported by an extensive literature review. In phase two the survey of the SMEs interviews with intermediary support organizations were conducted. As Sekeran(2000), observes, semi-structured face to face interviews gather qualitative empirical data and provide flexibility as they allow researchers to explore issues faced by respondents, generally not possible through questionnaires or telephone interviews.

Focusing on perceptions of the drivers and inhibitors of adoption of e-commerce technologies face-to-face semi-structured interviews with 17 SME owner/managers were conducted. Inhibiting factors, supporting activities and the general experience the organization faced during or prior to the adoption were discussed. Respondents, while providing descriptions of their e-commerce activities, contributed opinions regarding reasons for current usage levels along with perceptions of issues or factors acting as barriers to extend use.

A random sample from an Export Development Board (EDB) list, representing SMEs of varying size, type and market segments in various industry sectors were chosen. All respondents received the same set of open-ended questions a week before the interview for maximum autonomy in expressing views, and to prepare for the interview. One-hour long interviews were audio recorded and transcribed for analysis. Cross-case analysis was undertaken by organizing the data in a spreadsheet, with rows representing each SME and columns containing the data. Arranging the data into categories within a matrix-like structure is accepted as a useful technique for facilitating pattern matching of qualitative data (Yin, 1994).

Of the 17 organizations, service companies made up 87% percent of the participants. The remaining 23% were manufacturing companies. Of these, 35 % had a static Website mainly used for advertising though not updated regularly; none used it for buying or selling. Most (76%) had Internet and e-mail facilities, and 52% use the Internet for browsing and searching. E-mail was the preferred for overseas communication, with 62% on ADSL connections and 25% dial-up connections. Only 43% allow everyone to access the Internet. All owner/managers were male, and 80% had tertiary or professional qualifications.

Phase 2: Survey of SMEs Using Questionnaire

A survey instrument with questions using a 5 point likert scale was developed. Pilot testing to refine the instrument was conducted with three SME owner /managers in Sri Lanka, and with members of the Advanced Enterprise Information Management Systems (AeIMS) research group at the University of Western Sydney. The questionnaire covered: information about barriers internal to the organization (related to owner/manager, firm, return on investment) for not using or extending the use of e-commerce; barriers external to the organization (related to infrastructure, cultural, political, legal and regulatory) for not adopting or extending the use of e-commerce; internal and external support required by the organizations; usage of ICT and company demographics.

The questionnaire was administered in Colombo, the capital of Sri Lanka. Overall, 625 questionnaires were personally addressed to the owner/managing director. The Department of Census and Statistics in Sri Lanka helped select recipients using a random sampling technique from a database of 3,000 SMEs in the Colombo District and from the list of SMEs from Tradenet (an industry association). Follow-up efforts to non-respondents were made through phone calls and post, three weeks after the mail-out. Out of 168 total responses received, 139 usable responses provided a response rate of 23.8%. This is considered adequate for the analysis and comparable to response rates in the IS literature (Pinsonneault et al, 1993). Comparison of the analysis between the first and second round of respondents did not show any statistically significant difference. Therefore, it can be safely assumed that a non-response error is not present and the data obtained from the respondents are representative of the sample chosen.

Phase 3: Interviews with SME Intermediary Organizations

Investigating intermediaries' perceptions of "barriers" and "support" helps identify whether facilities provided address SME requirements. Of the seven interviewed, five were government-sponsored, one was in the government sector, and one was a non-governmental organization (NGO). Their views on existing SME barriers to e-commerce adoption, the services provided, and the success rate of the schemes were discussed. The range of services the intermediary organizations provide include: assisting SMEs with strategic implementation of e-commerce, technology transfer, conducting seminars and workshops to raise awareness, training, forming linkages with buyers and suppliers locally and overseas. Senior managers of intermediary organizations responsible for helping SMEs with e-commerce technologies participated in exploratory face-to-face semi-structured interviews.

RESULTS AND DISCUSSION

This section discusses findings of the interviews and the survey.

Barriers: Pilot Interviews

A majority (88%) of respondents ranked lack of awareness as the highest barrier, considered significant as the majority of owner/managers described themselves as basically computer literate. Knowledge of available technologies or suitability for effective use towards improved productivity for benefits was negligible. They appear confused with choices in software/hardware. Computers, were underutilized with adhoc purchases and isolated implementation shadowing any e-commerce strategy being a major concern for decision makers. Next, was cost of the Internet, equipment, and e-commerce implementation. Inadequate telecommunications infrastructure chosen by 83% was the third most frequently cited barrier chosen by the more advanced SMEs of e-commerce using e-mail and Internet. This group were more likely to have experienced problems. Unstable economy, political uncertainty, lack of time, channel conflict, lack of information about e-commerce and lack of access to expert help, was cited as barriers by 70% of respondents.

Preliminary Analysis of Survey Data

More than 75% of the respondents (96% males and 4% females) were either professionally qualified or graduates. T-test analysis showed no significant difference based on gender or level of education. There was consensus for support in various forms and directions to address the barriers faced in adopting e-commerce technologies.

Barriers and Support for SMEs

Of the tables produced, Table 2 identifies the top six internal barriers of nine listed. Table 3 shows external barriers, divided into Cultural, Infrastructure, Political, Social, and Legal and Regulatory. Tables 4 and 5 illustrate internal and external support needed.

Analysis of survey results reveal that lack of skills, lack of awareness of benefits and return on investments prevent SMEs from adopting e-commerce technologies, reinforced by "awareness and education" ranking top for support by nearly 90% of the respondents. This is not surprising for a developing country like Sri Lanka trying to implement technologies with limited knowledge.

Table 2. Internal barriers to using or extending use of e-commerce

Internal Barriers	Mean	Std	N	%
Staff lack required skills	3.88	1.35	120	66.6
Security concerns with payments over the internet	3.64	1.28	118	66.9
e-commerce cannot give a financial gain N= number of organizations	3.64	1.24	108	62.0%

Table 3. External barriers to using or extending use of e-commerce

External Barriers	Mean	Std	N	%
Cultural Barriers				
Lack of popularity for online marketing and sales	3.56	1.28	120	62.5
Infrastructure Barriers				
Low internet penetration in the country	3.78	1.09	125	71.2
Inadequate quality and speed of lines	3.63	1.06	130	70.8
Inadequate infrastructure in the country	3.52	1.22	125	62.4
Political Barriers				
Unstable economic climate in the country	3.73	.971	135	73.3
Changing regulations with each government change	3.72	1.12	135	71.9
Social Barriers				
Lack of information on e-commerce	3.59	1.04	133	69.1
No one-shop facility	3.50	1.19	127	54.3
No access to reliable expert help	3.25	1.10	130	52.8
Senior management in other sector lack ICT knowledge	3.24	1.05	123	52.8
Legal & Regulatory Barriers				
Little support for SMEs from government and industry associations	3.7	.96	128	64.0
Inadequate legal framework for business using e-commerce	3.68	.98	121	64.5
No simple procedures and guidelines	3.67	1.10	128	65.6
Lack of suitable software standards N= number of organizations	3.51	1.10	128	53.9

Table 4. Internal support for SMEs to use or extend use of e-commerce

Internal Support	Mean	Std	N	%
Awareness and education	3.91	.87	132	79.9
Guidance in overcoming risks associated with implementation	3.86	.92	129	78.0
Guidelines for appropriate hardware and software	3.78	.88	134	72.4
Advice and direction for ICT and e-commerce N= number of organizations	3.70	.91	135	70.4

Table 5. External support for SMEs to use or extend use of e-commerce

External Support	Mean	Std	N	%
Improve national infrastructure	4.04	.76	130	84.6
Provide financial assistance	3.97	.81	135	78.5
Provide tax incentives	3.97	.92	132	80.3
Improve ICT diffusion	3.95	.83	130	80.8
Government & industry sector to take leadership/promotion role	3.91	.91	134	75.4
Improve collaboration among SMEs	3.86	1.04	133	69.1
Improve low bank account and credit card penetration	3.83	.81	123	72.4
Enforce suitable software standards N= number of organizations	3.8	.97	132	74.3

This also reflects on other internal barriers, as awareness and education can, to a great extent, counter some barrier. Since the use of ICT in Sri Lanka is low, e-commerce faces inhibition and does not suit business transactions.

"Lack of popularity in online marketing" and "low Internet penetration" rate high in the list of external barriers. Improving ICT diffusion in Sri Lanka can address this problem. "Inadequate infrastructure" impedes SMEs as reinforced by their request for "improvement of national infrastructure" ranking very high on the support needed. SMEs in Sri Lanka are adversely affected by the high cost and unreliable service of infrastructure services such as electricity and telecommunications. The steps taken by the government to improve telecommunication facilities by breaking the telecommunications monopoly is noteworthy. Policy inertia and the lack of legal and regulatory framework also rank high and enforce constraints on SMEs. Policy reforms introduced by governments support the large export-oriented foreign direct investments leaving SMEs with ad-hoc policy prescriptions and weak institutional support (Task Force, 2002). The government's role in an overly bureaucratic regulatory system results in delays in its deliberations and is extremely costly (Task Force, 2002). Appropriate legal and regulatory framework would ensure that SMEs operate on a level playing field.

Social barriers come next. A one-stop shop facility helps SMEs access information, technology, markets, and the much needed credit facilities. This concept, implemented for export-oriented foreign direct investments (EOFDI) by the Board of Investments (BOI) found it to be successful. Being policy makers working towards progress of SMEs, senior management lacking in ICT knowledge is identified as an important constraint directly influencing operational efficiency of SMEs. Awareness building and education with regard to ICT and technologies would help alleviate this problem. Government, academia, and industry sectors can take leadership roles in promotion of ICT conducting awareness and training programmes, technical and non-technical catering to the needs of SMEs at grass-roots level. SMEs place a very heavy reliance on external advice and support. Such support and advice seem unavailable.

IT sophistication is defined as how a piece of IT is used with an appropriate process in an organization by investigating how people, processes, and technology interact (Ginige et al, 2001). Taking this indication, data was analysed to recognize the level of IT sophistication with internal and external business processes of SMEs and determine their position on the e-transformation road map. Two distinct new stages "No Website" on external processes and "Manual" on internal processes resulted from the analysis. In Sri Lanka,

Figure 3. Modified e-transformation road map for SMEs in developing countries

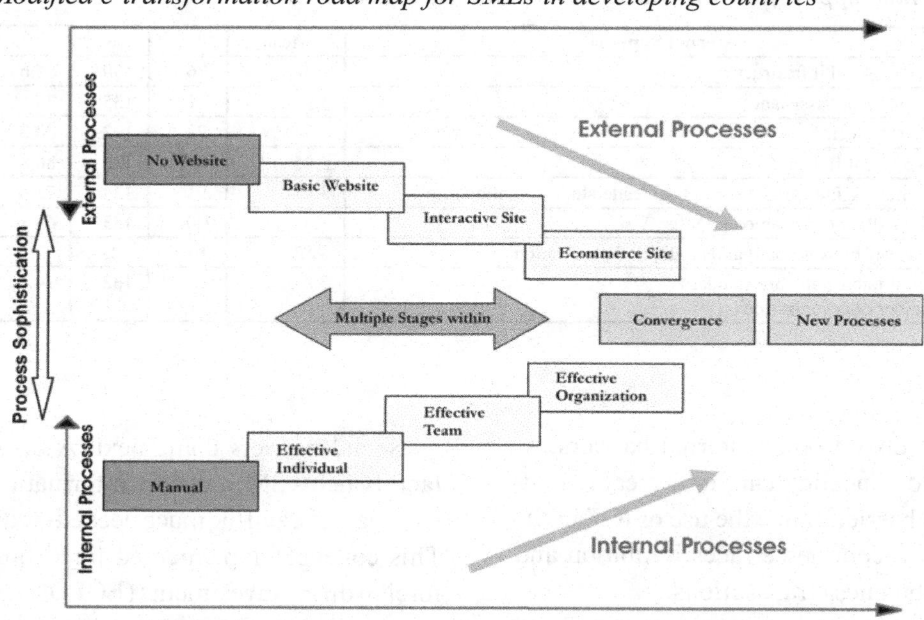

Figure 4. Detailed e-transformation road map with multiple sub stages within stages

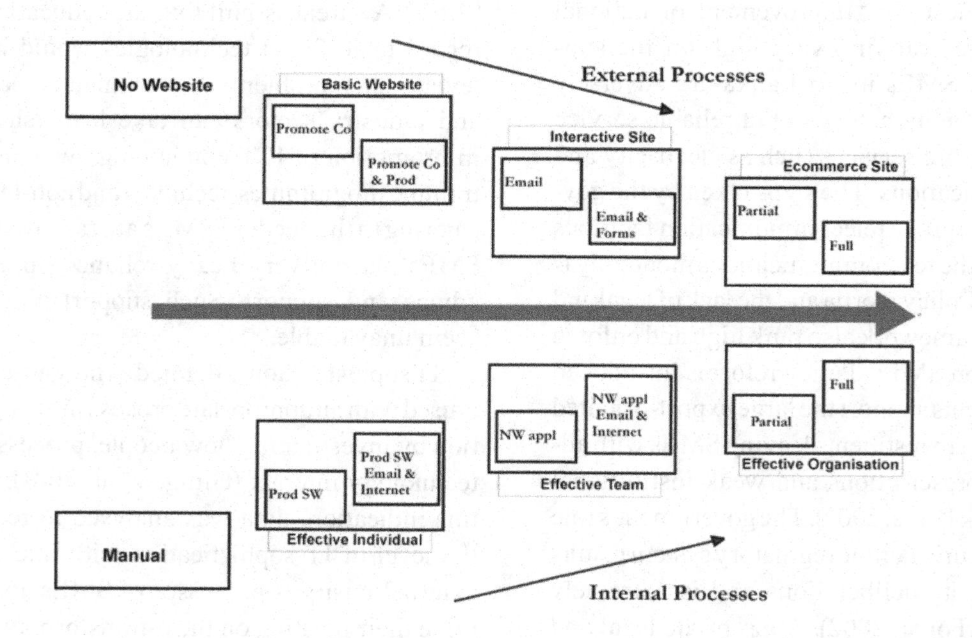

many organizations are yet to adopt computers in their business and small organizations fear hiring computer literate employees on high wages or losing trusted old hands to computers.

Extending the e-transformation road map (Ginige et al, 2001) accommodated new stages, with some stages consisting of multiple stages. The majority of the SMEs in this research were situated in the two middle stages, a few into the least and most sophisticated stages.

The proposed stage model, though it appears sequential is not so in reality. A company can enter at any stage and as awareness, technology, and support increases, a company can proceed to an advanced stage leapfrogging earlier stages in order to accelerate the e-transformation process. When this happens, it is anticipated that issues in all previous stages must be addressed.

Figure 3 shows the modified e-transformation road map in a developing country context. The original road map has been extended to incorporate two new stages; "no Website" on the external processes and "manual" on the internal processes.

Figure 4 depicts the multiple sub stages that can exist within a particular stage on the road map. Detailed analysis revealed that the SMEs do not possess all the characteristics incorporated in a particular stage. To illustrate this scenario multiple sub states were introduced within a main sage.

Table 6 below, describes main stages of the roadmap and the sub-stages within each main stage.

What Barriers are Predominant at a Stage?

Further statistical analysis was carried out on Internal Barriers and External Barriers to investigate if there is any dependency between the barriers/support and the levels of sophistication of the SMEs at different stages on the e-transformation roadmap. In order to achieve this Chi Square tests were carried out to investigate the barriers and support required with respondents at each stage. Some distinctive dissimilarity in the degree of prominence of these factors surfaced when the data was grouped according to the SME's IT sophistication.

Table 6. Stages of the e-transformation road map

External Stages	Stage No:	Stages within
No Website	1	
Basic Web Site	2	Promote company
		Promote company and products
Interactive Website	3	Has e-mail link to contact company (one way)
		Has 2 way communication, e-mail and facility for structured queries
E-commerce Site	4	Some e-commerce excluding financial transactions
		Full fledged e-commerce site
Internal Stages	**Stage No:**	**Stages within**
Manual	1	
Effective Individual	2	Use of Productivity Software
		Use of Productivity Software and e-mail /Internet
Effective Team	3	Use of Networked applications, share databases
		Use of Networked applications, share databases, use e-mail / Internet
Effective Enterprise	4	Some enterprise wide integrated applications
		Full use of enterprise wide integrated applications

Internal Barriers: Moving from No Website to E-Commerce Site

The following Tables illustrate the results of the Chi Square analysis carried out on the Internal Barriers and the associated support.

Support for Internal Barriers: Moving from No Website to E-Commerce Site

On a scrutiny of respondents' data, a clearer picture on the SMEs level of sophistication emerged. In keeping with our expectations, there are clear differences in the way SMEs at different levels of IT sophistication perceived the barriers and the necessary support. The internal barriers mentioned above broadly fall into categories of barriers namely: (a) barriers pertaining to owner/manager characteristics, (b) firm characteristics and (c) cost or return on investments. This reinforces the system of categorization of the internal barriers in the survey instrument.

Table 7 reveals that a lack of awareness about suitable technology, lack of skills and expertise within the staff and a lack of financial resources are the major barriers faced by SMEs on their way to ICT initiatives. Lack of awareness of technology continues to proceed to other stages too but fades as the company makes good progress on the way.

This observation makes good sense. An SME, by its very nature and with its low-level sophistication cannot claim to have staff with required IT skills or necessary expertise for an ICT uptake or e-commerce revision. Prananto, McKay and Marshall (2003) with their findings, strengthen this observation. Besides, a sound investment involving significant financial resources would be essential to recruit and retain staff with appropriate skills and expertise. Insufficient capital could hamper efforts to acquire or retain such staff. Therefore, SMEs are deficient with their resources. Besides, the SME owner/managers are under extreme pressure to mange the organization with limited resources, both physical and financial.

A lack of financial resources and time could reflect adversely on awareness building with a lack of awareness of technology contributing towards a pressing barrier even in the advanced stages. Already a lack of awareness of technology impedes progress of SMEs. There is a growing need to be educated with regard to technology, made aware of what technology is available and identify what technology is best for one's surroundings. The barriers seem to fade even further for SMEs trying to extend to a fully-fledged e-commerce site. With the adoption of advanced technologies and with time they appear to have overcome hurdles to address the internal issues hindering

Table 7. Chi square test for internal barriers

Internal Barriers to ICT	**Pearson Chi Sq**	**df**	**Asymp. sig(2 sided)**
Staff lack required skills	22.591	4	<.001
Lack of time to investigate	17.131	4	<.01
Lack of financial resources	15.427	4	<.01
Lack of awareness of suitable technology	9.551	4	<.05
Internal Barriers to -commerce	**Pearson Chi Sq**	**df**	**Asymp. sig(2 sided)**
Not suited to customer /supplier	14.3	4	<.01
Lack of required skills	12.647	4	<.05
Cannot give any financial gain	10.794	4	<.05
EC does not suit products/services	10.630	4	<.05

Table 8. Contingency table for internal barriers

Internal Barriers to ICT	**Stage 1-2**	**Stage 2-3**	**Stage 3-4**
Staff lack required skills	***39, 25.7 66.1%***	13, 18.7 30.2%	9, 16.6 23.7%
Lack of time to investigate	***35,24.6 59.3%***	16,17.9 37.2	7, 15.4 18.9
Lack of financial resources	***29, 19.9 53.7***	13, 15.1 31.7%	7, 14 18.4%
Lack of awareness of suitable technology	***19,14.2 32.2%***	12, 10.6 27.3	3, 9.2 7.9%
Internal Barriers to EC	**Stage 1-2**	**Stage 2-3**	**Stage 3-4**
Not suited to customer /supplier	***26,19.6 50.0%***	***18,17 40.0%***	7, 14.4 18.4%
Lack of required skills	***43, 35.7 79.6%***	29,29.1 65.9%	18, 25.1 47.4%
Cannot give any financial gain	***33,29.4 68.8%***	***27,24.5 67.5%***	16, 22.1 44.4%
EC does not suit products/services	***28, 19.7 54.9%***	14,16.6 32.6%	9, 14.7 23.7%

Table 9. Chi square test for support with external processes

Support	**value**	**df**	**Sig**
Assist SMEs with guidelines for HW/SW	13.001	4	<.05
Awareness building programmers	12.739	4	<.05

Table 10. Contingency table for support with external processes

Support	**Stage 1-2**	**Stage 2-3**	**Stage 3-4**
Assist SMEs with guidelines for HW/SW	46, 45.1 73%	30, 32.9 65.2%	32, 30 76.2%
Awareness building programmers	48,48.6 76.2%	38, 35.5 82.6	29, 30.9 72.5

them. As acquired knowledge is retained and as progression is witnessed, SMEs prepare for more difficult and complex problems in the advanced stages (Prananto et al, 2003).

With regards to factors impeding the adoption of e-commerce: the perception that e-commerce not suited to customers/suppliers is the most significant internal barrier, followed by lack of required skills, e-commerce cannot give any financial gain, and e-commerce does not suit products/services. As in the case for barriers for ICT, the Contingency Table shows that the SMEs seem to be having the maximum difficulty in getting started on e-commerce. Once they have taken the initial step, with time they seem to cope better with the issues they had in the initial stages.

SMEs would decide to host a basic Website only when they are positive, that e-commerce is suited for their products/services. Therefore, it does not seem to be a barrier beyond the initial stage. They seem to overcome the issues regarding skills with time. E-commerce not suited for customers/suppliers seems to be the most significant and pressing factors for the take-up of e-commerce and continues to have the same effect in the advanced stages. This is to be anticipated as a majority of the local customers and suppliers in Sri Lanka are not in favour of using e-mail let alone e-commerce. SMEs do not get any benefit by using e-commerce if the customers/suppliers are averse to it. Many SME owner/managers are not convinced that there is any financial gain in using e-commerce. Having a basic Website has not given them any new customers or sales. They are sceptical about extending the use of e-commerce to an interactive site. All these barriers seem to be less significant with the SMEs having an e-commerce site. They would only move into an e-commerce site when their customers/suppliers are ready to use the Web site for transactions, which definitely convinces the SMEs of the financial gains it would bring. The knowledge and experience acquired and retained through progression prepares the SME to deal with more complex and more difficult problems in the advanced stages (Prananto et.al, 2003).

External Barriers: Moving from No Website to E-Commerce Site

Table 11 illustrates the results of the Chi Square analysis carried out on the External Barriers and the associated support.

The external barriers for e-commerce fall into three major categories of external barriers previously identified in the proposed model and the survey instrument leading to reinforcing the system of categorization of the external l barriers in the survey instrument.

The barriers related to infrastructure and legal and regulatory environment highlighted in the survey instrument did not come up as significant. This could be attributed to many reasons. The Sri Lankan government has taken many steps to improve the telecommunication infrastructure of the country. The cost of telecommunication has become very much less with the invasion of mobile phones. Even though the speed is not up to the mark, access and reliability of telephone lines is far superior to the situation a few years ago. As majority of the SMEs are not using fully-fledged e-commerce, the issue of speed and quality of line has not become a pressing barrier for the SMEs. For the same reason the SMEs do not find legal and regulatory barriers a pressing issue.

The political barriers seem to loom high in the list, which is not surprising for a developing country like Sri Lanka, which goes through political uncertainties all the time. SMEs with their limited resources are cautious of investing in technology advancements, when there is uncertainty, which has adverse effects on the economy, legislations in the country. The SMEs also find it difficult to promote their Websites. This is to be expected as the culture in Sri Lanka and in many developing countries where shopping is considered a social activity, does not favour trading online. Another contributing factor, which is not discussed in the open, is evasion of tax. SMEs prefer to transact with cash, e-commerce does not give that flexibility.

Table 11. Chi square test for external barriers

External Barriers	Value	Df	sig
Unstable economic climate in the country	17.131	4	<.05
Constant change of government & rules an regulation	15.232	4	<.01
Difficult to promote Website	10.686	4	<.05
No access to reliable expert help	10.63	4	<.05
Lack of available information on e-commerce	10.045	4	<.05

Table 12. Contingency table for external barriers

External Barriers	Stage 1-2	Stage 2-3	Stage 3-4
Unstable economic climate in the country	53, 45.2 85.8%	29, 35 40%	28, 29.9 68.3
Constant change of government & rules an regulation	53, 43.9 85.5	26, 34 54.2	28, 29.1 68.3
Difficult to promote Website	25, 20 43.9	20, 16.5 42.6	6, 14.4 4.6%
No access to reliable expert help	35, 29.1 59.3%	25,23.2 53.2	12, 19.7 30.0%
Lack of available information on e-commerce	44.39 72.1%	39, 33.3 81.3%	21,28.4 51.2

Lack of access to reliable help is a significant barrier for SMEs. In Sri Lanka help is mostly not available, and the existing help either does not cater to the needs of SMEs, or SMEs are unaware it is available. Lack of information on e-commerce seems to be a pressing factor that deters SMEs from adopting the technologies. For a country like Sri Lanka still at a stage a little beyond infancy with regard to e-commerce this is to be expected. Proper strategic planning at national and industry level is fundamental in raising awareness among SMEs. A combined effort from government, industry sectors, and academia is vital.

Further analysis of the contingency Table 12 shows that the external barriers are more predominant at early stages. As in the previous case, barriers become less evident progressing to advanced stages. SMEs seem to be experiencing most of the external barriers in getting started on e-commerce and moving from a No Website stage to a Basic Website stage. Once they have taken the initial step, with time they seem to cope better with issues they experienced in the initial process.

The fact the SMEs have managed to host a basic Website means that they can extend it further to incorporate features for basic interactivity. The political barriers are not pressing when advancing to an interactive site but become a pressing issue when trying to adopt a fully-fledged e-commerce site. This could be because the SMEs have learnt to survive, and have found alternative techniques to rise above the problem. However, trading and particularly online trading is at stake when there is an unsteady economic and political environment hence these barriers prevail at stage 3 when SMEs try to advance to a fully-fledged e-commerce site.

The lack of reliable and expert help, lack of information on e-commence is still a continuing barrier when SMEs try to move from a Basic Website to an Interactive Website and even though it still remains an issue it does not seem to be as significant as in stage 1. Along with these two contributing factors, the cultural factor still deters the SMEs from promoting a Website to moving towards an interactive site. In Sri Lanka, use of Websites or computers for buying and selling is quite low and is almost non-existent especially outside the Colombo district. The practice of doing business electronically, dealing with non-cash payments, is not common for businesses in Sri Lanka. The SMEs' concerns about difficulties in promoting a Website stems from their perceived risk of e-commerce usage, lack of confidentiality or lack of trust of the credit card payments and the lack of Internet and computer penetration in the country. Creating awareness and promoting e-commerce at a national level would certainly help alleviate this barrier.

SMEs are faced with barriers moving beyond the Basic Website to an Interactive Site. They need to be informed about e-commerce, its applications, and benefits before they make a decision to adopt more advanced e-commerce. Having access to reliable help from the experts would assist and direct them in the decision making process. These two barriers become less evident in stage 3 (moving to a fully-fledged e-commerce site). With the adoption of advanced technologies and with time they seem to have overcome the issues hindering them.

Table 13 below shows awareness building, training and advice is most significant to SMEs in adopting the e-commerce technologies. For a developing country like Sri Lanka, little beyond infancy with regard to e-commerce support in these areas is essential.

Further analysis of the Contingency Table 14 reveals that there is a critical need for help for SMEs at all levels of IT sophistication. They need to be made aware of the available technologies, their benefits, and their applicability to business. Best practices success stories would help the SMEs in making informed decisions regarding adoption. The SMEs become familiar with the hardware and software once they have taken the initial move towards a Basic Website. However, they do require guidance with software and hardware when they advance to an e-commerce site.

Perceptions of SME Intermediaries

The intermediaries, with a consensus for awareness building programs at national level agree lack of awareness and lack of skills are major barriers for SMEs to adopt technologies. Training programs, workshops, and seminars conducted in the local language need to be especially designed for SMEs at grass roots level. Rather than training in ICT-specific skills the need for education of SMEs to impart the knowledge of the possibilities, accumulating from the adoption of e-commerce is vital. At a more advanced level, there is a requirement for training, coaching, and hands-on support in business change management to enable the SMEs to re-engineer their business.

Absence of a "one-stop shop" for advice and support is de-motivating and affects SMEs. It is fundamental to educate senior management of government organizations prior to providing support for SMEs with e-commerce. SMEs need not only technologies but also quality control and standards.

Inter-institutional coordination, developing staff, and institutional capacity are also vital.

Table 13. Chi square test for support with external barriers

Support	Pearson Chi Sq	df	Asymp.Sig (2 sided)
Assist SMEs with guidelines for HW/SW	13.001	4	<.05
Awareness building programmers	12.739	4	<.05

Table 14. Contingency table for support with external barriers

Support	Stage 1-2	Stage 2-3	Stage 3-4
Assist SMEs with guidelines for HW/SW	46, 45.1 73%	30, 32.9 65.2%	32, 30 76.2%
Awareness building programmers	48,48.6 76.2%	38, 35.5 82.6	29, 30.9 72.5

Table 15. Subset of barriers and support needed to move through stages

Type	Barriers	External Stage 1-2	External Stage 2-3	External Stage 2-3
Internal Barriers to ICT	Staff lack required skills	y		
	Lack of time to investigate	y		
	Lack of financial resources	y		
	Lack of awareness of suitable technology	y	y	
Internal Barriers EC	Not suited to customer /supplier	y	y	
	Lack of required skills	y	y	
	Cannot give any financial gain	y	y	
	EC does not suit products/services	y		
External Barriers to EC	Unstable economic climate in the country	y		
	Constant change of government & rules an regulation	y	y	
	Difficult to promote Website	y	y	
	No access to reliable expert help	y	y	
	Lack of available information on e-commerce	y	y	
Support	Assist SMEs with guidelines for HW/SW	y		y
	Awareness building programs	y	y	

Much effort seems replicated and wasted with public sector, private and non-governmental SME intermediary organizations working in isolation. The government is best equipped to reach rural SMEs at grass roots level. Tapping and utilizing all available strengths in a more coordinated manner would prove much more productive.

The results reveal that e-commerce technologies in SMEs are well diffused within the Colombo district as a means of communication and are beginning to be used for market development. Online transactions and payments are either non-existent or still in their infancy, limited by various internal and external barriers and lack of support to overcome them. Best practices among developing countries are limited and not widely publicized for others in the same regions to follow (Laosethakul and Boultan, 2007). Being aware of best practices, what works elsewhere, is important in formulating policies to foster e-commerce (OECD, 1998).

CONCLUSION

This chapter contributes by identifying a suitable framework for SMEs anxious to e-transform their organizations. Towards this it provides an understanding of the challenges faced by SMEs in Sri Lanka while presenting a comprehensive framework using the knowledge of the relative importance of factors that deter the adoption of e-commerce. It also discusses the necessary support activities to assist SMEs to overcome the barriers and better plan their e-transformation. SMEs could also use the framework for comparison with other SMEs involved in e-commerce, as it is strategically valuable for a company to compare oneself with competitors within one's own industry and within the e-commerce community.

In developing this framework, the difference between e-transforming SME organizations in the developing and developed countries and the focus on support activities needed in the developing were seriously considered. Whereas support is available in developed countries, and it is a matter of finding the appropriate support for a SME encountering barriers. In the developing countries this support is almost non-existent. Besides, raising awareness among SMEs and providing them with information is another necessity. The initial framework for eTransformation of SMEs in a developing country is proposed for trial towards validation.

This research contributes further by identifying the absence of a government and industry coordinated approach to providing support for SMEs, without addressing problems at a grass-root level. It is apparent that there is a need for more hands-on, customised delivery of information, assistance, and demonstration tailored to SMEs in developing countries. The trade associations, chambers of commerce, and government could promote the use of e-commerce through awareness campaigns. There is a crucial need for action by the government to influence the provision of such services. Governments also need to actively encourage the diffusion of e-commerce among SMEs as a way to improve competitiveness and access to new markets. They can help by raising awareness, (for example through road shows, Web sites, television, radio) demonstration and development centres, pilot project assistance, funding and training assistance It is encouraging to find the Sri Lankan government taking initial measures to broaden the use of ICT by SMEs and help improve access to skills providing necessary expertise for full participation in the digital economy. The government body, Information and Communications Technologies Agency (ICTA), established for this purpose shows further commitment, providing legitimate and positive leadership in developing an infrastructure to digitize Sri Lanka's economy. It also identifies External Barriers such as government policies, legal environment, and inadequate infrastructure to be beyond the control of the SME and need to be handled accordingly. The conceptual model developed identifies internal and external barriers while assessing necessary support to overcome obstacles.

The findings from this research should be significant to practitioners and owner/managers of SMEs. Firstly, owner/managers must be convinced of the benefits of e-commerce before they decide to fully embrace it. They also need to absorb e-commerce adoption into the objectives of their respective firms. With regard to policy makers, working towards policies with e-commerce adoption this study has several implications. They need to understand the value of government intervention as a regulatory body. The government must play a major role with a proactive approach to influence not only with behavioural changes responsible for technological innovations but also with a provision of necessary pre-requisites and infrastructure for SMEs. The government, as a regulatory body, needs to act as a standard setting and knowledge dispensing body. Similar issues have been resolved with Vietnamese SMEs, by the intervention of government, financial institutions, and large enterprises with support with policies and assistance programs (Huy and Filiatrault, 2006).

Promoting cooperation and trust among SMEs with clustering and collaboration provide specific support to SMEs to overcome some Internal Barriers, improve operating environment for more competition, transfer skills, and technology, and access wider markets. This concept is not popular in Sri Lanka, is ad-hoc and limited. Suitable policy interventions from government and active support from the private sector and the donor community are needed to address this issue (Task Force, 2002). The government needs to take leadership to facilitate a regulatory environment, improve national infrastructure and continue to help with ICT education. It can be argued that Institutional deficiencies play a major challenge in e-commerce development as found in the case in China (Martinsons, 2001). SMEs can follow the example set by the Chinese e-commerce companies by developing and leveraging relationships with involved parties, such as government agencies and banks, upon trust and mutual benefits thereby helping them to overcome regulatory, financial, and logistic issues (Laosethakul and Boultan, 2007).

As the research program unfolds, geographic and generic distinctions will be addressed, providing a clearer picture of e-commerce activity in different areas and within identified business sectors of Sri Lanka. The outcomes of this research could also be applied to other developing countries with similar business, infrastructure, and national culture.

REFERENCES

Akkeren, J. & Cavaye, A.L.M. (1999). *Factors affecting entry-level Internet technology adoption by small business in Australia: An Empirical Study.* Proceedings of the 10th Australasian Conference on Information Systems. Wellington, New Zealand, 1-3 December.

Anigan, G (1999). *Views on electronic commerce.* International Trade Forum, 2, 23–27.

Beatty R.C., Shim J.P & Jone M.C(2001). Factors influencing corporate Web site adoption: a time based assessment, *Information & Management* (38), 337–354.

Benbasat, I., Dexter, A.S., Drury, D.H. & Goldstein, R.C. (1984). A critique of the stage hypothesis: Theory and empirical evidence. *Communications of the ACM,* 27(5), 476-485.

Berryman, E. (1999). *Getting on with the Business of E-business.* PriceWaterhouseCoopers, USA.

Bhabuta, L. (1988). *Sustaining Productivity and Competitiveness by Marshalling IT. In Information Technology Management for Productivity and Strategic Advantage,* Proceedings of the IFIP TC8 Open Conference, Singapore.

Bingi, P., Mir A., & Khamalah J. (2000). The challenges facing global e-eommerce, *Information systems Management* 17(4), 26–35.

Bode, S & Burn, J.M.,(2002). Strategies for consultancy engagement for e-business development -a case analysis of Australian SMEs, S. Burgess (ed.), *Managing Information Technology in Small Business:challenges and solutions*, Idea Group, Melbourne, Australia, 227-245.

Burgess, L. & Cooper, J. (1999). A model for classification of business adoption of Internet commerce solutions, Global Networked Organizations: 12th International Bled Electronic Commerce Conference, Bled, Slovenia, June 7–9, pp. 46–58.

Chan, C. & Swatman, P. M. C., (2004). *B2B E-Commerce Stages of Growth: The Strategic Imperatives.* Proceedings of the 37th Hawaii International Conference on System Sciences,

Chau, S.B. & Turner, P. (2001). *A four phase model of EC business transformation amongst small to medium sized enterprises,* Proceedings of the 12th Australasian Conference on Information Systems. Coffs Harbour: Australia.

Chau,P.Y.K and Jim,C.C.F.(2002). Adoption of Electronic Data Interchange in Small and Medium Sized Enterprises, *Journal of Global Information management*,44,4, 332–351

Chong S. & Pervan G.,(2007). Factors Influencing the Extent of Deployment Electronic Commerce for Small-and Medium-Sized Enterprises, *Journal of Electronic Commerce in Organizations,* 5(1), 1-29,

Chong Sandy (2006). An empirical study of factors that influence the extent of deployment of electronic commerce for small- and medium-sized enterprises in Australia. *Journal of Theoretical and Applied Electronic Commerce Research* 1(2), ISSN:0718-1876

Cloete, E., S. Courtney, & J. Fintz (2002). Small businesses' acceptance and adoption of e-commerce in the western-cape province of South-Africa. *Electronic Journal on Information Systems in Developing Countries* 10(4), 1–13, http://www.ejisdc.org.

Corbitt, B., G. Behrendorf, & J. Brown-Parker. (1997). *Small and medium-sized enterprises and electronic commerce,* The Australian Institute of Management 14, 204–222.

Dedrick, J. & K.L. Kraemer (2001). China IT Report. *Electronic Journal on Information Systems in Developing Countries* 6(2), 1–10.

EBPG (2002). *Europe go digital: Benchmarking national and regional e-business policies for SMEs.* Final report of the EBusiness Policy Group, 28 June 2002.

El-Nawawy, M.A. & M.M. Ismail. (1999). *Overcoming deterrents and impediments to electronic commerce in light of globalisation: the case of Egypt,* Proceedings of the 9th Annual Conference of the Internet Society, INET 99, San Jose, USA.

Enns H.G. & Huff S.L.,(1999). Information technology implementation in developing countries: advent of the Internet in Mongolia, *Journal of Global Information Technology Management* 2(3), pp. 5–24.

Galliers, R.D. and Sutherland, A.R. (1994). Information Systems Management and Strategy Formulation: Applying and Extending the 'Stages of Growth' Concept. *In Strategic Information Management:Challenges and Strategies in Managing Information Systems*, R.D. Galliers and B. S. H. Baker (eds.),Butterworth-Heinemann Ltd., Oxford, 91-117.

Gallivan, MJ (1997). *Value in triangulation: a comparison of two approaches for*

Garcia-Murillo Martha (2004). Institutions and the Adoption of Electronic Commerce in Mexico. *Electronic Commerce Research*, 4, 201-219

Ginige A., Murugesan S. & Kazanis P.(2001). A Roadmap for Successfully Transforming SMEs in to E-Businesses, *Cutter IT Journal*,May 2001,Vol 14

Grant, S. (1999). *E-commerce for small businesses,* in Proceedings of the 2nd International Conference IeC ′99, Manchester, England, November 1–3, pp 65–72.

Huff, S. & P. Yoong. (2000). *SMEs and e-commerce: current issues and concerns. A preliminary report.* In Proceedings of the International Conference on E-commerce, Kuala Lumpur, Malaysia, 21 November 2000, pp. 1–5.

Huy Le Van & Filiatrault, P. (2006). *The Adoption of E-Commerce in SMEs in Vietnam: A Study of Users and Prospectors*, The 10th Pacific Asia Conference on Information Systems.

Iacovou, C.L., Benbasat, I. & Dexter, A.A. (1995). Electronic data interchange and small organizations: adoption and impact of technology, *MIS Quarterly*, 19, 4, 465-485.

Jeon B.N., Han K.S. & Lee M.J (2006). Determining factors for the adoption of e-business: the case of SMEs in Korea, *Applied Economics*, 38, 1905-1916.

Julien, P.A. & Raymond, L. (1994). Factors of New Technology Adoption in the Retail Sector. *Entrepreneurship: Theory and Practice*,18, 5, 79-90.

Jun,M. & Cai,S. (2003). Key Obstacles to EDI Success from the US Small Manufacturing Companies' Perspective, *Industrial Management and Data Systems,* 103, 3, 152-165

Kirby, D. & Turner, M. (1993). IT and the Small Retail Business, *International Journal of Retail and Distribution Management*, 21, 7, 20-27.

Knol, W.H.C. & Stroeken, J.H.M. (2001). The diffusion and adoption of information technology in small- and medium –sized enterprises through IT Scenarios, *Technology Analysis & Strategic Management,* 13(2),227-246.

KPMG (1997). *Electronic Commerce Research Report.* London, UK: KPMG.

Laosethakul , K., Boulton,W.,(2007). Critical Success Factors for E-commerce in Thailand: Cultural and Infrastructural Influences, *The Electronic Journal on Information Systems in Developing Countries* (http://www.ejisdc.org), 30, 2, 1-22.

Lawson, R., Alcock, C., Cooper, J., & L. Burgress. (2003). Factors affecting adoption of electronic commerce technologies by SMEs: an Australian study. *Journal of Small Business and Enterprise Development, 10(3)*, 265-276.

Ling, C.Y. (2001). *Model of factors influence on electronic commerce adoption and diffusion in small and medium enterprises,* ECIS Doctoral Consortium, AIS region 2 (Europe, Africa, Middle-East), 24-26 June.

Mahajan, V., Siriniwasan, R.& Wind, J. (2002). The dot.com Retail Failures of 2000: Were there any Winners? *Academy of Marketing Science Journal*, 16(3), 335-340.

Marshall, P., Sor, R. & McKay, J. (2000). An industry case study of the impacts of electronic commerce on car dealerships in Western Australia. *Journal of Electronic Commerce Research*, 1(1).

McKay, J., Marshall, P., and Prananto, A. (2000). *Stages of maturity for e-business: The SOG-e model.* Conference Proceedings of the 4th Pacific Asia Conference on Information Systems, Hong Kong University of Science and Technology, Hong Kong.

Mehrtens, J., Cragg, P.B. & Mills, A.M. (2001). A model of Internet adoption by SMEs. *Information and Management*, 39.165-176.

Mingers, J. (2000). 'The contribution of critical realism as an underpinning philosophy for OR/MS and systems', *Journal of the Operational Research Society*, 51(11), pp. 1256-70.

Mukti N.A.,(2000). Barriers to putting businesses on the Internet in Malaysia, *Electronic Journal of Information Systems in Developing Countries* 2(6), 1–6.

Nolan, R.L. (1973). Managing the Computer Resource: A Stage Hypothesis. *Communications of the ACM,* 16(7), 399-406.

O'Connor, J. & Galvin, E. (1998). Creating Value through E-commerce. *Financial Times*, Pitman-Publishing, London.

OECD (1998). *SMEs and electronic commerce*, Ministerial Conference on Electronic Commerce, Ottawa, Canada.

Panagariya, A. (2000). E-Commerce, WTO, and Developing Countries, *World Economy* 23(8), 959–979.

Pinsonneault, K. Kraemer (1993). Survey research methodology in management information systems: an assessment, *Journal of Management Information Systems* 10(2), 75–105.

Poon, S. (1999). *Management's role and internet commerce benefit among online small businesses,* in Proceedings of the 7th Conference on Information Systems, J. Pries-Heje, C. Ciborra, and K. Kautz, Eds. Copenhagen, Denmark: Copenhagen Business School, . 559-571.

Prananto, A., McKay, J., & Marshall, P. (2003). *A study of the progression of e-business maturity in Australian SMEs: Some evidence of the applicability of the stages of growth for e-business model.*7th Pacific Asia Conference on Information Systems (PACIS) 2003, University of South Australia,Adelaide, Australia.

Premkumar, G., Ramamurthy, K. & Nilakanta, S. (1994). Implementation of electronic data Interchange: an innovation diffusion perspective, *Journal of Management Information Systems*, 11, 157–86.

Rao, S. S. (2003). Electronic Commerce Development in Small and Medium Sized Enterprises: A Stage Model and Its Implications. *Business Process Management Journal*, 9(1), 11-32.

Rashid M.A., & Al_Qirim,(2001). N.A. E-commerce technology adoption framework by New Zealand small to medium size enterprises, *Research Letters in the Information and Mathematical Sciences, Institute of Information and Mathematical Sciences*, 2, pp 63-70.

Rayport, J.F., & Jaworski, B. J.(2003). *Commerce electronique*, Cheneliere / McGraw –Hill, Montreal (quebec), Canada, 652 pages

Schmid, B., K. Stanoevska-Slabeva, & V. Tschammer. (2001). *Towards the E-Society*: E-Commerce, E-Business, E-Government, Zurich, Switzerland, 13 October.

Sekaran. U. (2000). *Research Methods for Business – A Skill Building Approach*, 3rdEdition, John Wiley & Sons, Inc.

SLBDC, (2002). *Survey on E-Commerce Implementation in the SME Sector of Sri Lanka* Conducted by the SLBDC

Stroud, D. (1998). *Internet Strategies: A Corporate Guide to Exploiting the Internet*. London: Macmillan Press Ltd.

Tan J, Tyler, K., & Manica A. (2007). Business-to-business adoption of e-commerce in China, *Journal of Information & Management* 44, 332–351

Tan J., Tyler K. & Manica A. (2007). Business-to-business adoption of e-commerce in China, *Journal of Global Information management*,10,4,61-85

Tan, M., & Teo, T.S.H.(2000). Factors influencing the adoption of internet banking, *Journal of the Association of Information Systems* (1,5), pp.14

Task Force for Small & Medium Enterprise Sector Development Program (2002), *National Strategy for Small and Medium Enterprise Sector Development in Sri Lanka,*White Paper, Colombo

Thong, J. Y. L. (1999). An integrate model of information systems adoption in small business, *Journal of Management Information Systems*, 15, 187–214.

Tornatzky, L. G. & Fleischer, M. (1990). *The Process of Technological Innovation*, Lexington Books, Lexington, MA.

Travica B. (2002). Diffusion of electronic commerce in developing countries: the case of Costa Rica, *Journal of Global Information Technology Management* 5(1)

UNDP, Human Development Report (2004), retrieved July 2007 from http://hdr.undp.org/reports/global/2004

Wagner, B.A., Fillis, I., & Johansson, U.(2003). E-business and e-supply strategy in small and medium sized businesses (SMEs), *Supply Chain Management*, 8(4), 343 – 354.

Yin, RK (1994), *Case study research: Design and methods*, 2nd edn, Sage Publications Ltd, Thousand Oaks.

Chapter VI
E-Commerce in Developing Countries:
Impediments and Opportunities

Alev M. Efendioglu
University of San Francisco, USA

ABSTRACT

The number of Internet users around the world has been steadily growing and this growth has provided the impetus and the opportunities for global and regional e-commerce. However, as with Internet, different characteristics (infrastructure and socio-economic) of the local environment have created significant levels of variation in the acceptance and growth of e-commerce in different regions of the world. Our research on e-commerce development in China and the findings provide insights into some of the impediments for development and use of e-commerce. In this chapter, I present and discuss our findings, and propose some strategies for successful development of e-commerce in developing countries.

INTRODUCTION

As the number of Internet users around the world has steadily grown various studies have been conducted and models have been developed to identify diffusion of e-commerce in different environments. (Zwass, 1999; Wolcott, et. al. 2001; Travica, 2002; Hasan and Ditsa, 1999) These models have looked at "infrastructure" (e.g. connectivity hardware and software, telecommunications, product delivery and transportation systems) and "services" (e.g. e-payment systems, secure messaging, electronic markets, etc.) as the primary diffusion factors. Furthermore, Travica (2002) study has focused on Costa Rico and its culture, and Hasan and Ditsa (1999) have tried to identify and present possible cultural factors that may impact broad based adoption of Information Technology.

Industry based organizations have also been interested in diffusion of e-commerce in different countries and have also identified similar factors,

Copyright © 2009, IGI Global, distributing in print or electronic forms without written permission of IGI Global is prohibited.

and have rated these countries on their readiness for e-commerce. Most widely cited of these ratings are presented by IBM and the intelligence unit of The Economist (Economist Intelligence Unit, 2004), which define e-readiness by measurement in six distinct categories (1) Connectivity and technology infrastructure, (2) Business environment, (3) Consumer and business adoption, (4) Social and cultural environment, (5) Legal and policy environment, and (6) Supporting e-services.

In addition to infrastructural and business system issues, trust (I call this "transactional trust") has been identified as one of the critical issues that confront businesses that are new businesses or utilize new business models like e-commerce. One of the most widely studied cultural classifications was originally proposed by Hofstede (1980). His cultural framework consists of four dimensions identified as: individualism-collectivism, uncertainty avoidance, power distance, and masculinity-femininity. Even though Hofstede's framework was originally developed for national-level analyses, Oyserman *et al.* (2002) has shown that it can also be applied at individual levels. Further research by Doney *et al.* (1998) and Jarvenpaa *et al.* (1999) have suggested that individualism-collectivism effects the ways people form trust and may affect the users' willingness to trust online vendors. Other studies have also tried to find correlations between trust and experience with a new system, concept, or relationships, including a correlation to frequency of e-commerce activity, and other researchers have noted that trust may be significantly influenced by culture of a given society. (McKnight et. al., 1998; McKnight and Chervany, 2001; Lee and Turban, 2001) Grabner-Kraeuter (2002) observes and states that trust is "the most significant long-term barrier for realizing the potential of e-commerce to consumers", and others state that trust will be a "key differentiator that will determine the success of failure of many Web companies." (Urban et. al., 2000) Studies by Park (1993) and Keil *et al.* (2000) have focused on the impact of uncertainty avoidance on people's willingness to accept uncertainty, which is an unavoidable foundation of e-commerce.

To see the impact of these factors, especially the "influence of culture on acceptance and use of e-commerce in a developing country", we conducted a study in China. (Efendioglu and Yip, 2004) We selected China because it has unique social and cultural characteristics (Bond, 1986; Chen, 1993; Moore, 1967) and is a country with accelerated changes and growth in its economic systems, fueled and supported by both governmental and business entities.

In the following sections, the research and its findings are presented and discussed, and the changes that have taken place and their impact, since the completion of the study, are identified to provide lessons and to guide the development and use of e-commerce in other developing countries.

CHINA RESEARCH STUDY

The Efendioglu and Yip (2004) study group consisted of selected 252 individuals who would be considered to be a close match to e-commerce users in developed countries and were considered to be "early adopters" (people of means, access, and interest). Since the primary focus of the study was "impact of culture", we wanted to get the opinions of actual participants/users of e-commerce and wanted to eliminate the infrastructure problems as much as possible. The study participants resided and worked in different regions and for different types of organizations, and had different educational levels, professions, and gender. They held professional supervisory positions in their organizations and had much higher economic means than the average income levels for the local population.

The study participants were asked about their Internet usage to identify their familiarity with technology and their access to Internet, and their

Table 1. Study demographics (n=252)

GENDER		EDUCATION		AGE		ORGANIZATION		
Male	Female	BS Degree	Graduate	25-40 years	Over 40 years	MNC	DE*	JV
59.92%	40.08%	75.40%	13.49%	75.40%	7.54%	21.03%	63.49%	15.48%
* DOMESTIC ENTERPRISES including Private Enterprises, State Owned Enterprises (SOE), and University; MNC = Multi-National Corporation; JV = Joint Venture								

Table 2. Sample population (n=252) vs. e-commerce participants (n=166)

	Male*	Age <36 years*	Education (BS-GRAD)	Have Credit Card	Purchase in 12-mo	Purchase in 6-Mo
Total Population (%)	59.92%	79.37%	88.89%	86.51%	64.29%	65.88%
E-Commerce Participants (%)	55.42%	88.55%	88.55%	86.75%	97.59%	100.00%

*Differences not statistically significant.

e-commerce participation to determine their ability (access to type of medium used for payment) to pay (possession of credit cards) for e-commerce and whether they purchased any goods/services, using e-commerce, within the previous 12-month period (actual usage patterns). The respondents (166 out of 252 study participants) who indicated they had purchased goods/services were further asked about the frequency of their transactions during the previous 12- and 6-month periods, the products/services they purchased, highest total value of their single purchase, and their payment method (credit cards and other commonly used methods of payment in China) for these purchases. They were also asked to list their primary reasons for utilizing e-commerce and rate their overall satisfaction with the activity and to provide unstructured comments on what they consider to be impediments to the development of e-commerce in China and Chinese attitudes towards use technology as a means for commerce.

The participants were asked a set of questions (pervasiveness of e-commerce acceptance, choice of payment methods for electronic transactions, the purchased items, and evaluation of their experiences by e-commerce participants) to help us identify and clarify the culturally based behavioral patterns, especially as they related to their attitudes towards "transaction trust" and "debt", which are among the most critical foundations of e-commerce. Chinese culture does not condemn piracy and copying (counterfeiting and distribution of below par products is a major problem in China) and legal infrastructure is not sophisticated or organized enough to deal with some illegal activities, especially fraud, resulting in amplification of the prevailing lack of transactional trust between parties who do not know each other personally. As a result, Chinese rely on face-to-face contact (strong individual relationship and long term association between the parties, a concept described as "*guanxi*", which refers to a particular kind of social networking based on trust) and, to provide themselves with the necessary comfort level that they are making the right purchase, demand to have physical contact with the purchased good, before they pay for it. Furthermore, the current Chinese banking system is primarily designed to accommodate businesses, especially State Owned Enterprises (SOEs), and banks are primarily owned and used as tools by the Chinese government to further its economic and social aims, without much opportunity for the general public to easily acquire credit cards and use them in making retail purchases. As with most developing countries, Chinese financial institutions have not yet developed, do not encourage or support consumer lending practices, and continue to reinforce the principle of "buy when you have cash to pay", make debt unavailable, unknown and unacceptable, and further perpetuate the "cash society" characteristics.

The study respondents paid for their purchases in four major ways, cash/check (travel related purchases were paid at the time of use, e.g. hotel stay), COD (cash on delivery), credit card, and bank transfer. As can be seen in Table 3, in our study group, contrary to purchases made by U.S. consumers, credit card was not the most common payment method. This finding is also supported by the China Internet Network Information Center (CNNIC) surveys, which identify the top three payment methods as cash and carry (33.1%), online payment (30.7%), and post office transfer (30.0%). CNNIC, 2002; CNNIC, 2003)

With estimated RMB410billion (USD50 billion) in savings stashed away (most of it at homes), China still exhibits the characteristics of a cash society. According to Economist Intelligence Unit, Global Insights and McKinsey China's saving rate for 1997-2005 periods is 40.3 percent. (Pitsilis, Woetzel, & Wong, 2004) Our findings support this cultural characteristic. Even though 86.51 percent of our study group (218 respondents) had credit cards, only 19.28 percent of the e-commerce participants (32 out of 166 respondents) paid for their purchases using a credit card. These findings support the argument that Chinese consumers are conservative spenders and not willing to buy on credit as a matter of culture.

Our study participants identified specific infrastructure related impediments to full development of e-commerce in China. Among the most repeatedly mentioned issues were lack of credit cards (wide availability of them for the general public in China) and convenient payment means, poor distribution logistics, lack of specialized, trust-worthy online merchants of reasonable size (too many small players facing many bottlenecks and without necessary resources to set up e-commerce systems), imperfect legal system, and lack of large scale telecommunication transmission capability (broadband). They were especially concerned with issues related to "trust". As users of e-commerce, the primary *operational obstacles* for our study group, in the order of importance, were "Internet security", "lack of feel-and-touch associated with online purchases", "problems in returning products", and "selection" (product availability and breadth). Our research findings also show that "*transactional trust*" and related issues are major concerns for Chinese consumers conducting online transactions. Our respondents complained about existence of trust-worthy online merchants, and Internet security and credit card security. They were as wary of counterfeit products as western consumers are. As one Chinese gentleman put it "History and reality told us not to trust the system or the people's honor! E-commerce is a radical behavior that goes contrary to experience and culture. There is no "western honor system" in China." (Zhao, 2004)

OVERCOMING IMPEDIMENTS AND CREATING OPPORTUNITIES

As can be seen from Figure 1, the development, use and wide-spread acceptance of e-commerce require changes in three distinct areas: socio-

Table 3. Payment method (n=166)

Bank Transfer	Cash/Check	Cash On Delivery	Credit Card
8.43%	33.13%	39.16%	19.28%

economic behaviors favoring commerce, laws and governmental policies which support commerce, and infrastructure which enables physical exchange of goods and services. Our China study findings present the impact of specific issues which act as impediments to full development of e-commerce in developing countries (Efendioglu and Yip, 2004) and the way Chinese society and businesses have addressed some of these issues provide valuable lessons for addressing similar issues in other developing countries.

Socio-Economic Behaviors and Prevailing Cultural Characteristics

Doney *et al.* (1998) have argued that people in collectivist cultures (China is classified as a collectivist culture in Hofstede's 1991 publication) are more likely to form trust based on prior experiences or opinions of their in-group members. According to Wong and Tam (2000), in societies with little history of formal legal contracts, trust-based relationships are the only way of doing business and strangers are not to be trusted. For the Chinese, a strong individual relationship and long term association between the parties, "*guanxi*", provide a sense of community and enhances social bonding. (Davies and Lsung, 1995) and this "social bonding" acts as the foundation of trust between the sellers of products and services and the consumers of such.

It is very hard to develop a similar socio-economic entity using e-commerce, which is primarily based on a business model and a process that brings anonymity and distances the vendor from the customer, and depersonalizes the relationship between the sellers and the buyers of the product or service. Therefore, off-site transaction systems (like e-commerce, catalog sales, mail order systems) which require a trusting relationship (transaction trust) between the unseen vendor and the consumer requires a sophisticated consumer society, specific legal (consumer protection laws) and financial (consumer credit systems and social acceptance of credit cards as a payment mechanism) practices. Absence of these practices, coupled with inherent social and political characteristics of the developing countries, create cynical consumers and reinforce commerce systems where customer can see and check the product and the seller can get paid in cash, without any ambiguities about the product characteristics or collection problems that may accompany credit based payment systems.

In addition to general trust issues, raised under different economic and societal conditions, older

Figure 1. Influences on diffusion of e-commerce

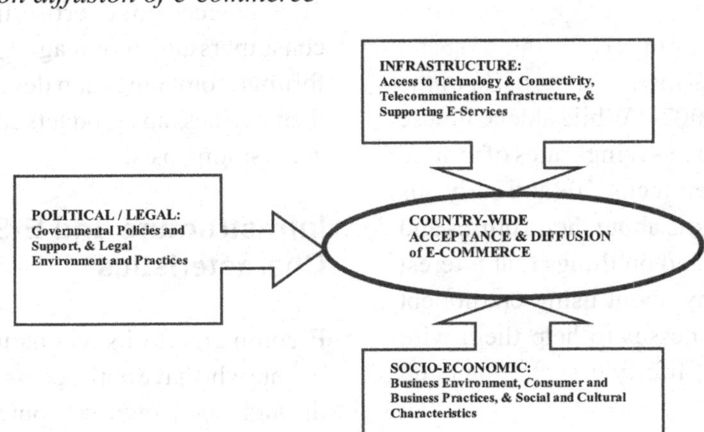

populations in developing countries are generally very conservative with their money and, if they have any means, customarily continue to "save for a rainy day". As a result, they exhibit high saving patterns and are afraid of making purchases using borrowed monies. The younger generations of consumers do not necessarily share the cultural biases of their parents and are more than willing to take advantage of available transactional mechanisms and are not as much concerned with their future needs. China presents an excellent example of this *generational cultural shift*.

In surveys and interviews the China Market Research Group (CMR) conducted, with Chinese youth between the ages of 18 and 28 in Shanghai, Beijing, and Guangzhou, more than 80 percent said they were willing to buy items online and over 70 percent said they would use a credit card if they could. This is supported by the increasing number of credit cards in circulation in China. In 2006, there were additional 15.6 million credit cards and 200 million debit cards in China, a big jump from 2004 when only 10 million credit cards were in circulation. Currently, there are around 50 million credit cards and more than 1.1 billion debit cards in circulation, yet another significant increase over 2006. CMR's interviews show that Chinese high savings rate is changing also changing, as Chinese are becoming more accustomed to a life of leisure and consumption rather than a hand to mouth existence that plagued many of them during the turmoil of the 50s an 60s. It is evident that Chinese youth are willing to spend and borrow as much as their counterparts in the United States. (Rein, 2007b) While older Chinese consumers still have high savings rates of around 40 percent, those in their teens, 20s and early 30s are much more optimistic about their futures and are more willing to spend on things that interest them. They are not shy about using credit/debt or Internet based businesses to help them with their consumer needs, lifestyle aspirations and expectations.

In China and other countries, a very large number of users of Internet are the younger generations who are familiar with and accepting of available technologies, and who trust the content of and information on the Internet more than traditional forms of advertisement. Internet and other telecommunications technologies (chats, cell phone based instant messaging, etc.) enable them to talk about what they like and dislike, including products and companies, and life in general. For example, during 2006, 70 percent of more than 111 million Internet users in China were under the age of 25 (Lemon, 2006), with approximately 120 million active blogs (short for Web logs). They spent a great deal of their online time (an average of 17 hours/week, as compared to developed countries like Japan, with 13.9hours/week, and United States, with 11.7hours/week) engaged in active discussion of products and advertising through blogs and BBS (bulletin board system) forums. This younger generation consumers seem to depend a lot on word of mouth and a circle of trust when choosing products. A Shanghainese woman who responded to CMR's interviews said, "I believe the bloggers and their ideas. They are my friends and will tell me the truth, unlike advertisements." (Knowledge@Wharton, 2007)

These fairly uniform characteristics of younger generations of all societies provide significant opportunities for businesses in developing countries. Cell phones, with their messaging capabilities can provide access to advertise directly to these young consumers and, by engaging them through online forums, companies can develop brand loyalty for their business and products and decrease consumer acquisition costs.

Infrastructure and E-Support Characteristics

E-commerce, by its very nature, is limited to those people who have both access to the Internet, either through their own computer or via an internet café, and a credit or debit card. As can be seen from the following user and access projections, access to Internet is becoming a non-issue in an accelerated fashion. In its "Worldwide On-line Population Forecast, 2006 to 2011," Jupiter Research (an Internet research and consulting firm) anticipates that by 2011, 22 percent of the Earth's population will surf the Internet regularly, with majority of the current users located in developed countries. In January 2007, there were 746,934,000 users worldwide, with approximately 30 percent (269,381,000 users) located in United States, Japan, Germany and U.K. and 18 percent (134,214,000 users) in China, South Korea and India. (Burns, 2007) At the end of 2005, China had 35.9 million broadband subscribers (second only to USA with 46.9 million subscribers) and is expected to surpass United States in subscribers in the next few years, with a projected 500 million subscribers by 2010. (Burns, 2005) eMarketer put the number of broadband households in China at 54.1 million and 81.4 million in 2007 and 2010, respectively. (E-Commerce News, 2007)

As with any business enterprise, an e-commerce business needs to ensure that it secures payment for goods sold and, to accomplish this, needs their customers to use credit and debit cards for payment, in addition to Internet connection and access. Unfortunately, majority of the populations in developing countries do not have access to these cards and the ones who have them cannot use them effectively due to insufficient and incompatible processing systems and centers. In developing countries, in addition to the payment for purchases, there are issues associated with physical distribution and the delivery of goods ordered on-line. If time is not of the essence, the normal postal service may be satisfactory but in other circumstances an express delivery company like DHL or FedEx will be needed, where the geographical coverage of these companies, particularly DHL and FedEx, may be limited or may not be available at all in developing countries. Even if these or other similar local companies are available, they would be comparatively expensive and significantly decrease the attractiveness of on-line shopping (or cutting into profit margins) for most consumers in developing countries.

If e-commerce is going to develop and flourish, businesses and governments of have to take the initiative and develop systems and processes to overcome these transaction infrastructure limitations. Some of the possible alternatives are provided by recent changes instituted in China. Lack of such infrastructure and a lack of broad availability of personal credit cards in China have created transaction payment systems that also utilize other payment methods, such as C.O.D (cash on delivery), cash at the time of purchase, and postal order (money order), to accommodate online purchases. In addition, some companies have developed non-traditional systems to streamline the way Chinese Web users to safely pay for their online purchases. An example of such a system is one that is offered by a Chinese company called "99bill", which enables buyers to make payments through their mobile phones (Chinese mobile phone users outnumber Internet users at almost 4 to 1) and immediately processes the online payment, with 1.6 million users after one year being in business. (Stout, 2005) In another system, Alipay, a subsidiary of a very large Internet service provider and search company Alibaba.com (which also owns the e-commerce company called Taobao.com), collects payments from buyers, holds the funds in escrow and then turns them over to sellers. (Johnson, 2007)

Another exchange mechanism called "*virtual currency*" was also started in China and, because of the lack of credit cards in circulation, and for many young Chinese consumers the first introduction to e-commerce comes through the use of the virtual currency. This exchange tool was created when an Internet chat company and an Internet game company decided to let gamers buy "*virtual Q coins*" to buy clothes and weapons for their game personas. It was a huge hit with the Chinese youth and gamers, and Xinhua News (the official Chinese News Agency) reported that the volume of virtual currency has reached several hundred million USD a year. The China Market Research Group (a Chinese research and consulting firm) projects a 30 percent growth in 2007. Currently, there are multiple *virtual currencies* available in China, which can be used to buy virtual products for use in games, vote for real world talent contests, purchase electronic cards (all using *Q coins*), watch movies and download music (using *Baidu currency* and Baidu Websites); and purchase real goods from Sina's online mall (using *U coins*). The mostly young users of virtual currency find it very "convenient" when buying things online and do not have to go through all the paperwork at Chinese banks to get a credit card. (Rein, 2007b)

Another infrastructure impediment for e-commerce in developing countries is the lack of efficient delivery systems and underdeveloped physical distribution infrastructure to move the goods from one location to another. These countries' poor logistic and distribution networks restrict how far apart sellers and buyers can be and make transporting or mailing products from the company warehouses to the customers very costly and time inefficient. The problems associated with physical distribution are further exasperated by consumers' inability to "touch and feel" (the need to physically evaluate the purchased product) the purchased goods, which as a foundation require a business system based on a trusting transfer relationship (*transaction trust*) between the unseen vendor and the consumer. Even though this business characteristic is not an issue in a developed country, with its sophisticated consumer society and accommodating specific business practices (consumer protection, liberal no-cost return policies, with penalties for deceptive advertising, standards for product quality, etc.), it can be a very important impediment in developing countries and pose significant challenges for the e-commerce industry in those countries.

Once again, there are opportunities to remedy some of these infrastructural impediments in developing countries, especially in the short-run, while giving the e-commerce industry the time it needs to establish itself. In countries where there is cheap and abundant manpower and there are inexpensive modes of transportation (e.g. bicycles, motor scooters, and small trucks, etc.), they can be effectively used as alternates to large scale distribution in close geographical areas. Local postal service and small and local private courier companies, those already have operations in major cities; can provide additional physical distribution services over larger geographical areas. In time, more efficiency (grouped deliveries, efficient modes of transportation, efficient routing systems, supply chain management tools, etc.) can be incorporated into the system to accommodate large scale shipments and a much wider geographic coverage. For example, during 2004 there were more than 1,000 couriers in Shanghai alone and when merchants, using local labor for delivery, instituted a delivery charge of 10 percent for purchases up to RMB800 (USD100) for deliveries, the most common delivery charge of RMB5 (barely enough to buy a can of Coca Cola in the store) was easily affordable by the city residents. Because the "*transactional trust*" (delivered products will be true to their advertised characteristics, e.g. quality, not counterfeit, etc.) is also a major problem in developing countries, a system similar to the one developed by the Chinese company called "EachNet" can be used to address these concerns. EachNet, through a feedback system like eBay's and a verification program, using a government database, verifies seller's national identity number and offers free insurance to buyers for their purchases. (Hoff, 2004)

Governmental Policies and Legal Environment Characteristics

In developing countries, unfortunately, it is very unlikely that the regulatory and legal environments will have the characteristics which are supportive of and conducive to e-commerce and other types of off-site business systems. Pressed by other issues and more urgent societal needs, governments in these countries take their time to institute reforms that enhance the economic system (legal changes that support business contracts, discourage counterfeiting, and encourage consumer credit and servicing by the banking industry, build telecommunication and transportation infrastructure, etc.). However, even in countries where e-commerce supportive regulatory environments are not fully developed, governments by their limited actions and short-term policies can help or impede the country's fledgling e-commerce industry. Once again, when we look at the developments in China, we can find examples of both of these types of governmental actions.

In 2004, Chinese government shut down 1,600 Internet cafes and fined operators a total of USD12 million as part of its campaign launched in March to reduce or eliminate sites that portray pornography, violence or other materials that Communist leaders have banned. (LeClaire, 2004) Given that Internet Cafes (used by 27 percent of Internet surfers in 2002) are the second most important locations to access Internet (Greenspan, 2002) and participate in e-commerce, even governmental actions such as this, with intentions and objectives unrelated to e-commerce, can have a significant negative impact on the e-commerce industry, by restricting access to technology.

On the other hand, there were two very significant recent governmental actions with very positive short-and long-term implications and impact. In 2006, the Credit Evaluation Center of the China E-commerce Association released a new rule, called the "Chinese Enterprise E-commerce Credibility Basic Regulation", to regulate the credit system of China's e-commerce market. This rule was first of its kind and the regulation covered enterprise authentication and validity, protection of users' personal data, and enterprises' online business behaviors. (ChinaCSR.com, 2006)

Around 750 million Chinese live outside of the main cities and are very reliant on cash (83 percent of all payment transactions compared with just 21 percent in the United States) for all of their economic activities, including receiving their wages and shopping. Furthermore, practically all rural transactions are cash based. In August 2006, to increase rural spending and to close the wealth gap with urban areas, the People's Bank of China directed domestic banks to devise a solution to bring about this economic and associated social change. One of the proposed systems is a SMS (secure messaging system) -based system which uses mobile phones to transfer funds from one account to another in seconds and send a confirmation message to the payer. (Bellens, Ip, and Yip, 2007) If instituted, such a system will enable rural consumers to make retail purchases, use the system to receive payments like salaries and wages, and eventually could be a tremendous opportunity for e-commerce to expand its operations over the vast countryside and will greatly enhance its broader diffusion.

CONCLUSION

There is no question that e-commerce in developing countries face significant cultural, infrastructural, and, in most cases, regulatory challenges and obstacles. Unfortunately, even though, with consorted efforts from businesses and governmental organizations, most of the infrastructural and regulatory issues can be resolved over relatively short time, the cultural issues might have to be addressed with much greater care and might require a generational transition for full fruition.

While these and other infrastructural and cultural impediments get resolved over time, business establishments and their professional groups in developing countries can play a significant role in providing interim solutions and services that address and overcome some of these issues and limitations. As the developing countries evolve into developed countries and their societies become more sophisticated and support more intricate and complex business systems, these interim steps and solutions for e-commerce can provide significant benefits, both to the participants and the country as a whole. We can easily see some of these impacts in the evolution of the e-commerce industry in China.

Efendioglu and Yip (2004) study results showed that younger Chinese customers have a greater propensity to use e-commerce (88.55 percent of the e-commerce participants were 35 years or younger in age) and this trend has continued over the years. As the Efendioglu and Yip (2004) study shows, there are signs of pervasiveness of technology acceptance among younger age groups in all societies and countries, developing as well as developed countries. For example, about 77 percent of young people (age 8-14) in USA shop on the Internet. (Burns, 2007a) Because the majority of Chinese online shoppers are young people living in large cities, and as they gain more economic power, they fuel a continued growth in the number of the e-commerce industry and online retailers. The number of Chinese buying products and services online increased from 2.08 million in 2001 to 20 million in 2006 (Rein, 2006) and to an estimated 6 million people per day in 2007. (Johnson, 2007)

The types of products sold online in China have also gone through a major transformation. The product mix has changed from computers sold to hard-core early adopters to women's and men's clothing, largest product category in 2004. (Hoff, 2004) At "Joyo" (an online retailer), the product mix ranges from books to electronics and between 2004 and 2006, the number of goods offered on Joyo's Website increased from 45,000 to 450,000 items. (Rein, 2006) The top selling products at Taobao.com (another online retailer) are cellular phones and accessories, cosmetics, notebook computers, digital cameras, jewelry, clothing, shoes, books and prepaid mobile phone cards, demonstrating the appeal of these sites to all kinds of consumers. (Johnson, 2007)

The increased number of consumers and the types of products available have also positively influenced and fueled the revenue growth of the industry. According to a comprehensive annual survey released by the Beijing-based Internet Society of China, a national industry business association, Chinese Internet users are spending on average RMB169.57 ($22) a month online, for payments to online services providers, shopping, and gaming and the yearly spending total of RMB276.8 billion (USD35.5 billion) for 2006 was up 47 percent from the 2005 figure of RMB187.653 billion (USD24 billion). (Chen, 2007) The change in the overall value of online shopping was mostly a result of increased number of participants (access to Internet and changing demographics of users), rather than increased volume of individual purchases. The findings of Efendioglu and Yip (2004) study showed that the average purchase value of 83.73 percent of purchases ranged in value from RMB50 to RMB500 ($6.00-$60), about the same amount spent in 2006. However, 2003 figures show that 2.1 percent of China's Web users had bought online (CNNIC, 2003) as compared to 8.5 percent penetration rate in 2005. (Chen, 2007) Registered online shoppers now number 43 million, and their purchases may hit USD6.4 billion in 2007, a leap of more than 60 percent over 2006. (Johnson, 2007)

As demonstrated by the positive changes in the growth of e-commerce in China, even in developing countries, small interim steps by businesses and other natural changes and developments (e.g. demographic changes) can reap significant benefits for the e-commerce industry. However, to overcome the broad-based infrastructure and cultural impediments, businesses should take a more active role to bring about an economically viable consumer society, encourage their governments to institute reforms that enhance the economic system (legal changes that support business contracts, discourage counterfeiting, and encourage consumer credit and servicing by the banking industry, built telecommunication and transportation infrastructure, etc.). Fortunately, as these businesses wait for more profound cultural changes to take hold (with the help of governmental actions and increasingly higher living standards) and online consumer critical mass to materialize to support large scale e-commerce, changes in telecommunications technologies, especially wide availability of cell phones and access to Internet, provide significant business opportunities for their online e-commerce activities.

The businesses in developing countries have an opportunity to directly move into technologies using "Web 2.0", including **Blogs** (short for Web logs, online journals or diaries hosted on a Web site), **Podcasts** (audio or video recordings—a multimedia form of a blog or other content), **Social networking** (systems that allow members of a specific site to learn about other members' skills, talents, knowledge, or preferences), and software systems that make it easier for different systems to communicate with one another automatically in order to pass information or conduct transactions. Most Web 2.0 tools are simple-to-use applications that are hosted offsite, which makes them easy to implement. The ease of utilizing these technologies is a major reason to explore them and gain the possible competitive and operational advantages which accompany these technologies.

Cell phones (which are available at much larger numbers than Internet access), with their messaging capabilities, can overcome some of the problems associated with lack of credit cards and fully developed online payment systems. Because younger generation consumers in most countries spend most of their time online and trust the content of the Internet more than traditional forms of advertisement, by engaging them through online forums, companies can develop brand loyalty for their business and products and decrease consumer acquisition costs. Local smaller businesses which sell similar products can form alliances with businesses in other cities and towns, even establishing loosely aligned franchises, and utilize the services of existing Internet Service Providers (ISP), acting as intermediaries, to develop national electronic storefronts with local distribution systems. Through these alliances, they can provide credit (issue local or alliance-wide credit cards) or continue to provide "cash-and-carry" services to the consumers who prefer to pay cash, overcome the local distribution problems (by transferring products among themselves) and address the customer concerns related to the "touch-and-feel" issues (counterfeit and below par products and problems with product returns).

There is no question that the unique social and cultural characteristics of developing countries, concepts associated with off-site exchange systems, and local infrastructure issues pose significant limitations and great challenges for the e-commerce industry in these countries and act as the major impediments to diffusion and broad acceptance of e-commerce. However, continual changes in demographics in these countries, coupled with technological innovations and developments in the telecommunications industries, provide some opportunities online merchants and can enable them to overcome some of these prevailing impediments. As in all economic environments, the companies that can search for, identify and utilize these opportunities will have significant advantages in the short-and the long run, as they develop online storefronts and participate in global e-commerce.

REFERENCES

China Internet Network Information Center, 2002. Semiannual Survey Report on the Development of China's Internet (1997-2002), Retrieved 11th September 2002 from the World Wide Web http://www.cnnic.net.ch/develst/2002-7e/5.shtml

China Internet Network Information Center, 2003. Semiannual Survey Report on the Development of China's Internet (1997-2003), Retrieved 20th September 2003 from the World Wide Web http://www.cnnic.net.cn/develst/2003-1e/444.shtml

The 2004 e-readiness rankings, Economist Intelligence Unit, 2004. Retrieved 20th April 2004 from World Wide Web http://graphics.eiu.com/files/ad_pdfs/ERR2004.pdf

Bellens, Jan, Chris Ip, and Anna Yip (2007). Developing a new rural payments system in China. McKinsey Quarterly (Web Exclusive), May 2007. http://www.mckinseyquarterly.com/article_print.aspx?L2=22&L3=77&ar=2002 Accessed on 5/2/2007.

Bond, M. H. (1986). The Psychology of the Chinese People, Hong Kong: Oxford University Press.

Burns, Enid (2005). U.S. Tops Broadband Usage, For Now. ClickZ Stats, November 14, 2005. http://www.clickz.com/showPage.html?page=3563966 Accessed on 7/2/2007.

Burns, Enid (2007). Internet Audience up 10 Percent Worldwide. March 6, 2007. http://www.clickz.com/showPage.html?page=36251683, accessed on /6/2007.

Burns, Enid (2007a). Kids Chores Turn Wired. May 14, 2007. http://www.clickz.com/showPage.html?page=3625858 Accessed on 7/10/2007.

ChinaCSR.com (2006). China Releases E-commerce Credibility Regulations. May 16, 2006. http://www.chinacsr.com/2006/03/16/362-china-releases-e-commercecredibility-regulation/ Accessed on 6/9/2007.

Hoff, Robert D. (2004). EachNet: Bringing E-Commerce to China. Business Week (Asian Cover Story), March 15, 2004. http://www.businessweek.com/print/magazine/content/04_11/b3874020.htm?chan=mz accessed on 7/4/2007.

Chen, Min (1993). Understanding Chinese and Japanese Negotiation Styles. International Executive 35: 147-159.

Chen, Shu-Ching Jean (2007). China Is No. 2 Online. Forbes.com, January 12, 2007. http://www.forbes.com/2007/01/12/china-internet-stats-biz-cx_jc_0112china_print.html accessed on 6/9/2007.

Davies, H. and Lsung, H. (1995). The Benefits of Guanxi: The Value of Relationships. Industrial Marketing Management 24: 207-213.

Doney, P.M.., Cannon, J.P., and Mullen, M.R. (1998). Understanding the influence of national culture on the development of trust. Academy of Management Review 23: 601-620.

E-Commerce News (2006). Is China the next eCommerce superpower? E-Commerce News, September 15, 2006. http://www.ecommercenews.org/e-commerce-news-009/0243-091406-ecommerce-news.html accessed on 6/9/2007.

Efendioglu, Alev M. and Vincent F. Yip (2004). Chinese Culture & E-Commerce: An Explatory Study. Interacting with Computers, Vol. 16/1, pp. 45-62, 2004.

Grabner-Kraeuter, S. (2002). The role of consumers' trust in online shopping. Journal of Business Ethics 39: 43-50.

Greenspan, Robyn (2002). China Pulls Ahead of Japan. E-Commerce Guide, April 22, 2002. http://www.clickz.com/showPage.html?page=clickz_print&id=1013841 Accessed on 6/29/2007.

Hasan, H. and Ditsa, G. (1999). The Impact of Culture on the Adaptations of IT: An Interpretive Study. Journal of Global Information Management 7-1: 5.

Hofstede, G.H. (1980). Culture's Consequences, Sage: Beverly Hills, CA.

Hofstede, G.H. (1991). Cultures and Organizations: Software of the Mind, McGraw-Hill: London.

Jarvenpaa, S.L., Tractinsky, N., Saarinen, L. and Vitale, M. (1999). Consumer trust in an Internet store: a cross-cultural validation. Journal of Computer-Mediated Communication 5(2): 1-29.

Johnson, Tim (2007). E-commerce soaring in China. McClatchy Newspapers, May 30, 2007. http://www.realcities.com/mld/krwashington/news/world/17300776.htm?source=rss&channel=krwashington_world accessed on 6/9/2007.

Keil, M., Tan, B.C.Y., Wei, K.K. and Saarinen, T. (2000). A cross-cultural study on escalation of commitment behavior in software projects. MIS Quarterly 24(2): 299-324.

Knowledge@Wharton, 2007. How To Tap Chinese Consumers? Market Online. http://www.forbes.com/2007/04/10/pepsico-dell-samsung-ent-sales-cx_kw_0410whartonchina_print.html accessed on 6/9/2007.

LeClaire, Jennifer (2004). China Cracking Down on Internet Cafes. E-Commerce Times, 11/01/04. http://www.ecommercetimes.com/story/37752.html Accessed on 6/9/2007.

Lee, M., & Turban, E. (2001). A trust model for consumers Internet shopping. International Journal of Electronic Commerce 6: 75-91.

Lemon, Sumner (2006). China's Internet industry potential is great, but most of its affluent population has yet to get online. IDG News Service, February 28, 2006. http://www.infoworld.com/archives/e-mailPrint.jsp?R=printThis&A=/article/06/02/28/75933_HNecommercechina_1.html accessed on 6/9/2007.

McKnight, D., & Chervany, N. (2001). What trust means in e-commerce customer relationships: An interdisciplinary conceptual typology. International Journal of Electronic Commerce 6: 35-59.

McKnight, D., & Cummings, L., & Chervany, N. (1998). Initial trust formation in new organizational relationships. Academy of Management Review 23: 473-490.

Moore, C. (1967). The Chinese Mind: Essentials of Chinese Philosophy and Culture, Honolulu: University of Hawaii Press.

Oyserman, D., Coon, H.M. and Kemmelmeir, M. (2002). Rethinking individualism and collectivism: evaluation of theoretical assumptions and meta-analyses. Psychological Bulletin 128: 3-72.

Park, H. (1993). Cultural impact on life insurance penetration: a cross-national analysis. International Journal of Management 10(3): 342-350.

Pitsilis, E. V., Woetzel, J. R.., & Wong, J. (2004). Checking China's Vital Signs. McKinsey Quarterly, Special Edition 2004. http://www.mckinseyquarterly.com/article_abstract.aspx?ar=1483&L2=7&L3=8&srid=63&gp=0 accessed on 2/12/2005.

Rein, Shaun (2006). China's Booming Online Sales. Posted on Sep 12th, 2006. http://china.seekingalpha.com/article/16768 accessed on 6/9/2007.

Rein, Shaun (2007a). Chinese Cozy Up to E-Commerce. Business Week, February 8, 2007. http://www.businessweek.com/print/globalbiz/content/feb2007/gb20070208_810426.htm accessed on 6/9/2007.

Rein, Shaun (2007b). China's Virtual, e-Commerce Currency. Posted on Jan 16th, 2007. http://china.seekingalpha.com/article/24227 accessed on 6/9/2007.

Rousseau, D.M., Sitkin, S.B., Burt, R.S. and Camerer, C. (1998). Not so different after all: a cross-discipline view of trust. The Academy of Management Review, 23(3): 393-404.

Stout, Kristie Lu (2005). China gears up for e-commerce boom. CNN, November 1, 2005. http://edition.cnn.com/2005/TECH/11/01/spark.china.payment/index.html accessed on 6/9/2007.

Travica, B. (2002). Diffusion of electronic commerce in developing countries: The case of Costa Rica. Journal of Global Information Technology Management, 5(1), 4-24.

Urban, G., & Sultan, F., & Qualls, W. (2000). Placing trust at the center of your Internet strategy. Sloan Management Review 42: 1-13.

Wolcott, P., & Press, L., & McHenry, W., & Goodman, S. E., & Foster, W. (2001). A framework for assessing the global diffusion of the Internet. Journal of the Association for Information Systems, 2(6), 1-53.

Wong, Y.H. & Tam, J. L.M. (2000). Mapping relationships in China: Guanxi dynamic approach. Journal of Business and Industrial Marketing, 15(1): 57–70.

Zwass, V. (1996). Electronic commerce: Structure and issues. International Journal of Electronic Commerce, 1(1), 3-23.

Zhao, Li Qin (2004). Author's personal interview with Mr. Zhao on his perceptions and use of Internet based commerce. The interview was conducted in Guangdong Province of China.

KEY TERMS

Cultural Dimensions: Identifying and classifying social foundations of a country using Hofstede's (1980) model.

Digital Economy: Economic system using Internet and technology for business transactions.

Electronic Commerce: Business to consumer exchange systems using virtual storefronts.

Online Shopping: Consumers using virtual storefronts and Internet to buy goods and services.

Technology Diffusion: Pervasive application and use of technology in everyday life.

Transaction Trust: Trust based exchanges between buyers and sellers of products and services. "Relational trust" as defined by Rousseau *et al.* (1998) applied to commerce.

Virtual Storefront: A commercial enterprise using Internet and Web servers to sell products or services.

Section III
E-Government in DCs

Chapter VII
E-Governance in Uganda: Experiences and Lessons Learned from the DistrictNet Programme

Victor van Reijswoud
Uganda Martyrs University, Uganda

Arjan de Jager
International Institute for Communication and Development (IICD), The Netherlands

ABSTRACT

E-governance is a powerful tool for bringing about change to government processes in the developing world. It operates at the crossroads between Information and Communication Technology and government processes and can be divided into three overlapping domains: e-administration, e-services and e-society. To succeed, e-governance must be firmly embedded in existing government processes; supported, both politically and technically, by the governments; and provide users with reasons to use these on-line domains. To maximize the impact, process change must be part and parcel of e-governance. This chapter presents and evaluates the ongoing DistrictNet e-governance programme in Uganda which was set up in 2002 to provide transparency at the local government level and improve the provision of public information using ICT. DistrictNet's achievements are presented and evaluated according to the criteria of the three domains of e-governance and their impact on government processes. On the basis of this evaluation, we elicit lessons that can be used to guide smaller programmes at the local government level in the developing world.

INTRODUCTION

In the developing world, Information and Communication Technology (ICT) is often welcomed as an important instrument for accelerated change. ICT programmes are used to increase the efficiency and effectiveness of organizations and

Copyright © 2009, IGI Global, distributing in print or electronic forms without written permission of IGI Global is prohibited.

to help align processes with best practices from the developed world.

Governments in the developing world are under a lot of international and national pressure to review and update their processes. Internationally, donors and governments in the developed world are urging governments of developing nations to increase transparency, support decentralization, decrease corruption and participate in global digital information sharing. Nationally, the private sector demands more openness and willingness to participate in transparent relationships, and citizens are asking their governments to provide better, faster services and to extend their information and service offerings to the rural areas. As a result of these pressures, governments in the developing world are challenged to change more than ever before (United Nations, 2003).

E-Governance is defined by the United Nations as "A government that applies ICT to transform its internal and external relationships" (United Nations, 2003). ICT allows a government's internal and external communication to gain speed, precision, simplicity, outreach and networking capacity, which can then be converted into cost reductions and increased effectiveness - two features desirable for all government operations, but especially for public services. ICT also enables 24/7 usefulness, transparency and accountability, as well as networked structures of public administration, information management and knowledge creation. In addition, it can equip people to participate in an inclusive political process that can produce well-informed public consent, which is, increasingly, the basis for the legitimacy of governments.

This chapter reports on the experiences of DistrictNet, an ongoing e-governance programme in the East African country of Uganda which tries to provide transparency at the local government level and to improve the provision of public information through the use of ICT. The implementation of this programme can be considered as an action based research with the goal to measure the impact evaluate this programme against a theoretical background, and also to draw practical lessons from the programme that could provide guidance to new e-governance programmes in the development context. After a short introduction to Uganda the chapter begins by providing some theoretical background for e-governance, which is important to better understand the objectives and design of the DistrictNet programme. In the section entitled 'DistrictNet–Uganda' we discuss the programme, focusing on its beginnings and its achievements so far. In the final section entitled 'Conclusions and Lessons Learned' we evaluate the programme in a larger context and elicit lessons learned from DistrictNet.

SHORT INTRODUCTION TO UGANDA

Uganda is one of the poorest countries in the world. In 2005, the per capita income was estimated to be approximately US$250. Life expectancy at birth remains low: 43 years in 2004, compared to 47 years in 1990. Similarly, infant and child mortality has not improved much over the same period and today remains at around 100 respectively 150 per 1,000 live births. Nevertheless, the country's firm commitment to poverty reduction, as spelled out in its Poverty Reduction Strategy, produced several positive results in the area of development, which brought the country closer to reaching the Millennium Development Goals:

- The number of adults with HIV/AIDS declined significantly over the last decade from about 18 percent in the early 1990s to 6.1 percent in 2005.
- Access to safe water increased from 54 percent in 2000 to 65 percent in 2005 in urban areas and from 50 percent in 2000 to 55 percent in 2003 in rural areas.
- Net enrolment rates for primary schooling increased from 62.3 percent in 1992 to 86 percent in 2005.

- Total youth literacy increased from 75 percent in 1995 to 81 percent in 2005.
- GDP per capita has grown on average by 3.6 percent since 1995.

The current telecommunications policy and regulatory environment was established through the telecommunications sector reforms which started in 1996: The monopoly of the former National Operator Uganda Telecom Ltd (UTL) was replaced by a system of limited competition (specifically in basic telephony services, cellular telecommunications services and satellite services) in which the licenses were issued to two National Telecommunications Operators and the creation of an independent regulator. Uganda Communications Commission (UCC: www.ucc.co.ug) is the regulator of the communications industry in Uganda. UCC regulates and promotes the developments in the communications industry. The result is a fast growing sector with three major telecom providers, 17 ISP's, about 10% of the population having a cell phone: Figures which compare positive to other countries in the region. Internet is still expensive mainly due to the high costs of the traffic (satellite!) from the ISP's in Uganda to the Internet backbone.

UNDERSTANDING E-GOVERNANCE

The work of governments is being reshaped by two ineluctable trends. The first is the movement away from centralized, vertical and hierarchical government machines towards polycentric networks of governance based upon horizontal interactions between diverse actors within complex, multi-layered societies. The second trend is the rapid introduction of ICT aimed at the transformation of the generation and delivery of public services. The concept of e-governance is the convergence between these two trends (Coleman, 2005).

In order to get a better understanding of the potential impact of ICT on government processes, we need to start with a general overview of the role that ICT and Information Systems can play in the optimization of organizational processes, transcending the traditional perception of ICT as mere technology. We then identify types of e-governance and e-governance, describe the status of e-governance internationally, and conclude with guidelines for successful e-governance programme design and implementation.

ICT for Change

Information and Communication Technology are important initiators and drivers of change in an organization. The use of ICT creates new possibilities, and ultimately ICT has the potential to reinvent organizations and their services (Leer, 2000).

Dennis and Haley Wixom (2000) identify three strategies for the implementation of ICT in an organization:

1. business process automation (BPA)
2. business process improvement (BPI)
3. business process reengineering (BPR)

The three approaches have an increasing impact on the organization. The goal of BPA is to increase the efficiency of the work of the users. It does not intend to change the work in an organization, but automates the existing processes. In the development context, this often implies that manual processes are supported or replaced by automated processes. For example, data is no longer stored in paper files, but a database management system is introduced to manage information; however, the same information as before is stored, without considering its quality and usefulness. The goal of BPI is to reconsider the processes used and information stored, and to improve upon them by introducing some moderate changes that are generally incremental or evolutionary in nature. The new practice is enhanced both through making the users more efficient and by changing how processes work in order to make them more effective. In practical terms, this means that processes are examined carefully to see whether existing problems can be eliminated during the introduction of ICT. However, BPI does not lead to completely new processes or new tasks within an organization, since it builds on the existing processes. BPR[a] focuses on the fundamental and critical rethinking of an organization's processes . Following the introduction of new ICT, the organizational processes are evaluated, changed or eliminated, and new processes are added in order to improve performance in terms of costs, service delivery, quality and speed. In the development context, we observe in many e-governance programmes a focus on the first-time introduction of ICT. This opens up new horizons and allows organizations to deliver new ICT-enabled services that they have not previously been able to offer. It is important to realize, though, that in this introductory or implementation context, BPR can be very technology-driven.

Although business process automation, improvement and reengineering are often considered in a private-sector context, their focus is definitely not limited to the private sector. Rather, they are general concepts for increasing the efficiency and effectiveness of organizations. While ICT is not essential to these concepts, nowadays it lies is at the heart of most practical initiatives.

Domains of E-Governance

Heeks (2001a) identifies three main domains of e-governance, based on taxonomies proposed by Ntiro:

1. **E-administration:** Improving government processes
2. **E-services[b]:** Connecting individual citizens with their government
3. **E-society:** Building interactions with and within the civil society

The main purpose of the e-administration is to improve the internal workings of the public sector by cutting process costs, managing the process performance, creating strategic connections within the government bodies, and creating empowerment. Shortening the lead time for passport applications from two weeks to one day is an example of e-administration. E-service initiatives focus mainly on improving the relationship between the government and its citizens by increasing the information flow be-

Figure 1. Overlapping domains of e-governance (adapted from Heeks, 2001)

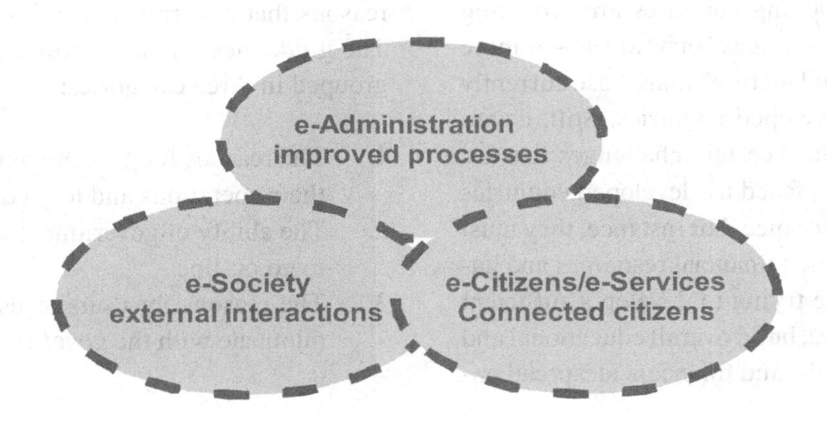

tween them – which, notably, involves two-way communication – and improving the service levels of government towards its citizens. Public service institutes offering citizens the opportunity to apply for business licenses through a government Website is one example of e-services. E-society initiatives extend on the previous e-services domain by focusing on institutional stakeholders, such as private sector service providers, other public agencies, and not-for-profit and community organizations. In addition, e-society focuses on building long lasting partnerships and social/economical communities: for example, through the creation of a business community portal.

Practically speaking, the three domains of e-governance are seldom separate in their implementations; rather, they involve overlapping activities as part of the same initiative (Heeks, 2001). To put it more strongly: good e-governance programmes must take into account all three domains.

Where is E-Governance Now?

The United Nations' *World Public Sector Report 2003: E-Governance at the Crossroads*, prepared by its Department of Economic and Social Affairs, provides three main conclusions on the current status of global e-governance. First, using an extensive survey, the report concludes that developing countries are creating and implementing e-governance applications similar to those currently used in developed countries. In fact, says the survey, developing countries are providing "information and services" that "are as – or more – sophisticated and mature" than those currently used in some developed countries. Still, developing countries face certain challenges that are greater than those faced by developed countries in pursing e-governance. For instance, they must contend with limited financial resources and human capital while trying to develop a sufficient ICT infrastructure, build overall educational and technological skills, and finance widespread on-line access to rural areas and other under-served populations.

In describing the methodology for their Telecommunication Infrastructure Index, the United Nations report admits to placing less weight on the use of mobile technologies than on a country's personal computer density, number of Internet users, number of telephone lines, and on-line population. Regardless of this, there is evidence that developing countries are addressing e-governance implementation issues through the innovative use of currently available technologies, including radio, television and mobile technologies.

The two additional conclusions of the United Nations report are, first, that both developed and developing governments have made little use of on-line transaction services, and secondly, that participation in e-governance ranges from "rudimentary" to non-existent. Finally, the report asserts that there is no single strategy for achieving e-governance success, as governments must respond to the specific needs of their particular societies. These conclusions and assertions present areas of opportunity where developing countries can pursue their e-governance strategies through practical, innovative applications.

Guiding Principles for Successful E-Governance

In its 2003 report, the United Nations defines guiding principles for success which include the reasons that governments and users go on-line. The guidelines for successful e-governance are grouped in three categories:

1. The reasons for governments to use ICT in their operations and to go on-line.
2. The ability of governments to use ICT and to go on-line.
3. The reasons for users to use ICT to communicate with the government

Ad 1: The following compelling reasons are identified for the government to use ICT in its operations and to go on-line:

- **Priority development needs that require government involvement**. E-governance applications are best embedded in areas that are perceived as closely related to the priority development needs of the society. This approach creates broad support, making it easier to overcome inherent difficulties and to sustain attention, commitment and funding.
- **Efficiency and effectiveness as key success criteria of government involvement**. It is best if the role that the government plays in such areas is judged partly or predominantly by factors that ICT can bring. The link between ICT applications, optimization of government operations and achievement of important social development goals is a very convincing argument for the continued development of e-governance.

Ad 2: The ability of a government to use ICT in its operations and to maintain a successful on-line presence depends on a number of factors:

- **The availability of (initial) funding.** Even initial pilot e-governance operations should start with a good understanding of the costs involved and with assured funding that follows careful analysis of opportunity cost. Whenever advisable and feasible, funding should be treated as a business investment and should carry expectations of returns.
- **Skills and culture of the civil service**. Civil servants must be able (through ICT, change and programme management and partnership-building skills) and willing to support e-governance, or at a minimum, must be eager to learn and change. The culture prevailing in the civil service determines the assessment of expected loss of jobs, prestige or power that e-governance applications might impose upon individual civil servants and thus the eventual strength and effectiveness of the anti-change lobby (if any such lobby exists).
- **Co-ordination.** The necessary "backroom" co-ordination and effort - within and between government agencies - must take place before any e-governance application goes on-line in order to avoid duplication, assure interoperability and meet the expectations of users.
- **Legal framework.** E-Governance introduces unique legal requirements and these should be realized and dealt with early in the process.
- **ICT infrastructure.** Infrastructure needs should be assessed against the background of requirements and desired results of e-governance development plans. An insufficient assessment risks underestimating requirements and limiting results, or alternatively overestimating requirements and leading to the possibility that ICT infrastructure will simply become expensive and idle office equipment.
- **Political leadership and long-term political commitment.** The chief executive officer of the public sector must be committed to e-governance, must lead and build broad support for it, and must be eager to learn. This commitment generates the all-important positive signals that the civil service needs to receive from its top leadership.
- **Public engagement.** The public should have a personal stake in e-governance development. Their engagement should be reinforced by actively, genuinely and continuously soliciting people to participate in the development of e-governance applications so that these are custom-crafted to the way people live and work.

- **Plans for the development of human capital and technical infrastructure.** There should be a vision and plans for closing the existing gaps in ICT skills and access. Otherwise, neither the public administration nor the citizenry can hope to become ICT literate and capable, which are important ingredients for e-governance success.
- **Partnerships.** Early on, the government should involve business firms and civil society organizations (CSOs) as its partners in securing financial resources, skills improvement, better access and adequate capacity to service the ICT network. However, partnerships should never be forged at the cost of transparency, accountability or the economic soundness of investments.
- **Monitoring and evaluation.** Setting clear responsibilities and realistic benchmarks for e-governance development, as well as for its transparent monitoring, is an important ingredient for eventual success and helps build the overall transparency and accountability framework in the public sector.

Ad 3: Finally, there must be compelling reasons for the *users* of e-governance to go and stay on-line:

- **Perception of added value**. Any design of an e-governance development must incorporate a calculation of the added value that the application intends to bring to individual users. This calculation should be congruent with the needs, desires and/or expectations of the users.
- **Access and skills.** It should be made easy in terms of time, cost and effort for the potential users of e-governance to actually use it. Imaginative solutions for increasing the level of this ease of use must be part of any e-governance development plan. They should include, but also transcend, attention to individual access and skills.
- **Privacy and security.** Security and privacy concerns - culturally defined as they are - must be addressed early on, openly and with demonstrated professional aptitude. The public is likely to expect a breakdown in this area and news (even informal) of even one breakdown in privacy or security is bound to become a huge setback with long-lasting consequences.

Model for Evaluation

It is important to evaluate the performance of e-governance programmes in the developing world. Limited, often temporary funding requires governments to implement the 'first time right' approach. Most of the evaluations are quantitative and founded in the ontological tradition of science, like the longitudinal survey published in the United Nations' *World Public Sector Report 2003* and the work on e-governance and e-commerce by the Institute of Development Policy and Management (see, for example, Heeks, 2001; Molla, 2004). Few qualitative and epistemological studies on e-governance have been reported.

In this chapter we will focus on the evaluation of an e-governance programme that started in 2002 in Uganda and has gone through the first pilot cycle. Information about the programme has been collected through document analysis, interviews and participative observations in the context of an "Action Research" arrangement (Argyris et al, 1990; Baskerville, 1999).

DistrictNet is analyzed along the lines of the theoretical framework presented above:

1. The programme is analyzed according to the criteria associated with its domains (e-administration, e-services and e-society) and the levels to which the programme has supported (automated) or changed existing processes and/or introduced new processes (that is, its engagement with the BPA, BPI and BPR strategies defined by Dennis and

Haley Wixom). Figure 2 below presents a growth model.

2. The programme is also analyzed along the guidelines of successful e-governance programmes as identified by the United Nations. This measurement is related to the principles outlined earlier under the heading 'Guiding Principles for Successful e-governance' and is used to identify the 'Lessons Learned' presented at this chapter's conclusion.

We assume, based on the work of Heeks (2001a, 2001b), that meaningful e-governance optimizes the operations of the government (through e-administration) and supports human and societal development (by implementing e-services and e-society). In line with the United Nations' *World Public Sector Report 2003*, we consider e-governance that does not result in an optimization of the government processes to be 'wasteful' and e-governance that has very limited or no impact on the development objectives of the country at large to be 'pointless'.

DISTRICTNET: UGANDA

Over the past fifteen years, Uganda has shown a remarkable recovery from economical, social and political turmoil. However, in spite of this recovery, Uganda is still a poor country and the penetration of ICT and level of Internet use is low (see National Indicators in Table 1).

It is against this background that the District Administration Network programme (DistrictNet) started in 2002, with the general aim of introducing ICT to improve transparency of the local government and to improve communication within districts to support decentralization (Weddi, 2005). The programme was focusing initially on supporting e-administration, and the possibilities of e-services were to be investigated during programme implementation. E-society was not within the scope of the programme

However, the overall development objective supported by this programme is government decentralization[c]. Until May 2005, the programme was fostered by Uganda's Ministry of Local Government (MoLG), and the initial investments

Figure 2. E-governance development cycle

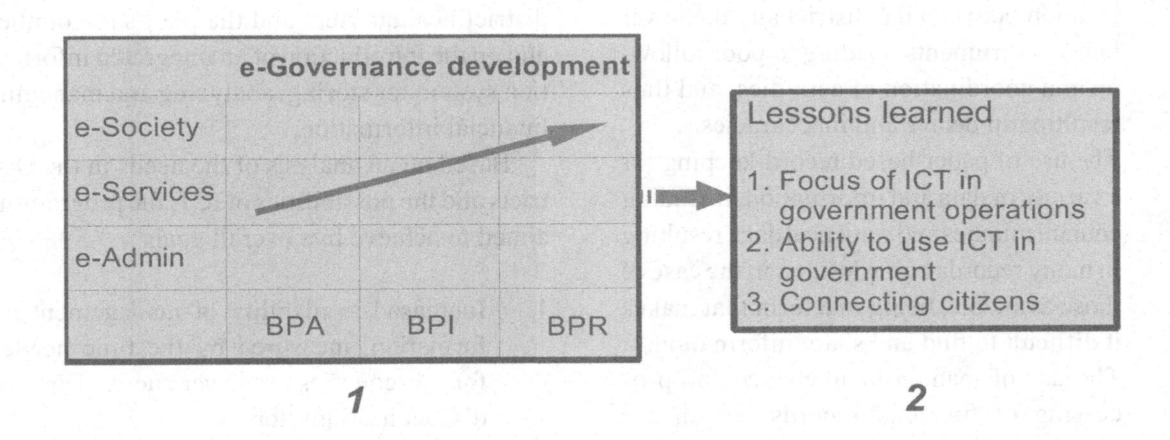

Table 1. National indicators of Uganda. In: Tusubira et al., 2005.

National indicators Uganda	
Population (000.000)	28.6
Poverty (% of population below $1 per day)	26.8
Adult literacy rate (% ages 15 and over)	68.9
Urban population (% of total population)	14.9
Surface area (000 km2)	241
Computer usage and Internet	
Ownership of computers (% urban/rural)	3.5/0.4
Internet access (% urban/rural)	4.2/0.1

and running costs were financially supported by DFID through the International Institute for Communication and Development (IICD) in conjunction with the MoLG.

Set-Up of DistrictNet

The idea for DistrictNet emerged from a round-table conference[d] organized by IICD in March 2001. The workshop was themed "ICT for Rural Development" and brought together participants from rural and up-country institutions in public and private sectors. Workshop participants identified the following problems at the district and sub-county local government levels[e]:

1. The lack of a convenient mode of communication between the district and the lower local governments, leading to poor follow-up and coordination of activities, and thus resulting in delays and inaccuracies.
2. The use of paper-based record-keeping for a variety of data and information, including council minutes and statistical data, resulting in many records being lost, or, in the case of those available, being in a form that makes it difficult to find and share information.
3. The use of manual maintenance and processing of financial records, which are consequently often out-dated and inaccurate, leading to reduced transparency and accountability.
4. The numerous reports that have to be prepared manually and submitted from lower local governments to the district, and then from the district to central government ministries, leading to slow and often inaccurate processing
5. The limited access to important information: for example, on government policies; government, donors and NGO programmes that are planned or ongoing; general development information on agriculture, health, etc.

In order to address these problems, the introduction of ICT at the district and lower local government levels was proposed. Emphasis was put on data and voice communication between the district headquarters and the pilot sub-counties and on the introduction of an integrated information system for storing, analyzing and managing financial information.

Based on an analysis of the needs in the Districts and the possibilities of ICT, the programme aimed to achieve five overall goals[f]:

1. Increased availability of management information, measured by the time needed for sub-counties to answer queries from the district headquarters.
2. Increased coordination between headquarters and sub-counties, measured by the volume of data/communication.

3. Reduced costs of coordination between headquarters and sub-counties, measured by the amount of physical travel by officers.
4. Improved IT skills, measured by the usage of the systems.
5. Increased availability of public information, measured by the amount of information spread through notice boards, radio, and Websites, as well as the number of information requests by the citizens and the number of queries answered.

The DistrictNet programme was initially designed to be implemented in four districts in Uganda (Mbarara, Lira, Mbale and Kayunga), covering the country's west, north, east and central regions. The Kayunga district was selected because of the unique challenges caused by its remote location. Uganda consists of 76 districts,[g] which are further divided into sub-counties (with over 900 in the country) and then into parishes. The selected districts were characterized by their long-term political commitment; in addition, the geographical breadth of the programme was chosen to provide a base for its evolutionary growth, based on the premise that pilot districts would inform neighboring districts about their achievements, in the end leading to regional capacity development. Within the four districts, eleven sub-counties were selected for participation.

Proposed Technical Solution

The proposed technical solution envisaged to realize DistrictNet was, for the most part, simple and straightforward. To improve the communication between the offices in the district, voice and data communication links were needed to connect all the offices in the district headquarters, some of which are as far as two kilometers apart. A client-server based Local Area Network (wired and wireless) was to provide the communication in the headquarters. Within the headquarters, PCs were installed with standard office applications (Microsoft suite), Logics (an Access based Management Information System developed by MoLG in conjunction with development partners), Geographical Information System software (Arcview) and financial software (Navision, which was chosen in part because it was already in use in one of the districts).

The connection from headquarters to the sub-counties was less straightforward, and the solutions were determined on the basis of three parameters:

1. access to a landline connection.
2. access of the sub-county offices to the electricity grid.
3. the distance from the sub-county to the headquarters.

Table 2. Up-country connectivity solutions in the DistrictNet programme. The last column lists the amount of times each solution was selected in the programme proposal.

1	Land Line	An external modem is used for the data exchange	7
2	Mobile phone I	Mobile phone with data accessories and associated software	4
3	Mobile phone II	As above with additional antenna	2
4	Broadband wireless	Wireless access to HQ LAN where the sub-county is within a 15 km range and with line-of-sight.	1
5	HF radio with data comm	Radio set with antenna, power supply, modem	6

Four sub-counties were selected because they were not connected to the electricity grid and consequently alternative energy sources, such as solar energy panels, would be used. Overall, the programme identified five different options for data and voice communication (see Table 2).

Implementation of DistrictNet

The implementation of DistrictNet was designed as a pilot programme to prove the concepts and to build a body of knowledge. IICD supported the formulation and implementation of the programme via research, strategic advice, capacity development (in ICT skills and soft skills) and general programme management. While the technical solution as such can be classified as "technically simple" the programme was not easy to implement mainly because of lack of capacities and the change management required within the organizations. At the start of the programme, there was virtually no experience with the use of ICT at local government levels. Some ICT programmes had been implemented in Uganda, but all at the central government level. Of course, the programme was aligned with the plans of the Uganda Communications Commission (UCC), the regulator in Uganda, to spread Internet connectivity to District centres, and with those of the Local Government Development Program (LGDP-I) to restructure government structures to better address the national goals of economic growth and poverty alleviation.

The implementation plan of the programme can be characterized as "phased" (Shelly et al, 2001) but executed simultaneously at four locations (i.e., the four districts). The whole programme plan - from design, through procurement, implementation, training and evaluation - was expected to take one year. However, although it was projected to start in May 2002, the programme did not take off until February 2003. At the time of writing, the pilot phase is about to be finalized.

Soon after the programme's kick-off, the ICT infrastructure implementation began and the massive training programme was started up. Local Area Networks (LAN), e-mail and internet services were purchased and installed to establish the first connectivity between the offices in the Headquarters and between the Headquarters and the offices in the sub-counties.

The implementation of the ICT infrastructure in the four districts did not move at the same pace in each. As expected, implementation in the Kayunga district, because of the specific challenges caused by the district's geographical location, initially moved more slowly than in the other locations. From the start it was acknowledged that training and capacity development were key factors to the success. In each district a number of training programmes were implemented such as computer appreciation, computer literacy, maintenance of ICT equipment (for a minimum of 3 staff members per district), Website development (for a minimum of 3 staff members per district).

The impact of the programme was monitored in an intense way: Staff members and beneficiaries were asked to take part in monitoring and evaluating the services provided by the programme on an annual basis. The results were analyzed (by IICD) and then brought back to the staff members and beneficiaries for a participatory feedback session in order to improve the quality and to fine-tune the services of the programme.

DistrictNet and E-Administration

At the start of the programme, the basic data was collected at parish level and forwarded to sub-county administration. The sub-county's responsibility was to collect and compile all data from the parishes, and then forward it to District HQ. Then, the District HQ, like the sub-county administration, checked the data for completeness and forwarded it to MoLG, where digital recording took place. All data was in hard-copy form, and was physically transported by road. In order to ensure uniformity, standardized forms were used at all levels. The process is depicted in Figure 3.

Several problems occurred in this process. In the first place, the data which was collected at the parish level took a long time before reaching District HQ and MoLG. We observed information backlogs of three to six months. Secondly, data was lost in transport, never reaching the District HQ and MoLG, for reasons that were not very clear. Indeed, some data was never collected properly in the first place. For example, in one district less than 20% of the information required for budget and planning reached the MoLG. This implied that in 80% of the sub-counties, the planning and budgeting process was seriously undermined. These two problems guided the programme design.

Currently, the basic data is still collected at the parish level and forwarded to sub-county administration using the same hard-copy standard forms. The first change was implemented at the sub-county level: the eleven pilot sub-counties are now responsible for the digitization of data. After digitizing the data and checking its completeness, the sub-counties then forward the data via e-mail and/or floppy disk to District HQ, resulting in a timely delivery of the data needed for planning and budgeting purposes.

The third change was implemented at District HQ, where District Planners (who were trained to use data analysis tools) now perform data analysis and provide timely feedback to the sub-county administration and the parishes.

A fourth change is in the improvement in lead times for the data's arrival at MoLG, as the four pilot districts are now able to transfer their information electronically to MoLG. Moreover, MoLG can now work much more efficiently and effectively because it is no longer responsible for digital recording, thus allowing more time for analysis and informed decision-making. The process is depicted in Figure 3.

In the reverse feedback flow, the decision was made to send relatively little information, using low-end tools, to provide feedback from MoLG to the District HQ and from District HQ to lower local government levels. This feedback mechanism enables lower-level governments to finalize their planning and budgeting processes. This process still needs (and deserves!) further development, and much more staff training is required. However, at this stage we can say that the system is a unique example of e-administration and e-services for East Africa, and it has had an enormous impact on the government planning in

Figure 3. Business process improvement in DistrictNet

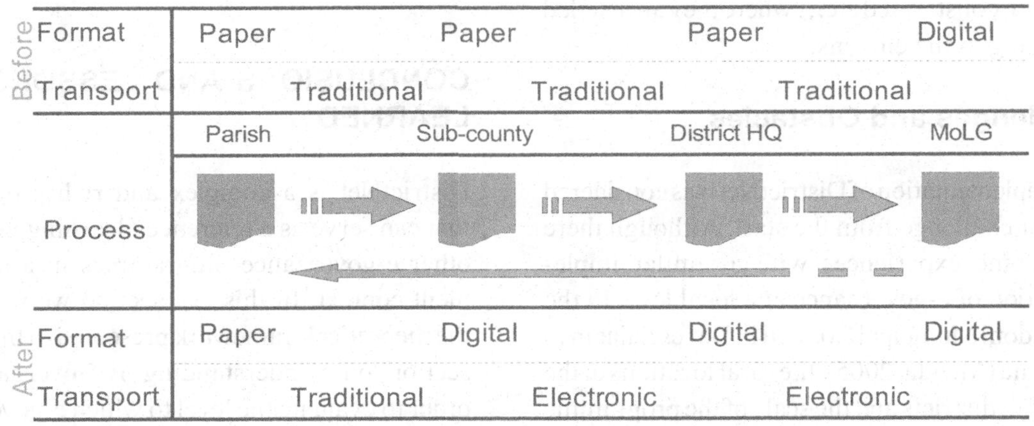

		Parish		Sub-county		District HQ		MoLG
Before	Format	Paper		Paper		Paper		Digital
Before	Transport		Traditional		Traditional		Traditional	
	Process							
After	Format	Paper		Digital		Digital		Digital
After	Transport		Traditional		Electronic		Electronic	

the four pilot districts. The support for decentralization supported through ICTs deserves further documenting and dissemination.

DistrictNet and E-Services

Efforts to offer direct information services to the citizens of the four pilot districts began in 2004. In this respect it should be mentioned that Uganda is a strongly decentralized country, which is a "disadvantage" for implementing e-services in that most governmental information services (e.g. business licenses, tax forms and information) are already available to the citizens in hard-copy form at the sub-county level. As a result, offering these types of services in electronic form is not among the programme's direct priorities.

DistrictNet and E-Society

E-society was, and is not, within the scope of the programme. DistrictNet was to focus on e-administration and e-services. As a result, this domain has not yet been developed nor evaluated.

Summarizing: The programme has a strong but indirect impact on the citizens of the 4 pilot districts. Since the staff members of the districts are enabled to do heir work much ore efficient and much more effective, proper planning and budgeting can take place leading to a more transparent environment n which schools are build, where roads are constructed etc... where they are needed according to the citizens.

Challenges and Obstacles

The implementation of DistrictNet was considered a major challenge from the start. Although there were some experiences with a similar implementation of e-governance at a local level in the Kinondoni Municipal Council in Dar es Salaam in Tanzania (Menda, 2005), the rural locations of the four pilot districts and the scale of the programme posed some new and unexpected problems.

In the implementation phase, the importance of large-scale continuous capacity development became immediately apparent. The levels of professional technical ICT knowledge (i.e., the knowledge to implement an ICT infrastructure) as well computer literacy (the ability to operate the computer and its applications, as well as awareness of the opportunities ICT creates in organizations) proved to be lower than anticipated. When combined with the huge staff turn-over in local governments, this circumstance demanded the establishment of continuous training programmes at the District HQ. In addition, the implementation of the ICT infrastructure began slowly, and the implemented solutions were inadequate. This problem was caused in part by the fact that the Districts themselves did not take up ownership of the programme until May 2005, when it was decided to make the districts directly responsible for implementation. This shift in responsibility improved the quality of implementation greatly.

Another problem was that DistrictNet faced significant delays in the implementation of e-services because of a strong technological focus at the start of the programme. Decisions needed to be taken on the type of hardware, software and network connections that were suitable in the programme's rural context. Not until the discussions on the type of technology to be used were concluded could the programme proceed to the level of e-services.

CONCLUSIONS AND LESSONS LEARNED

DistrictNet is a complex and rich programme that can serve as a reference / learning model for other e-governance programmes in a development context. In this last section we will apply the theoretical framework presented in the earlier section on 'Understanding E-Governance' in order to evaluate the level to which e-governance has been implemented in the programme. On the basis of the evaluation, we will formulate some lessons learned that can guide other e-governance programmes at local government levels.

E-Governance Implemented

In the section entitled 'Understanding E-Governance', we developed a matrix to determine the focus of e-governance and the level to which the processes in the organization are affected. We postulated that meaningful e-governance programmes optimize the processes of the government and human and societal development. In order to evaluate whether this has taken place, the three focus areas of e-governance (e-administration, e-services and e-society) need to be considered, as do the levels to which the government processes are automated, improved or redesigned (BPA, BPI and BPR). What can we conclude for the DistrictNet programme in Uganda?

The design of DistrictNet allows the programme to extend to all three areas of e-governance, supporting the processes at the local and sub-country levels by offering new services for the citizens, and by creating the conditions for the eventual involvement of business communities and non-governmental and community organizations. The programme is designed not only to automate existing processes, but also to emphasize the improvement of processes. For instance, the budgeting and planning processes underwent radical improvement. The old budgeting and planning processes have been re-structured and optimized, and the new processes have created dramatic improvements in efficiency and effectiveness, thanks to the use of ICT. Similar positive results were recorded for the information sharing of the sub-counties with the Chief Administration Officer and District Planner.

Most of the initiatives were problem-driven. Hence, the programme has so far had very little space for e-society initiatives. Some actions for e-society were integrated in the development of a new communication structure for information sharing through the newly established Websites (each of the pilot districts has a Website offering generic information about the district).

The programme has had the most impact at the e-administration and e-services levels. The programme was able to optimize and, where possible, restructure processes in these two areas of e-governance. However, the programme has so far not been able to re-design processes at the e-services level. The results of the programme are plotted in Figure 4.

Lessons Learned

To conclude this chapter, we want to elicit some lessons learned from the DistrictNet programme in Uganda. We focus our lessons through the three

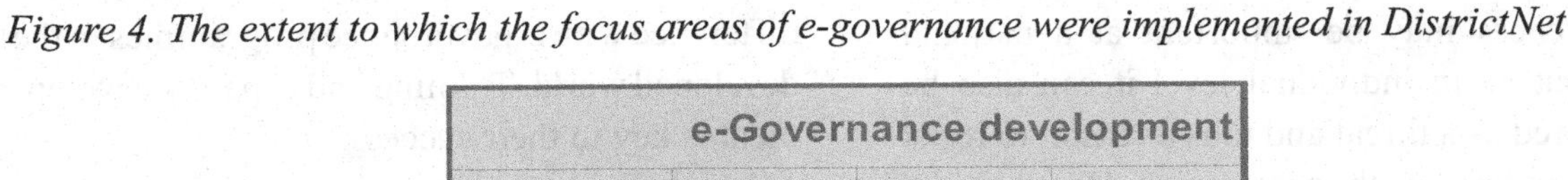

Figure 4. The extent to which the focus areas of e-governance were implemented in DistrictNet

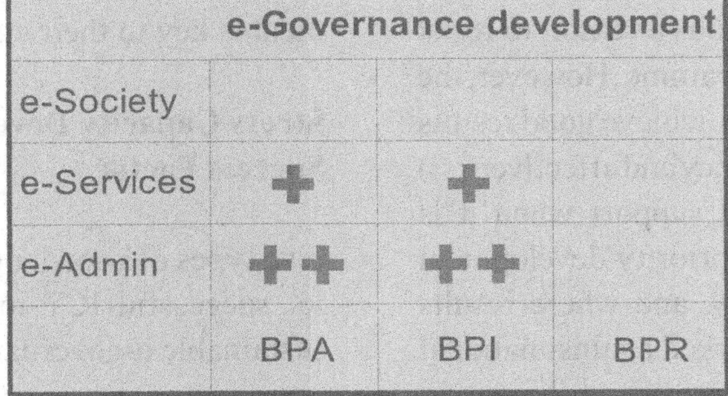

main categories identified in the United Nations' *World Public Sector Report 2003*. In addition to the points raised in the UN report, we identify six new lessons in three categories:

1. Focus of ICT in government operations
    - Think big, but begin small
    - Create feedback loops in e-governance programmes
2. Ability to use ICT in government
    - Stress capacity development as a key success factor
    - Recognize that fighting technology takes time
3. Strategies for connecting citizens
    - Emphasize that information is a commodity
    - Ensure content availability and usage

The six lessons are explained in the three categories below.

Ad 1. Focus of ICT in Government Operations

DistrictNet presents a good example of embedding the introduction of e-governance in the larger context of priority development needs in a country (in this case, the government's decentralization programme). As DistrictNet shows, e-governance programmes are complex and need constant attention and care. Improvement in efficiency and effectiveness may be important at a national level, but at an individual level it can also be considered as a threat and thus a reason to resist or even undermine the programme. However, the programme is most likely to achieve good results (i.e. improvements in efficiency and effectiveness) and constant attention and support when it is part of the success of high priority development programmes in the country, and where results of individuals are benchmarked against national development goals.

Think Big, But Begin Small

Gradual and phased implementation of the programme is the key to success. In other words: Think big, but begin small. DistrictNet has been designed as a pilot programme. The main goal was to build knowledge and gain experience. New programmes should build on these experiences because the underlying idea of the pilot is to create a nation-wide e-governance network. It is important to integrate this goal in the design of the next phases of this pilot programme.

Create Feedback Loops in E-Governance Programmes

In countries like Uganda, civil servants at the local levels are often asked to gather data but seldom receive feedback on the impact of their data-collecting activities. A good feedback mechanism in an e-governance programme creates a tool to provide the local levels with information, and the improved information position of the officers at the local government levels enhances their commitment to the introduction of e-governance.

Ad 2. Ability to Use ICT in Government

Our observations from the DistrictNet programme show that in a development context the ability of local governments to design, implement, use and maintain e-governance in action should not be over-estimated. This might be an important difference with e-governance programmes in the developed world. Training and capacity development is key to their success.

Stress Capacity Development as a Key Success Factor

Five types of knowledge and skills are necessary for successful ICT implementation, as well as sustainable e-governance:

1. Professional technical knowledge to implement and to maintain the technical infrastructure.
2. Professional business knowledge to guide and check the quality of the suppliers implementing and maintaining the technical infrastructure (tendering, quality control, Service Level Agreements).
3. Computer literacy at the government level, such as basic knowledge about how to operate the computers and their applications, and an understanding of the role ICT can play in the improvement of work processes.
4. Computer literacy among users, such as basic knowledge about how to operate the computers and e-governance applications.
5. ICT change management skills among management and administrators.

Professional knowledge may be available in the country; however, this knowledge is less likely to be found at the level of the local governments, and is seldom found in the rural areas. As a result, obtaining quality ICT consulting services is difficult. Computer literacy is often defined as the ability to use office applications; however, e-governance programmes also demand that staff have a good understanding of the role that ICT can play in their organization and in their work. In the developing world, the level of computer literacy among the people in the rural areas is extremely low (see also Table 1). Consequently, in the design and implementation of an e-governance programme, one cannot assume any level of computer literacy. Training in the programme should focus on developing the skills to operate and maintain the applications used in the e-governance programme, as well as on educating people about the possibilities of ICT for government operations. When ICT solutions are outsourced, business-related skills such as supplier and contract management are vital, since the quality of service of ICT suppliers in rural environments is often low.

Training should not be purely technology-driven or organization-focused. In a rural setting, the introduction of ICT does not automatically lead to the use of the new tools. Resistance, fear and lack of understanding need to be managed carefully and skillfully to persuade the users to use the new ICT. Training can serve as a tool to change the attitudes of users in the organization. It is advised that the training simulates the day-to-day working practice as anticipated in the desired situation. Training should not be limited to the borders of the organization, but should also include community leaders and potential champions in the communities. Their role is vital for carrying knowledge to the surrounding communities.

Recognize that Fighting Technology Takes Time

In DistrictNet's initial stage of implementation, the primary focus was on developing the ICT infrastructure to enable e-administration and e-services. Often in e-governance, the primary focus is on these technical aspects, and the organizational and social aspects are treated with less priority. It takes time to change this technology-focused attitude, and the issue needs to addressed from the start of the implementation process.

Ad 3. Strategies for Connecting Citizens

Connecting the citizens to the programme is probably the biggest challenge, especially with the local government in rural areas. One of the reasons for the success of DistrictNet is that it has been using traditional means combined with modern (ICT-enabled) strategies to distribute information to the citizens. In the excitement of introducing new technology, programmes tend to forget to include the traditional means for information distribution, such as radio, television, bulletins, bulletin boards, and even word-of-mouth. The traditional communication channels are the first ways to make use of the new ICT-based communication channels.

In Uganda, as in many parts of Africa, mobile telephony is gaining rapid acceptance as a means of spreading information (see, for example, the wide range of information services offered through SMS). The reach of mobile telephony has increased dramatically in recent years and has penetrated deep into the rural areas of Africa (Scott et al, 2004). The design of DistrictNet could benefit from a closer integration of mobile telephony with the ICT-enabled solutions. The spread of information to citizens through a special (free) SMS service could have increased the e-services dimension of the programme.

Emphasize that Information is a Commodity

The success of e-administration and e-services programmes relies heavily on the quality of data and information. The availability of quality data and information is too often taken for granted. Programmes must remember that information is a commodity:

- The quality of data should be monitored, while the quantity of data at higher levels has to be reduced.
- Information is not "just lying around"; it should be derived from the right datasets. Therefore, lobbying at all levels, and especially at the political level, is needed to ensure that the necessary data can be collected and used.
- Incentives should be in place for data generation at lower local government levels (e.g.: direct outlets of data should be present at the level at which the data is being collected).

The DistrictNet programme taught us that potential users can be trained to use the services offered and that the staff members of the programme can be trained in basic ICT applications, project management, and financial management. At the operational level, the rule that "people learn when they see how they can use their skills and knowledge" was proved valid once again.

The difficulty is in training the staff members how to use the data at a more strategic level, so they can transform the data into useful information and knowledge. Thus, two critical factors in good governance programmes are the creation of information flow procedures and the development of solid training programmes in information management.

In DistrictNet, an information flow toolkit for Information Officers at Higher Local Government Level was provided during training sessions. The kit was developed in a participatory way.

Ensure Content Availability and Usage

The availability of information is key to keeping momentum in an e-governance programme, and the way the users employ this information is the measurement for success. Access to information, and thus the success of ICT programmes, is determined by:

1. *Awareness*: Do the potential staff members and end-users know the services exist?
2. *Connectivity*: Are the services and information available?
3. *Affordability*: Can government administration and the citizens afford the access to the information without external financial support?
4. *Capability*: Do the potential users and the staff members of the programme have the skills required for access?
5. *Sustainability*: Will similar services be available in the (near) future?

DistrictNet experiences show that the content needs careful management in order to keep citizens attached to the programme. We have noticed that centralized management of local information does not work as the information is not in line with the local needs and is often outdated or arrives too late to be useful.

Conclusion

DistrictNet has created a wealth of experiences and provides a rich model of reference for other e-governance programmes in Africa. The programme is a showcase of what e-governance in rural areas can look like. New technologies have been introduced and tested, and the programme has provided evidence that the introduction of ICT at the local government level can lead to major improvements in performance. At the same time, the programme shows that the low penetration of ICT skills and equipment in countries like Uganda limits the way such initiatives can move into e-administration and e-services, and makes e-society unreachable for the moment. Governments need to continue their efforts to develop an ICT infrastructure and to increase the penetration of ICT skills among their citizens, especially concentrating their efforts on the rural areas, while development partners should establish more research programmes to ensure the successful implementation and support of ICT.

REFERENCES

Argyris, C., Putnam, R., & McLain Smith, D. (1990). *Action Science: Concepts, Methods, and Skills for Research and Intervention.* San Francisco: Jossey-Bass.

Baskerville, R. (1999). Investigating Information Systems with Action Research. *Communications of the Association of Information Systems,* 2(19).

Bitwayiki, C., & de Jager, A. (2004). *Building Capacity for Embedding: The DistrictNet Uganda Programme.* IICD / capacity.org. Retrieved from http://www.capacity.org and http://www.iicd.org.

Coleman, S. (2005). *African e-governance: Opportunities and Challenges.* Commission for Africa. Retrieved from http://www.commissionforafrica.org.

Dennis, A., & Haley Wixom, B. (2000). *Systems Analysis and Design: An applied approach.* New York: Wiley.

Hammer, M., & Champy J. (1993). *Reengineering the Corporation: A manifesto for business revolution.* New York: HarperCollins.

Heeks, R. (2001a). Understanding e-governance for Development. *I-Government Working Papers No. 11.* Manchester, United Kingdom: University of Manchester, Institute for Development Policy and Management. Retrieved May 2007, from http://www.man.ac.uk/idpm.

Heeks, R. (2001b). Building e-governance for Development: A Framework for National and Donor Action. *I-Government Working Papers No. 12.* Institute for Development Policy and Management, University of Manchester. Retrieved May 2007, from http://www.man.ac.uk/idpm)

IICD. (2004). *The ICT Roundtable Process: Lessons Learned from facilitating ICT-Enabled Development.* The Hague: International Institute for Communication and Development.

Kintu, M.J.R., & Mbeine, E. (2004). *Output to Purpose Review DistrictNet Uganda.* FIT Uganda. Retrieved from http://www.iicd.org.

Leer, A. (2000). *Welcome to the Wired World: Tune in to the Digital Future.* Pearson, Harlow/London.

Menda, A., *Computerising Local Government in Tanzania: The Kinondoni Experience.* iConnect Online, 2005. (www.iconnect-online.org)

Molla, A. (2001) The Impact of eReadiness on eCommerce Success in Developing Countries: Firm Based Evidence. *Development Informatics Working Papers No. 18.* Manchester, United

Kingdom: University of Manchester. Institute for Development Policy and Management. Retrieved from http://www.man.ac.uk/idpm.

Scott, N., Batchelor, S., Ridley, & J., Jorgensen, B. (2004). *The Impact of Mobile Phones in Africa. Commission for Africa.* Retrieved from http://www.commissionforafrica.org.

Shelly, G., Cashman, T.J, & Rosenblatt, H.J. (2001). *Systems Analysis and Design.* Boston: Course Technology/Thomson.

Tusubira, F.F., Kaggwa I., & Ongora J. (2005). In: A. Gillwald (Ed.), *Towards an African e-Index: Household and Individual ICT Access and Usage across 10 African Countries.* The LINK Centre, Wits University School of Public and Development Management.

United Nations. (2003). *World Public Sector Report 2003: E-Governance at the Crossroads.* New York: United Nations, Department of Economic and Social Affairs.

Weddi, D. (2005). *Transforming Local Government: E-Governance in Uganda.* iConnect Online, Retrieved from http://www.iconnect-online.org.

ENDNOTES

[a] The term Business Process Reengineering has attracted enormous attention through Michael Hammer and James Champy's book *Reengineering the Corporation* (1993). In this chapter we do not promote their radical reengineering approach, but consider BPR as a means to fundamentally reconsider the tasks and responsibilities of an organization, and the processes and tools by which an organization may implement these tasks and responsibilities. That is, ICT can be used to trigger BPR.

[b] The original taxonomy of Ntiro, adapted by Heeks, identifies e-citizen and e-services as two separate classes. In this chapter we prefer to use the term e-services only, which includes the class of e-citizens.

[c] DistrictNet programme proposal, 11th February 2002.

[d] The Roundtable Conferences organized by the International Institute for Communication and Development are conferences oriented towards mutual and participative programme formulation. For more information on the roundtable concept, see (IICD, 2004).

[e] Mentioned in the programme proposal of DistrictNet, 11th February 2002.

[f] In the original programme, eight expected outcomes were defined (as described in Kintu, Mbeine, 2004), but some of them showed so much overlap that we have grouped them together.

[g] In 2005 the number of districts was increased from 52 to 76 by "local governmental reorganization"

APPENDIX: LOCAL GOVERNMENT ADMINISTRATIVE STRUCTURE IN UGANDA

Figure 1. Local government administrative structure

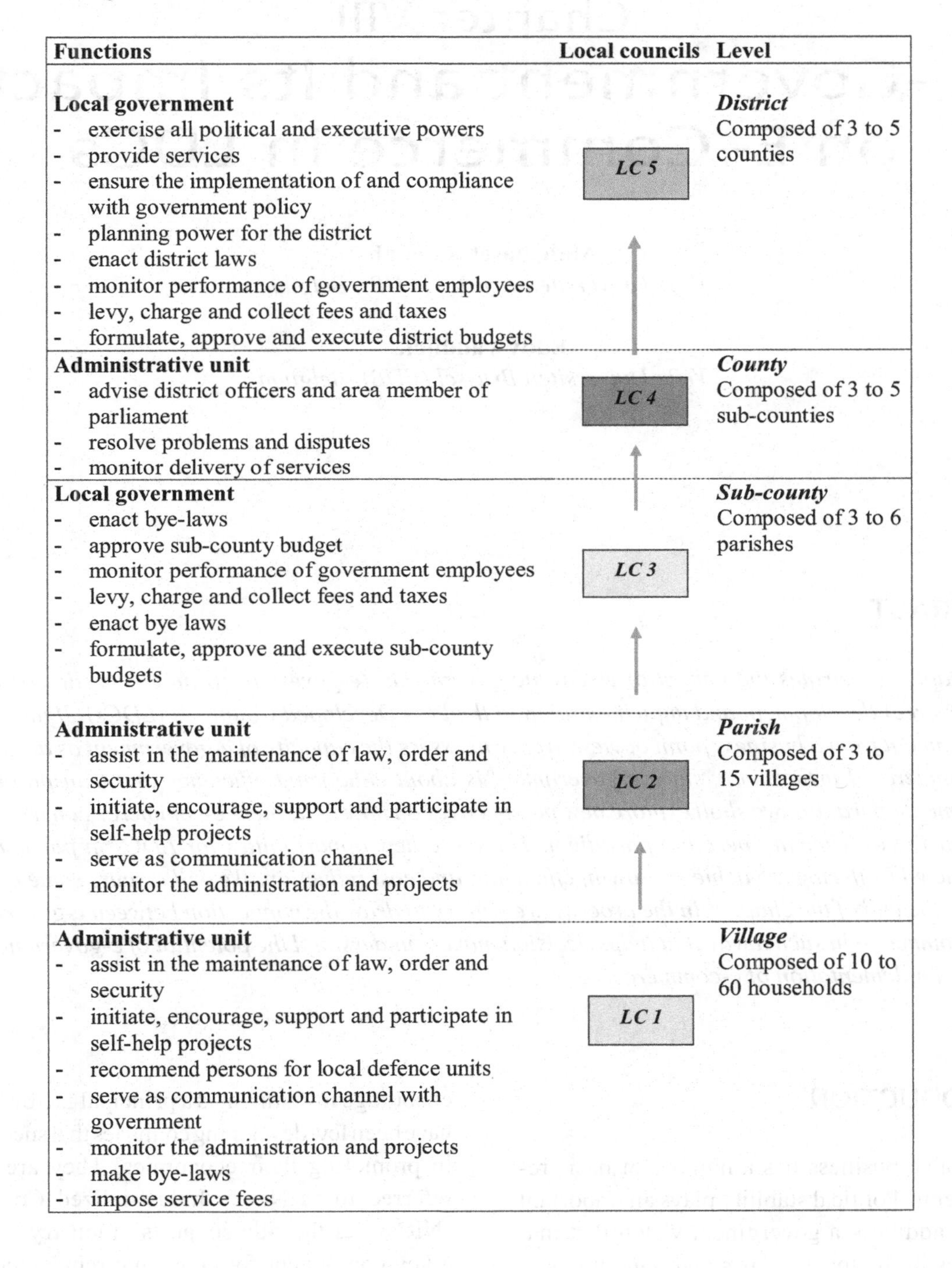

Functions	Local councils	Level
Local government - exercise all political and executive powers - provide services - ensure the implementation of and compliance with government policy - planning power for the district - enact district laws - monitor performance of government employees - levy, charge and collect fees and taxes - formulate, approve and execute district budgets	*LC 5*	***District*** Composed of 3 to 5 counties
Administrative unit - advise district officers and area member of parliament - resolve problems and disputes - monitor delivery of services	*LC 4*	***County*** Composed of 3 to 5 sub-counties
Local government - enact bye-laws - approve sub-county budget - monitor performance of government employees - levy, charge and collect fees and taxes - enact bye laws - formulate, approve and execute sub-county budgets	*LC 3*	***Sub-county*** Composed of 3 to 6 parishes
Administrative unit - assist in the maintenance of law, order and security - initiate, encourage, support and participate in self-help projects - serve as communication channel - monitor the administration and projects	*LC 2*	***Parish*** Composed of 3 to 15 villages
Administrative unit - assist in the maintenance of law, order and security - initiate, encourage, support and participate in self-help projects - recommend persons for local defence units - serve as communication channel with government - monitor the administration and projects - make bye-laws - impose service fees	*LC 1*	***Village*** Composed of 10 to 60 households

Chapter VIII
E-Government and Its Impact on E-Commerce in LDCs

Abdelbaset Rabaiah
Vrije Universiteit Brussel (VUB), Belgium

Eddy Vandijck
Vrije Universiteit Brussel (VUB), Belgium

ABSTRACT

This chapter illustrates the impact of electronic government (e-government) on electronic commerce (e-commerce) development and implementation in the Less Developed Countries (LDCs). It introduces e-government from a business point of view. We try to assess the capacity of e-government as an enabler to e-commerce. Furthermore, since e-government is about enhancing efficiency and transparency of government operation; we shall explore new perspectives on how and where e-commerce can avail from this shift in government operation paradigm. There are new opportunities for LDCs in particular to utilise new IT offerings to achieve growth, efficiency, and cost reduction. We will discuss some of these towards the end of the chapter. In the process, we will try to draw the connection between e-government and e-commerce in such a way that helps decision makers understand the potential of e-government for a better implementation of e-commerce.

INTRODUCTION

Sustainable business has a number of basic requirements. Political stability plays an important role. In addition, a government vision that materialises in the form of laws and regulations to encourage investment is a principal factor. There have been few developing countries that succeeded in promoting their economies. They are often referred to as Newly Industrialized Countries (NICs). As the title suggests "Industry" is still a key component for economic renaissance. To

Copyright © 2009, IGI Global, distributing in print or electronic forms without written permission of IGI Global is prohibited.

maintain quality and competitive industry; knowledge is needed. In the information age, the world witnesses a shift towards Knowledge Economy. In today's global economy, knowledge has become a key component to drive innovations in business. Innovation is necessary for survival amidst the fierce competition. Technology advances rapidly and knowledge is needed in every step of the production process.

Having a good economy goes hand-in-hand with human development. Business cannot thrive in a poor environment neither when the majority of the labour force is unskilled or illiterate. It is our mission in this chapter to provide some important guidelines curb such deficiencies. These suggestions will enlighten decision makers to make informed decisions in order to achieve economic growth. In particular, we will explore the rule of government in giving rise to e-commerce.

According to the UN, the digital divide between north and south is widening. The problem is getting worse as the living environmental conditions are deteriorating in many LDCs. Poverty and famine strike harder. This leaves governments in a position where they strive to meet urgent human needs. In spite of this reality, we will see how savvy governments can wisely seek development through innovative solutions. We will mention some examples of implementation.

One major government responsibility is to try to reduce the digital divide. Reducing the digital divide means that knowledge becomes more and more ubiquitous which impacts all sectors in a society. Knowledge is very much needed for every society. LDCs in particular experience severe lack of professional knowledge. Governments should utilise ICT to promote good living of the society. They should perceive themselves as an enabler to other sectors like business. Public partnership with the private sector is vital. Each government must provide facilitation for building a solid ICT infrastructure. This should be part of their national strategy. Governments themselves should engage in digitizing their operation internally and externally. This has great benefits, as we shall later in the chapter. E-government has a profound impact on e-commerce. This is the main focus area of this chapter.

PREVIOUS STUDIES

Most hitherto research efforts were carried out by scholars who looked at electronic government (e-government) from government perspective. Many research papers were published by scholars involved already in government projects. There has been some serious research in on Public-Private Partnership (PPP) (e.g. Wood-Harper et al, 2004). These papers served largely to stress the importance of PPP as well as to suggest new theories on how to enhance this relationship. Some other research effort on the other hand focused on challenges faced by LDCs in the process of establishing e-government (e.g. Heeks, 2002, Ndou, 2004...etc.)

While most research is single case-based (e.g. Zukauskas & Kasteckiene, 2002) this chapter tries to fill the void by looking globally at how e-government and Electronic Commerce (e-commerce) can prop up one another. In the course of this study, we will introduce e-government from a new perspective and explain how its establishment can really achieve development through the encouragement of investment and the support it provides for the private sector. It is the first attempt to scrutinise the impact of e-government on e-commerce and development in LDCs.

This chapter is more than just exploring the relationship between e-government and e-commerce. It serves as an augmented guide to e-government. It introduces some new ideas for enhancing e-government. LDCs environment is kept in mind while writing the chapter. Whenever possible, reference is made in relation to opportunities and challenges attributed for LDCs.

DEFINITION OF E-GOVERNMENT

In today's world, Internet and the World Wide Web have become a norm of our daily lives. Many of us are attached to the Web and the related services to such an extent that it has occupied a sizable portion of our social lives. We turn to the Web to check our e-mails, view the latest news, communicate with friends in different ways (text, sound, video, virtual reality...etc.), do shopping, listen to music, watch movies, read books, do blogging...etc. With these online services, the Internet has become so indispensable in the modern societies. We use the Internet to interact not only with friends but also with work colleague, professional partners...etc. To this reality, it is no longer acceptable for people of today to still interact with their government the old way they used to fifteen or twenty years ago. We are living in a cyber world within the real one. In the cyber world, data are stored, transferred and processed electronically. Speed and accuracy are the criterion. e-business, e-learning, e-commerce, e-government, e-participation, e-shopping...etc, are thriving and are at the tips of peoples' tongues.

It is safe to say that governments are lagging behind businesses when it comes to online service offering for plenty of reasons. Above all, governments prioritise accuracy and credibility rather than speed (Rabaiah et al, 2006). This puts them on their guard to implementing online services. Nonetheless, some governments excelled in offering online services. According to the research group Gartner, Canada has taken the lead by transforming most of their services into electronic. They were ranked as *trendsetters* transcending all other governments of the world for the last few years.

During the last decade, most world governments have been intensively involved-albeit in varying degrees-in establishing their own online electronic services and creating new ones. The purpose is to keep up with the de facto advancements in information and communication technology (ICT). Some governments were quite successful; others have bungled for plenty of reasons. Most of them launched promising projects to move their services online (or at least some of them.) The official term to describe these projects was e-*government Initiatives*. But what exactly is e-government? There are a number of definitions that vary in complexity. The following are some workable definition of the term e-government according to some high-ranking organizations:

United Nations (UN)
E-government is defined as utilizing the Internet and the world-wide-Web for delivering government information and services to citizens.

World Bank
E-government refers to the use by government agencies of information technologies (such as Wide Area Networks, the Internet, and mobile computing) that have the ability to transform relations with citizens, businesses, and other arms of government.

Global Business Dialogue on Electronic Commerce
Electronic government refers to a situation in which administrative, legislative and judicial agencies (including both central and local governments) digitize their internal and external operations and utilize networked systems efficiently to realize better quality in the provision of public services.

Gartner
E-government is the continuous optimization of service delivery, constituency participation and governance by transforming internal and external relationships trough technology, the internet and new media.

To put it briefly, e-government is all about offering online services. From the citizens point of view this elevates the level of services of the government. The only requirements for him or her to utilise such services are to have access to the Internet and to possess enough skills to use them. From the government's point of view, however, this entails many challenges to make the online services credible, secure and efficient. This also implies that they will work hard to bridge their back office and front office systems and consider all the risks.

As we shall see later, e-government is not just a technical problem; in fact, IBM and hp have long developed complete software packages for e-government implementation that is said to be applicable. Many factors decide the success or failure of e-government initiatives.

E-GOVERNMENT AS A CATALYST FOR E-COMMERCE

Undeniably, e-commerce plays an important role in development. It increases efficiency of the commercial transactions. It facilitates buying and selling over the Internet. The added convenience of conducting business online gives a strong boost for commercial activities of small and big business institutions as well as the customers. Such an environment is obviously attractive to investors. The business sector as a result will grow. For this reason, e-Japan (Japanese e-government initiative) has set e-commerce the next priority after the establishment of an ultrahigh-speed network infrastructure. According to e-Japan, e-commerce is not just the digitisation of paper-based transactions but rather a creation of new modes of transactions that are never thought of before.

Unfortunately, though, e-commerce does not come without irritants. There are many challenges that need to be overcome before e-commerce thrives. One such challenge is the technical infrastructure. An online business transaction is normally conducted between two financial institutions: typically the bank of the seller where the account is credited and the bank of the buyer where the account is debited. If we seek to have a real e-commerce system running nationwide then there must be a common infrastructure utilised by financial institutions.

Common financial infrastructure per se is not the ultimate remedy. It will not function efficiently and securely without regulations. To this, we believe that governments must actually lead on three fronts:

- Establishing the technical infrastructure
- Setting forth regulations in consultation with the private sector
- Piloting e-commerce operation

The Central Banks plays the most important role in building the common infrastructure. It assures inter-operability, efficiency, trust, and accessibility through the common infrastructure and effectuated regulations and guidelines. In many LDCs, each private bank use its own money transfer forms, bank number formats, communication protocols, modus operandi…etc. This diversity in similar bank functionalities makes it difficult for fast, accurate and efficient cross-operation on the national level. In the United States, for examples, the central bank (The Federal Reserve) acts both as an operator and as a regulator of the e-payment system. Regulating the work of financial institutions is meant to reduce risks and build up trust in conducting online transactions. A security breach or operation failure can severely adversely affect customer's trust in e-Payment systems. Proper legislations must be passed to regulate:

- Digital signatures
- Authentications certificates
- Privacy laws
- E-Payment and E-Money guidelines etc…

The Canadian government has built a Secure Channel Network (SCNet) in order to provide secure access to online governmental services.

Later on, a Common Services Roadmap was devised on top of SCNet to support e-commerce operation. In addition, the Canadian government has introduced its basic authentication system called e-pass. E-pass is basically based on public key infrastructure (PKI) technology. The Federal information and communication technology (FEDICT), which is responsible for realising the Belgian e-government's initiative, has also introduced similar authentication system, called (e-ID).

In fact, e-government brings about efficiencies and cost reductions not only for internal government operation but also for businesses. They both become more responsive. In other words, the benefits are mutual. We will delve into more details in connection to this later in the chapter. E-government reach out to e-commerce has a dramatic positive impact on development. It allows the latter to grow quickly by facilitating operation and access to common ICT infrastructure.

E-GOVERNMENT VERSUS E-BUSINESS

It is a fact that businesses are faster than governments when it comes to employing new technologies. This has to do with the competition in the business environment. Technology plays a major role in the operation of businesses. Application of technology is classified into automation, business process re-engineering, business re-conceptualization. The impact of IT can affect the very core of business architecture: the business model. Businesses have been able to gain superior experience in technological implementation. The question is, can governments benefit from such an experience and adopt similar approaches? The following sections explore this possibility in some detail.

The Roadmap to Success

Each profit organization must follow a model in order to achieve profit. A model comes first before anything else in a project. The adopted model should lead institution's activities, allocation of its resources, design of all processes...etc. If a company fails to achieve the projected profits then most likely the business model followed or part of it was inappropriate or it was not implemented correctly. But what exactly is a business model? There is no one universally agreed upon definition for a business model. Slywotzky (1996) defines a business model as "*the totality of how a company selects its customers, defines the tasks it will perform itself and those it will outsource, configures its resources, goes to market, creates utility for customers and captures profit*". A similar yet a more improvised definition by Bouwman (2002): "*A business model provides a description of the roles and relationships of a company, its customer, partners and suppliers, as well as the flows of goods, information and money between these parties and the main benefits for those involved, in particular, but not exclusively the customer*". The last definition is more specific as it describes facets of a business model. This goes in line with the proposition of (Osterwalder & Pigneur, 2002). They identify four main elements of any business model: product; customers; suppliers and partners; and processes that lead to profit. Thus, any business model must provide detailed descriptions of these basic components.

Businesses have adapted to the fast-changing environment in which they operate. They have become flexible in their operation. They have also become more responsive to changes in the business environment. Governments, in contrast, face no such competition. There operation environment is radically different. Instead of, customers, suppliers and partners, we speak of politics, constituency demands. These elements must be reflected in the e-government model. E-government is a continuous optimisation of services. The optimisation process takes government policies as input. Then through research and development, better solutions are introduced. A feedback from the constituency is observed and is looped back to R&D and finally information is disseminated to the respective parties either within or outside the government.

Can E-Government use E-Business Models and Technology Platform?

The purpose of establishing a government entity (GE) is different from that of establishing a firm. The nature of each is different and the models of operation of each of them will thus be different. Another study (Grönlund 2004) has revealed the following discrepancies between the two:

- A firm aims at maximising profit but a government furnishes its citizens with services and maintains stability and well-being of the society. The latter is obviously not a clearly defined goal.
- Citizenship (relationship between a citizen and the government) is very different from consumership (relationship between the customer and the firm). The paradigm of relationship management is different.
- A government follows legal and policy processes while firms normally have administrative and technical ones.
- Business value drives business whereas constituents' needs drive government actions.

That said; the implementation of IT in business is different from that in government. This difference is manifested as:

- In governments, the technical orientation is focused on e-government, e-workflow (Processes), and e-democracy (e-participation and e-voting) whereas the focus is on e-commerce, e-business, outsourcing and integration for businesses.
- For interoperability and data sharing across levels and among braches, obstacles are mostly legal, political, and social, while technical aspects are being the least (Scholl 2005).
- Decision-making in businesses is central and leaves little place for empowerment of employees. This leads to managerial, organizational, and technical problems.

While information sharing among GEs improves transparency, they are reluctant to share information for many reasons. This has very much to do with the stiff bureaucracy in their working environment. Government units operate like silos where cross-functional processes barely exit. Each unit maintains a sort of autonomous status and specific processes, which are not very well integrated with other processes in government units or GEs. This causes inefficiency in productivity. It restrains transparency as well. If bureaucracy is so strong in GEs and can threaten cross-functional processes and system integration then whatever model tailored for e-government should at least cope with it. It must provide solutions to minimise the possible failure due to bureaucracy. The model should fit factual situation of governments a not impose changes on politics.

Most businesses nowadays implement cross-functional processes and abandon silos style of operation to make a more flattened and thus flexible and efficient workflow (Laudon 2006). This methodology cannot be directly applied to GEs as the emphasis for the latter is correctness and credibility rather than speed and efficiency.

Table 1 summarizes these differences.

In short, "A government is not a firm". Similarly, e-government and e-business cannot be approached the same way. Borrowing successful models from business does not necessarily mean that they will also work well for governments.

Table 1. Differences between government and business, adapted from Grönlund (2004)

Criteria	Business	Government
Aim	Maximize Profit (Clearly Defined)	Well-being of Society (Stability)
Driver	Business Value	Constituents' Needs
Processes	Administrative/Technical	Legal/Political
Clients Relationship Paradigm	Consumership	Citizenship
Operation	Centralized	Decentralized/Autonomous
Emphasis	Efficiency, Profitability	Correctness, credibility

Figure 1. E-government development process

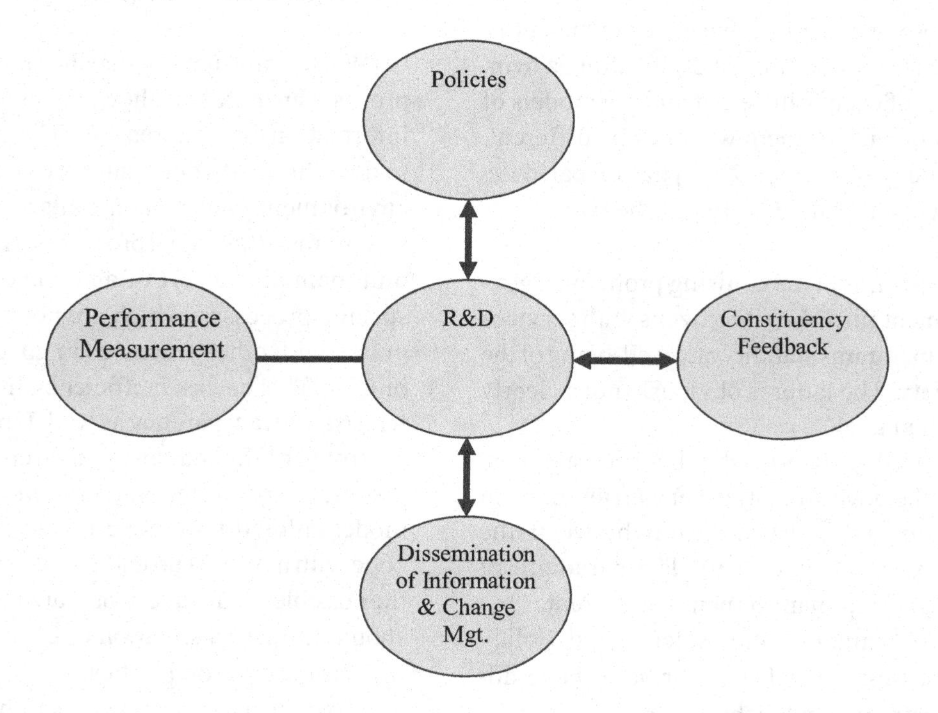

As we can see in Figure 1 the research and development (R&D) unit within the government constitutes the core of the e-government development process. It is normally a committee of specialists formed prior to the launch of the e-government initiative. It orchestrates efforts of all government units to help them join the transformation towards an e-government. In its operation, this unit sticks to policies set forth by the government. Such policies govern, among other things, the way technology is implemented. Policy shift can seriously jeopardise e-government implementation. This makes it more difficult for the R&D unit to develop efficient solutions in e-government than in business. E-government projects require continuous political support of the highest levels. By contrast, stiff government policies do not exist in business.

Constituency demands (public opinions) and employees' level of satisfaction are recorded through the feed back process as suggested in Figure 1. Such demands are responded to in the next iteration of design update. If a change to a part of the e-government architecture is brought about then the description of the change in terms of new capabilities added or efficiencies or procedures must be communicated to the people concerned (citizens, businesses or public servants). In addition, change management in the affected agencies must be carried out carefully. Without considerate change management it is not very uncommon that the new implementation fails.

E-GOVERNMENT STRATEGY

An e-government strategy is a detailed long-term plan that ushers success of the whole e-government project. It incorporates details on procedures and actions. Milestones, solutions to problems, answers to challenges are all well articulated. Planning to all scenarios is part of the e-government strategy. This augmented strategy can have sub strategies prepared and carried out by each subsidiary of the central government.

First, government must have a vision and a political will to launch its e-government initiative. This vision is necessary, as it will be always the motto of the executive committee. It will always be referred to during implementation later on. It manifests political will. From this vision, the committee is held accountable to lays out the mission statement, which is normally more expressive than the vision and contains further details. From the mission statement the committee highlights strategic objectives of the whole endeavour. It is important for the committee to be able to measure the performance and advancement of the project. If an objective is not measurable, it is hardly attainable. Next, the critical success factors are identified. The committee will then assign a taskforce to work on each objective. Unlike the committee, a taskforce's lifetime is limited to the completion of the task assigned to it. An example is a team of security experts working to lay out the security plan.

It is very important to set phases in the framework. E-government is obviously a large-scale project that must be planed carefully. The stakes of failure are high. Besides, it is evolutionary in nature. It cannot happen immediately by just procuring a new hardware platform or a software system. Divide-and-conquer or incremental approach is the best methodology to tackle such a huge endeavour. As such, the whole project is divided and is perceived as a collection of smaller sub-projects. The whole framework should be designed in such a way to minimize the effect of one sub-project failing on the overall evolution.

E-government is essentially sought to satisfy three fundamental objectives: constituency services; operation proficiency; and political return. These objectives should be taken into account when putting together the e-government strategy and implementation framework.

Constituency Services

Government customers (citizens and businesses) solicit a responsive government. They demand effective ways of interaction with their government just as they do with business. They need ubiquitous information, better and faster communication channels, carry out online transactions, and practice political participation electronically (e-participation). Pressure from citizens and businesses pushes governments to establish e-government services.

Operational Proficiency

Most citizens especially in the developed countries use the Internet quite often to access a plethora of services. They expect their government to provide online services in a similar manner. It is no longer suitable to continue to use the same traditional manual procedures/processes. Therefore, governments should re-engineer and streamline their processes to allow online services. In fact, e-government projects caused serious alterations to laws and regulations adopted by governments worldwide. It allowed for simplified processes. Governments expect the new technology to bring about a higher level of efficiency, transparency and effectiveness.

Political Return

There are short-term and long-term political returns from the effectuation of e-government. On the short-term, the new efficiencies expected from e-government will have a dramatic impact on cost reduction. The cost reduction is multifaceted. The government will save time and money because it will use fewer resources and faster processes.

The long-term return on investment is development, be it human development, business development...etc. In the end, standards of living will become higher. Political will is a key component for the success or failure of any e-government initiative. This is quite challenging in an environment where political influences of all the players is so strong. A rigorous and continuous attempt to convince politicians and get them involved in the projects is crucial. Therefore, such short and long-term returns on investment must be clearly highlighted by the e-government committee.

In many cases, governments chose to engage in e-government for their national esteem. Some of them declare to be the number one country of e-government implementation like Canada, for example. Others do not want to be left behind. They just want to follow the tide and show their posing presence.

CHALLENGES FACING E-GOVERNMENT

The blessing of e-government does not come about without irritants. The battle must be fought on a number of levels. Each level poses unique challenges. These levels can be generally divided into political, social, legal and technical.

Political Challenges

Realisation of e-government must first address political challenges. This is where the whole project starts. If the political will does not exist, such a large-scale project will never see light. E-government initiatives face many glitches on the road of implementation. Political support is vital at every step. Governments with rigorous e-government vision and enthusiasm (e.g. Canada) have excelled. The lack of political commitment can fail the project at the earliest stages.

However, political enthusiasm must be translated into seamless planning and dedication of all kinds of resources (monetary, skills, time, efforts, empowerment, training, education...etc). It is not enough to have political will and a strategic vision although these are the primary components for success.

Social Challenges

Social challenges are different for developed and developing countries. People in developed countries are more familiar with technology than those of the developing countries. Jumping to advanced technological solutions might cause a technological shock to many people in LDCs. If technology becomes readily available and yet the masses are incapable of using it then we have achieved nothing. The whole would be considered a failure because it would fail to achieve its goal. An assessment of public readiness for e-government within a country must be made. Computer literacy surveys should be carried out. A plan must then be put together to raise computer literacy through awareness campaigns. Gulf Arab states have excelled in human development during the past decade. They have developed state-of-the-art training centres for this purpose.

Many LDCs are plagued with illiteracy. If locals are hopelessly illiterate then radio broadcasts that draw information from the Internet can be a forthcoming source of information. The latter, after all, can take many forms and disseminated in different ways including radio broadcast. Local radio stations are much popular than one can imagine especially in developing countries where not everybody can have a computer at home. Prices of radio sets are much lower than personal computers. Besides, simplicity of operation is far more convenient. This makes it well suited for illiterates.

Digital Divide

A very noticeable socio-technical concern is the digital divide. It exists in all societies but it is more severe between the north and the south on the global level. Digital divide has three dimensions:

- **Education and skills:** In this context, the digital divide is simply the gap between those who possess knowledge and skills in ICT and those who do not. This is a major challenge to governments especially if the number of those who need education and training is huge. The whole e-government is in vein if a large sector of the population is computer and Internet illiterate. Clearly, the solution is to start training as many people as possible utilising educations centres like schools and universities after normal working hours. There are many examples of governments who took on this approach. IT Centres of Excellence are usually established to provide training and certification. Universities and schools can assume this rule. The government of Canada has provided public Internet terminals where anybody can use them freely to access the Internet. Computer labs at schools are also open to the public after normal working hours.
- **Web access***:* if people are well educated on using computer and Internet technologies there is still another challenge. Citizens must be able to access the Internet. For this reason, the government with the help of telecom companies must provide the necessary backbone connections and broadband Internet access. There are normally discrepancies in penetration rates between rural and urban areas. Broadband wireless access (e.g. WiFi, WiMAX, HSDPA, 3G…etc.) can be a quick remedy to this. This type of communication is easily installed and spans across large areas where no infrastructure is present. Another challenge is to provide access to people with disabilities. It is the government's responsibility to configure there online services in such a way that they are accessible by blind, deaf and people with other kinds of disabilities. In some cases, special hardware and software must be procured.
- **Poverty:** The last problem of digital divide is low-income and poverty. People in many LDCs cannot afford subscription fees, hardware cost…etc. This would marginalise them and prevent them from the treats of improved and convenient services of e-government. However, with a national strategy that aims at economic development, this problem can be curbed. In a number of countries dial up connection has become free. In the Palestinian Territories, citizens have free dial-up access.

Privacy and Security

Government should demonstrate to its citizens that their privacy is preserved. Laws must be modernised to assimilate the new advancements in ICT. Privacy laws should be secluded by the constitution. LDCs have fallen behind in this regard. Privacy and security must be a core component of e-government implementation. They must not be added later on. They should be well thought out from the beginning. Furthermore, they must be reviewed constantly. Digitised processes must incorporate security measures and be privacy-sensitive. If not taken into consideration, private information is at stake. Manipulation of voting results, for example, can be possible in the absence of unblemished measures. This ushers disastrous consequences.

Hacker attacks must be taken extremely seriously. Dedicated secure intranets protected by multiple levels firewall security are normally used in e-governments. The open Internet should never be used to carry out G2E or G2G transactions.

In addition to citizens' privacy and security, proper service continuity plans must be prepared and simulated. This guarantees continuous availability of critical services in severe conditions.

With advent of e-government, identity theft becomes even more catastrophic. Stolen credit card numbers is already a big issue in e-commerce with billions of dollars stolen each year. But the losses are just financial. In e-government, the term "Identity Theft" will be literally possible if no careful measures are applied especially at the level of authentication. Transactions carried out at a government's portal are completely different from that of a shopping Website. They involve sensitive documents like passports, identity cards, birth certificates…etc. Some of the top sensitive processes (e.g. changing names) must be verified the traditional way.

Corruption

As with all new inventions, e-government can be misused. Corrupt politicians can use e-government in a bad way. All information including transactions is captured on government's servers. It is possible, in principle, to find out to which a certain individual has given his or her vote. If corrupt people have gained power, they can even change results without anybody knowing about them. This is a great threat to democracy. Therefore, legislations alone are not a deterrent. They must be backed by practical solutions to such problems.

Legal Challenges

The role of a government is to practice governance and maintain the well-being of the society. In contrast, the role of business is to achieve maximum profit with least cost. This huge difference in role has its influence on processes. For a government process, a number of strict considerations have to be taken into account at design time and at run time.

Government processes follow delicate legal constraints. Legal constraints come first in the planning of government processes. After all, government is supposed to enforce law and order. Failure to do so ushers corruption and even chaos. Corruption in a government has far severer impact on the population than that in a business. Governments -especially democratic ones- make sure that they abide by the law. Corruption and lack of transparency has severe political and social consequences. With this ugly formula, there is no way to address accountability. Furthermore, persecution and bias can become so widespread.

When developing technical solutions in the course of e-government implementation, legal issues must be taken into account strictly. Governments do not enjoy the same level of flexibility as businesses do. In the process, a review of current laws and regulations can be reviewed in light of the new advancements in operation. Retarding laws can be flagged for alteration or update for more efficiency.

Technical

Technical Hitches and glitches are countless. Building technical solutions from scratches normally faces challenges, hindrances or failures. Some governments choose to employ tested solutions but may discover later that they were ill-suited for their needs. In some other cases technical problems might be so challenging that they halt the whole project's implementation. Research and Development (R&D) is usually setup to work on such problems. Therefore, R&D must be an integral part of e-government implementation (see Figure 1).

BENEFITS OF E-GOVERNMENT

It is important to enumerate the benefits of implementing e-government. In fact, failure to state the benefits clearly will be a primary obstacle realizing e-government. Decision makers will not be convinced unless they realise the expected benefits. Governments are supposed to invest and spend money wisely and in the right place. Remember that businesses are more willing to invest in new technologies. They are ready to accept a higher level of risk for competitive reasons. This is not evident in governments. We will now introduce a number of benefits of e-government implementation.

Political and Governance Benefits

E-government facilitates a healthy political life in the society. Rural and remote regions will have better penetration rates. Access to relevant information will not only be limited to large cities. The more the number of people will have access to government information and services the better informed they will be. In addition, when citizens are more informed about the political process they can participate effectively. This is good for development.

The new electronic channel will increase participation in the political process. Electronic participation (e-participation) makes it more convenient for citizens during elections. It also saves the government and businesses money, as citizens do not have to leave their workplaces to go for voting. Diminishing human involvement in the processes reduces corruption and produces fewer errors.

Economic Benefits

The resulted efficiencies from e-government have positive effects on the economy:

Operational Efficiency and Cost Reduction

E-government is more than just automation of government services. Some processes will have to be re-engineered for the new channel. Responsiveness across government agencies will be faster. Complexity of operation and organization will be reduced. This leads to better management of resources. In addition, the new channel is much cheaper than traditional channels. Sending an e-mail is much quicker and costs nothing compared to snail mail. Up to 40% cost reduction can be reached. Besides, once information is electronic it is faster to search. On the other hand, electronic information sharing can reduce costs, duplication of efforts and inconsistencies. A proper clustering and taxonomy of information accompanied by syndicating different contents to different users must be adopted.

Codifying knowledge is very important to keep the "memory" of the government. Information can be accessed easily after a long time when it is encoded in an electronic form. Information is easily converted from one format into another. If it remains on paper, it will never be accessed and manipulated remotely. Moreover, it would be very tedious to dig a pile of paper files in a government archive to look for an old official document (I once did!).

Electronic services are self-service by nature at least for the first stages in the process. This leads to up to 90% reduction of Clerical work. Loads on the shoulders of public servants in front offices are reduced. Intelligent expert systems can handle large volumes of online requests at ease. They minimise chances of human errors as well.

Effect of E-Government on Competitiveness

The use of ICT will surely increase productivity for businesses especially if ICT is used throughout all the production phases. The increased productivity drives competitiveness. In the end, when all competitors use efficient solutions, end products will have higher quality. Production costs will be lower and end prices will diminish. The lower the process the more satisfied consumers will become. They can save the money for other expenses. This will have some effect on the overall development. There would be more money to spend on education and health.

E-government can play an important role to increase competitiveness on three aspects:

- The establishment of a common IT infrastructure would essentially increase e-competency among local businesses. Companies will deploy advanced IT systems to gain a competitive advantage. The use of connected systems will become a new field of for competitiveness. The level of service, as a result, will increase.
- Better taxation policies: such policies must always have competitiveness in mind. The taxation system should encourage competitiveness among companies.
- Direct government spending: By building the necessary infrastructures and public services
- New efficient regulations: e-government requires changing old inefficient regulation, laws, and legislations.

Consumers Convenience and Cost Reduction

E-government, by definition, should improve services. The quality of services would be better at reduced response times and cost. It is even possible to offer brand new services. For citizens and businesses, the savings are significant. Because of one-stop online services, an individual will no longer have travel for different government agencies to get a service done. He or she will not stand in line again. Furthermore, services are available 24/7, which allows the citizen to ask for a service at the time of his or her convenience without interruption to his daily work. Less travel journeys mean huge energy savings countrywide. Since the government becomes more responsive, the time needed to complete a service is dramatically reduced and as the adage says: "time is money" it implies further cost savings.

Another convenience for a citizen is that he or she can track the status of his or her application online without paying anything. This will save citizens the cost of phone calls otherwise. Similarly, it will save the government a lot of working hours for help desk operators.

As mentioned earlier, to use electronic services, individuals must possess ICT skills. This could be a by-product of e-government. People will be thrilled to use the convenience of the new technologies. In the end, the total number of ICT-knowledgeable people will increase because of ICT training. This reflects on their chances of getter better jobs with their new knowledge in ICT.

Cost savings apply to business too. As interaction with the government has a new cheaper channel, they will reduce costs. In addition, electronic procurement (e-procurement) and online supply chain management will allow small companies to bid at lower costs.

Social Benefits

Enhanced transparency, accountability, efficiency and democracy will have positive effects on the society as a whole. These are important ingredients of social developments. Besides, there are other qualities of e-governments, which are hard to quantify. It is hard, for instance, to measure the effect of citizen satisfaction in government services. Satisfaction will surely change the mode of individuals and perception of their government for the better. The negative view of government bureaucracy will abolish.

The developed ICT infrastructure should provide room for new innovative projects in health, education, agriculture…etc.

Impact of E-Government on E-Business

E-government and e-businesses face similar technical and regulatory challenges. Partnership will result in joint effort that has a synergic effect. Government will be deeply involved and can understand business needs better. This will reflect on government strategies. They would abolish retarding regulations and laws that limit e-business. The government will need to joint-venture the private sector to outsource services, especially ICT. This will increase cooperation of both sectors. Each sector will understand better the needs of the other. The two sectors will come closer to the notion of partnership.

IMPROVING E-GOVERNING IN LDCS

E-government requires abundant resources to function properly. Unfortunately, many LDCs are plagued by scarcity of monetary resources. There are almost always huge deficits in yearly budgets. The budget of an LDC is in many cases a fraction of its developed counter-parts. For example, Egypt is a home of some 80 million people. It is about three times the geographical area of Germany, which has a population of 82 millions. Even though, the budget of Egypt is less than 1 % of that of Germany for the year (2006).

Despite abundant resources in many developed countries on the other hand, little is being shifted towards e-government. That's why we still see some developed countries with lower maturity level of e-government implementation.

Some LDCs (particularly in sub-Saharan Africa) suffer from famine. Clearly, these governments strive to furnish citizens with only the necessities. Little or nothing is virtually left in many cases for e-government. Yet, LDCs can still reach some basic level of e-government implementation with relatively little investments. The gains from such small investments can improve governance and facilitate operation to some extent. In this section, we will introduce some practical applications that can help both developed and under-developed countries. All of these applications require relatively low investment.

On the implementation level, the best policy it to follow the "Divide and Conquer" methodology. As e-government is a large scale endeavour it cannot be approached as a single project but rather as a collection of sub project. This minimises the risks of failure. It is also advised to implement e-government in an incremental approach. This way, the results will be felt quicker. As soon as a sub-project is ready, it can be set operational regardless of the completion of other projects. Many governments actually perceive e-government as a collection of projects as in the case of Belgium. However, it is very important that interoperability is always taken into account. Each project must follow the same guidelines for integration. *Data portability* is key for any e-government project if we are to have a *connected* government.

Online Presence

Though online presence is the simplest form of e-government, it is essential since it makes information available for the pubic. It is simple and cheap enough to enrich static Web pages with database connectivity. This allows for customised and dynamic content. The Web pages in this case draw their key content from a database.

E-Mail

The idea behind electronic mail or e-mail is very simple yet this is a very efficient and useful tool. It is so trivial that in many cases it is overlooked by system designers who look for more sophisticated solutions. Such sophisticated solutions, however, do not come without cost. Normally, they come at huge costs and require aggressive maintenance.

E-mail constitutes a major two-way communication channel of service delivery in e-government. Compared to other forms of communication, e-mail is more formal similar to a fax in this sense. Its asynchronous nature makes it quite beneficial for e-government application. It incurs huge savings nation-wide as it replaces traditional phone calls. There is no need for amplified help desk staff to answer clients' phone calls. On the other hand, it costs almost nothing to send an e-mail with all sorts of attachments. It is a service that is naturally accessible 24/7.

E-mail systems are simple and easy to setup. Their installation costs are negligible. It does not require maintenance and updating costs and efforts as do other state-of-the-art systems. Furthermore, many hardware systems come e-mail ready out f the box (think about PDAs, Smartphones...etc). An e-mail system can be accessed across different hardware and software platforms. This tool can really be used to provide G2G, G2E, G2B and G2C interactions at reasonably low cost. This makes it a precious tool for LDCs.

Simplified Knowledge Management

State-of-the-art knowledge management systems (KMS) are generally very expensive. A commercial KMS license can cost between US$ 150,000 to 1 million. Cost of ownership is even multiple times larger (Wagner et al, 2003). But some simplified KMS can be both simpler and cheaper. They call for less maintenance and updates. It is simple enough to create a directory of professionals with their field of specialty and expertise in a database and then make it accessible via Web pages. It is equally possible to make a list of requirements, conditions, exceptions...etc of a process. This helps cherish the government's unit memory and knowledge. In addition, information for investors can prove beneficial to draw investment. Also posting CVs for graduates with the same simple technique can contribute to the reduction of unemployment.

ICT can be utilised to build virtual communities (Wang et al, 2003). A virtual community is a cyber aggregation of people who share common interests. Underlying technologies can vary from e-mail to chat rooms to online forums to work groups...etc. Virtual communities serve as a dissemination engine of information and knowledge. A government, after all, must find some way to disseminate information among employees in a fast, reliable and cheap manner.

Pubic Private Sector Partnership

One way in which a government can enhance its online service offering is through public-private partnership (PPP). Unlike outsourcing private companies, PPP means that both government and the private companies share profits as well as risk through a contractual agreement. Many countries face difficulties in approving budgets. PPP can help getting e-government projects across. PPP can rid governments from financing, maintaining and managing infrastructures of certain online services. It can also innovate online service offerings, as new ideas are likely to immerge from a business partner.

PPP is not something new, in many countries contractual agreements were signed between governments and private partners to build and run hospitals, prisons, power plants…etc. Some other governments collaborate with private companies to support the army. For example, half the American security personnel in Iraq belong to private companies. What is new, however, for PPP in e-government is service delivery. Institutions from the private sector can devise, run and maintain governmental online services. This leads to enhancing government services quite noticeably.

Private companies, however, seek profit. It is imperative for PPP to be tempting to both parties. There are different sources of profit. The following are some opportunities:

- Revenues in the form of subscription fees for the automated services
- Revenues from transaction fees
- Advertisements on the e-government portal

There are two caveats that must be dealt with properly when drafting the contractual agreement. The government must make sure that no personally-identifiable information can be disclosed by the private partner. The rule of thumb is that privacy of customers must be preserved by the private partner as if the information or service is maintained by the government itself. Also it is important to make sure that the level of security provided is as high as the government itself would allow it to be.

An example of PPP is TexasOnline. This is the online portal for the state of Texas. The government of Texas has collaborated with a private company (BearingPoint) to devise, manage and run online services. With a $23 million investment, the company could achieve profits of $1 billion. This profit was shared by BearingPoint and the government on the bases signed agreement.

In order to promote the use of e-government services further, some countries have set up E-Government Centres of Excellence (E-Gove COE). Such centres increase awareness though special campaigns. They provide piloting and spearheading of innovation. In addition, E-Gov COE encourage competitiveness among government units. E-Gov COE might be perceived as the factory for e-government development where research and testing can take place and if a system is ready, it is populated to the other government units. This is where best practises churn out. This way such centres increase readiness for e-government. They can also be the glue for a strong public-private partnership.

When resources are available, many applications can be implemented to enhance e-government. Among these are:

- Geographical information systems (GIS): Providing spatial services.
- E-procurement: Electronic management of public tendering.
- Client-centric approach: Services are designed and implemented not according to government units' needs and constraints but rather clients' (citizens and businesses) needs.
- Client relationship management (CRM): Managing relationships with clients electronically and offering customised services for individuals.
- Increasing the number of servers
- Implementing boadband network
- Extending e-government with mobile government (m-government) and ubiquitous Government (u-government)
- E-authentication (Smartcards)
- Enhancing security
- Protecting privacy
- Identity management projects

EXTENSIONS TO E-GOVERNMENT

E-Government has witnessed major advancements during the last decade. New breakthroughs in wireless communications, satellite industry and geographical information systems (GIS) have brought about new opportunities for innovative e-government applications. The applications were significant enough to become new disciplines within the context of e-government. Mobile government (m-government), geographical (GIS/GPS) government (g-government), and ubiquitous government (u-government) will be introduced immediately. We shall explore the potential of these advanced and ubiquitous technologies. They have direct impact on the daily life of citizens/businesses, as they make possible exalted services on the go.

M-Government

Cellular networks and handheld devices have achieved high penetration rates worldwide. Mobile operators have invested in new markets worldwide. According to Gartner, revenue from mobile services will peak at almost $55 billion in 2008. GSM, GPRS and EDGE alone will account for $24.6 billion. In the Middle East and Africa, revenue from sales of mobile network infrastructure grows annually at a rate of 12% for 2005 to 2010, bringing the annual total to $8.5 billion. This constitutes a large portion of their economies. With the availability of such an advanced infrastructure, related services and economies will tag on. Installing and updating cellular networks are faster and easier than traditional landline networks. They can span large distances in remote areas.

Around 991 million mobile units were sold globally in 2006, a 21% increase over 2005. In the Eastern Europe, Middle East and Africa 52.4 million units were sold in the 4th quarter of 2006. This was 13% higher than that of 2005 of the same period. There is currently a high demand for refurbished mobile phones in emerging markets. By 2008, ultra-low-cost handsets will account for about half of all basic phones sold in regions with emerging economies.

Functionality of current mobile devices has been expanded. An MP3 player, a digital still and video camera, a GPS navigator, an FM radio, a TV and a computer processor can all be crammed into one palm-sized device today. Such devices are typically equipped with diverse communication channels. In addition to regular cellular communication, they can be hooked up other devices through Bluetooth, WiFi, WiMAX, 3G, HSDPA, IR…etc. Adding their capacity to house software applications makes these devices superior pocket tools. with They can access the Web in different ways and through any communication channel. They have their own operating systems. They can be used to do e-commerce easily. Such converged devices have been given different nomenclatures. Smartphones, PDA phones, PocketPCs, or recently Computer Phones (Cellular UMPCs). The differences in naming conventions can be confusing but they are certainly powerful mobile gadgets. On the global level, Smartphone and PDA shipments grew 42.7% in 2006 compared with 2005 (Gartner Dataquest, 2007). Their sales are expected to continue to grow through 2010.

This remarkable penetration rate of handheld devices together with the expansion of wireless networks have ushered the beginning of mobile government (m-government). Mobile government (m-government)

> *is a strategy and its implementation by the government to provide information, deliver services, engage citizens and improve efficiency through mobile devices (Sang et al 2006).*

This makes it an extension to e-government to mobile platforms. In other words, it is about delivering government services and information through wireless communication networks to end users who use mobile media like mobile phones, Smartphones, PDAs, Laptop computers, UMPCs…etc. This will practically allow access to government services anytime and anywhere. M-Government leverages the convenience and flexibility to a new level. It furnishes citizens and businesses with a practical way to access government services. In addition, the government would able to reach out to a larger number of people through mobile devices. An example is sending short text messages (SMS) to the masses in case of Tsunami or similar threats. Despite the obvious advantages, there are some issues to be addresses. Among these is security. Mobile devices can be easily stolen or tapped into, especially with the abundance of insecure WiFi networks. This puts private information at risk. Another challenge for the government is to customise their services for mobile phones' tiny screens, limited memory, small keypads and underpowered processing capabilities. This means re-designing their portals or employing rendering techniques.

G-Government

With GIS, soliciting data becomes more efficient. Governments can design their Websites to allow for spatial data search. An example is searching for the nearest governmental services. The way search results are displayed makes it quite convenient for citizens, businesses and other government units. Instead of having the results displayed in tabular form, they are layered on maps. A citizen for instance can easily look for garbage collection facilities in his/her area. Businesses can discover the local industrial or commercial sites, real estate agents, transportations facilities…etc. On the government-to-government level, g-government can lead to more efficient cross-agency cooperation. Examples include cross-jurisdiction activities like fire-fighting, crime investigation…etc. All of these services are offered 24/7. As these services are carried out via Web applications, governments can save costs by reducing the number of staff in call centres. The city of Sacramento in the United States reported to have saved an estimate of $1.8 million per year by offering GIS-enabled Web services. Up to 500 people were serviced by their Website daily.

Combining g-government with m-government can bring e-government to an elevated level of services. About 12.7 million in-vehicle GPS navigation systems were made in 2005, and the figure for 2010 will be 30 million (Gartner Dataquest, 2006). By the end of 2010, almost 40% of handsets will support GPS. As in the case of location-based commercial services, governments can offer their services for individuals, businesses and government employees on the move. A citizen for example, can be automatically put through to the closest police station to his current location to report a crime or an accident. In the United States, mobile phone manufacturers will be obliged to include a GPS module for a better 911 service (emergency service).

U-Government

The rapid advances in wireless communications, feature-rich and omni-connected handheld devices, nanotechnology, interoperability…etc will all bring us closer and closer to ubiquitous government (u-government). U-government is the ultimate form of e-government. In u-government services offered are really accessible anywhere anytime in plenty of ways never thought before. U-government stems from ubiquitous computing. The latter describes a paradigm shift where many computational devices and systems collaborate to carry out ordinary tasks without overall systems knowledge of such tasks. Smart devices (e.g. Smartphones, smart cards…etc) are becoming widely used. Nanotechnology might bring us cheaper, intelligent and ever connected inventions that make government service delivery unrestricted by time, place or means. This is sometimes referred to as *Ambient Intelligence*. With time, technologies become more advanced, efficient, faster, smarter and cheaper. Transmission of information would be seamless, timely and cheap and in various forms never reckoned possible.

Today, there are some examples of u-government. Many governments have developed digital identity cards and passports. They make it more efficient and convenient to update personal information. Digital passports are anticipated to increase efficiency and security at airports. Many cell phones are capable of accessing Websites anywhere anytime using broadband wireless connections. This, though, is only the beginning to offering full u-government services. Mobile phones are recently announced to replace boarding passes at airports.

Such technologies bring new challenges. Privacy is traditionally an issue here. There should be rigorous regulations to make sure of safe usage of such advanced technologies. Security also becomes more challenging. These two challenges have been and will always be persistent with any new technology.

LDC-Specific Environment Characteristics

Generally speaking, there are economic, political, cultural, and demographic differences between developed and underdeveloped countries. There is an obvious difference in ICT readiness. On top of that, there are mild to severe differences in levels of education and wealth. These differences reflect as well on the company levels.

(Austin, 1990) has studies this issue in details in his book" Managing in Developing Countries - Strategic Analysis and Operating Techniques". He mentioned that developing countries are plagued by the following:

- Governmental controls
- Rampant inflation and devaluation
- Cumbersome bureaucratic procedures for obtaining import licenses
- Skill scarcity
- Difficulties with training new employees on new technology
- Lack of political stability
- Scarcity in logistics

The latter point hinders any outsourcing plans in local regions. There are fewer advanced and reliable industries or business in certain fields. For instance, if a company wants to outsource backup of its data chances are slim of finding a local company that can do that.

Any company willing to operate in an LDC must be aware of what the local environment can bring about. The hardest part in their quest is getting the right information from their credible sources. It is a major setback to stumble across an unforeseen law or regulation that may draw an end to a project. This is where e-government can really be of great benefit to foreign as-well-as local investors. E-government would presumably make all sorts of information easily accessible for investors. This is one good reason why e-government can drive development in an LDC.

Differences in culture can bring some risks to business. Employees from different cultures working together must really understand each other's differences on the personal and on the professional levels. In addition, Level of Service of each joint-venturing or outsourcing company must be compatible to some extent. If a company with a high level of service or maturity liaise with another of a lower level then expectations from each are different. In many cases, this leads to a standstill in operation. This can dangerously put a project on halt.

Besides, working in politically unstable environment adds a severe threat to the mix. Unlike in the developing countries, geopolitical situation in LDCs must always be monitored closely as it affects operation of companies directly. Political risk assessment here is necessary.

Investing in an LDC must not be understood as fruitless. On the contrary, there are important opportunities that companies need to hunt. Many

LDCs have plenty of skilful workforces that are well-trained and low-paid which is a practical formula for maximising returns on investment. On the demographic front, many LDCs are heavily populated. Investing in low-priced but large volume products and services can prove lucrative. The caveat here is to account for the new different kinds of risk in advance and to curb them with appropriate measures.

The Learning E-Government

We have seen the impact of e-government on e-commerce. Nevertheless, there is just the opposite effect. E-government can learn from businesses. In fact, many of the solutions adopted by e-governments today are the best-tested solutions that were implemented in businesses. Business solutions can form a testing environment for e-government. Despite our arguments earlier in the chapter about differences between governments and businesses, we believe that government can benefit from experiences of the private sector. It is true that there are differences but there are also similarities. We do not call for directly implementing business solutions to governments but rather to promote government learning from business. Albert Gore and Scott Adams argue in their book "Businesslike Government: Lessons Learned from America's Best Companies" that governments can learn a lot from business practises. The authors stress that innovation in e-government can stem from the working force (the government employees) who know risk, mistakes and opportunities of e-government. They call for the stimulation of government employees to innovate.

Some scholars have identified possible private sector's participation in establishing operating e-government projects (e.g. Zukauskas & Kasteckiene, 2002). Private companies can participate in building the infrastructure needed to support online services as mentioned earlier. The can also provide the public sector with their expertise. In addition, they can directly carry out transactions on behalf of the public sector. Another form of participation is to joint-venture projects with the public sector in the form of packaged public/private sector solutions. Finally, Business can affect government in an indirect way. Since citizens are now used on buying products and services over the Internet, they would expect something similar from their government. Hopefully, this would put some pressure on governments to offer online services.

OPPORTUNITIES FOR LDCS

We have introduced enough information that should familiarise the reader with e-government. In preparation of this material, we have always had LDCs in mind. In this section, we will discuss impact of e-government and the related technologies on development of LDCs. Can e-government hold some opportunities for LDCs in particular? We will show that LDCs can avail from e-government and ICT in a way that was not possible for developed countries. To make development a priority, it must be embedded in the e-government strategy from its initiation. The strategy should have answers on how to fight poverty and achieve development on different levels.

ICT as an Enabler for Business

ICT for Business must go hand-in-hand with ICT development and fighting poverty. ICT must be available and affordable to the public in order to achieve development yet there are certain considerations to be taken into account. Introduction of ICT in LDCs must be carefully planed and managed.

These technologies must be market-driven as much as possible and wherever is possible. This will meet demands efficiently. They should have multi-stakeholders with vigorous government involvement. Government should perceive itself as a pioneer and a leader. This should be part of its strategy. This would achieve faster and concrete development. Governments of LDCs can adopt the following policies.

Open-Source Software

People in LDCs have mostly lower-incomes. It is necessary for the implemented technologies to be affordable. There are certain technologies that are efficient enough to serve a certain purpose yet they cost far less than others do. Budgets of a typical LDC are only a fraction of that of Developed Countries. Not only money is scarce but also these countries are stifled by heavy debts. Procurement of ICT, therefore, must be considerate.

An example of such technologies is open-source software. As the name implies, source code of this kind of software is available to anybody. This software has virtually no cost to own. Open-source operating systems, programming languages, desktop applications…etc can be owned without paying extra money. There are several advantages for adopting open-source strategies:

- LDCs need to buy many computers for schools, laboratories…etc. In many cases, software that is shipped with these computers can exceed the price of the hardware. Using open-source OS and office applications can cut down expenses sharply.
- Students studying computer science or IT can avoid paying a lot of money for owning commercial software. Java for example is an open-source programming language that is both powerful and free.
- Open-source software encourages innovation. An open-source OS for example can be tailored specifically for certain usage. Modules can be developed to provide extended functionalities.
- Locally developed solutions are more convenient with open-source. Buying locally-developed solutions means less drain of precious hard currency.

Software Industry

It is industry that achieves sustainable development and prosperity for a nation. The new term to describe a developed LDC is "newly *industrialised* country" or NIC. Industry, however, can be in any field. Some countries have excelled in certain industries whereas other developed other kinds of industries. Among traditional industries (machinery, high-tech, agriculture, medical…etc) Software industry is conceivably the most profitable for LDCs. Software industry does not require any raw materials as input. It only needs innovative human brains.

There are many programmers graduating every year from universities in LDCs. These programmers are low-salaried compared to their peers in the developed countries. Thus, LDCs can achieve better returns on investments.

Knowledge Economy

In today's economy, knowledge is a key component of any business or industry. To this, modern economy is referred to as "knowledge economy". Therefore, institutions employ knowledge management systems to capture and codify knowledge. The good news is that this knowledge has become easy to get thanks to the Internet. Knowledge is available in different and rich forms. It easily transferable and storable. The Internet has made information equally accessible by all. Whether you live in an LDC or in a DC you will always be able to gain access to the same information. Many conferences and journals publish scientific research finding on the Internet. There is either very little fee or even no fees at all to read them. This is a very good opportunity to explore the latest developments in a certain field. This opportunity has never been so abundant throughout history.

Quality information and knowledge can be utilised for development. One problem is that individuals in LDCs normally pay more to access the Internet than their counterparts in DCs. This has to do much with poor ICT infrastructures. Governments should work with private sector to lower access costs.

Leapfrogging

According to Wikipedia, Leapfrogging is,

a theory of development in which developing countries skip inferior, less efficient, more expensive or more polluting technologies and industries and move directly to more advanced ones.

Leapfrogging can be performed in any field: technological, social, political...etc. For example Freeman (2005) discusses the prospects of human resource (HR) leapfrogging. He argues that LDCs can achieve a competitive advantage by utilising their huge low-waged working force of scientists and engineers. Quantity can in some cases of research and development (R&D) outweigh quality. Superiority of DCs stems from two factors: technological infrastructure and skilled labour. This skilled labour though comes at a price as these workers are high-waged. If we are going to apply economics to R&D, which is attributed to produce new innovative products, then we can see that by employing more under skilled but low-waged workers LDCs can become quite competitive with DCs.

In this section, we will focus on technological leapfrogging. According to the technological leapfrogging theory,

under certain social, economic, and technological conditions, communities or countries can jump several steps to reach a higher level of technology production and consumption and attain parity with countries at the top of the ladder in that particular domain. (Brezis and Tsiddon 1998)

LDCs can perform technology leapfrogging by using the latest and most efficient technologies. LDCs have little or no technologies in place.

Leapfrogging can be practiced by LDCs as well as DCs. DCs can leapfrog to new and efficient technological tools or systems. Even companies can leapfrog competitors to new technological solutions. After all, companies are about achieving maximum rate of return. If new proven solution is adopted by a small and fast-growing company then it can achieve a higher "rate of return" than an old company which has already invested in a less efficient solution. New mobile operators in a certain country find it easy to offer new services than old ones. This is because they do no have old systems installed. This is not always successful though. The company must have some input requirements to make the shift. Among these are availability of market niche, training, skills, leadership, vision, and commitment. The aim for LDCs, however, is different. They seek to build an efficient infrastructure that can bridge the divide with DCs or to reduce it to say the least.

Benefits of Leapfrogging

There are a number of acclaimed benefits of practicing leapfrogging. Among these are:

- **Access to information:** With the implementation of new efficient IT infrastructure, it is contingent that the Internet penetration rate will be boosted. Government strategy must encourage this and become a catalyst for the private sector. There will be a great social impact on the society. Mentality shift of people of LDCs will accelerate pace towards modernization. Now the people have access to transparent information through the net, means that they are empowered to participate vigorously in the political process and can influence government policies. It is true that not all people in LDCs may have access to computers because many of them are illiterate or poor. As mentioned earlier, one solution to this serious limitation might be local radio stations. Such stations can draw relevant and up-to-date information from the Internet and broadcast it to the locals. An example of such implementation took place in India. Illiterate farmers working in remote villages learn about the latest prices of agricultural products through loud speakers announced by the local radio, which in turn obtain the up-to-date prices from the Internet. In such a way, they can sell their goods at the latest prices.

- **Human development:** The impact of ICT on human development is critical. Implementation of innovative ICT solutions in fields like education, health, economy, agriculture, transportation…etc can have great benefits on sustainable development. Distance learning can provide a good opportunity for people in remote areas. Video conferencing allows professors from universities in DCs to lecture students in universities of LDCs. This is particularly important for LDCs witnessing conflicts where students might not have the chance to leave their homes or villages.
- Farmers can benefit from the Internet to get relevant and timely information to help them in all stages of cultivation. Farmers will be more productive and efficient if they are more informed.
- Physicians can follow up their patients' conditions though cell phones whenever a local clinic is not available. Some gadgets available today can measure patients' blood pressure, sugar level, heart rate…etc and can transmit data wirelessly to medical centres.
- Technology leapfrogging has a huge impact on the economy. Businesses in LDCs can employ e-commerce and can thus have access to worldwide markets at lower costs. They can also better manage their supply of raw materials. E-commerce allows local businesses to go global and joint venture multi-national companies. They can act as outsourcers to foreign companies with the help of technology.
- Employing new technologies to transportation can result in elevated safety and efficiencies. Hi-tech control systems in railways, airports, highways, waterways…etc can reduce accidents due to human errors. They can better handle congestions much more efficiently. Inside cities, the use of fully actuated traffic lights manages circulation much more efficiently and thus reduces green gas emissions, which are harmful to the environment.
- **Conservation of resources by using the most efficient technologies:** Costs should now be decreased and revenues should be increased
- **Bridging the digital divide:** Now that both DCs and LDCs use the same, efficient technologies they can have better cooperation on different levels: economy, cooperation, information and skills interchange…etc.

Technology leapfrogging must be practised carefully. If people affected are unprepared then this might lead to what is referred as "Technological Shock".

In the summary of the Third United Nations Conference on the Least Developed Countries held in Brussels 2001, it was stressed that the major challenge to for LDCs in embracing e-commerce was not technical. Technology and infrastructure were not found to be the most demanding challenges. Business culture and practices were simply inconsistent with successful e-Business strategies adopted by DCs.

From this brief discussion, we can see how important technology leapfrogging is to human development. The list can go on and on for every sector in the LDCs.

Wireless Access Opportunities

Wireless communications provide a communication platform that can be setup quickly. They are cost and power effective because of wire elimination. This communications infrastructure can be utilised in many ways. In general, it helps establish a connected society. Broadband wireless communications can reach Internet access speeds of up to (1) Gbps towards 2009 (WiMAX 802.16m standard). These gigabit mobile networks can have many useful applications. They can be used for remote medication, distance education video conferencing…etc.

This communication infrastructure is accompanied by a wave of wireless devices of different kinds and specs. Many of these ultra portable devices are laden with capacities to do so many things despite their miniaturised size. They can even transcend desktop computers in terms of functionality. The ultra mobile PC (UMPC) is a full-fledged computer that fits the palm of a hand.

Availability of these highly capable mobile devices combined with broadband wireless communications create a huge new market where different sorts of businesses can thrive. Not only can wireless communications and the related technologies be used for development, but they can also support innovative business applications. As mentioned earlier, there is a high penetration rate of mobile phones even in LDCs. These mobile devices vary in complexity and applications they support. Simple DTMF (dual tone multi frequency) and SMS based applications can reach out the masses. In Jordan, for example, some parking services in the capital Amman have started to receive reservations via SMS. In addition, many banks offer SMS services to their clienteles. Clients can request banking services through their mobiles phone. They can receive short bank statements or results of transactions right on their phones screens. Companies can offer ring tones, short video clips, images…etc for a fee to mobile users.

These are just some examples of mobile-based businesses and services. The list is endless. What is amazing about mobile business is that a mobile device is actually an incessant point of service (POS). This is not the case for traditional POSs. A customer cannot be at a retailer's place or in front of his or her computer or TV anywhere and any time. Yet the overwhelming majority of customers always carry their cell phones with them wherever they go. This means mostly a non-stop business channel for companies.

REFERENCES

Anthopoulos, L., & Tsoukalas, I. (2005). A Cross Border Collaboration Environment, as a Means for Offering Online Public Services and for Evaluating the Performance of Public Executives. *Proceedings of the 2005 IEEE International Conference on e-Technology, e-commerce and e-Service (EEE'05) on e-Technology, e-commerce and e-Service*. pp.: 622-627. ISBN: 0-7695-2274-2.

Austin, J. (1990). *Managing in Developing Countries: Strategic Analysis and Operating Techniques*. Free Press. ISBN 0029011027.

Barnickel, N., Matthias, M. & Schmidt, K. (2006). Interoperability in eGovernment Through Cross-Ontology Semantic Web Service Composition, *Workshop on Semantic Web for eGovernment of ESWC 2006*, 11-14 June 2006, Budva, Montenegro. pp 37-47.

Belanger, France Carter, Lemuria D. Schaupp, & L. Christian (2005). U-government: A framework for the evolution of e-government. *Electronic Government, an International Journal*, *2*(4), 426-445(20).

Bochicchio, M., & Fiore, N. (2005). Supporting the Conceptual Modeling of Web Applications: The MODE Project. *Proceedings of the 19th International Conference on Advanced Information*

Networking and Applications. Volume 1. pp.: 495-500. ISBN ~ ISSN:1550-445X, 0-7695-2249-1.

Bonnet Ph., Bressan S., Leth L., & Thomsen B. (1996). Towards ECLiPSe Agents on the Internet, Proceedings of the 1st *Workshop on Logic Programming Tools for Internet Applications*, Bonn, Germany, 1996 – pp 1-9.

Bouwman, H. (2002). The Sense and Nonsense of Business Models. *International workshop on business models*, Lausanne.

Brezis, Elise S. & Daniel Tsiddon (1998).Economic Growth, Leadership and Capital Flows: The Leapfrogging Effect. *Journal of International Trade & Economic Development*, 7 (September), 261-277.

Darrell, M. (2005). *Global E-Government Report*.

E-Japan (2001). http://www.kantei.go.jp/foreign/it/network/0122full_e.html. Last visted: Nov 6 2007.

Gartner Dataquest (May 2007).

Grönlund, Å. (2005). *What's In a Field – Exploring the eGoverment Domain*. Örebro University. Sweden. 0-7695-2268-8/05 IEEE.

Heeks, R. (2002). E-Government in Africa: Promise and Practice. iGovernment Working Paper Series. Institute for Development Policy and Management.

Jenny Y.Y. Wong, Dickson K.W. Chiu, & Kai Pan Mark. (2007). Effective e-government Process Monitoring and Interoperation- A Case Study on the Removal of Unauthorized Building Works in Hong Kong, *Proceedings of the 40th Hawaii International Conference on System Sciences*. 1530-1605/07, IEEE.

Kafka Report (2006). Available at http://www.kafka.be. Last visited March 1, 2007.

Laudon, K., & Laudon, J. (2006). *Management Information Systems*. 9th Edition.

Layne, K., & Lee, J. (2001). Developing fully functional E-government: A four stage model. *Government Information Quarterly*. VOL 18; NUMBER 2, pages 122-136.

Mugellini, E., Khaled, O.A., Pettenati, M.C., & Kuonen, P. (2005). eGovSM metadata model: towards a flexible, interoperable and eGovernment service marketplace. e-Technology, e-commerce and e-Service, 2005. EEE apos;05. *Proceedings. The 2005 IEEE International Conference on*. Volume, Issue , 29. pp.: 618-621. Digital Object Identifier 10.1109/EEE.2005.67.

Ndou, V. (2004). E – Government for Developing Countries: Opportunities and Challenges. *The Electronic Journal on Information Systems in Developing Countries*.

Rabaiah, A., Vandijck, E. & Musa, F. (2006). Abstraction of e-government. *Proceedings of the IADIS International Conference E-Commerce*, Barcelona, Spain, pp. 27-34. ISBN: 972-8924-23-2.

Richard Freeman (2005). *Human Resource Leapfrogging*. The Globalist. Available at: www.theglobalist.com/StoryId.aspx?StoryId=4759. Last visited: June 24, 2007.

Sang M. Lee, Xin Tan, & Silvana Trimi (2006). M-government, from rhetoric to reality: learning from leading countries. *Electronic Government, an International Journal*. Issue: Volume 3, Number 2/2006. pp.:113-126.

Scholl, H. (2005). *Interoperability in e-government*: More Than Just Smart Middleware. IEEE Computer Society, USA.

Slywotzky, A. (1996). *Value Migration*, Harvard business school press.

Spahni, D. (2004). Managing Access to Distributed Resources. *IEEE Computer Society*, USA.

Summary of the United Nations Conference on the Least Developed Countries (2001). *The Digital Economy: Integrating the LDCs into the Digital Economy.* A/CONF.191/L.15. Brussls, Belgium, 14-20 may 2001.

Osterwalder, A., & Pigneur, Y. (2002). An E-Business Model Ontology for Modelling E Business. *15th Bled Electronic Commerce Conference*, Bled.

Themistocleous, M., & Irani, Z. (2005). Developing E-Government Integrated Infrastructures: A Case Study. *IEEE Computer Society*, USA.

Traunmüller, R., & Wimmer, M. (2002). Web Semantics in e-government: A Tour d'Horizon on Essential Features. Institute of Applied Computer Science, University of Linz. *IEEE Computer Society*, USA.

Wagner, C., Cheung, K., Lee, F., & Ip, R. (2003). Enhancing E-Government in Developing Countries: Managing Knowledge through Virtual Communities. The Electronic Journal on Systems in Developing Countries. 14, 4, 1-20.

William E., & Lewis, D. (1992). *Higher Education and Economic Growth.* Kluwer Academic Publishers. ISBN: 978-0792392354.

Wood-Harper, T., Ithnin, N., & Ibrahim, O. (2004). *Effective Collaborative Partnership for Malaysian Electronic Government Service Delivery.* Proceedings of the 6th international conference on Electronic commerce. Delft, The Netherlands. ISBN:1-58113-930-6.

Zukauskas, P., & Kasteckiene, A. (2002). *The Role of E-Government in the Development of the New Economy in Lithuania.*

Section IV

National Culture and E-Commerce Adoption in DCs

Chapter IX
Cultural Interpretation of E-Commerce Acceptance in Developing Countries:
Empirical Evidence from Malaysia and Algeria

Zakariya Belkhamza
Universiti Malaysia Sabah, Malaysia

Syed Azizi Wafa
Universiti Malaysia Sabah, Malaysia

ABSTRACT

Global deployment in information and communication technology requires understandings of the cultural constraints in technology acceptance and usage behavior. Prior research indicates that the salient technology acceptance models may not be applicable to all cultures since empirical support was mainly obtained from North America and developed countries. There has been little research done on technology acceptance and usage behavior in the context of developing countries which exhibit distinctive cultural differences from developed countries. The purpose of this study is to test the cross-cultural applicability of technology acceptance model in two developing countries, Malaysia and Algeria, and to investigate the influence of cultural values on the acceptance of e-commerce. The four cultural values of individualism/collectivism, power distance, uncertainty avoidance, and masculinity/femininity identified by Hofstede are posited to comparatively explain the e-commerce acceptance in the context of the two countries. Only uncertainty avoidance was found to moderate the relationship between perceived usefulness and intention to use e-commerce, whereas the other three national culture dimensions did not moderate the relationship, which validate the longstanding notion of important cultural differences between Malaysia and Algeria and show that those differences extend to the e-commerce context.

Copyright © 2009, IGI Global, distributing in print or electronic forms without written permission of IGI Global is prohibited.

INTRODUCTION

Internet has always been considered as an open platform of e-business activities with its global connectivity, which makes it an important factor to incorporate the international dimension of the cross-culture studies in the information technology and e-commerce adoption literature. Globally, previous research has shown that developed countries and developing countries differ in terms of e-commerce use and the level of behavior toward its usage, and the factors shaping that behavior (Dewan and Kraemer, 2000).

In spite of many studies on the technology acceptance, the line of research has yet to reach a satisfactory level of extension beyond the boundaries of the developed countries, although a number of research has been done on countries such as Taiwan (Shih, 2004), Algeria (Belkhamza and Syed Azizi Wafa, 2006), Kuwait (Rouibah and Hamdy, 2006) and Saudi Arabia (Al-Gahtani et. al., 2007). However, given the ongoing rapid globalization of business and systems, there is pressing need to learn more about the impact of culture on information technology and e-commerce acceptance around the world. Cultural differences that exist between different countries may affect the organization's ability to adopt and implement e-commerce. It is important then for managers to learn about the cross-cultural differences that exist in the adoption of e-commerce. Such knowledge can make the difference between success and failure in implementing new technologies, as well as to allow the process of collaborate sharing of experience in the discipline.

This research analyzes e-commerce by employing the two constructs of TAM – perceived usefulness and perceived ease of use. The aim of this study is to investigate what cultural factors lead the behavioral intention toward e-commerce use. Further, in order to account for the increasing globalization of e-commerce, this research also addresses how national culture influence intention to use e-commerce. We address the last question by including an examination of the cultural dimensions of the Dutch psychologist Geert Hofstede, drawing upon his categorization of national societies (1980). Malaysia and Algeria were chosen for this study because they represent nearly reverse positions on three important cultural dimensions.

CULTURE AND INFORMATION AND COMMUNICATION TECHNOLOGIES

The study of the relationship between culture and information technology has taken several directions in cultural anthropology. The reference discipline of anthropology provides additional insight as well as support for focusing on the relationship between cultural and information technology. Anthropologists like Bertolotti (1984) points out that the culture of a country or region greatly affects the acceptance of technology through its beliefs and values about modernization and technological development. Thus, ignoring the cultural context can result in delays or, at worse, failures in information technology adoption process (Matta and Boutros 1989).

Straub (1994) suggests that cultural factors have a significant effect on technology diffusion process ranging from evaluation to adoption, use and performance. Burn (1995) believes that cultural values affect the efficacy of technology transfer across national boundaries. Particularly, culture is considered to be the most important factor in technology transfer from industrialized countries to developing ones. As the way technology is perceived and used in organizations is embedded in certain cultural environment, successful information technology implementation across cultures addresses both the technological readiness and the wider cultural and national setting within which the organization operates (Cummings and Guynes, 1994; Tricker, 1988; Robey and Rodriguez-Diaz, 1989).

Limaye and Victor (1991) argue that although information technology in business organizations around the world would converge, the conveyed meaning and the outcomes of information technology use may remain culturally oriented. There have been ample evidences in information systems literature on cultural differences regarding to the perception and use of information technology, and the way it is managed and transferred.

Since information technology design conveys the cultural elements inherent in its environment, successful information technology deployment, development, user acceptance and use in a different culture would require understanding of the cultural factors that account for the possible gaps in related behaviors (Hofstede, 1980).

UNDERSTANDING BEHAVIORAL BELIEFS AND ATTITUDES

According to Ajzen and Fishbein (1980), external variables influence beliefs associated with performing a behavior, which in turn shape attitudes toward performing a behavior. Attitude, however, influences the behavior itself. As articulated in the theory of reasoned action (TRA), these relationships will be predictive of behavior when the attitude and belief factors are specified in a manner consistent with the behavior to be explained in terms of time, target and context (Ajzen and Fishbein, 2005; Fazio and Olson, 2003). Within the information technology management literature, these ideas have taken shape in the form of technology acceptance model (TAM), which has been widely applied to understand attitude about the use of technology, and to predict the adoption and use of information technology. The attitude construct in TAM represents attitude toward the behavior of using technology.

Davis' goal in developing TAM was to provide a theoretically justified explanation of the determinants of technology acceptance across a wide range of applications and user populations (Davis, 1989). A key purpose of TAM is to provide a basis for tracing the impact of external factors on internal beliefs, attitudes, and intentions as reference for managerial intervention. TAM was formulated in an attempt to achieve these goals by identifying a small number of fundamental variables dealing with determinants of computer acceptance, and, at the same time, adopting TRA's well-established logic chain of belief–attitude–intention-behavior as the basic theoretical relationships among these variables. One of the salient contributions of TAM is the development of the two key beliefs that specifically account for technology acceptance.

The original TAM (Davis, 1986) postulates that actual usage behavior is solely affected by intention, which is in turn influenced by attitude and perceived usefulness, while attitude is jointly determined by perceived usefulness and perceived ease of use.

However, TAM later excludes the attitude of the user (Davis et. *al.*, 1989), due to its weak influence on usage and its weak direct link with perceived usefulness. The researchers argue that people might intend to use a technology because it was useful even though they did not have a positive attitude toward using. Their study tested the original version of TAM on the voluntary usage of a word-processing package by 107 first year full-time U.S. MBA students. Findings suggested that perceived usefulness and perceived ease of use fully mediated the influence of external variables; that perceived ease of use affects perceived ease of use, and that intention is an indicator of usage (Venkatesh and Davis, 2000; Gefen and Straub, 2000)

Recently, scholars have begun to explore the link between culture and technology user acceptance and have indicated that national culture affect user technology acceptance (Gefen and Straub, 1997; Rose and Straub, 1998; Srite, 2000; Straub, 1994; Straub et. *al.*, 1997; Straub et. *al.*,

2002; Ho et. al., 1989). For example, TAM did not explain user acceptance in a study conducted in Asia, along with Straub, Keil and Brenner's (1997) finding of the non-applicability of TAM in Japan, contrary to the generally supportive evidence reported in North America.

Since different technology acceptance patterns existed when cultural differences are taken into account, technology must adapt to new cultural environments to be accepted. TAM-based studies also found that gender difference, viewed as part of cultural difference, has significant impact on technology user acceptance (Venkatesh and Morris, 2000). Gefen and Straub (1997) found that men and women differ in their perceptions of e-mail acceptance. They called for future research to include gender in IT diffusion models along with other cultural effects.

CONCEPTUAL DEVELOPMENT

Cultural Differences

The importance of culture on various aspects of management and organizational behavior has long been recognized, along with being a major concern in much of the earlier work in anthropology. The cultural environment for certain behavior is found to have a significant impact on one's values, beliefs, and attitudes (Brislin, 1993). Various disciplines have defined culture differently. According to Kroeber and Kluckhohn's (1952) review of culture, over 150 different definitions of culture have been proposed in the literature. The wide range of connotations in culture includes the beliefs, value system, norms, traditions, myths, and structural elements of a given organization, tribe, or society, that exists at different social levels. An individual usually belongs to cultural groups at different levels at the same time. One may carry many layers of "mental programming" depending on situational states. The different levels of culture include: (1) national or country level; (2) a regional and/or ethnic and/or religious and/or linguistic affiliation level; (3) a gender level; (4) a social class level; (5) an organizational level; (6) an individual level (Hofstede, 1991; Lu and Lu, 1995).

In different academic disciplines, researchers tend to define culture based on their respective backgrounds. As a result of this practice, the effects of culture on human performance have been generally described rather than actually defined.

The most widely accepted cultural framework is based on the research of Hofstede (1980). He posited that cultural differences manifest themselves through different aspects of the national culture. He looked at values and attitudes of workers and managers in over forty countries in a multinational company. Based on a survey using nationality as a precursor of culture, he identified individualism, power distance, uncertainty avoidance and masculinity as significant cultural value dimensions. After a decade of further study, he proposed a fifth dimension—time orientation.

In view of academic and theoretical perspective, the effects of culture on technology diffusion have been studies by information systems researchers (e.g. Straub et. *al*., 1997; Kettinger, 1997). Several studies assert that culture plays a significant role in information technology diffusion (Ein-Dor and Orgad, 1993). Hofstede's (1980, 1991) studies are well-known in the cultural dimension values, and deemed important in information technology diffusion as well as in global research. The major motivation behind this classification framework is that it is able to establish the degree to which cultural environment systematically influence employees' attitudes and behavior. According to Hofstede, culture is a set of shared assumptions representing the system of socially constructed meanings and preferences of a group (Hofstede, 1980; Schein, 1985). This cultural framework has also received strong empirical support. Most of the cultural research in information systems literature has adopted the framework of Hofstede's cultural dimensions or cultural values because of its extensive validating support (Kumar et. al., 1993; Jordan, 1994). In particular, Hofstede's research on cultural dimensions has been regarded as a major theoretical foundation for exploring the impact of cultural differences on the adoption and diffusion of IT-based innovations such as e-mail (Straub et. al., 1997).

Power Distance

Power distance is a core cultural value distinctive in the workplace, capturing the extent to which unequal distribution of power in organizations is accepted. High power distance societies tend to be hierarchically ordered, while low power distance societies tend to be egalitarian (Ho et. al., 1989). In a high power distance culture, superiors and subordinates consider each other as unequal in power, and contacts between superiors and subordinates are to be initiated only by superiors. It is common that subordinates defer to superiors and avoid questioning their authority (Watson et. *al*., 1994). Status differences among individuals are pronounced in high power distance countries, but are less significant in low power distance cultures (Tan et al., 1998). High power distance values indicate that hierarchical structures and centralized decision making are the organizational norms that help preserve the existing social order and its related distribution of power.

For example, Teng et. al., (2000) found that while decision decentralization appears to facilitate business process reengineering success in a low power distance culture (i.e., the U.S.), decision centralization is related to success in a high power distance culture (i.e., Taiwan). This finding suggests that innovation diffusion in a high power distance culture may depend on certain mandate from the top management.

Straub et. al., (1997) found that higher power distance country show low technology adoption. People who have low power distance are likely to be more willing to take new responsibilities that are essential to the business process reengineering through e-commence acceptance (Grover et. al., 1995). On the other hand, people with high power distance will be reluctant to accept empowering initiatives with respect to both physical and information-based activities. Specifically, low power distance perception would influence the antecedents of technology adoption, because empowering initiatives would affect the belief of computer ability of the organization member according to social cognitive theory (Bandura, 1986; Compeau and Higgins, 1995).

In high power distance cultures, technology could threaten the hierarchy, which reflects the existential inequality between higher-ups and lower-downs because it suggests decentralization (Hofstede, 2001). Conversely, in low power distance cultures individuals are more interdependent whatever their ranks in the hierarchy; therefore, they will be more favorable to information technology, which doesn't contradict their perception of power distribution. Thus, it is hypothesized that:

Perceived ease of use has a greater influence on intention to use e-commerce in low power distance culture than in high power distance culture

Perceived usefulness has a greater influence on intention to use e-commerce in low power distance culture than in high power distance culture.

Uncertainty Avoidance

Hofstede defines uncertainty avoidance as the degree to which members of society feel uncomfortable with uncertainty and ambiguity. He argued that uncertainty avoidance is related to anxiety that is the general feeling of anxiety when confronted with problems or challenges. Computers and database can reutilize jobs, and telecommunication products such as e-mails, telephones, fax machines, and cell phones can reduce uncertainties in communication (Bagchi et. al., 2003). Given that surprise and uncertainty are though to be an adverse state for individuals who desire ownership, organizational members will use formal information sources that are attributed and proven to reduce these uncertainties. Increased feedback-seeking behavior with formal sources will be beneficial to reduce these uncertainties.

Uncertainty avoidance is believed to lead to a reduction of ambiguity and predictable structures. In uncertainty avoiding societies there are many formal laws and/or informal rules controlling the rights and duties in the work place. Individuals with weak uncertainty avoidance tend to have low stress and therefore higher in their subjective feeling of well-being, while individuals with strong uncertainty avoidance tend to have high stress levels and therefore the subjective feeling of anxiety (Hofstede, 1991).

Individuals who perceived they are in an organization with high uncertainty avoidance without anxiety of control or instruction would perceive that system is easy to use. Transaction cost theory (Williamson and Masten, 1995) shows the possible linkage between uncertainty avoidance and perceived ease of use, where uncertainty reflects the inability to predict relevant contingencies. it has been found that those having high uncertainty avoidance are averse to technologies that present ambiguities and unnecessary complexities in their use. Thus, perceived ease of use is a very important variable to such individuals. The hypothesis supported is therefore:

Perceived ease of use has a greater influence on intention to use e-commerce in high uncertainty avoidance culture than in low uncertainty avoidance culture.

However, individuals who are high in uncertainty avoidance, the use of media such as Web sites to conduct shopping present ambiguities and uncertainties that impact on perceptions of usefulness (Straub et. al., 1997). The lack of face to face interaction with a vendor, the inability to touch and feel any physical products that are to be purchased, and the uncertainty surrounding the privacy and security of personal information are all instances where ambiguity and uncertainty arise. These will be of greater concern to those high in uncertainty avoidance. Thus, the hypothesis supported is:

Perceived usefulness has a lesser influence on intention to use e-commerce in high uncertainty avoidance culture than for in low uncertainty avoidance culture.

Individualism/Collectivism

Generally, individualism refers to the extent to which members of a culture view themselves as distinct persons, rather than as part of a collective (Hofstede, 1980). Erez and Earley (1987) suggest that the individualistic versus collectivistic orientation of a society has profound implications for how individuals work. Individualism-collectivism has consistently featured in many empirical studies as the most important dimension of cross-national culture.

Hofstede (1980) notes that in individualistic cultures, people tend to place greater emphasis on personal time and emotional independence from their work. Individualists usually value challenge and autonomy on the job and encourage individual initiative. Paralleling with their search for personal fulfillment, individuals high in individualist value tend to be more non-conformist and less loyal to the group than people from collectivistic cultures. In conclusion, a more individualistic culture tends to encourage personal initiative, where people tend to be more non-conformist, searching for personal fulfillment and emotional independence.

Individuals with collectivism are integrated into strong cohesive group, valuing the group's well-being more that individual desires (Ford et. *al*., 2003). People holding collectivist values will be more concerned about the maintenance of the group cohesiveness, and they are expected to show more interest in e-commerce adoption. Chung and Adams (1997) suggest that countries reflecting more collectivist tenancies such as China, or Korea may actually adopt collaborative software such as enterprise resource planning more effectively that individualistic cultures like those of the US or Australia. Haythornthwaite and Wellman (1998) found that, in strong ties such as collectivism, e-mail-based communications were increased as supplements to face to-to-face communications. Thus, high collectivism with strong ties of social network would positively influence on individual's belief of both usefulness and ease of use:

Perceived usefulness has a greater influence on intention to use e-commerce in high collectivism culture than in low collectivism culture

Perceived ease of use has a greater influence on intention to use e-commerce in high collectivism culture than in low collectivism culture

Masculinity/Femininity

Masculinity/femininity is linked to the sex roles society assigns to its people. It captures the extent to which "masculine" values such as assertiveness and success prevail over "feminine" values that focus more on the quality of life. Hoffman (1972) points out that men are motivated by achievement needs to a greater extent than women. Hofstede (1980) found men usually rate the two classic extrinsic motivators of "advancement" and "earning power" as more important than women, while women rate the importance of service aspects and physical environment more highly than men. This is consistent with Minton and Schneider's (1980) conclusion that men may be more task-oriented than women, paralleling the finding that men's work role, accomplishment or eminence is typically their most prominent concern, while the family role is often of only secondary importance (Barnett and Marshall, 1991; O'Neil, 1982)

Drawing on the view that gender is a fundamental aspect of culture, Gefen and Straub (1997) studied a sample of 392 female and male respondents via a cross-sectional survey to test gender differences that may relate to beliefs and use of computer-based media. Findings indicate women and men differ in their perceptions but not in the use of e-mail.

At an individual level, masculinity is associated strongly with importance attached to earnings, recognition, advancement and challenge (Hofstede, 1991). However, in organizations, this dimension reflects whether the organization will be task-oriented (i.e. high masculinity) or people-oriented, emphasizing the quality of life and the environment (i.e. low masculinity). The masculine emphasis on tasks suggests that people with high masculine values are more concerned with the usefulness of a given technology, regardless of whether it is easy or difficult to use (Srite, 2000).

Masculinity pertains to being assertive, tough, task oriented and focusing on material success (Hofstede, 1980; Robichaux and Cooper, 1998). From this perspective, perceived usefulness is related to masculinity through assessment on the instrumentality of performing a behavior. Perceived usefulness of a technology has been closely related to mental representation that links goals to specific actions that are instrumental for achieving those goals (Davis, 1989, 1993; Davis et. *al*., 1992; Venkatesh and Davis, 2000). Masculinity captures goal orientation and affects usefulness perception through an assessment process linking instrumental acts (i.e., using a technology) to goals (i.e., improving task performance). Taylor and Hall (1982) indicate that masculine scales correlate highly with instrumental behaviors. Therefore, individuals with high masculine value may be more concerned with usefulness or work goals than those holding lower masculine value.

Thus, it is hypothesized that:

Perceived usefulness has a greater influence on intention to use e-commerce in masculinity culture than in femininity culture

Perceived ease of use has a greater influence on intention to use e-commerce in masculinity culture than in femininity culture.

CULTURAL DIFFERENCES IN MALAYSIA AND ALGERIA

The choice of Malaysia and Algeria for this study was based on three main factors. First, the cultural value orientations between these two cultures differ, especially on power distance and uncertainty avoidance, where the difference is significantly noticed, that may give us two distinct benchmarks to test our hypotheses in these two developing countries. For example, it has been found that Algeria is a highly collectivistic society, with a high tolerance for uncertainty, and with a relatively low power distance, relatively higher masculinity than Malaysia, which is an individualistic society, higher on power distance structure and relatively lower on tolerance for uncertainty (Hofstede, 1980, 1991). Second, while trade between Malaysia and Algeria has increased substantially, there have been very few cross-national studies of marketing practices and consumer behavior between Malaysia and Algeria. This study may contribute to address this deficit in the comparative international marketing research. Finally, both Malaysia and Algeria represent significant and growing online consumer populations and are potential future online markets.

RESEARCH METHOD

Questionnaires were distributed personally and through the post mail to the selected travel agents and tourism organizations. Due to the internationalization of this study, the questionnaire distributed in Algeria has been translated into French to facilitate the response and avoid any inaccurate that may occur due to the lack of understanding English. The questionnaire distributed in Malaysia was in English. Due to the busy activities of most travel agents, some of the returns from the respondents were delayed. Follow-up telephone calls or e-mail reminders were carried out to ensure respondents complete answering the questionnaire.

For Malaysia, out of the 120 initial participants, 28 questionnaires were returned undeliverable, 92 responses were obtained, resulting in an effective response rate of 76%. For Algeria, out of 120 surveys sent out, 32 were undeliverable, and 88 final responses resulted, for a rate of 73% percent.

DEMOGRAPHICAL PROFILE OF THE RESPONDENTS

A summary of the respondent's profile is shown in Table 2. The results show that various tourism companies in Malaysia and Algeria are well represented. More than half of responses (52%) are from executive directors and top managers,

Table 1. Cultural index scores (Hofstede 1980, 2001)

	Power Distance	Individualism	Uncertainty Avoidance	Masculinity
Malaysia	104	26	36	50
Algeria	80	38	68	53

Table 2. Respondent's profile

No	Profile	Description	No. of Respondent	Percentage %
1	**Type of organization**	Travel Agent	90	50.0
		Tourism Organization	47	26.1
		Tour operator	41	22.8
		Diving operator	2	1.1
2	**No. of years business was established**	Less than 1 year	0	0
		1-2 years	4	2.2
		3-5 years	40	22.2
		More than 5 years	136	75.6
3	**Number of employees**	Below 5	25	13.9
		5-50	142	78.9
		51-100	5	2.8
		101-200	0	0
		Over 200	8	4.4
4	**Primary Job function**	Owner/manager	103	57.2
		Major shareholder/non- manager	24	13.3
		Minor shareholder/non-manager		
		Owner/non-manager	19	10.6
		Minor shareholder/Manager		
			18	10.0
			16	8.9
5	**Position in the company**	Executive/ Top management	93	51.7
		Middle Management		
		Supervisory	38	21.1
		Administrative/ Clerical/ Technical	31	17.2
			18	10.0
6	**Annual Income (Before Tax)**	Less than $20,000	8	4.4
		$20,000 - $29,999	21	11.7
		$30,000 - $39,999	26	14.4
		$40,000 - $49,999	7	3.9
		$50,000 - $59,999	4	2.2
		$60,000 - $69,999	21	11.7
		$70,000 - $79,999	55	30.6
		$80,000 - $89,999	28	15.6
		$90,000 - $99,999	10	5.6
7	**Country of Origin**	Malaysia	92	51.1
		Algeria	88	48.9

followed by 22% of middle managers, 18% supervisors, the remaining 10% are from technical and clerical position of the company. The results also show that most of respondents own and manage the company business with a percentage of 58%, 10% of respondents own the business but do not manage it, about 14% are major shareholders of the business and 11% are minor shareholders. These respondents are in important positions in the organizations, which enable them to provide reliable information about the e-commerce adoption of the organization as they are the main key in the decision making. In response to the type of the tourism organization, 50% of the respondents

Table 3. Reliability test

Section	Variables	Source	Questions	Cronbach's Alpha
1.	Intention to use e-commerce	Pavlou, 2003 Ndubisi and Jantan,2003	(10 Questions)	0.88
2.	Perceived usefulness	Davis, 1989	(4 Questions)	0.79
3.	Perceived ease of use	Davis, 1989	(4 Questions)	0.90

Table 4. Description of variables for compiled samples

No	Variables	N	Mean	Standard Deviation
1	Intention to use e-commerce	180	3.52	0.64
2	Perceived usefulness	180	3.65	0.62
3	Perceived ease of use	180	3.41	0.74

Table 5. Description of variables for Algeria and Malaysia samples

No	Variables	N		Mean		Standard Deviation	
		Malaysia	Algeria	Malaysia	Algeria	Malaysia	Algeria
1	Intention to use e-commerce	92	88	3.67	3.65	0.54	0.30
2	Perceived usefulness	92	88	3.65	3.64	0.74	0.46
3	Perceived ease of use	92	88	3.75	3.04	0.71	0.58

are travel agents, 48% are tourism organizations and tour operators, 2% of them are specialized in diving operations. The duration for which business has been established was measured in years with the majority (76%) of the organizations established for more than 5 years, 3-5 years (23%), and 3% for newly established company in less than 2 years. The size of the organization was measured using number of employees and the results reveal that majority of the organizations are small and medium enterprises which employ from 5 to 50 employees with percentage of 79%, 3% are employing from 51-100, 4% are large organizations with more than 200 employees.

The results further show that all respondents have been using information technology in their company, only 3% of the respondents have not yet involved in e-commerce and internet technology, other respondents` rate vary between 2 to 5 years which show good significant aspect of the actual usage.

RELIABILITY MEASUREMENT

Cronbach's alpha analysis was performed to determine the reliability of the results, which is the extent to which a variable or set of variables is consistent in what it is intended to measure (Gefen et. *al.*, 2000). Table 3 shows a summary of all variables as well as Cronbach's Alpha coefficient, and sources from where the questionnaire items were adapted.

Cronbach's alpha range of acceptance is in a value from 0 to 1. The acceptance level of .60 and below is considered not reliable (Hair et. *al.*, 1998).

The Cronbach's alpha coefficient for intention to use e-commerce is .88. The intention variables consists of 10 questions which test the reliability of all questions in gathering responses that hold well established scale. Perceived usefulness and perceived ease of use have scale of 0.79 and 0.90 respectively with no question dropped. As the Cronbach's alpha values for all the constructs in the datasets of both Malaysia and Algeria are generally greater than 0.60 as suggested by Hair et. *al* (1998), we conclude that the scales can be applied for the analysis of the datasets with acceptable reliabilities.

MEAN VALUES OF COMPOSITE VARIABLES

All of the variables have mean values of 3 and above, the highest mean value is for intention, perceived usefulness with 3.52, 3.65 respectively. Perceived ease of use has a closer mean value of 3.41. This indicates that the tourism organizations in both Malaysia and Algeria have positive awareness and attitude towards the adoption of e-commerce on their organizations and with good intention towards its usage.

Table 5 shows separate mean values for Malaysia samples and Algeria samples, Malaysia samples shows to have high mean values for intention to use e-commerce, perceived usefulness and perceived ease of use.

HYPOTHESES TESTING

In order to examine the proposed hypotheses, a set of two linear regressions was employed. In each case, all variables in a block were entered in a single step. As shown in Table 4, results for the combination of both countries broadly support the role of the measured variables in explaining usage intention of e-commerce. Tables 6 and 7 give separate results for Malaysia and Algeria respectively. Results were explained according to the relationship between the variables in each country, in which the culture dimensions were conceptualized.

As shown in Tables 6 and 7, the results indicate that the relationship between perceived usefulness and intention to use e-commerce in Malaysia is significant (B= 0.50, p= 0.00), but in Algeria, the

Table 6. Results of regression analysis of the research model for Malaysia

	Unstandardized Coefficients		Standardized Coefficients		
	B	Std. Error	Beta	t	Sig.
(Constant)	2.22	0.26		8.32	0.00
Perceived sefulness	0.50	0.13	0.70	3.72	0.00
Perceived ease of use	-0.19	0.14	-0.26	-1.38	0.16

Dependent Variable: intention

Table 7. Results of regression analysis of the research model for Algeria

	Unstandardized Coefficients		Standardized Coefficients		
	B	Std. Error	Beta	t	Sig.
(Constant)	2.04	0.55		3.65	0.00
Perceived sefulness	0.15	0.17	0.10	0.85	0.39
Perceived ease of use	0.37	0.14	0.31	2.62	0.01

results show no significance between the relationship (B =0.15, p = 0.39)

The results therefore show that the notion of perceived usefulness having a greater influence on intention to use e-commerce in low power distance culture than in high power distance culture does not hold true, as well as in the collectivism and masculinity cultures, where perceived usefulness in Algeria does not show any significant effect on the intention toward the use of e-commerce.

However, the results confirm that perceived usefulness has a lesser influence on intention to use e-commerce in high uncertainty avoidance culture than in low uncertainty avoidance culture. The influence of uncertainty avoidance was found to exist with respect to both perceived usefulness and perceived usefulness would lead to suggest that a culture with high uncertainty avoidance such as the Algerian culture, would exhibit a weaker orientation toward e-commerce usefulness-intention relationship (Choi and Geistfeld, 2004). These findings call for attention in understanding benefits of e-commerce adoption based on cultural., rather than cognitive and norms criteria.

Concerning perceived ease of use, all the hypotheses of the study were confirmed to be true; the results showed that it has a greater influence on intention to use e-commerce in low power distance culture than in high power distance culture, as well as in uncertainty avoidance, collectivism, and masculinity cultures, as the results show no significant relationship between perceived ease of use and intention to use e-commerce in Malaysia (B= -0.19, p= 0.16), and significant relationship for Algeria (B =0.37, p = 0.01).

Another point to notice is that masculinity scores may simply not differ enough between the two countries to capture a strong moderating effect, especially given the small sample size. Nonetheless, there is still directional evidence for the moderating role of masculinity that remains to be validated by future cross-cultural research in countries with high masculinity differences, or with larger sample sizes.

In sum, the role of cultural differences was found to be a noteworthy moderator in the proposed e-commerce acceptance model, emphasizing the role of cultural aspects in multi-national e-commerce research. It is suggested therefore to look more into the social influence on the behavioral intention (Bandyopadhyay and Fraccastoro, 2007)

The findings of this study provide some interesting findings. It was not expected that only uncertainty avoidance would moderate the relationship between perceived usefulness and intention to use e-commerce, whereas the other three national culture dimensions did not moderate the relationship.

This study tries to set the stage for grounding the four important cultural dimensions, uncertainty avoidance, power distance, collectivism and masculinity in a well accepted model in the information systems adoption, the technology acceptance model, and then making applications in a cross-cultural context. Empirical results validate the longstanding notion of important cultural differences between Malaysia and Algeria and show that those differences extend to the e-commerce context. Results of this research additionally suggest that different research models of e-commerce are appropriate for different cultural contexts, and support previous studies as well. (Malhotra and McCort, 2001)

THEORETICAL AND MANAGERIAL IMPLICATIONS

This study contributes to our understanding of the global e-commerce. A main contribution is that a set of interrelationships between important factors that tend to be associated with usage intentions of e-commerce was specified, justified, and empirically validated. Another important contribution of this research is the placement of fundamentally important variables – perceived usefulness and perceived ease of use, as determinants of e-commerce adoption, drawing from well-established models of technology acceptance.

E-commerce provider companies could use the preliminary insights developed here to modify their approaches, depending on the culture they are targeting. For example, e-commerce companies attempting to penetrate and assist the Algerian e-commerce companies should focus on creating and fostering a secure e-commerce image, and investigate the attitude of those organizations. The Malaysian culture, similar to that of Algeria, exhibits a strong relationship between usefulness and usage intention. It should be important therefore to make it a business priority to establish a strong local identity and presence in the local country.

LIMITATIONS AND SUGGESTIONS FOR FUTURE RESEARCH

Some limitations should be mentioned, which call for future investigation. First, much of e-business behavior might occur because of habituation as opposed to intentional behavior (Limaye et. *al.*, 2001). This research did not account for habitual business behavior. For example, for many organizations, online business is gradually becoming a habit as opposed to being driven by thoughtful deliberation. Therefore, examining this factor may reveal interesting aspects of e-commerce adoption.

Future research should also aim to enhance the predictive power of the proposed model, by eliminating unnecessary variables that compromise its parsimony, or considering the interaction effects of other cultural dimensions, such as long-term orientation, which Hofstede and Bond (1988) later combined into his research. This could be added to the model as another cultural moderator, and may provide a deeper and richer understanding of e-commerce in the global setting by conducting studies in multiple countries with different degrees of cultural variation across Hofstede's dimensions. Finally, the issue of small sample size, due to low response rate could also be dealt with in future research. The fact that the response rates for the two countries were 120 respondents in both Malaysia and Algeria might also have impacted the results and should be addressed with further data. Besides expanding sample size, future research could also imply the model to other fields such as retails business and other e-commerce activities, in order to accumulate the findings with robust ground of empirical evidence.

REFERENCES

Ajzen, I., & Fishbein, M. (1980). *Understanding attitudes and predicting social behavio*r, Englewood Cliffs, NJ: Prentice Hall.

Ajzen, I., & Fishbein, M. (2005). The influence of attitudes on behavior. In D. Albarracín, B. T. Johnson, & M. P. Zanna (Eds.), *The handbook of attitudes*. (pp. 173-221). Mahwah, NJ: Lawrence Erlbaum

Al-Gahtani, S. S., Hubona, G. S. and Wang, J. (2007). Information technology (IT) in Saudi Arabia: Culture and the acceptance and use of IT. *Information & Management*. 44(8), 681-691

Bagchi. K., Cerveny. R., Hart. P. & Peterson. M. (2003). *The Influence of national culture in Information Technology product adoption*, In Proceedings of the 9th Americas Conference on Information Systems (AMCIS), AIS, 112- 131

Bandura, A. (1986). *Social foundations of thought and action: A social cognitive theory*. Englewood Cliffs. Prentice-Hall.

Bandyopadhyay, K., & Fraccastoro, A. F. (2007). The effect of culture on user acceptance on Information Technology. *Communications of the Association for Information Systems*. 19(23), 522-543.

Belkhamza, Z., & Syed Azizi Wafa, S. K. W. (2006). Evaluation of the effect of perceived system risk on the intention to use e-commerce: An empirical study on tourism organization. In Proceedings of *Le 3ième Ecole Informatique de Printemps – EIP'06. Sécurité Informatique: Tendances et Applications.* (pp.189-198). INI. Algiers.

Barnett, R. C., & Marshall, N. L. (1991). The relationship between women's work and family roles and their subjective wellbeing and psychological distress, in (eds) *Women, Work and Health: Stress and Opportunities*, M. Frankenhaeuser, V. Lundber, and M.A.Chesney. (pp. 111-136). Plenum, New York.

Bertolotti, D. S. (1984). *Culture and Technology.* Bowling Green, OH: Bowling Green State University Popular Press.

Brislin, R. (1993). *Understanding culture's influence on behavior.* Harcurt Brace College, Publishers. Orlanda Florida.

Burn, J. M. (1995). The new cultural revolution: The impact of EDI on Asia. *Journal of Global Information Management.* 3(4),16-23.

Chung, I. K., & Adams, C. R. (1997). A Study on the characteristics of group decision making behavior: Cultural difference perspective of Korea Vs US. *Journal of Global Information Management*, 5(3), 18-29

Choi, J. & Geistfeld, L.V. (2004). A cross-cultural investigation of consumer e-shopping adoption. *Journal of Economic Psychology*, 25 (6), 821-83

Compeau, D. & Higgins, C. (1995). Computer self-efficacy: Development of a measure and initial test (in Theory and Research). *MIS Quarterly.* 19(2) 189-211.

Cummings, M. L. & Guynes, J. L. (1994). Information system activities in transnational corporations: A comparison of U.S. and Non-U.S. subsidiaries. *Journal of Global Information Management*, 2(1), 12-27.

Davis, F. (1986). *Technology acceptance model for empirically testing new end-user information systems: theory and results*, unpublished doctoral dissertation, MIT.

Davis, F. D. (1989). Perceived usefulness, perceived ease of use and user acceptance of information technology. *MIS Quarterly,* (13) 3, 319-340.

Davis, F. D. (1993). User acceptance of information technology: system characteristics, user perceptions and behavioral impacts. *International Journal of Man-Machine Studies,* 38, 475-487.

Davis, F. D., Bagozzi, R. P., & Warshaw, P. R. (1992). Extrinsic and intrinsic motivation to use computers in the workplace. *Journal of Applied Social Psychology*, 22, 1111-1132.

Davis, F. D., Bagozzi, R. P., & Warshaw, P.R. (1989). User acceptance of computer technology: A comparison of two theoretical models. *Management Science*, 35(8), 982-1003.

Dewan, S., & Kraemer, K. (2000). Information technology and productivity: evidence from country-level data. *Management Science*, 46(4), 548-562

Ein-Dor, P., & Orgad, M. (1993). The effect of national culture on IS: implications for international information systems. *Global Journal of Information Management*, 1(1), 33-44.

Erez, M., & Earley, P. C. (1987). Comparative analysis of goal-setting strategies across cultures. *Journal of Applied Psychology*, 72, 658-665.

Fazio, R. H., & Olson, M. A. (2003). Implicit measures in social cognition: Their meaning and use. *Annual Review of Psychology*, 54, 297-327.

Ford, D. P., Connelly, C. E., & Meister, D. B. (2003). Information systems research and Hofstede's Culture's Consequences: An uneasy and incomplete partnership. *IEEE Transactions on Engineering Management,* 50(1), 8-26

Gefen D., & Straub, D. W. (2000). The relative importance of perceived ease of use in IS adoption: A study of e-commerce adoption. *Journal of the Association for Information Systems,* 1(8), 1-30

Gefen, D., Straub, D. W., & Boudreau, N. C, (2000). Structural equation modeling and regression: guideline for research practice. *Communications of the Association of Information Systems,* 4(7), 1-79.

Gefen, D., & Straub, D. W. (1997). Gender differences in the perception and use of e-Mail: an extension to the technology acceptance model. *MIS Quarterly*, 21(4), 389-400.

Grover, V., Golsar, M.D. & Segars, A. (1995). Adopters of telecommunications initiatives: a profile of progres-sive US corporations. *International Journal of Infor-mation Management,* 15(1), 33-46.

Hair, J. F., Jr., Anderson, R.E, Tatham, R. L, & Black, W.C. (1998). *Multivariate data analysis with readings*. 5th Edition. Englewood Cliffs, NJ: Prentice Hall.

Haythornthwaite, C., & Wellman, B. (1998). Work, friendship and media use for information exchange in a networked organization. *Journal of the American Society for Information Science,* 49(12), 1101–1114.

Ho, T. H., Raman, K. S., & Watson, R.T. (1989). Group decision support systems: the cultural factor. *Proceedings of the Tenth Annual International Conference on Information Systems.* Boston. pp.119-129.

Hoffman, L.W. (1972). Early childhood experiences and women's achievement motives. *Journal of Social Issues,* 28(8), 129-155.

Hofstede, G., & Bond, M. H. (1988). The Confucius connection: from cultural roots to economic growth. *Organizational Dynamics,* 16(4), 4-21.

Hofstede, G. (1980). *Culture's Consequences: international differences in work-related values.* CA: Newbury Park, Sage.

Hofstede, G. (1991). *Cultures and organizations: software of the mind,* McGraw-Hill, London.

Hofstede, G. (2001). *Culture's Consequences,* 2nd Ed., Sage, Thousand Oaks, CA.

Jordan, E. (1994). *National and organisational culture:their use in information systems design* (Report). Hong Kong: City Polytechnic of Hong Kong. Faculty of Business.

Kettinger, W. J. (1997). The use of computer-mediated communication in an intraorganizational context. *Decision Sciences,* 28(3), 513-555.

Kroeber, A., & Kluckhohn. C. (1952). *Culture: a critical review of concepts and definitions,* Peabody Papers, 27(1).

Kumar, S. Nicol, D. M., & Rude, D. E. (1993). *The State of cross-cultural decision making research: A critique and foundations for future research* (Working paper). University of Houston. Department of Management.

Limaye, M., & Victor, D. (1991). Cross-cultural business communication research: State of the art and hypotheses for the 1990's. *Journal of Business Communication,* 28(3), 277-299.

Limaye, M., Hirt, S. G. & Chin, W.W. (2001). Intention does not always matter: the contingent role of habit on IT usage behavior, *In Proceedings of The 9th European Conference on Information Systems, Bled, Slovenia,* 27-29 June, pp. 27-9.

Lu, M., & Lu, D. H. (1995). Cultural impact on information systems: a framework for research. Waiman Cheung ed. *Selected Essays on Decision Sciences,* The Chinese University of Hong Kong. pp.20-30.

Malhotra, N. K., & McCort, J. D. (2001). A cross-cultural comparison of behavioral intentions models: theoretical considerations and an empirical investigation. *International Marketing Review*, 18(3), 235-269

Matta, K. F., & Boutros, N., (1989). Barriers to electronic mail systems in developing countries. *Computer & Society*, 19 (1), 1-6

Minton, H. L., & Schneider, F. W. (1980). *Differential Psychology*. Waveland Press, Prospect Heights, IL.

Ndubisi, N. O., & Jantan, M. (2003). Evaluating IS usage in Malaysian small and medium-sized firms using the technology acceptance model. *Logistics Information Management*, 16(6), 440-450.

O'Neil, J. M. (1982). Gender-role conflict and strain in Men's lives: implications for psychiatrists, psychologists, and other human-service providers. *Men in Transition: Theory and Therapy*. K. Solomon and N. B. Levy (eds.), Plenum, New York. pp.5-44.

Pavlou, P. (2003). Consumer acceptance of electronic commerce: integrating trust and risk with the technology acceptance model. *International Journal of Electronic Commerce,* 7, 69-103.

Robey, D., & Rodriguez-Diaz, A. (1989). The organizational and cultural context of systems implementation: Case experience from Latin America. *Information & Management*, 17, 229-239

Robichaux, B. P., & Cooper R. B. (1998). GSS participation: a cultural examination. *Information & Management*, 33, 287-300.

Rose, G., & Straub, D. (1998). Predicting general IT use: applying TAM to the Arabic World, *Journal of Global Information Management,* 6(3), 39-46

Rouibah, K., & Hamdy, H. (2006). Does instant messaging usage impact students' performance in Kuwait? *In Proceedings of the IASTED International Conference Networks and Communication Systems*, 29-31 March, Chiang Mai Thailand

Schein, E. H. (1985). *Organizational Culture and Leadership*. Jossey-Bass, San Francisco. CA.

Shih, H. P, (2004). Extended technology acceptance model of internet utilization behavior. *Information & Management,* 41(6), 719-729

Srite, M. D. (2000). *The influence of national culture on the acceptance and use of information technologies: an empirical study*. Doctoral Dissertation. The Florida State University.

Straub, D. (1994). The effect of culture on IT diffusion: e-mail and fax in Japan and the U.S. *Information Systems Research*, 5(1), 23-47.

Straub, D., Keil, M., & Brenner, W. (1997). Testing the technology acceptance model across cultures: a three country study. *Information & Management*, 33(1), 1-11.

Straub, D., Loch, K., Evaristo, J. R., Karahanna, E., & Srite, M. (2002). Toward a theory-based measurement of culture. *Journal of Global Information Management*, 10(1), 13-23.

Tan, B. C. Y., Wei, K., Watson, R. T., Watson, R. T., & Walczuch, R. M. (1998). Reducing status effects with computer-mediated communication: evidence from two distinct national cultures. *Journal of Management Information Systems*, 15(1), 119-141.

Taylor, M. C., & Hall, J. A. (1982). Psychological androgyny: theories, methods, and conclusion. *Psychological Bulletin*, 92, 347-366.

Teng, J. T. C., Fiedler, K. D., & Grover, V. (2000). A cross cultural study on the organizational context of process redesign initiatives: U.S. vs. Taiwan. *Journal of Global Information Management*, 3(3), 7-28.

Tricker, R. I. (1988). Information resource management: a cross cultural perspective. *Information & Management*, 15, 37-46.

Venkatesh, V., & Davis, F. D. (2000). A theoretical extension of the technology acceptance model:

Four longitudinal field studies. *Management Science*, 46(2), 186-204.

Venkatesh, V., & Morris, M. G. (2000). Why don't men ever stop to ask for directions? gender, social influence, and their role in technology acceptance and usage behavior. *MIS Quarterly*, 24(1), 115-140.

Watson, R., Ho, T. H., & Raman, K. S. (1994). Culture: a fourth dimension of group support systems. *Communications of the ACM*, 37(10), 45-55.

Williamson, O. E., & Masten S. E. (1995). *Transaction cost economics. theory and concepts,* Edward Elgar, Aldershot.

Chapter X
Cultural Differences, Information Technology Infrastructure, and E-Commerce Behavior:
Implications for Developing Countries

Ahu Genis-Gruber
TOBB University of Economics and Technology Ankara, Turkey

Bedri Kamil Onur Tas
TOBB University of Economics and Technology Ankara, Turkey

ABSTRACT

E-commerce has been a widely used mean to purchase goods and services all over the world. This study investigates the role of cultural differences and information technology infrastructure on usage of e-commerce in developed and developing countries. As shown in Genis-Gruber and Tas (2007) cultural differences are expected to play a major role on e-commerce behavior especially in developing economies. In order to identify cultural differences, we use Hofstede's classification. We classify the countries according to these indices and their technological and economic development. We make several cultural comparisons among various countries and we empirically investigate whether these cultural differences play a significant role on e-commerce behavior. We implement OLS and fixed effect regression methods. Using dummy variables and interaction variables, we estimate the effect of cultural differences on e-commerce purchases and other e-commerce variables. Besides the effects of cultural factors, we also investigate the effects of information infrastructure and education level of the countries. We conclude that cultural dimensions play an incremental role on e-commerce and relationship between infrastructure and e-commerce. We control for several other factors like information infrastructure and education level, and use different econometric techniques to achieve our results.

Copyright © 2009, IGI Global, distributing in print or electronic forms without written permission of IGI Global is prohibited.

INTRODUCTION

In the latest era, the constant acceleration in the usage of high-speed Internet has led to a significant surge in various ways of getting goods in a limited period of time. In this sense, e-commerce, which is defined as all business activities that use Internet technologies,[1] has been a widely used mean to purchase goods and services all over the world. The major increase in e-commerce usage enables people to reach the products that they want in a global environment and compare the goods and products not only in local but in global dimensions. On the companies' sides, once a company is connected to Internet retailing, the company becomes an international company. The key factors that conduct the route of their activities are trust to sellers, cultural perception of buyers, language and infrastructure.

In the literature, trust in e-commerce activities is a challenging concept. There are several studies in the literature that show the importance of trust trait as a part of culture on e-commerce activities. Gefen (2000) stated trust as a critical factor influencing the successful rise of e-commerce. Strategy implementation in various cultures has distinctive differences. The study by Lynch and Beck (2001) present the implications and traits for successful strategies and that geographical and cultural difference should be taken into account. They show that Internet buying behavior shows differences depending on user experience, home country and region. Trust is a fundamental part of culture that influences the usage of e-commerce. Grabner-Kraeuter (2002) presents that trust is the long-term barrier for realizing the potential of e-commerce to customers. Teo and Liu (2005) indicate the importance of trust for online purchases. Gefen and Heart (2006) empirically investigate whether the effects of predictability and familiarity on trust beliefs differ across national cultures and conclude that trust beliefs differ across national culture. In this study, trust and trust beliefs, trustworthiness, in U.S. and Israel and conclude that trust beliefs differ across national culture are further analyzed. Trust, by Alm and Melnik (2006) is stated as a dependent on the personal reputation and image of the party, which is one of the critical and vital factors for e-commerce success. Efendioglu (2005) states in his paper that in e-commerce transactions, trust extends beyond the buyer and seller to institutions including online payment firms, banks, credit card companies and the Internet provider. Whereas Cheng (2006) shows that, parties loose trust when the exchange relationship by collecting irrelevant information of the other party without informing them, exploits. Knezevic et.al. (2006) mentions in their paper that the restrictions for e-commerce improvement are basically the perceptions about e-commerce in the culture. Wu and Chang (2006) state the importance of transaction trust on e-commerce. Genis-Gruber and Onur (2006) show that trust, as a proxy for culture, affects Internet retailing. Schneider (2007) mentions the importance of trust generation in order to compete with traditional retail sales. Goldstein and O'Connor (2001) mention the importance of virtual trust for online transactions.

Many studies in the literature focus on the effects of trust beliefs on e-commerce. Since different cultures have different levels of trust perceptions, countries with different cultural properties should have different levels of e-commerce. Trust affects the intensity of going online and willing to give personal information. Lack of trust results less online transactions, as retail shopping is expected to replace it. As giving personal financial data is not essential during a retail sales, cultures with less trust to unknown are expected to divert their consumption to traditional shopping. This study provides the empirical evidence for this hypothesis by directly analyzing the effects of cultural properties on usage levels of e-commerce and interaction of e-commerce and information technology infrastructure.

This study is making two main contributions to the literature. First, this study is one of the first studies that directly examines the effects of culture on e-commerce. We provide empirical evidence that cultural differences play a vital role on e-commerce activities. This study uses four different indices to identify cultural differences. Thus, this study considers several different dimensions of cultural differences and it is an extensive study in that sense. Second, we investigate the relationship between e-commerce and information infrastructure and examine the implications of this relationship on developing countries like Middle East and Nordic African (MENA) countries and specifically Turkey. These analyses also provide support for the previous literature which claims that national culture should be included in e-commerce studies. The results of this study have many policy implications.

MOTIVATION

The classification of cultures represented in this study, depends on the methodology of Hofstede's. Hofstede classifies the countries according to their rankings in his five dimensions; Individualism (IND), Uncertainty Avoidance Index (UAI), Masculinity (MAS), Power Distance Index (PDI), and Long-Term Orientation (LTO).

The first dimension, Individualism (vs. Collectivism) Index, stands for the degree to which individuals feel themselves belong to the groups. In an individualist culture, everyone should take care of themselves; everyone is responsible for himself and core family. Whereas in collectivist cultures, people are born into groups with which they share a strong "group belonging" feeling. People are expected to care about the group and the perception of the group is an important issue during decision making process. In order to sustain the "group belonging", the ideas of the group are taken into account and behavior patterns are leant from childhood on. In such an environment, we expect that individuals and enterprises make more online purchase and use e-commerce more intense than in collectivist societies. As the ideas of the group are not a vital issue for the individual's decision, the purchase process completion is expected to process faster and more rational.

H1: In individualist countries, individuals and enterprises make more online purchase and use e-commerce more intense than in collectivist countries.

Second dimension of Hofstede is Uncertainty Avoidance Index (UAI). The index contends with the tolerance of the society for unexpected situations, how tolerant the members of the culture are to uncertain and not-planned situations. In cultures with Weak UAI, anxiety levels are low. In Weak UAI cultures, aggression and emotions are not supposed to be expressed. In order to minimize the uncertainty and unexpected situations, strict rules and regulations are applied. In Strong UAI cultures, people are more tolerant of different opinions, relative fewer rules are applied. People within these cultures are more reflective. In this point, we hypothesize that cultures with Strong UAI have lower Internet purchase than Weak UAI cultures. Online purchase requires trust to the seller, which is hard in Internet environment. Cultures that try to avoid uncertainty are expected to use less e-commerce activities. The empirical results support this hypothesis.

H2: Countries with Strong UAI have lower Internet purchase than Weak UAI Countries.

Third dimension of Hofstede is Masculinity (vs. Femininity) Index which stands for the distribution of the roles in the society. Masculine roles are expected to be assertive, tough and material whereas feminine roles are expected to be more tolerant, modest and life quality concerned. As a result of our study, this index turned out not to impact Internet purchases significantly.

H3: Masculinity Index does not impact e-commerce activities.

Fourth dimension of Hofstede, Power Distance (PDI) Index informs the dependence relationship in a culture. In Small PDI cultures, limited dependence of subordinates on bosses is monitored, emotional distance is small, and subordinates are likely to ask their bosses for consultation. Whereas in Large PDI cultures, counter dependence between the subordinates and bosses are seen, emotional distance is large; subordinates are unlike to approach their bosses directly. Thus, we predict that PDI can also play a role on e-commerce activities. We find supporting results for this hypothesis.

H4: Power Distance Index might effect online transactions and Internet usage, which increases the possibility of e-commerce activities.

Fifth dimension is Long-Term Orientation (vs. Short-Term Orientation) endures traditional values, social obligations. Also this index can be combined with the perceptions of culture towards Internet usage, which lead to e-commerce activities.[2]

H5: Long Term Orientation Index is expected to influence e-commerce activities.

We use Eurostat and Internet World Stat dataset of ITU. By implementing our empirical model, we have shown that cultural traits play an essential role for e-commerce activities and on the relationship between e-commerce and information infrastructure. These findings have many practical implications for development of e-commerce especially for developing countries.

OVERVIEW OF CULTURAL AND INFORMATION INFRASTRUCTURE DIFFERENCES ACROSS COUNTRIES

As shown by Hofstede, different countries have different cultural properties. Genis-Gruber and Tas (2007) proposes that cultural properties of a country significantly effects e-commerce behavior. This study also shows that information infrastructure, like PC ownership, Internet usage, telephone ownership, of a country is also a significant factor of e-commerce. We provide evidence that the usage of information infrastructure is affected by culture. The empirical study also shows that relationship between information infrastructure and e-commerce is affected by cultural dimensions. In this section, we provide an overview of cultural differences and information structure in different regions of the world and MENA countries[3].

Cultural Differences

As mentioned above, it has been shown empirically and theoretically that cultural differences play an incremental role on e-commerce behavior of individuals. Hofstede's cultural dimensions are widely used to measure and identify cultural properties of different countries. Comparison of cultural dimensions shows that different countries have various cultural properties.

Figure 1 display the average of Hofstede's cultural dimensions by region. It can easily be seen from Figure 1 that in the different regions of the world countries have various cultural properties. For example, the individualism index of Asian countries is very low compared to Oceania countries.

Table 1 presents descriptive statistics for all of the countries that Hofstede analyzed. There are 68 countries from different regions of the world examined by Hofstede. The statistics presented

Figure 1. Regional comparison of cultural dimensions

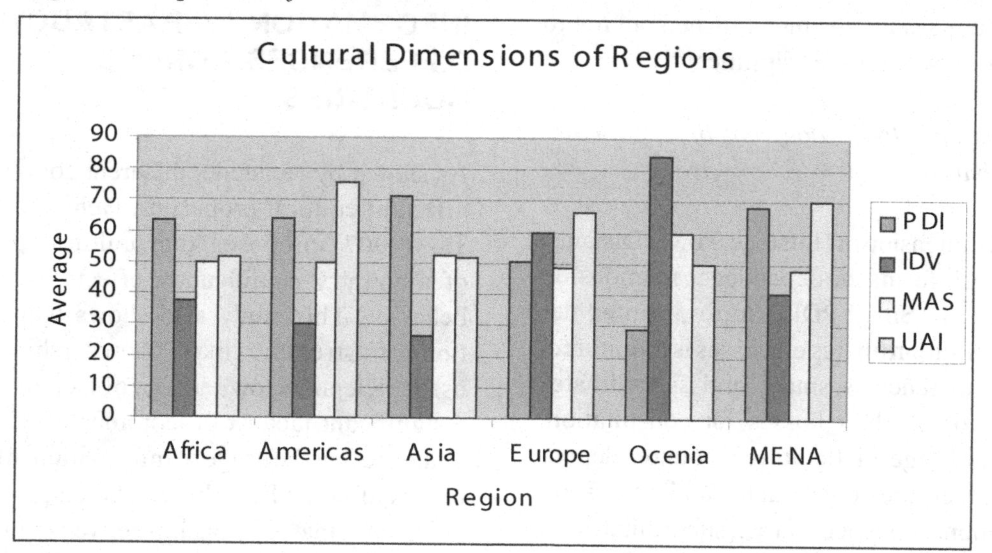

Table 1. Cultural dimensions of all countries

Cultural Dimensions	Mean	Standard Deviation	Minimum	Maximum
PDI	59.3	21.8	11	104
IDV	43.4	24.1	6	91
MAS	50.5	18.7	5	110
UAI	66.4	23.7	8	112

in Table 1 indicate that all four cultural dimensions are very different across different regions and different countries. The tables in Appendix A display a detailed description of the descriptive statistics for different regions.

Information Infrastructure

Information infrastructure of a country is one of the fundamental components of e-commerce. Without a well-working infrastructure, an Internet economy can not survive. Thus, the information infrastructures of countries significantly affect e-commerce in that country. Section 6 investigates the relationship between information infrastructure and e-commerce. In this section, we show that the different countries have significantly different information technology infrastructures. We use the percentage of Internet users in the population as an indicator for information technology infrastructure.

Figure 2 shows the average Internet user percentage for the countries in different users. The averages are calculated using year 2005 data for 209 countries provided by International Telecommunication Union (ITU). Figure 2 presents that information infrastructure differs significantly among different countries. In African countries the average is close to 5% where in Europe, it is almost 40%.

Table 2 displays descriptive statistics of percentage of Internet users at different regions of

Figure 2. Regional comparison of Internet users

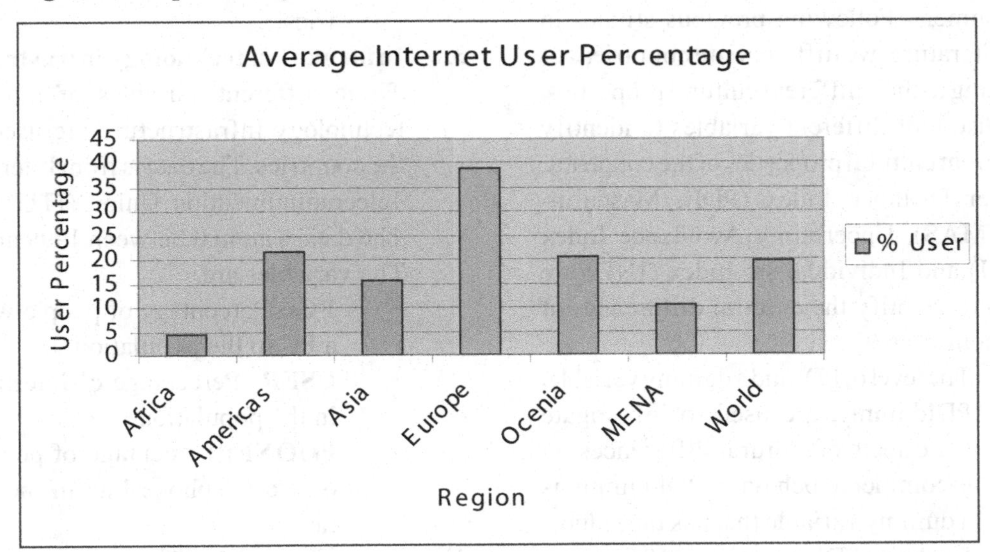

Table 2. Properties of Internet users percentage for regions (2005)

Region	Mean	Standard Deviation	Minimum	Maximum
Africa	4.58	6.35	.19	28
Americas	21.8	17.8	1.69	67.9
Asia	15.6	18.3	0.06	68.4
Europe	39	18.7	6	76.2
Oceania	20.5	24.9	0.84	70.4
MENA	10.6	9.3	0.14	31.1
World	19.6	20.5	0.06	76.2

the world. Table 2 shows that some regions like Europe and Americas have developed information infrastructure (Internet users) compared to other regions like Africa. Information infrastructure has very different properties at different parts of the world. Since development of e-commerce depends on adequate information infrastructure, e-commerce behavior will be different at different regions.

DATA

The data used in this chapter can be separated into four sections: e-commerce, cultural indicator variables, technology infrastructure and control variables.

1. **E-commerce[4]:** E-commerce variable is the dependent variable in our regressions. The e-commerce data is taken from Eurostat information society statistics. Internet purchases by individuals purchasing via Internet and/or networks other than Internet variables are used in our analysis. The variables contain the percentage of individuals and enterprises that purchase online. Data is annual and between 2002 and 2006.
2. **Cultural indicator variables:** This chapter investigates the effects of cultural dif-

ferences on the e-commerce behavior of consumers. Following previous studies in the literature, we differentiate countries according to their different cultural properties. We use four different variables to identify different cultural properties of the countries. Power Distance Index (PDI), Masculinity (MAS), Uncertainty Avoidance Index (UAI) and Individualism Index (IND) are used to identify the cultural differences of the countries.

- The level of PDI and a dummy variable, PDIdummy, are used to investigate the effects of cultural differences on e-commerce behavior. PDIdummy is a dummy variable that has the value 1 for strong PDI countries and 0 for weak PDI countries. So, the coefficients of PDI and PDIdummy indicate the difference in strong and weak UAI countries.
- MAS is the level value of Masculinity MASdummy is a dummy variable that has the value 1 for masculine countries and 0 for feminine countries. The coefficients of MAS and MASdummy indicate the difference in strong and weak UAI countries.
- Both the level of UAI and a dummy variable, UAIdummy, are used to investigate the effects of cultural differences on e-commerce behavior. UAIdummy is a dummy variable that has the value 1 for strong UAI countries and 0 for weak UAI countries. So, the coefficients of UAI and UAIdummy indicate the difference in strong and weak UAI countries.
- Level of IND and INDdummy are used. INDdummy is a dummy variable that has the value 1 for individualist countries and 0 for collectivist countries. The coefficient of IND and INDdummy shows the difference in individualist and collectivist countries.

3. **Information technology infrastructure[5]:** Three different variables of information technology infrastructure are used for all the countries. The data is from International Telecommunication Union (ITU) dataset. The data is annual between 1999 and 2005. The variables are,
   - **PCs:** Percentage of people who own a PC in the population
   - **USER:** Percentage of Internet users in the population
   - **PHONE:** Percentage of people who own a telephone line in the population
4. **Control variables:** We use control variables to concentrate on the cultural effects. There are variables that affect e-commerce other than culture, like GDP and education level of a country. Countries considered in this study have different levels of GDP and education. The difference in the e-commerce levels could be caused by these differences in GDP and education. Thus, we control for GDP and education by adding them into our regressions as regressors.
   - **GDP:** Per Capita Gross Domestic Product.
   - **EDUC:** The education level of a country can affect the use of e-commerce. We used the percentage of mathematics, science and technology enrolments and graduates variables from Eurostat Education and Training data set.

The selection and construction of e-commerce, information technology infrastructure and education level variables is mainly limited by data availability. Eurostat provides a detailed dataset on e-commerce for all EU countries between 2002 and 2006. This cross-country dataset gives us the opportunity to investigate the effect of cultural differences. Different countries have different levels of cultural indicators and e-commerce. We analyze how much of the different levels of e-commerce behavior among different countries are caused by cultural differences. The choice of dependent and independent variables do not affect our main results since we control for other variables that can affect e-commerce and the dependent variable (e-commerce) correctly measures cross-country differences in e-commerce. Usage of alternative measures[6] for (e-commerce) will only change the coefficients but the effect of cultural differences will still be significant.

METHODOLOGY

To test our hypothesizes, we used Ordinary Least Squares (OLS) and Panel Data Regression with fixed effects methods. The dependent variable is e-commerce. The independent variables are cultural indicator variables (PDI, MAS, UAI and IND), information infrastructure (PCs, USER, PHONE), GDP and education level (EDUC). The significance of the coefficients of the cultural indicator variables indicates that cultural differences are an important part of e-commerce behavior. The regressions are run with different sets of independent variables and different cultural indicator variables. GDP and EDUC are included in the regressions as control variables.

The following regression equation is estimated using OLS:

$$y_{i,t} = \beta_0 + \beta X_{i,t} + \varepsilon_{i,t}$$

Where $y_{i,t}$ is e-commerce variable (Internet purchases by individuals and enterprises), $X_{i,t}$ contains the control variables (GDP and EDUC), information infrastructure variables (PCs, USER, PHONE) and the cultural indicator variable (PDI, MAS, UAI and IND).

The following regression equation is estimated using the fixed effects estimator:

$$y_{i,t} = \beta_i + \beta X_{i,t} + \varepsilon_{i,t}$$

Where β_i is the fixed effects term that indicates that differences across countries can be captured in differences in the constant term. $y_{i,t}$ is e-commerce variable (Internet purchases by individuals and enterprises), $X_{i,t}$ contains the control variables (GDP and EDUC), information infrastructure variables (PCs, USER, PHONE) and the cultural indicator variable (PDI, MAS, UAI and IND). Both the level of cultural indicator variables and a dummy variable that takes the values of 1 if cultural indicator index is larger than 50 and 0 otherwise are used. The regressions with level of indicator variables show us how changes in the cultural indicator levels affect e-commerce behavior. Such as the effect of one point increase in PDI level of a country on e-commerce of that country can be calculated using coefficient of PDI in the regression with cultural indicator levels.

The regressions with cultural indicator dummy variables (PDIdummy, etc.) investigate the e-commerce differences between countries with weak and strong cultural indicators. A country is defined to have weak cultural properties if cultural indicator is below 50 and strong cultural properties if cultural indicator is above 50. For example Uncertainty Avoidance Index score of Turkey is 85 and Turkey is referred as Strong U.A. culture and UAI score of Denmak is 23 which is referred as Weak U.A. Using the coefficient of the dummy variable, we can analyze how e-commerce differs among countries with weak and strong cultural indicators.

To investigate the effect of cultural differences on the relation between infrastructure and e-commerce we use interaction variables. Interaction variables are constructed by multiplying the culture dummy variable with infrastructure variable. The coefficient of the interaction variables shows the effect of culture.

INFORMATION TECHNOLOGY INFRASTRUCTURE AND E-COMMERCE BEHAVIOR:

Section 3 shows that infrastructure of different countries varies among different countries. Using data from Eurostat this section empirically investigates the relationship between infrastructure and e-commerce. Data for the European countries is used because reliable data about e-commerce for all European countries is available for a wide time period. Once the relationship between information technology infrastructure and e-commerce behavior is identified, the implications for developing countries can easily be determined.

Table 3 reports the results from OLS regressions of percentage of individuals purchase online (ecommerce) on different sets of information infrastructure variables (PCs, USER, PHONE). The coefficients of the following regression equation are estimated.

$$\text{E-commerce} = \beta 0 + \beta 1\text{USER (or PCs or PHONE)} + \beta 2\text{GDP} + \beta 2\text{EDUC}$$

t-statistics are displayed in parentheses below the coefficient estimates. The last row displays the R-square. The data is annual. One star next to the standard errors denotes that the coefficient is significant at 5%. Two stars denote that the coefficient is significant at 1%.

Table 3 presents regression results of Internet purchases by individuals as dependent variable with different sets of independent variables. Table 3 investigates the effect of information infrastructure identified by different variables (USER, PHONE, EDUC) on e-commerce, thus the coefficients of these variables are of interest. Each column represents a different regression specification (different variable to identify infrastructure). The regressions are also run without GDP because GDP is highly correlated with infrastructure variables which might cause multicollinearity problem. From Table 3, we can conclude that all infrastructure variables are significant and the coefficients are positive. Thus, infrastructure positively affects Internet purchases by individuals. A better information technology infrastructure will cause an increase in

Table 3. Internet purchases by individuals: Effect of information infrastructure, GDP and education (analysis of EU countries)

	Internet Purchases by Individuals				
	1	2	3	4 (Fixed Effect)	5 (Fixed Effect)
PCs	0.313 (5.88)**			0.257 (3.82)**	
USER		0.265 (4.16)**			0.269 (2.87)**
PHONE			0.112 (2.26)*		
GDP	0.267 (3.96)**	0.419 (7.05)**	0.449 (5.96)**	0.410 (5.17)**	0.364 (3.93)**
EDUC	0.039 (0.89)	0.117 (2.72)**	0.195 (4.44)**	0.155 (0.55)	0.104 (0.33)
Constant	-8.663 (2.92)**	-15.938 (5.01)**	-27.115 (3.88)**	-17.947 (0.99)	-13.853 (0.69)
Observations	78	78	78	78	78
R-Square	0.77	0.73	0.69	0.70	0.66

continued of following page

Table 3. continued

	Internet Purchases by Individuals				
	1	2	3	4 (Fixed Effect)	5 (Fixed Effect)
PCs	0.478 (13.28)**			0.355 (4.45)**	
USER		0.554 (8.85)**			0.451 (4.88)**
PHONE			0.336 (8.66)**		
EDUC	-0.034 (0.78)	0.050 (0.94)	0.229 (4.35)**	0.798 (2.57)*	0.389 (1.12)
Constant	-3.804 (1.29)	-13.029 (3.22)**	-50.416 (7.21)**	-57.471 (2.83)**	-32.721 (1.48)
Observations	78	78	78	78	78
R-Square	0.72	0.55	0.54	0.53	0.56

e-commerce. Education variable is not significant for most of the regression specifications suggesting that education level does not play that much important role on e-commerce. Also, the R^2 is very high especially when the control variables are added to the regression.

CULTURE AND E-COMMERCE

The previous section shows that information infrastructure is an essential component of e-commerce. This chapter also claims that the cultural properties of countries significantly affect e-commerce behavior. This section investigates and answers two main questions:

- What is the relationship between different cultural properties (PDI, IND, MAS, and UAI) of a country and the level of e-commerce in that country?
- How do cultural properties affect the relationship between information infrastructure and e-commerce?

The Effect of Power Distance Index (PDI)

Table 4 presents regression results of Internet purchases by individuals as dependent variable with different sets of independent variables. Table 4 investigates the effect of culture identified by PDI and information infrastructure identified by USER on e-commerce, thus the coefficients of these variables are of interest. Each column represents a different regression specification. Both the level of PDI and a dummy variable to identify strong PDI country are used.

Table 4 reports the results from OLS regressions of percentage of individuals purchase online (ecommerce) on information infrastructure variable (USER), cultural indicator variable (PDI or PDIDummy) and other control variable (EDUC). The coefficients of the following regression equation are estimated.

$$\text{e-commerce} = \beta 0 + \beta 1\text{PDI} + \beta 2\text{PDIDummy} + \beta 3\text{USER} + \beta 4(\text{USER*PDIDummy}) + \beta 5\text{EDUC}$$

Table 4. The effect of power distance index (PDI) on e-commerce and the relationship between information infrastructure and e-commerce behavior: Evidence from EU countries

	Internet Purchases by Individuals			
	1	2	3	4 (Fixed Effect)
PDI	-0.110 (2.04)*			
PDIDummy		-5.373 (2.06)*		
USER	0.460 (6.19)**	0.429 (5.18)**	0.465 (6.54)**	0.523 (5.42)**
USER*PDIDummy			-0.179 (2.26)*	-0.472 (2.24)*
EDUC	0.085 (1.58)	0.075 (1.37)	0.072 (1.33)	0.521 (1.38)
Constant	-5.701 (0.98)	-6.778 (1.26)	-8.273 (1.76)	-39.340 (1.68)
Observations	66	66	66	66
R-Square	0.62	0.62	0.63	0.63

Power Distance Index (PDI) that is the extent to which the less powerful members of organizations and institutions (like the family) accept and expect that power is distributed unequally. PDIDummy is a dummy variable which is 1 if PDI index is larger than 50 and 0 otherwise. As before, t-statistics are displayed in parentheses below the coefficient estimates. The last row displays the R-square. The data is annual. One star next to the standard errors denotes that the coefficient is significant at 5%. Two stars denote that the coefficient is significant at 1%.

Regression specifications 1 and 2 (columns 1, 2) show that power distance (PDI) cultural characteristics of a country is an important and significant part of e-commerce in a country. The coefficients of PDI and PDIDummy are significant and negative indicating that e-commerce and PDI are negatively correlated.

Regression specifications 3 and 4 analyze how different cultures use information infrastructure for e-commerce. In other words, the effect of culture on the relationship between infrastructure and e-commerce is investigated. The interaction variable, USER*PDIDummy, examines that relationship. The coefficient of USER*PDIDummy is significant and negative. Both OLS and fixed effects regressions have similar results. This result indicates that PDI significantly affects the relationship between infrastructure (USER) and e-commerce. When the PDI level of a country is higher then the coefficient of USER is lower. Thus, culture (PDI) has two effects.

1. PDI directly effects e-commerce. Countries with high PDI level conduct less e-commerce.
2. Indirectly, PDI affects how people use information technology infrastructure. The relationship between infrastructure and e-commerce depends on PDI level of that country.

The Effect of Individualism (IND)

Table 5 presents regression results of Internet purchases by individuals as dependent variable with different sets of independent variables. Table

Table 5. The effect of individualism (IND) on e-commerce and the relationship between information infrastructure and e-commerce behavior: Evidence from EU countries

	Internet Purchases by Individuals			
	1	2	3	4 (Fixed Effect)
IND	0.127 (1.82)			
INDDummy		-1.540 (0.45)		
USER	0.471 (6.36)**	0.553 (7.36)**	0.610 (2.95)**	-0.327 (0.47)
USER*INDDummy			-0.062 (0.37)	0.794 (1.21)
EDUC	0.065 (1.13)	0.112 (1.80)	0.113 (1.70)	0.538 (1.20)
Constant	-17.368 (4.20)**	-14.825 (3.73)**	-16.159 (2.80)**	-39.859 (1.47)
Observations	66	66	66	66
R-Square	0.61	0.60	0.60	0.60

5 investigates the effect of culture identified by IND and information infrastructure identified on e-commerce. Each column represents a different regression specification.

Table 5 reports the results from OLS regressions of percentage of individuals purchase online (ecommerce) on information infrastructure variable (USER), cultural indicator variable (IND or INDDummy) and other control variables EDUC. The coefficients of the following regression equation are estimated. USER is percentage of Internet users.

E-commerce = β0+ β1IDV + β2INDVDummy+ β3USER + β4(USER*INDDummy) + β5GDP+ β6EDUC

Regression specifications 1 and 2 (columns 1, 2) show that individualism (IND) cultural characteristics of a country is not significant for e-commerce in a country. The coefficients of IND and INDDummy are not significant. Regression specifications 3 and 4 show that individualism does not affect the relationship between infrastructure and e-commerce.

The Effect of Masculinity (MAS)

Table 6 presents regression results of Internet purchases by individuals as dependent variable with different sets of independent variables. Table VI investigates the effect of culture identified by MAS and information infrastructure identified on e-commerce. Each column represents a different regression specification.

Table 6 reports the results from OLS regressions of percentage of individuals purchase online (ecommerce) on information infrastructure variable (USER), cultural indicator variable (MAS or MASDummy) and other control variables EDUC. The regression equation is:

E-commerce = β0+ β1MAS + β2MASDummy+ β3USER + β4(USER*MASDummy) + β5GDP+ β6EDUC

Masculinity (MAS) versus its opposite, femininity refers to the distribution of roles between the genders which is another fundamental issue for any society to which a range of solutions

Table 6. The effect of masculinity (MAS) on e-commerce and the relationship between information infrastructure and e-commerce behavior: Evidence from EU countries

	Internet Purchases by Individuals			
	1	2	3	4 (Fixed Effect)
MAS	-0.035 (0.90)			
MASDummy		0.127 (0.06)		
USER	0.506 (6.82)**	0.539 (7.19)**	0.544 (8.03)**	0.514 (5.05)**
USER*MASDummy			0.022 (0.44)	0.186 (0.72)
EDUC	0.109 (1.94)	0.098 (1.66)	0.093 (1.64)	0.107 (0.26)
Constant	-12.323 (2.65)*	-14.657 (3.59)**	-14.831 (3.73)**	-17.313 (0.70)
Observations	66	66	66	66
R-Square	0.60	0.59	0.60	0.59

are found. MASDummy is a dummy variable which is 1 if MAS index is larger than 50 and 0 otherwise.

Regression specifications 1 and 2 (columns 1, 2) show that masculinity (MAS) cultural characteristics of a country is not significant for e-commerce in a country. The coefficients of MAS and MASDummy are not significant. Regression specifications 3 and 4 show that masculinity does not affect the relationship between infrastructure and e-commerce.

The Effect of Uncertainty Avoidance (UAI)

Table 7 investigates the effect of culture identified by UAI and information infrastructure identified by USER on e-commerce, thus the coefficients of these variables are of interest.

The table reports the results from OLS regressions of percentage of individuals purchase online (ecommerce) on information infrastructure variable (USER), cultural indicator variable (UAI or UAIDummy) and other control variables EDUC. The regression equation is:

$$\text{E-commerce} = \beta 0 + \beta 1\text{UAI} + \beta 2\text{UAIDummy} + \beta 3\text{USER} + \beta 4(\text{USER*UAIDummy}) + \beta 5\text{GDP} + \beta 6\text{EDUC}$$

Regression specifications 1 and 2 (columns 1, 2) show Uncertainty Avoidance (UAI) is an important and significant part of e-commerce in a country. The coefficients of UAI and UAIDummy are significant and negative indicating that e-commerce and UAI are negatively correlated. This result is inline with out hypothesis since the level of uncertainty in e-commerce is perceived to be higher than the traditional means of commerce.

Regression specifications 3 and 4 analyze how different cultures use information infrastructure for e-commerce. In other words, the effect of culture on the relationship between infrastructure and e-commerce is investigated. The interaction variable, USER*UAIDummy, examines that relationship. The coefficient of USER*PDIDummy is significant and negative. Both OLS and fixed effects regressions have similar results. This result indicates that PDI significantly affects the relationship between infrastructure (USER) and

Table 7. The effect of uncertainty avoidance index (UAI) on e-commerce and the relationship between information infrastructure and e-commerce behavior: Evidence from EU countries

	Internet Purchases by Individuals			
	1	2	3	4 (Fixed Effect)
UAI	-0.084 (2.24)*			
UAIDummy		-6.555 (3.72)**		
USER	0.517 (8.05)**	0.521 (8.71)**	0.598 (9.45)**	0.494 (3.46)**
USER*UAIDummy			-0.139 (3.38)**	0.026 (0.16)
EDUC	0.061 (1.09)	0.077 (1.53)	0.076 (1.47)	0.221 (0.58)
Constant	-6.144 (1.15)	-8.065 (2.03)*	-11.814 (3.18)**	-22.032 (0.92)
Observations	66	66	66	66
R-Square	0.62	0.67	0.66	0.58

e-commerce. When the PDI level of a country is higher then the coefficient of USER is lower. Thus, culture (PDI) has two effects.

1. PDI directly affects e-commerce. Countries with high PDI level conduct less e-commerce.
2. Indirectly, PDI affects how people use information technology infrastructure. The relationship between infrastructure and e-commerce depends on PDI level of that country.

SUMMARY OF THE EMPIRICAL RESULTS

This study empirically investigated three main issues:

1. The relationship between information technology infrastructure and e-commerce.
2. The effect of different cultural properties (PDI, IND, MAS, UAI) of a country on the level of e-commerce in that country.
3. The effect of cultural properties on the relationship between information infrastructure and e-commerce.

Using datasets from Eurostat, Internet World Stat dataset of ITU and Hofstede's cultural dimension indices, we get the following results in Sections 2, 7 and 8:

- Information technology infrastructure and cultural dimensions are different among countries and regions of the world.
- There is positive relationship between information technology infrastructure and e-commerce behavior. Better infrastructure promotes e-commerce.
- Besides information infrastructure and education level, cultural properties play an essential role in e-commerce behavior. Power Distance Index (PDI) and Uncertainty Avoidance Index (UAI) are significant cultural dimensions that affect e-commerce. PDI and UAI negatively induce e-commerce. Countries with high PDI and UAI levels conduct less e-commerce independent of

their infrastructure and education level. Masculinity (MAS) and Individualism (IND) are not significant cultural factors.
- Cultural dimensions impact the connection between information technology infrastructure and e-commerce. Usage of information infrastructure for e-commerce depends on the cultural properties. PDI and UAI negatively affect the relationship between infrastructure and e-commerce.

As a result, both the information technology infrastructure and cultural dimensions should be taken into account when analyzing e-commerce behavior. We find supporting evidence for hypotheses H2, H3 and H4. We reject the hypotheses H1 since individualism does not affect e-commerce. H5 is not analyzed because of lack of available data.

POLICY IMPLICATIONS

The results of this empirical study have several results for e-commerce policy implications. As Kenny (2002) argues, Internet is expected to impact economic growth. Thus, policymakers would like to promote e-commerce adoption. The results of the previous sections indicate that investing in information technology infrastructure is not enough to promote e-commerce. Policymakers should take into account the cultural dimensions. For example, in a country with high Uncertainty Avoidance Index (UAI), people will be more reluctant to conduct e-commerce behavior compared to a country with low UAI. Also, policymakers should consider Power Distance Index (PDI) while implementing e-commerce policies.

Usage of information infrastructure for e-commerce depends on the cultural properties. PDI and UAI negatively affect the relationship between infrastructure and e-commerce. The policymakers should not only focus on the aspects of e-commerce like infrastructure and legislation and neglect the cultural differences and cultural properties. The policies designed to promote e-commerce will not achieve its intended goals if cultural dimensions are not taken into consideration. The empirical results suggest that cultural properties especially UAI and PDI of a country should be examined carefully. Then, improvements in information infrastructure should be designed. Also, the policymakers should implement policies to alter the cultural properties of countries which significantly affect e-commerce. For example, in a high UAI country, the government can run advertisement campaigns about the security of the means of e-commerce like making transactions online using a credit card. Also, the quality of the product delivered through e-commerce can be guaranteed in these countries to promote trust in e-commerce. As a result, ignoring cultural properties of a country while promoting e-commerce will decrease the efficiency of the policies significantly.

The results of this study have implications for investors. Before investing in e-commerce related business in a country, the investor should carefully analyze the cultural properties of that country besides factors like infrastructure, GDP and education level. Ignoring the effects of cultural dimensions will give misleading results. As mentioned above, cultural dimensions have both direct and indirect effects on e-commerce. Careful study regarding the culture of the country will lead to the patterns of general e-commerce behavior in that particular society.

CASE STUDY: TURKEY

In order to specify our study, we decided to implement our model to a specific country and Turkey is analyzed by using Hofstede's classifications.[7]

- Power Distance Index score of Turkey is 66 and is referred as Large P.D. culture.

- Individualism Index score of Turkey is 37 and is referred as Collectivist culture.
- Uncertainty Avoidance Index score of Turkey is 85 and is referred as Strong U.A. culture.
- Masculinity Index score of Turkey is 45 and is referred as Feminine culture.

Under these classifications, Turkey is expected to use less e-commerce compared to other countries that score opposite on the scale. As our model suggests that countries with Strong Uncertainty Avoidance prefer to complete their purchase process mutually, they avoid online transactions. Also, countries that have large P.D. culture tend to make fewer online transactions. Our empirical results suggest that, in Turkey, development of information technology infrastructure will affect e-commerce less than the countries with different cultural properties.

Table 8 presents e-commerce and IT infrastructure of Turkey. E-commerce behavior in Turkey more than doubled from 2003 to 2004. Same increase can also be seen in the percentage of Internet users.

CASE STUDY: MENA COUNTRIES

Average Hofstede's classifications for MENA countries are as the following:

- Average Power Distance Index score of MENA is 68.5 and is referred as Large P.D. culture.
- Average Individualism Index score of MENA is 40.5 and is referred as Collectivist culture.
- Average Uncertainty Avoidance Index score of MENA is 70 and is referred as Strong U.A. culture.
- Average Masculinity Index score of MENA is 48.25 and is referred as Feminine culture.

Table 8. E-commerce and infrastructure of Turkey

Year	E-commerce (Number of Online Transactions)[1]	PCs	USER	PHONE	GDP
1999	.	3.28	2.23	38.77	2847
2000	.	3.66	3.66	50.6	2941
2001	.	3.9	5.05	55.54	2146
2002	.	4.27	6.12	60.07	2622
2003	3534678	4.68	8.42	65.69	3412
2004	7617446	5.13	14.15	74.54	4187
2005	.	5.56	15.31	85.51	5016

Table 9[8]. Average infrastructure statistics of MENA countries

Year	PCs	USER	PHONE	GDP
1999	4.1	2.3	17.6	4327
2000	4.5	3.2	21.9	5428
2001	4.9	4.1	25.1	5654
2002	5	5.5	27.1	5384
2003	7.8	7.9	35	5632
2004	7.4	9.1	37	5858
2005	9.7	10.6	44.3	7332

MENA countries and Turkey have very similar cultural properties. Under these classifications, MENA countries are expected to use less e-commerce compared to other countries that rank opposite on the scale. In MENA countries, development of information technology infrastructure will affect e-commerce less than the countries with different cultural properties.

Table 9 presents that information infrastructure of MENA countries is consistently improving. E-commerce is expected to increase related to the development in the infrastructure.

CONCLUSION

In this study, we show the importance of cultural traits and information technology infrastructure on e-commerce behavior. We provide empirical evidence that differing cultural traits affect e-commerce behavior and the relationship between infrastructure and e-commerce. We use Hofstede's classification of cultures. We demonstrate that countries with strong UAI and PDI have lower Internet purchases than the ones with weak UAI and PDI. Our analysis considering the differences between Individualistic and Collectivist cultures conclude that Individualism dimension does not impact on-line purchases. Also, Masculinity is not an important factor for e-commerce behavior. As a controlling factor, education parameters and GDP are taken into account.

This study has three main results. First, information infrastructure and e-commerce behavior is positively related. Second, UAI and PDI are important cultural dimensions that affect e-commerce. High PDI and UAI countries conduct less e-commerce. Finally, UAI and PDI impact the relationship between infrastructure and e-commerce negatively.

First result is expected since information infrastructure reflects the availability and accessibility to means of e-commerce. Better infrastructure promotes e-commerce. As explained in the motivation section and supported by our empirical analysis people with high UAI conduct less e-commerce. The main reason for this result is Online purchase requires trust to the seller, which is hard in the Internet environment. The final result indicates that infrastructure is not the only factor for promotion of e-commerce but cultural dimensions should be taken into account while implementing policies.

For future research, the underlying reasons of the impact of cultural dimension on e-commerce will be analyzed. Also other cultural classification models like Trompenaars (2003), Gesteland (2002) and Hall (1990) can be implemented to the model and other aspects on cultural classification can be tested.

REFERENCES

Alm & Melnik (2005). Sales and tax decision to purchase online. *Public Finance Review, 33*(2), 184 (29).

Cheng et.al, (2006). Consumer acceptance of the Internet as a channel of distribution in Taiwan: A channel function perspective. *Technovation, 26*(7), 356 (9).

Efendioglu et.al, (2005). E-commerce in developing countries: Issues and Influences. *2005 IBEC Annual Conference, Honolulu, Hawaii*, P.6-9

Gefen et.al, (2006). On the Need to Include National Culture as a Central Issue in e-commerce Trust Beliefs. *Journal of Global Information Management, 14*(4), 1-30.

Gefen, (2000). E-Commerce: The Role of Familiarity and Trust. *Omega, 28*(6), 725-737.

Genis-Gruber & Onur, (2006). The Effect of Cultural Perception on E-Commerce. In *Proceedings of IADIS International Conference E-cCommerce 2006, Barcelona*, P.346-350.

Gesteland (2002). *Cross cultural business behavior.* Copenhagen Business School Pr; 3rd edition.

Grabner-Kraeuter, (2002). The role of customer's trust in online shopping. *Journal of Business Ethics 39*, 43-50

Goldstein et.al, (2001). Navigating between Scylla and Charybdis: Will e-commerce help solve problems that are dogged developing countries for decades, or will a widening digital divide entrench them still further in a vicious circle of poverty?", *OECD Observer, 72*(3).

Hall, (1990). *Understanding Cultural Differences.* Intercultural Press.

Hofstede, (2005). *Culture and Organizations: Software of Mind.* McGraw Hill, USA.

Hofstede, (2007). Website of Geert Hofstede.

Kenny, (2002). The Internet and economic growth in LDCs: A case of managing expectations?" UNU WIDER Paper No. 2002/75

Knezevic, Boris R. & Vidas-Bubanja, Marijana, (2006). *Analysis of Electronic Commerce Adoption in Serbia*, Available at SSRN: http://ssrn.com/abstract=941390

Lynch & Beck, (2001). Profiles of Internet buyers in 20 countries: Evidence for region-specific strategies. *Journal of International Business Studies, 32*(4), 725-748.

Schneider, (2007). *Electronic commerce.* Thompson Canada, P.5 &P. 33

Teo & Liu, (2005). Consumer trust in e-commerce in the U.S., Singapore and China. *The International Journal of Management Science*, P.22-38.

Trompenaars, (2003). *Business across cultures.* Capstone

Wu & Chang, (2006). The effect of transaction trust on e-commerce relationships between travel agencies. *Tourism Management 27* (2006), P.1253-126.

ENDNOTES

1. The number of online transactions data for Turkey is from Interbank Credit Card Center (BKM) of Turkey. Data is only available for 2003 and 2004. http://www.bkm.com.tr/istatistik/eticaret_istatistikleri.html
2. Schneider,G.,2007, Electronic Commerce, Thompson Canada, pp.5
3. The LTO index is calculated for very few countries. Thus, an empirical analysis will not give reliable results. Because of lack of data, we do not conduct empirical analysis to examine effect of LTO on e-Commerce.
4. MENA countries consist of: Algeria, Bahrain, Comoros, Djibouti, Egypt, Iran, Iraq, Jordan, Kuwait, Lebanon, Libya, Mauritania, Morocco, Oman, Qatar, Saudi Arabia, Somalia, Sudan, Syria, Tunisia, Turkey, United Arab Emirates, and Yemen.
5. The percentage of individuals and enterprises that purchase online to measure e-commerce is used to measure e-commerce. Data availability is the main reason for the selection of this item from the Eurostat dataset. Alternative measures of e-commerce do not exist in the dataset. We believe that this variable is appropriate for our study since it takes into account differences in population among countries and measures differences in e-commerce behavior in different countries. This variable could also be described as a measure of "e-commerce diffusion". This variable indicates usage of e-commerce in different countries thus it shows cross-country differences in attitude and approach to e-commerce which can be

described as behavioral tendencies towards e-commerce.

[6] There are several different ways to measure IT infrastructure. To make sure that our results are not affected by the selection of different measures we used all alternative measures (PCs, USER, PHONE) in our analysis. By IT infrastructure we mean the accessibility of the means of e-commerce. The measures we use especially PCs and USER indicate the availability and accessibility to devices to conduct e-commerce.

[7] Eurostat only contains "Internet purchases by individuals purchasing via Internet and/or networks other than Internet variables" as a measure of e-commerce. Alternative measures do not exist.

[8] Score above 50 indicates that cultural dimension is strong and score below 50 indicates that cultural dimension is weak.

[9] E-Commerce data is not available for many MENA countries. So, we do not report e-Commerce in this table.

APPENDIX A

The tables below display the descriptive statistics of PDI, IDV, MAS and UAI for countries in different regions.

Properties of Cultural Dimensions for Different Regions

PDI

Region	Mean	Standard Deviation	Minimum	Maximum
Africa	63.3	14	49	77
Americas	64.4	18.9	35	95
Asia	71.5	14	54	104
Europe	50.4	21.7	11	104
Oceania	29	9.9	22	36
MENA	68.5	9.2	58	80

IDV

Region	Mean	Standard Deviation	Minimum	Maximum
Africa	37.3	24.2	20	65
Americas	30.3	24	6	91
Asia	26.7	12	14	48
Europe	60	17.1	27	89
Oceania	84.5	7.8	79	90
MENA	40.5	4	37	46

MAS

Region	Mean	Standard Deviation	Minimum	Maximum
Africa	50	11.5	41	63
Americas	50.1	15	21	73
Asia	52.6	14.3	34	95
Europe	48.7	25.2	5	110
Oceania	59.5	2.1	58	61
MENA	48.3	5	43	53

UAI

Region	Mean	Standard Deviation	Minimum	Maximum
Africa	51.6	2.5	49	54
Americas	75.6	22.4	13	101
Asia	52	22.7	8	92
Europe	66.5	25.1	12	104
Oceania	50	1.4	49	51
MENA	70	10.9	59	85

Chapter XI
Mobile-Commerce Intention to Use via SMS:
The Case of Kuwait

Kamel Rouibah
Kuwait University, Kuwait

Samia Ould-Ali
Kuwait University, Kuwait

ABSTRACT

With the widespread use of mobile phones in the Arab world, companies, including banks, are offering different communication channels for their customers to access their services. Among these channels, this study investigates the level of intention to use SMS for banking transactions. To reach this objective the study compares the explanatory power of six technology adoption models to predict SMS intention to use. These models are: the theory of reasoned action, the theory of panned behavior, the technology acceptance model, the decomposed theory of planed behavior, Nyvseen's et al., (2005) model, and a new model proposed by the authors. A convenient sample of 171 users in Kuwait was used to compare these models using regression analysis. Results show that the decomposed theory of planned behavior has the largest explanatory power, followed by the new proposed model. Results also reveal that the technology acceptance model and the theory of reasoned action have the least explanatory power. These results provide researchers and practitioners with some insights on the adoption of SMS. For researchers, such insights would be useful in understanding the adoption phenomenon, while for practitioners, such insights would provide some basis for adopting certain policies to promote adoption.

Copyright © 2009, IGI Global, distributing in print or electronic forms without written permission of IGI Global is prohibited.

INTRODUCTION

With the widespread use of new ICT around the world, studies dedicated to mobile services adoption have increased. Advancements in mobile technologies hold the promise to reshape the way professionals and individual work. With the help of these technologies, both employees and individuals can break free from the bounds of spatial and temporal constraints, being able to use the technology to work, to socialize and perform transactions anywhere and anytime. A number of past studies focused on different services offered by mobile devices such as mobile payment (Rouibah 2007), camera mobile payment (Rouibah and Abbas 2006) and SMS (Turel et al., 2007; Rau et al., 2008; Hsu et al., 2007; Peevers et al., 2008; Okazaki and Taylor 2008; Rau et al., 2008). SMS is short for Short Message Service which is a communications protocol allowing the interchange of short messages between mobile telephony devices. While several studies focused on SMS adoption, no study focused on this technology to conduct banking transactions. One key advantage of SMS is that it can capitalize on the "always on" trend, in which people have access to the Internet virtually the entire day. SMS also allows for more interactivity with the consumer than traditional media (Okazaki and Taylor 2008).

SMS technology is an enabler of mobile commerce, which is a part of mobile commerce. E-commerce refers to buying and selling goods, services, and information via computer networks (mostly Internet). Mobile commerce (noted henceforth as m-commerce) refers to the use of the Internet for purchasing goods and services and transmitting messages using wireless mobile. Over the past few years, m-commerce, has emerged as an efficient alternative to conduct transactions via mobile devises. Even though m-commerce represents a small fraction of e-commerce, that percentage has been steadily growing over the last five years. From less than $2 billions in 2000, it has reached $ 69 billions in 2005 and will reach 88 billions by 2009 (Juniper Research 2007). The growth is facilitated by the cost reduction of used communication channels. According to Kamel and Assem (2003), the cost of banking transactions handled by different communication channels are as follow: $2.5 for transactions in physical bank's branch, $1 by telephone, $0.4 by ATM, $0.24 by SMS, and $0.1 by Internet.

In order to shed light on factors that may affect m-commerce, this study only focuses on the intention to use SMS in the banking sector. Four main reasons lead to focus on this subject. *First*, the growing influence of SMS has attracted significant attention. As a convenient and low-cost mobile communication technology, SMS is experiencing rapid growth (see Figure 1). This figure shows that the number of SMS sent between 2001 and 2007 has grown exponentially. Growth of SMS use is also observed in China where Chinese send 750 million SMS daily (SMS Research and Statistics 2005). *Second,* SMS has several benefits. It can be used to conduct bank transactions and mobile payment such as M-net. This is a mobile payment technology that is recently introduced in Kuwait, which enables users to conduct transactions based on their mobile devices. *Third*, although millions of dollars have been spent on building mobile banking systems (including usage of SMS), reports on mobile banking show that potential users may not be using the systems, despite their availability. *Fourth*, searching the academic literature through *ScienceDirect* reveals few SMS adoption articles and none of these were dedicated to the use of SMS for banking transactions (Karlsen et al., 2001; Kasesniemi and Rautiainen, 2002; Reid and Reid 2004; Nysveen et al. 2005; Yan et al., 2006; Baron et al., 2006; Turel et al., 2007; Rau et al., 2008; Hsu et al., 2007; **Peevers** et al., 2008; Okazaki and Taylor 2008; Rau et al., 2008).

Figure 1. Total number of SMS in the Middle East and Asia (in Billions) (Instat 2007)

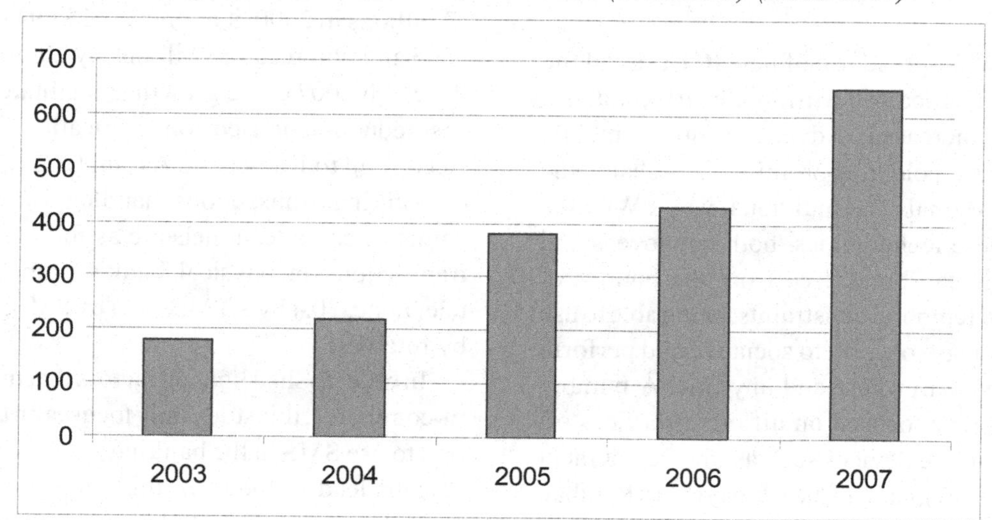

Research Questions and Objectives

While many reports indicate that the mobile Internet market will be huge, little is known about which actors most influence user's adoption of SMS. Technology adoption is defined as the potential user's predisposition toward personally using a specific technology This study aims to shed light on this issue. Over the last past twenty years, there has been considerable research that predicts whether individuals will accept and voluntarily use information and communication technologies (hereafter ICT). While several ICT adoption models have been proposed, little research has been focused on comparing the explanatory power of these models, including: the theory of acceptance model (TAM) (Davis 1989), the theory of planned behavior (TPB) (Ajzen 1991), the theory of reasoned actions (TRA) (Ajzen and Fishbein 1980), the decomposed theory of planned behavior (DTPB) (Taylor and Todd 1995), Nysveen's et al. (2005) model, and the integrated model (Yi et al., 2006).

While these models used different constructs, there is little evidence to show which constructs contribute more to the behavioral intention to use SMS. Therefore, this study aims to answer the following questions: What factors lead potential customers to use SMS services for banking transactions? Is it merely the characteristics of the technology itself (ease of use and usefulness)? Are individuals also influenced by pressure of social norms of their environment, their predisposed tendency to try out a new technology, or the cognitive and situational resources required for its effective utilization (attitude, cost)? If these factors are indeed important in the adoption decisions of potential users, are they interrelated? If so, how are they related and what are the mechanisms through which they achieve their effects on the adoption decisions? What is the best model in tern of explanatory power?

Such questions have widespread practical and theoretical ramifications because the expected benefits from the investments in ICT are realized only when these technologies are fully adopted by their intended users.

Therefore, the study aims to achieve the following: explore the factors critical to SMS adoption for banking transactions; compare the relative importance of six ICT adoption models in order to determine which is the most predictable of SMS adoption; and examine the causal relationships among different variables on SMS adoption behavior.

Significance of the Research

The major contributions of this study are as follows: (1) this study is useful for banking planners and marketers. These two groups must be aware of the primary concerns of customer's intention to use SMS. Such knowledge can help banks to increase the adoption of SMS services and, (2) marketing staff can understand the critical influences on customer adoption, and knowledge about the reasons for resistance to SMS services adoption among potential users is relevant for marketers. Based on the study findings, marketers should be able to justify expenditures that promote and enhance SMS usage or a variety of applications and how to attract more potential customers.

Why the Study Focused on SMS in Kuwait?

Kuwait is the focus of this study because it is rare among the twenty two Arab countries in that it has achieved a high IT/ICT penetration achieved amongst the GCC countries (see Table 1). For example, PC penetration was 23.66% (third after Saudi Arabia and UAE), internet penetration rate was 27.6%, (second after UAE), and mobile phone penetration was 93.86 (second after UAE). In addition, the GDP per person is the second highest ($31860) after Qatar. Kuwait was ranked third behind the United Arab Emirates and Qatar in term of utilizing ICT`s to provide and improve access to basic social services (UN World Development Indicator 2007). It is also ranked fifth in term of e-government technology readiness behind the United Arab Emirates, Bahrain, Jordan, and Qatar.

This study focuses on SMS adoption in Kuwait for two main reasons: *First*, the growth of mobile phone usage is faster than that of the Internet. The penetration rate of the mobile phone is approximately 93% while Internet penetration is 26.6%. *Second*, there is a paucity of knowledge about how ICTs are used in the Arab world. Very few studies have focused on ICT including instant messaging in Kuwait (Rouibah 2008) and adoption of new communication technologies (ATM, phone banking, Internet banking and credit cards) in the banking sector in Egypt (Kamel and Assem 2003). In addition, studies have shown that culture seems to play a significant role in ICT adoption in the Arab world. In succeeding to show the effect of culture on IT adoption, Loch et al., (2003) called for additional research to shed light on other ICT (beyond the Internet) in the Arab world.

Online banking and mobile banking services (based SMS) are offered by all ten national banks

Table 1. Basic ICT indicators in the GCC countries (World Development Indicator 2007)

Indicator	Year	Kuwait	Bahrain	Oman	Qatar	Saudi Arabia	UAE
Country area (sq km)	-	17,818	694	309,500	11,521	2,149,690	77,700
Population (thousands)	2000	2190	672.0	2442.0	606.4	20660.7	3247
	2005	2535.4	726.6	2566.9	812.8	23118.9	4533.1
GDP per capita ($)	2000	17222	11861	8135.	29290	9120	21740
	2005	31860.6	17773	9460.	52239	13399	28611
PC penetration rate	2000	11.41	14.13	3.30	14.85	6.29	12.31
	2005	23.66	16.65	4.60	16.36	36.66	18.75
Mobile penetration rate	2000	21.73	30.61	6.63	19.93	6.65	43.98
	2005	93.86	100	51.93	88.17	57.53	100
Internet penetration rate	2000	6.85	5.95	3.68	4.95	2.23	23.5
	2005	27.6	21.3	11.10	26.9	6.86	30.82

in Kuwait (Industrial Kuwait Bank, Ahli Bank, Gulf Bank, Burgan Bank, Commercial Bank of Kuwait, National Bank of Kuwait, Kuwait Bank and Middle East, Kuwait Finance House, Real Estate Bank, and Bubiyan Bank). These banks offer wireless alerts about changes in customers' account on their wireless devices that support text messaging. Customers can also check their account balances, transfer funds between savings and other accounts, and pay their mobile phone and Internet usage charges. Enrolled customers can also make some transactions such as paying prepaid cards for online shopping and online trading transactions to sell and buy shares in the Kuwait Stock Exchange. Customers may complete these transactions SMS-based anywhere and anytime without having to visit their bank. The Ministry of Interior in Kuwait allows citizens to check and pay online traffic violations using their wireless devices based-SMS. Kuwait Airways, the national airline carrier, uses SMS technology to acknowledge its customers about its services such as information about customer flights (departure and arrival), confirmation of booking, flight delays, and additional information about any unexpected events. Moreover, Kuwait University allows students to pay registration and courses fees via SMS. Investment companies use SMS to inform their customers about changes of their investments.

There are two mobile operators that offer SMS in Kuwait: MTC and Al Wataniya, which are two international Kuwaiti companies operating in a number of Middle eastern countries and Arica. These two companies provide a variety of services including local, international SMS, Wchat SMS (SMS with unknown users), Reuter news via SMS, MissU (i.e. a reminder about miscalls even mobile phone is switched off).

The usage of SMS is very high in Kuwait. Between 640 and 660 millions of SMS were exchanged in 2007, 80% are local and 20% are international, which totalize a total volume of $59 millions. The following table provides the prices of SMS use in the Gulf Cooperative Countries (GCC). These numbers reveal that prices in Kuwait are among the highest one in GCC, which may suggest that price is an important determinant of SMS use.

The remainder of this chapter is organized as follows: Section 2 reviews past studies on SMS as well as existing models in the field of IT adoption as well as discusses past comparison studies in this field; section 3 describes the research method

Table 2. SMS prices in Gulf Cooperative Council countries (in $ cents)

Gulf Countries	Mobile operator	Prepaid		Subscription	
		Local	International	Local	International
Kuwait	MTC	6.9	17.2	6.9	17.2
	Al Wataniya	6.9	17.2	6.9	17.2
	Batelco	8.4	8.4	6.6	6.6
	MTC	8	8	5.3	6.6
Oman	Oman Mobile	2.6	13	2.6	13
	Nawras Telecom	2.6	13	2.6	13
Qatar	Qtel	11	16.5	6.8	16.5
Saudi Arabia	Al Jawwal	8	12	8	12
	Mobily	6.7	13.3	6.7	13.3
	Bravo	-	-	6	16
	MTC	?	-		-
Unite Arab Emirates	Itisalat	8.2	24.5	8.2	24.5
	Do	8.2	24.5	8.2	24.5

and presents the research methodology; section 4 lists the analytical results; and section 5 presents conclusions, as well as discussing the implications of the findings of this study.

THEORY AND BACKGROUND

Past Literature Review on SMS Adoption

In order to review the relevant literature, the authors searched the ScienceDirect database using the descriptors "SMS", "acceptance of SMS", and "adoption of SMS" that were found in the title or the abstract of the paper. The search resulted in 822 papers, which were published between 1985 and 2008. Of these papers, 12 were published in journals and focused on SMS acceptance/adoption.

While many studies focused on different services of mobile devices, few studies studied SMS adoption. Karlsen et al., (2001) studied the effect of text messaging amongst teenagers. Kasesniemi and Rautiainen, (2002) studied SMS in Finland, and found that teenagers wrote more formal messages when texting a person outside their social circle. Reid and Reid (2004) studied the psychological drivers behind SMS among key user groups and their implications for the design of mobile phone interfaces. The study didn't adopt any solid ICT adoption theory, but, they studied types of SMS usages and gender preferences. Nysveen et al. (2005) investigated the motivational factors that affect intention of potential customers to use mobile chat services through the moderation effects of gender in Norway. The authors proposed a model that is a combination of TAM and TRA. Results of their study suggested that social norms and intrinsic motives (such as enjoyment) are important determinants of intention to use among female users, whereas extrinsic motives (such as usefulness and expressiveness) are key drivers among male users. The findings put renewed focus on non-utilitarian motives and illuminate the role of gender in technology adoption. Yan et al., (2006) developed a model for user adoption of SMS in China, which posit that various factors (usefulness, ease of use, and social norm) impact user adoption of SMS. Baron et al., (2006) critically examined the current definitions of key constructs of the technology acceptance model in a consumer technology-based service. The authors undertook two qualitative research studies that encouraged consumers to reflect upon their SMS behavior. The research highlights the inadequacy of a concentration on simple and single adoption of technology where technology is embedded in a consumer community of practice. The existence of counter-intuitive behaviors, technology paradoxes, and intense social and emotional elements in actual SMS usage all point to the need for a review of the definition of the key TAM constructs. Rau et al., (2008) studied the effects of mobile communication technology (SMS, e-mail, and online forum) on student learning in education, based on a comparative investigation of 176 students in Taiwan. Leung (2007) studied the motives of social usage of SMS and its impact on interpersonal mediated communication on 532 college students in Hong Kong. He found that respondents use SMS for entertainment (seek enjoyment and stimulation and have fun), for affection and socialization (channel for expressing appreciation, showing care for the feelings of another person, giving encouragement, sending goodnight messages to loved ones). Results revealed that showing affection was an important motivation for students to use SMS. Fashion was found the third factor while convenience (ease to use) and low cost was ranked the fifth factor. Results show that students who made the heaviest use of SMS were motivated by its convenience, low cost, and utility for coordinating events. Turel et al., (2007) examined the adoption of SMS by 222 young adult users using a combination of marketing and information system perspective – a modified technology. The authors found that emotional value (enjoyment and feel good) followed by value or money (quality services) exert the strongest effect on perceived value of SMS; this affects behavioral intention to use SMS, which in turn affects current usage. Rouibah (2007) studied factors that affect mobile payment Mnet technology in Kuwait, which is SMS-based with 175 users. He found that perceived usefulness and enjoyment driven are two important factors of intention to use Mnet. Okazaki and Taylor (2008) examined the factors associated with the intention of multinational corporations operating in Europe to implement SMS advertising. Hsu et al., (2007) examined the factors that influence the adoption of MMS/SMS with 207 online users in Taiwan. The proposed model was empirically evaluated by using survey data collected from 207 users concerning their perceptions. Results indicate that perceived usefulness was the major driver for MMS/SMS intention to use while perceived ease of use has no significant affect for potential users. **Peevers** et al., (2008) studied the usability of three types of SMS message input format (abbreviations, numbers and fee-form) to carry banking services with 74 users in the UK. Results found that the older age group found all three versions in general to be less usable than the younger age group.

Finally while few studies have focused on SMS adoption, no study focused on its usage in the Arab world, and none study concentrated on it usage to carry banks transactions. Moreover, very few papers used well-know theories, including TAM (Yan et al., 2006; Baron et al., 2006, Rouibah 2007; Turel et al., 2007), TAM and TRA (Nysveen et al., 2005), the innovation diffusion theory (Hsu et al., 2007), and uses & gratification (Leung 2007).

Other Related Literature Review on ICT Adoption Models

Theory of Reasoned Action (TRA)

In TRA, two factors that contribute to behavioral intention (noted BI) are determined: Attitude toward the behavior (noted ATT) and subjective norm (noted SN) (Ajzen and Fishbein 1980). Attitude refers to an individual's positive or negative feeling about performing the target behavior. Subjective norm is defined as a person's perception that most people who are important to him or her think that he or she should or should not perform the behavior and his or her motivation to comply with the specific referents. In the IT field, TRA has been used as the basis to test several technologies and spans a variety of subject areas, e.g. word processing (Davis et al., 1989) and e-banking (Shih and Fang 2004; Shih and Fang 2006). A particularly helpful aspect of TRA from an information system perspective is that attitude and subjective norm are theorized to mediate the effect of external variables on intention to use new IT (Davis et al., 1989). Empirical support of three studies (Davis et al., 1989; Shih and Fang 2004; Shih and Fang 2006), however, failed to find a significant relationship between SN and BI. In addition, no study tested TRA on SMS, except Nysveen et al., (2005) who used a combination of TRA and innovation diffusion theory.

Theory of Planed Behavior (TPB)

TPB is an extension of the TRA model due to the limitation of TRA to deal with behavior which individuals have incomplete volitional control (Ajzen 1991). According to TPB, people's actions are determined by their intentions, which are influenced by their *perceived behavioral control* (noted PBC), besides attitude and SN. PBC refers to the perception of internal and external resource constraints on performing the behavior. Control beliefs reflect the perceived difficulty (or ease) with which the behavior may be affected and perceived facility acts as an important weighting (Ajzen 1991). In the case of SMS, control beliefs refer to knowing how to perform transactions via mobile devices and facility refers to external resource constraints, such as time and money. Abundant empirical evidence exists that suggests TPB effectively explains individual intentions in adopting several new ICT including but not limited to: Computing recourse center (Taylor and Todd 1995), telemedicine technology (Chau and Hu 2001), and Internet banking (Shih and Fang 2004). Empirical findings provide mixed results. Shih and Fang (2004) failed to find a significant relationship between PBC and BI. Moreover, other studies did not found SN to play a significant effect on BI (Mathieson 1991; Chau and Hu 2001; Shih and Fang 2004). Moreover, no study used PB to test SMS adoption.

Technology Acceptance Model (TAM)

Based on the TRA, Davis (1989) developed the TAM model. It states that an individual's system usage is determined by BI, which is, in turn, is determined by his attitude toward the behavior, which in turn is determined by two beliefs: perceived usefulness (noted PU) and perceived ease of use (noted PEOU). PU refers to the extent to which a person believes that using the technology will improve his or her task performance. PEOU refers to the extent to which a person believes that using the system will be free of effort. TAM is the most widely applied model and was used to explain or predict the motivational factors underlying users' acceptance of technologies. Many studies applied TAM to a variety of technologies while five comparative studies have compared TAM to other competing model: e-mail (Davis 1989), spreadsheet (Mathieson 1991), university computing resource center (Taylor and Todd 1995), telemedicine (Chau and Hu 2001; and e-banking (Shuh and Fan 2004). Moreover, only two studies applied TAM to SMS adoption (Yan et al., 2006; Baron et al., 2006). However, the authors used a qualitative approach.

The Decomposed TPB

Based on TAM and TPB, Taylor and Todd (1995) decomposed the belief structures in the TPB and proposed the decomposed TPB (noted DTPB). According to the authors, people's decisions vis-à-vis a new technology are determined by their intentions, which are influenced by their *perceived behavioral control (PBC)*, besides attitude and *subjective norm (SN)*. Attitude toward the behavior is determined by PU and PEOU. Taylor and Todd (1995) tested the new proposed model with 786 potential users of a computer resource center business in Canada. They found it has more explanatory power than TAM and TPB. Similar to PB, no study used this model to study the adoption of SMS adoption.

Nysveen's et al. (2005) Model

Nysveen et al. (2005) proposed a modified model that is based on TAM, TRA, and non-utilitarian motives (including perceived enjoyment and perceived expressiveness). The authors proposed BI to depend on attitude toward the technology, image (which is similar to image construct), perceived enjoyment, PU, PEOU, and normative pressure (subjective norm- SN). In testing the model, the authors examined antecedent of intention to use mobile services (text messaging, contact, payment, and gamming). Results indicate the following: All external and latent variables exert effect on BI to use mobile service; perceived enjoyment, PU, PEOU, and normative pressure (subjective norm) have a direct effect on BI to use SMS services; perceived enjoyment exerts the strongest direct effect on BI while normative pressure exerts the weakest effect on BI; and the model for females (71%) was found to explain more variance than males (68.2%). Rouibah and Abbas (2006) studied determinant of camera mobile phone adoption in Kuwait. They found perceived enjoyment and perceived usefulness play the most important effect on camera mobile usage.

The Modified Integrated Model

Yi et al., (2006) developed a new integrated model that combined three well-known models (TAM, TPB and the innovation diffusion theory) (Rogers 1983). The proposed model considers an individual's system usage to be determined by BI, which is, in turn, is determined by PBC, PU, PEOU, and SN. The authors removed attitude from their model and considered PBC to be determined by personal innovativeness "*willingness of an individual to try out any new IT* " while PEOU depended on PI and result demonstrability "*tangibility of the results of using an information technology*". The authors posit PU to depend on image (similar to perceived expressiveness of Nysveen et al., 2005), result demonstrability, PEOU and SN. Yi et al., (2006) posited SN to depend on PI. Finally, Yi et al., (2006) posit image to depend on SN and PI. In addition, while Yi et al., (2006) tested successfully this model with 222 users in USA using PDA technology, we decided to modify this model to account the following. Personal innovativeness and result demonstrability were removed from the model because SMS is a relatively not a new technology, and its result demonstrability is obvious. Attitude was also included in order to compare its effect within different previous models.

Past Studies on Model Comparison

Despite much research which has separately investigated the previous ICT adoption models, little evidence is available about their comparison (Davis et al., 1989; Mathieson 1991; Taylor and Todd 1995, Chau and Hu 2001; Shih and Fang 2004).

Davis et al., (1989) compared TAM with TRA in studying usage of a word processing program. Their data provided mixed support for the two specific theoretical models. They found that attitude had a strong significant influence on BI; attitude only partially mediated the effects of beliefs (PU and PEOU) on BI; and subjective norm had no significant effect on BI. The confluence of TRA and TAM led to the identification of a more parsimonious causal structure based on only three theoretical constructs: BI, PU and PEOU. Social norm as an important determinant of behavioral intention was found to be weak in this case. Mathieson (1991) compared TAM with TPB. The results indicated that the two models explained BI very well.

Taylor and Todd (1995) compared the DTPB model with the TAM and TPB. The addition of subjective norm, PBC and the decomposition of beliefs provided some additional insight into behavioral intention. Taylor and Todd (1995) found the explanatory power (R^2) of DTPB is 60%, TPB is 57%, and TAM 52%. Chau and Hu (2001) compared TAM, TPB and DTPB in understanding physicians' usage of telemedicine technology. The results illustrated that DTPB explained 42% of the variances; TAM explained 40%; and TPB explained 32% in the adoption of the telemedicine technology. PU was a significant determinant of attitude and BI, in both TAM and DTPB. PEOU did not have any effects on PU or attitude in all models. The findings suggested that instruments that have been developed and repeatedly tested in studies involving end-users and business managers in ordinary business settings may not be equally valid in a professional setting (e.g. physicians). These results were found after Chau and Hu (2001) accounted an additional variable (compatibility) as a determinant of PEOU and PU, which is defined as "*the degree to which an innovation is perceived as consistent with the existing values, past experiences, and needs of potential adopters*". However, this variable will not be included in this study since SMS is now compatible with all our tasks and cultures, as the focus of the paper was to use the original DTPB.

Shih and Fang (2004) compared TRA to TPB and DTPB models. The authors found that the DTPB model has better explanatory power for behavioral intention, attitude and subjective norm than the TRA and TPB model. The path from subjective norm to BI failed to achieve significance in either models (TPB and TRA). In addition, they found that the variance explained by TPB (53%) is better than that of TRA (46%).

Analysis of past studies reveals the following: *First*, there is no agreement on which factors most affect BI to use new technologies. *Second*, according to the authors' knowledge, there is none past study that compares the six models (TRA, TPB, TAM, DTPB, Nysveen's et al. (2005) model and Yi et al., (2006) except Venkatesh et al., (2003), which focused on a different objective. *Third*, while Venkatesh and Davis (2000) stated that TAM has become well established powerful model for predicting user adoption, Ajzen (2001) pointed out the ability of TPB to provide a very useful theoretical framework for understanding and predicting the adoption of new technologies. This is in line with previous studies that called for substantial research to address the limitation of these three models (Chau and Hu 2001).

RESEARCH METHODOLOGY

Before questionnaire distribution, this study subjected the user perceptions' scale to an intensive validation procedure to determine both *reliability* and *validity*. To keep the length of the instrument reasonable, the shortened version of the scales was used here (see annex 1).

Instrument Development and Data Collection

An empirical investigation of current SMS users was conducted. The questionnaire consisted of two parts. The first solicited demographic information such as age, sex, type of wireless devices owned and number of years at his/her college. The second presented questions pertaining to the studied models as well as type of SMS usage for transactions. The questions related to variables in the six models.

The four-page survey consisted of 38 questions, each representing a component of the research model. All the variables in the research model were operationalized using standard scales (five points) from past literature on technology adoption.

A structured questionnaire was administrated to users over a period of two months. The technique of sampling was the non-probability convenient sampling method. It was used because it was a viable alternative due to the constraint of time, speed, cost and convenience in order to obtain enough respondents. The questionnaires were distributed to students and collected by hand to speed up the collection process.

To address face validity (questionnaire for validity, i.e. what variables are intended to measure, completeness, i.e. each variable includes all relevant observations, and readability/understandability), a group of business professors and students were asked to read and refine the questionnaire. Based on the collected feedback, several items were changed to better reflect the purpose. This pretest examination provided reasonable validity of the scale items.

Target subjects were students from ages sixteen and above, and who had completed banking transactions using SMS. This is in line with previous studies on SMS (Turel et al., 2007). Questionnaires were distributed to a group of 250 students at a leading College of Business Administration in Kuwait. Of this number, 171 questionnaires

Table 3. Reliability of the measure

Variables	Observation	References	Mean	SD	N	Cronbach α
Image (IM)	IM 1	Nysveen et al., (2005)	4.00	1.26	171	0.95
	IM 2		3.75	1.25	171	0.95
	IM 3		3.75	1.17	171	0.95
	IM 4		3.67	1.23	171	0.95
Perceived Enjoyment (PE)	PE 1	Heijden (2003)	3.82	1.04	171	0.95
	PE 2	Heijden (2004)	3.87	1.08	171	0.95
	PE 3	Heijden (2004)	3.87	1.08	171	0.95
	PE 4	Davis et al., (1992)	3.97	1.00	171	0.95
Perceived Usefulness (PU)	PU 1	Rouibah (2008)	4.01	0.95	171	0.95
	PU 2		4.05	0.96	171	0.95
	PU 3		4.05	0.90	171	0.95
	PU 4		4.15	0.87	171	0.95
	PU 5		3.73	0.61	171	0.96
Perceived Ease of Use (PEOU)	PEOU 1	Davis et (1989)	4.01	0.82	171	0.96
	PEOU 2		4.00	0.92	171	0.95
	PEOU 3		4.06	0.94	171	0.95
	PEOU 4		4.11	0.88	171	0.95
Subjective Norm (SN)	SN 1	Taylor and Todd (1995)	3.82	1.12	171	0.95
	SN 2		3.91	1.00	171	0.95
	SN 3		3.87	1.11	171	0.95
Attitude toward use (ATU)	ATU 1	Davis (1989)	3.91	1.18	171	0.95
	ATU 2		3.96	1.00	171	0.95
	ATU 3		3.98	1.08	171	0.95
	ATU 4		4.01	1.02	171	0.95
	ATU 5		4.07	0.95	171	0.95
Perceived behavioral control (PBC)	PBC 1	Taylor and Todd (1995)	4.01	0.88	171	0.95
	PBC 2		3.99	0.81	171	0.95
	PBC 3		3.89	0.86	171	0.95
Behavioral Intention – (BI)	BI 1	Venkatesh and Davis (2000)	4.00	0.97	171	0.95
	BI 2		4.04	0.92	171	0.95

were completed from a non-random population of young adults.

Reliability of the Measure

In order to ensure that the variables (research constructs) were internally consistent, reliability assessment was carried out using Cronbach's alpha. A low value (i.e. α close to 0) implies that the variables are not internally related in the manner expected (Hair *et al.*, 1998). Reliability analyses show all variables exhibit Cronbach's alpha values between 0.95 and 0.96. Accordingly, all the reliability test results in this study exceed 0.60, recommended as the lower limit of acceptability (see Hair *et al.*, 1998), ensuring that the items for the respective variables in this study are reliable. Table 3 shows that all the eight variables had mean values higher than three, indicating that, on the average, most respondents agreed to the items set in the questionnaire.

Measures

The measures used to operationalise the variable constructs included in the investigated models

Table 4. Profile of respondents

Variable	Description	Number	Frequency
Gender	Female	97	56.7
	Male	74	43.3
	Total	**171**	**100**
Education	< 1 year	7	4.1
	1–2 years	15	8.8
	2- 3 years	58	33.9
	3 – 4 years	61	35.7
	More than 4 years	30	17.5
	Total	**171**	**100**
Student/Employee	Student	95	55.6
	Employee	76	44.4
	Total	**171**	**100**
Mobile Phone	Yes	168	98.2
	No	3	1.8
	Total	**171**	**100**
PDA	Yes	6	3.5
	No	165	96.5
	Total	**171**	**100**
Pen-Based	Yes	2	1.2
	No	169	98.8
	Total	**171**	**100**
Pager	Yes	28	16.4
	No	143	83.6
	Total	**171**	**100%**
GPA	N.A	5	2.9
	Below 1	11	6.4
	From 1 to less than 2	48	28.1
	From 2 to less than 3	67	39.2
	Above 3	40	23.4
	Total	**171**	**100%**

and the questionnaire were mainly adapted from previous studies, with minor wording changes to tailor them to the use of SMS in the banking field. Items for PU, PEOU, and BI were adapted from Davis (1989). Items for attitude, subjective norms, and perceived behavioral control were from Taylor and Todd (1995). In addition, image and perceived enjoyment were reused from Nysveen et al., (2005). Moreover, constructs common to the examined models were measured using the same scale, an approach suggested by Taylor and Todd (1995). All items were measured using a 5-point Likert-type scale with anchors on *strongly agree* and *strongly disagree* respectively.

RESULTS AND DISCUSSION

Demographic Data and Behavior of Respondents with SMS Usage

Table 4 and 5 provides demographic and users' behavior with regard to SMS usage in Kuwait.

Table 4 indicates that the percentage of female respondents (56.3%) is larger than that of male respondents. 55.6% of respondents are students while 44.4 % are students who worked per time. 62.3% have spent less than three years at their college. 98% of the respondents owned a mobile phone, 16.1% owned a pager, while a very small

Table 5. Type of SMS use in the banking sector

Type of SMS use	Mean	SD
Pay registration fees	4.7	1.02
Check my bank's account	4.5	1.07
Use SMS instead of calling the call center	4	1.1
Check latest transactions	3.85	0.89
Transfer money between accounts	3.2	1.2
Purchase mobile prepaid card	2.99	1.3

Table 6. Factor analysis

Component	Factor 1	Factor 2	Factor 3	Factor 4	Factor 5	Factor 6	Factor 7	Factor 8
IM 1			0.739					
IM 2			0.754					
IM 3			0.780					
IM 4			0.794					
PE 1				0.682				
PE 2				0.780				
PE 3				0.769				
PE 4				0.691				
PU 1	0.591							
PU 2	0.633							
PU 3	0.781							
PU 4	0.784							
PU 5	0.626							
PEOU 1		0.686						
PEOU 2		0.682						
PEOU 3		0.726						
PEOU 4		0.713						
SN 1							0.808	
SN 2							0.770	
SN 3							0.798	
ATU 1					0.776			
ATU 2					0.759			
ATU 3					0.853			
ATU 4					0.900			
ATU 5					0.839			
PBC 1						0.798		
PBC 2						0.819		
PBC 3						0.700		
BI 1								0.741
BI 2								0.735

percentage owned a PDA (3.5%) or pen-based device (1.6%).

Table 5 reveals five type of SMS usage in banking transactions. It indicates that respondents use SMS mostly to pay their university registration fees, followed by checking their bank's account. Use of SMS instead of calling the call center of their banks is ranked third, while using SMS to purchase mobile prepaid card is ranked the last one.

Factor Analysis

Factor analysis was conducted to confirm the existence and relevance of the existing variables. A total of six factors with *eigenvalues* greater than 1.0 were identified. These factors explained 73.39 of the total variance. Table 6 ensures construct validity. This pattern of validity is consistent with prior research (Davis 1989; Mathieson 1991, Taylor and Todd 1995; Chau and Hu 2001).

Regression Analysis

After the factor analysis was performed, regression analyses were carried out to determine the relationships between variables of the models. Different regressions were computed depending on the model used. For TAM, Nysveen's et al., (2005) model, DTPB, and the new proposed model, three regressions were run successively for PU, ATT and BI. For TPB and TRA, only one regression, goodness of fit from the ANOVA table, was carried out to estimate BI.

Predicting Behavioral Intention Using TRA

Figure 2 indicates that attitude toward behavior and subjective norm have a positive direct effect on BI to adopt SMS in the banking sector, with $ß = 0.370$, $t = 5.250$, $p < 0.01$ and $ß = 0.264$, $t = 3.742$, $p < 0.01$ respectively. Attitude plays a more significant role in predicting BI than subjective norm. Results also reveal that 27% of the variation in the BI to use SMS is explained by these two variables. These results are similar to those of Davis et al., (1989) in the use of MS Word, but are smaller than Shih and Fang (2004 and 2006) for e-banking adoption. Therefore, TRA is still valid in the case of SMS.

Predicting Behavioral Intention Using TPB

Figure 2 shows only two variables (attitude and perceived behavioral control) exert a positive direct effect on BI, successively with $ß = 0.164$, $t = 2.636$, $p < 0.01$ and $ß = 0.576$, $t = 8.986$, $p < 0.01$ successively. However, subjective norm has no effect on BI. Moreover, 50.4% of the variation in BI is caused by the two variables (ATT and PBC). This variance is smaller than that of Mathieson (1991) in the usage of spreadsheet, Taylor and Todd (1995) in the case of competing resource center usage, and Shih and Fang (2004) in the case of e-banking. However the variance explained by this study model is larger than that of Chau and Hu (2001) in telemedicine adoption. Moreover, it can be observed that TPB produces more variance than does TRA. In addition, PBC seems to play the strongest direct effect on BI. This result reveals that attitude loses its dominance in TPB in favor of PBC. Accordingly, TPB is not fully valid in predicting SMS in the banking sector.

Predicting SMS Adoption Using TAM

Predicting behavioral intention using TAM: Figure 2 indicates that the three variables (attitude, PU and PEOU) exert a significant positive and direct effect on BI with $ß = 0.204$, $t = 3.264$, $p < 0.01$; $ß = 0.197$, $t = 3.151$, $p < 0.01$, and $ß = 0.518$, $t = 8.303$, $p < 0.10$ successively. The three variables contribute to explain 33.7% of the total variance in BI. Three observations can be highlighted. *First*, the effect of PEOU on BI is the strongest followed by attitude, and then by PU. *Second*, the effect of PEOU on BI is over 2.6 times that of the effect of PU on BI, which contradicts the trends in prior TAM research (Legris et al., 2003). *Third*, the explanatory power of TAM is less than that of TPB but higher than TRA. In addition, results reveal that the variance explained is smaller than those of Davis et al. (1989), Mathieson (1991), Taylor and Todd (1995) and Chau and Hu (2001).

Figure 2. Regression results of the six tested models

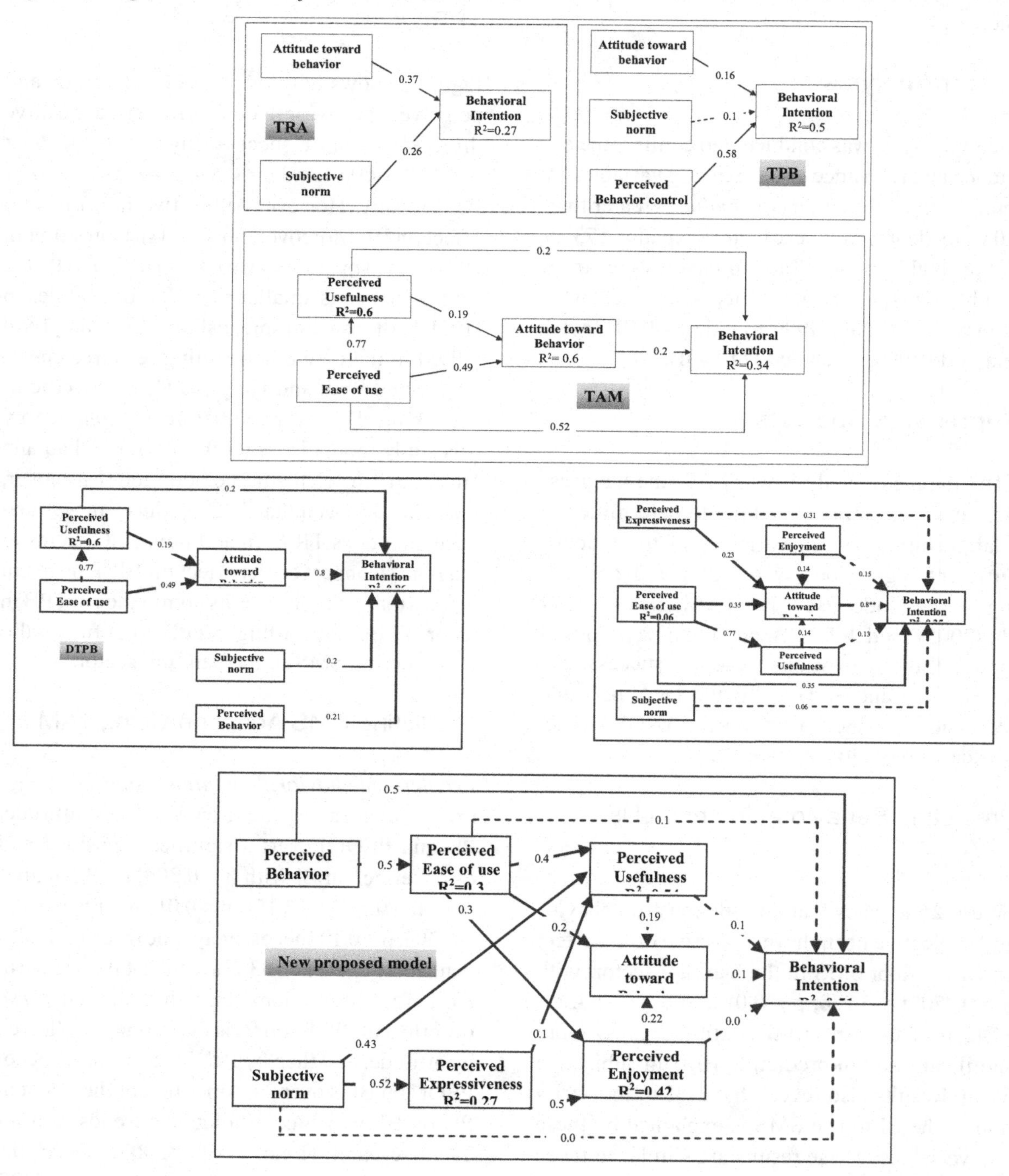

Predicting attitude and PU: Figure 2 indicates that PEOU (ß = 0.493, t = 7.523, p < 0.01) exerts more influence on attitude than does PU (ß = 0.197, t = 2.921, p < 0.01). These two variables contribute to explain 27.1% of the total variance in attitude to adopt SMS. Moreover, the results indicate that PEOU affect positively PU (ß = 0.774, t = 15.882, p < 0.01) and PEOU contributes to explain (R^2= 60%) of the variance of PU. This is in line with much prior TAM research.

Predicting SMS Adoption Using the DTPB

Predicting behavioral intention using: Figure 2 indicates that the four variables (attitude, PU, SN and PBC) exert a positive effect on BI with ß = 0.795, t = 27.402, p < 0.01; ß = 0.121, t = 4.131, p < 0.01; ß = 0.200, t = 6.211, p < 0.01; and ß = 0.205, t = 6.423, p < 0.01 successively. The four variables contribute to explain 86.3 % of the total variance in BI. The following observations can be highlighted. *First*, the effect of attitude on BI is the strongest followed by PBC, which reveals that attitude gains its dominance over PBC when PU and PEOU are integrated in the DTPB. *Second*, the explanatory power of decomposed TPB is higher than the three previous models (TRA, TPB, and TAM). *Third*, the variance explained by the study model is higher than any previous study that used DTPB including Taylor and Todd (1995), Chau and Hu (2001), and Shih and Fang (2004).

Predicting attitude and PU using DTPB: Similar to TAM, the results of Figure 2 indicate that PEOU exerts more influence on attitude (ß = 0.493, t = 7.523, p < 0.01) than does PU (ß = 0.191, t = 8.921, p < 0.01). These two variables contribute to explain 27.1% of the total variance in attitude. Similarly to TAM, results indicate that PEOU is a determinant of PU (ß = 0.774, t = 15.882, p < 0.01) and PEOU contributes to explain (R^2= 60%) of the variance of PU. This is in line with much prior TAM research.

Predicting SMS Using Nysveen's Model

Predicting behavioral intention using SMS: Figure 2 indicates that only three out of six variables of Nysveen's et al., (2005) model (perceived enjoyment, attitude, and PEOU) exert a positive direct effect on BI with ß = 0.152, t = 4.32, p < 0.01; ß = .169, t = 2.719, p < 0.01; and ß = 0.345, t = 3.921, p < 0.01 successively. These variables contribute to explain 34.7 % of the total variance in BI. The three variables that did not posit any significant relationships are perceived image (ß = 0.090, t = .923, p < 0.01), PU (ß = 0.128, t = 0.901, p < 0.01), and SN (ß = 0.056, t = 0.694, p < 0.01). The following observations can be highlighted. Among variables that have significant relationships with BI, PEOU exerts the strongest effect. This result contradicts previous findings of Nysveen et al., (2005) who found that perceived enjoyment exerts the strongest effect on BI for female users and perceived Image for male users. The effect of attitude on BI is minimized with the absence of PBC. Social norm has no effect on BI as was the case of TRA in Nysveen's et al., (2005) model for male users. Moreover, the explanatory power of Nysveen's et al., (2005) model is higher than TRA and TAM, but less than TPB, and DTPB. Finally, the application of Nysveen's et al., (2005) model on SMS intention to use SMS in Kuwait produces slightly different results than in Norway and the variance explained by its application in Kuwait is far less than its application in Norway for female (71%) and male users (68%).

Predicting attitude and PU using SMS: Figure 2 indicates that among the four variables that are hypothesized to affect attitude: perceived image (ß = 0.225, t = 2.291, p < 0.01), perceived enjoyment (ß = 0.042, t = 0.381, p < 0.01), PU (ß = 0.137, t = 2.038, p < 0.01), and PEOU (ß = 0.347, t = 4.094, p < 0.01), only three variables exert a significant influence on BI. These are: perceived image, PU and PEOU. Among these variables, PEOU exerts more influence on attitude, followed by image. The three variables contribute to explain 30.5% of the total variance in attitude. Similarly to TAM, results indicate that PEOU is a determinant of PU (ß = 0.774, t = 15.882, $p < 0.01$) and PEOU contributes to explain (R^2= 60%) of the variance of PU.

Predicting SMS Using the New Proposed Model

As stated in the literature review, this new model is based on previous of the unified model proposed by Yi et al. (2006).

Predicting behavioral intention using the new proposed model: Figure 2 indicates that only two out of the six variables positively affect BI. These are PEOU (ß = 0.138, t = 2.297, $p < 0.01$) and PBC (ß = 0.558, t = 7.624, $p < 0.01$). The two variables contribute to explain 51.2 % of the total variance in BI. This is similar to the results of Yi et al., (2006) even though the current study removes two constructs from their study (personal innovativeness and result demonstrability) and included attitude in the modified model. Four variables did not posit any significant relationships which are: Perceived enjoyment (ß = 0.047, t = 0.658, $p < 0.01$), attitude (ß = 0.112, t = 1.919, $p < 0.01$), PU (ß = 0.116, t = 1.890, $p < 0.01$) and SN (ß = 0.047, t = 0.658, $p < 0.01$). The following observations can be highlighted. *First*, among the two variables that have significant relationships with BI, PBC exerts the strongest effect. *Second*, the variance explained by this new model is higher than TRA, TAM, TPB, and Nysveen's et al., (2005), but less than of DTPB.

Predicting attitude, PU, PE, PEX and PEOU using new model: Figure 2 indicates the three variables that are hypothesized to affect attitude all have significant influence on BI: PU (ß = 0.187, t = 2.574, $p < 0.01$), perceived enjoyment (ß = 0.221, t = 3.038, $p < 0.01$), and PEOU (ß = 0.284, t = 4.073, $p < 0.01$). Among these three variables, the effect of PEOU is stronger than that of PU and perceived enjoyment. In addition, the three variables explain 17.4% of attitude's variance.

With regard to PU, the three variables image (ß = 0.192, t = 3.578, $p < 0.01$), SN (ß = 0.426, t = 7.549, $p < 0.01$) and PEOU (ß = 0.408, t = 7.085, $p < 0.01$) all have significant influence on PU. These three variables explain 53.6% of the total variance of PU. SN plays the strongest effect on PU followed by PU. This result contradicts most studies (in particular TAM findings). With regard to perceived enjoyment (PE), the two hypothesized variables: image (ß = 0.510, t = 8.546, $p < 0.01$) and PEOU (ß = 0.318, t = 5.328, $p < 0.01$), have significant influence on PE. These variables explain 42% of the total variance of PE. However, the results show the effect of image is larger than that of PEOU. Finally, PBC positively affects PEOU (ß = 0.552, t = 8.599, $p < 0.01$) and explains 30% of the total variance of PEOU.

Figure 1 illustrates the significant relationships in the six models.

In summary, the best explanatory model is the DTPB (R^2=86.3%), followed by the new proposed model (R^2= 51.2%), TPB (R^2=50.4%), Nyvseen's model (R^2=34.7%), TAM (R^2= 33.7%) and TRA (R^2=27%).

Discussion

This study partially supports findings of three previous studies that used TRA (Davis et al., 1989; Shih and Fang 2004; Shih and Fang 2006) in that it found attitude exerts the strongest effect on BI. However, the current study contradicts these three studies since it found a positive direct effect between SN and BI, while the three previous studies failed to find such a relationship.

Davis et al., (1989) found that in TRA attitude had a strong significant influence on behavioral intention, and it was second after PU in TAM. Their findings on subjective norm were consistent with this study, as they found subjective norm had no significant effect on behavioral intention, and TAM explains more variance than does TRA. Mathieson (1991) found attitude had the strongest effect on BI, but it was second after PU in TPB. His findings on subjective norm contrasted with this study, as it found subjective norm had no significant effect on BI. In addition, it found TAM to have more explanatory power than did TPB. Shih and Fang (2004) also found that attitude was a significant determinant of behavioral intention, but subjective norm was not. Taylor and Todd (1995) suggest that the link between subjective norm and behavioral intention may be due to perception of the real consequences associated with use. However, this finding is contradicted by Shih and Fang's (2004) research.

Results discrepancy between this study and previous could be interpreted in light of two factors: technology used and culture. The used technology in this study is SMS in Kuwait, while it was e-banking in Taiwan (Shih and Fang 2004 and 2006) and office automation system in USA (Davis et al., 1989). Moreover, this study is performed in Kuwait, where the culture play a different role than in the west.

Finally, with regard to past studies on SMS, this study shows that perceived value of SMS in terms of behavioral control was found to be a stronger predictor of intention to use SMS in the three models (TRA, DTPB, Nysveen's model), which is in line with previous studies on SMS (Turel et al., 2007) who found that value for money is highly correlated with perceived value of SMS, which in turn positively affects intention to use SMS.

CONCLUSIONS

This study compares the explanatory power of six technology adoption models to predict Short Message Service (SMS) intention to use in Kuwait. These models are: TRA, TPB, TAM, DTPB, Nyvseen's et al., (2005) model, and a new model proposed by the authors.

Contributions

There are four major contributions of this chapter. First, this study succeed to show that TRA, TAM, TPB, and DTPB are all valid in predicting intention to use SMS in another region/ culture not yet investigated, application of Nysveen et al., (2005) model is, however, not valid in Kuwait. *Second*, this study suggest that DTPB model produces the highest explained variance, followed by the model proposed by the authors in this chapter, and followed by the TPB model. TRA and TAM show the least explained variance, which call or further studies in order to replicate these results in other regions/ culture. *Third*, results indicate the absence of a dominant factor (i.e. variable that exerts the strongest effect on behavioral intention to use SMS) across the six models, which call for caution when applying different technology adoption models across different cultures and regions. The last contribution of this study is the application of SMS in a specific context related to banking sector.

Limitations

The limitations mostly relate to external validity, since the population of SMS users were from only one school in one country and a convenience sampling method was utilized. While recent studies (e.g. King and He 2006) confirmed the value of using students as surrogates for professionals in some technology adoption, the results are only generalisable for young Kuwaiti adults. The results of this study are, therefore, exploratory in nature and should be interpreted with caution.

Research Implications

This study has several implications for both research and practice.

Form a research perspective, This study is different from previous ones since it focuses not a single model but on different technology adoption models, and suggest the following.

First, this study suggests conducting a replication of this study in Arab Gulf Cooperative Council countries in order to confirm the implications of these results because o two reasons: (a) these countries are geographically related and culturally similar in term value, of language, and history, and (b) because in term of wealth they are very rich countries (see Table 1) and mobile penetration rate is one of the highest in the world (NStat 2007).

Second, perceived factors that have a strong impact on intention to use SMS varied across the six models. SMS is attitude driven in the three models (TRA, DTPB, Nysveen model) and behavioral control driven in two models (TPB, and new modified model), and perceived ease of use driven in TAM. This demonstrates that the use of a single model is not enough to fully understand the complex phenomena of technology adoption. The use of joined psychological and MIS viewpoints may provide more insight on this complex issue..

Third, Although this study discusses the application of six different adoption models of SMS in Kuwait, and integrates different constructs, the best variance is 86% which is explained by four variables in the decomposed theory of planed behavior. Thus, more than 14% remain unexplained, which call for additional research, and to integrate more constructs related to social and human aspect.

This study also provides practical insights for industry. Understanding what drives the adoption of SMS is critical to foster technology diffusion (Loch et al., 2003). This study suggests three applications: two related to mobile commerce and one related to social use of SMS.

First, this study suggests promoting the use of SMS in mobile commerce. Since the study succeeds to show that perceived behavior control (related to money and time) in three adoption model, this study suggest to develop new services/ applications that will fulfill this need and increase SMS use. For example, mobile operators are encouraged to develop information systems for mobile devices that allow potential customers to compare prices while they shop. Shoppers equipped with mobile phones can access the envisioned system, which is similar to mysimon.com, a leading comparison shopping agent. Then, as they shop, they can sent an SMS to the mobile operator, in order to request prices in the store to those available elsewhere.

Second, this study succeeds to show that ease of use is also a driver of SMS use in other technology adoption. This study also encourages to develop services/ application that achieve this need. With the increased trend toward location based commerce. This refers to delivery of applications and services for users based on their specific location, local mobile operators are encouraged to proposed innovative services with this regard. Example of services may include identification of the nearest gasoline station or a specific restaurant (such as Italian foods) with parking and entertainment for kids in a specific area/location. According to a 2003 European survey, 56%, 55%, and 46% of mobile users received SMS ads in Germany, the UK, and Spain, respectively (Tongeren et al., 2004). By 2009, the aggregate growth in the United States and Europe will exceed $1 billion, with the increasing availability of multimedia content (TMC Net, 2008). This is likely to happen as Google has expressed its intention to penetrate this market with its open source operating system for mobile phones and the creation of a consortium that includes 33 mobile telecommunication companies around the world. This suggests that the adoption of SMS advertising is beginning to grow and may have the potential to become an important new mode of interactive marketing communication.

Third, with the increase use of SMS in the Arab countries, its social usage in a variety of circumstances such as congratulations, birthdays, condolences, Islamic holidays (e.g. Eid and Ramadan) is also increasing. The day before the holly

Islamic Ramadan (the 12th of September 2007), 18 millions of SMS were exchanged in Kuwait by the first leading mobile telecommunication company based in Kuwait, 90000 MMS, and 35 millions of phone calls (Quotation of senior executives of MTC). During period of Islamic pilgrimage of 2007, 1 billion of SMS were sent out of Saudi Arabia in period of 10 days, 4 millions of phone calls were given. In Kuwait, every year 1 billion of SMS are sent annually, this study is therefore useful for companies willing to tape into these opportunities. Mobile phone designers are encouraged to design customized products that satisfy the unique features of Arab and Islamic culture. Examples of features may include designing predefined SMS (Arabic or English languages) for such purposes, or for allowing customers to voice record their SMS and then send them as attached SMS.

REFERENCES

Ajzen (1991): The theory of planned behavior. *Organizational behavior and human decision processes, 50*(2), 179-211

Ajzen, I. & Fishbein, M. (1980). *Understanding attitudes and predicting social behavior.* Englewood Cliffs, NJ: Prentice Hall.

Ajzen, I. (1991). The Theory of Planned Behavior. *Organizational Behavior and Human Decision Processes, 50*, 179-211.

Ajzen, I. (2001). Nature and operation of attitudes. *Annual Review of Psychology, 52*, 27–58.

Baron, S., Patterson, A. & Harris, K. (2006). Beyond technology acceptance: understanding consumer practice. *International Journal of Service Industry Management, 17*(2), 111-136.

Chau, P. Y. K. & Hu, P J. (2001). Information technology acceptance by professionals: A Model comparison approach. *Decision Sciences, 32*(4), 699-719.

Davis, F. D. (1989). Perceived usefulness, perceived ease of use and user acceptance of information technology. *MIS Quarterly, 13*, 983-1003.

Davis, F. D., Bagozzi, R. P., & Warshaw, P. R. (1989). User Acceptance of Computer Technology: A Comparison of Two Theoretical Models. *Management Science, 35*, 982-1003.

Davis, F. D., Bagozzi, R. P., & Warshaw, P. R. (1992). Extrinsic and intrinsic motivation to use computers in the workplace. *Journal of Applied Social Psychology, 22*(14), 1111- 1132.

Hair, J. F. Jr, Anderson, R. E., Tatham, R. L., & Black, W. C. (1998). *Multivariate data analysis* (5th ed.). Englewood Cliffs, NJ: Prentice Hall.

Heijden Van Der, H. (2003). Factors influencing the usage of Websites: the case of a generic portal in The Netherlands. *Information & Management, 40*(6), 541–549.

Heijden Van Der, H. (2004). User acceptance of hedonic information systems. *MIS Quarterly, 4*, 695-704.

Hsu C., Lu H., and Hsu H., (2007) Adoption of the mobile Internet: An empirical study of multimedia message service (MMS). *Omega 35*(6), 715-726.

Instat (2007), *SMS in the Middle East and Asia.* Retrieved May 9, 2007 from http://www.instat.com/

Juniper Research (2007). *M-Commerce Hot Spots, Part 1: Beyond Ringtones and Wallpaper.* Retrieved May 9, 2007, from http://www.ecommercetimes.com/story/ebiz/57109.html

Kamel, S., & Assem, A. (2003). Assessing the Introduction of Electronic Banking in Egypt Using the Technology Acceptance Model. *Annals of Cases On Information Technology*, 1-25.

Karlsen, M. E., Helgemo, I., & Gripsrud, M. (2001). *Useful, cheap and fun: A survey of teenagers demands for mobile telephony.* Norway: Telenor R&D.

Kasesniemi E. E. L. & Rautiainen P. (2002). Mobile culture of children and teenagers in Finland. In J.E. Katz and M. Aarkhus (Editors), *Perpetual Contact* (pp. 170-193). Cambridge: CUP.

King, W. R. & He J. (2006). A meta-analysis of the technology acceptance model. *Information & Managemen, 43*, 740–755.

Legris P., Ingham J., & Collerette P. (2003). Why do people use information technology? A critical review of the technology acceptance model. *Information & Management 40*, 191–204

Leung, L. (2007). Unwillingness-to-communicate and college students' motives in SMS mobile messaging. *Telematics and Informatics, 24*(2), 115-129.

Loch, K. D., Straub, D. W., & Kamel, S. (2003). Diffusing the Internet in the Arab World: The Role of Social Norms and Technological Culturation. *IEEE Transactions on Engineering Management, 50*(1), 45-63.

Mathieson, K. (1991). Predicting user intention: comparing the technology acceptance model with the theory planned behavior. *Information systems research, 2*(3), 173-1991.

NStat (2007). *ICT in the middle east.* Retrieved 25th August 2007.

Nysveen, H., Pedersen P. E. & Thorbornsen, H. (2005). Intention to use mobile services: Antecedents and cross-service comparison. *Journal of the Academy of Marketing Science, 33*(3), 330-346.

Okazaki, S., & Taylor C. R. (2008). What is SMS advertising and why do multinationals adopt it? Answers from an empirical study in European markets. *Journal of Business Research, 61*(1), 4-12.

Peevers G., Douglas G. & Jack M. A. (2008). A usability comparison of three alternative message formats for an SMS banking service. *International Journal of Human-Computer Studies, 66*(2), 113-123.

Rau, P. P., Gao, Q., & Wu, L. (2008). Using mobile communication technology in high school education: Motivation, pressure, and learning performance, *Computers & Education 50*(1), 1-22.

Reid, F. J. M. & Reid D. J. (2004). Text appeal: The psychology of SMS texting and its implications for the design of mobile phone interfaces. *Campus-Wide Information Systems, 21*(5), 196-200.

Rogers, E.M. (1983). *Diffusion of innovations.* New York: Free Press.

Rouibah, K. (2008). Social usage of instant messaging by employees outside the workplace in Kuwait: A structural equation model. *IT and People, 21*(1), 34-68.

Rouibah, K., & Abbas, H. (2006). Modified technology acceptance model for camera mobile phone adoption: Development and validation. *17th Australian Conference on Information System*, 6-8 December 2006, Adelaide, Australia.

Rouibah, K., (2007). Does mobile payment technology Mnet attract potential consumers: A Kuwaiti Study. In M. Toleman, A. Cater-Steel, and D. Roberts (Editors), *18th Australian Conference on Information System.* 199-211, Queensland, Australia, 4-5 December 2007.

Shih, Y., & Fang K. (2006). Effects of network quality attributes on customer adoption intentions of Internet Banking. *Total Quality Management & Business Excellence, 17*(1), 61-77.

Shih, Y., and Fang, K., (2004). The use of a decomposed theory of planned behavior to study Internet banking in Taiwan, *Internet Research 3*(14), 213-223.

SMS Research and Statistics (2005). *Chinese send 750 million SMS daily.* Retrieved December 31,

2007 from http://smschronicle.com/?q=taxonomy/term/12

Suh, B. & Han, I. (2002). Effects of trust on customer acceptance of Internet banking, *Electronic Commerce Research and Applications, 1*(3/4), 247-63.

Taylor, S., & Todd, P. A. (1995). Understanding information technology usage: a test of competing models. *Information System Research, 6*(2), 144-174.

TMC Net. (2008). 2006 Will Be the Year of Mobile Advertising Experimentation. *TMC net news* (2006), March 16. Retrieved December 3, 2008, from http://www.tmcnet.com/usubmit/2006/03/16/1465460.htm

Tongeren, v. M. Lussanet. de, Favier J. & Jennings R. (2004). Mobile campaigns that don't annoy: how should marketers create successful SMS campaigns? *Trends. Forrester research* March 8, Web http://www.forrester.com

Turel, O., Serenko A., & Bontis N., (2007). User acceptance of wireless short messaging services: deconstructing perceived value. *Information & Management, 44*(1), 63-73.

Venkatesh, V. & Davis, F. D. (2000). A theoretical extension of the technology acceptance model: Four longitudinal studies. *Management Science*, 46(2), 186-204.

Venkatesh, V., Morris, M. G., Davis, G. B., & Davis, F. D. (2003). User acceptance of information technology: toward a unified view. *MIS Quarterly, 27*(3), 425-478.

World development Indicators (2007). Retrieved June 23, 2007, from Internet database. Web: http://devdata.worldbank.org/

Yan, X., Gong M., & Thong J. Y. L. (2006). Two tales of one service: user acceptance of short message service (SMS) in Hong Kong and China. *Info, 8*(1), 16-28.

Yi, M. Y., Jackson J. D., Park J. S., & Probst J. C. (2006). Understanding information technology acceptance by individual professionals: toward an integrative view, *Information & Managemen,t 43*, 350-363.

APPENDIX 1: CONSTRUCT MEASUREMENT

Image

- SMS is something I often talk with others about or use together with others.
- SMS services is something I often show to other people.
- I express my personality by using SMS.
- Using SMS gives me status.

Perceived Enjoyment (PE)

- I find SMS entertaining.
- I find SMS pleasant.
- Using SMS is exciting.
- It is fun to use SMS.

Perceived Usefulness (PU)

- Using SMS make me save time when staying in contact with friends and family.
- SMS make me more social and available.
- SMS make me a person it is easier to stay in contact with.
- SMS make my contact with others better.

Perceived Ease of Use (PEOU)

- Learning to use SMS is easy to me.
- It is easy to make SMS do what I want them to do.
- My interaction with SMS is clear and understandable.
- It is easy to understand and interpret SMS.

Subjective Norm

- People important to me think I should use SMS.
- It is expected that people like me use SMS.
- People I look up expect me to use SMS.

Attitude Toward Use

I found SMS

- Good/bad
- Wise/foolish

- Favorable/unfavorable
- Beneficial/harmful
- Positive/negative

Perceived Behavioral Control (PBC)

- I am able to use SMS.
- I have the resources to use SMS.
- Using SMS is wise.

Intention to Use

- I intend to use SMS to perform transaction banks.
- The next six months I intend to use SMS frequently to perform transaction banks.

Section V
Strategies for Successful E-Commerce Development in DCs

Chapter XII
An Economic Framework for the Assessment of E-Commerce in Developing Countries

Ayoub Yousefi
King's University College at the University of Western Ontario, Canada

ABSTRACT

This study presents a theoretically-based model for economic analysis of electronic commerce in developing countries. The Porter diamond model is adopted for proper economic examination of the factors that affect e-commerce. The model not only captures the factors as the driving forces of e-commerce, but also facilitates the assessment of e-commerce and identification of the global competitive advantages of the firms. The new model can be used as a framework for better policymaking by the public and private sectors and to predict changes in the rapidly expanding e-commerce in the global environment, especially in developing countries.

INTRODUCTION

Globalization in the latter half of the twentieth century has been driven primarily by the advancements in information and communication technologies (ICTs) and electronic commerce. The enormous surge in e-commerce in the recent past has significantly altered the ways in which business is conducted around the world. The e-commerce as a new phenomenon is in fact a reference to all markets in which exchanges are facilitated by digital networks. The new market opportunities brought about by e-commerce have forced firms to find digital solutions for becoming more competitive in the global marketplace.

Due to the rapid expansion of the digital marketplace and diffusion of information, e-commerce has been growing in scale and scope faster than the pace of research devoted to the study of the organizational development, regulatory, and

Copyright © 2009, IGI Global, distributing in print or electronic forms without written permission of IGI Global is prohibited.

institutional aspects of this new phenomenon. Today, the scope of e-commerce comprises the electronic labor market, electronic procurement, electronic money, and electronic entertainment, among other enterprises. As such, e-commerce means different things to different people, rendering a clear-cut definition somewhat problematic. VanHoose (2003) makes a distinction between e-commerce and e-business. E-commerce is defined to capture any process that entails exchanging ownership of or rights to use goods and services via electronically linked devices that communicate interactively within networks. On the other hand, e-business includes a firm's internal coordination, decision-making, and implementation processes in its production, marketing, and management functions by using electronic networks. Kauffman and Walden (2001) suggest a broader definition of e-commerce, in which digital goods play a focal role. Digital goods, also known as information goods, exhibit some characteristics that are substantially different from those of traditional goods sold on the Internet. In particular, when a physical product is searched for and bought on the Internet, it becomes a digital-physical bundle (1).

Kauffman and Walden (2001) maintain that the research on e-commerce is the "business" of business schools and suggest a multi disciplinary approach to e-commerce. In this study, however, we identify three major benefits from recasting the principles of e-commerce as a new medium of exchange within the wider context of the traditional theory of trade:

First, e-commerce marks the beginning of a new era in the history of international trade where production, marketing, sales, and distribution occur in the digital marketplace. By the end of 2005, according to Sherif (2006), more than 25 percent of the global trade had been carried out through the digital economy. In fact, e-commerce and cross-border e-commerce, in particular, is radically changing the landscape of international business. In the context of international trade literature, such a substantial change requires a fresh interpretation of such concepts as tariffs, quotas, and intellectual property rights.

Secondly, the Internet and other ICT- related media, called digital opportunities, have the potential to reduce barriers of the free trade and create a somewhat frictionless, but not perfect, business environment. Although some potent impediments to the free flow of trade remain today, the Internet through wired or wireless networks has virtually wiped out national boundaries and eliminated the distance between trading partners in different nations in the global economy. According to Mann et al. (2000) the Internet has reduced friction in the marketplace in three dimensions: time, distance, and information, resulting in lower costs for new firms to enter and exit from an industry.

Thirdly, the new medium of exchange appears to have implications for developing countries that are expectedly different from those in developed countries. Although developed countries have pioneered e-commerce and, in general, enjoy a higher volume of trade than developing countries, there are significant variations in the rate and pattern of usage and the expected benefits within each group. Despite all trading nations can potentially gain from these opportunities, developing countries are expected to gain, in the long run, more than developed countries since they are deeply inside the current technological circle (Panagariya, 2000).

The rest of this chapter is organized as follows: Section 2 reviews the e-commerce literature with particular attention to its foundation in economics. Section 3 adopts the Porter theory of firms' global competitiveness to provide a suitable framework for the economic analysis of e-commerce. Section 4 presents the conclusions and explains contributions of the study.

LITERATURE REVIEW

E-commerce literature has been growing rapidly in a number of interrelated dimensions by covering, primarily, business-related topics in relation to ICTs (the wired and wireless networks), and the Internet (2). The relatively recent body of literature on e-commerce identifies a wide range of factors encompassing numerous socioeconomic, cultural, and institutional factors affecting operations and the progress of e-commerce around the world. Sherif (2006) presents a recent comprehensive survey of the status of a number of developing countries in relation to various aspects of e-commerce such as strategies, challenges, and opportunities. Clearly, these conditions appear to vary substantially from one nation to another and across firms depending on the industry structure, state of the technology, and geographic locale.

International trade has long been viewed to enlarge trading nations' production and consumption capacities and provide access to scarce resources without which poor nations would be unable to grow. In addition, the continued expansion of trade is expected to equalize returns to factor prices between nations, promote greater international equality and, in the long run, bring about economic growth. The emergence of the so-called digital opportunities and specifically the e-commerce has altered the landscape of this debate and led some to believe that the gap between poor and rich countries might shrink at an even faster pace than before as developing countries gain access to these technologies. However, there are those who hold an opposing view on this matter. Ferran and Salim (2006), for instance, argue that such equalization tendencies are far from happening as deficiencies in business practices caused by inadequate transportation, organizational, and payment infrastructures overwhelm the sole importation and installation of physical ICT capital. Similar concern has been raised by Mansell (2001), which examines the claim that using ICTs and particularly the Internet will facilitate success of firms in developing countries in international markets. The study concludes that unfavorable institutional setting and the lack of ICT-related skilled labor force hinder the success of e-commerce and long-term economic growth for most developing countries.

The literatures of the Internet and e-commerce are both integral parts of a broader body of ICTs literature. It is interesting to observe that researchers from different disciplines, even non-economists, are showing an increasing interest in understanding the economic foundations of ICTs in an attempt to answer questions concerning costs and benefits of ICTs. Bakos and Kemerer (1992) review six areas of economic theory that have been identified as a reference discipline for the systematic analysis of ICTs. McKnight and Bailey (1997) focus more closely on pricing models for the Internet, which is operational and economically efficient. The study also reminds the industry leaders, academics, and policymakers of the lack of a proper economic framework of the Internet services and the policy assessment of the Internet. In particular, the study invites scholars of technology, economics, and policymakers to cooperate in an interdisciplinary study of the Internet economics.

Studies by Tapscott (1996) and Harbhajan and Varinder (2005) attempt to explain the way digital economy operates. That is, how in the new economy enterprises organize their activities and how they are linked to one another. Shapiro and Varian (1999) focus on information economy and elaborate on the pricing of information goods, which tend to have zero marginal cost. Similarly, Liebowitz (2002) examines the network economy especially the basic Internet economics. Finally, Kauffman and Walden (2001) offer a comprehensive review of a broad-based literature on e-commerce from the perspective of a multi discipline research and a multilevel framework for conceptual analysis.

The spread of e-commerce over many different jurisdictions necessitates multinational protocols and agreements by all trading nations. Because no single international body can afford to address the multitude of e-commerce issues, many such organizations have stepped forward to help facilitate and promote e-commerce in specific ways. Mann et al. (2000:144) tabulate international, regional, and other mandated organizations based on their devotion to different e-commerce issues such as standards, information security, taxes, etc. Among international institutions, the World Trade Organization (WTO) assumes a major responsibility in promoting a fair and secure operating framework for all parties (WTO, 1998). In addition, UNCTAD's Electronic Commerce Branch routinely carries out studies to investigate the impact of e-commerce and the Internet technologies on developing countries and assist them in adopting proper national polices and strategies (UNCTAD, 2001-2004).. In particular, UNCTAD assists developing countries with the establishment of a legal and regulatory framework compatible with international standards and protocols in order to protect intellectual property rights.

From the existing relatively new literature of e-commerce the following two conclusions are in order: First, the pioneering efforts and their contributions are commendable. But as with any first-generation research, these studies fail to establish a coherent relationship among the wide spectrum of factors affecting e-commerce by overlooking the importance of the interconnectedness and synergy among them. Secondly, the literature fails to identify an adequate framework for the assessment and analysis of the e-commerce based on an appropriate economic model.

In aim of this study is to fill the aforementioned gap in the literature by suggesting an economic framework that can be used for proper assessment of the e-commerce in developing countries. It should be emphasized that a business based on the Internet to remain viable, it must be as competitive as businesses on the traditional bricks-and-mortar markets. In other words, for trade taking place in an imaginary medieval marketplace or in today's cyber marketplace, competitive advantages of the trading partners still remain the primary basis. Our proposed model can be used in identifying the basis for firms' competitive advantages given the particular characteristics of the e-commerce.

MODEL

The objective of this study is to present an economic framework for proper economic examination of the factors that contribute to the firm's competitive advantage in electronic marketplaces. The model considers the demand-side conditions, industry structure, and the economy as a whole. To achieve this objective, the Porter (1990) theory of global competitiveness is adopted as a new conceptual model for effective analysis of e-commerce. Porter's seminal theory of global competitiveness is in the tradition of the classical theory. It can also be considered as a natural extension of Adam Smith's Absolute Advantage (1937), David Ricardo's Comparative Advantage (1963), and Heckscher-Ohlin's (1983) general equilibrium factor endowment theory. However, Porter argues that the classical theory of international trade based on natural factor endowment is not comprehensive enough to fully express a firm's competitive advantage. The contribution of Porter's theory of global competitive advantage to the classical theory can be summarized as follows:

First, in today's global business environment firms are endowed with the opportunity to achieve global competitive advantages by obtaining market information, factors of production, and technology from international markets. Porter questions the viability of the natural-factor-driven competitiveness in favor of acquired-factor and technology-driven competitive advantage (3). In other words, competitive advantage should not be taken as an intrinsic characteristic of a nation.

Secondly, unlike the classical factor endowment theory that attributes competitiveness to the nations, Porter argues that competitive advantages and trade opportunities accrue to individual firms regardless of the competitive position of their domestic or host countries. Strategic management scholars argue that global competitiveness at the aggregate level for a nation does not necessarily correspond to the global competitiveness at the individual firm level (Whinston, et al. 1997). From the point of view of a specific firm, innovations in an unrelated industry might actually turn out to be harmful because they tend to drive up the prices of general-use factors of production in domestic economy.

Thirdly, Porter's theory identifies four inter-related key conditions commonly referred to as the Porter Diamond, a reference to its diamond shaped diagram. The intuition for the diamond shaped model is that it captures the interaction and synergy among the four conditions as depicted Figure 1. From theoretical perspective, the model incorporates all the related factors including global supply and demand, industry structure, levels of competitions in the input and output markets, and strategies adapted by rivals into a general equilibrium framework

In summary, the success of e-commerce depends, in general, on a given set of conditions internal and external to a firm, including global competitiveness of the domestic economy. This, in turn, is made possible by the interplay of the four interrelated and mutually reinforcing key conditions as follows:

I. Factor Conditions
II. Demand Conditions

Figure 1. The Porter Diamond

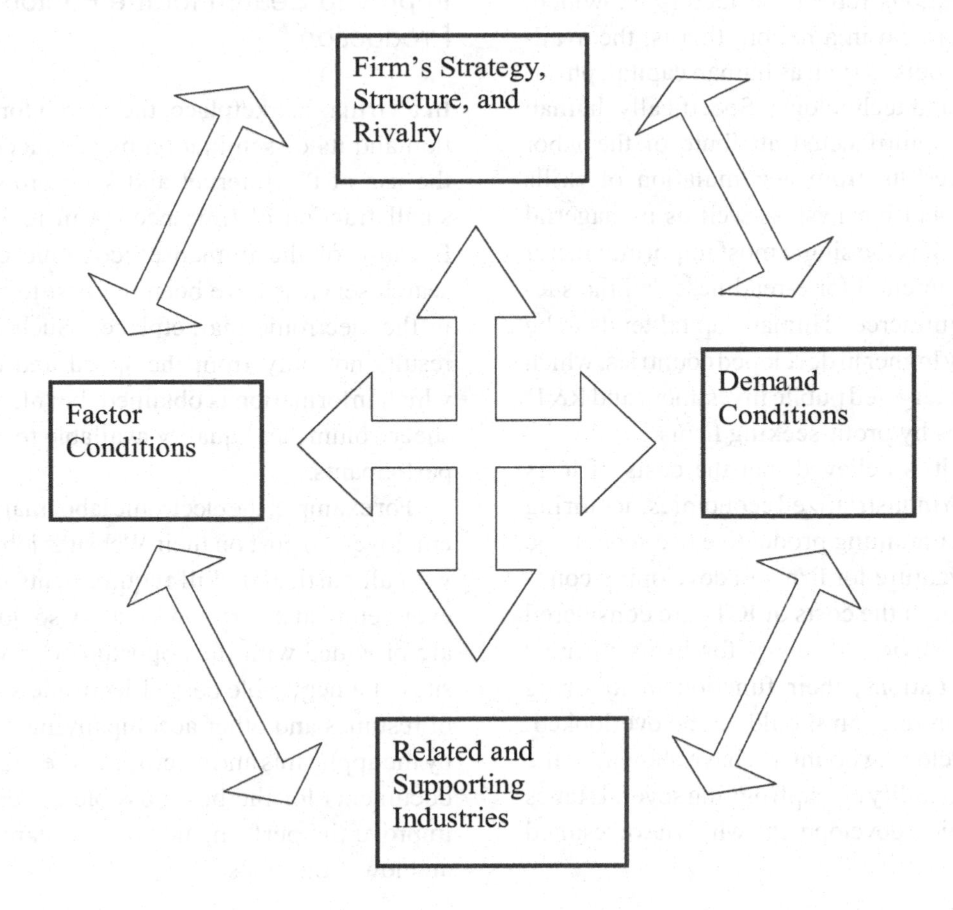

III. Related and Supporting Industries and Firm Structure
IV. Company's Strategy, Organizational Structure and Rivalry.

The model suggests that all four conditions should be favorable for a firm to achieve global competitiveness in a particular country. However, shortage of a specific factor in the home country does not inhibit firms from achieving a competitive advantage. Evidently, however, these conditions can be influenced by the pertinent government policies. In what follows we reexamine the wide range of factors identified in the literature to group them in one of the aforementioned four key conditions.

Factor Conditions

Factor conditions reflect the factor-endowment position of a firm in a nation; that is, the availability of resources such as human capital, physical capital, and technology. Specifically, human capital is a multifaceted attribute of the labor force that results from accumulation of skills in international business as well as managerial knowledge. It is the single most important factor that is instrumental for e-readiness and the success of e-commerce. Human capital tends to be significantly higher in developed countries, which results from targeted public investment and R&D expenditures by profit-seeking firms.

Despite it is believed that the costs of ICTs are falling in industrialized economies, acquiring ICTs and maintaining productive use seem to be a costly adventure for firms in developing countries. Although the costs of ICTs are considered substantial barriers to entry for firms in most developing nations, their function in lowering the cost of production should not be overlooked. Finally, developing countries have shown, in the past, the possibility of leapfrogging several stages of technological development, which have resulted from substantial R&D investments in developed economies over time.

The factors that have been discussed above are relevant to all markets and are by no means unique to e-commerce. However, e-commerce is not merely a linear extrapolation of the traditional commerce nor an alternative distribution system. Electronic commerce takes place in markets in which the producers, consumers, intermediaries, and all processes undergo fundamental changes. Because of such a phenomenal environment, the factors take on different functions requiring a new perspective for their analysis. Similarly, to better understand the way this market operates, its dynamics should be reexamined by considering special features of the factors being used. Figure 2 summarizes some important characteristics of the factor conditions relevant to e-commerce:

Improved Search for the Factors of Production

In a virtual marketplace, the search for information and its dissemination by producers require the use of the Internet and Web browsing at a small fraction of time needed in real markets. Because of the immense economic efficiency, search services have been the first to be offered in the electronic marketplace. Such efficiency results not only from the speed and ease with which information is obtained, but also from the sheer volume and quality available to all market participants.

For example, the electronic labor market allows employers to post on their Websites job openings with all particular skill requirements more than ever before at a very low cost. Also, job seekers are provided with the opportunity to visit these sites at a negligible cost. Electronic submission of résumés and other accompanying documents by the applicants and electronic screening of such documents for the best possible match seem to improve the performance of the search process and lower the costs.

Figure 2. The Porter Diamond model: Basis for comparative advantage

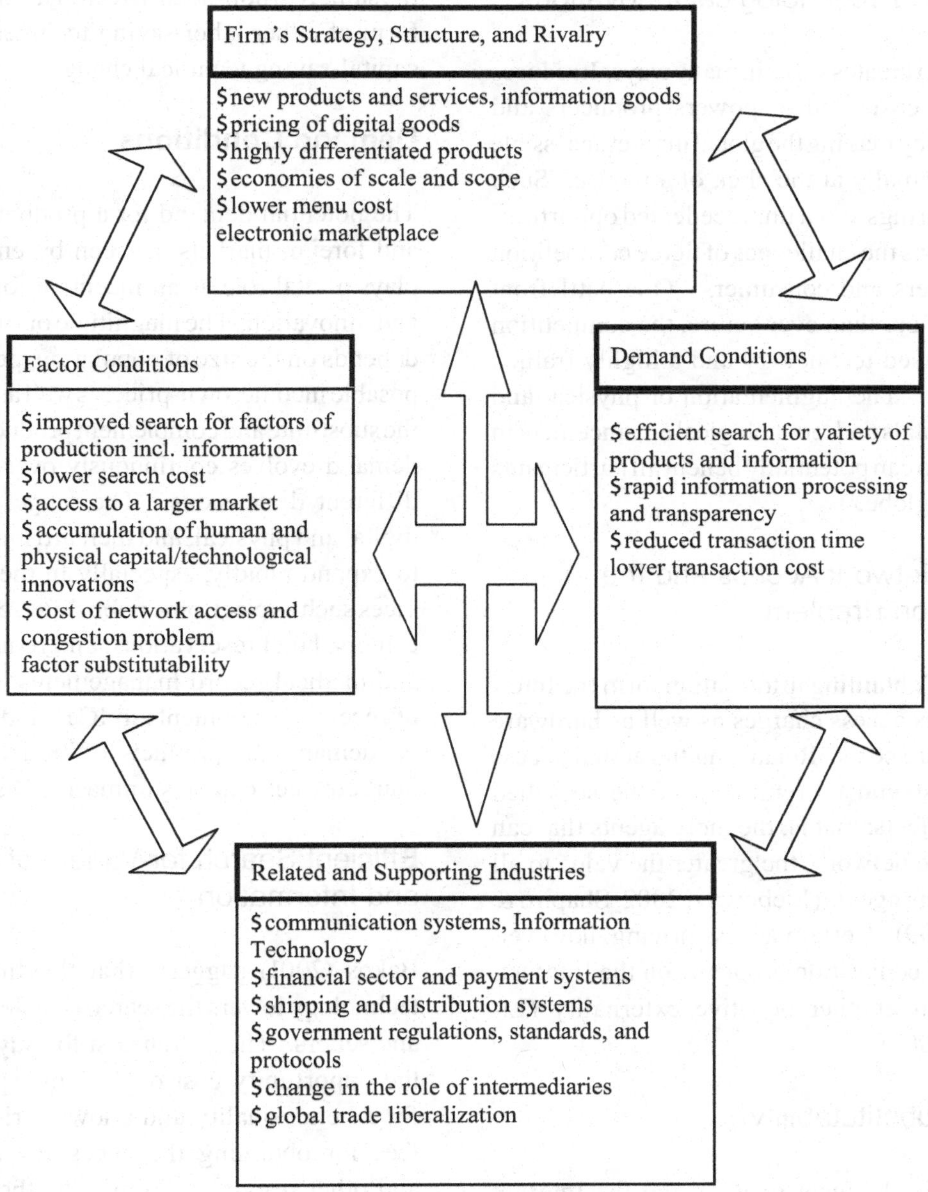

Firm's Strategy, Structure, and Rivalry

- new products and services, information goods
- pricing of digital goods
- highly differentiated products
- economies of scale and scope
- lower menu cost

electronic marketplace

Factor Conditions

- improved search for factors of production incl. information
- lower search cost
- access to a larger market
- accumulation of human and physical capital/technological innovations
- cost of network access and congestion problem

factor substitutability

Demand Conditions

- efficient search for variety of products and information
- rapid information processing and transparency
- reduced transaction time

lower transaction cost

Related and Supporting Industries

- communication systems, Information Technology
- financial sector and payment systems
- shipping and distribution systems
- government regulations, standards, and protocols
- change in the role of intermediaries
- global trade liberalization

Access to a Larger Market

The electronic marketplace is confined neither by spatial nor geographical boundaries. Given the appropriate infrastructures and logistics, firms can participate and compete in such an environment, which brings about both unprecedented opportunities and huge challenges for firms in developing countries.

Accumulation of Human and Physical Capital and Technological Innovations

The Internet creates value in many ways. It reduces the search costs and empowers producers and consumers by making the global market accessible to them virtually at the click of a mouse. Such openness brings about unprecedented opportunities as well as the challenges of fierce competition for producers and consumers. One battlefront involves, more than ever before, the competition over advanced technology and a highly trained labor force. The augmentation of physical and human capitals and technological advancement in one location can potentially benefit all participants across the globe.

Cost of Network Access and the Congestion Problem

The cost of obtaining information form the Internet includes access charges as well as hardware and software costs. Regarding the actual access cost, one should be reminded of the so-called network effects; that is, the more agents that can log onto the network, the greater the value to all participating agents (Liebowitz, 2002; Shapiro & Varian, 1999). Certain access pricing, however, can lead to congestion problems on the Internet, resulting in another negative externality (Liebowitz, 2002).

Factor Substitutability

The fast development of ICTs and the Internet inevitably results, to some extent, in substitution among the Internet and e-commerce-specific capital, labor, and other nonspecific forms of capital. This, in turn, can affect the cost of e-commerce activities with cross-sectional and economy-wide consequences. The capital now forming around the Internet and e-commerce can, in principle, lead to one of the following dynamics: (a) neutral technical change where the ratio of inputs remains the same, (b) non-neutral technical changes in the form of either labor-saving technical change or capital-saving technical change.

Demand Conditions

The potential demand for a product in the local and foreign markets, as seen by entrepreneurs, plays a vital role as an incentive for investment and innovation. The magnitude of such a demand depends on the size of population, per-capita disposable income, own-price, as well as the prices of the substitute and complement products. Potential demand evolves continuously over time and in different dimensions. The range of products, digital and physical, and their attributes continue to expand rapidly, especially in the area of services such as electronic publishing, customer call centers, hotel reservations, and remote financial and medical record managements. The impact of recent developments in ICTs and the Internet on demand for products offered in electronic marketplaces can be summarized as follows:

Efficient Search for Variety of Products and Information

Bakos (2001) suggests that the Internet-based technology lowers the search cost for both buyers and sellers. The search cost for buyers includes the opportunity cost of the time spent looking for a better quality and a lower-priced product, fees for obtaining the necessary information, and other resources. Similarly, the search cost for sellers includes the opportunity cost of the time and the effort spent identifying the potential buyers and disseminating information about the products through advertising and sales media. With positive impacts on both sides of the markets, the Internet-based technology appears to improve efficiency and boost demand. Finally, the efficient search and advertising processes can reinforce each other and potentially dampen prices in electronic marketplaces compared to those in the traditional markets.

Rapid Information Processing and Transparency

The fast-paced electronic marketplace enables consumers to search for, compare, and, in some instances, negotiate the best possible price. Likewise, producers can access a larger market and a wider range of audiences to whom the products can be sold. Given that all processes relating to search and negotiation can be stored electronically, easier follow-ups and a more transparent system should be expected. Such an environment reduces the risk of market failure by lowering information asymmetry about product characteristics such as price, quality, and the like.

Reduced Transaction Cost

Transaction costs arise from the opportunity cost of the time spent negotiating and reaching an agreement about the price and other aspects of the product and to ensure that the terms of the contract are fulfilled. The rapid transmission of information, the possibility of tailoring the terms of the contract to satisfy objectives of all parties involved, and the continuous electronic monitoring of the progress of the contracts are expected to lower the total transaction costs. It should be noted that such a positive momentum behind the demand is a feature unique to electronic markets, which makes them distinguishable from the traditional markets.

Related and Supporting Industries and Firm Structure

Marketing apparatus, banking and transportation industries, and other infrastructures are the prerequisites for the profitable operation of a firm. Such a business environment coupled with factor conditions helps to determine a firm's competitive advantage. The e-commerce literature sums up the supporting industries collectively as a capacity to benefit, e- readiness, or e-business climate. The terms, however, appear to be interrelated and can be used interchangeably. E-readiness, for instance, is a reference not only to favorable factor conditions, but also to interconnected systems as the foundation for the vitality of e-commerce in a nation (Molla, 2006) (4). As a result, e-readiness flourishes from the existence of financial and banking services, currency convertibility, agreements governing mutual access to foreign markets, supportive regulatory and institutional setting, and other "soft factors" such as political support (5). However, e-readiness should not be seen as immune from the existing body of complex tariff and non-tariff trade barriers of nations. Among non-tariff barriers, foreign exchange restrictions, health and environmental safety requirements, and the multitude of idiosyncratic barriers can hinder e-commerce activities.

Better understanding of the competitive advantage of a firm in e-commerce requires an in-depth examination of the related and supporting industries individually, which is beyond the scope of this study. Nonetheless, specific impacts of these industries on e-commerce, listed in Figure 2, are briefly discussed below.

Communication Systems, Information Technology

The existence of communication infrastructure and affordability of accompanying services lead to better connectivity that facilitates e-commerce. Connectivity which involves fast-paced flow of information among sellers, intermediaries, and buyers results in efficiency not only in the physical goods markets, but also in the digital goods markets. In spite of efficiencies, the flow of personal and business information in the cyberspace suffers from of the lack of perfect information security. Information security is a reference to the network of safeguard measures that prevent personal and business information from falling into the wrong hands. Most studies conclude that the security concern remains a contentious issue and the most important obstacle in e-commerce. The higher is the lack of information protection mechanisms, the higher would be the perceived risk of losing valuable information to competitors, which, in turn, lowers the willingness to participate in e-commerce.

Financial Sector and Payment Systems

One of the by-products of the Internet is the development of electronic money; that is, a digital note capable of storing value and making it available to the holder at any place and any time. The systems of electronic money have shown to have the potential of replacing cash and other traditional forms of money as a superior medium of payment. The development makes transactions easier and lowers transaction costs for buyers and sellers in the traditional and electronic markets. With the online debt-discharging capability, electronic money, which has become a substitute for cash in the traditional markets, is virtually the only medium of payment in e-commerce. In addition, the emergence of the new medium of payment and the ensuing changes in the payment systems has extensive macroeconomic consequences. The changes provide opportunities as well as challenges for the conduct of monetary policy by the central banks.

Shipping and Distribution Systems

E-commerce relies on the traditional shipping and distribution systems for the delivery of physical products and on electronic delivery of digital goods, and often on both systems. On the Internet, the delivery of digital goods is handled by the Internet Service Providers (ISP) and facilitated by the universal resource providers (URL) and the stateless communication procedure, hyper text transfer protocol (HTTP). Typically, digital technology allows products to be distributed quickly at a very low cost, (Shapiro & Varian, 1999). Clearly, the shipping and distribution apparatus of e-commerce is inseparable from the Internet infrastructure. However, a separate and in-depth study of the complex systems of shipping and distribution in e-commerce seems an obvious need.

Government Regulations, Standards, and Protocols

Undoubtedly, government policies affect developments in communication networks, shipping and distribution systems, and other infrastructures that indirectly impact e-commerce. Mann et al. (2000) explain the relevance of these infrastructures within a wider context of e-commerce. The nature of information goods necessitates government involvement for protecting intellectual property rights, information privacy, and fair competition (Shapiro & Varian, 1999). In addition, the jurisdictional overlap of e-commerce makes it impossible for national governments to pursue their own policies unilaterally. Public debate concerning the extent of government involvement has been controversial and will continue for a foreseeable future. That is, as new technological developments keep unfolding, government's involvements through supervision and regulatory power over ICTs and e-commerce should not weaken any time soon.

Changes in the Role of Intermediaries

Along with the progress of e-commerce, the role of intermediaries appears to be shifting and less certain for the future. One of the roles of the intermediaries in the traditional goods markets is to warehouse products between wholesalers and retailers to optimize the flow of goods, resulting in minimized transportation and distribution costs (Whinston et al., 1997). Thus, intermediaries can in fact eliminate the need for direct access to the original suppliers that reduces duplicated shipping traffic, lowers search cost, and enhances network efficiency. A similar distributive efficiency of online intermediaries is out of the question since the distance between buyers and sellers is no longer an issue. After all, producers of digital products need to send only one copy to a wholesaler or a retailer without facing distribution costs. However, online intermediaries are capable of lowering distribution costs in a different way by collecting, processing, and storing information in one place that is accessible to all interested parties.

As a result of these changes, a number of markets have exhibited some degree of disintermediation. On the other hand, new forms of intermediation have emerged to provide bundles of services in markets such as travel, tourism, and real estate (Bakos, 2001). Brousseau (2002) examines the reasons for the existence of commercial intermediaries in the digital market environment and draws attention to the economics of commercial intermediation. The study points out that the digital networks cannot eliminate intermediation services, but give rise to a new generation of intermediaries. These changes have shown to have a sizable impact on the transaction costs and significant role in the evolution of e-commerce.

Global Trade Liberalization

As mentioned earlier, the jurisdictional overlap of e-commerce defies unilateral approaches to e-commerce. Because no government can individually afford to address all of the e-commerce issues, a number of international organizations have taken on the coordination, standards, security, and other aspects of e-commerce. Mann et al. (2000) tabulate international organizations based on the nature of their involvements in different areas of e-commerce.

The World Trade Organization is known to have a dual support of the development and progress of e-commerce. On one hand, WTO has played an instrumental role in trade liberalization since its establishment in 1995. To this end, WTO facilitates international trade by providing its signatories with a forum to negotiate agreements and resolve trade disputes (WTO, 1998). On the other hand, WTO is actively involved in regulatory processes and external enforcement of competition in the telecommunication sector; that is, WTO's role in trade liberalization cannot be separated from its impact on the regulatory framework, standards, and protocols of e-commerce.

Company's Strategy, Organizational Structure and Rivalry

The managers of firms need to be fully mindful of the fact that local conditions and organizational settings affect the level and intensity of rivalry within an industry. Rivalry, as an integral part of the business process, can strengthen firms' competitive advantages by putting pressure on firms to augment investment and upgrade their production processes. Firms will realize that, unlike in a closed market, in the global market environment pressure comes from all directions around the world. It is important to note that for developing countries, the nature of rivalry and strategy might take a different form than those of developed countries. Although firms can indeed skip several stages of e-commerce development, they will still face an uphill battle in conquering a niche market within the global markets for their products (Sherif, 2006).

According to Porter (1990), rivalry, especially a domestic one, is a major contributor to the global competitiveness of a company. In addition to these conditions that apply to all markets, further elaboration on the characteristics of digital goods and economic principles relevant to a firm's strategy, structure, and rivalry in e-commerce is given next.

Pricing of Digital Goods

The pricing mechanisms of digital goods have received a fair amount of researchers' attention and close scrutiny. Shapiro and Varian (1999) present a classic textbook example of e-commerce economics that focuses on the information and technology markets. Topics range from the cost of producing information and network effects, to the pricing of digital goods. A host of particularities of information goods creates a competition atmosphere different from that of the traditional markets. For instance, Shapiro and Varian (1999) suggest that firms should focus not only on their competitors but also on their collaborators. In addition firms need to form alliances and ensure compatibility of their products.

Highly Differentiated Products

The intense competition in information goods markets fueled by the power of the Internet lowers marginal cost so much that the marginal cost pricing of some digital goods becomes untenable. However, the unique product characteristics and the market structure of the information goods make product differentiation much easier than in the traditional markets. Consequently, it becomes much easier for firms to distinguish themselves from their competitors (Shapiro & Varian, 1999; Whinston et al., 1997).

Economies of Scale and Scope

Economies of scale refer to the decline in a firm's long-run average cost of production as scale of production expands. Economies of scope, however, arise when a firm produces two or more goods and services at a cost lower than that of individual firms can produce the same goods and services separately. According to (VanHoose, 2003), access to a large market, product differentiation, and network externalities are the preconditions for economics of scale and scope. Many high-tech products and information goods have a substantial development and set-up costs. However, these products produced in different varieties and huge numbers can illustrate the economies of scale and scope.

Lower Menu Cost

In the traditional markets, firms need to manually mark and re-mark prices and in some department stores even unit by unit. In the electronic marketplaces, firms have the opportunity to post and alter prices with simple updates to their databases. This implies a lower menu cost and a lower nominal price rigidity or stickiness in these markets. As a result, price changes in online markets for commodities such as books, software, compact discs, and digital products are expected to be more frequent than those in the traditional markets. Tang et al. (2001) compared the pricing behavior of six major online branches of the traditional CD retailers with six top specialized Internet retailers. The study found that menu costs are not as negligible in the online markets as one may claim. However, the magnitude and implications of the menu cost in markets involving e-commerce remain to be fully investigated (6).

The combination of lower menu costs and search costs is expected to lead, on one hand, to further competition and lower prices in some segments of the market and, on the other hand, to product differentiation and price discrimination in other segments (7). Bakos, (2001) and Shapiro and Varian (1999) provide numerous examples of tailored products and price discrimination in the digital goods markets.

Electronic Marketplace

Technology-based electronic markets behave markedly differently from the traditional markets. The former operates beyond spatial, temporal, and geographic boundaries by offering new types of products with transactions in real time. Participants in such an environment must inevitably adapt a new set of organizational and procedural rules. For instance, Bichler et al. (2001) argue that market designers and participants in e-commerce should encounter different matching mechanisms and negotiation strategies.

For firms to enjoy a global competitive advantage, they need to internalize both the domestic and foreign conditions, as stylized by the four-condition Porter diamond model. Moreover, success in the global markets depends on the harmony and synergy among these conditions. For instance, factor abundancy alone cannot lead to innovation and competitive advantage, unless there is a sufficient force of rivalry in the market and a potential high demand on the horizon.

Finally, according to Porter (1990), governments must play an important role to ensure that the four conditions are in place and function simultaneously and efficiently. Specifically, governments need to level the playing field by promoting rivalry, abstaining from direct cooperation, and the creation of monopoly powers. The governments should engage in harmonizing practices at the international level and make available useful information and other facilities that are deemed permissible by the pertinent international bodies. In a sum, the structural deficiencies and bottlenecks of e-commerce in developing countries, as seen by Ferran and Salim (2006), could be avoided should the continual assessments of e-commerce are carried out based on the Porter's diamond model adopted in this study.

CONCLUSIONS AND POLICY IMPLICATIONS

The Internet and technology-based e-commerce have transformed the nature of conducting business around the world. This, in turn, has resulted in changing in market structure and reshaping industries, giving birth to the concept of "New Economy." Although the Internet has altered, to some extent, the way in which forces of demand and supply manifest themselves in the digital marketplace, this study supports the previous findings that the basic principles of economics continue to be powerful tools for analyzing the basis of competitive advantage, prices, and choices in e-commerce.

This study illustrates that Porter theory of global competitive advantage (1990) is an appropriate model for the examination of the factors that affect e-commerce. The adopted model provides a solid microeconomic theoretical framework to identify firms' competitive advantages and to formulate better policies involving e-commerce. The model can be used for the assessment and better understanding of growth of e-commerce and its implications for the fast-paced globalization process of the world economy. It can also be instrumental in examining the factors which are hindering growth of e-commerce in developing countries. In other words, the framework not only makes economic analysis easier, but also facilitates economic development policy making for developing countries. Specifically, these countries can benefit from using the suggested framework for enterprise development and helping them to become more competitive in the digital marketplace.

Although dynamic interactions among the four conditions leading to sustainable competitive advantage are not fully detailed here, this study provides a blueprint for a conceptual economic framework for the assessment of and policymaking involving e-commerce in developing countries. For future research, the proposed economic model of e-commerce needs to be extended on both the theoretical and empirical levels. For developing countries, however, special attention should be given to the ICT-skilled labor force, structural deficiencies as well as institutional bottlenecks. In addition, changes in the search characteristics of the labor market and the resulting decline in search costs, substitution among e-commerce-specific capital, labor, and other nonspecific forms of capital, and the reduction in menu costs are few examples of a promising research agenda.

REFERENCES

Bakos, J. Y. (Winter 2001). The emerging landscape for retail e-commerce. *The Journal of Economic Perspectives*, 15 (1), 69-80.

Bakos, J.Y., & Kemerer, C.F. (September 1992). Recent applications of economic theory in information technology research. *Decision Support Systems*, 8 (5), 365-386.

Bichler, M., Field, S., & Werthner, H. (2001). Introduction: theory and application of electronic market design. *Electronic Commerce Research*, 1 (3), 215-220(6).

Brousseau, E. (2002). The governance of transactions by commercial intermediaries: an analysis of the re-engineering of intermediation by electronic commerce. *International Journal of the Economics of Business*, 9 (3), 353-374.

Ferran, C., & Salim, R.(2006). Electronic business in developing countries: the digitalization of bad practices? In Sherif, K. (Ed.), *Electronic business in developing countries: opportunities and challenges* (pp. 1-33). IDEA Group Publishing.

Harbhajan, K., & Varinder, P. S. (2005). *Digital economy, impacts, influences and challenges*. IDEA Group Publishing.

Kamel, N. M. (2006). International e-commerce: language, cultural, legal, and infrastructure issues, challenges, and solutions. In Sherif, K. (Ed.), *Electronic business in developing countries: opportunities and challenges* (pp. 45-62). IDEA Group Publishing.

Kauffman, J. R., & Walden, A. E. (Summer 2001). Economics and electronic commerce: survey and directions for research. *International Journal of Electronic Commerce*, 5 (4), 5-116.

Levy, D., Bergen, M., Dutta, S., & Venable, R. (August 1997). The magnitude of menu costs: direct evidence from large U.S. supermarket chains. *Quarterly Journal of Economics*,112, 791-824.

Liebowitz, J. S. (2002). *Re-thinking the network economy: the true forces that drive the digital marketplace*. AMACOM: A Division of American Management Association.

Mann, L. C., Eckert, E. S., & Knight, C. S. (July 2000). *Global electronic commerce: a policy primer*. Washington, DC: Institute for International Economics.

Mansell, R. (2001). Digital opportunities and the missing link for developing countries. *Oxford Review of Economic Policy*, Vol. 17, No. 2, 282-295.

McKnight, W. L., & Bailey, P. J. (November/December 1997). Internet economics: when constituencies collide in cyberspace. *Internet Computing IEEE*, 1 (6), 30-37.

Molla, A. (2006). E-readiness and successful e-commerce diffusion in developing countries: results from a cluster analysis. In Sherif, K. (Ed.), *Electronic business in developing countries: opportunities and challenges* (pp. 214-233). IDEA Group Publishing.

Ohlin, B. (1983). *Interregional and international trade*. Cambridge, Mass: Harvard University Press.

Panagariya, A. (2000). E-commerce, WTO and developing countries. *The World Economy*, 23 (8), 959-978.

Porter, E. M. (1990). *The Competitive advantage of nations*. New York: The Free Press.

Ricardo, D. (1963). *The Principles of political economy and taxation*. Homewood, Ill: Irwin.

Shapiro, C., & Varian, H. R. (1999). *Information rules: a strategic guide to the network economy*.

Boston, Massachusetts: Harvard Business School Press.

Sherif, K. (Ed.), (2006). *Electronic business in developing countries: opportunities and challenges*. IDEA Group Publishing.

Smith, A. (1937). *The wealth on nations*. New York: The Modern Library.

Tang, F-F., & Lu, D. (2001). Pricing patterns in the online CD markets: an empirical study. *Electronic Markets*, 11 (3) 171-185(15)

Tapscott, D. (1996). *The digital economy, promise and peril in the age of networked intelligence*. McGraw-Hill.

UNCTAD (2001- 2004). *E-commerce and development report.*

UNCTAD (2000). *Building confidence: electronic commerce and development.*

VanHoose, D. (2003). *E-commerce economics*. South-Western, a Division of Thomson Learning.

Whinston, B. A., Dale, O.S., & Choi, S-Y (1997). *The economics of electronic commerce*. Macmillan Technical Publishing.

WTO (1998). *Electronic commerce and the role of the WTO.*

Zwass, V. (Fall 1996). Electronic commerce: structures and issues. *International Journal of Electronic Commerce*, 1 (1), 3-23.

ENDNOTES

1. It is noteworthy to bear in mind that information is, to a varying degree, a key component of all goods and services, as well as production processes. In addition, new products seem to contain more information than the traditional products and the information content accounts for one of the important elements of product differentiation.
2. Zwass (1996) provides a historical account of e-commerce evolution. Although the traditional e-commerce has been conducted by the use of information technologies centering on the electronic data interchange (EDI) over separate and proprietary networks, the contemporary e-commerce whose driving force is the Internet is based on an open and non-proprietary protocol.
3. Porter divides the factors of production into four categories: (1) Basic or endowed; e.g., natural resources, climate, semi-skilled, and unskilled labor, (2) Advanced or created; e.g., skilled labor, and acquired capital and technology, (3) General or multiple-use, and (4) Special or specific-use. According to Porter (1990), the advanced factors which are created by human activity are missing from the classical factor proportion theory as a powerful driving force of sustained competitive advantage.
4. Although the concept of e-readiness has a record in the literature, it has recently gained researchers' attention in relation to e-commerce in developing nations. For a full explanation of the external e-readiness as a pre-requisite condition for successful expansion of e-commerce, see Molla (2006).
5. Mansell (2001) remind us of the importance of favorable institutional setting, ICT-related skilled labor force, and other requirements for the adoption of e-commerce. Lack of such factors in most developing countries has been shown to hinder the success of e-commerce and long-term economic growth.
6. Levy et al. (1997) provides some empirical evidence on the magnitude of menu cost in the traditional markets.
7. Although the Internet can potentially boost forces of competition in most segments of

the electronic marketplace, other forms of market structure such as monopoly and monopolistic competition may prove equally powerful in shaping the dynamics of these markets.

Chapter XIII
Guidelines for Preparing Organizations in Developing Countries for Standards-Based B2B

Lena Aggestam
University of Skövde, Sweden

Eva Söderström
University of Skövde, Sweden

ABSTRACT

B2B development has been faster in the developed world comparing to developing countries. This chapter proposes a "tool" for managing CSF in B2B settings. The tool is in the form of guidelines, which are concrete and detailed, and which enable a more clear view of actions needed during the preparation stage of B2B projects. We argue that developing countries seldom have the luxury of affording failure in new B2B ventures, but that they instead must learn from the mistakes already made by the developed countries. Thus, our proposed guidelines are based on an existing framework and experiences made in the developed countries. The guidelines are furthermore discussed with regard to the specific problems and conditions that developing countries face. Much work still remains, and problems still must be resolved. From a global perspective, this is important for all of us!

INTRODUCTION

It is no secret that electronic business between organizations (B2B) is constantly picking up speed and adoption throughout the world. B2B can be defined as the use of Internet and Web-technologies for conducting interorganizational business transactions (Teo and Ranganathan, 2004). So

Copyright © 2009, IGI Global, distributing in print or electronic forms without written permission of IGI Global is prohibited.

far, its development has been faster in the developed world than in developing countries (Hawk, 2004; García-Murillo, 2004; Uzoka and Seleka, 2006). In the former, B2B is adopted and used for competitive and collaborative reasons to a larger extent than in developing countries. In particular, the developing world often lacks the infrastructural, economic and socio-political framework to develop e-commerce in comparison to the developed countries (Uzoka and Seleka, 2006). Furthermore, power distance must be considered, since it indicates the ability for organizations to affect change in government. The higher the distance, the faster industry – including e-commerce – can grow (Sparks et al, 2007).

Through the use of B2B, companies in developing countries can create and sustain competitive advantage, get access to new and better suppliers and customers, etc (Wood, 2004). Proper attention to specific conditions of these countries can prevent negative effects and slow e-business adoption (García-Murillo, 2004). However, a successful B2B development project requires proper management of different types of Critical Success Factors (CSF). CSF are: "*the conditions that need to be met to assure success of the system*" (Poon and Wagner, 2001, p.395). CSFs can be categorised as emerging from economic, technological or organizational issues (Ewusi-Mensah and Przasnyski, 1994). Planning considerations should focus on important organizational factors, because they influence the other factors. Circumstances in the developing countries also reveal the importance of trying to resolve organizational factors such as confidence and trust in order to establish a corporate culture where the benefits of sharing are viewed as important and natural. Leaders initiate this process by imposing his/her beliefs, values, and assumptions, but culture only arises when the assumptions of individuals lead to shared experiences (Schein, 2004). Thus, developing a culture is a long-term process, and the importance of planning and preparation is clear. Currently, the lack of means for dealing with CSF is accentuated by the fact that many B2B projects fail. Additionally, specific conditions in developing countries such as capacity of organizations to absorb, use, and adapt advances in science and technology must be studied (Salman, 2004). Organizations in developing countries must prepare themselves well to avoid pitfalls and achieve the full benefits of B2B. This is no different compared to developed countries. The difference is that developing countries lack suitable resources for such preparations, with regard to poverty, and inadequacy and instability of various resources in developing countries (Agoulu, 1997; Roy and Biswas, 2007; Purcell and Toland, 2004), together with low B2B maturity. There are barriers to e-commerce such as: low income levels, low literacy rates, lack of payment systems that support online transactions, and cultural resistance to online transaction-making (Ho et al, 2005). Our work contributes to better preparatory routines in organizations in developing countries.

This chapter proposes a "tool" for managing CSF in B2B settings. The tool is in the form of guidelines, which are concrete and detailed, and which enable a more clear view of actions needed during the preparation stage of B2B projects. The guidelines can be used during the planning stage of B2B in order to prepare the organization for managing CSF in this context. They are built on experiences in developed countries, and will hence enable organizations in developing countries to avoid redoing the same mistakes. The specific conditions of developing countries are taken into consideration by specific referencing when each guideline is discussed in terms of how they help to alleviate problems. The target audience is B2B project managers, since they are in charge of making the B2B venture happen.

BACKGROUND

Collaboration is a necessity to survive in the business world regardless of geographical location.

Developing countries should strive in this direction. In order to set the scene for the guidelines, we first give some background information on B2B, developing countries, and a framework for managing CSF. The guidelines are developed from these areas.

B2B

B2B is defined as the use of Internet and Web-technologies for conducting inter-organizational business transactions (Teo and Ranganathan, 2004). This section will introduce B2B, and elaborate on an implementation model used as the basis for the work presented in this chapter.

Introduction to B2B

To a great extent, B2B is conducted using standards to simplify cooperation (Ersala et al, 2002; Hasselbring, 2000; Ghiladi, 2003). Standards are guidelines for how to structure and manage communication and information sent between organizations (Söderström, 2004). They enable a common language between partners, as well as automation of relevant business processes. However, the associated technology is often complex and expensive, which in itself can be an obstacle for developing countries to enter into world-wide B2B. One reason is that the standards used are flexible and general, and hence difficult to implement (Jakobs et al, 2001). It takes time and resources. Standards should therefore be used with as many partners as possible to be a justifiable option. This requires some economies of scale for quality (Motwani et al, 1999), and is in itself is a problem for small organizations, which may not have that many partners. Adopting B2B is a strategic choice, and partner relationships must be carefully managed (Thompson and Ranganathan, 2004).

B2B Standards Implementation Model

As a point of origin in our analyzis, we use a model of the B2B standards implementation process developed by Söderström (2004). The three main phases are: preparation, architectural and consolidation. *Preparation* concerns activities for planning and preparing projects and architectural work. *Architectural* work concerns making changes to processes and technology to incorporate the standard into the existing infrastructure. Finally, *consolidation* concerns launching the standard, as well as evaluating and maintaining the system and expanding its use. Our focus is the *preparation* phase, since careful planning and proper management features are best determined therein. Preparation includes four sub-steps (Figure 1): strategic planning, process analysis, partner alignment, and project planning. The order between the steps is not necessarily the same at all times, and some activities may be conducted parallel (double-headed arrows).

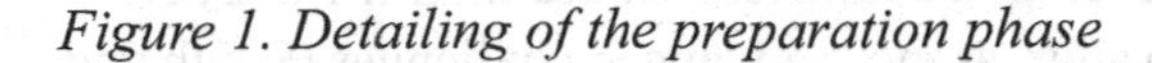
Figure 1. Detailing of the preparation phase

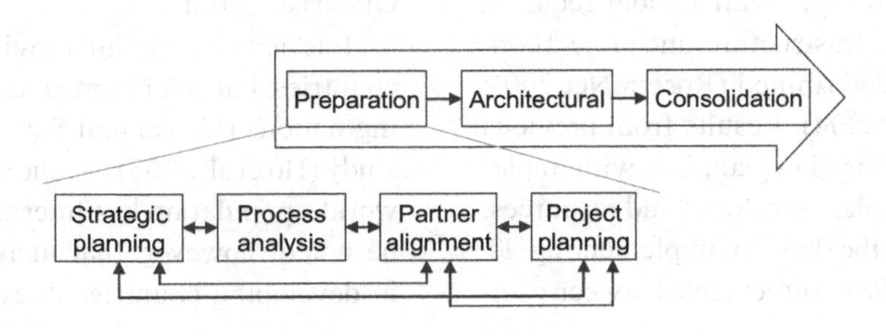

In brief, the four steps contain:

1. **Strategic planning:** Standards and B2B must be part of the business strategy, in order to identify how they can help achieve the business plan (Ramsey, 1998), create new markets, redefine old ones and enable inter-operability (Bolin, 2004). The lack of strategic vision is a major barrier to justifying IT investments (Love and Irani, 2004). Top management commitment is a necessity (Premkumar et al, 1994). Stakeholders from different organizational levels must be involved early to achieve implementation success.
2. **Process analysis:** Business processes must be analyzed in order to identify, prioritise and orchestrate which processes to include (Söderström, 2004), which enables a deeper understanding of the organization and its processes (Kosanke and Nell, 1999). Hence, business processes help define project scope regarding which processes to support (Ersala et al, 2002), and how and which part(s) of the organization that will be affected.
3. **Partner alignment:** B2B partners must identify with whom to trade (Intel, 2003; Söderström, 2004). Partners may have different levels of maturity, and hence varying experience in standards use. Agreements include what, where, how, and scope (WebMethods, 2003). Common goals must be set, responsibilities, time span and resources established, and a commitment given by each partner, for example through Trading Partner Agreements (TPA).
4. **Project planning:** Details about required technology, infrastructure, and project conduction are determined (RosettaNet 2001; Söderström, 2004). Results from previous phases are utilised in planning, with implementation goals, milestones and resources. Planning is the key to implementing IT (Ramsey, 1998). Agreements between project participants are important to resolve open issues and prepare execution options.

This model is the most detailed implementation model of its kind for B2B. It is based on an extensive literature survey, as well as on empirical material from standards developers, standards users and creators of standards-based software.

Developing Countries

One basic difficulty compared to developed countries is the vast population and degree of illiteracy in developing countries. The developed world consists of 20% of the world's population of which 96% are literate, while 30% of the remaining population in the developing countries still are illiterate (Agoulu, 1997; Hawk, 2004). Developing countries also suffer from poverty, as well as inadequacy and instability of various resources (Agoulu, 1997; Roy and Biswas, 2007; Purcell and Toland, 2004). In a literate world, information is a basic resource that is spread with high speed. In a population where illiteracy is vast, traditional practices remain (Agoulu, 1997; Goodman, 1991). The lack of new technology and an appropriate good infrastructure for communication and information spreading in developing countries is also evident (Agoulu, 1997; Sadowsky, 1993; Singh and Gilchrist, 2002; Purcell and Toland, 2004; Tan et al, 2007). The consequences are effects on if and how e-business is regarded and practiced. Therefore, many developing countries still struggle with basic technology functions, while developed countries can use their infrastructure to address more advanced challenges (Singh and Gilchrist, 2002).

Internet use is fairly evident in developed countries, but is far more uncommon in developing nations (Uzoka and Seleka, 2006). An ITU study (Ho et al, 2005) has shown that 11,8% of the world's population has Internet access. It should be noted, however, that increased Internet use in developing countries does not automatically mean an increase in e-commerce adoption, even if this is the case in developed countries (Sparks et al, 2007). In the latter, e-commerce is more well spread and advanced (Hawk, 2004; García-Murillo, 2004; Uzoka and Seleka, 2006). One potential reason is that even though Internet use can be widespread, e-commerce activities are sometimes not as popular (see for example Meskaran & Ghazali on e-commerce in Iran). Empirical evidence also still lag behind theoretical developments (Kshetri, 2007). One contributing factor behind this may be that more basic needs such as food and clean water are of a more primary concern than investments in new technologies. Sharing information between companies and partners in B2B is essential. However, this requires a culture in which the benefits of sharing over protecting assets are important and natural. Such a culture does not exist to the same extent in developing countries compared to in developed ones (Jennex et al, 2004). Still, developing countries may have at least one advantage compared to developed countries, in that they do not have the broad availability of different mechanisms for delivering goods and services. This availability may reduce the benefits of electronic networks, Developing countries can hence get higher payoff faster (Sadowsky, 1993).

Table 1 presents an overview of the problems mentioned concerning developing countries and e-business. Each problem has been given an identifier, which will be referenced when discussing the guidelines. Firstly, many people are not aware of what information can do for them, and what they can use it for. Since information in developed countries is the "nerve" of society, this problem must be addressed. A related aspect is that oral culture still dominates these countries, making written communication something for the "elite". Face-to-face commerce is also preferred in many countries, such as India. Incorporating electronic meetings and trading into traditional culture and traditions therefore faces great challenges. Neither should replace the other, but consideration must be taken to the conditions and culture of the specific countries.

A proper infrastructure for conducting and reaching B2B benefits is essential. Infrastructure not only refers to technology, even if this is important, but also to financial infrastructure, and access to the adequate infrastructure. All perspectives are needed. It also places requirements on the knowledge and skills required for the population, both in terms of the people working with the B2B systems, and the customers that are to use them. It also concerns lack of management knowledge,

Table 1. Problems for developing countries related to e-business

Problem	Reference
People are often unaware of the need for information, and do not exploit information as much as they could (A)	Agoulu, 1997
Oral culture dominates, written communication is "elitistic", and commerce is preferred face-to-face (B)	Agoulu, 1997; Hawk, 2004; Mwangi, 2006; Kshetri, 2007
Lack of proper infrastructure, both technical, financial and access to (C)	Hawk, 2004; Sadowsky, 1993; Singh and Gilchrist, 2002; Purcell and Toland, 2004; Uzoka and Seleka, 2006; Kshetri, 2007; Sparks et al, 2007;
Lack of qualifications, in staff as well as customers (D)	Hawk, 2004; Sadowsky, 1993; Jennex et al, 2004; Singh and Gilchrist, 2002
Lack of an advanced legal system (E)	Hawk, 2004; Uzoka and Seleka, 2006; Mwangi, 2006; Kshetri, 2007; Sparks et al, 2007
Security and trust issues are not resolved (F)	Jennex et al, 2004; Uzoka and Seleka, 2006; Meskaran & Ghazali, 2007
Unsure quality in products, and unstable markets (G)	Motwani et al, 1999; Wood, 2004; Uzoka and Seleka, 2006

which is needed for B2B success. The management level concerns company-internal management, as well as government/national management. In the latter, the legal system must be evolved to enable handling of new situations due to B2B.

Trust is an essential aspect of collaborations, and an important part of the culture needed for successful B2B. Lack of trust and doubts about security are problems that all countries face. However, developing countries do not have as many mechanisms and cultural features in place as developed countries do. Meskaran and Ghazali (2007) claim most developing countries have a collectivistic culture, in which the level of trust is lower than for those countries in which individualistic culture dominates. An understanding of culture helps to develop more suitable strategies to improve trust.

Lastly, several literature sources mention that the developed world has doubts concerning the quality of products and the stability of markets in developing countries. Some doubts may origin simply in inexperience in trading with these countries, others from different quality control systems, etc. These problems are not exclusive to, and may not be of the same dignity in all developing countries. Still, they must be addressed. Our work concerns how companies and organizations can better prepare themselves for standards-based B2B. Since developing countries are our centre of attention, we will return to discussing how our suggestions and guidelines help alleviating and/or reduce these problems later on in the chapter.

The Framework for Managing Critical Success Factors

The framework is developed on a generic level in order to fit all kinds of information systems (IS) development. It is based on organizational success factors and should be used during planning to prepare an organization for a project. We choose this framework since B2B systems are IS, and since this framework, to the best of our knowledge, is the only one focusing on CSF from a preparation point of view. Furthermore, a cornerstone in the framework is to motivate the users and let them understand what the project is about, how it is going to affect them etc. This contributes to trust, which must be encouraged in particular in developing countries.

Critical Success Factors: The Framework Base

CSFs are conditions that must be met to avoid failure. The analysis of the factors emerging from organizational issues shows four different CSF (Aggestam, 2004):

- To learn from failed projects
- To define the system's boundary, both for the whole system and for relevant subsystems
- To have a well defined and accepted objective that aligns with the business objectives
- To involve, motivate and prepare the "right" stakeholders.

The factor *To learn from failed projects* is a prerequisite whether an organisation is to better perform projects as for example a B2B. Thus, the framework does not explicit need to take this into consideration. Furthermore, for less developed countries it is important to avoid redoing the mistakes already made by the developed counterparts. The reminder of this chapter will elaborate on each of the three remaining CSF.

The System's Boundary

This factor concerns business borders, and not technical ones. Knowing what the system is and defining its boundary is a prerequisite for addressing all success factors and a performing a successful B2B implementation. The system's boundary constrains what needs to be considered and what can be left outside (van Gigch, 1991). Identifying the boundary triggers an active discussion about what the actual system includes, which related systems and subsystems there are, etc. Related systems may also offer resources in exchange for something.

The Stakeholders

Organizational change is risky, but risk can be minimised by having the right kind of persons on your team (Champy 1997), and to identify important stakeholders and discover their requirements (Kotonya and Sommerville 1997). How well an IS will work in an enterprise depends on the user involvement in the development process (Cherry and Macredie, 1999; Pohl, 1998; Sutcliffe, Economou and Markis, 1999; Saiedian and Dale, 2000; Browne and Ramesh, 2002). The success of the involvement depends on how well people work and communicate (Saiedian and Dale 2000), and communication gaps do exist. According to Champy (1997) stakeholders across the organization have two needs during organizational change: Confidence in the management and knowledge about the meaning of the change. Commitment from the top is crucial if the project affects a large part of the organization (Milis and Mercken, 2002). Strong sponsorship is required even before a project is launched to it being initiated and seeded resources (Poon and Wagner, 2000), and confidence in the management is essential (Proccacino et al, 2001).

The Objective

A successful IS should meet common business objectives (Ewusi-Mensah and Przasnyski 1994, Milis and Mercken 2002). When the IS strategy reflects organizational objectives, supports business strategies, recognizes external forces and reflects resource constraints, then the organization more likely uses IS strategically (Kearns and Leder 2000). Defining the goal is fundamental (Clavadetcher 1998) and organizational change must begin here (Champy, 1997). A comprehensive project definition gives a common vision, a co-operation base, terms of reference and prevents boundaries from extending beyond intended limits (Milis and Mercken 2002). An organization should be examined from different perspectives (Pun 2001) which in turn is a prerequisite for defining the goal. We use Bolman and Deal's (1997) four complementary views/frames (Table 1), but complement them with a fifth frame – *Neutral* – in order to capture the neutral perspective of the organization in terms of mission (service or manufacture), business plan, size (both turnover and number of employees), ownership (private or public) and so on. The frames are summarised in Table 2.

The Neutral frame can be thought of as a starting point for the other frames, because facts from this frame limits an organization and consequently organizational change, and it also limits and influences the other frames. Also the Structural frame focuses on explicit facts about the organization as e.g. rules and policies. The Human resource, Political and Symbolic frames, on the other hand, help to understand and gain knowledge about the organizational culture which is an important influence factors regarding if the B2B project will be a success or not.

The way an objective will be defined and formulated depends on the level of inquiry at which it has been considered (van Gigch 1991, Beyer and Holtzblatt 1998, Leffingwell and Widrig 2000). Discussions about objectives, often only take place at the action level and/or what-to-do level, but according to van Gigch (1991) all three levels (why, what and how) are necessary. This is in accordance with Bubenko (1993) who claims that the HOW part should be linked to the WHY and WHAT parts. The framework based on the presented organizational factors is presented in next section.

Table 2. Overview of the four-frame model, adapted from Bolman and Deal (1997)

	Structural frame	Human resource frame	Political frame	Symbolic frame
Metaphor for organizations	Factory or machine	Family	Jungle	Carnival, temple, theatre
Central concepts	Rules, roles, goals, policies, technology, environment	Needs, skills, relationship	Power, conflict, competition, organizational politics	Culture, meaning, metaphor, ritual, ceremony, stories, heroes
Image of leadership	Social architecture	Empowerment	Advocacy	Inspiration
Basic leadership challenge	Attune structure to task, technology, environment	Align organizational and human needs	Develop agenda and power base	Create faith, beauty, meaning

The Framework for Managing CSF

We argue that preparation based on organizational factors is necessary to increase the chances of success when organizations in developing countries engage in B2B projects. To the best of our knowledge, no other framework takes this point of view. The framework, see Figure 2, stresses a flexible outset adaptable according to stakeholder type, and should be used in planning to prepare the organization for managing CSF in future activities. The framework should also be used iteratively on different levels of abstraction: first to the whole project ("the system") and then to identified critical parts ("subsystems"). However, we will use a sequential order in this chapter for simplicity.

The target organization should define the system's boundary and relevant subsystems. Next, the objective must be defined, and relevant stakeholders identified. The objective should be analyzed and described from different complementary frames and at different levels of detail. It should always support the business objective, which requires IS- and business strategies to be clearly aligned. The goal descriptions can be thought of as a tool box aiming to be used in the motivation process.

Relevant stakeholders should be motivated and prepared for future participation and involvement in the ISD process. User participation refers to user activities, while user involvement is more a subjective psychological state of individuals. Stakeholder groups are probably a mix of the two. Both motivation and preparation must thus be adapted to the various types of stakeholders. The motivation process should focus on stakeholder knowledge and confidence needs. They feel confident and motivated by a a description of the objective that is adapted to them and explained in a way that they understand how it will affect them and why the project is important. The most suitable stakeholder description should be chosen, which could mean more than one description. User participation and user involvement is a communication process. The preparation process should thus focus on educating stakeholders about concepts to make future communication easier and more effective.

These processes aim to meet stakeholder needs about confidence and knowledge about changes. This will contribute to positive, motivated and prepared stakeholders, a prerequisite for user involvement and participation, and consequently for reaching user satisfaction with the system. Using the framework results in a clear, well defined and accepted objective, and in positive, motivated and prepared stakeholders which is critical for all types of projects, including a B2B-project.

Figure 2. A framework to support the information systems development process

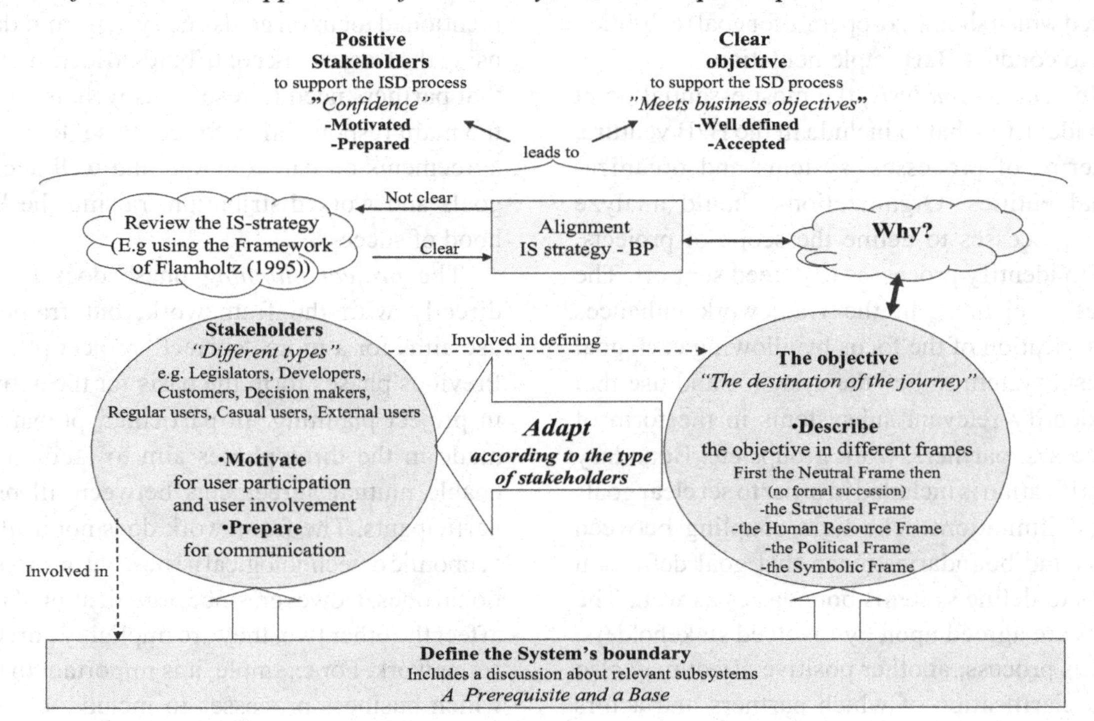

MAPPING THE CSF FRAMEWORK TO THE B2B SETTING

The mapping of the CSF framework to B2B originates from the descriptions of the implementation phases with the intention to identify matches between them and the framework. Since the framework is based on organizational CSF and has a planning and preparion view, the main matches are found in the three sub-steps: strategic planning, process analysis, and partner alignment (see Table 3). The leftmost column presents the four implementation phases, the middle column includes a brief description of key points therein, and the rightmost column includes comments of in what way the framework can assist in preparing for B2B implementation planning.

Starting with *strategic planning*, the two central issues are: the need for an updated business strategy, and the inclusion of relevant stakeholders. The strategy determines where the organization is heading and which operations matters, and the standards-based solution must be duly incorporated. The framework emphasizes the important why-perspective by stressing the necessity of clear and accepted goals. Commitment from top management is another central building block. This is where strategy is determined and operations are set towards meeting goals. The framework also emphasizes the identification of critical parts such as departments, partners, systems, work groups, processes etc. and their alignment between and to the goals. If the strategic perspective is not clear, the strategy or what is included in the parts must be revised. Identifying critical parts and their relationships includes delimiting the IS by clearly identifying and stating systems boundaries, the whole system and critical sub systems, and to include relevant stakeholders in its preparation. In the implementation model, a cross-functional/

cross-organizational, implementation team is suggested which should co-operate for goal realisation and to conduct B2B implementation.

In *process analysis*, the most essential point is to identify what to include in the B2B venture, in terms of processes, systems and organizational entities. Organizations should analyze their processes to define the scope of projects, and to identify processes that need support. The iterative element in the framework enhances identification of the focus by allowing each goal and subsystem to be "the system", and use that to identify relevant subsystems in the form of processes, partners, work groups etc. Boundary identification is included in order to set clear goals and delimitations. The tight coupling between goals and boundaries mean that goal definition helps to define systems boundaries as well. The goals are agreed upon by involved stakeholders. In this process, another positive effect may also be a clarification of which partners and actors there are to include.

Partner negotiations (or partner alignment) are essential to establish what to do, why, by whom, with what means, and when. Clear responsibilities make better ground for project success. Besides the mentioned focus on goals and system boundaries, using the framework contributes to identify issues that partners need to resolve as well as who has the main responsibility for doing so. Results are agreements on e.g. common and well accepted goals and work distribution, raising the likelihood of success.

The *project planning* phase does not deal directly with the framework, but framework use aims for a more "correct" project planning. Previous phases form the basis for the activities in project planning. In particular, preparations made in the three phases aim to facilitate and enable mutual agreements between all project participants. The framework does not deal with economic or technological issues, but on organizational ones. However, since organizational issues affect the other two, they are implicitly part of the framework. For example, it is important to know which business processes to include to be able to establish needed economic and technological resources.

Our previous work has resulted in generic guidelines (Aggestam and Söderström, 2006).

Table 3. Relating B2B standards implementation preparation to Aggestam's (2004) framework

Phases	Description	Framework
Strategic planning	An updated business strategy is essential when implementing B2B standards. As many relevant stakeholder as possible should be involved early on.	It is essential to have a clear and accepted goal, supporting the why perspective. Strengthens the need to identify critical departments, partners, work groups, systems etc. Emphasises relations and alignment between goals, included stakeholders, and identified sub-systems.
Process analysis	Identifying what (parts of) business processes.	The goal and systems boundaries are tightly coupled, and presuppose one another. Contributes to identify important sub-systems/parts of the organization and enhance where to focus.
Partner alignment	The common goal needs to be agreed on and committed to. Responsibility and resource commitment must be agreed upon. To identify requirements placed on each partner	The goal and system boundaries need to be identified. Contributes to identify relevant issues to resolve between partners. Contributes to achieving well accepted goals.
Project planning	Make a detailed plan based on the results from the previous phases.	Is not explicitly managed within the framework, but results from previous phases can be utilized as a basis for project planning.

These will be developed into more concrete ones in the coming sections. The three most relevant phases of the B2B standards preparation stage, Strategic planning, Process analysis and Partner alignment, will be used as the main structure. Sub-sections are created for each main aim with a summarizing table. Each table provides the existing generic guideline to the left, and specific guidelines to the right. Problems in developing countries will be discussed. The identifier of each problem (Table 1) is referenced in the discussion.

CONCRETE GUIDELINES FOR STRATEGIC PLANNING

Based on the mapping (Table 4) three aims can be identified explaining why the framework is useful in B2B standards implementation concerning strategic planning:

- To achieve clear and accepted goals in relation to an updated business strategy
- To identify critical parts as departments, stakeholders etc
- To explicitly define how these critical parts relate to one another and to the goals and the strategy.

For each of these aims, we will elaborate on a more generic level on what to do in order to reach them (Aggestam and Söderström, 2006). The generic guidelines are then concretized into more detailed ones, with a specific reference to developing countries and how help them alleviate their specific problems. It should be noted that strategic planning concerns work conducted internally in an organization.

To Achieve and Describe Goals in Relation to an Updated Business Strategy

The guidelines are summarised in Table 3. When describing the goals of a B2B project in relation to an updated business strategy, different perspectives are needed. The framework for preparation (Figure 2) makes a clear contribution by empha-

Table 4. Guidelines to achieve clear and accepted goals in relation to an updated business strategy

Guidelines	Detailed guidelines
Discuss from different views how the goals of the standards implementation project are useful in helping the organization to achieve its general business goals (G-1)	The goals of B2B should be described from the following frames using a why-perspective: - Neutral: increase the number of standards-based B2B transactions with more partners, to increase the chances of reaching e-business benefits - Structural: identify and describe how the organization needs to change when implementing B2B, in terms of technology, rules, structure, management, etc., to ensure a suitable infrastructure - Symbolic: plan a launch event to contribute to incorporating B2B into the corporate culture - Political: describe how staff at different levels are affected by the changes, and how to achieve collaboration, to get everyone in the organization to work towards a common goal - Human resources: describe what competences that need to be developed to ensure sufficient knowledge on all organizational levels, to ensure that the benefits of B2B are reached
If necessary, review the existing strategy and reformulate the strategy to incorporate the use of standards as a strategic tool (G-2)	Incorporate text on (B2B) standards and their usefulness into the business strategy, to motivate management Define a process for how the strategy and standards perspective therein can be updated on a regular basis.

sising the five frames. The B2B goals should be described in each frame including a why-perspective, as illustrated in Figure 2. Developing countries currently have a low e-business rate, and therefore benefit naturally from all frames since they contribute to creating a culture for sharing and conducting e-business. This takes time, and must be initiated early on. Developing countries may have the advantage of not having to battle already existing cultures. The detailed guidelines thereby address the problems A, B, C, D and F: They clarify the meaning of information, raise the competence level and make written communication accessible for more people, contribute to increase the willingness to share, contribute to creating a clear infrastructure on several levels, emphasise education, and by conducting B2B with known partner, they increase the likelihood of partners trusting the transactions made.

It is also important to review and revise the existing business strategy to align it better with the B2B intents. The detailed guidelines thereby address the problems C and G by incorporating standards in the business strategy, the number of automated transactions can increase. Standards are then managed more systematically and transactions are consistent, which potentially raises their quality. Standards are made part of the corporate culture, contributing to the change of perspective.

To Identify Critical Parts where the Initial Anchoring Work should Start

The first generic guideline in this aim concerns the identification of bottle-necks. These, such as the lack of competence regarding B2B standards, can be identified from the goal descriptions and systems boundaries. By comparing them with the general problems (Table 1), priorities can be made of the importance of the problems. The detailed guidelines (Table 5) thereby address the problem A: since it makes people aware of the meaning and importance of information.

The problem priority list (*what* to do) can assist in the creation of an action list (*how* to do) for removing obstacles, which must be accompanied by a time plan and the assignment of responsibilities. The detailed guidelines thereby address the problems A, B and D since they contribute to raising the awareness of the importance of information and planning. For example, responsibilities must be assigned to ensure the completion of tasks. Furthermore, the staff competence level is raised, and the oral culture is affected in a long-term perspective.

In all activities planned based on the priorities, the goals must be explained to the stakeholders in such a way so that they firstly, understand the project, and secondly, how the project affects them. This results in the stakeholders trusting

Table 5. Guidelines to identify critical parts where the initial work should start

Guidelines	Detailed guidelines
Analyze the goal descriptions to discover potential "bottle-necks", in terms of people, organizations or systems (G-3)	Identify where the bottle-necks are, both from general problems, and from the company's specific conditions, to increase the chances of reaching the goals and to remove unnecessary obstacles Prioritise the problems based on their importance and consequences, to ensure that the limited resources are directed towards the most important actions
Plan explicit actions to ensure the inclusion and motivation of "bottle-necks" residing inside the organization (G-4)	Based on the priorities create an action list, a time plan and responsibility assignments, to ensure that actions are made in a reasonable timeframe, and to enable follow-up actions. An example is to plan education activities in, for example, Internet technology
Use the adapted goal descriptions in order to motivate critical stakeholders (G-5)	Use the goal descriptions in activities such as education, meetings, launch events, etc., to motivate relevant stakeholders on different organizational levels

the efforts and the management. The detailed guidelines thereby address the problems A and C since they make the needs explicit, and give access to information and an infrastructure.

To Explicitly Define Relations Between Goals, the Strategy, Stakeholders, etc.

The second and third aims are similar, since both concern why B2B is an important effort, and how things relate. While the second concerns bottlenecks, this aim concerns the relationships between goals, strategies and stakeholders. The generic guideline (Table 6) is focused on relationships, both in terms of identification and awareness. Written documents and oral meetings are needed in all situations. In developing countries, however, the oral tradition is – as mentioned – prevailing, and written communication is elitistic. By face-to-face discussions, people can participate regardless of their reading skills, which contributes to trust and inclusion.

The detailed guidelines thereby address the problems A, B and C: They show the importance of written information as a point of origin, create an awareness of the importance of a common view and to share information to achieve this. However, discussions are grounded in the oral tradition and residing culture, which should increase the chance of identifying and anchoring goals. Furthermore, the guidelines provide a clear view of goal relations, which increases the chances of developing a good infrastructure that is accessible to the right users.

CONCRETE GUIDELINES FOR PROCESS ANALYSIS

Based on the mapping (Table 2) three aims can be identified explaining why the framework is useful in B2B standards implementation concerning process analysis:

- To have a clear view of the organization's business processes
- To identify what business processes to include, and to motivate and prepare relevant stakeholders
- To identify what systems that support the business process

These aims are derived from the tight coupling needed between goal and system boundaries, and from the identification of what processes and other sub-parts on which to focus. Similarly to the former section, we elaborate on a more generic level on what to do in order to reach the aims and concretize them into more detailed actions. It should be noted that process analysis concerns work conducted internally in an organization.

To have a Clear View of the Organization's Business Processes

In B2B standards implementation, different business processes are included, such as: procurement, order, invoice and payment (Söderström and Pettersson, 2003). To have a clear view of which these processes are, and which of them that are the

Table 6. Guidelines to explicitly define relations between critical parts

Guidelines	Detailed guidelines
Use goal descriptions and discussion seminars to identify relations between goals and raise the awareness of the same (G-6)	The project leader reviews the goal descriptions and makes a draft describing goal relations, to provide a basis for discussion Organise at least one seminar with relevant stakeholders to model and discuss around the goals, to get a common view of goals, to find what goals affect what other goals and how, and to identify what stakeholders affect/are affected by the goals

most relevant for the future project is important. Guidance is provided by the results from the strategic planning phase in terms of e.g. bottle-necks. The initial step is to map the situation "today" (AS-IS), which is done by studying documents and existing models, talking to relevant people, observe the work, and then construct up-to-date models (see Table 7).

These guidelines address the problems B and F: they use the oral culture to extract information and lay the foundation for a solid written documentation (Agoulu, 1997). They can also assist in removing prejudices and assumptions, and thereby increase the trust in co-workers and their ways of working.

The results from the AS-IS-modeling should be mapped to the goal descriptions from strategic planning in order to identify the desired future (TO-BE). Here as well, a combination of written documentation and oral discussions should be used as a basis. Note that it is essential to disseminate the TO-BE models to everyone involved, for commitment purposes. The detailed guidelines thereby address the problems C and D: They contribute to increasing the modeling skills of the staff, and since they utilize a combination of oral and written information to disseminate information and ensure commitment. Discussions during development and anchoring of the models can be conducted orally, while the end product can be shared in a written format.

To Identify what Business Processes to Include, and to Motivate and Prepare Relevant Stakeholders

From the identification of relevant processes, this aim is focused on which processes to include in the B2B venture (see Table 8). This is essential, by removing irrelevant or low-priority processes, and focusing on the right ones. In developed countries, many projects have failed because not proper attention has been paid to the *right* processes, i.e. on prioritized processes. Furthermore, most organizations do not learn from their failures; but make the same mistakes over and over again (Ewusi-Mensah and Przasnyski, 1995, Lyytinen and Robey, 1999). This is one mistake developing countries can avoid by doing it right from the beginning. The detailed guidelines thereby address the problem G: they secure quality in a long-term perspective since the business processes and goals are audited and defined more clearly.

Motivational actions of different kinds are also important to enable trust and a common purpose among the people involved in the prioritized pro-

Table 7. Guidelines to enhance a clear view of the business processes

Guidelines	Detailed guidelines
Model the business processes according to the current situation (AS-IS) (G-7)	Study existing documents of for example work and process descriptions, to establish a basis for AS-IS process models
	Speak to different stakeholders on different levels, to obtain their view and a more up-to-date perspective on how the work actually is conducted
	If possible, participate in and observe the work done
	Use the results to create process models, preferably through joint discussions, to get a basis for discussion with relevant stakeholder groups
Model the business processes according to the desired future situation (TO-BE) (G-8)	Identify how the organization and work should be structured by originating from existing process models, identified bottle-necks, and documentation from strategic planning, to establish an up-to-date process view
	Develop new process models, preferably via discussions, to document the process view
	Anchor the models in all levels of the organization, to ensure commitment

cesses. In terms of the framework, the symbolic perspective comes into play here, since it is not enough to simply distribute written information or just to inform. Some levels of emotions must be included. The detailed guidelines thereby address the problems A and B: They contribute to create awareness of the importance of information, and to creating a common culture with a focus on sharing information and data.

To Identify what Systems that Support the Business Process

The guidelines is summarised in Table 9. Besides processes, it is also relevant to identify which systems that are critical, based on the priorities made. Do we need to make any IS/IT investments or do we have what we need? Are our systems in accordance with the strategy? If this work identifies a need for investments, it is really important that this is aligned to all relevant strategies, including the IT/IS strategy.

The activities needed are the same as for identifying and listing processes. In developing countries, the lack of a proper infrastructure, of for example a technical nature, is clear (Kshetri, 2007). This may seem to be a problem, but it can be an advantage. Since there are only a few legacy systems, little effort is needed to integrate new systems with old ones, and there is instead a chance for the companies to start fresh. It is hence possible to learn from mistakes and experiences in developed countries, and our guidelines are one way to do so.

The detailed guideline thereby address the problem A, C and F: They provide greater opportunities in managing and using information, provide a more stringent and clear infrastructure to enable e-business, and the overview of the IT systems can be used to identify potential security problems.

CONCRETE GUIDELINES FOR PARTNER ALIGNMENT

Based on the mapping (Table 2) three aims can be identified explaining why the framework is useful in B2B standards implementation concerning partner alignment:

- To establish partner readiness
- To establish legal contracts
- To form cross-organizational teams

These aims are derived from the need to resolve important issues between partners, and preparing

Table 8. Guidelines to identify what processes to include and to motivate and prepare relevant stakeholders

Guidelines	Detailed guidelines
Identify, list and prioritise processes to include in B2B by pairing each goal description with the TO-BE process models (G-9)	Use goal descriptions and identify all processes mentioned therein, to obtain a goal perspective Map the results to the TO-BE models to ensure that the rights relations and processes have been identified Compare the matching results to the priority list, to ensure that efforts are made in the rights areas and in the right order
Take specific actions must to motivate the personnel involved in the selected processes to participate in the project (G-10)	Use the results and identify what staff to involve, to ensure that all relevant staff will be involved in the project Plan events to inform, discuss and commonly plan what to do next, to ensure that everyone feels involved, and to incorporate the project into the corporate culture

Table 9. Guideline to identify supporting systems

Guidelines	Detailed guidelines
Identify what IT systems that support the business processes and list relevant systems (G-11)	Use the revised list of processes and identify what parts of the organization that is affected, to ensure that the most critical processes are included Identify what IT-systems that are used in these organizational parts Discuss if the organizational parts that lack IT-support can be made more efficient by implementing systems

Table 10. Guidelines to establish partner readiness

Guidelines	Detailed guidelines
Establish common B2B project goals in a meeting with all partners (G-12)	Discuss what goals the company has with B2B, and develop a dictionary of central concepts and definitions, to be well prepared for common discussions Negotiate on what common goals the B2B project should have based on the separate corporate goals, to establish common grounds
Identify what the project will require from each partner in terms of preparation and work (G-13)	Define what resources and competences that each partner should contribute to the project, what activities to perform and when, and what responsibility assignments to have, to ensure commitment and successful project completion
Establish readiness by matching requirements and internal preparations (G-14)	Based on the mutually established grounds, each partner should review and plan internal project preparations

for a successful project. Similarly to the former sections, we elaborate on a more generic level on what to do in order to reach the aims and concretize them into more detailed actions. It should be noted that partner alignment concerns external work between organizations.

To Establish Partner Readiness

Partner alignment is all activities involving more than one organization. Basically, it concerns a lot of rework, but this time with the external perspective in mind (see Table 10). Readiness refers to organizations' awareness of what they become involved in, what human and technological resources it will require, as well as how much time it will demand. Common project goals should be established in joint meetings, where negotiations take place based on internally relevant goals. The detailed guidelines thereby address the problems A, B and D: They concern a better understanding and use of common documents, participating representatives enhance their respective knowledge, and face-to-face meetings are the basis for creating a sense of commonality and acceptance of the ways of working of others.

Based on the common goals, the contributions of each partner in terms of resources, competences, activities, etc. must be clarified. Followingly, mutual agreements on responsibilities are necessary. The detailed guidelines thereby address the problem B: they contribute to strengthen the sense of commonality and the corporate culture of collaborating across borders. Lastly, requirements should be matched against conducted internal preparations, to establish what remains to be done to enable the external connection. Possible actions should be planned to address shortcomings. The detailed guidelines thereby address the problem B: they contribute to strengthen the corporate culture of collaborating across borders.

Lastly, requirements should be matched against internal preparations, to establish what remains to be done to enable the external connection. Possible actions should be planned to address shortcomings. The detailed guidelines

Table 11. Guideline to establish legal contacts

Guideline	Detailed guideline
Establish connections between legal expertises to draw up contracts (G-15)	Use existing attorneys or legal connections to discuss the B2B project, to establish solid contracts and secure the conditions for the own company

Table 12. Guidelines to form cross-organizational teams

Guidelines	Detailed guidelines
Agree on the team structure and boundaries in terms of number of people, skills required, mandate, resource requirements, etc (G-16)	Document what competences that are needed to succeed with B2B based on the previous agreements, to establish a suitable project organization
Assign appropriate team members based on internal preparations in other phases (G-17)	Internally identify and assign suitable persons to the project, based on contracts and agreements, and create jointly a written agreement on the commitment of each partner, to ensure a successful project result

thereby address the problem B: they contribute to strengthen the corporate culture of collaborating across borders.

To Establish Legal Contracts

All legal issues need to be resolved by involving legal expertise to draw up the contracts (see Table 11). If "skeleton agreements" exist within an industry, or if standards exist on either a national or an international level, these should be used. This issue highlights the need for a legal system nation-wide that takes B2B collaborations into account.

The detailed guideline thereby addresses the problem E by ensuring a correct and legally valid collaboration effort.

To Form Cross-Organizational Teams

In the case of cross-organizational teams, stakeholder identification helps facilitate the management of organizational relationships in standards implementation, and the joint teams enable orchestration of implementation activities (see Table 12). The previously developed priority list can facilitate the task. The partners should jointly establish what competences that are needed in the project, using the readiness assessments. If one or more such competences are missing, actions must be taken. The detailed guidelines thereby address the problem B: by maintaining the culture of meeting face-to-face, and by stimulating written culture through the documentation work.

Based on the agreements on needed competences, a project team is established with representatives from each partner. The written agreement is crucial in this step, not the least to ensure that the legal agreements (contracts) with the respective commitments are followed and obtained. The detailed guidelines thereby address the problem B by here as well maintaining the culture of meeting face-to-face, and by stimulating written culture through the documentation work.

CONCLUDING REMARKS

Preparation is always important in organizational development projects. Developing countries seldom have the luxury to afford failure in new ventures like in business-to-business. Thus, they should have the possibility to learn from developed countries and hence not redo mistakes already committed by developed countries. By careful preparation, the risk of failure can be reduced, and our guidelines are one approach to use. They aim to prepare the organization from the perspective of CSF, and provide means for dealing with these in B2B. All organizations and nations must prepare themselves well to achieve B2B benefits and gains. Still, our guidelines can help developing countries in particular, since project managers (our target audience) can practically implement them because they:

1. Are based on actual experiences in developed countries
2. Have been developed from factors of critical importance
3. Are technology-neutral and can hence be used in planning regardless of infrastructural platform used
4. Can be directly implemented in ongoing projects
5. Can be easily adjusted to *all* types of preparatory/planning projects in B2B
6. Can help organizations to achieve a long-term e-business perspective and increased maturity to perform B2B projects

The guidelines are based on an existing framework for ISD, and are therefore in themselves also proof of that existing tools and methods for ISD can be useful in B2B development. The literature on developing countries also shows that the guidelines are suitable to the existing culture in these countries since issues such as the willingness to adopt Internet technologies (Kshetri, 2007), and the collectivistic culture which includes low trust levels, (Meskaran & Ghazali, 2007), can be addressed. This is necessary to get commitment to the B2B project, and in developing countries in particular in order to raise the maturity of written communication, and to resolve security and trust issues.

In the guidelines, specific references have been made to problems (Table 1) that are particularly important or present in developing countries. Table summarize these references. All problems are addressed to some extent, showing fit of the guidelines to alleviate problems such as lack of proper infrastructure, qualifications and advanced legal systems. The latter (see e.g. Hawk, 2004) can, in a way, be used as an advantage, since developing countries can "start over" and create a suitable and updated legislation to begin with. We therefore argue that the proposed guidelines are one way to give developing countries a real chance to come closer to the developed countries in terms of B2B maturity and increased electronic business use.

It should be noted that the guidelines proposed are not explicitly connected to processes, phases or steps in relation to time. The motivation is that firstly, they vary between projects, and secondly, they must be adaptable according to for example project and company size, and maturity level. As experience grows, the time required for each step is also likely to be reduced. Future work will need to address the weaknesses of our guidelines. These include firstly that they are focused on organizational aspects. Complementary methods and/or guidelines must therefore be developed to cover for example economical and technical aspects.

Table 13. Problems in developing countries versus the guidelines

Problem	Guidelines
A	G-1, G-3, G-4, G-5, G-6, G-10, G-11, G-12
B	G-1, G-4, G-6, G-7, G-10, G-12, G-13, G-14, G-16, G-17
C	G-1, G-2, G-5, G-6, G-8, G-11
D	G-1, G-4, G-8, G-12
E	G-15
F	G-1, G-7, G-11
G	G-2, G-9

Secondly, the guidelines lack elements for measuring the effects. In a long-term perspective this is a difficult issue to resolve. The Neutral frame does provide valuable contributions to measuring, and potential measuring points include the number of B2B transactions, changes in strategies, number of agreements, and B2B partners. The measuring should be performed *before* preparation as well as during and after the project, after for example 6 months, and after 1 year.

Finally, we can conclude that the proposed guidelines enable the developing countries to climb on the B2B maturity staircase, even though using the guidelines will not take them to the top. There is still work to be done and further problems to be solved. With the words of Becker (2007, p.233): "*Under the right conditions, entrepreneurs in developing nations can launch locally viable Internet ventures with real value, but many developing nations also face very real constraints in harnessing the Internet economy.*" In our global world, all countries irrespectively of financial status or literacy degree have a contribution to make on the "e-scene". We hope our work will encourage others to address the issues of developing countries and their e-commerce/B2B adoption. Empirical evidence must be gathered, guidelines be tested, and efforts made to reduce the gap between the developed and developing worlds. From a global perspective, this is important for all of us!

REFERENCES

Aggestam, L. (2004). A Framework for supporting the preparation of ISD. *Proceedings of the Doctoral Consortium, held in conjunction with the Conference on Advanced Information Systems Engineering* (CAiSE'04).

Aggestam, L. & Söderström, E. (2006). Managing Critical Success Factors in a B2B Setting. *IADIS International Journal on WWW/Internet, Vol.4, No.1,* 96-110.

Aguolu, I. (1997). Accessibility of information: a myth for developing countries? *New Library World, Vol.98, No.1132,* 25-29.

Bastöe, P. Ö. & Dahl, K (1996). *Organisationsutveckling i offentlig verksamhet.* Utbildningshuset Studentlitteratur.

Becker, K. (2007), The impact of e-commerce and information technology in developing countries, In Krishnamurthy and Isaias (eds.), Proceedings of the IADIS International Conference e-Commerce, December 7-9, Algarve, Portugal, pp.230-235

Beyer, H. & Holtzblatt, K. (1998). *Contextual Design Defining Customer-Centered Systems.* Morgan Kaufman, Publishers Inc.

Bolin, S. (2004). The Nature and Future of ICT Standardization. Retrieved June 21, 2004, from: http://www.sun.com/software/standards/natureandfuture_ICT.pdf

Bolman, L.G. & Deal, T.E. (1997). *Nya perspektiv på organisation och ledarskap.* Andra upplagan, Lund, Studentlitteratur.

Browne, G. J. & Ramesh, V. (2002). Improving information requirements determination: a cognitive perspective. *Information and Management,* 1-21.

Bubenko jr, J.A. (1993). Extending the Scope of Information Modelling. *4:th International Workshop on the Deductive Approach of Inforamtion Systems and Databases, Lloret, Costa Brava, (Catalonia), Sept 20-22 1993.* Departmentd de Llenguatges i Sistemes Informaticsn Universitat Politecnica de Catalunya, Report de Recerca LSI/93-25, Barcelona (http://www.dsv.su.se/~janis/jbpaper/library/bib.htm)

Champy, J. A. (1997) Preparing for OC In Hesselbein, F., Goldsmith, M. & Beckhard, R. (1997). *The Organiszation of the Future.* Jossey-Bass, Publisher San Francisco,

Cherry, C. & Macredie, R.D. (1999). The Importance of Context in Information System Design:

An assessment of Participatory Design. *Requirements Engineering, 4* 103-114.

Clavadetcher, C. (1998). *User involvement: key to success.* IEEE SoftWare March/April.

Crick, F. & Koch, C. (2003). A framework for conscious. *Nature neuroscience, Vol6, no 2,* 19-126.

Ersala, N., Yen, D. & Rajkumar, T. (2002). Enterprise Application Integration in the electronic commerce world. *Computer Standards & Interfaces,* 2189, 1-14.

Ewusi-Mensah, K & Przasnyski, Z.H. (1994). Factors contributing to the a bondonment of information systems development projects. *Journal of Information Technology, 9,* 185-201.

Ewusi-Mensah, K & Przasnyski, Z.H. (1995). Learning from abandoned information systems development projects. *Journal of Information Technology, 10,* 3-14.

Flamholtz, E. (1995). Managing Organisational Transitions: Implications for Corporate and Human Resource Management. *European Management Journal vol.13, No1,* 39-51.

García-Murillo, M. (2004). Institutions and the Adoption of Electronic Commerce in Mexico. *Electronic Commerce Research, 4,* 201-219.

Ghiladi, V. (2003). The Importance of International Standards for Globally Operating Businesses. *International Journal of IT Standards & Standardization Research, Vol.1, No.1, Idea Group Publishing,* 54-56.

Goodman, S. (1991). Computing in a Less-Developed Country. *Communications of the ACM, vol.34, no.12,* 25-29.

Hasselbring, W. (2000a). Information System Integration. *Communications of the ACM, June, vol.43, no.6,* 33-38.

Hatch, M. J. (1997). *Organisation Theory Modern, Symbolic, and Postmodern Perspectives.* Oxford University, Press.

Hawk, S. (2004). A comparison of B2C e-commerce in developing countries. *Electronic Commerce Research, 4,*181-199.

Ho, S., Kauffman, R. and Liang, T-P. (2005), A growth theory perspective on the international diffusion of e-commerce, In Proceedings of the International Conference on E-Commerce (ICEC'05), August 15-17, Xi'an, China, pp.57-65

Intel (2003). Collaborative RosettaNet Implementation: Intel and Fujitsu streamline e-Business automation across the supply chain. *Intel Information Technology White Paper, October.*

Jakobs, K., Procter, R. & Williams, R. (2001). The Making of Standards: Looking Inside the Work Groups. *IEEE Communications Magazine,*.2-7.

Jennex, M., Amoroso, D. & Adelakun, O. (2004). E-commerce infrastructure success factors for small companies in developing economies. *Electronic Commerce Research, 4,* 263-286.

Kearns, G.S. & Leder, A.L. (2000). The effect of strategic alignment on the use of IS-based resources for competitive advantage. *Journal of Strategic Information Systems 9,* 265-293.

Kosanke, K. & Nell, J. (1999). Standardisation in ISO for enterprise engineering and integration. *Computers in Industry, 40,* 311-319.

Kotonya, G & Sommerville, I. (1998). *Requirements Engineering.* ISBN 0-471-97208, WILEY.

Kshetri, N. (2007), Barriers to e-commerce and competitive business models in developing countries: A case study, *Electronic Commerce Research and Applications,* 6 (2007), pp.443-452

Leffingwell, D. & Widrig, D. (2000). *Managing Software Requirements A unified Approach* .Addison, Weasley.

Love, P. & Irani, Z. (2004). An exploratory study of information technology evaluation and benefits management practices of SMEs in the construction industry, *Information & Management, In press.*

Meskaran, F. & Ghazali, M. (2007), B2C in Iran: A case study to improve trust in developing countries, In Krishnamurthy and Isaias (eds.), Proceedings of the IADIS International Conference e-Commerce, December 7-9, Algarve, Portugal, pp.129-136

Milis, K. & Mercken, R. (2002). Success factors regarding the implementation of ICT investments projects. *(Article in Press) Elsevier Science BV.*

Motwani, J., Youssef, M., Kathawala, Y. & Futch, E. (1999). Supplier selection in developing countries: a model development. *Integrated Manufacturing Systems, vol.10, no.3,* 154-161.

Mwangi, W. (2006). The Social Relations of e-Government Diffusion in Developing Countries: The Case of Rwanda. *Proceedings of the 2006 international conference on Digital government research, ACM International Conference Proceeding Series, vol.151, San Diego, USA,* 199-208.

Pohl, K. (1998). Requirements engineering: An overview. *CREWS Report Series CREWS-96-02.*

Poon, P. & Wagner, C. (2001). Critical success factors revisited: success and failure cases of information systems for senior executives. *Decision Support Systems 30,* 393-418.

Premkumar, G., Ramamurthy, K. & Nilakanta, S. (1994). Implementation of Electronic Data Interchange: An Innovation Diffusion Perspective. *Journal of Management Information Systems, Fall, Vol.11, No.2,* 157-186.

Procaccino, D.J., Verner, J.M., Overnyer, S. P. & Darter M. E. (2002). Case study: factors for early prediction of software development success. *Information and Software technology 44 (2002),* 53-62

Pun, K-F. (2001). Cultural influences on total quality management adoption in Chinese enterprise: An empirical study. *Total Quality Management, Vol.12 Issue 3,* 323, 20p.

Purcell, F. & Toland, J. (2004). Electronic Commerce for the South Pacific: A Review of E-Readiness. Electronic *Commerce Research, 4,* 241-262.

Ramsey, J. (1998). Developing an IT Strategy. *Computer Bits, 8 (8).* Retrieved August, 1998 from http://www.computerbits.com.

RosettaNet (2001). Case Study: Arrow and UTEC replace EDI-based purchase order process with RosettaNet standards. *Case study report.* Retrived 20 February, 2004 from http://www.rosettanet.org/RosettaNet/Doc/0/D074294MUC4KJD8GF7HQL8RE67/Arrow_case_study.pdf.

Roy, S. & Biswas, S. (2007). Collaborative ICT for Indian Business Clusters. *Proceedings of the WWW 2007 Conference, May 8-12, Banff, Alberta, Canada,* 1115-1116.

Sadowsky, G. (1993). Network connectivity for developing countries. *Communications of the ACM, vol.36, no.8,* 42-47.

Saiedian, H. & Dale, R. (2000). Requirements engineering: making the connection between the software developer and customer. *Information and Software Technology 42),* 419-428.

Salman, A. (2004). Elusive challenges of e-change management in developing countries. *Business Process Management Journal, vol.10, no.2,* 140-157.

Schein, E.H. (2004). *Organisational culture and Leadership (3rd edition).* John Wiley & Sons, Inc. ISBN: 0-7879-6845-5.

Singh, J. & Gilchrist, S. (2002). Three layers of the electronic commerce network: challenges for the developed and developing worlds. *Info, vol.4, no.2,* 31-41.

Sparks, R., Desai, N., Thirumurthy, P. & Kistenberg, C. (2007), An analysis of e-commerce adoption between developed and developing countries: A holistic model, In Krishnamurthy and Isaias (eds.), Proceedings of the IADIS International Conference e-Commerce, December 7-9, Algarve, Portugal, pp.11-18

Sutcliffe, A.G., Economou, A. & Markis, P. (1999). Tracing requirements problems in the requirements engineering process Requirements. *Engineering, 4,* 134-151.

Söderström, E. & Pettersson, A.H. (2003). The Use of B2B Process Standards. *Proceedings of the 15th International Conference on Advanced Information Systems Engineering Forum* (CAiSE Forum 2003), 121-124.

Söderström, E. (2004). *B2B Standards Implementation: Issues and Solutions.* PhD Thesis, Department of Computer and Systems Sciences, Stockholm University, Akademitryck, ISBN 91-7265-942-4.

Tan, J., Tyler, K. & Manica, A. (2007). Business-to-business adoption of eCommerce in China. *Information & Management, 44,* 332-351.

Thompson, T. & Ranganathan, C. (2004). Adopters and non-adopters of business-to-business electronic commerce in Singapore. *Information & Management, Vol.42,* .89-102.

Uzoka, F.-M. & Seleka, G. (2006). B2C E-Commerce Development in Africa: Case Study of Botswana. *Proceedings of the Electronic Commerce conference (EC) Ann Arbor, Michigan, USA,* 290-295.

Van Gigch, J.P. (1991). *System Design Modeling and Metamodeling.* New York, Plenum Press.

WebMethods (2003). GEAR 6 RosettaNet Implementation Guide: Project Planning Guide, *Whitepaper.*

Wood, C. (2004): Marketing and e-commerce as tools of development in the Asia-Pacific region: a dual path. *International Marketing Review, vol.21, no.3,* 301-320.

Chapter XIV
A Proposed Template for the Evaluation of Web Design Strategies

Dimitrios Xanthidis
Ciber, University College London, UK, DEI College, Greece, & NYC College, Greece

David Nicholas
Ciber, University College London, UK

Paris Argyrides
University College London, UK

ABSTRACT

This chapter is the result of a two years effort to design a template aiming at standardizing, as much as such a task is feasible, the evaluation of Web sites. It is the product of a few publications in international conferences and journals. A thorough review of the international literature on the subject led the authors to conclude there is a very large number of opinions, thoughts and criteria from different professionals involved, directly or indirectly, with the process of designing a good Web site. To make matters even more complicated there are a number of different terms used by various scholars, scientists and professionals around the world that often refer to similar, if not the same, attributes of a Web site. However, it seems that all these differences could boil down to a systematic approach, here called evaluation template, of 53 points that the design strategies of the Web sites should be checked against. This template was tested on a significant number (232) of Web sites of Greek companies and proved it can be used to evaluate the quality of Web sites not only by technology experts but by non-experts alike. The evaluation template, suggested here, is by no means the solution to the problem of standardizing the process of evaluating a Web site but looking at other work done on the subject worldwide it is a step ahead.

Copyright © 2009, IGI Global, distributing in print or electronic forms without written permission of IGI Global is prohibited.

INTRODUCTION

Despite the fact that in many developing countries internet access and e-commerce was not introduced until very recently (Xanthidis and Nicholas, 2004), the world is, clearly, moving towards the digital platform (Figure 1 – Greece in the red circle) with a rapidly increasing number of companies in these countries hosting Web sites. The question is whether these Web sites meet the international standards concerning a site's functionality. A preliminary research of large on- or off-line universities' libraries and governmental Web sites revealed that there are a number of different professions involved in the process of designing a good Web site, e.g. managers, marketing people, information technology experts, lawyers, ethnologists, all having different opinions regarding the functionality and appearance of a good Web site. However, it also proved it is possible to design a template that incorporates the main points of all these different views.

A critical parameter affecting the way people interact with a Web site is its structure, overall design and layout. A poorly designed Web site might lead to accessibility problems as well as reduced interest to navigate through it causing reluctance to visit the site again. Even though professional firms design many Web sites, there is, still, a substantial amount of work done by people with limited knowledge on how a well-designed Web site should be regardless of the fact these technology experts have the know-how to build any e-commerce solution, from a simple to a very sophisticated one.

The main problem in most cases where an evaluation of a Web site is required is the lack of certain systematic methodology to follow. This is exactly what this chapter is all about. A simple yet comprehensive, straightforward yet seen from four different angles, approach of how a Web site could be evaluated based on a number of criteria gathered from many different sources, scholars, scientists and academics, worldwide. Noone can claim to have found the solution to a problem so complex that it involves a variety of different professions not limited to the information and telecommunications technology. However, the discussion that this template has be subject to in three international conferences leads the authors that it is, indeed, a small step ahead toward the solution to the problem.

BACKGROUND

In a highly competitive environment, such as the Web, with billions of sites online and thousands added every day (D-Lib Magazine, 2003) designers/developers consider important that Web sites are attractive and inspire trust to the users so as to cause them to revisit. Therefore, once decisions have been made as of what features and functionalities the e-commerce solution should include the technology experts come into play in order to realize the solution into a good Web site. Based on extensive review of the international literature four categories of features and functionality are considered key for the successful implementation of an e-commerce strategy: user-interface design, globalization and customization, accessibility and availability, security and privacy. This section identifies, describes and analyzes the issues that comprise each category.

Stickiness

In the internet, billions of Web sites exist and even thousands are added every day (Trends…, 2003; Faster…, 2002). Designers and developers consider it important that their Web sites be attractive and inspire trust in users. This is reflected by the amount of time repeatedly spent visiting a site; a practice known as stickiness, a combination of "content, usability and personalization" and other issues, each one to be evaluated and measured on its own merit (Stickiness…, 2000).

Figure 1. Global Internet penetration 2006

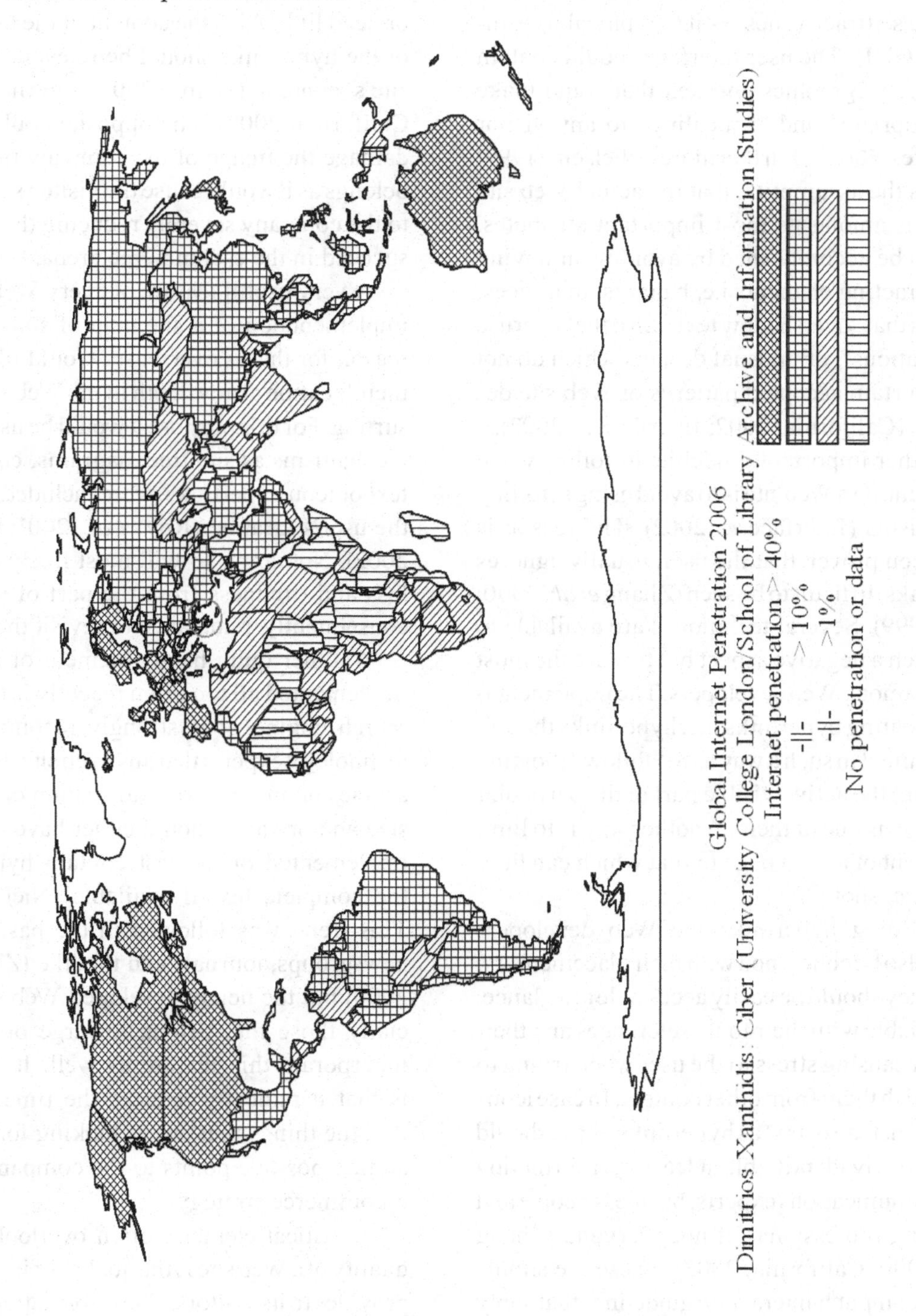

Arguably the most important element of a Web site's attractiveness is its graphical user interface (GUI). The user interface should contain a mixture of graphics and text that could make it "appropriate" and "appealing" to any visitor (Sutcliffe, 2002). Furthermore, Nielsen (1999) supports the assumption that the actual Web site content is among its most important attributes. This can be accomplished by avoiding annoying and distracting elements i.e. banners, marquees, graphics that "overshadow text", also the "overuse of animations", or unusual designs which do not follow certain accepted patterns of Web site design, etc (California, 2002; Interface..., 2002).

Another important guideline to follow when implementing a Web site is to avoid using scrolling mechanisms (Interface..., 2002). The reason is it has been proven that the user, usually, ignores hyperlinks difficult to be seen (Zhang *et al.,* 2000; Iowa, 1999). Several techniques are available to avoid such a negative aspect but two are the most popular among Web developers. The implementation of floating hyperlinks, i.e. hyperlinks that are programmed in such a way as to "follow" (floating on screen) the active/visible part of the particular Web page, is one of them. Another way is to limit the content of a Web page to that which can fit in one screen shot.

Regarding hyperlinks the Web developers should also be concerned with their placement and style. They should be easily accessible at a glance, and readable with their font preferences and their style not causing stress to the user when trying to distinguish them from other content. In case icons are used instead of text as hyperlinks, these should be, intuitively identifiable at least by information and communications experts, business people and marketing professional, if not everyone (Zhang *et al.,* 2000; California, 2002). These are simple human-computer interaction guidelines that apply in the case of Web sites as well.

One of the essential requirements for every Web site is to avoid having undefined objects as the targets of any of its hyperlinks, meaning that none of the hyperlinks should lead to a missing or dead link. Also the content of the target object of the hyperlinks should be relevant to the Web site's content (Helm, 2001; Internet..., 2002; California, 2002). The opposite could seriously damage the image of the company the Web site belongs as it would cause the visitor's lack of trust to the company severely reducing the chances to succeed in the e-commerce arena.

A very useful feature of every Web site is the implementaion of a site map of some sort. The reason for that is every user would like to know their location at any depth in the Web site they are surfing. For this purpose it would be useful if such mechanisms as site tree diagrams, composed of text or icon hyperlinks, were included displaying the user's location (Roy *et al.,* 2001; California, 2002). Not doing so will most likely cause time loss and tiredness from the part of visitor and, consequently, reluctance to revisit the site.

Another quite handy element of a Web site implemented all too often recently is the internal search engine. It is strongly recommended by technology experts that any Web site that includes articles or any type of information of significant size and/or value should either have this feature implemented or at least contain hyperlinks to the complete text if available (Nielsen, 1999). This trend was followed in the past by online newsgroups, journals and the like (Zhang *et al.,* 2000) but the newly developed Web sites, especially those that belong to large organization, incorporate this feature as well. Its advantage is that it radically reduces the time needed to find the things that one is looking for in the site adding positive points to the company's overall e-commerce strategy.

A critical element, often overlooked, of the quality of a Web site is the quality of information it provides to its visitors. The information displayed should be extracted from the most accredited and accurate source (Zhang *et al.,* 2000). Additionally, it should be updated regularly to eliminate the possibility of any outdated content, product specifications or "past-due elements" (Katerattanakul and Siau, 1999). Otherwise, failure to comply with the aforementioned criteria will cause a direct impact on the consumer's behavior towards the corporation i.e. misbelief of the information presented (Katerattanakul and Siau, 1999).

Finally, a very easily implemented feature with surprising positive influences on the visitors' behavior is any mechanism that would allow for visitor feedback. A Web site should allow visitors to comment on its strengths and weaknesses (Zhang *et al.,* 2000) as well as provide a two-way communication channel (Katerattanakul and Siau, 1999), by means of online surveys, e-mail link, feedback forms (Interface…, 2002; Evaluating…, 2004). It would help the visitor feel that it's ideas, comments, remarks are important and taken seriously under consideration.

Customization and Globalization

A Web site's success depends not only on features such as the aforementioned, but also on its global (or local) perspective, meaning its attractiveness and usefulness to populations in different geographic regions, a feature often referred to as globalization. The reason is people in different parts of the globe behave in different ways to various stimulations triggered by a Web site because they live in different cultures, practice different religions and communicate using various languages and symbols (Hanrahan and Kwok, 2001). Furthermore, it would be quite helpful to clarify, through the Web site, legal and/or customs particularities that might affect a visitor's engagement in e-commerce activity when using the Web site of a company based in another country than the one the individual resides. This factor could cause positive first impressions to some populations or culture shock to others. Therefore, the strategy followed in designing the site should address whole populations (Rutherford, 2000).

In order to achieve the above a Web designer/developer has to take under consideration certain realities. First, it is a false assumption that English is the internet's dominant language. Indeed several studies and surveys reveal other languages are used more by the internet users (Xanthidis and Nicholas, 2004; Communicate…, 2000). A company that wishes to attract multilingual audiences should include them in their e-commerce strategy as alternative target audience in addition to the English speaking internet users (Hanrahan and Kwok, 2001). Then, the color used for the background is another issue that affects users' positive or negative reactions. Recent surveys revealed that different colors have different connotations for different regional populations (Zhang *et al.,* 2000; Hanrahan and Kwok, 2001). One such example is the case of China where red is the dominant color (Anderson and Fell, 2003) and has several meanings including the symbolism that the person whose name is written in red is dead, or about to die, or on the other hand expresses such happy moments of life as birthdays, weddings etc. and in general is considered good luck.

A third key point to seriously consider when developing a Web site with global prospects is that users should also be informed about the legal framework related to taxation and import/export procedures in case products are to move in or out of a country (Rutherford, 2002). The reason for that is it is not rare to have sanctions imposed to a country from the part of the international community or have the a ban on certain products from the part of a country's government. Finally, online ordering forms should include a "universal address" format i.e. instead of using the U.S. term "zip codes" use the universal "postal codes" (Housley, 2004), and allow for the selection of various countries and their corresponding addresses.

On the other hand, the developer must address each individual's preferences as well. This is called customization or "adaptive interfaces" (Ardissono *et al.,* 2002) and refers to a Web site's built-in facility to identify a user's preferences even before any interaction takes place between the user and the site and present information in a way that is tailored by the users' preferences (Svet, 2003) and knowledge. Some scholars, scientists, professionals and generally experts in the field use the term personalization instead of customization. Most of the times they mean the same functionalities and just occasionaly they distinguish the two referring to the former when focusing in Web site content and to the latter when focusing in Web site interface and design. These variations in the way a Web site appears or as of the content presented to different user profiles can be created using forms, queries, cookies or other mechanisms and stored in databases.

A few added features could yield some more positive points towards achieving personalization and/or customization. For example, the different payment options accepted i.e. credit cards, money orders, various types of checks, etc., should be listed somewhere and a detailed description of the specific procedures followed both by the visitor and prospect customer of the company and by the representatives should be provided (Hanrahan and Kwok, 2001; Housley, 2004). Also, a currency converter should be implemented to facilitate quick conversion between currencies (Housley, 2004; Hanrahan and Kwok, 2001). These are very easily implemented features and quite useful helping visitors' decision towards engage in e-commerce transaction but are, once again, quite often overlooked.

Availability, Hardware/Software Requirements, Accessibility

The introduction of new types of electronic devices such as personal digital assistants (PDAs), new generation mobile phones, also called cellular phones, with embedded internet capabilities, etc., in addition to the personal computers and laptops (notebooks) all having different abilities of presenting content to their user has lead the companies to find ways to make their Web sites available to different platforms and operating systems. The advent of mobile commerce in several digital economies worldwide has just stressed this need even further.

The main problem to be tackled is that a Web site display is primarily hardware/software dependent. Imagine the enormous problems that arise when a Web site designed in 1200x1600 in 32-bit color is viewed in the 120x240, 256-color display of a PDA or a mobile phone. It would, simply, be unreadable. In order to address this issue professionals suggest the design of a Web site that is available and its content prenentable by any type of electronic device. Currently, it appears that there are no tools available that actually convert a Web site's layout for different device usage but there are tools that help create accessible code [Macromedia…, 2004; Bohman, 2003; Sullivan, 2004). The recommended way of dealing with platform diversity is to separate layout design and content by having different layout templates, or "style sheets" for the same content, depending on the specific device (Nielsen, 1999; Accessibility…, 2004).

Closely related to the type of electronic device, the operating system and the browser platform, but mainly to the internet connection speed available is the time required for a Web page of a Web site to be loaded. This is a crucial factor when evaluating the Web site. Slow response speed, i.e. the time required to load a page inside a Web site, of more than 7-10 seconds, could be annoying (California, 2002) and discourage internet users to revisit.

No doubt the biggest challenge for every Web site designer/developer is to implement it in such a way as to make it accessible for persons with disabilities. A Web site should be designed not only with the media through which it is viewed in mind but its viewers as well. People with disabilities such as limited vision, hearing or mobility could find it difficult to navigate in a site filled with "graphically intense" content i.e. fairly large amounts of different colors and graphics. Too much color could be a problem for a person who is "visually impaired" person since it may make the content hard to read (Universal…, 2004). For that reason it is suggested to host a second or even third version of the Web site, customized for persons with disabilities (McManis *et al.*, 2001).

There are a number of guidelines to follow for versions of Web sites for viewers with various types of disabilities. The first is that if tables are used in which text is contained, then a logical grouping must be followed since most screen readers and magnification software may not read the text correctly. Text in cells must be separated into paragraphs to assist reading software (Making…, 2002; Pyatt, 2004). Additionally, include the functionality of providing textual description of images and "non-textual elements" in the case where browsers are configured not to display images, or the person who is using the browser uses a screen reader that cannot "read" images (Making…, 2002).

In the most likely event that a Web site includes "motion and animation" this should be at a frequency of less than 2Hz or more than 55Hz, as within this frequency range an animation may "trigger epileptic seizures" to individuals with related health problems (Making…, 2002; 30; Iowa, 1999). Finally, it would be quite useful to ensure that the site contains a mechanism that may trace the utilization of a screen reader or any other related tool and/or has also the ability to identify a change in language and adjust accordingly (Making…, 2002).

Some other issues related to accessibility and availability are the following:

- Text that is available through JavaScript i.e. pop-up windows, should also be available for users with JavaScript disabled and for users utilizing screen readers since screen readers may not read text contained in JavaScript (Pyatt, 2004).
- Frequently Asked Questions (FAQ) should be implemented together with a Help Topics feature. Accessibility covers matters that deal with user problems, not just hardware. Online guides, help topics and support reduce user stress to solve potential problems and increase the ease of navigating the Web site (Roy et al., 2001).

The main problem with the implementation of the features mentioned just above is the overall costs associated with it both in terms of time but most important in terms of money. To make matters worse the returns of investment are far from sufficient enough as the internet users' population that would be addressed by such sophisticated sites is a very small part of the overall online population. This is the main reason even large multinational corporations are reluctant in realizing such types of Web sites despite the various directives towards this goal from government organizations or nations like the European Commission and the U.S. department of Justice just to name a couple.

Security, Privacy, Legal and Ethical Issues Involved in Internet Marketing

Security, privacy, legalities and ethics are probably the most discussed technologies issues, nowadays. Several studies were conducted to clarify how they affect large corporations' successful or failed strategies to attract digital consumers (Privacy…, 2002). Currently, the most effective way to tackle this problem is to apply available mechanisms, in the form of software packages, aiming to protecting and securing valuable and sensitive data and restricting access to vulnerable systems (Benjamin *et al.*, 1998).

Unfortunately, it is a proven fact that there is no bulletproof mechanism to ensure complete defense against the various types of threats e.g. spyware, viruses including Trojan horses among other malicious programs/scripts, adware, even cookies used improperly by unauthorized people, etc. Then, it is on the developer's judgment to decide which of the available mechanisms should be used and how to ensure the success of internet strategies without compromising their visitors' privacy and keeping security, legal and ethical issues properly addressed. This is a goal very difficult to achieve. On one hand the more visitors' data a company keeps recorded the more effectively it will present a customized Web site tailored to their needs. On the other hand this causes many compromises in terms of the visitors' personal privacy and quite possibly of their personal computer security from malicious software. The following guidelines address the majority of these issues except all those that are not directly connected to the Web e.g. television/radio marketing.

First, in order to ensure the visitor's privacy Web sites should not collect sensitive information from users' PCs without their consent. In those cases where it is decided as necessary to collect such information the visitors should be clearly informed as of the use of the information. Personal data is most often collected through the use of cookies, spyware, and other related mechanisms. It is not always possible to directly confirm existence of such mechanisms like spyware and computer viruses. However, there are a number of anti-spyware and anti-virus software available which can be used by internet users to quite successfully block any attempts to compromise their personal computers' security and their own privacy.

Second, aiming to further protect visitors' personal financial data e-commerce Web sites at the transaction level (Xanthidis and Nicholas, 2007) should implement security protocols and services, like SSL (Secure Socket Layer), SET (Secure Electronic Transaction) to name the most widely used, to ensure safe transactions over the Internet (Verisign, 2002). Furthermore, in those cases where e-mails are exchanged between the company's representatives and their Web site's visitors it could help if the latters' e-mail addresses were protected or masked via some type of scripts, forms, buttons, etc. to help defend against spam bots' attempts to identify e-mail addresses while crawling the Web.

Looking from the opposite site that of the owner of the Web site things are a little more complicated in those cases where the site is somehow connected with the company's intranet. In that case, the company's information and communication technology experts must ensure that no unauthorized person is allowed to enter Web pages restricted to authorized access. This could be achieved by implementing log-in procedures to authenticate a visit to such pages.

Finally, in every Web site like in every other software a message should be present to inform the reader that the material is an official document bound by relevant international copyright laws (Fishman, 1994).

METHODOLOGY

The aim of this work was to develop a systematic methodology for the evaluation of Web sites which would be as simple as possible yet comprehensive enough to include all those elements discussed in the previous section with straightforward answers while the evaluation takes place. The authors, then, came up with an evaluation template which comprises of 53 questions divided, not equally, into four categories called dimensions each one tackling the issues discussed earlier. It was also decided to use only dichotomous questions and avoid all other types, i.e. multiple answer, semantic differential, likert scale valued, ranked ordered. The rationale behind this decision is the idea to have a template as binary in nature as possible, one that any individual could use, even not having a significant technology background, limiting subjective judgement as much as possible. Also, the authors wanted to design in a way to make the evaluation of any Web site, no matter how large or complicated, quite feasible as of the time required. The results can be seen in the next four tables (see Table 1, Table 2, Table 3, Table 4).

In order to test the template the authors selected for evaluation a quite significant in size sample

Table 1. Evaluation template: Dimension I: Stickiness

1.		Lack of tendency to use scrolling mechanisms.	Yes = 1	No = 0
2.		**Hyperlink placement/style**		
	i.	Hyperlinks easily accessible (at a glance)?	Yes = 1	No = 0
	ii.	Presence of floating hyperlinks (embedded in bars)?		No = 0
	iii.	Font properties (name, size, bold/no bold, color) of the text hyperlinks distinguishing them from the rest of the text?	Yes = 1	No = 0
	iv.	Icons used in graphical type hyperlinks intuitively identifiable, i.e. do they represent the target object or are they misleading?	Yes = 1	No = 0
3.		**Hyperlink target/content**		
	i.	Tendency NOT to have dead hyperlinks in the site (use home page)?	Yes = 1	No = 0
	ii.	Hyperlinks lead to relevant pages?	Yes = 1	No = 0
4.		**Site maps**		
	i.	Presence of any type of site map, i.e. site tree diagram, drop-down menus, etc.?	Yes = 1	No = 0
	ii.	Mapping mechanisms informative as to the actual depth in which the user navigates?	Yes = 1	No = 0
5.		**Web site user interface attractiveness**		
	i.	Appropriate and appealing?	Yes = 1	No = 0
	ii.	Lack of distracting and annoying elements?	Yes = 1	No = 0
6.		**Information quality and completeness**		
	i.	Any "read more" hyperlinks available clarifying possibly broad, unclear or unknown topics to the reader?	Yes = 1	No = 0
	ii.	Is the information provided in the Web site signed and, thus, credible?	Yes = 1	No = 0
	iii.	Is the information provided updated on a reasonably expected timeliness?	Yes = 1	No = 0
	iv.	Any internal search engine available?	Yes = 1	No = 0
7.		**Visitor's feedback enabled and online help available**		
	i.	E-mail links available to the visitors?	Yes = 1	No = 0
	ii.	Online surveys available?	Yes = 1	No = 0
	iii.	Feedback forms available?	Yes = 1	No = 0
	iv.	On line help available (e.g. FAQs, etc.)?	Yes = 1	No = 0

of the Web sites of 232 medium-large companies from the 15 sectors of the Greek economy, public and private, either "local" (Greek) or international with subsidiaries in the country (see Appendix). It took between 15' and 20' to evaluate each site and the evaluation period started on 11/5/2005 and ended on 30/6/2005. The answers to the evaluation questions were quite straightforward, binary in nature, a fact that simplified the process. In several cases during the evaluation, i.e. appropriate and appealing, we found it was somewhat subjective to determine/measure the Web site but in broad lines our decision was in general agreement with what any person would value as an appropriate and appealing Web site. This holds true despite the fact that people coming from different backgrounds may view this issue under another perspective.

One aspect we found to be problematic was the measurement of the *time availability* of a Web site. This would be possible by monitoring the site's online status on a 24/7 basis or alternatively by examining a detailed specification and possible the logs files of the hosting server. Human resource and time constraints of this part of the study prohibited us from doing the first. Furthermore, the fact that the server and network specifications and/or their log files were not available to us did not permit to follow the second path.

Table 2. Evaluation template: Dimension II: Customization and globalization

1.	**Languages supported (cocacola.com is worldwide)**			
	i. English		**Yes = 1**	**No = 0**
	ii. Spanish		**Yes = 1**	**No = 0**
	iii. Chinese		**Yes = 1**	**No = 0**
	iv. French		**Yes = 1**	**No = 0**
	v. German		**Yes = 1**	**No = 0**
	vi. Other (Greek, Turkish, Arabic, Hebrew, Japanese, etc.)		**Yes = 1**	**No = 0**
2.	**Colors used:** Is Web site color related with the cultural background (Western, Asian, etc) of the targeted population?		**Yes = 1**	**No = 0**
3.	**Issues related to globalization**			
	i. Briefing/information provided concerning import/export and taxation issues?		**Yes = 1**	**No = 0**
	ii. Any restrictions applicable for a commodity to be exported/imported to/from certain countries?		**Yes = 1**	**No = 0**
	iii. Any list of countries to which import/export restrictions apply?		**Yes = 1**	**No = 0**
	iv. Any information provided about available shipping/ delivery options?		**Yes = 1**	**No = 0**
4.	**Level of customization the Web site achieves**			
	i. Level 0: No customization		**Yes = 1**	**No = 0**
	ii. Level 1: Content → display information based on previous user interaction and preferences stored in log files.		**Yes = 1**	**No = 0**
	iii. Level 2: Suggestive → display information on relevant or competitive commodities/ services.		**Yes = 1**	**No = 0**
	iv. Level 3: Informative → display further clarifications on issues not in the sphere of the user's knowledge.		**Yes = 1**	**No = 0**
	v. Level 4: Design format → lets the user permanently decide the layout of the Web site as it appears in his/her browser.		**Yes = 1**	**No = 0**
	vi. Level 5: Language and Culture → identifies the user's of language and culture preference based on the IP address of the user's system or on the user's selection of a region/country from a map/list available.		**Yes = 1**	**No = 0**
5.	**Payment – shipping/billing options**			
	i. List of different payment options available?		**Yes = 1**	**No = 0**
	ii. Detailed description of each payment option available?		**Yes = 1**	**No = 0**
	iii. Currency converter available?		**Yes = 1**	**No = 0**
	iv. Use of the universal "postal code" instead of the regional "zip code"?		**Yes = 1**	**No = 0**

ANALYSIS AND RESULTS

Web Site Design/Stickiness

Initially, concerning Web site design issues, the study showed that developers in Greece follow the internationally accepted standards of what a nice looking Web site should be like (Figure 2). Indeed, the majority of developers (142/232; 61.21%) tend to avoid the use of scrolling mechanisms which proved to have a negative impact in the Web site's attractiveness. In all but 3 cases (229/232; 98.7%) the hyperlinks were found to lead to relevant pages and in all but 6 (226/232; 97.4%) the hyperlinks did not lead to a dead end. If icons are used to represent the hyperlinks, the selections were found to be intuitively identifiable in 216/232 cases (93.1%). When text was the basis for the hyperlinks, the font properties were quite helpful in distinguishing it from the rest of the objects on the Web sites in 204/232 of the cases (87.9%). In general, the hyperlinks could be found easily at a glance in 167/232 of the cases (71.9%).

Table 3. Evaluation template: Dimension III: Accessibility, availability, hardware/software requirements

1.	Is the Web site accessible (Platform Compatibility)		**Yes = 1**	**No = 0**
2.	Is the Web site optimized for users with a mental or physical handicap?		**Yes = 1**	**No = 0**
3.	**Hardware/ Software/ Network requirements**			
	i.	Time required loading the Web site's home page?	**<10" = 1**	**No = 0**
	ii.	Web site displayed properly, i.e. no horizontal scrolling mechanisms, no twisting of objects, etc., in different display resolutions?	**Yes = 1**	**No = 0**
	iii.	Option to download and install "third party" components required to view the Web site, e.g. activeX, flash players, different fonts, etc.	**Yes = 1**	**No = 0**

Table 4. Evaluation template: Dimension IV: Security, privacy

1.	**Security**			
	i.	Authentication required to login into possible intranet part of the site?	**Yes = 1**	**No = 0**
	ii.	If transactional or interactive what protocol are they using (None, SSL, SET, Other)?	**Yes = 1**	**No = 0**
	iii.	What is the cipher strength?	**Yes = 1**	**<128 = 0**
	iv.	On-line anti-virus scanner available?	**Yes = 1**	**No = 0**
	v.	Web site expires after a pre-defined amount of idle time?	**Yes = 1**	**No = 0**
2.	**Privacy**			
	i.	Avoid the use of tracking/identifying mechanisms i.e. cookies, spyware, etc, without the consent of the user?	**Yes = 1**	**No = 0**
	ii.	Privacy statement?	**Yes = 1**	**No = 0**
	iii.	Masked e-mail addresses through scripts, forms, buttons, etc?	**Yes = 1**	**No = 0**

Concerning the presence of any sort of distracting and annoying elements, findings were quite positive again as in 212/232 cases (91.3%) no such elements were found and in general the user interface of the Web sites was found to be appropriate and appealing in 215/232 cases (92.6%). The only problem related to site interface was that in the majority of the Web sites floating hyperlinks were not present (152/232; 65.5%).

The problems started when more technical details were evaluated (Figure 3). One of the central components of any Web site, the site map, was only found in 85/232 (36.6%) of the Web sites. More technical mapping mechanisms that could provide information as of the depth in which the visitor navigates were even more seldom utilized (10/232; 4.3%). As far as online help made available to visitors is concerned, unfortunately, such a feature was only available in one site (1/232; 0.4%). The same can be said of the availability – lack, rather – of online surveys with only 2 sites implementing such feedback mechanisms for the visitors (2/232; 0.8%).

The most surprising element of the findings, however, was that only 156/232 sites (67.2%) incorporated the very easy to implement and almost obvious to include e-mail link for the visitors and, also, less than half the Web sites (106/232; 45.6%) made a feedback form available to visitors. The information was updated quite regularly in 227/232 cases (97.8%), however, it is signed – and, hence, credible – in only 32/232 cases (13.8%). There is the projection of providing more information in 134/232 sites (57.8%) through the utilization

Figure 2. Web site evaluation from a technical viewpoint. Dimension 1 - Stickiness

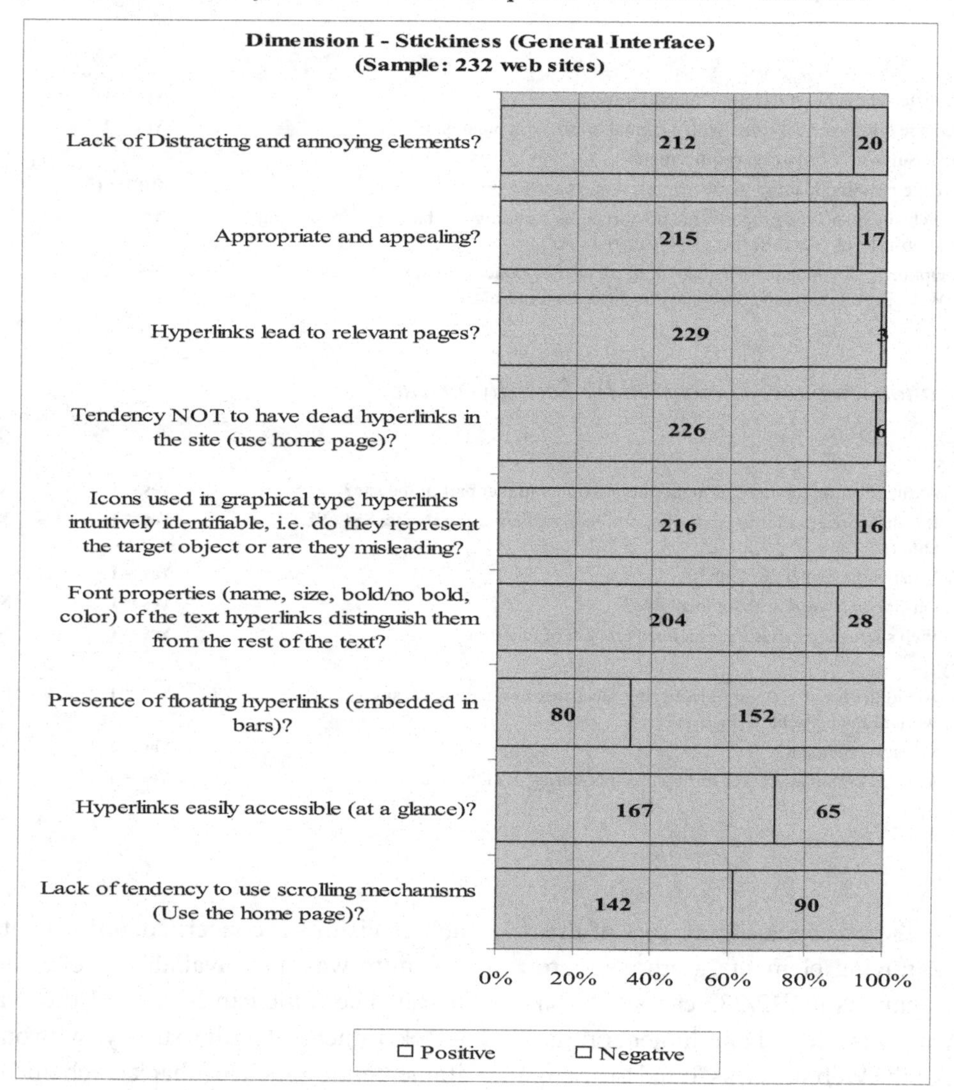

of "read more" hyperlinks and 88/232 of those (38.0%) included an internal search engine.

Customization and Globalization

It was quite obvious that except Greek (211/232; 90.95%), the only other language seriously considered and used when developing Web sites was English (178/232; 76.72%). All the rest, i.e. Spanish (7/232; 3.01%), French (7/232; 3.01%), German (8/232; 3.44%) and Chinese (3/232; 1.29%), included into our study, were seldom used mainly in specific cases of companies which probably had some business or other relations to certain groups of people in parts of the world.

In terms of the colors used, they were found to be appropriate (231/232; 99.57%) in connection with the populations of visitors targeted (based

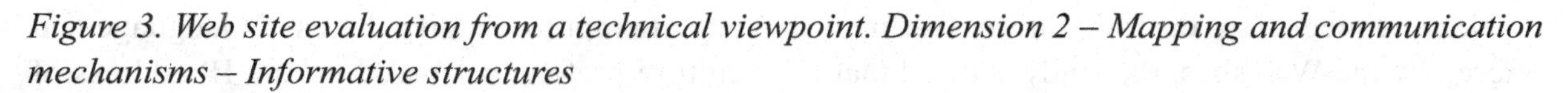

Figure 3. Web site evaluation from a technical viewpoint. Dimension 2 – Mapping and communication mechanisms – Informative structures

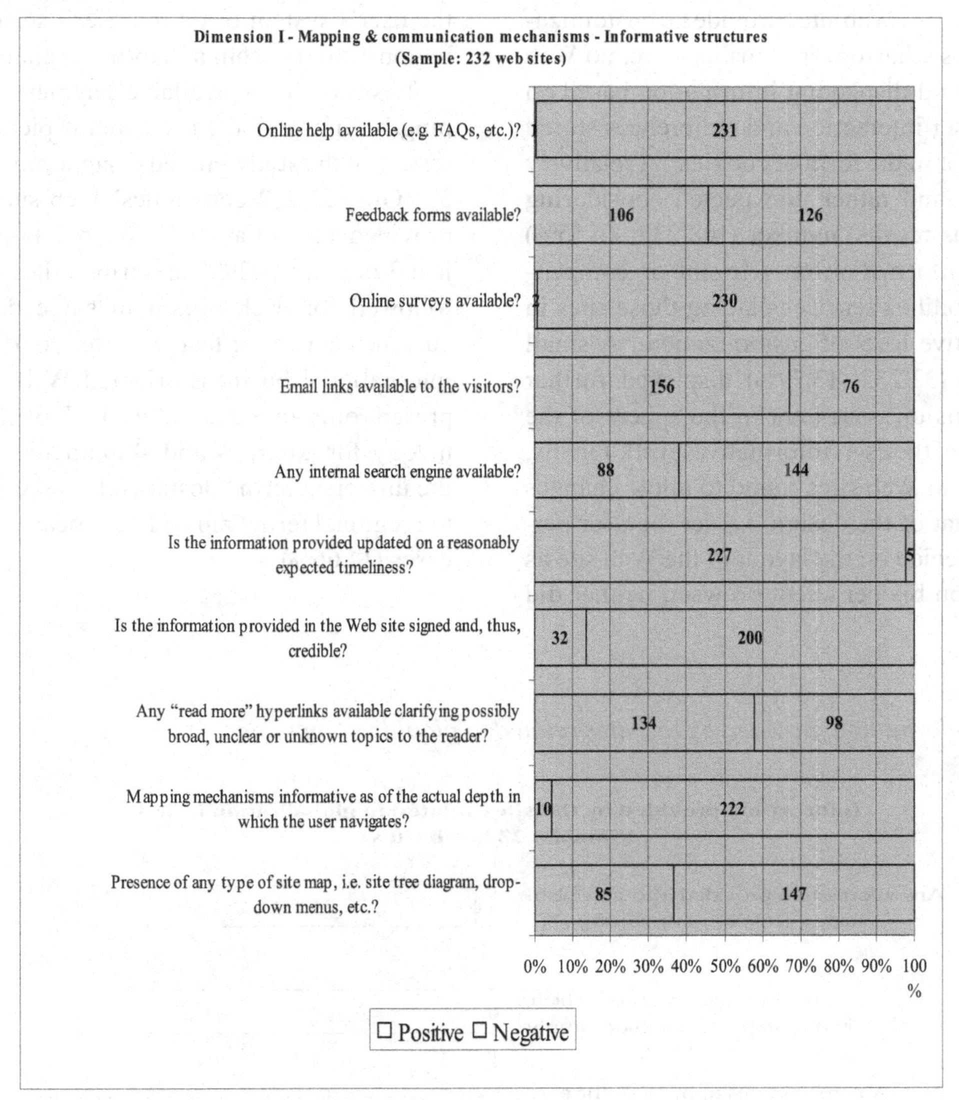

on the assumption that the language in which the text was written reflected the mother tongue and culture of the visitor targeted). However, it was also realized that this last conclusion was not based on enough evidence and it would be very interesting to see how things would change if, say, a large proportion of the targeted population were Chinese-speaking people.

Finally, only the executives of a handful of companies seem to take things seriously as only in 10/232 cases (4.31%) was there some kind of briefing about import/export and taxation matters, and only in 11/232 Web sites was information provided on shipping/delivery options (4.34%). No discussion can be made about providing lists of countries or commodities for which certain imports/exports restrictions apply (Figure 4).

Next, concerning customization features offered by the Web sites, the study showed that 89/232 (38.36%) Web sites provide no customization features whatsoever. Furthermore, no Web site was found displaying information based on previous user interaction and preferences stored in log files or in the form of cookies. A relatively significant (and rather unexpected considering the previous results) number (108/232; 46.55%) displayed information on relevant or competitive commodities/services placing those sites in the suggestive level of customization. A small percentage (32/232; 13.79%) displayed further clarifications on issues not in the sphere of the knowledge of the user (informative level). Finally, there were no Web sites found to allow changes in the format of the design, i.e. let the user permanently decide on the layout of the Web site as it appears on his/her client browser, neither did any attempt to identify the user's language and culture preferences based on the IP address of the user's system or on the user's selection of a region/country from a map/list available.

Last, as far as available payment and shipping/billing options, the general picture of the results of the study proved disappointing (Figure 5). Only 21/232 companies' Web sites (9.05%) provided a list of available payment options and just 3 of them (1.29%) described the steps to be followed for each option in some detail. The currency converter feature, often found in many international business-oriented Web sites, was present only in 3/232 (1.29%). Universal terminology for payment and shipping/delivery, e.g. the universal term "postal code" used instead of the regional term "zip code", appeared in 34/232 cases (14.66%).

Figure 4. Information provided by the sites related to globalization issues

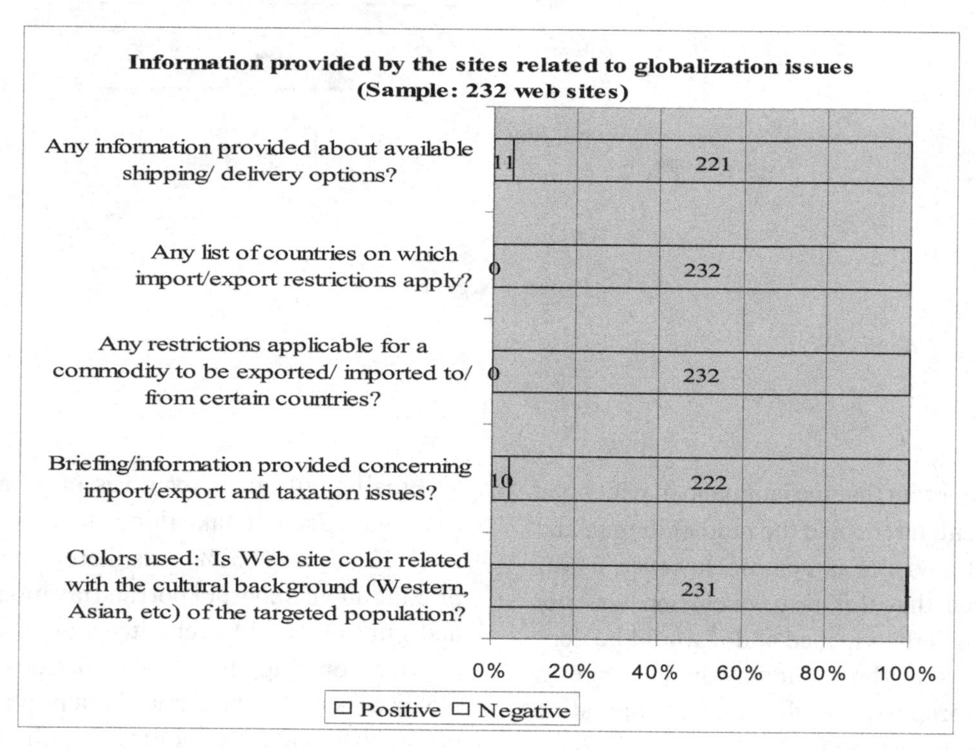

Figure 5. More globalization issues faced

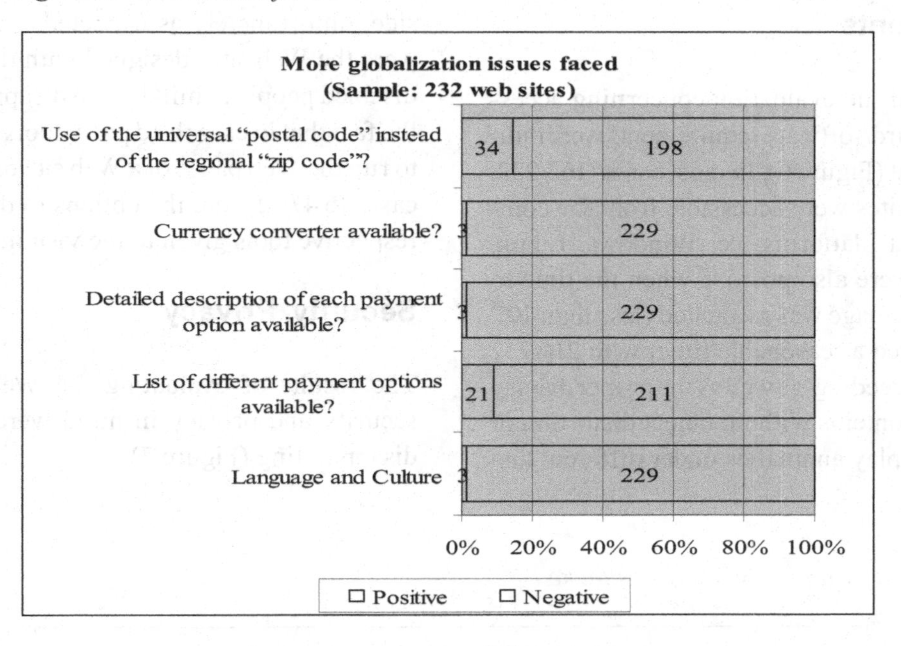

Figure 6. Accessibility and availability issues

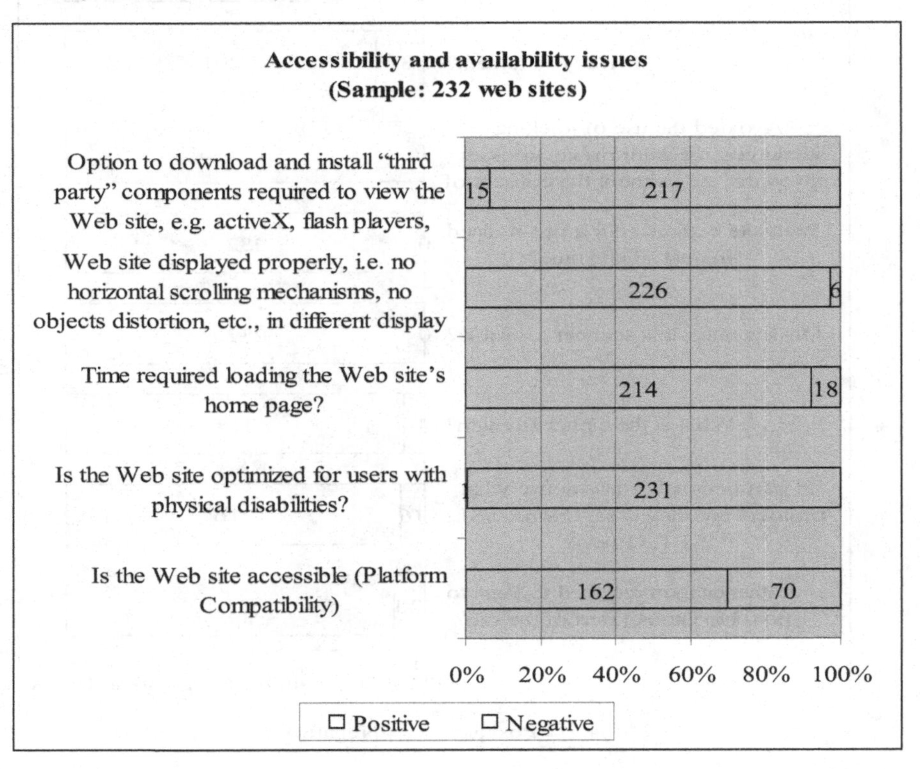

Accessibility, Hard/Software Requirements

The results of the evaluation concerning accessibility and hard/software requirements were radically different (Figure 6). In most cases (162/232; 69.83%) the sites were accessible from the common different platforms, i.e. Windows, Linux. The results were also positive when the time to load the home page was evaluated (less than 10'' was considered a reasonable time) with 214/232 (92.24%) succeeding, as well as the proper display of the page contents without object distortion or any other display anomalies under different display resolutions (226/232; 97.41%). On the negative side, unfortunately as expected, only in 1 case were the Web sites designed with the physically disabled people in mind. Also disappointing was the fact that in case third party tools were needed to run the Web pages of a Web site only in 15/232 cases (6.47%) were the options to download the respective tools given to the visitors.

Security, Privacy

The results of evaluating the Web sites with security and privacy in mind were completely disappointing (Figure 7).

Figure 7. Security and privacy issues tacked

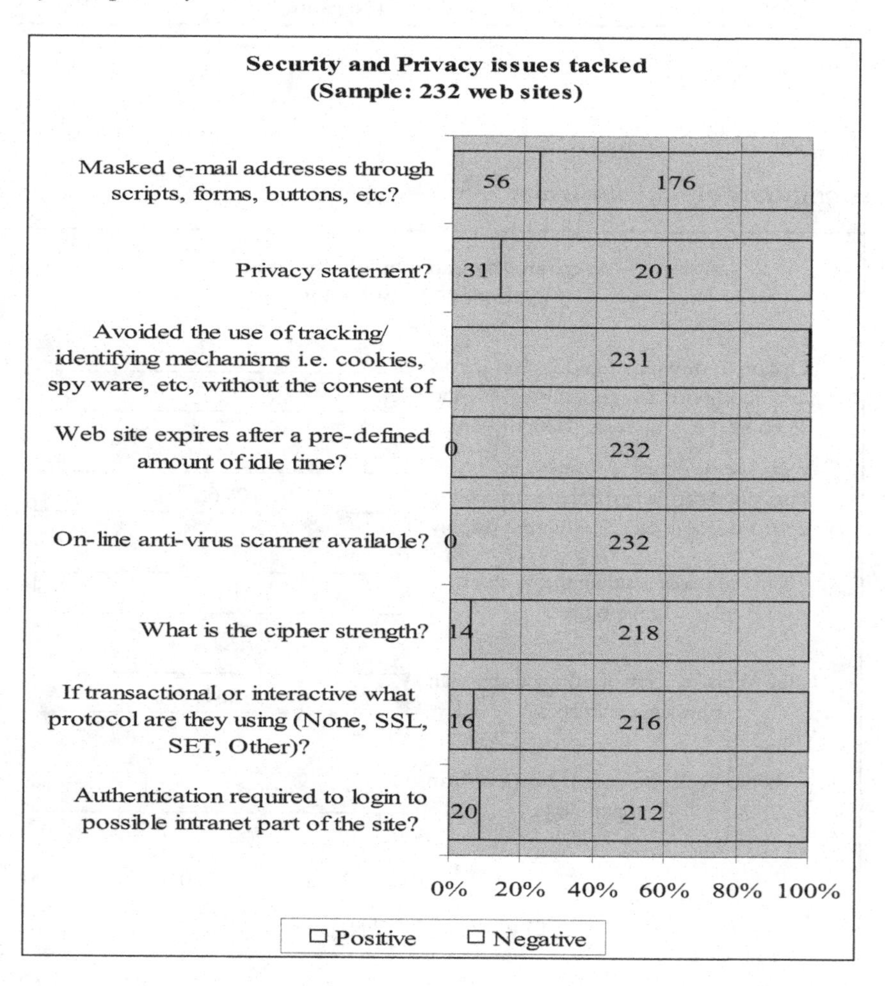

On the one hand, security concerns should be tackled but very little was found be undertaken in this direction. Only 20/232 (8.62%) sites had some kind of authentication process running when a visitor requested to access to the companies'/organizations' intranet. Even less were the sites (16/232; 6.90%) protected by a security protocol like SSL, SET, etc. The cipher strength for the sites protected by such protocols was less than 128 (very low indeed) in 218/232 cases (6.03%). No on-line anti-virus scanner was available and no expiration time after a specific amount of idle time (as suggested for security purposes) was present and/or activated.

On the other hand, concerning the visitors' privacy, the study showed a tendency to avoid tracking/identifying mechanisms, like cookies, spy ware, etc. (231/232 cases; 9.57%) but there is serious doubt this was a conscious decision on the part of the companies' executives or lack of technical expertise required to implement it. Additionally, only 31/232 sites were found (13.36%) with a privacy statement (an utterly simple feature to realize), and only 56/232 (24.14%) cases of Web sites with masked e-mail addresses through scripts, forms, buttons, etc. for privacy-related reasons.

IMPLICATIONS

It is quite possible after all, although very difficult, to put together all bits and pieces that make up the puzzle of what suggests a good Web site, be it a simple one or a very sophisticated. The number of the elements to be evaluated is significant, of course, but limited enough to make the whole idea of evaluating a Web site feasible as of time and effort required. Furthermore, the nature of the questions of the template is such that allows even non-experts of the field of e-commerce to use it for their evaluation of their Web sites.

The template introduced in this chapter could be used as a "marking scheme" for the assessment of all different types of Web sites by information and communication technology (ICT) experts in a systematic way. It could also be used by business and other professionals as a suggestion, a rule of thumb indeed, of how could or should their companies' Web sites be implemented to meet their online strategies. The main reason the template can deliver both the aforementioned goals is that the questions to be answered carry on them the "correct" approaches of how to address each of the issues related to the development of a Web site. Therefore, it is quite straightforward that every positive answer adds one positive point to the overall design of the site with any negative answer pointing to its weaknesses.

LIMITATIONS: FURTHER RESEARCH

The authors used a number of Greek Web sites to test this systematic methodology that the suggested evaluation template represents. Despite the poor performance of the rather large local information society in e-commerce activity it was possible to use this template to draw useful conclusions for the quality of the Web sites and their effect in e-commerce growth in the country. The authors selected the Greek Web sites for reasons of physical proximity to the companies (Greek residence). However, it would be quite interesting to test the same methodology on the Web sites of companies in the developed digital economies and those of the underdeveloped countries as well just to see if it is applicable in those cases as well. Also, the methodology was tested on medium-large companies' sites. It would help to see if and how much applicable it would be in the case of small companies as well.

Apparently, like in every other field of information and communications technology this effort is not over. This is only a measurement template. The next step, parallel to updating the template with new ideas and insight from professionals all over the world, is to work towards clarifying the metric against which the various results of measurement should be checked. There could be certain numerical results that distinguish a poor designed Web site from a better one and then from a very good one. Probably such a distinction is more complicated as it depends on certain variables including but not limited to the type of the Web site, e.g. information level up to full e-commerce solution, the progress towards the digital economy in the country of the company that owns the site, and others.

CONCLUSION

It should be underlined once again that the task of designing a comprehensive template/formula that could be used to evaluate Web sites looking from different viewpoints based on the various professions involved is extremely difficult, but proven feasible. The pieces of the puzzle are many and as the technology changes they change with it. However, there are a few facts that helped achieve our goal of designing the proposed evaluation template.

First, despite the quite significant, some could consider it rather large, number of 53 elements of a Web site to be evaluated they can be organized into categories each one addressing completely different viewpoints. This is the reason the authors called them dimension as it is like looking into the same structure from different angles. Second, it is proven that with just a little difficulty it is possible to answer the questions of the template in a straightforward binary way that leaves very little or no room to different and subjective interpretations of the quality of features implementing while addressing each specific issue. Third, it is proven possible to have a numerical result of the evaluation, although, by itself this cannot lead to safe conclusions as of the quality of the Web site overall but only to relevant suggestions. Finally, the time required to use this template to evaluate any Web site is very reasonable, less than 20' per site, regardless of the quality, type or size of the Web site.

The authors do not claim they found the ideal solution to the problem. What was proposed in this chapter is the result of the ongoing process of reviewing, adjusting and incorporating different ideas and thoughts into a template as little technical as possible in order for anyone to be able to use it even if that person is not an ICT expert. The authors opened a path which they believe could lead to a systematic way of assessing the quality of Web sites. The thing that encourages them to move further this type of research is the positive and insightful comments received in the conferences where this methodology is presented.

REFERENCES

Accessibility on the Web (2004). International Center for Disability Resources on the Internet [online], Available: www.icdri.org [accessed: December 2004].

Anderson, B., Fell, J. M. (US Government Export Portal) (2003). Taming the Red Dragon: Getting in and Succeeding in China, Available: www.export.gov/comm_svc/pdf/RedDragon.pdf [accessed: 2004].

Ardissono, L., Goy, A., Petrone, G., Segnan, M. (2002). Personalization in B2C interaction. *Communications of the ACM, 45*(5) (May 2002).

Benjamin, R., Gladman, B., Randel, B. (1998). Protecting IT systems from cyber crime. *The Computer Journal, 41*(7), 429-443. Available: www.cs.ncl.ac.uk/research/pubs/trs/papers/631.ps [accessed: December 2004].

Bohman, P. (2003). *Using Opera to check for accessibility.* Available: www.Webaim.org/techniques/articles/opera [accessed: 2004].

California State University, Sacramento (2002). *Web Design Principles.* Available: www.csus.edu/uccs/training/online/design/d_principles.htm.

Communicate in your customers' language (2000). WorldLingo Press Releases [online], Available: www.worldlingo.com/company_information/pr20000625_01.html [accessed: November 2004].

D-Lib Magazine (2003). *Trends in the Evolution of the Public Web.* Available: www.dlib.org/dlib/april03/lavoie/04lavoie.html [accessed: 2004].

Evaluating Web Pages: Techniques to apply and questions to ask (2004). UC Berkeley – Teaching Library Internet Workshop [online], Available: www.lib.berkeley.edu/TeachingLib/Guides/Internet/Evaluate.html [accessed: December 2004].

Faster Growth Heightens Web Class Divide (2002). TRN (Technology Research News) [online], Available: www.trnmag.com [accessed: December 2004].

Fishman, S. *Software Development: A legal guide,* Nolo Press, Berkeley, 1994, First Edition.

Hanrahan, M., Kwok, & Wei-Tai (2001). *A New Connectivity - How Technology is Changing the Marketing World.* Available: iaa2001.atalink.co.uk/html/p026.htm [accessed: 2004].

Helm, J. C. (2001). *Web based Application Quality Assurance.* Available: sce.cl.uh.edu/helm/Helm_html/papers/QW2001_PaperJune0101.pdf [accessed: 2004].

Hirsh, L. (2002, February 25). *Online Shopping and the Human Touch, E-Commerce Times: The E-Business and Technology Supersite* [online], Available: www.ecommercetimes.com/.../16483.html [accessed: December 2004].

Housley, S. (2004). *Web site Globalization.* Available: www.onevision.co.uk/xq/ASP/id.1072 [accessed: 2004].

Iowa University (1999). Designing accessible Web sites booklet, Available: www.uiowa.edu/infotech/WebAccess.htm [accessed: 2004].

Interface Design (2002). *Web Style Guide 2nd Edition* [online], Available: www.Webstyleguide.com/interface/user-centered.hmtl [accessed: December 2004].

Internet Guide (2002). Canada Government [online], Available: www.cio-dpi.gc.ca/ig-gi/m/wsm-msw/wsm-msw_e.asp [accessed: December 2004].

Katerattanakul, P., Siau, K. (1999). Measuring Information Quality of Web sites. In *Proceedings of the 20th International Conference of Information Systems* [online], Charlotte, North Carolina, United States, Available: portal.acm.org [accessed: December 2004].

Macromedia – Accessibility (2004). Macromedia [online], Available: www.macromedia.com/macromedia/accessibility [accessed: December 2004].

Making your Web sites Accessible with Microsoft FrontPage (2002). Microsoft Corporation [online], Available: www.microsoft.com [accessed: December 2004].

McManis, B. L., Ryker, R., Cox, K. C. (2001). An Examination of Web Usage in a global context. *Industrial Management and Data Systems, 101*(9), 470-476.

Nielsen, J. (1999). User interface directions for the Web. *Communications of the ACM, 42*(1), 65-72.

Novell (2004). *Securing your Web site.* Novel [online], Available: www.novell.com/documentation/nw6p/index.html [accessed: December 2004].

Privacy and Data Sharing. A Performance and Innovation Report (2002). Cabinet Office (UK

Government – Department of Constitutional Affairs) [online], Available: www.foi.gov.uk/sharing/pubs.htm [accessed: December 2004].

Pyatt, E. J., Pennsylvania State University (2004). Creating Accessible Web Sites, [accessed: Dec. 2004].

Roy, M. Christine, Dewit, O., Aubert, B. A. (2001). The impact of interface usability on trust in Web retailers. *Internet Research: Electronic Networking Applications and Policy, 11*(5), 388-398.

Rutherford, E. (2002). *How to Avoid Global Website Disasters.* Available: www.cio.com/research/.../111400_disaster.html [accessed:2004].

Stickiness in an eTailing environment (2000). Northwestern University [online], Available: www.medill.northwestern.edu/imc/studentwork/projects/Sticky/index.htm [accessed: November 2004].

Sullivan, N. (2004). *Why design accessible Websites.* PostDiluvian Org. [online], Available: postdiluvian.org/~nicole/work/why.php [accessed: December 2004].

Sutcliffe, A. (2002). Heuristic Evaluation of Website Attractiveness and Usability. *Proceedings of the 35th Hawaii International Conference on System Sciences* [online], Available: csdl2.computer.org/comp/proceedings/hicss/2002/1435/05/14350137.pdf [accessed: December 2004].

Svet, B., State University of New York, Buffalo (2003). *Personalization and Customization in eCommerce.* Available: www.cse.buffalo.edu/~sbraynov/seninar2003/presenttations/lecture.pdf [accessed: 2004].

Thelwall, M. (2000). Commercial Web sites: lost in cyberspace? *Internet Research, 10*(2), 150-159.

Trends in the Evolution of the Public Web (2003). *D-Lib Magazine* [online], Available: www.dlib.org/dlib/april03/lavoie/04lavoie.html [accessed: November 2004].

Universal Web Site Accessibility Policy for State Web Sites – Version 4.0, (2004). State of Connecticut Web site Accessibility Committee [online], Available: www.cmac.state.ct.us/access/policies/accesspolicy40.html [accessed: December 2004].

Verisign (2002). *Guide to securing your Web site for business.* Verisign [online], Available: www.verisign.com/resources/gd/secureBusiness/secureBusiness.html [accessed: December 2004].

Xanthidis, D., & Nicholas, D. (2007). A pilot qualitative study of eCommerce practices and attitudes of medium-large companies' executives in Greece. *WSEAS Transactions on Information Science and Applications, 4*(2), 354-361.

Xanthidis, D., & Nicholas D. (2004). Evaluating internet usage and ecommerce growth in Greece. *Aslib Proceedings, 56*(6), 356-366.

Zhang, X., Keeling, B. K., & Pavur, J. R. (2000). Information Quality of commercial Web sites Home Pages: An explorative analysis. *ACM* [online], Available: portal.acm.org [accessed: November 2004].

APPENDIX

Companies: http://www.presspoint.gr/sectors.asp
(Sources: ASE (Athens Stock Exchange): companies in blue background, Presspoint.gr: companies in white background)

Sector 1:	Food, beverages and tobacco industry	Web Site
1.	Coca Cola Greece S.A.	www.cocacola.gr/
2.	Chipita International A.B.&E.E.	www.chipita.com
3.	Katseli & Sons A.B.E.E.	www.katselis.gr
4.	Eurofarma A.B.E.E.	www.evrofarma.gr
5.	CMA	www.cma-greece.gr
6.	Diageo	www.diageo.com
7.	Intercatering	www.intercatering.gr/
8.	Kraft Foods	www.kraftfoods.gr/
9.	Nestle Hellas	www.nestle.gr/online
10.	Athens Beers S.A	www.amstel.gr/
11.	Alatini S.A.	www.allatini.com.gr
12.	Vasiliou Wines	www.vassilioudomaine.gr/
13.	Delta Ice Creams S.A.	www.delta.gr/
14.	Dodoni Ice-Creams A.B.E.E	www.dodoni.com.gr/
15.	ELAIS S.A. Olive products businesses	www.elais.gr/
16.	Pedestrians Union	www.pezaunion.gr/
17.	Thraki S.A	www.thraki-sa.gr
18.	INO S.A.	www.inowines.gr/
19.	Kanakis ST. A.B.E.E.	www.stelioskanakis.gr/
20.	Kri-Kri Milk Company A.B.E.E.	www.krikri.gr/
21.	Lazaridis Wines S.A.	www.domaine-lazaridi.gr/
22.	Mevgal S.A.	www.mevgal.gr/
23.	Mega Farm	www.megafarm.gr/
24.	Melisa - Kikizas	www.melissa-kikizas.gr/
25.	Mparmpa Stathis Foods S.A.	www.geniki-trofimon.gr/
26.	Louli Mills S.A	www.loulisgroup.com
27.	Nostimo A.E.B.E	www.musses.gr/
28.	Xifias Fish S.A	www.xifias.gr/
29.	Chatzikraniotis & Sons	www.xatzikranioti.gr/
Sector 2:	Chemical industries	Web Site
1.	Veterin A.B.E.E.	www.veterin.com/
2.	PLIAS A.B.&E.E.	www.plias.gr/
3.	Druckfarben Hellas S.A.B.E.	www.druckfarben.gr/
4.	Ballis Chemicals A.E.B.E.	www.ballis.gr/profile
5.	Kerakoll Hellas	www.kerakoll.com/
6.	Neochimiki L.V. Lavrentiadis A.B.E.E.	www.neochimiki-lavrentiadis.gr/
7.	Famar S.A.	www.famar.gr/
Sector 3:	Transport equipment manufacturing	Web Site
1.	Neorion Shipyards S.A	www.neorion-shipyards.gr/
2.	Sfakianakis S.A.B.E.	www.suzuki.gr/
3.	Petropoulos, P., S.A.&B.E.	www.petropoulos.com/
4.	Hyundai Hellas	www.hyundai.gr/hyundai/
Sector 4:	Financial sector	Web Site
1.	Alpha Leasing S.A.	www.alpha.gr/introen.html

2.	Progress Funds S.A.	www.progressfund.gr/
3.	New Millennium Investments A.E.E.X.	www.newmillenniumaeex.gr/
4.	Dias fund A.E.E.X.	www.diasfund.gr
5.	Altius Investments S.A.E.X.	www.altius.gr/
6.	Credit Petropoulakis	www.credit-sec.gr/
7.	Eurocapital Financial Services	www.athenstock.com/
8.	EuroXX Finance	www.euroxx.gr/
9.	Investor ΕΠΕ	www.investor.gr/
10.	Aspis Bank	www.aspissec.gr/
11.	Eurodynamics S.A.E.X.	www.eudynamics.gr/
Sector 5:	Insurance and pension funding services	Web Site
1.	Ethniki Insurance .A.E.Γ.A.	www.ethniki-asfalistiki.gr/
2.	Agrotiki Insurances S.A.	www.agroins.com/
3.	Phoenix Metrolife S.A	www.phoenix-metrolife.com/
4.	Aspis Pronia S.A. General Insurances	www.aspis.gr/
5.	Europisti S.A.Γ.A.	www.europisti.gr/
6.	Alico AIG Life	www.alico.gr/
7.	ING Hellas	www.ing.gr/
8.	International Life Group	www.inlife.gr/
9.	Megaservice Ltd.	www.megaservice.gr/
10.	Eurobrokers S.A.	www.eurobrokers.gr/
11.	Interamerican Insurance S.A.	www.interamerican.gr/
12.	Syneteristiki ΑΕΕΓΑ	www.syneteristiki.gr/
Sector 6:	IT services	Web Site
1.	Logicdis S.A.	www.logicdis.gr
2.	Ipirotiki Software & Publications S.A.	www.ipirotiki.gr/
3.	Compucon Computer Applications A.B.E.E.	www.compucon.gr/GR/
4.	Logismos S.A.	www.logismos.gr/
5.	01 Pliroforiki A.E.	www.01p.gr/
6.	ABC Professional Services S.A.	www.abc.gr/
7.	ACE Advanced Applications S.A.	www.ace.gr/
8.	ACOM S.A.B.E.	www.acom.gr/
9.	Actis Information Systems S.A.	www.actis.gr/
10.	Active Computer Systems E.Π.E	www.active.gr
11.	Adacom S.A	www.adacom.com
12.	Ahead Rm A.E	www.aheadrm.com
13.	Algo Systems S.A.	www.algo.com.gr
14.	Alpha Grissin INFOTECH S.A.	www.alphagrissin.gr/
15.	Alpha IT S.A	www.alphait.gr/
16.	Alphyra Hellas	www.alphyra.gr/home/
17.	Altasoft	www.altasoft.gr/
18.	American Computers & Engineers Hellas S.A.	www.ace-hellas.gr/
19.	Anixter Greece Network Systems	www.anixter.gr/
20.	Apollo	www.apollo.gr/
21.	Areia S.A.	www.areianet.gr/
22.	Arion Software	www.arion.gr/
23.	Binary Logic Computers E.Π.E	www.mmpi.net/
24.	Cardisoft S.A.	www.cardisoft.gr/
25.	Datablue S.A.	www.datablue.gr
26.	Hipac S.A.B.E.	www.hipac.gr/
27.	Infomap S.A.	www.infomap.gr/
28.	Mantis IT S.A.E.	www.mantis.gr/

29.	Gnomon IT S.A.	www.gnomon.com.gr/
Sector: 7	Communications and Telecommunications Services	Web Site
1.	Vodafone – Panafon S.A.E.T.	www.vodafone.gr
2.	Forthent S.A.	www.forthnet.gr
3.	Lanet S.A.B.E.T.	www.lannet.gr/
4.	Intersat S.A.	www.intersat.gr/
5.	Algonet Telecommunications S.A	www.algonet.gr
6.	Chorus Call Hellas S.A.	www.choruscall.com/
7.	Com-Tonet S.A.	www.com-tonet.gr
8.	Cosmoline S.A.	www.cosmoline.com/
9.	Hellas Sat S.A.	www.hellas-sat.net/
10.	OTEGlobe	www.oteglobe.gr/
11.	Plural A.E.T.B.E.	www.plural.gr/
12.	Stet Hellas Telecommunications A.E.B.E	www.tim.gr/
13.	Teledome	www.teledome.gr/
14.	Telepassport Hellas	www.telepassport.gr/
15.	Tellas Telecommunications S.A	www.tellas.gr/
16.	Unitel Hellas S.A	www.unitel.gr/
17.	Uunet Hellas	www.gr.uu.net/
18.	Vivodi Telecommunications S.A	www.vivodi.gr/
19.	VoiceWeb S.A.	www.voiceWeb.gr/
20.	Winet	www.winet.gr/
21.	Newsphone Hellas A.E.E.	www.newsphone.gr/
22.	Mediatel Telephone Information S.A.	www.mediatel.gr/
23.	Cosmote Mobile Telecommunications S.A.	www.cosmote.gr/
24.	Q-Telecom	www.myq.gr/
Sector 8:	Health and social services	Web Site
1.	IASO S.A.	www.iaso.gr
2.	Euromedica S.A	www.euromedica.com.gr/
3.	Ygeia Diagnostic & Therapeutic Center, Athens S.A	www.hygeia.gr/
4.	Medicon Hellas A.E.	www.mediconsa.com/
5.	Biorehab Hellas	www.biorehab.gr/
6.	Gerolimatos Group of Companies	www.gerolymatos.gr/
7.	Thessaloniki Psychiatric Hospital	www.psychothes.gr/
Sector 9:	Media and printing (newspapers)	Web Site
1.	Lampraki Press Group S.A.	www.dol.gr/
2.	Kathimerini S.A.	www.kathimerini.gr
3.	Inform P. Lykos S.A	www.lykos.gr/
4.	Imako Media Net Group S.A.	www.imako.gr/
5.	Technical Press S.A	www.technicalpress.gr/el/
6.	Alpha Satellite TV S.A.	www.alphatv.gr/
7.	Filalthis	www.filathlos.gr/
8.	MAD TV Productions	www.mad.gr/
9.	Ellinika Grammata Publications	www.ellinikagrammata.gr/
10.	Asfalisi Net	www.asfalisinet.gr
11.	Amalthia Publications S.A	www.euro2day.gr/
12.	Alter TV S.A.	www.alter.gr/
13.	Greek Radio Television S.A.	www.ert.gr/
14.	Click FM ΕΠΕ	www.klikfm.gr/
15.	OPAP S.A.	www.opap.gr/
16.	Mega TV S.A	www.megatv.com/
17.	Alupress S.A	www.alupress.gr/

18.	Biokosmos News	www.bioshop.gr/
19.	Compupress S.A.	www.compupress.gr/
20.	Direction Publications S.A	www.direction.gr/
21.	Europress Publications	www.europress.gr/
22.	Knowledge Systems S.A.	www.business2005.gr/
23.	Metamedia	www.metohos.com
24.	Motor Press Hellas AEE	www.chip.gr/
25.	Newspaper Direct Hellas	www.newspaperdirect.gr
26.	Northmedia Publications	www.city231.gr/
27.	Option Press S.A.	www.optionpress.gr/
28.	Smartpress S.A.	www.smartpress.gr/
29.	Travel Times Publishing ΕΠΕ	www.traveltimes.gr/
Sector 10:	Metal/machinery manufacturing – Mineral and Cement	Web Site
1.	ELVAL S.A.	www.elval.gr/
2.	Metal Company Arkadias Cr. Rokas A.B.E.E.	www.rokasgroup.gr/
3.	Profil Pipe Company S.A.	www.tzirakian.com/
4.	FITCO S.A.	www.fitco.gr/
5.	S & B Industrial Minerals S.A	www.s.andb.gr/
6.	Naxos Marbles AEBE	www.naxos-marble.com/
7.	Pavlidis Marbles & Granites S.A	www.pavlidismg.com/
8.	F.H.L. H. Kyriakidis Marbles - Granites A.B.E.E.	www.fhl.gr/
9.	Betanet A.B.E.E.	www.betanet.gr/
10.	Heracles Cements Group	www.aget.gr/
11.	Iktinos Hellas S.A.	www.iktinos.gr/
12.	Mathios Refractories S.A	www.mathios.gr/
13.	Sidma S.A.	www.sidma.gr/
14.	Metka Metal Constructions Hellas S.A.	www.metka.gr/
15.	Grecian Magnesite AMBNEE	www.grecianmagnesite.com/
16.	Spider Metal Industry S.A.	www.spidersa.com/
17.	MEVACO A.B.E.E.	www.mevaco.gr/
Sector 11:	Education	Web Site
1.	Alba	www.alba.edu.gr/
2.	Alexander	www.alexanderinst.gr/
3.	Andim	www.andim.gr/
4.	Business Training Center	www.btc.com.gr/
5.	Centre of European Management Studies (CEMS)	www.cems.gr/
6.	Compact S.A.	www.compact.gr/
7.	Delta Singular Training S.A.	www.ds-training.gr/
8.	Didacta Training Group	www.didacta.gr/
9.	ECDL Hellas S.A.	www.ecdl.gr/
10.	Icon International Training	www.icon.gr/
11.	Infotest	www.certification.gr/
12.	Inte*learn	www.intelearn.gr/
13.	ITEC S.A.	www.itec.edu/
14.	New York College	www.nyc.gr/
15.	Proseed	www.proseed.gr/
16.	Akmi IEK	www.iek-akmi.gr/
17.	American College, Hellas	www.acg.edu/
18.	Xinis Educational Group	www.xinis.com/
19.	Crete Educational Institutes	www.sport-tourism.com/
20.	Aegean University	www.aegean.gr/
21.	Omiros Training Group	www.omiros.gr/

22.	Futurekids S.A S.A.	www.futurekids.edu.gr/
23.	Piraeuos University, Department of Industrial Management and Technology	www.tex.unipi.gr/
Sector 12:	Retail	Web Site
1.	Atlantic Supermarket A.E.E	www.atlantic.gr/
2.	Duty Free Shops, Greece S.A.	www.dutyfreeshops.gr/
3.	Promota Hellas S.A	www.promota.gr/
4.	AS Company S.A.	www.ascompany.gr/index.jsp
5.	Expert Suppliers S.A.	www.experthellas.gr/
6.	Glorybook-Economist Co.,Ε.Π.Ε.	www.glorybook.gr/
7.	Metro AEBE	www.metro.com.gr/
8.	Metropolis	www.metropolis.gr/
9.	Moda Bagno N. Varveris S.A.	www.modabagno.gr/
10.	Multirama A.B.E.E.	www.multirama.gr/
11.	Oriflame	www.oriflame.gr/
12.	Sara Lee Coffee and Tea Hellas S.A.	www.bravo.gr/
13.	Tupperware Hellas S.A.	www.tupperware.gr/
14.	Vadas A.E.B.E.E.	www.vardas.gr/
15.	Vassilias S.A.	www.vassilias.gr/
16.	Eikona – Ixos A.E.E	www.e-h.gr/
17.	Electornici Athens A.E.E.	www.electroniki.gr/
18.	Interflora S.A	www.interflora.gr/
19.	Kotsobolos A.E.B.E.	www.kotsovolos.gr
20.	Marinopoulos Group	www.marinopoulos.gr/
21.	Plaisio Computers A.E.B.E.	www.plaisio.gr/
22.	Hatzigeorgiou S.A	www.hatz.gr/
Sector 13:	Tourism [Hotels]	Web Site
1.	Louis Hotels	www.louishotels.com/
2.	Loutraki Club Hotel Casino	www.clubhotelloutraki.gr/
3.	Metropolitan Hotel	www.chandris.gr/
4.	Park Hotel Athens	www.athensparkhotel.gr/
5.	Rodos Park Suites Hotel	www.rodospark.gr/
6.	Astir Palace Vouliagmenis A.Ξ.E.	www.astir.gr/
7.	GEKE S.A.	www.president.gr/
8.	Divans Hotels Group	www.divanis.gr/
9.	Ioniki Hotels S.A.	www.ionianhe.gr/
10.	Capsis Tourist Group S.A.	www.capsis.gr/
11.	Porto Carras	www.portocarras.com/
Sector 14:	Government	Web Site
1.	Greek Parliament	www.parliament.gr
2.	National Administration Center	www.ekdd.gr
3.	Peiraias District	www.nomarhiapeiraia.gr
4.	Ministry of development	www.ypan.gr
5.	Ministry of foreign affairs	www.mfa.gr
Sector 15:	Business services	Web Site
1.	Promaxon S.A	www.procom.gr/
2.	Forever Print Recycling	www.foreverprint.gr/
3.	Euroconsultants S.A	www.euroconsultants.com.gr

Section VI
Case Studies on E-Commerce in DCs

Chapter XV
Electronic Commerce Reality in Tunisia

Jameleddine Ziadi
Jendouba University, Tunisia

Abderrazzak Ben Salah
University of Tunis El Manar, Tunisia

ABSTRACT

This chapter has as an aim the identification of the present reality of the e-commerce activity in Tunisia and the challenges its faces. After giving an overview on the e-commerce birth in the country, it focuses on two distinct experiences: First, the e-commerce transactions via the Tunisian Post Office (known as the ONP) and secondly the e-commerce operations via the Banking Association (known as the SMT). While exploring the general scheme of the two different techniques notably concerning the relation with the merchants' commercial Websites (CWS), it gives statistics related to the evolution of transactions in this field. We depart from that point to discuss the general situation of the Tunisian e-commerce activity, to explore the problems it faces and to give potential solutions for its real expansion and development in the country. In this regard, we believe that the spread of use of bank cards and other forms of electronic payments would make citizens used to those forms and would constitute therefore the real takeoff point of the e-commerce activity.

INTRODUCTION

The world economic activity is based on exchange in different fields and sectors (exchange of products, services, information, etc.). Due to the increasing use of computer and telecommunication networks, the electronic commerce has become a market reality with a considerable turnover (about 300 000 US $ of turnover per minute in international electronic commerce).

Copyright © 2009, IGI Global, distributing in print or electronic forms without written permission of IGI Global is prohibited.

This new kind of commerce is progressively replacing the traditional commercial methods and is currently the essential tool of communication between individuals and enterprises in all over the world.

The electronic commerce consists in the use of computer (hardware and software) means and telecommunication networks (Internet being the reference network) to buy and sell goods and services. In order to do these commercial exchanges (operations of buying/selling), there must be a third party of trust to guarantee those kind of transactions that are made through the Internet network and not face to face as in the traditional commerce. This third party can be a financial institution or an administrative institution and would have therefore a crucial role in ensuring electronic transactions.

In this regard, Tunisia was among the few African countries which began the execution of transactions and electronic payments via the Internet. Tunisia was also the first Arab country to be connected to this worldwide network and the use of Internet has been since generalized to all citizen categories. Special measures (such as the "family PC initiative" that consists in offering special prices to private citizens) has increased the number of Internet users. Also, the spread of public Internet spaces ("*publinets*") has participated in this growth. Besides, strong competition between Tunisian Internet service providers (the existence of different connection kinds has helped to increase this competition) and the improvement of telecommunication infrastructure, have participated in improving the quality of services (High flow of the Internet (*ADSL*) has permitted rapid navigation and file downloads).

The universities, the administrations under State-control and especially the private enterprises were the first to get benefit from this new technological reality by creating static Websites at the beginning and dynamic ones after that, and this in order to improve services offered to their customers. Among these enterprises, we note mainly banks and commercial enterprises that were rapid to improve their B to C (Business to Consumer) services in order to participate in the new communication methods and take therefore their place in the electronic market.

Also, Tunisia was pioneer in the jurisdiction concerning electronic commerce. Indeed, several decrees regarding this field were established and the creation of the ANSE (*Agence Nationale des Certification Electronique*) in 2000 and the ANSI (*Agence Nationale de Sécurité Informatique*) in 2001, have also played a positive role in the coordination of the electronic commerce activity in the country.

THE BIRTH OF THE ELECTRONIC COMMERCE IN TUNISIA

The first step towards the expansion of the e-commerce activity in Tunisia took place at the University. The first e-commerce experiences were carried out in the ISET campus (*Institut Supérieur de l'Enseignement Technologique en Télécommunications*) and in the EST campus (*Ecole Supérieure des Télécommunications*). These two institutions are under the joint direction of the Ministry of Communication and Technology and the Ministry of High Education. Students were invited to make their inscriptions at the university on line by using electronic cards for payment (through the E-Dinar service created by the Tunisian Post in 2000); this experience has been very successful. Since then, The Ministry of High Education extended this new way of on-line inscriptions to all students and university institutions.

The Tunisian Post Initiative

The Tunisian Post, known as the ONP (*Office National des Postes*) had the intention to profit from this experience and enlarge the same technological infrastructure in the trade sector since it is the owner of the electronic payment system, posses the databases of E-Dinar cards and is responsible of their creation.

The first commercial Website (CWS) of the ONP had as an objective to assure electronic payments of the gas and electricity consumption bills (of the STEG: *Société Tunisienne d'Electricité et du Gaz*), of telecommunication bills (of the *Tunisie Télécom*), of water consumption bills (of the SONEDE: *Société Nationale d'Eau et de Distribution d'Eau*) and also the on-line purchase of Internet connection cards. The ONP initiated these activities using the Web site: http://www.fatouranet.poste.tn.

But the real CWS of the ONP was done through the site "*fleurs de la poste*" (http: //www.e-fleurs.poste.tn) that was a real commercial activity consisting in selling flowers online (that's to say the real B to C: the customer buys the product, pays on line and then he receives the product at home).

Description of the General Scheme of E-Commerce Transactions via the ONP

The customer is not in direct relationship with the ONP as described in Figure 1 (the only case in which the ONP is the third party of trust is when it is at the same time the merchant; that is when the customer wants to purchase flowers through the Website that belongs to the ONP (http: //www.e-fleurs.poste.tn). Nevertheless, even in the case when the customer is in a relation with another merchant's Website, and although he does not perceive the presence of the ONP, the latter remains always active and thanks to it the electronic payments are assured.

The Connection Between the CWS of the Merchant and the Server of the ONP via Internet

In every CWS of any merchant, there must be installed the M kit (a software designed by the ONP engineers). As illustrated in Figure 2, this M kit is responsible of the secured connection with the principal server of the ONP and guarantees the authenticity of the CWS of merchants (by exchanging some parameters with the Kit server installed in the principal server of the ONP).

The data exchanges between the merchant's CWS and the ONP must pass through a fire wall to filter all accesses to the principal server of the ONP according to the kind of the electronic card used for payment (post card or bank card). The requests go through another fire wall before reaching the database server of the E-Dinar cards or other.

If a bank card is used in payment, the verification of its data is transferred via a private bank server to the SMT (*Société Monétique de Tunisie*), which is an association that includes all Tunisian banks and the ONP).

Figure 1. General scheme of e-commerce transaction via the ONP

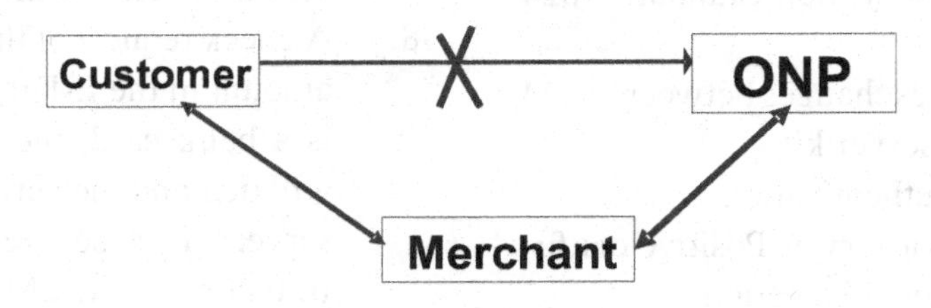

Figure 2. Global path of the connection between the merchant's CWS and the ONP via the Internet

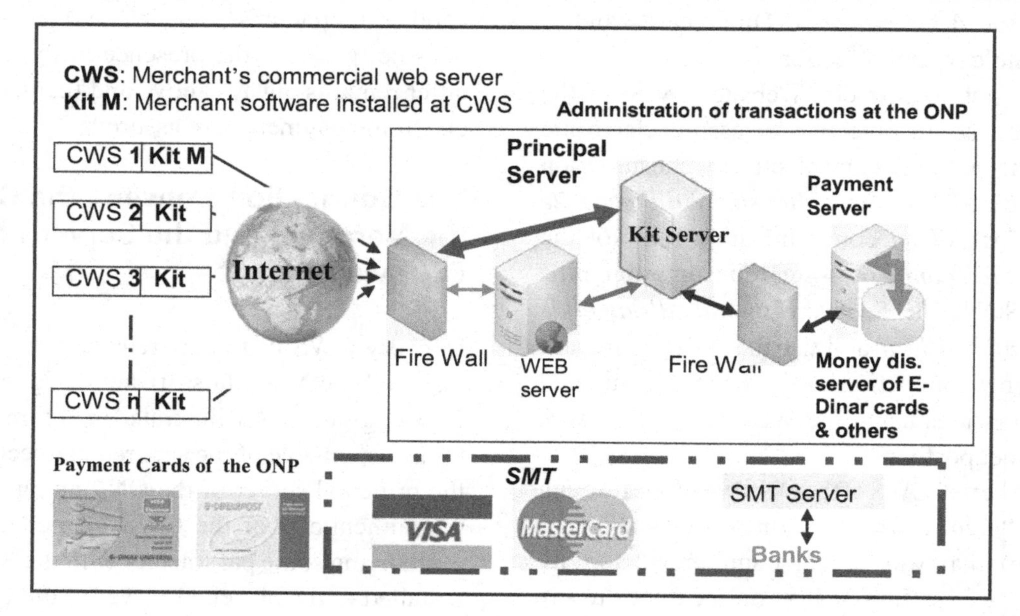

Steps of an Electronic Payment Transaction Between the Customer and the Merchant

1. Visit of the CWS and choice of product(s) or service(s), creation of the chosen products' order, typing of the payment card, verification of information on the final form and finally the making of the order (in http mode)
2. Connection TCP/IP of the CWS through the M kit (of Plug in type, special scripts, installed by the ONP) with the ONP principal server (server Kit) in SSL secured mode (Secure Session Layer) with encoding data by DES (Data Encryption Standard 1024 bits) for:
   - Parameters exchanges between the M kit and the server kit
   - Merchant authentication
3. Response of the kit server: Positive confirmation or cancelled connection
4. Web page display in secured mode Https (SSL) through a merchant certificate obtained from an authority of certification (international "Verisign", another authority or the National Agency of Electronic Certification *(ANCE)*), RSA encryption -128 Bytes- to insert the payment card number and the confidential code.
5. Reading of the displayed information, insertion of the payment card number and the confidential code before validating.
6. Data insertion in the merchant's database (without the customer's card number) to reach the purchase action.
7. Data redirection towards the ONP payment server to achieve the transaction.
8. A check request of the card validity and the amount in the E-Dinar cards database. If it is a bank card, the ONP principal server will demand the verification from the SMT server via a secured private connection. In that case, the SMT will use its banking server.

The ONP can manage transactions through VISA cards and MasterCard with a special server attested by VISA.

9. Response (confirmation or cancellation),
10. Response results display:
    - False card number, new number required
    - Bad confidential code, new code required
    - Not enough money, transaction cancelled
    - Payment authorization: The displayed page is a proof that the payment was achieved (printing of that page to save it as a proof if there would be any litigation, a kind of payment invoice of the product(s))
11. End of transaction, redirection towards the merchant's Web site (this step is not shown in Figure 3, it's a sort of marketing action to encourage the customer to buy more products from the same Web site).

Survey of Transactions Made by the ONP

The purchases are directly displayed on the screen of the merchant's Web server and he is obliged to provide the product(s) to the customer at the delivery address (according to the customer choice when filling the order).

The merchant can display and manage all his transactions via a Web interface due to his login and password and the transaction numbers (reference of the validate order – step 6 – saving in his database, see Figure 3).

The day after transactions are reached by the ONP, the service concerned in the administrative direction of the SMT sends by post a paper of transaction inventory to the merchant for account-

Figure 3. Transaction and electronic payment process between the customer and the merchant via the ONP

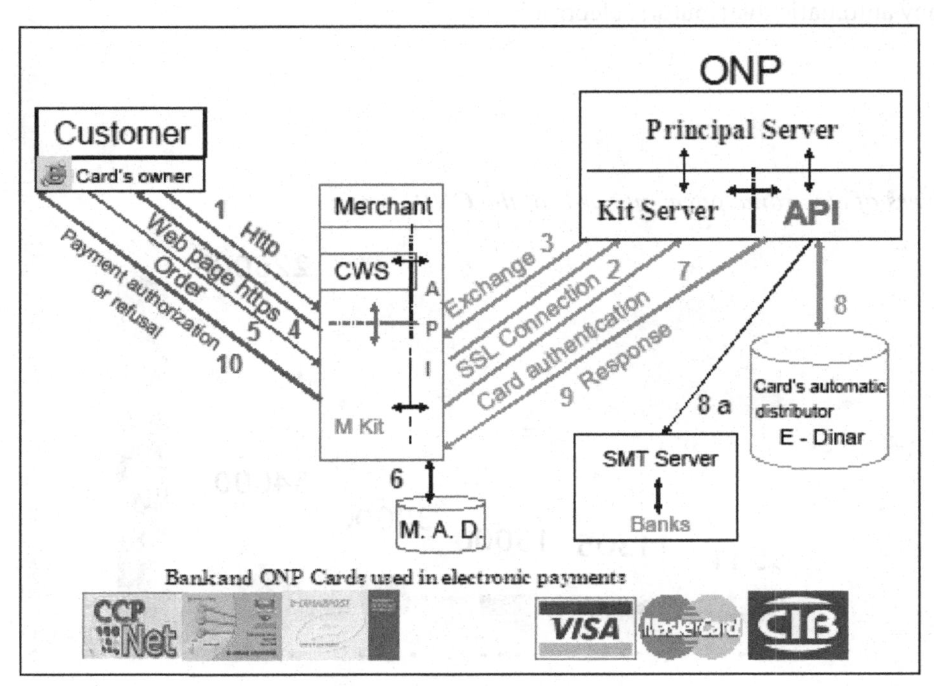

ing. The money is debited from the customer's account and deposited in the merchant's account (if he has a post account), otherwise by a bank transfer order to his bank.

If there's any connection problem (break in the tenth step with a payment authorization), the customer must claim to the ONP (that he did not watch the payment confirmation) to have a proof of transaction (if the money was really debited from his account); the ONP must also give to the customer an invoice related to the transaction (via e-mail or post).

STATISTICS RELATED TO THE ONP CARD

Card Types and Users' Evolution

The ONP has created many types of payment cards in order to satisfy card users. The E-Dinar card can be a kind of electronic pocket-money and can play the role of a prepaid card, it is anonymous and multi-functional. The card of the electronic Dinar *"universel"* is like an ordinary bank card used in money automatic distributors, electronic payments and the Internet. This card is rechargeable and especially secured by a confidential code and a personal password.

The number of cards' users has increased drastically, from 3541 in 2001 to 226000 in October 2006 as shown in the following figure.

Benefits of Electronic Payments via the ONP

The benefits of this new way of payment have touched many categories and many fields. The following lines highlight some of these benefits:

- 332000 university inscriptions
- 16700 driving licensees
- 7900 Hand/Foot games (selling of tickets)
- 2000 invoice payments: *STEG/SONEDE/TELECOM*
- 390 handicraft shops,
- 136 travel agencies,
- 60 CWS (of merchants online).

Figure 5 shows the rapid increase of electronic payments via the ONP

Figure 4. Users of electronic payment cards of the ONP

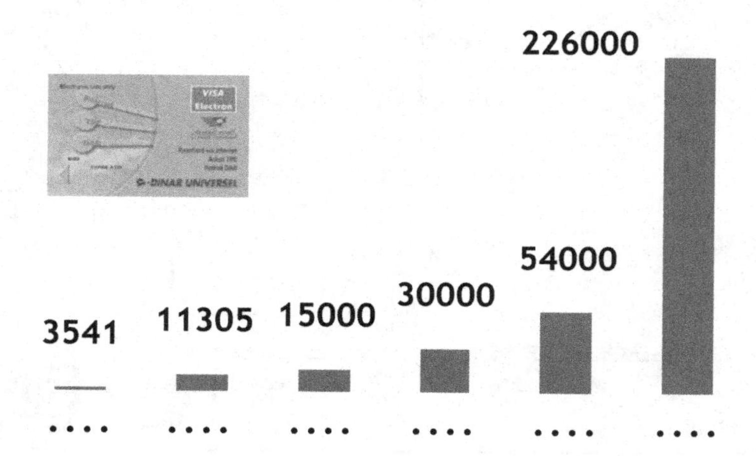

DESCRIPTION OF THE GENERAL SCHEME OF AN E-COMMERCE TRANSACTION VIA THE SMT

Contrary to the process of transactions via the ONP in which the customer is not connected directly to the ONP Web site, in this case however, and as it is illustrated in Figure 6, the customer is connected to the SMT server at the beginning of the electronic payment.

The Connection Between the Merchant's CWS and the SMT Server via Internet

Using a navigator, the customer can connect to the CWS of any chosen merchant, as it is illustrated in the figure below. After the choice of one or more products and at the moment of the order and payment, the customer is redirected to a secured server (named the SPS: *Serveur de Payment Sécurisé*) of the SMT where the data of his bank card will be verified. After that the merchant will be informed about the achievement of the transaction.

The following figure shows the steps of the electronic payment transaction via the SMT.

The Steps of Achieving an Electronic Payment Transaction Between the Customer and the Merchant via the SMT

1. Purchase and validation of the order in the merchant's Web site
2. Redirection towards the payment page of the SMT' SPS server
3. Typing of the bank card data
4. Treatment at the SMT server level
5. An authorization request from the bank to the buyer
6. A response return to the SPS: Payment authorization or not (typing error of the card number, code or not enough money)
7. Sending of the payment authorization result to the merchant and the customer

The Authentication Steps of the Merchant's Website by the SMT

1. The order validation by the customer produces a request of payment by the merchant to the SMT
2. The SPS server verifies the validity of the received information

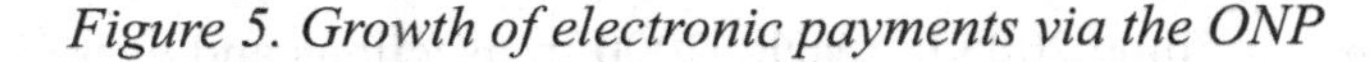

Figure 5. Growth of electronic payments via the ONP

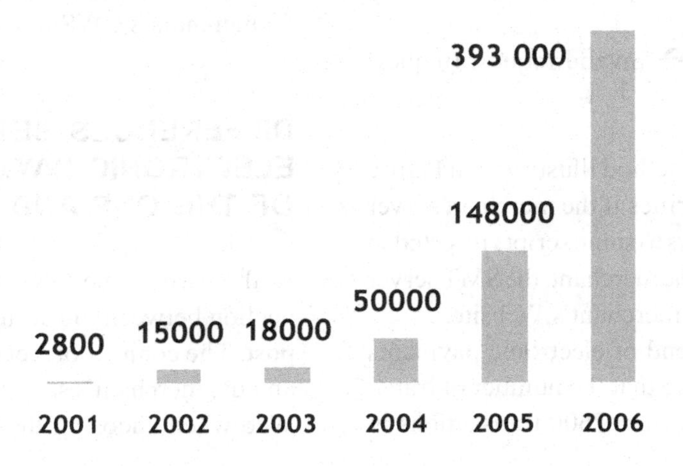

Figure 6. General scheme of the e-commerce transaction via the SMT

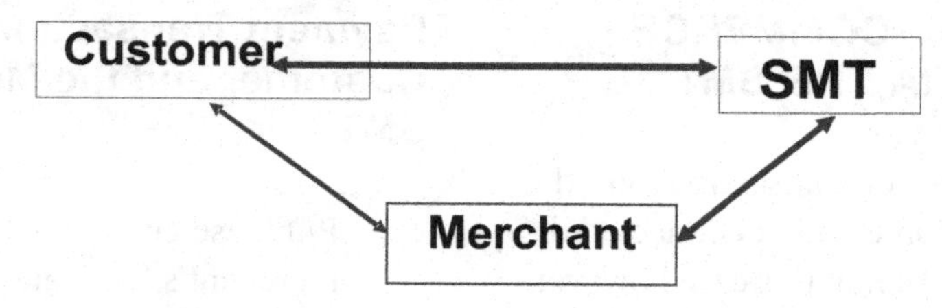

Figure 7. Running of electronic payment transaction between the customer and the merchant via the SMT

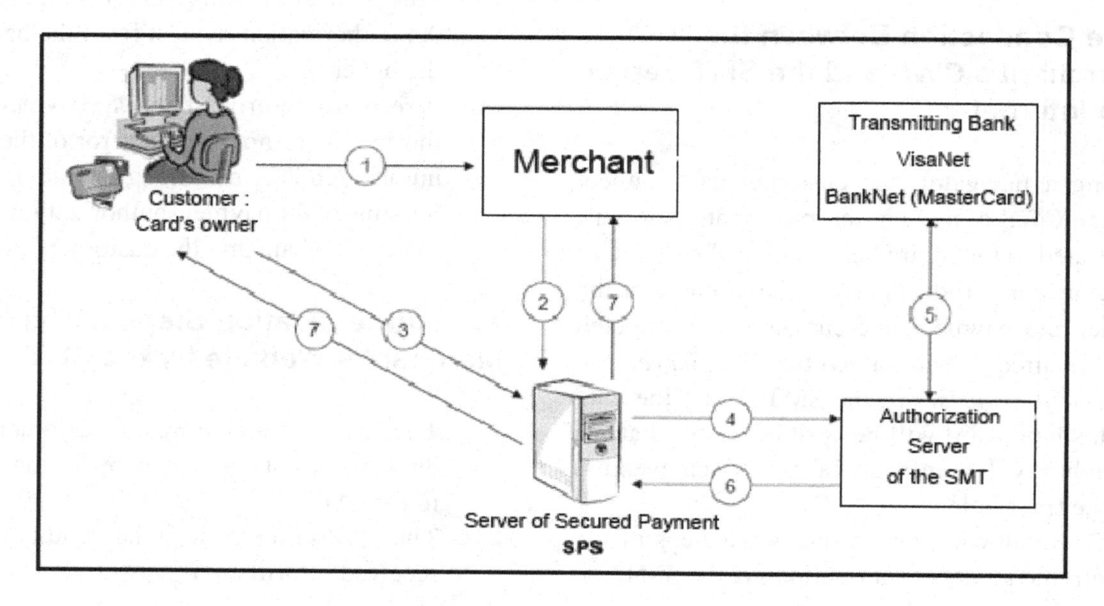

Valid information ➔ a payment authorization request

Invalid information ➔ invalid request (request cancellation)

By the Call Back method illustrated in Figure 8, the SMT server verifies if the merchant server is the right one. Thanks to some scripts inserted in the Web site pages of the merchant, the SMT server is able to certify this merchant's Website.

Looking at the trend of electronic payments via the SMT, we notice that the number of transactions has increased from 7600 transactions in June 2005 to reach 52000 transactions and over 50 merchant's CWS in October 2006.

DIFFERENCES BETWEEN THE ELECTRONIC PAYMENT SYSTEM OF THE ONP AND THE SMT

In the case of the ONP, there is no direct connection between the customer post and the ONP post. The connection between the customer post and the merchant's server is in http mode via the Web when choosing the product(s) and is done

Figure 8. Merchant's Website authentication by the SMT

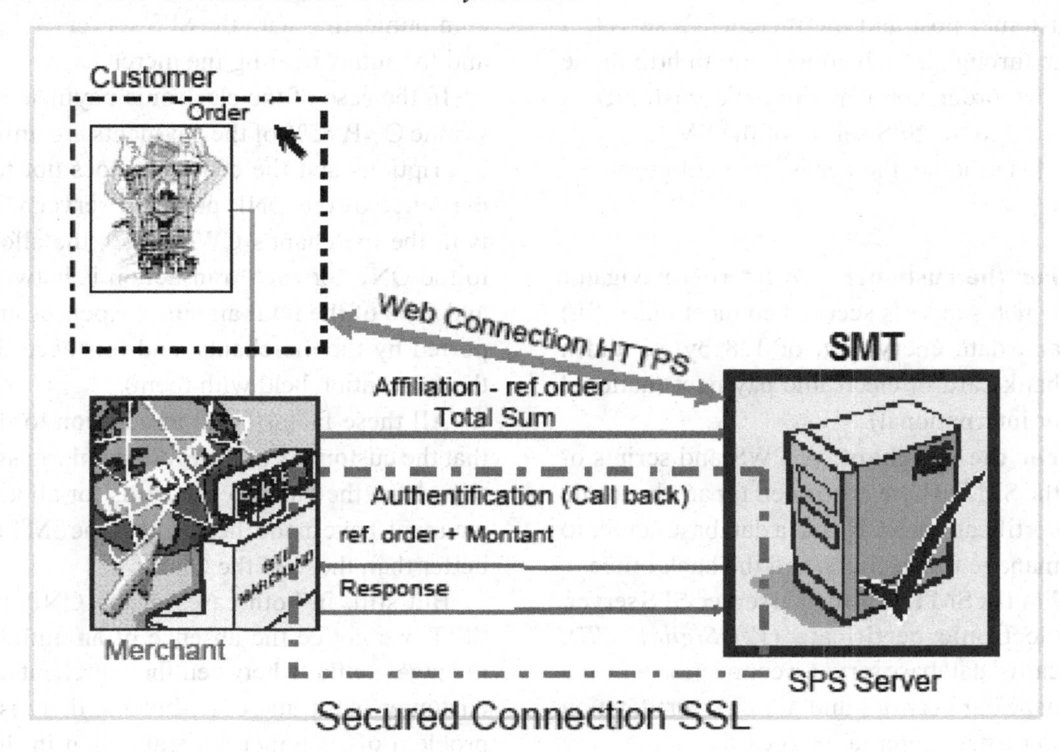

through a Web secured connection in http mode (SSL) with RSA data encryption (128 bytes). For that, the merchant must have an electronic certificate to ensure such connection. The confidential data of the customer (number of the payment card and confidential code) are not saved by the merchant. Concerning the connection between the merchant's server and the ONP server, it is a TCP/IP secured connection in SSL mode with DES encryption (1024 bytes), and is done through an M kit software application installed in the merchant's server.

In this scheme, the necessary configurations are:

- **For the customer:** An Internet navigator which supports the secured connections (SSL) and the data encryption of 128 bytes; and a post or bank card of electronic payment (national or international).
- **For the merchant:** A CWS, M Kit software, an electronic certificate (*ANCE*) and a database server to manage transactions and back office.
- **For the ONP:** A principal server, A Kit server, an electronic certificate (*VeriSign/ANCE*), a database server, E-Dinar cards and a VISA Certificate to manage international cards.

In the case of the SMT, there are three-dimensional connections: The connection between the customer post and the SMT server is done through a Web secured connection in http mode (SSL) with RSA data encryption (128 bytes). The connection between the merchant's server and the SMT server is done through the CWS. It is a secured connection SSL (Electronic certificate VeriSign/ANCE) and some scripts are inserted by the SMT in the merchant's Web site pages to authenticate the merchant. Concerning the connection between the customer post and the merchant's server, it is done through a Web connection in http mode and after order confirmation; the customer is redirected to the SPS server of the SMT.

In this scheme, the necessary configurations are:

- **For the customer:** An internet navigator which supports secured connections (SSL) and data encryption of 128 bytes; and a bank card of electronic payment (national or international).
- **For the merchant:** A CWS and scripts of the SMT. There is no need for an electronic certificate (ANCE) and a database server to manage transactions and the back office
- **For the SMT:** A principal server, SPS server, electronic certificate (*VeriSign/ANCE*), cards' database server, a connection with the banking network and a VISA certification to manage international cards.

LESSONS LEARNT FROM THE CASE STUDIES: THE RESULTS AND LIMITATIONS

The ONP is the first actor in the e-commerce field in Tunisia (since 2001), the SMT activity begun later in June 2005. There is more security in the electronic payment system via the ONP than via the SMT. However, the electronic payment system via the SMT is more flexible. Indeed, the merchant who works with the ONP must have an electronic certificate (from the *ANCE* or from the *VeriSign*). In the case of SMT, merchants do not need such a certificate. Also, on the merchant's CWS of the ONP, there must be installed the M Kit - it takes much time to install it according to the enterprise's network architecture, the number of the staff, the operating system, the different applications, etc.-. In the case of the SMT, only some scripts must be inserted in the merchant's Web site pages for communicating with the SPS server of the SMT and for authenticating the merchant.

In the case of the electronic payment system via the ONP, 85% of the payments are university inscriptions and the customer does not feel the existence of the ONP payment server when he is in the merchant's CWS. Also, the allowance to the ONP for each transaction is between 5% and 10% of the total amount (expenses are supported by the merchants, and this according to the convention held with them).

All these factors, and in addition to the fact that the customers of the SMT -banking association- have the habit to use cards for all kinds of payment, have made the results of the SMT clearly better than those of the ONP.

But still, in both cases of the ONP and the SMT, we notice the absence of an authority to manage conflicts between the merchant and the customer in a fraud case. Indeed, there is a real problem of customer authentication in the case of a potential fraud. We notice also a lack of jurisdiction in the electronic payment field in general and a reluctance of acceptance of print screen and e-mails as a proof for accounting in addition to the absence of judges specialized in this particular field.

CONCLUDING

At the technical level, in spite of the possibility to do electronic payments and transactions via the Internet network (it works well with the ONP and the SMT), the turnover remains, however, far away from the merchants' expectations (and this in comparison with the turnover obtained with traditional commercial ways).

Some time is needed, however, since this is only the beginning of the electronic commerce in Tunisia. Much more efforts must be done by the government to encourage this new way of living by inciting citizens to use bank cards or other means of payment in order to have the habit not to use always cash money. Then, accordingly, electronic payment via the Internet would increase.

The professionals in this field can also play an important role in encouraging the citizens to buy and sell via the Internet. Indeed, it is really a big market and there is a lot of money to earn (Currently, about 300 000 US $ of turnover per minute in international electronic commerce).

The bankers must find solutions (such as free cards) in order to encourage more citizens to use bank cards, because in our opinion this represents the real takeoff point of the e-commerce (that is the habit to use bank cards; it must be indeed a national custom). In the United States, for instance, bank cards were used since the twenties of the last century and in Europe since the sixties.

The merchants must carry much more efforts for better use of technologies in order to increase sales via the Internet, and this for example by making discounts for online buyers since it is still a new market open to them.

Concerning the technological level, Tunisian competencies (engineers of computer networks, programmers and software developers, specialists of computer security, etc...) have shown that they possess the same know-how of their counterparts in developed countries (The United States, Europe, etc.).

Generally, despite the general lack of positive results in the field of Tunisian e-commerce, we are very optimistic concerning its future since there is a real political desire for spreading the use of new technologies in all sectors (there would be therefore more jurisdictions able to fill in the present vacuum). There must be however better awareness in all fields related to e-commerce to the importance of encouraging customers to use this technology since they represent the basis of the development of this new way of trade.

REFERENCES

Andrieu, O., & Lafont D. (1996). *Internet et l'Entreprise*, Paris: Editions Eyrolles.

Annual reports of the National Office of Posts, Tunis: ONP Publication

Bernstein,T., Bhimani, A.B., Schultz, E., & Siegel, C. (1997). *Sécurité Internet pour l'Entreprise*, Paris: International Thomson Publishing.

Bordage, S. (2001). *Conduite de Projet Web*, Paris: Editions Eyrolles.

Chernaouti, H.S. (2000). *Sécurité Internet, Stratégies et Technologies*, Paris: Editions Dunod.

Danda, M. (2001). *La Sécurité sur leWeb*, Paris: Microsoft Press.

JORT: Official Journal of the Republic of Tunisia: Various Articles; notably: Law n° 2000-57 (June, 13, 2000), JORT n° 48 p.1456; and Law n° 2000-83 (August, 9, 2000), JORT n° 64 p. 1887.

Kaplan, D. (2000). *Guide du Commerce Electronique* , Paris: Editions Servidit.

Langlois, M., & Gasch, S. (2001). *Le Commerce Electronique B to B de l' EDI à l'Internet*, Paris: Editions Dunod.

Macdonnel, J., & Perkins, D. W. (1996). *L'avantage Internet pour l'Entreprise*, Paris: Editions Dunod.

Marchand, R., Agnoux, H., & Chiaramonti, C. (1999). *Applications EDI sur l'Internet, Commerce Electronique B to B* , Paris: Editions Eyrolles.

Monteiro da Rocha, P., & Boutain, F. (2000). *Net Entreprises réussir on line,* Paris: Compus Press.

Reboul, P. (1999). *Le guide du Commerce Electronique*, Paris: Publi-U-Editions.

Reboul, P., & Xardel ,D. (1997). *Commerce Electronique*, Paris: Editions Eyrolles.

Ziadi, J. (2005). Vers une approche originale de la pratique e-manageriale pour les entreprises Tunisiennes. *International Journal of Management and Technologies, 1*, 137-158.

Chapter XVI
Electronic Commerce in China: Can We Wake Up the Giant?

Hongxiu Li
Turku School of Economics, Finland

Reima Suomi
Turku School of Economics, Finland

ABSTRACT

This chapter introduces the four sets of prerequisites for successful electronic commerce (e-commerce) development, including national factors, related and supporting industries, firm strategy, structure and rivalry factors and demand conditions. It introduces the present condition of e-commerce development in China and explores the four sets of prerequisites in China. It aims to find the influential factors which impede e-commerce development in China. In this chapter, a four-level approach is taken, in accordance with the four sets of prerequisites of e-commerce development. The four aspects are mirrored against the current situation in China, and some suggestions are put forward on the four aspects. Understanding the e-commerce development in China based on the four sets of prerequisites of e-commerce development can offer some guidance to less developed countries, which have the similar conditions in their e-commerce development.

INTRODUCTION

China might not be a typical less developed country, but it is a very convincing "living laboratory". Even though the total resources of China are huge compared with all other less developed countries, the huge size of the country is a big challenge for all aspects of development. Resources per capita are not necessarily any larger than in many other less developed countries. If the Chinese can turn e-commerce into a success story, it should not be a "mission impossible" even for smaller, less

Copyright © 2009, IGI Global, distributing in print or electronic forms without written permission of IGI Global is prohibited.

developed countries. To wield a mariner phrase, smaller ships should be even faster to turn around if needed.

E-commerce in China has grown at an astonishing rate since 1993 when the Chinese government took the first step towards implementing electronic commerce (e-commerce) through a series of "golden projects". According to the 20th statistical survey report on the Internet development in China released by China Internet Network Information Centre (CNNIC), the number of Internet users in China has reached 162 million and the number of Websites has arrived at 918,000 by the end of June in 2007 (CNNIC, 2007).

E-commerce in China is multiplying almost as fast as Internet users in China. According to the survey conducted by iResearch centre in China, the revenue generated in business-to-business (B2B) e-commerce in China has arrived at $169 billion in 2006, which takes nearly 95% of the total e-commerce avenue in China in 2006 (iResearch, 2007). The Chinese e-commerce market will continue to expand and perhaps total as much as $654.3 billion by 2010 (CCID, 2006). In China, B2B is still the main e-commerce model, and business-to-consumer (B2C) and consumer-to-consumer (C2C) takes a small size in the e-commerce market.

E-commerce development in China is in line with the rate of adoption theory and the industry life cycle theory, which describes the IT diffusion process as initially proceeding through a slow, gradual growth period, followed by dramatic and rapid growth, then gradual stabilization (Klepperer & Graddy, 1990). Currently, the U.S. is still the largest global Internet market, which takes nearly half of the global Internet market. Analysts predict that with the second largest user population and double-digit economic growth, China could potentially take the place of the U.S. to become the largest Internet market in the world (Du, 2006).

Though e-commerce in China has developed in the past several years, it falls behind some developed countries because of various obstacles. There is a call for research on the obstacles and useful strategies to help China to live up to its great potential in e-commerce and catch the developed countries.

Our research question is

What are the prerequisites for China to implement successful electronic commerce?

This chapter discusses the current condition of e-commerce development from four perspectives – the national factors; related and supporting industries; the strategy and structure and rivalry factors of the firm; and the conditions of demand. It aims at finding the barriers in e-commerce development in China from these four perspectives. In this chapter, a four-level approach is taken in accordance with the four sets of prerequisites of e-commerce development. The four aspects are mirrored against the current situation in China, and some suggestions are put forward on the four aspects to push e-commerce development and live up to its potential. This study focuses on e-commerce development in China. It offers some guidance on e-commerce development for less developed countries, which have similar conditions in their e-commerce development. The study is based on a literature study and contains no direct own empirical research.

FACTORS INFLUENCING E-COMMERCE DEVELOPMENT

E-commerce is a newly developed industry in the world. Its development has been influenced by different factors. As Porter (1998) identifies in his "National Diamond of Competitive Advantage", there are four sets of prerequisites for a successful national industry development: national factors; related and supporting industries; firm strategy, structure and rivalry; and demand conditions (Porter, 1998). The theoretical context of the four

Table 1. Factors influencing e-commerce development

The Porter factors	Our list for e-commerce
National factors	Telecommunications infrastructure Government regulations Talent supply
Related and supporting industries	Payment systems Logistics systems
Firm strategy, structure and rivalry	Managing and organizing e-commerce
Demand conditions	Consumer demand for e-commerce Business demand for e-commerce

sets of prerequisites introduced by Porter (1998) can explain e-commerce development in China as well. For e-commerce, we interpret the Porter factors as follows, based on an exploratory study of the basic factors in the four sets of prerequisites in e-commerce development in the literature review, summarized in Table 1.

National factors mainly refer to the infrastructure, talent and the related regulations in e-commerce industry, which are closely connected with the state strategies and measures. The related and supporting industries of e-commerce are mainly connected with the presence of the associated logistics and financial industries. The strategy, structure and rivalry of the firm denote how companies are managing and organizing their business to push e-commerce. Demand conditions refer to the nature of the demand for e-commerce products or services, where consumer and business demand form two distant areas (Chen & Ning, 2002). The four sets of prerequisites are vital for the e-commerce development in China. In our paper we establish an e-commerce system, which illustrates the roles of the four sets of prerequisites in e-commerce development in China, including national factors, related and supporting industries, firm strategy, structure and rivalry factors and demand conditions. Our following discussion on the e-commerce development in China is based on the four perspectives in e-commerce.

METHODOLOGY

This research aims to explore the issue on e-commerce development in China, including its current development, constraints and its future developing strategies from national perspective, related and supporting industries, firm strategy, structure and rivalry and demand perspective. In this chapter both qualitative and quantitative approaches have been employed. The study issue is investigated based on qualitative information and early evidence related to e-commerce in China. Our research is exploratory in nature. In the study we have also used some quantitative data related to e-commerce in China, including some past empirical researches related to e-commerce. The main sources are the statistical survey reports on e-commerce from CNNIC, iResearch, and some other governmental organizations or research centres in China.

ANALYSIS OF E-COMMERCE IN CHINA

E-commerce development requires mutual efforts from government, related and supporting industries, firm strategy, structure and rivalry, and demand. Their various roles in e-commerce development cannot be ignored.

The National Factors Perspective

Economic development has become a major goal for Chinese government. The Chinese government regards information technology (IT) as a new point of economic growth of the national economy. It welcomes the potential economic gains that e-commerce and the Internet bring to the Chinese economy and tries to propel the development of e-commerce in China by establishing the infrastructure, cultivating demanded talents and issuing regulations related to e-commerce (Haley, 2002)

Telecommunications Infrastructure

In China, the Chinese government has put effort into building its technical infrastructure to push e-commerce. Since 1993, a series of "Golden Projects" funded by the Chinese government have been implemented in China, e.g., Golden Bridge, Golden Gate, Golden Card, Golden Tax and so on (Chen, Gillenson et al. 2002). The Chinese electronics and telecommunication industry has developed quickly from 2000 to 2005. Its avenue has increased rapidly, taking nearly 8.8 per cent of the GDP growth in China in 2005. China Telecoms, the largest company in the telecommunications industry, has made great progress in its service during the past 10 years. Its cable network has increased to 4.259 million square kilometres in 2006, and its community of Internet users has also increased greatly in the past several years, comprising leased line connections, dial-up connections, broadband, and mobile connections (MII, 2007). According to CNNIC statistics, the total international bandwidth of China reached 312,346 M by the end of June in 2007, with an increase of 45.8 per cent as compared to 2006 (CNNIC, 2007). In China, dial-up and leased line connections are shrinking, while broadband connections have stably maintained their leading position.

In China the telecommunication market is held by the state-owned four companies: China Telecom, China Mobile, China Unicom and China Netcom. No foreign and private enterprises are permitted to get into the market. A strong monopoly has been created in telecommunication market, which results in the high service fee with less satisfied service in telecommunication industry. Complaints to the services of telecommunication industry can be listed as the top ten complaints in China every year. It is a big issue to deal with in e-commerce development, since good Internet service is one of the basic requirements of e-commerce.

Though the Chinese government has put great efforts into infrastructure construction, an imbalance in infrastructure construction in various areas exists in China. The infrastructure in large cities is better than in the countryside, and in areas with better economic development, better than in the areas where it is slow. For example, in West China, its economic development is falling behind that in the east, south and north of China, and its infrastructure construction is also falling behind in other areas.

In spite of the significant progress of technical infrastructure for e-commerce in China, Internet access is still a severe constraint for e-commerce development, including its speed and cost. The Chinese government has currently tried to invest to improve its Internet access speed while cutting down on expense for Internet users. The average cost for Internet users per month is about $10 in 2007, which is less than in 2006. However, it is still much more than what Internet users are willing to accept as based on the average income level in China (CNNIC, 2006 & 2007).

Government Regulations

Because of the characteristics of Internet, being virtual and open to everyone worldwide, some immoral behaviour even including crimes occur on the Internet, which damage interest on the part of the state and pose a risk to national security. The emerging global network is highly problematic with respect to its regulation (Trappey & Trappey, 2001). Not only China but other countries as well are facing these problems. In the wake of the increased use of new information technology in business, the adoption of a legal framework to regulate e-commerce is particularly important for China's economic development (Yan, 2005). The Chinese government has drafted some regulations and policies on Internet usage and e-commerce since 1996. These regulations and policies focus on Web access, domain name regulation, Internet content regulation, encryption regulation and so on (Kennedy, 2000a; Lo & Everett, 2001). The Chinese government has issued some regulations or laws on e-contract, e-signature, taxation, authentication and so on to help push e-commerce development. In 2005, the Electronic Signature Law was issued in China. It is a set of rules to deal with the most activities in e-commerce and have generated the most legal work in e-commerce in China (Yan, 2005).

However, the supporting legal system on e-commerce in China cannot solve some problems and uncertainties. The development of e-commerce calls for an adequate administrative and legal environment (Ho & Chen, 1999; Rosen, 1999; Chen & Ning, 2002; Markus & Soh, 2003; Stylianou, Robbins et al. 2003; Chen & Ning 2002; Srivastava & Thomson, 2007).

Access Regulation

The Administration of International Link-ups of Computer Information Networks, Tentative Provisions (Computer Link-up Provisions) were promulgated in February 1996 and amended in May 1997, which set up a four-tier system for access to the Internet and designated MII as the ultimate gatekeeper for transmission to and from the World Wide Web. At the top of this system is the international gateway that is operated by Ministry of Information Industry (MII). The second tier of the system is made up of four government Internet Service Providers (ISPs) known as interconnected networks: CHINANET (administered by MII); CHINAGBN (administered by the Ministry of Electronics Industry); CERNET (administered by the Ministry of Education) and CASNET (administered by the Chinese Academy of Sciences). The third tier is made of private sector ISPs or connected networks. These connected networks can only link to the Internet through the four government-interconnected networks. Private sector ISPs must have a link-up business permit from one of the four government ISPs before they can offer services to users. The final tier is Internet user, which can be individuals, legal persons or organizations. Individual clients can obtain Internet access either indirectly from private providers or directly from one of the four government ISPs (Kennedy, 2000b). Once connected to the Internet, Internet users must register with the local public securities authorities within 30 days according to the Work of Record of Computer Information Systems Linked to Foreign Networks Circular and the Internet Security Regulations.

Domain Name Registration

CNNIC handles the registration and administration of all domain names in China. The domain name rules, issued by the State Council, stipulate that domain names are available on a first-come, first-served basis. Web companies that intend to register domain names in China must meet certain requirements: (1) the applicant must be a registered organization in China (in the case of a foreign enterprise it must have a branch or representative office in China); (2) the main domain name server must be in China; (3) the proposed domain name should not include an enterprise name or a trademark registered by a third party in China (Wang 2001).

China's domain name system is facing some problems. Firstly, due to the popularity of dot.

com domain names, some Chinese companies prefer a dot.com registration to a dot.cn one. Since October 1999, companies have been able to apply for a dot.com or a dot.cn registration. Secondly, at present CNNIC does not have effective mechanisms to deal with disputes over domain name registration. CNNIC does not have the responsibility to check whether a requested domain name violates the trademark or existing usage rights belonging to another organization. If the owners of companies' name or trademarks raise objections to the proposed domain name registration, they must themselves provide evidence of registration to CNNIC.

Encryption

Encryption is considered as an important element of the infrastructure for electronic commerce. The emergence of strong encryption products and the expanded application and impact of encryption on the daily lives of citizens have alerted many governments to public safety, law enforcement, and national security risks associated with encryption. China is also one of them. In China, the National Commission on Encryption Code Regulations (NCECR) is the organization to monitor the domestic use of encryption. In October 1999, the PRC State Council issued the Commercial Use Encryption Management Regulations (Encryption Regulations). On November 8, 1999, the State Encryption Management Commission (SEMC) announced the implementation of the Encryption Regulations. Under these regulations, all foreign companies must obtain approval from NCECR for their use of imported encryption products, while local companies are only allowed to use Chinese-made, state-approved ones. The main reasons driving the Encryption Regulations are to keep Chinese national security and public safety (Rayburn & Conrad, 2004).

The Secrecy Regulations

The State Secrets Bureau under the Ministry of State Security issued the State Secrecy Protection Regulations for Computer Information Systems on the Internet (Secrecy Regulations) on January 1, 2000. The Secrecy Regulations prohibit the dissemination, storing, and processing of state secrets by Internet-connected computer systems. The Internet police are charged primarily with combating Internet crimes ranging broadly from pornography to the dissemination of state secrets. The regulations cover all activities conducted through the Internet. All local Internet content providers (ICPs) are now obliged to routinely censor the content of their Web and expunge politically sensitive material.

Personal Data Privacy and Security

Basically there are no legal guarantees of privacy on the Internet in China. Privacy is always a big concern in e-commerce for consumers. Consumers did not recognize the importance of privacy when e-commerce was first introduced in China. With the penetration of Internet into people's life, consumers concern more and more about their privacy when they are required to offer their personal data to business companies in their visits to some business Websites or in their online shopping process, for example e-mail address, bank account information and so on. Currently in China the Public Pledge of Self-Regulation and Professional Ethics for China Internet Industry issued by the Internet Society of China is the main regulation to protect customer privacy. It is not the legal guarantee for consumer privacy. The increased awareness of Internet privacy by both privacy advocates and legislators in China calls for legal privacy policies in order to protect consumer privacy. China can learn from the U.S. and European Union on the issue of privacy, which have already achieved success in privacy protection with legal systems.

Consumer Protection Regulation

In e-commerce, consumers are at risk. Some illegal behaviour in e-commerce can infringe on consumers' benefits, e.g., fraud, bad quality of products or services offered by online sellers and so on. In China, the Chinese government has issued the Law on the Consumer Benefits Protection in 1993, which is to protect consumer benefits. This law is also applicable in e-commerce in China. Consumers can turn to the State Administration for Industry and Commerce and local Administration for Industry and Commerce if their benefits have been infringed in e-commerce adoption. In China, the Consumer Association is also an organization which protects consumer benefits, doing so according to the Law on the State administration for Industry and Commerce. Consumers can send their complaints to the Consumer Association and get assistance in finding solutions. Though there are laws and related organization to protect consumer benefits in e-commerce, they cannot solve all the problems which occur as related to consumer benefits in e-commerce. To issue detailed consumer protection laws or regulations in e-commerce is important in protecting consumer benefits in e-commerce.

Talent Supply

The rapid growth of e-commerce imposes an increasing demand for professionals with the knowledge of e-commerce in network economy times. In China, there is a high demand for high-level talents with technology and business knowledge in e-commerce, including middle-class managerial staff, accountants and the staff in some secondary and base government organizations, as well as senior managerial staff.

Currently, e-commerce education in China supplies some talents in e-commerce field. Before 2000, no higher education institution in China offered e-commerce by subject or programme, though the demand for talent in e-commerce was quite great at the time. In 2001, the Ministry of Education in China awarded 13 Chinese universities the possibility to recruit students in an e-commerce major. Until the present time, almost all the universities in China have offered the study of e-commerce for a bachelor's degree, master's degree and doctorate (Zhang, 2005). Chinese higher education institutions have cultivated a considerable amount of talent in the e-commerce field and have contributed to the development of e-commerce in China.

Although success in e-commerce education has been achieved and talents in e-commerce have been cultivated during the past several years, there is a gap between the supply and the demand of e-commerce professionals in either quality or quantity aspects. Though there are more students enrolled in different e-commerce programs in China, it is still far below demand because of the rapid increase of e-commerce application in enterprises and the quick enhance of demand for professionals in e-commerce field. Meanwhile, though e-commerce education can cultivate professionals in e-commerce in China, their knowledge is unable to meet the requirements of enterprises. Some of them are good at technology without managerial knowledge, or versed in business without knowledge in technology, which eventually results in the coexistence of supply over demand and demand over supply for e-commerce talents in China.

The Related and Supporting Industries Perspective

E-commerce needs the support of financial industry and logistics industry, which help customers to complete payment in their online transaction process and offer delivery services after the transactions. In China, the payment systems and the logistic services cannot meet the requirements of e-commerce. There is no centralized Chinese bank system and electronic payment system with credit cards or debit cards, hampering e-commerce transactions (Ho & Chen, 1999; Steinert-Threlkeld, 2000; Haley, 2002; Markus & Soh, 2003; Stylianou, Robbins et al. 2003; Tan & Ouyang, 2004; Wang, Yen et al. 2004). Meanwhile, the logistics system in China is inefficient, which impedes e-commerce development as well (Haley, 2002; Wang, Yen et al. 2004).

Payment Systems

The importance of online payment is unassailable in e-commerce. In e-commerce, the ownership of goods can be transferred only when the payment has been finished. One of the advantages of e-commerce is its convenience and quickness without face-to-face business. Internet purchases are generally credit card-based transactions, which is a quite direct contrast to the cash-based consumer culture in China. The most common method of payment among Chinese online shopping sites is cash payment upon the delivery and receipt of ordered goods, which reflects the Chinese culture of cash-based payment.

A statistics survey about the payment methods for online shopping among the Internet users in China shows that 73.8% would like to pay online with credit cards or debit cards, 28.1% by cash and carry; 15.2% by bank transfer, 12.4% by post offices remittance and 2.0% by other methods. About 21.7% of them regard inconvenient payment as one of the important barriers for them not to shop online (CNNIC, 2006).

Although analysts agree that e-commerce growth in China will be great, higher growth is stymied by the lack of nationwide credit card network. The use of credit cards requires an infrastructure capable of handling electronic payments. China's substandard electronic payment infrastructure creates a somewhat formidable obstacle. In China, twenty banks have issued their own bankcards and most of the bankcards are debit cards. Cash, instead of credit cards, is the dominant payment method, which stems from the lack of a credit system. In China, the phenomena of bilking or defaulting on bank loans exist among the enterprises, which may stem from regime-related malpractice or the unhealthy legal system.

According to the statistics conducted by China Unionpay, about 1 billion bankcards have been issued in China including debit card and credit card (Netease, 12.08.2006). Most debit and credit cards can be used to pay online. It is common that 3 to 5 bank cards are held on hand by Chinese people. In China, bank cards can only be accepted by the issuing bank in the issuing province. No national bank cards are issued in China. Compared to debit cards, the amount of credit cards issued in China is still very small. According to the statistics of China Unionpay, about 10 million credit cards had been issued in China until the end of 2004 (Netease, 12.08.2006). On the one hand, some lack credit cards to pay online in China. On the other, those who have credit cards worry about the potential risks of using their credit cards to pay online (Chen, 2007; Ren, 2007).

China lacks a centralized settlement system. In China, various banks issue their own credit cards, and the cards can only be used in certain shops, restaurants and hotels, etc. All the commercial banks in China do their business in their own way. It results in various protocols being used in various banks. In China, there are four main commercial banks offering online payment service, i.e., China Construction Bank, Industrial and Commercial Bank of China, Bank of China and Agricultural Bank of China. Different technological standards are used in the banks in China, which prevents them from cooperation with each other. Moreover, it also lowers the entire online service quality of banks in China. In China, payment systems remain a major bottleneck to e-commerce development. The Chinese government still needs to take effective measures to develop the payment systems.

Logistics Systems

Another severe constraint on the development of e-commerce in China is the inefficient logistics systems. The local logistics system in China is poorly developed. China's primitive and unreliable distribution capabilities present additional difficulties to the development of e-commerce in China for large-scale B2B and small-scale B2C transactions (Cao, 2007; Chen, 2007). In fact, the development of delivery and transaction infrastructures is beyond the reach of Internet companies in China. Many e-commerce companies in China are forced to outsource distribution service. The Chinese Post Office is one alternative channel, which covers 2300 cities in China and 200 cities abroad. However, it seems unable to meet the need of e-commerce in China. The Chinese postal system is inefficient and lacks staff skilled in e-commerce. Some foreign competitors have joined in this industry, but the cost they charge is excessively high for ordinary online shoppers or enterprises. Currently, it is impossible for some manufacturing enterprises and major retailers in China to realize JIT supply chain management successfully.

In online shopping, people would usually prefer to choose low-price delivery methods. Postal delivery seems to be the best alternative for consumers in China. A survey on delivery service for online shopping conducted by CNNIC shows that most Internet users would like to choose the postal system in China to offer delivery service (CNNIC 2006). Underdeveloped transportation infrastructure, fragmented distribution systems, limited use of technology in the distribution and logistics sector, regulatory restrictions and local protectionism all result in the inefficiency and unreliability of logistics in China. The logistics service still needs more time to develop and meet the requirements of e-commerce.

The Strategy, Structure and Rivalry Perspective of the Firm

Enterprises play an important role in e-commerce development. Organizational factors exert a strong impact on e-commerce development, such as the perceptions of e-commerce, the degree of information technology application, management model, and executive support and so on (Stylianou, 2003).

In China, the application of computer in business is lagging behind some developed countries. Most Chinese enterprises use computers initially just to store information or deal with text work which lacks the ability to process and deal with information. With the penetration of the Internet into business and society, more and more Chinese enterprisers are trying to conduct business through the Internet. They have linked up with the Internet and have built up Websites or at least have a Webpage. Most Chinese enterprises release their product or service information, conduct transaction and implement their marketing through the Internet. They target at achieving more benefits and gaining a strategic competitive advantages in competition (iResearch, 2007), which is based on their application of modern information technology in their business. Obviously, the importance of e-commerce has been recognized by the Chinese enterprises.

As we have mentioned above, B2B in China is the main e-commerce model in the nation. Compared to other e-commerce models, B2B has achieved better development. In China, catalogue, auction, transaction and community are the main B2B business models. The third-party e-commerce platform (3PECP) has become popular and some enterprises have got successful in their 3PECP business, for example Alibaba (www.alibaba.com), HC360 (www.hc360.com) and Globalsources (www.globalsources.com). In China, there are about 30 million SMEs. The 3PECP offers good online transaction platforms for them. According to the statistical results released by iResearch centre in 2007, nearly 28% of Chinese SMEs in China are using the 3PECP as their e-commerce platform (iResearch, 2007), which can help SMEs to overcome budget and technology difficulties in their application of e-commerce.

Though B2B in China has achieved success to some degree, some organizational factors, e.g., the lack of an R&D budget for e-commerce, traditional management ideas, the lack of support from executives and a deficiency of talent, strongly influence negative e-commerce development in China. In addition, though some enterprises have adopted e-commerce in their business, not all of them have achieved success in their e-commerce. Some of them do not arrive at their goal, i.e., achieve more benefits and competition superiority in the competitive market. It is mainly due to their lack of right strategies in e-commerce development: for example, how to build customer trust and loyalty in the online transaction given the high risks and uncertainties, how to improve service quality, and so on. In B2C e-commerce in China, customers always worry about security risks and the reliability of enterprises in case of fraud in online business transactions.

How to develop e-commerce seems to be a significant issue for Chinese enterprises. Currently, literature on e-commerce is booming. A qualitative approach was adopted in order to achieve an appreciation of the strategies of e-commerce development from the perspective of enterprises and develop a set of appreciation variables in e-commerce development strategies. Some literature on e-commerce development strategies has been explored in the study and we attempted to extract 10 basic guidelines for Chinese enterprises to develop their e-commerce, based on the exploratory study on e-commerce developing strategies in literature. These are summarized in Table 2.

In the e-commerce environment, the customer should not be offered just what he/she seems to look for at the first place. The customers must

Table 2. Guidance for e-commerce from e-commerce literature

Guidance
Offer complete product packages for sale (Bakos, 1998; Grover and Ramanlal, 1999; Slywotzky, 2000).
Build customer trust (Friedman, Kahn et al. 2000; Schoder and Yin, 2000; Rose, 2000).
Build a user community (Stauss, Chojnacki et al. 2001; Gustafsson, Roos et al. 2004).
Provide contact points (Olson and Olson, 2000).
Keep the customer alert and informed (Olson and Olson, 2000).
Update the site constantly (Huang, 2000).
Appreciate customer loyalty (Atkins, 1998; Prahalad and Ramaswamy, 2000).
Focus on user interface design (Huang, 2000).
Establish security (Jones, Wilikens et al. 2000)
Establish entry point to your site (Joachimsthaler and Aaker, 1997; Aaker and Joachimsthaler, 2000; Carr, 2000; Grover and Yeng, 2001).
Consider and avoid channel conflict (Cordell, 1994; Andaleeb, 1996; Weiss and Kurland, 1997).

be offered supplementary products and complete personalized product packages. As Bakos (1998) puts it: "The ultimate objective is to provide customized services according to individual preferences, whether expressed or inferred. Increased selling effectiveness comes from being able to design appropriate products to address the needs of individual consumers, and then being able to identify the moment when a customer's purchasing decision is most likely to occur..." (Bakos, 1998, pp.37). The customers must be able to specify the product they want by themselves, even in the case of traditional physical product offerings. Slywotzky (2000) introduces the concept of "Choiceboard" as a metaphor for the platform for the production of personalized service and product offerings. There is also in-depth discussion on whether product customisation will benefit buyers or sellers more (Grover & Ramanlal, 1999). In principle, customers might want tailored products, but tailoring them too much makes product and price comparisons impossible, as has been the case in, for example, airline fares (Dennett, Ineson et al. 2000). The presence of too many choices can lead to confusion, also leading to greater transaction costs, which could potentially deter people that are not very savvy in using technology or people who are not patient enough.

Customer trust is an absolute necessity for successful e-commerce (Friedman, Kahn et al. 2000; Schoder and Yin, 2000). The basic properties of a secure transaction are that the ordered products and services will come as ordered, and that the payment takes place in an ordinary manner. For example, credit card data must not be used for other purposes, and the credit card data must run over secured connections. One important element in trust is that the customers feel that data on their buying behaviour must not be distributed without their consent. E-commerce companies must assure customers that their privacy in this respect in order to maintain trust (Rose, 2000).

Building a user community will greatly expand the possibilities for successful e-commerce. User communities have several beneficial characteristics (Stauss, Chojnacki et al. 2001). Through virtual communities customers can discuss product offerings with each other, and the customers can see that even other people trust the service offering. Of course, virtual communities do not exist merely for the purpose of joining customers in electronic commerce. Virtual communities can help to create personal relationship in cyberspace, which also represent a social aggregation. User communities will exchange ideas and experiences over products and services, and satisfied customers will attract more customers to the products and services. User community is also a good channel to help build customer loyalty (Gustafsson, Roos, & Edvardsson, 2004).

One part in the security feeling of customers is that they have contact points to real people if needed, and through other media than only the Web. It is necessary to reintermediation or the reintroduction of people to online interaction in e-commerce transaction in order to ensure services. (Olson & Olson, 2000).

Keeping the customer informed and aware of the proceeding of his/her transaction is of immense importance. Technologies like e-mail can help foster trust by responding to requests in a timely manner (Olson & Olson, 2000). If customer contact is not continuously maintained, the customer will lose the sense of activity and feel disappointed.

Visiting a Website must be rewarding. The user must have access to true and recent information, and expects to find the newest information from the Website. The user must be able to conduct the transactions s/he wishes through the Website. For example, all the product and service offerings marketed through other channels must also be available on the Website. This is why it is important that the contents are up-to-date and updated constantly (Huang, 2000).

Customers must be rewarded for their loyalty to a Website. Various regular customer programmes serve this goal. Atkins (1998) introduces the concept of appropriability. Appropriability refers to the ability of stakeholders to retain the financial benefits that arise through the exploitation of an innovation (Atkins, 1998) for themselves. In other words, the benefits from e-commerce must also touch the customers in terms of lower prices and transaction costs. Giving attention to the customer is important as well: for enterprises, in addition, engaging in dialogue with a diverse and evolving customer base in multiple channels can place a high premium on organizational flexibility (Prahalad & Ramaswamy, 2000).

User interface design is of primary importance even in e-commerce, since clients can always turn to other sites if the user interface is not feasible. Building a Website is a compromise between simplicity and robustness leading to complexity (Huang, 2000). According to the Huang, in some cases designing virtual shopping environments that are perceived as complex, large-scale and crowded can, however, help promote the image of leading-edge corporations (Huang, 2000).

Security is a key concern for the customer and the seller as well. The standards and norms for secure Websites are quite established ones, but customer reactions to security must not always be correlated to the absolute level of security: the customer can feel that an insecure site is secure and vice versa. The customer must have a feel of privacy, and feel absolutely safe that his/her money will not be lost in the transaction. The cry for absolute security would nevertheless be naive. As Jones, Wilikens et al. (2000) state, the requirements concerning security, reliability, and availability in e-commerce must be made by trading off costs and benefits and identifying acceptable levels of risks (Jones, Wilikens et al. 2000).

Only very strong brands enjoy a constant flow of customers without massive marketing (Joachimsthaler & Aaker, 1997; Aaker & Joachimsthaler, 2000). Others will have to cater for entry points and gateways to their Websites. Positioning the e-commerce site to portals and other Websites is of immense importance (Carr, 2000; Grover & Yeng, 2001).

Especially for industries that are very dependent on external agents and retailers, the issue of channel conflict can be of major importance (Andaleeb, 1996; Weiss & Kurland, 1997). The usual consideration is that if the producer of the goods or services itself enters retail activity, the current external marketing channels would suffer and react poorly to the situation. Especially important, these considerations have come now during the Internet era (Cordell, 1994). In tourism, travel agents are a powerful market force, and keeping them satisfied for any company in travel business is of key importance.

The Demand Perspective

In the e-commerce market, the demand can be classified into two kinds: the demand from individual customers (B2C) and the demand from enterprises (B2B).

Consumer Demand for E-Commerce

In China, the demand of individual customers in the e-commerce market is still very low compared to the B2B market in the nation, though it will have great potential in the years to come. In China, consumption behaviour and the attitude of individual customers has greatly impacted B2C development in China. According to the statistics on the purpose of using Internet from CNNIC, 76.3 percent of Internet users in China use the Internet as an information source, 69.8 percent use it as a communication tool, 68.5 for entertainment, and 25.5 percent for online purchasing. Only one-fifth of Internet users in China would like to use online bank (CNNIC, 2007). Individual customers would still like to turn to traditional channels to purchase products or services. According to the 19th survey of CNNIC, the main barriers for individual customer not to shop online are mainly security risk, the lack of credit cards, and the lack of trust (CNNIC, 2007).

According to the statistics released by CNNIC, though the number of Internet users in China has increased quickly, the 162 million Internet users only account for 12.3 percent of the total Chinese population of nearly 1.3 billion. Although China has a large number of Internet users and a fast expansion speed, compared to the penetration of the Internet in developed countries and the average penetration rate – 17.6 percent – the overall penetration of the Internet in China is still quite low and offers vast potential for development (CNNIC, 2007).

In addition, some personal factors have impact on individual customers in their e-commerce application, including IT knowledge, e-commerce knowledge and e-commerce communication. It is necessary to offer more public education in the e-commerce field to improve the knowledge and skills of individual customers which will help individual customers to clearly recognize the benefits of e-commerce and attract more and more individual customers to adopt e-commerce in their lives. The recognition of e-commerce benefits is a strong driver for customers to use e-commerce, though there are barriers which impede them from adopting e-commerce.

Business Demand for E-Commerce

As mentioned above, in China B2B is the main e-commerce model. B2B has developed quickly there in the past ten years and continues to grow at a high rate. Before 2007, information services were the main content in the B2B arena, which is mainly servicing SMEs in China. B2B has turned to transaction and services since 2007, not only servicing SMEs within China, but also the large-sized Chinese enterprises.

There is a high demand for B2B in the international business market in China. As above mentioned, in 2006 B2B has generated an avenue of $169 billion, 67.2 percent of which derives from international business. China is a large country with high competition capability in some industries in international business. It is the global manufacturing centre. In international business, e-commerce has become a highly accepted business model because of its convenience and efficiency in business transaction. The international business increase in China provides an important impetus to demand for B2B e-commerce in China.

The furious competition in the international market obliges Chinese enterprises to apply e-commerce in their business. The competition between enterprises is always furious. Chinese enterprises are trying to save costs and improve efficiency in their business in order to survive, given such fierce competition. Applying e-commerce in their business is one of their business strategies due to the benefits and advantages of e-commerce in cost-saving and high efficiency.

Though there is a high demand for B2B e-commerce in China, some barriers impede its development. Some of the barriers have been mentioned above. In addition, lack of trust is another sizeable barrier in B2B e-commerce, since commercial fraud always occurs in China.

Based on the above discussion on the four perquisites of e-commerce development in the nation, it is obvious that e-commerce development in China is the result of mutual efforts from the Chinese government, related and supporting industries and the strategy, structure and rivalry and demand with respect to the firm. E-commerce development in China has not developed as well as in some developed countries, because of some barriers existing in these four aspects.

DISCUSSION AND CONCLUSION

In China, there are increased numbers of Internet users and an improved information infrastructure. The payment system and logistics system are improving. The perceptions of e-commerce in enterprises are changing, and people's consciousness of e-commerce is expanding. All these conditions are together accelerating e-commerce development in China. Compared to the e-commerce development in some developed countries, e-commerce in China is still in its formation stage. There are some barriers which impede e-commerce development in China. From the perspective of the national factor, the existing barriers are unbalanced infrastructure construction in different areas, the lack of an adequate administrative and legal environment, and the lack of e-commerce skills. The lack of centralized bank systems and online payment systems, as well as the inefficient logistics systems in China, represent the barriers existing in related and supporting industries. With regard to the firm's strategy, structure and rivalry perspective, the lack of an R&D budget on e-commerce, traditional management ideas, lack of support from executives, and no appropriate strategies for the application of e-commerce serve to impede e-commerce application in Chinese enterprises. As far as demand goes, the lack of trust and credit cards in addition to security risks act as the main barriers in their e-commerce adoption for individual customers, in addition to the scarcity of e-commerce knowledge and the popularity of traditional consumption behaviour. Lack of trust in business is the barrier in B2B for Chinese enterprises. The barriers existing in e-commerce development have impeded the rapid development in China. Some strategies still need to be taken to eliminate the barriers to e-commerce development in China.

From the perspective of national factors, some state strategies should be taken to break the monopoly system in the telecommunication industry, and a competition mechanism should be adopted which can offer better telecommunication industry service with even lower service fees to Chinese clients. In addition, Chinese government should enhance the issuing of related laws and criterions related to e-commerce in order to regulate e-commerce transactions. Investing more in the infrastructure construction in the countryside and West China as well as balancing e-commerce in various areas in China is also what the government should focus on. The Chinese higher education institutions should cooperate and communicate more with enterprises, which can help them to understand what talents are needed for Chinese enterprises and resolve the gap between demand and supply in the e-commerce talent market. In addition, international cooperation is also a good way for Chinese higher education institutions to cultivate e-commerce skills to meet the demand for e-commerce expertise in China.

From the related and supporting industries perspective, establishing centralized bank systems and establishing the online payment system with high security is very important in China, which can change the customer's attitude on payment in online transactions and push online bank applications in the lives of Chinese people. Online payment can really make customers enjoy the convenience of e-commerce in their life. In addition, it will be an effective strategy to utilize the postal system in China to offer logistics services in e-commerce, given its advantages, since China is a large country with a wide geographical sphere; whereas the post office covers almost all of China. In addition, improving the efficiency of the logistics service with the modern IT is crucial, which can make the delivery service in e-commerce visible and increase the confidence and trust in online business transactions.

With regard to the strategy, structure and rivalry perspective on the part of firms, there are two different sides. For those enterprises which have not applied e-commerce in business, it is imperative for them to change their perceptions and attitudes to e-commerce by learning from other enterprises which have applied e-commerce successfully in their business. In addition, the driving force from the Chinese government should not be underestimated in the e-commerce development in China, since the entire industry development is closely related with the state strategies of the Chinese government. Those enterprises that have applied e-commerce in their business should follow the guidance discussed above to improve their e-commerce service quality and obtain competition-based advantage in the furious competitive market. In addition, e-commerce should be adopted in the complete business process of enterprises gradually – not only in sales and marketing, but also in the material purchasing and manufacturing process.

As far as the demand perspective goes, given the penetration of Internet, people can easily accept it as an important tool in their lives, which includes shopping, learning and so on. Whether a customer accepts e-commerce or not largely depends on change in the environmental factors discussed above, including national criteria, the related and supporting industries and the strategy, structure and rivalry factors particular to the firm. With the popularization of higher education in China and advertisements and promotion related to e-commerce from both the Chinese government and Chinese enterprises, knowledge and skills in e-commerce will not be an appreciable obstacle for customers.

Based on the above discussion, it can be concluded that though e-commerce in China has developed in China, e-commerce in China is still in its initial stage. Compared to some developed countries where e-commerce has developed very well, it will take more time for China to go into the next stage of e-commerce, due to the different circumstances in China. E-commerce development requires the mutual efforts of the Chinese government, the supporting financial and logistics industries, enterprises and customers. The development of e-commerce in China should go step-by-step, but cannot be completed in a short time. In other words, there is still a long way for China to go.

E-commerce development in China can be typical in less developed countries. This chapter explores the e-commerce development from four different perspectives, including the current condition, the barriers and developing strategies. This chapter can offer some guidance on e-commerce development for some less developed countries. Some strategies which have been used successfully in e-commerce development in China may also be valuable for other less developed countries as well. A summary of the top 10 issues to be addressed if e-commerce is to be developed in less developed countries is provided in Table 3.

Table 3. The top 10 issues to be addressed if e-commerce is to be developed in less developed countries

The Porter factors	Our list for e-commerce	Top issues for countries
National factors	Telecommunications infrastructure Government regulations Talent supply	1 To cater to telecommunications infrastructure 2 To cater to regulation on Internet access 3 To cater to regulation on domain name registration 4 To cater to regulation on data privacy and security 5 To educate enough people in business issues and IT technology issues 6 To cater to consumer protection regulation
Related and supporting industries	Payment systems Logistics systems	7 To allow a decent banking and payment infrastructure to develop 8 To see to the infrastructure of physical distribution
Firm strategy, structure and rivalry	Managing and organizing e-commerce	9 To develop incentives for companies to engage in e-commerce
Demand conditions	Consumer demand for e-commerce Business demand for e-commerce	10 To cater to Internet access by private persons

REFERENCES

Aaker, D. A., & Joachimsthaler, E. (2000). The brand relationship spectrum: The key to the brand architecture challenge. *California Management Review*, 42, 8-23.

Andaleeb, S. S. (1996). An experimental investigation of satisfaction and commitment in marketing channels: The role of trust and dependence. *Journal of Retailing, 96*(1), 77-93.

Atkins, M. H. (1998). The role of appropriability in sustaining competitive advantage - an electronic auction system case study. *Journal of Strategic Information Systems, 7*(2), 131-152.

Bakos, Y. (1998). The emerging role of electronic marketplaces on the Internet. *Communications of the ACM, 41*(8): 35-42.

Cao, J. X. (2007). Logistics service in e-commerce in China. *Management Exploration,* 3, 17-18.

Carr, N. G. (2000). Hypermediation: Commerce as clickstream. *Harvard Business Review,* January-February, 46-47.

Chen, J.-J. (2007). The difficulties and strategies in e-commerce development in China. *Technology & Management*, 2, 14-16.

China Market Information Centre (CCID). (2006). B2B market will continue develop in China. Retrieved June 14, 2007, from http://news.ccidnet.com/art/1032/20060214/428239_1.html

Chen, L.-D., Gillenson, M. L., & Sherrell, D. L. (2002). Enticing online consumers: An extended technology acceptance perspective. *Information & Management, 39*(8), 705-719.

Chen, S., & Ning, J. (2002). Constraints on e-commerce in less developed countries: The case of China. *Electronic Commerce Research, 2*(1, 2), 31-42.

China Internet Network Information Center (CNNIC). (2006). The18th statistical survey report on Internet development in China. Retrieved June 14, 2007, from http://www.cnnic.net.cn/uploadfiles/doc/2006/7/19/103601.doc

China Internet Network Information Centre (CNNIC) (2007). The 19th statistical survey report on the Internet development in China. Retrieved June 18, 2007, from http://www.cnnic.cn/download/2007/cnnic19threport.pdf

China Internet Network Information Centre (CNNIC) (2007). The 20th statistical survey report on the Internet development in China. Retrieved July 13, 2007, from http://www.cnnic.cn/uploadfiles/pdf/2007/7/18/113918.pdf

Cordell, V. V. (1994). Information exchange and the diffusion of computer based information technologies in U.S. and Japanese distribution channels. *Journal of Euromarketing, 3*(3, 4), 161-175.

Du, J. (2006). E-commerce development in the world in 2005. Retrieved June 12, 2007, from http://www.istis.sh.cn/list/list.asp?id=2853

Friedman, B., Kahn, P. H. J., & Howe, D. C. (2000). Trust Online. *Communications of the ACM, 43*(12), 34-40.

Grover, V., & Ramanlal, P. (1999). Six myths of information and markets: Information technology networks, electronic commerce, and the battle for consumer surplus. *MIS Quarterly, 23*(4), 465-495.

Grover, V., & Yeng, J. T. C. (2001). E-commerce and the information market. *Communications of the ACM, 44*(4), 79-86.

Gustafsson, A., Roos, I. & Edvardsson, B. (2004). Customer clubs in a relationship perspective: A telecom case. *Managing Service Quality, 14* (2/3), 157-168.

Haley, G. T. (2002). E-commerce in China changing business as we know it. *Industrial Marketing Management*, 31, 119-224.

Ho, C., & Chen, J. (1999). The prospects of B2B e-commerce in China's Internet industry. *Business Forum, 24*(3, 4), 62-69.

Huang, M.-H. (2000). Information load: Its relationship to online exploratory and shopping behavior. *International Journal of Information Management*, 20, 337-347.

IResearch. China B2B e-commerce research report. Retrieved June 14, 2007, from http://www.iresearch.com.cn/html/B2B/detail_free_id_45218.html

Joachimsthaler, E., & Aaker, D. A. (1997). Building brands without mass media. *Harvard Business Review*, January-February, 39-50.

Jones, S., Wilikens, M., Morris, P., & Masera, M. (2000). Trust requirements in e-business. *Communications of the ACM, 43*(12), 81-87.

Kennedy, G. (2000a). China rushes to catch up with the Internet. *International Financial Law Review*, 19, 36-42.

Kennedy, G. (2000b). E-commerce: The taming of the Internet in China. *The China Business Review*, July-August, 34-39.

Klepperer, S, & Graddy, E. (1990). The evolution of new industries and the determinant of market structure. *Journal of Economics, 21*(1), 27-44.

Lo, W. C. W., & Everett, A. M. (2001). Thriving in the regulatory environment of e-commerce: A guanxi strategy. *SAM Advanced Management Journal*, Summer, 17-24.

Markus, L., & Soh, C. (2003). Structural influence on global e-commerce activity. *Journal of Global Information Management, 10*(1), 5-12.

Ministry of Information Industry (MII). The report of telecommunication industry in China in 2006. Retrieved June 14, 2007, from http://www.cnii.com.cn/20070108/ca398639.htm

Netease. (12.08.2006). The pain after the happiness of pay with credit cards. Retrieved June 16, 2007, from http://finance.163.com/06/0812/12/2OAT80T800251SBB.html

Olson, J. S., & Olson, G. M. (2000). i2i Trust in e-commerce. *Communications of the ACM, 43*(12), 41-44.

Payton, F. C., & Brennan, P. F. (1999). How a community health information network is really used. *Communications of the ACM, 42*(12), 85-89.

Porter, M. E. (1998). *Competitive advantage: Creating and sustaining superior performance*. New York, the U.S.: Free Press.

Prahalad, C. K., & Ramaswamy, V. (2000). Co-opting customer competence. *Harvard Business Review*, January-February, 79-86.

Rayurn, J. M. & Conrad, C. (2004). China's Internet structure: Problems and control measures. *International Journal of Management, 21*(4), 471-480.

Ren, R. (2007). The constraints and developing strategies in e-commerce in China. *Market Modernization, 491*(1), 134-135.

Rose, E. (2000). Balancing Internet marketing needs with consumer concerns: A property rights framework. *Computers and Society*, June, 20-24.

Rosen, D. H. (1999). Hype versus hope for eCommerce in China. *The China Business Review*, July-August, 38-41.

Schoder, D., & Yin, P.-L. (2000). Building firm trust online. *Communications of the ACM, 43*(12), 73-79.

Slywotzky, A. J. (2000). The age of the Choiceboard. *Harvard Business Review*, January-February, 40-41.

Srivastava, A., & Thomson, S. B. (2007). E-Business law in China: Strengths and Weaknesses, *Electronic Markets, 17*(2), 126 – 131.

Stauss, B., Chojnacki, K., Decker, A., & Hoffmann, F. (2001). Retention effects of a customer club. *International Journal of Service Industry Management, 12*(1), 7-19.

Steinert-Threlkeld, T. (2000). China holds Internet dragon by tail. *Inter@ctive Week, 7*(19), 86-91.

Stylianou, A. C., Robbins, S. S., & Jackson, P. (2003). Perceptions and attitudes about eCommerce development in China: An exploratory study. *Journal of Global Information Management, 11*(2), 31-47.

Tan, Z., & Ouyang, W. (2004). Diffusion and impacts of the Internet and e-commerce in China. *Electronic Markets, 14*(1), 25-35.

Trappey, C. V., & Trappey, A. J. C. (2001). Electronic Commerce in Great China. *Industrial Management & Data Systems, 101*(5), 201-209.

Wang, J.-Y. (2001). The Internet and e-commerce in China: Regulations, judicial views, and government policy. *Computer and Internet Law,* 18, 12-30.

Wang, X., Yen, D. C., & Fang, X. (2004). E-commerce development in China and its implication for business. *Asia Pacific Journal of Marketing and Logistics, 16*(3), 68-83.

Weiss, A. M., & Kurland, N. (1997). Holding distribution channel relationships together: The role of transaction-specific assets and length of prior relationship. *Organization Science, 8*(6), 612-623.

Yan, W. (2005). The electronic signatures law: China's first national e-commerce legislation. *Intellectual Property & Technology Law Journal, 17*(6), 6-10.

Zhang, X.-F., Li, Q., & Lin, Z.-X. (2005). E-commerce education in China: Driving forces, status and strategies. *Journal of Electronic Commerce in Organizations*, July-September, 1-17.

Chapter XVII
Evolution of Electronic Procurement in Egypt: Case of Speedsend.com

Sherif Kamel
The American University in Cairo, Egypt

ABSTRACT

Emerging information and communication technology is driving transformation and change in the cyberspace. Speed, competition and globalization are key factors for development and growth in the reengineered global business environment where electronic business promises to grow in volume helping the digital economy to mature and dominate. This chapter demonstrates the case of an Internet startup that capitalized on the opportunities presented by the information economy. Since its establishment in 2001, the business2business platform of speedsend.com pioneered the electronic procurement industry in Egypt through a customized Web-based platform. The transformation of classical emerging markets challenges into opportunities has been a critical success factor that related to all building blocks of the business venture including technology infrastructure deployment, community awareness, information availability, and cultural adaptation of the online business amongst others. The owners of Speedsend.com developed a set of models to drive down procurement costs while providing a practical and reliable electronic solution that can boost enterprise procurement efficiency and effectiveness and that could be appealing to a community that is known for being resistant to change and not really mature in terms of information technology adoption, diffusion and adaptation. The case focuses on the models deployed by speedsend.com demonstrating the internal and external challenges faced and lessons learnt.

EVOLUTION OF ELECTRONIC PROCUREMENT

The Internet is an enabler to many online applications that renders organizational processes more effective and more efficient (Pani & Agrahari, 2007). One of these applications is the procurement process that has traditionally involved slow and manual procedures for handling procurement transactions (Hawking et al, 2004). eProcurement

Copyright © 2009, IGI Global, distributing in print or electronic forms without written permission of IGI Global is prohibited.

refers to the electronic acquisition of goods and services in a firm (Turban et al, 2006). eProcurement has had an increasingly important role in business2business (B2B) commerce (Philips & Piotrowicz, 2006). Moreover, with the continuous improvement in information and communication technology (ICT) and especially Internet-related technologies, opportunities emerge to make procurement for goods and services more transparent and efficient (Carayannis & Popescu, 2005). eProcurement has been advocated as a tool that can improve competencies and performance.

It is important to note that eProcurement has received tremendous attention from both researchers and practitioners alike (Pani, 2007). The reasons for such focus are numerous however; one can include the positive implications on process quality, total procurement cost, user satisfaction and system responsiveness (Subramaniam & Shaw, 2002). The implementation of eProcurement in private enterprises has resulted in savings in the range of 10-15% of procurement value (Somasundaram, 2007). However, a challenge remains constant among various eProcurement implementation and that relates to human resistance (Angeles, 2006). eProcurement practice is not well-established or documented in the context of emerging economies (Yamamoto & Karaman, 2007). Therefore, the case of Speedsend.com tries to demonstrate the initiation, development and implementation of a business2business procurement venture in the context of an emerging economy, Egypt (Kamel, 2000a & 2000b). The case shows the different stages of development as well as the various challenges and opportunities that faced the founders of the promising Internet startup.

SPEEDSEND: EGYPT LEADING EPROCUREMENT PLATFORM

It was 10am on a rainy morning in Cairo (Egypt) in February 2006. While the rain drizzled outside his office window, Ahmed El-Sherif looked out the open doorway of his office and stared at the increasing number of employees, whose offices were on the same floor of his office, not taking into account the other two full floors that were occupied by the rest of the firm employees. What started out, as a business operation with only two people in 2001 was now rapidly approaching 95 staff members and counting.

As Speedsend.com co-founder, partner and sales director, El-Sherif mind was occupied with many concerns. Together with co-founder Mohamed Hussein, they had an unwavering goal of formulating their exit strategy, which guided the firm efforts since its foundation. In El-Sherif words, *"we wanted to setup a firm with a proven premium tested business model to valuate it and sell it at the end"*. According to El-Sherif, in order for them to reach their desired goal, they decided to build a company with a premium business model which would provide effective means of managing and controlling corporations' procurement processes. Moreover, both of the cofounders wanted to gain an advantage from existing and emerging technology as an accelerator for their business, and that was to be accomplished by the firm being an online electronic procurement-servicing firm.

Speedsend.com aim was to develop a set of comprehensive products that provide companies of all sizes with both process and cost benefits making the firm the leading "office consumables" online supplier and a one-stop-shop platform for all businesses. The aim of Speedsend.com was to provide an IT-based solution using electronic business that can radically alter the ways in which firms interact with their suppliers and positively improve both their efficiency and effectiveness (Phillips, 2003). Consequently, the firm aspired to become Egypt largest B2B eDistributor of indirect goods with high turnover and ones consumed regularly by businesses. Since the inception of the firm and with a changing economy, Speedsend.

com was faced with a number of challenges. This included uncertainty of financial markets, internal financial limitations, and technological constraints, adaptation of the business model and threat of the emerging financially secure competitors. Therefore, the challenge was exactly how Speedsend.com could best deliver their promises remained a key question for its founders.

Exhibit 1. Local market dynamics

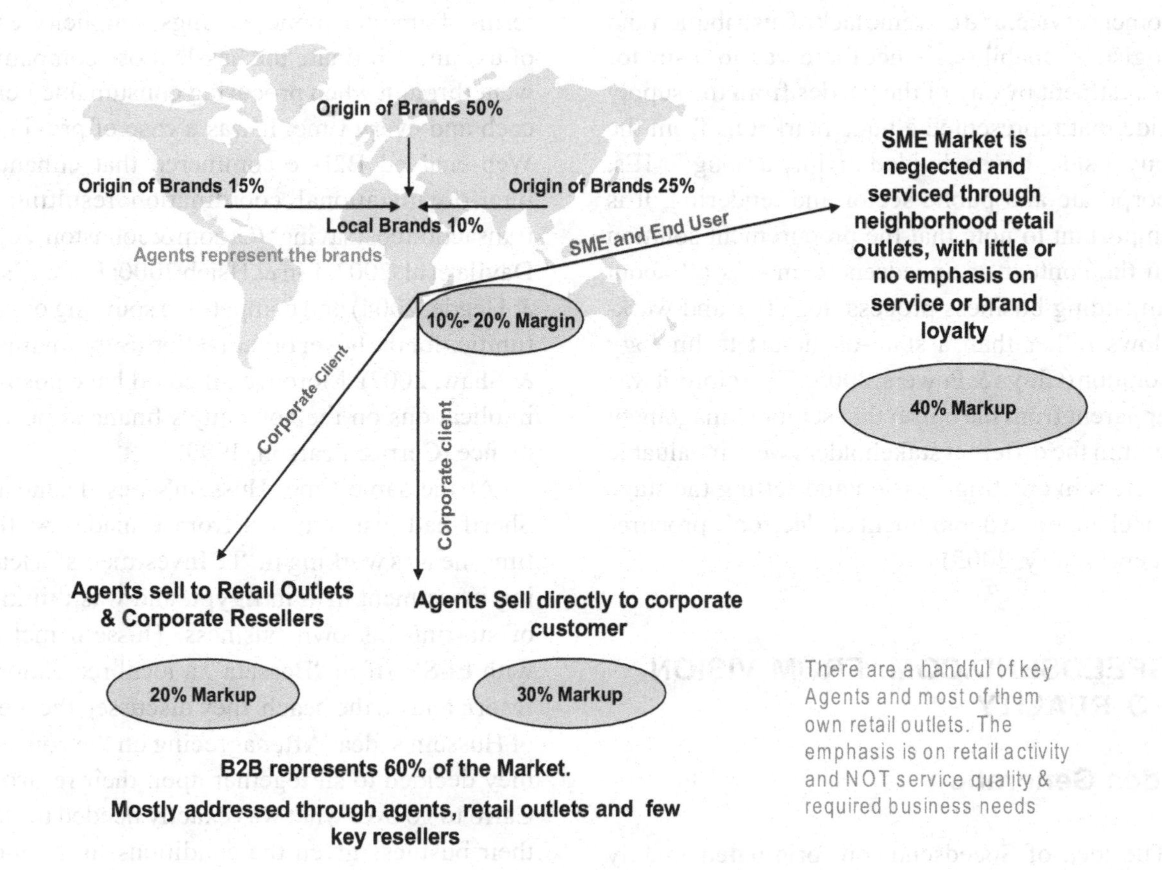
Origin of Brands 50%
Origin of Brands 15%
Origin of Brands 25%
Local Brands 10%
Agents represent the brands
SME and End User
10%- 20% Margin
Corporate Client
Corporate client
SME Market is neglected and serviced through neighborhood retail outlets, with little or no emphasis on service or brand loyalty
40% Markup
Agents sell to Retail Outlets & Corporate Resellers
Agents Sell directly to corporate customer
20% Markup
30% Markup
B2B represents 60% of the Market.
Mostly addressed through agents, retail outlets and few key resellers
There are a handful of key Agents and most of them own retail outlets. The emphasis is on retail activity and NOT service quality & required business needs

LOCAL MARKET STRUCTURE AND DYNAMICS

Whether Speedsend.com operations were online or offline (move-to-the-net or born-on-the-net), the fact remained that the firm was competing within the office supplies market in Egypt. A market characterized by being very fragmented and dominated by traditional competitors such as agents, retailers, and stationary stores among other players. In 2006, Speedsend.com had a market share of 0.01% and the rest of the market was dominated by traditional stakeholders who controlled the office supply market (American Chamber of Commerce in Egypt, 2002). Primary agents sold the products to retail outlets and corporate reseller and/or directly to corporate entities if they had their own retail outlets. Retailers then sold to corporate entities as well as small and medium-sized enterprises (SMEs). Exhibit 1 demonstrates local market dynamics. The office supplies market was a double-edged sword. On the one hand, it is characterized by having a high turnover, with massive volumes of sales and high percentage of revenue and regular consumption rate. However, on the other hand, it is a highly fragmented and specialized retail outlets market. A market where there is little emphasis on customer service, and extreme lack of distribution and logistics capabilities, since there was no desire for investment by any of the parties from the supply side that represented a huge market as from the buyer side, it was divided mainly among SMEs, corporate and public sector and tendering. It is important to note that the procurement solution in the context of Speedsend.com was all about amending business process, logistics and workflows rather than a state-of-the-art technology solution (Ghiya & Powers, 2005). Therefore, it was apparent from the outset that senior management within the different stakeholders were invaluable factors in creating a vision and setting the stage for change and deployment of electronic procurement (Avery, 2005).

SPEEDSEND.COM: FROM VISION TO REALITY

Idea Generation

The idea of Speedsend.com originated in July 2000, when its cofounder, Mohamed Hussein while working in the marketing department of MobiNil, one of Egypt leading mobile services operators. The idea came to him when he started receiving memorandums from top management requesting all departments to reduce their spending and consumption of stationary since the company was spending approximately 45,000 US dollars per month on these consumable goods. The above-mentioned scenario was a typical situation found in many other firms operating in Egypt. Hussein hence realized that an opportunity resided, since there was a need to establish a more controlled procurement purchase system. It was then that he felt he could realize his ambitions to become an entrepreneur. Moreover, with the growth of the Internet and the growing number of people utilizing Web services, he visualized the idea of an online B2B eProcurement platform that would serve companies and benefit them in terms of time and money savings, simplicity, ease of use and eliminate the hassle those companies went through when procuring consumable items each and every time. It was a case of providing Web-enabled B2B e-commerce that enhances inter-organizational coordination resulting in transaction cost savings (Croom & Johnston, 2003; Davila et al, 2003; Lin & Hsieh 2000; Radovilsky & Hegde, 2004) and competitive sourcing opportunities for the buyer organization (Subramaniam & Shaw, 2002). Moreover, it could have positive implications on the company's financial performance (Carr & Pearson, 1999).

At the same time, Hussein's best friend El-Sherif had just returned from Canada. At that time, he was working in "IT Investments" a leading investment firm in Egypt, and was thinking of starting his own business. Hussein met up with El-Sherif in "Bassata", a local recreational resort, and on the beach, they discussed the merit of Hussein's idea. After agreeing on the concept, they decided to sit together upon their return to Cairo to go over what was exactly needed to start their business given the conditions in the local marketplace. The key issue was how to blend state-of-the-art IT with local culture, values and habits to be able to render the venture a success in the digital economy.

Business Model

In August 2000, Hussein and El-Sherif met to develop the business plan for the new venture, a process that took over a month of hard work. Their idea started with having a Web-based application that would serve companies by allowing them to buy all their consumable goods and office supplies that was needed online, while the payment would be made offline based on cash upon delivery. The whole idea behind the business was to use electronic business technology as a means of gaining competitive advantage. Consumables goods were especially chosen due to their high turnover, regular consumption and relative ease of shipping and handling. They knew that the eProcurement process is somewhat different from classical procurement (Podlogar, 2007).

Taking into consideration the novelty of such an idea in Egypt, they came up with a business model that was flexible to change. The plan was to develop a model that is capable to adapt to change and market shifts as well as decentralized allowing staff to respond quickly to customer needs (Neilson et al, 2000). Moreover, the processes constituting the business model were to be very simple, which involved online ordering through Speedsend.com by identified individuals from the client's side (through a username and password) and the online transmission of the order to Speedsend.com. The order would then be transferred to Speedsend.com employees responsible for order fulfillment either from the firm warehouses or from its suppliers. The next day the order would be delivered to the exact destination by the firm van. Payment was to be made offline after a specific agreed upon number of days as per the contract signed between Speedsend.com and the buying party. The offline payment was important for the success of the model due to the local market conditions related to online payment and the current slow penetration rate in the community. Exhibit 2a demonstrates Speedsend.com eBusiness model and exhibit 2b shows a simplified illustration of Speedsend.com business process.

The business model of Speedsend.com offered ease of use and control for the client, creating value through expected costs savings, simple process, control over cost and procedures, and improving quality of decision-making. The speed of service and the huge number of different stock keeping units (SKU), along with the insufficient technology acceptance of the market were the main constraints of the business model. The main revenue stream was created through the selection, ordering, and final fulfillment of service. Additionally, cost streams were created through warehousing, product purchase, delivery process, and resources development. Resources were mainly concentrated in warehousing, human resources development, and technology platform development. Through the development of the resources operating the business, the dynamics of the business model were defined. One particular important dynamic was the mix between online and offline activities capitalizing on the benefits of a blended model. Online activities were concentrated in the online ordering process, product display, automated approvals, reporting module, and internal communications. While offline operations were composed of supplier operations and selling operations. Blending and mixing both operations and keeping a certain service level were considered the main risks involved in the model. However, such blend was utilized as attempt to adapt technology to serve the local market.

The future changes in the business model were expected to be many and diversified as the acceptance level of technology in Egypt was projected to improve and entrance of new market segments was projected. Accordingly, the components of Speedsend.com business model had to be built with an expansion plan to offer enough flexibility for management to change or transform the original business model if needed. Finally, the technology platform that was considered the building block of the business model, required

Exhibit 2a. SpeedSend e-business model

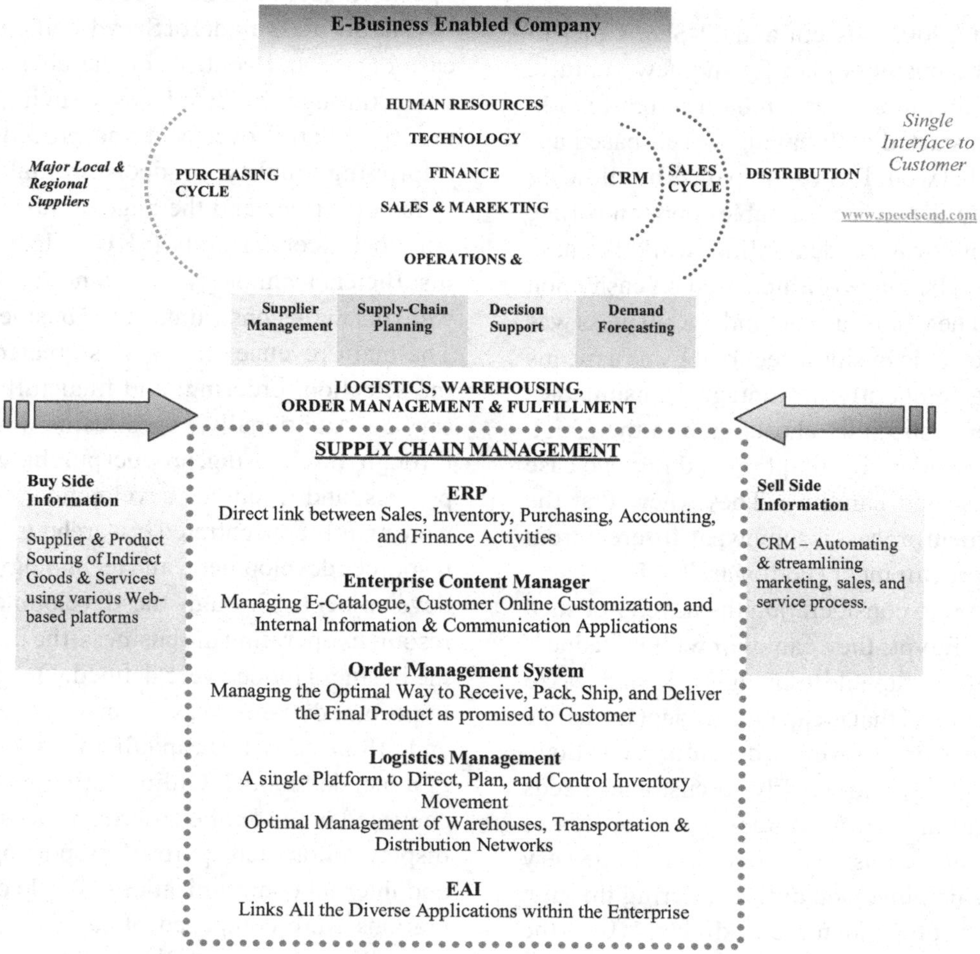

E-Business Enabled Company

Major Local & Regional Suppliers

PURCHASING CYCLE

HUMAN RESOURCES

TECHNOLOGY

FINANCE

SALES & MAREKTING

OPERATIONS &

CRM

SALES CYCLE

DISTRIBUTION

Single Interface to Customer

www.speedsend.com

Supplier Management | Supply-Chain Planning | Decision Support | Demand Forecasting

LOGISTICS, WAREHOUSING, ORDER MANAGEMENT & FULFILLMENT

Buy Side Information

Supplier & Product Souring of Indirect Goods & Services using various Web-based platforms

SUPPLY CHAIN MANAGEMENT

ERP
Direct link between Sales, Inventory, Purchasing, Accounting, and Finance Activities

Enterprise Content Manager
Managing E-Catalogue, Customer Online Customization, and Internal Information & Communication Applications

Order Management System
Managing the Optimal Way to Receive, Pack, Ship, and Deliver the Final Product as promised to Customer

Logistics Management
A single Platform to Direct, Plan, and Control Inventory Movement
Optimal Management of Warehouses, Transportation & Distribution Networks

EAI
Links All the Diverse Applications within the Enterprise

Sell Side Information

CRM – Automating & streamlining marketing, sales, and service process.

major financial investments that were not expected to be regained quickly. Consequently, a delayed effect had to be taken into consideration while planning the financial aspect of the model.

Value Proposition

Hussein and El-Sherif were perceptive enough to comprehend that before even going through with their business idea, the value clients would gain from doing business with their company had to be clearly outlined. After a series of mentally consuming meetings, they came up with the benefits companies would realize if they chose to eProcure their consumable goods through their potential company. These benefits are demonstrates in Table 1.

Initial Financing

After developing the business plan, the business model, and agreeing on the customer benefits, the next step involved financing the firm that was to be established. After a thorough financial analysis,

Exhibit 2b. Speedsend.com business process

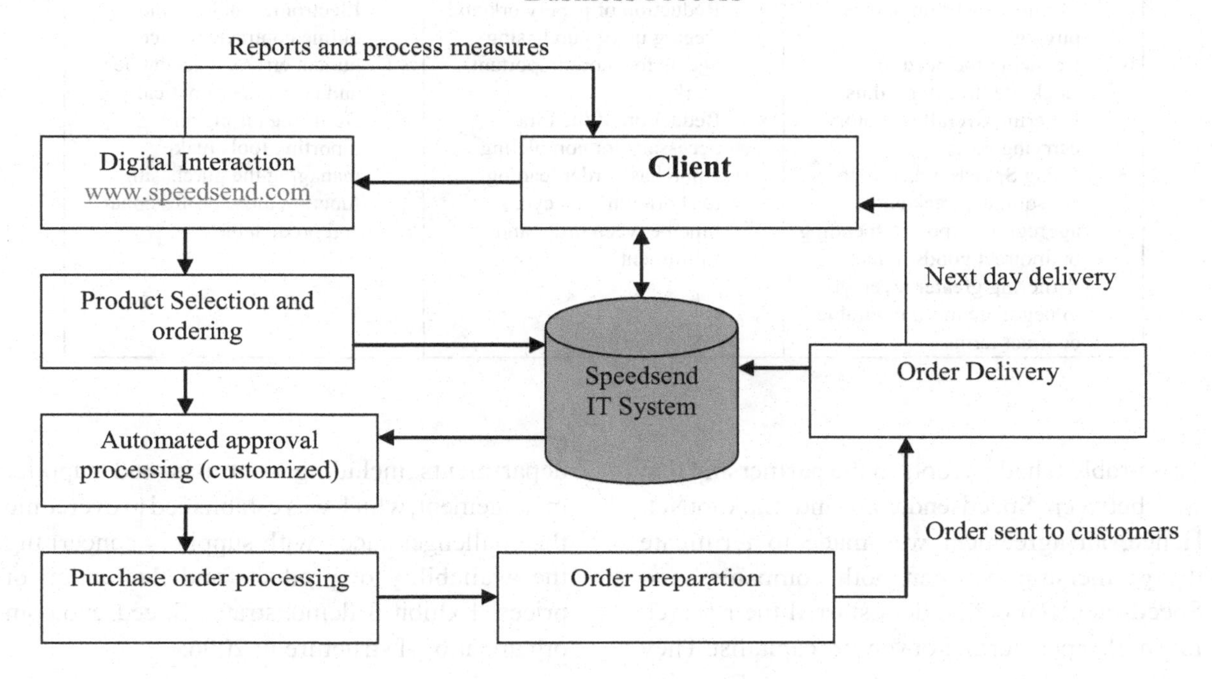

it was evident that in order to finance the project, 175,000 US dollars was needed in capital to be paid over a one-year period. During that time (December 2000), Egypt was going through a depression and no investor was willing to invest in an Internet startup, as it was perceived as a risky business with great uncertainty. Hussein and El-Sherif went to LinkdotNet[1] and met with its CEO Khaled Bishara, presented their business idea and invited him to become their partner in their promising business venture. After exhaustively analyzing the merit of the business opportunity presented, LinkdotNet signed a memorandum of understanding with Speedsend.com. In January 2001, a shareholders agreement was signed where LinkdotNet share amounted to 51% and it was to provide both financial support and technology expertise. The remaining 49% of the shares were divided equally between Speedsend.com cofounders. Hussein and El-Sherif were responsible for managing the business altogether. Speedsend.com was established as a legal entity with 175,000 US dollars in capital in June 2001 and in September of the same year, Speedsend.com Website was completed and the company was ready to start its operations (www.speedsend.com).

Speedsend.com Growth

In October 2001, Speedsend.com successfully finalized its first online sale to LinkdotNet and gradually the company started to build its reputation in the local market trying to sell the business idea and service to various clients. The business was growing slowly, and although Speedsend.com increased its capital by 175,000 US dollars in 2003, the business growth rate remained slow. From September 2004 until August 2005, Speedsend.com was a company that was merely surviving with minimal progress and no significant profits.

Table 1. Speedsend.com partner benefits

Cost Savings	Productivity Improvements	Efficiency Increases
• Elimination of unplanned buying • Reducing the need to stockpile inventory, thus lowering overall inventory carrying costs • Using Speedsend.com to consolidate, track and aggregate corporate spending on indirect goods, thus garnering greater leverage to negotiate more favorable contract terms	• Reduction of paperwork and freeing up of purchasing agents for more important work • Reduction of the time necessary for completing a purchase order leading to shortening the cycle time between order and fulfillment	• Electronic catalogs and online contracts reduce human errors, inaccuracies and reworks dramatically • Built-in auditing and reporting tools make managing the purchasing function more professional and predictable

This problem had its roots in the partnership that was between Speedsend.com and LinkdotNet. Hence, an agreement was made to terminate the partnership between both companies and Speedsend.com cofounders started their search for another partner and/or venture capitalist. They successfully managed to attract three Egyptian prominent businesspersons, to become partners and members of the board of directors, along with the initial cofounders. Hussein and El-Sherif were the only board members active in Speedsend.com management. The new board members had a diversified collection of expertise in financial management, organizational development, and project management. To lift Speedsend.com from the stagnant state it dwindled into, an additional influx of 350,000 US dollars were injected into the company, thus increasing the company capital to 700,000 US dollars. Speedsend.com was divided among the five board members equally, with each one owning 20% of the company shares. Speedsend.com new management structure led the company to great success and the company started acquiring new major clients, opening new branches and investing in more warehouses to meet the increasing clients' requests. With this expansion, they started recruiting more employees. Furthermore, as sales grew and clients' demands increased, the company started establishing new departments including contracts and supplier management, which was established to overcome the challenges faced with suppliers concerning the availability of products and fluctuation of prices. Exhibit 3 demonstrates Speedsend.com organizational structure in 2006.

Internal Operations and Capabilities

Ordering Cycle

Speedsend.com clients were offered a unique solution for their ordering process. The management of the company recognized the different modes, procedures, and regulations that each client had. Some clients assigned a specific person, department, or purchase panel for the ordering of the needed requirements. As for other clients and companies, they preferred to centralize purchasing through one department (gateway) and consequently, that department managed and distributed other departments' requirements. Accordingly, Speedsend.com set up its online modules to respond to each client-purchasing mode or way that was a challenge but the only way to cater to clients needs. When dealing with Speedsend.com, every ordering process passed through general steps that could be described as follows: (a) clients log onto Speedsend.com

Website through a user name and password, (b) clients select the products, quantities, and other variables of the orders, (c) clients send the orders through the Website and (d) Speedsend.com receives orders and act accordingly.

Clients could set different options through the initial service agreement with Speedsend.com. They could permit direct ordering for all employees or for a selected few, set approvals rules, or blend both ways into a unique ordering process that was aligned with the client's specific internal purchase policy and organization rules. Speedsend.com electronic ordering module had many features that complemented the customer ordering process. It had an electronic approval system where approvals were automated, online reporting module that allowed customers to track their purchasing pattern and generated purchasing reports, an integration with the customer's ERP solution (if available) which allowed a smooth ordering process within the customer's IT environment, and customized Webpages for each client for easy product selection and order development. Once a customer order was placed, the order and its specification were transmitted to Speedsend.com and stored in its database. The order took its route within the internal IT platform of Speedsend.com for approvals and regular checks. The order was then sent to inventory for dispatching the required products and the delivery cycle started. The process of internal ordering processing was fully automated and the ordering management system was totally linked to the logistics system to ensure smooth and quick flow of information leading to decreasing cycle time for the entire procurement process (Poirier & Bauer, 2001).

Purchase Cycle

Speedsend.com developed a supplier management system to streamline the process of purchasing; however, there were multiple processes involved in the purchasing cycle. The two most important aspects were demand forecasting and cash-to-cash management cycle. In the startup of Speedsend.com, suppliers were very reluctant to give stock on credit to Speedsend.com, as they were skeptical of the success of the business model coupled with the low ordering quantities. As the quantities increased and the model proved successful, this resulted in building suppliers trust; Speedsend.com was able to leverage better credit limits (45 days) which improved its cash-to-cash cycle dramatically. The type of suppliers Speedsend.com dealt with was non-IT oriented and distant from adopting an online IT-based environment, which set a huge challenge for Speedsend.com business model. Therefore, it was important for them to understand the impact of technology and gain competency in making a business case for eProcurement (Presutti, 2003). Suppliers did not only have a slow paper oriented system, they refused to change it.

Accordingly, the electronic cycle was broken and products were purchased using a non-digital mode. Although Speedsend.com team entered the newly purchased product into their computing environment, which re-linked the entire system, yet they purchased it from suppliers in a non-electronic manner, which added to the processing time and increased costs. The final and most challenging aspect of purchase management was demand forecasting which was regularly fluctuating. Over purchasing would result in overstock and cash flow problems, and under purchasing would result in under stock, which consequently would decrease Speedsend.com service level from the clients' point of view. Speedsend.com relied heavily on historical data of purchases done by their clients, hence developing a purchasing pattern for each client and combining all patterns to come up with the demand estimate or the purchasing pattern that would help Speedsend.com stock accurately according to real demand. Management also put around 10-15% overstock for unplanned or sudden demand fluctuations. The electronic nature of the buying (ordering) cycle of Speedsend.com clients, gave Speedsend.com

Exhibit 3. Speedsend.com organizational structure in 2006

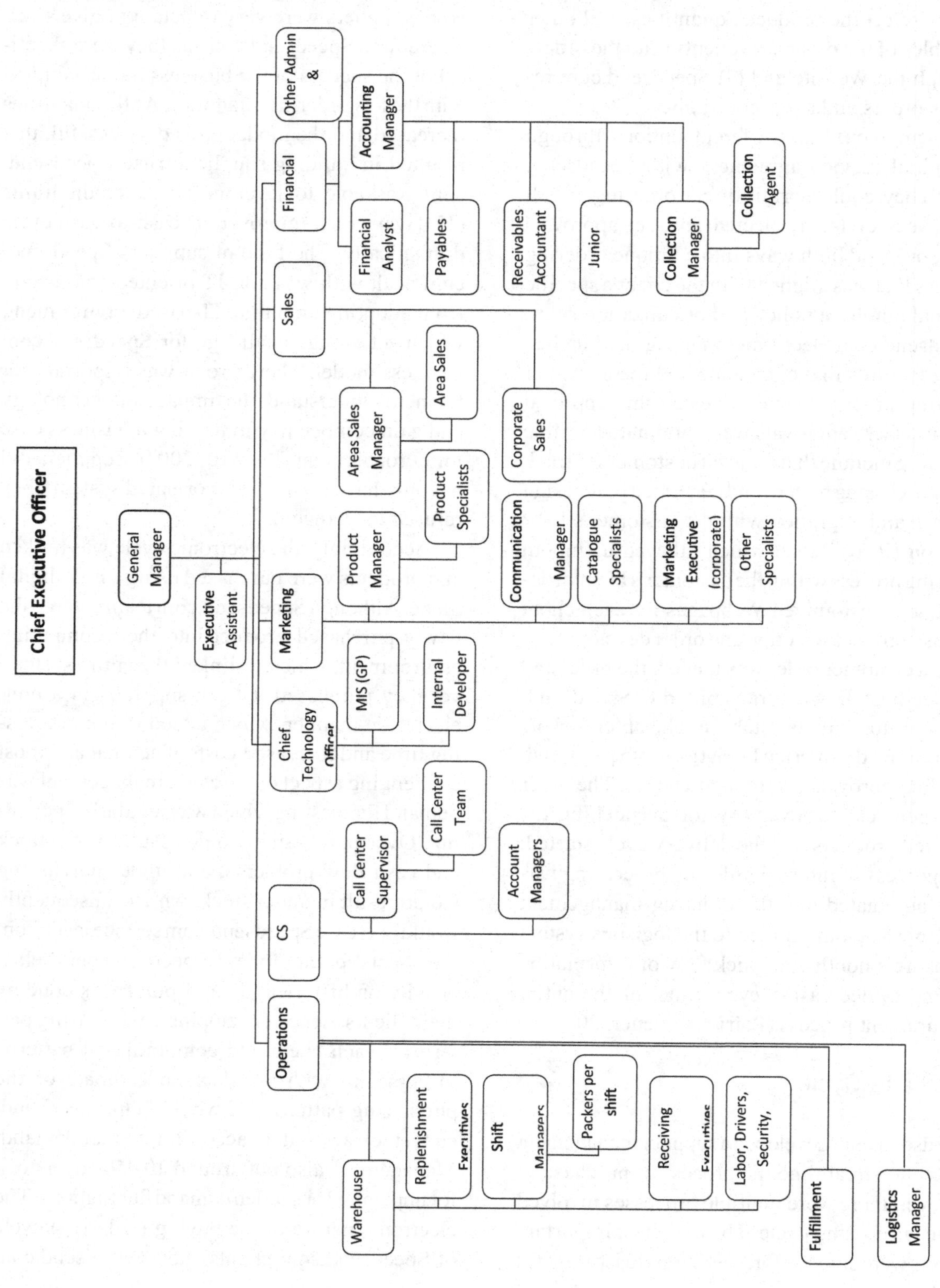

and its clients an edge in having on-time accurate information on the purchasing pattern and demand based on the reduction in purchasing cycle time enabled (Davila et al, 2003; Lin & Hsieh 2000; Radovilsky & Hegde, 2004).

Enterprise Content Management

Speedsend.com relied on its Website for processing customer orders and delivering a major portion of their services. Customer service representatives were very active and participated in developing customer satisfaction, yet the Website was the main customer interface, which put a huge importance on the performance of the Website. One important component that Speedsend.com management focused on in the company's Website was the ease of use and information provision. The more the Website was easy and provided useful information for customers the more it delivered customer satisfaction. Internal communication was critical to service processes. The speed of information flow as well as accuracy was an essential ingredient to service excellence. Accordingly, Speedsend.com used an advanced enterprise content management system that enabled the company to manage its electronic catalog, customer online customization process, and internal communication applications.

Customer Service

Speedsend.com operations focused on customer service more than observers could expect. Customer service was considered a customer retention point at Speedsend.com. Management believed that by servicing customers before, during and after the purchase, the company's value to customers increased and hence improved customer retention rate and built a shield against current and future competition. By 2006, Speedsend.com was employing seven customer service representatives to service its 2000 users covering 35 major clients. Speedsend.com customer service executives performed multiple tasks such as following-up customer orders to ensure fulfillment at the optimum service level, solving customer problems, answering customers questions, processing special request for customers, gathering post purchase satisfaction data, and developing relationship with clients. For each client dealing with Speedsend.com, there was a dedicated customer service agent catering to his/her daily needs. Such customer service agent in turns reported to an account manager. As the customer base grew, the number of customer service agents increased to ensure service level achievement and customer satisfaction. Moreover, account managers played a more superior role by performed prices negotiations, product line sales, understood customer needs, found new ways to integrate more with clients, and maintained the overall account status of customers. Such modality in dealing with clients and the development of such partnerships leads to closer and longer connections with business partners (Komp Leonard, 1999).

Training

Speedsend.com had a complete training and orientation program for the sales, customer service, and marketing and personnel departments. The training covered the basic requirements to understand the business model, operations, and customer interaction processes. However, due to the importance of employees' quality and the company's internal knowledge, management was always developing new training areas for almost all functions within the organizational structure. A cycle of three weeks was needed to prepare a new hire for flawless job functioning. Human capacity development was perceived as a vital building block for the success of Speedsend.com. This related to technology and non-technology related elements such as customer service, non-technology bound customer handling technology-based processes as well as operating a hybrid model of online and offline logistics.

Warehousing and Delivery

Warehousing and inventory management system were key components for effective operations of Speedsend.com. Warehousing represented a valve for Speedsend.com operations as well its contribution to the operational cost structure. Speedsend.com owned two warehouses of 1,000m^2 in space located in Cairo; an additional warehouse of 3,000m^2 was added in 2006. Inventory management operated through the Speedsend.com ERP system, which linked the ordering, delivery, and purchasing processes together.

To deliver its promises to its clients, Speedsend.com had to maintain a strong delivery arm in order to fulfill customer orders on time. Two important elements were involved in Speedsend.com delivery process; (a) on-time delivery that was critical in building customer satisfaction through a second day delivery model and (b) delivery cost that represented an important element within Speedsend.com business model. By 2006, Speedsend.com operated 10 delivery trucks to cover its annual 14400 orders to its 35 corporate clients with an average of 300 orders per week. Speedsend.com integrated a delivery system module within its ERP system to enable management of the complex delivery process to achieve customer requirements and at the same time keep costs level at minimum.

Online Information Dissemination

Online product catalog was vital for customer interaction. It helped Speedsend.com sell its current products, new products, and learn about customer preferences. The product catalog was the only interface Speedsend.com had with its customers. Accordingly, updating and managing the catalog was critical to customer satisfaction and service level. Speedsend.com updated its online catalog twice a year. The product selection process took about 6 months to complete. It involved dialog with both international brand owners such as HP, 3M, Imation and Stabilo, etc, as well as Speedsend.com local agents or distributors. The update process was seen as being slow due to the pace of the negotiation process having different offline and online channels in dealing with vendors. The operation took place inside and outside of Egypt. All the above-mentioned steps and communications slowed the operations of updating the catalogs. However, the clients' needs were changing in a slower pace, which balanced the scenario for Speedsend.com.

Website

Both the cofounders of Speedsend.com were focused on ensuring that the company's Website and interface that clients interacted with when dealing with Speedsend.com evoked feelings of simplicity, ease of use and at the same time exuded attractiveness and professionalism. Speedsend.com chose live and vivid colors, mainly red, light blue and shaded light grey, to represent their corporate identity, which made the site appear very attractive, professional and visually appealing. The graphics used on the Website were simple and slightly animated. The color scheme was easy to the eye and the icons used were innovative and attractive. On the home page, Speedsend.com highlighted its slogan "Simplifying Life at Work" to emphasize their competitive advantage in facilitating and simplifying the process of indirect goods procurement and management. Speedsend.com divided the Website into two types of interfaces, an interface accessible by all visitors and another accessible only by a username and password unique for each client doing business with Speedsend.com. The first interface, which could be accessed by all visitors, only displayed information about Speedsend.com. This interface did not allow visitors to purchase anything from Speedsend.com; however, it offered them the option to request a demo of the actual eProcurement site in order to experience the online buying process and to view the products and services offered by Speedsend.com and their prices. The main aim of this interface was to disseminate information about the company, help build Speedsend.com brand image and identity as well as attract potential clients. The interface was very simple, informative, attractive and easy to navigate. Moreover, the interface featured very cohesive and organized page content. It addressed most of the questions and concerns that Speedsend.com target customers could have and enticed interested companies to start using Speedsend.com. Finally, the site offered customer support through e-mail and telephone to respond to any visitor's inquiries or requests.

The second interface, which is the actual eProcurement site, could only be accessed by Speedsend.com clients. This section displayed all Speedsend.com products and services, allowing clients to navigate through them, choose the products that they would like to order, and then finally set their order. The site was very comprehensive, visually appealing in a professional context, well organized, as well as easy to navigate with a user-friendly interface. It also facilitated the purchasing process for clients by offering them a variety of search options for items such as searching by the brand, by the type of e-catalogue or by the category of product. Moreover, the Website offered clients a number of options such as the ability to create a favorites list of the items that were regularly purchased; receive reports of their consumption figures and patterns; view promotions on various items and allowed senior personnel within a client's organization to modify and approve their employees' orders before being processed by Speedsend.com. Exhibit 4 shows sample snapshots of Speedsend.com

SpeedSend Strategies

Sales Strategy

An integral part of Speedsend.com sales strategy was to go after the premium leaders of select industries, and use its partnership and close alliance to lure in other prominent companies within the same industry. For example, in the banking industry, Speedsend.com successfully signing with Citibank resulted in eventually acquiring HSBC as a customer. Similarly, establishing a very close relationship with British Gas helped Speedsend.com acquire BP and ExxonMobil as customers. Exhibit 5 demonstrates a sample of Speedsend.com customers. *"Acquiring industry leaders is our gateway to others in the industry"*, said El-Sherif. After carefully studying the local culture, the cofounders of Speedsend.com learnt that one of the key factors of success is building on interpersonal relationships and networking. Based on this fact, Speedsend.com management decided to use a direct sales approach to enable them to build strong business relationships and acquire new customers. Exhibit 6 demonstrates Speedsend.com achievements to date.

Speedsend.com sales strategy was divided into 3 components that addressed the company's target market, their products and their value proposition.

Retention and Client Growth Strategy

Through a dedicated customer service representatives' force, Speedsend.com aimed at growing its customers' sales from 1,050,000 million US dollars to 1,400,000 US dollars

Product Development Strategy

Through an innovative marketing department, Speedsend.com planned to grow its current existing product range, which will lead to sales of 500,000 US dollars from its current product range and sales mounting to 150,000 US dollars from new product developments

New Client Acquisition

Utilizing an aggressive sales strategy, Speedsend.com aimed at generating sales of 650,000 US dol-

Exhibit 4. Snapshot of SpeedSend Website

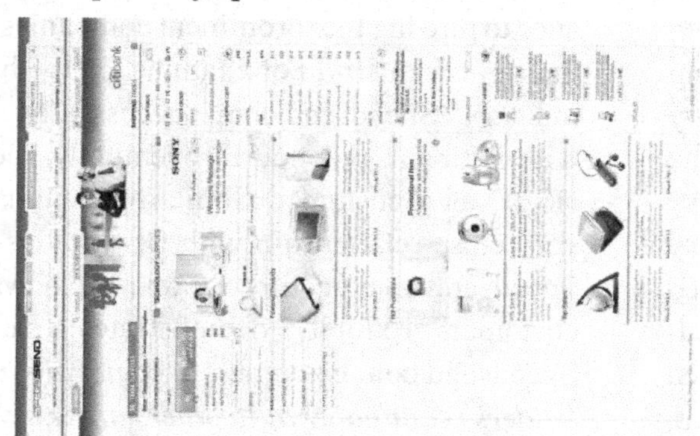

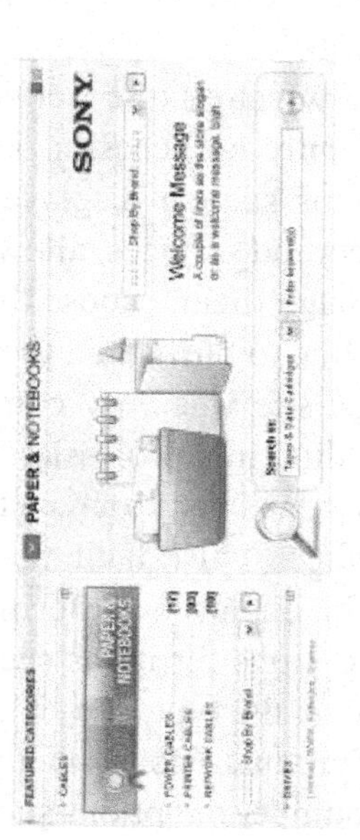

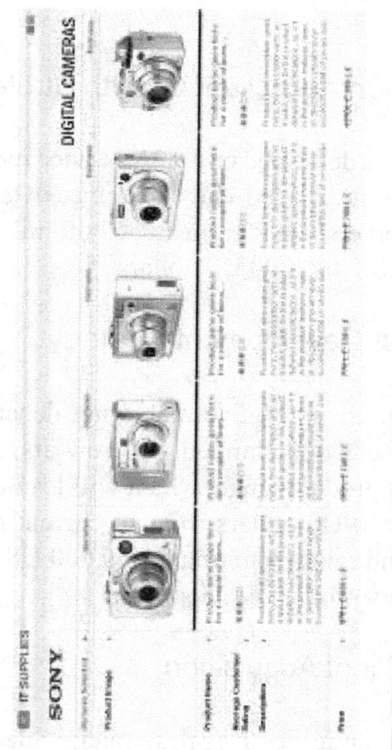

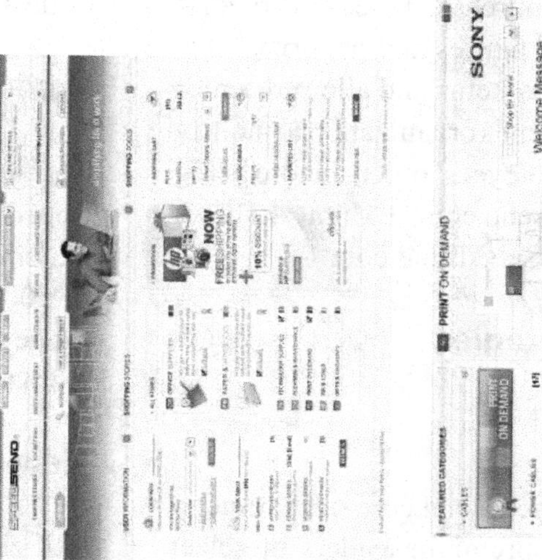

Exhibit 5. Some of Speedsend.com major corporate clients

- Al-Ahram Beverages Company
- Amiral
- BP
- British Gas
- Citibank
- DHL
- Egyptian Cement Company
- Exxon Mobil
- General Motors Corp.
- GlaxoSmithKline
- HC Securities and Investments
- HP
- HSBC
- LinkdotNet
- Master Foods
- McDonald's
- Mentor Graphics
- Microsoft
- Nile City Investments
- NSGB Bank
- Orascom Construction Industries
- Orascom Telecom
- Procter & Gamble
- Schlumberger
- Shell
- Travco

Exhibit 6. Speedsend.com achievements reached by 2006

- Over 2000 users from over 35 corporate clients
- Over 300 orders fulfilled weekly (next business day delivery)
- Over 2000 products
- 35 primary source suppliers
- 10 delivery vehicles covering a city of 18 million
- 3 warehouse facilities

Award Winning Technology
Speedsend.com won the Microsoft Gold Certificate for e-commerce in 2001–2002 and the Microsoft Egypt Award for best e-commerce solution in 2002–2003

Strategic Partnerships with Leading Business Communities in Egypt
Speedsend.com collaborated with Nile City Business Community, a premiere business community in Cairo, and the Smart-Village Business Community, Egypt's technology business park

HP Business Partner
SpeedSend signed a Select Business Partner Agreement with HP to be the first official ePartner selling HP Supplies in the Middle East

Certified Xerox Corporate Business Re-seller

Strategic Alliances
Speedsend.com underwent a strategic alliance with "Lyreco", a French company ranked amongst the first worldwide business2business distributors of office supplies. Moreover, Speedsend.com signed another strategic alliance with Sahara Press in 2005

lars from new corporate sales and sales mounting to 1,120,000 US dollars from SME sales.

Although Speedsend.com above-mentioned future growth and sales strategies were based upon sound analysis of the situation on hand and the company's capabilities, the question still remain unanswered on whether Speedsend.com will be able to deliver on its objective or not? How the company is planning to grow? Should it offer new channels? Should it develop a backward integration activity? Should it expand into new products in Egypt, go regionally or aim for a global outreach? There are multiple scenarios for the future and choosing the appropriate strategic direction will be the biggest challenge facing Speedsend.com.

Challenges

Demand Forecasting

Up until 2006, this remained the biggest challenge facing Speedsend.com as the company promised its clients next business day delivery. In Egypt, product availability and distribution systems were chaotic. In order to deal with this obstacle, Speedsend.com had to carry 25 days on hand stock to ensure order fulfillment deadlines were met. Carrying such levels of inventory imposed a big drain and constraint on the company.

Internal Communication

Communication remained a major challenge for Speedsend.com and the larger the company got, the larger this challenge became. For Speedsend.com, internal communication was important to their success as their departments coordinated and communicated with each other in the fastest and most efficient way to fulfill their "next business day delivery" promise. There was no room for communication gaps or lags. Thus, the business model needed to support consistently the efficiency of internal communication amongst the different departments.

Personnel Challenges

In many cases, what could make or break a company are the people working in that company. The quality of employees is very important. For Speedsend.com to succeed, management always had to be on the lookout for the right type of employees. Speedsend.com was always on the lookout for people who could take the initiative, be creative and carry the business forward with a vision similar to the owners' vision. On the other hand, the trade off was the high cost that was involved in recruiting and hiring those people. The higher the quality of employees a company wants to hire, the more one must be willing to pay.

Technological Challenges

The speed of developing new technology to match the business needs was becoming critical for both, the customer interface and the internal efficiency of the model. From a customer perspective, Speedsend.com was introducing technological changes to meet customer needs. However, Speedsend.com had to keep the balance between this business requirement and keeping the technology simple and not too complicated. From the internal system perspective, technological changes should be continuously offered to overcome system breakdowns, but unfortunately, this required huge financing. Some of the technological challenges could be obviously handled by providing good financing to support the model. Nevertheless, there were other challenges imposed that could not be handled by the company. For example, the broadband of the country was a problem. Some clients had low broadband levels so doing business with them was hard. Some clients were uneducated customers (i.e. no English, computer and internet literacy). Thus, conducting business with them was even harder. Consequently, Speedsend.com was evaluating the idea of "Arabizing" their portal.

Business Model Divide

The breakdown of Speedsend.com business model into offline and online operations represented a challenge for management in order to keep service level as promised to customers while making profits. Offline operations were presented in the heart of the supply chain (Suppliers). The search, evaluation, and actual operations with any given supplier were done offline, except of abroad vendors. However, operations were still done offline with local distributors, which disabled or slowed the model's operations, hence potentially increasing costs and disrupting the flawless flow of operations. The sales cycle and the initial contact with potential clients were done offline as the internet awareness, technology acceptance, and trust of online operations in Egypt was still too low. Balancing the fast-paced technology platform of Speedsend.com business model with the slow paced offline process without affecting the service level and cost structure was and remained to be a great challenge for Speedsend.com.

SWOT ANALYSIS

Table 2 demonstrates SpeedSend SWOT analysis as envisioned by the management of the company.

COMPETITION

Competition for Speedsend.com took mainly the form of traditional competition models. It ranged from large to small distributors, agents and stationary retailers, varying in sizes and number of branches. Big customers were served through monthly contracts, yet the majority of the market was using retail shopping to satisfy their consumables and office supplies needs. However, by 2006, some retailers, big importers, and distributors had started to adapt basic brochure internet models to promote their business. Branasouse and Kassem store in Egypt (www.kassemstore.com) was an example of such a player. Although in 2006, the Branasouse Website was a primitive Website used to display products and price (which were mostly outdated); the store is an example of a market player who should be considered as a future competitor for Speedsend.com.

Figure 1.

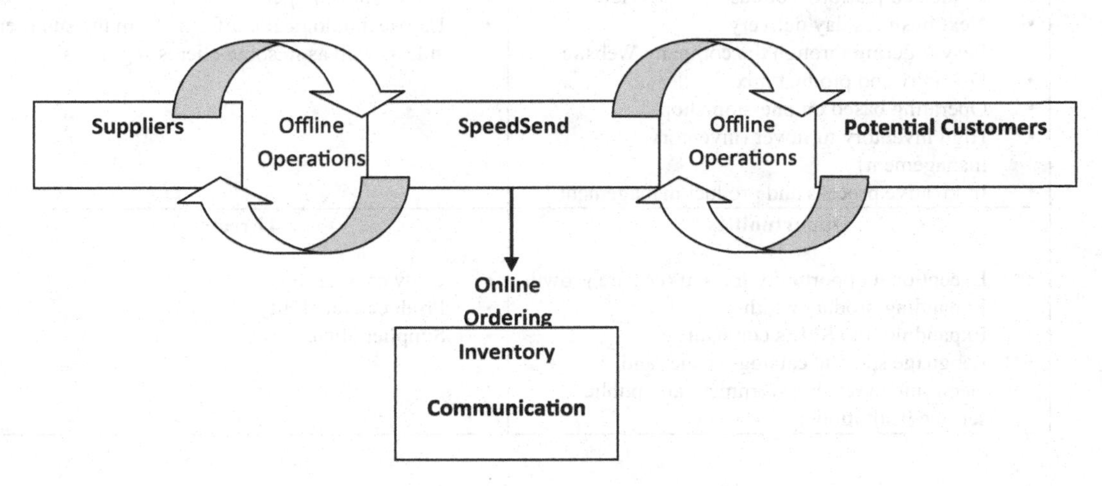

SPEEDSEND FINANCIALS

Speedsend.com financials give an insight on how the company was performing. As shown in Exhibit 7 (Figure 1), in 2006 Speedsend.com was experiencing growing revenues that reached 3.8 million US dollars. Their revenue streams were solely coming from the sales of products and services; however, in 2006 Speedsend.com management was planning to offer advertising spaces on their Website. Thus, a new revenue stream was expected. Moreover, Speedsend.com management was planning to request rebates from mother companies of international brands, such as HP and Xerox, when they reached a specific volume of sales for their products. It is noteworthy here to highlight how suppliers were increasingly trusting Speedsend.com and how the company was gaining weight in the market. When Speedsend.com started, back in the year 2000, they had to pay their suppliers in cash. No supplier trusted them enough to give them favorable payment terms as they the company's success was doubted. This mistrust lasted until 2003. After that, the company started getting some credit terms from some suppliers and by time, Speedsend.com was able to establish itself in the local market and achieve high volume of sales.

This consequently enabled them to gain the confidence of suppliers, and thus gaining more favorable payment terms. Successfully, in 2006 Speedsend.com was able to reach an agreement with its suppliers. This agreement entailed dealing with all suppliers on credit basis. (See Exhibit 7, Figure 2). Further illustrating the increasing trust and confidence factor in Speedsend.com is the comparison shown in Exhibit 7 (Figure 3). When comparing the company payables in the year 2002 to those of year 2006, a tremendous increase is seen, as Speedsend.com were allowed 55 days for their payables compared to 0 days in the year 2002. This reflects the great credibility that Speedsend.com had gained along those years. When looking at the company receivables, the graph shows that the number of days decreased from 47 days in the year 2002 to 38 days in 2006. This further proves the increasing power and control that Speedsend.com was getting in the market. (See also Exhibit

Table 2. SWOT analysis

Strengths	Weaknesses
• Utilizing technology to create a truly sustainable company • Dedicated platform for customer service • Next business day delivery • Easy ordering through the company Website • Diversity and product mix • Operating based on one-stop-shop • High inventory turnover (inventory management) • Innovative process and product management	• Resource limitation (lack of asset and a human resource base for expansion) • Under funded operation • Low technological platforms from the suppliers side as well as in some clients segments
Opportunities	**Threats**
• Exceptional opportunity for marketshare growth • Expanding product width • Expanding into SMEs companies • Language specific catalogs (paper and electronic to reach government and public service institutions)	• Copy cat market • Product availability • Supplier alienation

8a and 8b for Speedsend.com historical and projected income statement)

WHAT IS NEXT?

In 2006, Hussein and El-Sherif were contemplating how they would be able to achieve their growth objectives. Together, they came up with several strategies that they believed were suitable in helping achieve Speedsend.com ambitions. Those strategies relate to a number of organizational elements that could be demonstrated as follows:

- **Customer acquisition:** Setting up a specialized sales force that could acquire customers from different market segments
- **Ordering mediums:** Facilitating different ordering mediums for clients by utilizing the Web, creating a call centre and distributing paper catalogues
- **Business communities:** Branding Speedsend.com as the premium partner for the business community through unique customer service, customization and technology deployment
- **Expanding local market coverage:** Establishing a sales vehicle in different cities in Egypt including, but not limited to, Alexandria, Ismailia, Hurghada, Sharm El-Sheikh
- **Product line expansion:** Increasing the average order value per client by increasing the number of products that are offered to customers such as furniture, giveaways, printing, accounting forms and unique industry products
- **Introducing branded products:** Capitalizing on Speedsend.com branded paper by increasing the number of Speedsend.com branded products that can lead to higher margins
- **Warehousing and distribution facility:** Introducing state-of-the-art warehousing facility that can accommodate customer needs and product growth as well as increasing the number of vehicles required to cover a wider geographic market
- **Human resources:** Hiring and training qualified professionals who can grow all aspects of the business
- **Technology:** Investing in technology to support logistics, customer service and inventory management thus allowing Speedsend.com to maintain and grow its competitive edge

REFERENCES

American Chamber of Commerce in Egypt (2002) Information Technology in Egypt, Business Studies and Analysis Center, April

Angeles R (2006) Business-to-business E-Procurement Corporate Initiative: A Descriptive Empirical Study, ICEC Conference, Fredericton, NB, Canada, pp. 391-402

Avery S (2005) Intel Goes Global with Indirect Buying Strategy, Purchasing Magazine, April

Carayannis E G and Popescu D (2005) Profiling a Methodology for Economic Growth and Convergence: Learning from the EU eProcurement Experience for Central and Eastern European Countries. Technovation, Volume 25, Number 1, January, pp. 1-14

Carr A S and Pearson J N (1999) Strategically Managed Buyer-Supplier Relationships and Performance Outcomes. Journal of Operations Management, Volume 17, Number 5, August, pp. 497-519

Croom S Johnston R (2003) E-service: Enhancing Internal Customer Service through eProcurement, International Journal of Service Industry Management, Volume 14, Number 5, pp. 539-555

Exhibit 7. Speedsend.com financials

Chart A

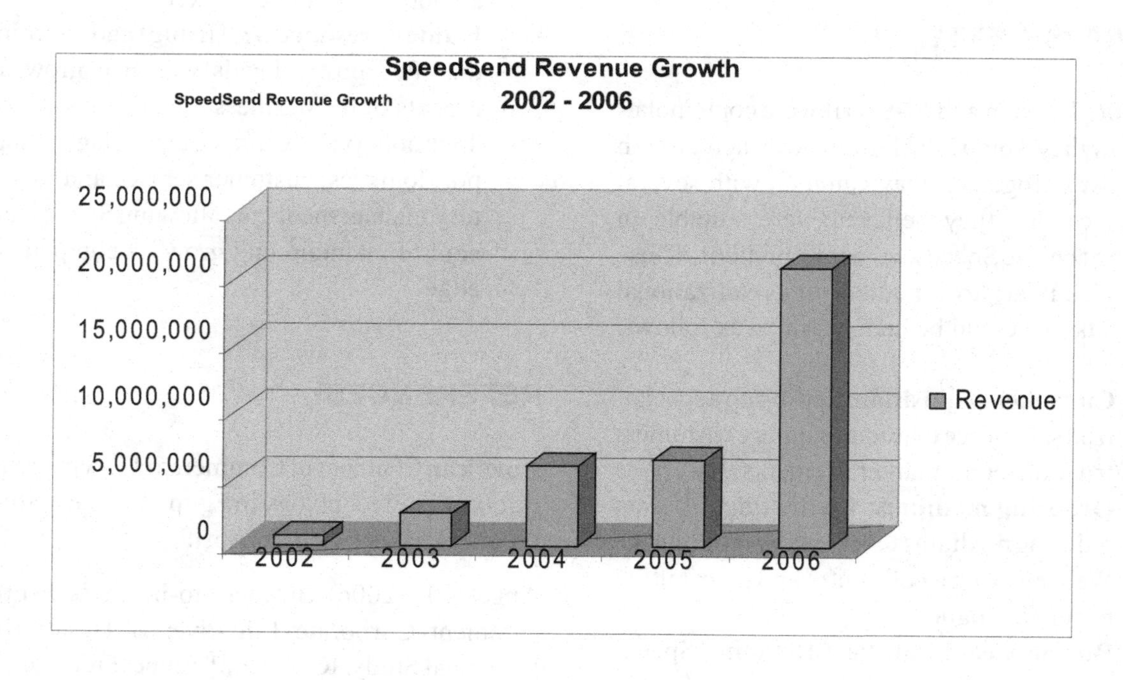

Chart B

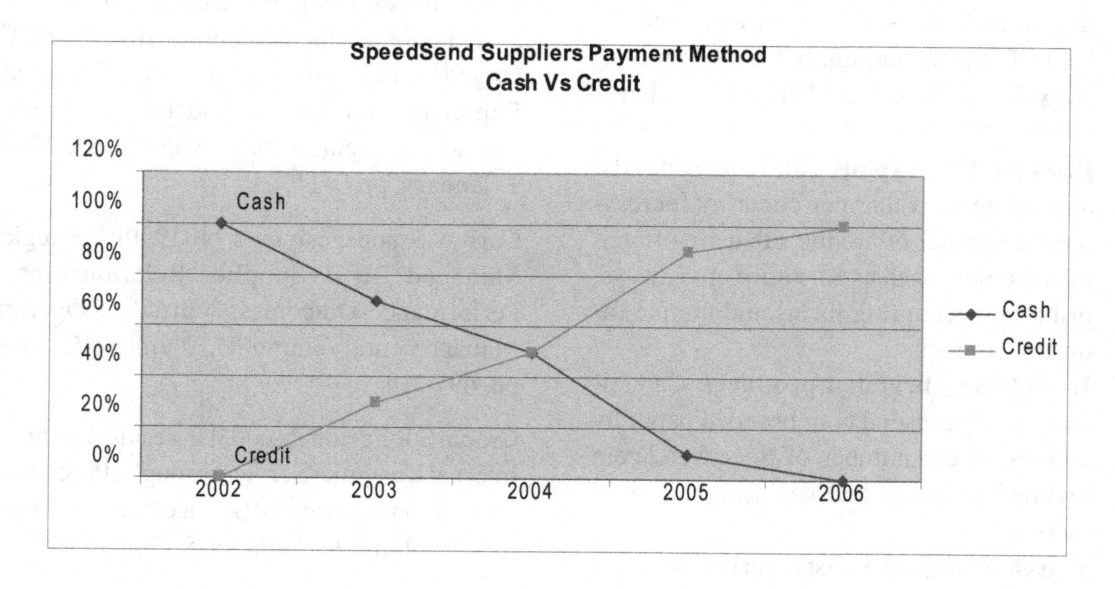

Exhibit 7. Speedsend.com financials

Chart C

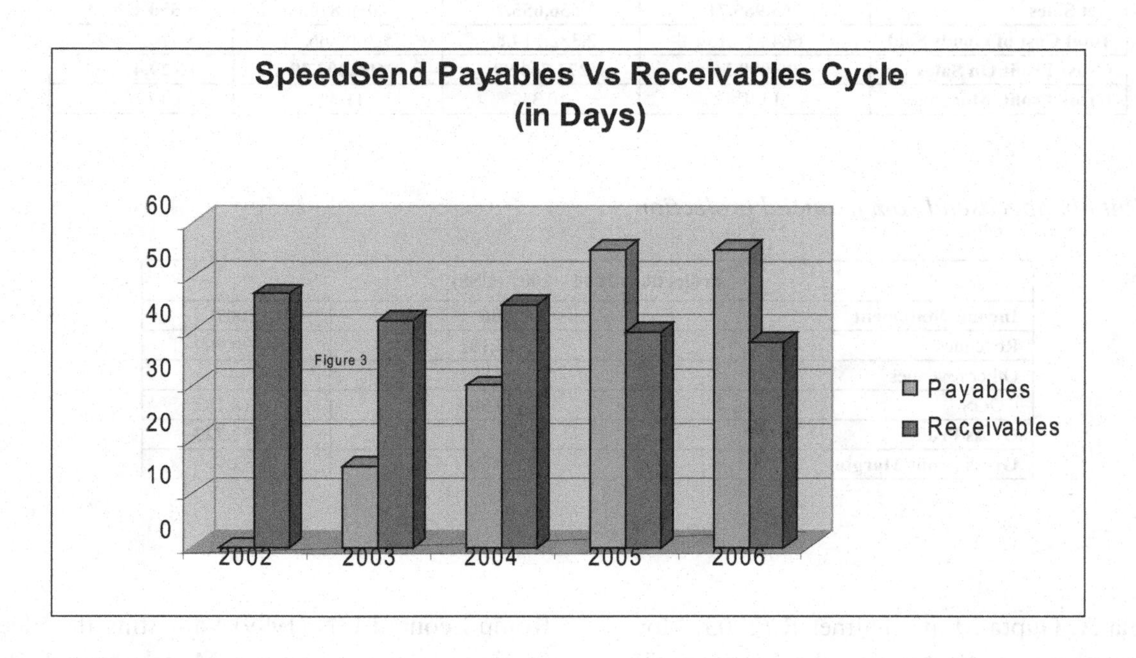

Chart D

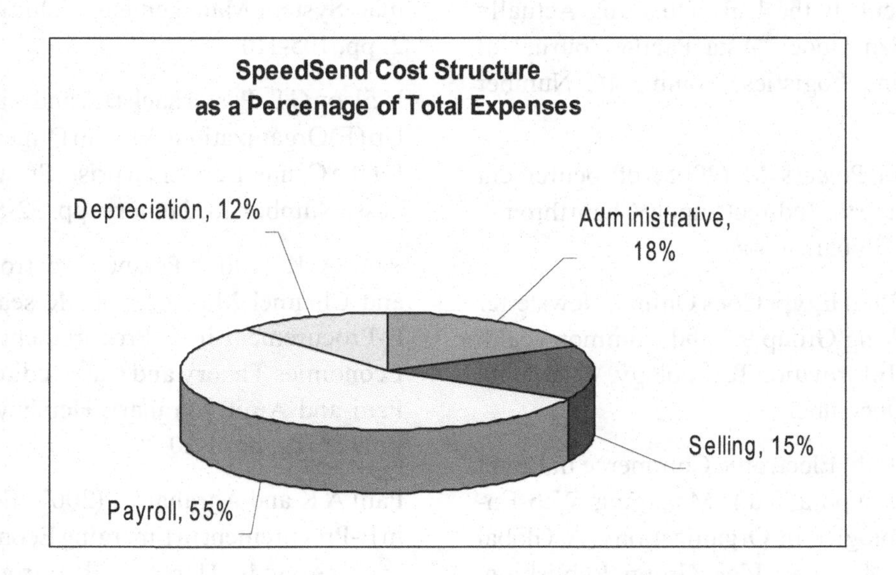

Exhibit 8a. Speedsend.com financial history

	Jan 2001-Dec 2002	Jan-Dec 2003	Jan-Dec 2004	Jan-Dec 2005
Net Sales	**763,985.71**	**2,656,655.75**	**6,050,870.00**	**6,550,424.21**
Total Cost of Goods Sold	664,886.15	2,382,914.85	5,360,666.71	5,420,946.24
Gross Profit On Sales	**99,099.56**	**273,740.90**	**690,203.29**	**1,129,477.97**
Gross Profit Margin	13.0%	10.3%	11.4%	17.2%

Exhibit 8b. Speedsend.com financial projection

Projections 2006 – 2007 (US$)		
Income Statement	**2006**	**2007**
Revenues	3,818,182	9,090,909
Other revenues	-	-
COGS	3,130,909	6,818,182
Gross Profit	**687,272**	**2,272,727**
Gross Profit Margin	18.00%	25.0%

Davila A, Gupta M and Palmer R (2003) Moving Procurement Systems to the Internet: The Adoption and Use of e-Procurement Technology Models, European Management Journal, Volume 21, Number 1, February, pp. 11-23

Hawking P, Stein A, Wyld C D and Foster S (2004) E-Procurement: Is the Ugly Duckling Actually a Swan Down Under. Asia Pacific Journal of Marketing and Logistics, Volume 16, Number 1, pp. 3-26

Ghiya K and Powers M (2005) eProcurement – Strengthening the Indirect Supply Chain through Technology Globalization

Kamel S (2000a) Egypt Goes Online, Newsletter of IFIP Working Group 9.4 and Commonwealth Network for Information Technology, Volume 10, Number 3, December

Kamel S (2000b) Electronic Commerce in Egypt in M. Khosrowpour (ed.), Managing Web-Enabled Technologies in Organizations: A Global Perspective, Hershey: Idea Group Publishing, pp. 210-232

Komp Leonard L N (1999) Validating the Electronic Commerce Success Model through the Supply Chain Management Model. Doctoral Dissertation, University of Arkansas

Lin B and Hsieh C T (2000) Online Procurement: Implementation and Managerial Implications, Human System Management, Volume 19, Number 2, pp. 105-110

Neilson G L, Pasternack B A and Visco A J (2000) Up (E)Organization! A seven Dimensional Model for the Center Less Enterprise, Strategy and Business, Number 18, January, pp. 52-57

Pani A K (2007) Perspective from IOIS, EDI and Channel Management: Research Issues in E-Procurement in E-Procurement in Emerging Economies Theory and Cases edited by Ashis K Pani and Amit Agrahari, Hershey: Idea Group Publishing, pp. 1-20

Pani A K and Agrahari A (2007) E-Procurement in E-Procurement in Emerging Economies Theory and Cases (eds), Hershey: Idea Group Publishing, pp. vi-xiii

Phillips P A (2003) E-Business Strategy: Text and Cases, McGraw-Hill, Maidenhead, England

Philips P and Piotrowicz W (2006) E-Procurement: How Does it Enhance Strategic Performance? Working Paper Series Number 113, Kent Business School, April

Poirier C C and Bauer M J (2001) E-Supply Chain: Using the Internet to Revolutionize your Business, San Fransisco: Berrett-Koehler Publishers

Podlogar M (2007) E-Procurement Success Factors: Challenges and Opportunities for a Small Developing Country in E-Procurement in Emerging Economies Theory and Cases edited by Ashis K Pani and Amit Agrahari, Hershey: Idea Group Publishing, pp. 42-75

Presutti W D (2003) Supply Management and e-Procurement: Creating Value Added in the Supply Chain, Industrial Marketing Management, Volume 32, Number 3, April, pp. 219-226

Radovilsky Z and Hegde G V (2004) Factors Influencing e-Commerce Implementation: Analysis of Survey Results, Journal of Academy of Business and Economics, Volume 4, Number 1, March, pp. 29-37

Speedsend.com Company Reports (2007) www.speedsend.com (Website) last accessed 25 July

Somasundaram R (2007) Challenges in Implementation of E-Procurement in the Indian Government in E-Procurement in Emerging Economies Theory and Cases edited by Ashis K Pani and Amit Agrahari, Hershey: Idea Group Publishing, pp. 76-100

Subramaniam C and Shaw M J (2002) A Study of the Value and Impact of B2B E-Commerce: The Case of Web-Based Procurement. International Journal of Electronic Commerce, Volume 6, Number 4, Summer, pp. 1940

Turban E, King D, Viehland D and Lee J, Electronic Commerce: A Managerial Perspective, Pearson-Prentice Hall, Upper Saddle River, NJ

Yamamoto G T and Karaman F (2007) Barriers to E-Procurement Adoption: The Turkish Case in E-Procurement in Emerging Economies Theory and Cases edited by Ashis K Pani and Amit Agrahari, Hershey: Idea Group Publishing, pp. 101-125

ENDNOTE

1. LinkdotNet is one of the largest Internet Service Providers in Egypt. The company was formed as a merger between In-Touch Communications, the first ISP in Egypt established in 1992 and Link Egypt, a company established in 1995 to provide turnkey Internet services and solutions. In June 2000, the two joined forces to become LinkdotNet

Chapter XVIII
The State and Development of E-Commerce in Serbia

Borislav Jošanov
Higher School of Professional Business Studies, Novi Sad, Serbia

Marijana Vidas-Bubanja
Belgrade Business School, Serbia

Emilija Vuksanović
University of Kragujevac, Serbia

Ejub Kajan
High School of Applied Studies, Serbia

Bob Travica
University of Manitoba, Canada

ABSTRACT

The authors of this chapter constructed and published multidimensional model for the evaluation of e-commerce diffusion in any country. According to this model qualitative research of conditions for e-commerce penetration in Serbia was conducted. Serbia is located on an important geographical location in Southeast Europe. After Yugoslavia's falling apart and a decade of stagnation, Serbia came to a road of economic changes and it became an economy in transition – it was pronounced the leading reformer in 2005 by The World Bank. Our main finding is that the process of diffusing e-commerce in Serbia is still on the waiting list, but different states are found for different layers of this multidimensional model. Some good experiences found in Serbia's e-commerce practice are mainly from the B2C e-commerce, while a strategy of B2B e-commerce could be a catalyst for pulling together the facilitating conditions and engaging Serbia in global electronic economy.

Copyright © 2009, IGI Global, distributing in print or electronic forms without written permission of IGI Global is prohibited.

INTRODUCTION

This study is the result of the wide research which investigated the conditions for **diffusion of e-commerce in Serbia**. For developing countries like **Serbia**, e-commerce can be noticed as a compelling strategy and a paramount opportunity for economic development. The ongoing globalization process has the strong driving force in a "revolution in information technology" which has led to the emergence of a "global informational capitalism" (Castells, 2000). Each developing country which tends to be a part of the global capitalist economy has to be a part of international electronic networks. Our question which we appointed before our research was: how Serbia responds to these opportunities and challenges?

Serbia is one of the most important crossroads of Europe, featuring important roads and railways (USAID, 2007). Flows of row materials from the east and south used to cross Serbian territory on their way to the industrialized European countries, and the finished goods used to follow the opposite direction. The economic turmoil in the 1990s has seriously challenged its capability of integrating into the global digital economy. Significant transitory moves in last seven years brought Serbia to the position of the leading reformer in 2005, according to the investigation of The World Bank (2005). This chapter will try to analyze the conditions for diffusing e-commerce in Serbia today.

MAIN FACTS ABOUT SERBIA

Serbia is an old European country and a new member of world community, still waiting for the final definition of the borders and the integration into international community. Main characteristics of Serbia are given in Table 1. Separation processes left strong scarf on economy and social values in Serbia.

Thinking about conditions for diffusion of **e-commerce** in Serbia, the authors of this study conducted an integral investigation based on a previously defined multidimensional **model** (Travica et al, 2006). After more than a decade of stagnation Serbia is on the road of economic and political changes. It is located on an important geographical location, on the crossroads between north and south, and east and west of the Europe. That is the reason why Serbia is one of the significant crossroads of Europe, featuring important international roads and railways. This characteristic raises the importance of Serbia in the period of economic restructuring of Europe, triggered by the fall of the Berlin Wall in 1989. Flows of raw materials from the east and south would naturally cross Serbian territory on their way to the industrialized west and north Europe, and the finished goods would follow in the opposite direction. While enjoying this potential role of a geographic chain link, Serbia slid into a political and economic turmoil in the 1990s, which has seriously challenged its capability of integrating into the global electronic economy (Dinkić, 1995). NATO attacks in 1999, which destroyed bridges, main factories and a lot of transport infrastructure, made the situation even much worse. On the other hand, Serbia makes significant transitory efforts. The World Bank has rated Serbia as the "leading reformer in 2005." These reasons motivated our study.

This research has one restriction: as the part of Serbia called Kosovo is under the international governance lead by the United Nations and it is now completely autonomous, it is excluded from this research.

Serbia used to be the largest federal unit in a country called Yugoslavia (meaning: the country of Southern Slavs), which stretched from Greece to Austria and Italy. Although situated in Eastern Europe, Yugoslavia was never part of the Eastern Block. Contrary to it, Yugoslavia boasted a hybrid economic system in which major firms were

Table 1. Characteristics of Serbia

Area	88,361 square kilometers
Population	9,800,000 (July 2007 est., 7,800,000 excl. Kosovo)
Larger cities	Belgrade (the capital, 1.6 million), Novi Sad (500,000), Niš (250,000), Kragujevac, (175,000) and Subotica (120,000)
GDP	$44.83 billion; $4,400 per capita (excl. Kosovo)
GDP Composition	57.9% services, 25.5% manufacturing, 16.6% agriculture
Inflation Rate	18% (2005)
Unemployment Rate	31.6% incl. Kosovo (Kosovo 50%)
Brain Drain	More than 200,000 with undergraduate and higher education
Telephones	2,685,000 (2004) mobile 5,229,000 (2005, excl. Kosovo)

government-run, while private small and medium size enterprises operated across industries—from agriculture, to transportation, tourism, and to software/hardware production. The political system, however, mirrored the model of the Eastern single-party monopoly, while boasting larger individual freedoms. Yugoslavia's social system was also unique in its capability of balancing enormous differences concerning the economic power of its federal units and the cultural traditions of its many ethnic and religious groups. At a high benchmark level, Yugoslavia was scoring high annual rates of economic growth and played a role of bridging the political east and west, and north and south. Peculiar as it was, Yugoslavian system had long been in operation due to a combination of internal and external political factors, up until winds of change hit Yugoslavia and Europe in the late 1980s.

In the changed international environment of the 1990s, Yugoslavia disintegrated along the borders of its federal units and locations of different ethnic groups, through processes of secession with violent aspects. Serbia fell into a period of hardship, as our analysis will repeatedly point out. The hallmark of the 1990s period was governance that lacked economic and political wisdom needed for adaptation to the changed environment. Serbia plunged into international isolation, economic embargo, and an overall decline. The final blow came in 1999, when the Clinton administration moved NATO's air force into a campaign against Serbia, which decimated the already unraveled economy. Serbia entered the new millennium with its economy being half the size of that in 1990 (The World Factbook, 2007).

Hundreds of thousands of refugees from war-thorn parts of the former Yugoslavia and from Kosovo ended up in Serbia. In these days, after all efforts for their return, we found information, according to UNHCR, that in Serbia are 100,651 refuges from Croatia, 46,951 refuges from Bosnia and Herzegovina and almost 246,391 internally displaced people from Kosovo, what makes the largest population of refuges and IDP in Europe today (The World Factbook, 2007) ibid.

A political turnover in 2000 finally put a bar to the reign of entropy. Serbia joined the line up of the developing countries presenting economies in transition, and began searching for its place in the new world.

We believe that the combination of geographical importance and the unleashed economic changes qualifies Serbia's e-commerce situation as an important topic with potential contributions to theory and practice in the areas of international information systems, e-commerce/business, and management. The present study has investigated the conditions for diffusion of e-commerce in Serbia. Serbia sits on a geographical location that is important for international trade. After a decade of stagnation and seclusion, indications of change show up in the economy and other areas in Serbia (Travica et al, 2007). For developing countries, e-commerce presents a compelling strategy and a paramount opportunity for economic development. The other argument could be found by relating the ongoing process of globalization to a "revolution in information technology" that has led to the emergence of a "global/informational capitalism." To be part of the global capitalist economy, a developing country, as any other, has to be capable of acting in international electronic networks.

LITERATURE REVIEW AND METHODOLOGY

The study of **e-commerce** in developing countries is interesting for the researchers in the recent years (Palvia et al., 2002; Kamel, 2006; Wolcott et al., 2001). By definition, the theme of e-commerce sits at the intersection of IS research and business/management research. With this anchoring, researchers have been giving different emphases to particular issues, such as culture, regulatory environments, strategies, diffusion models, industry analysis, outsourcing, supply chains, electronic marketplaces, organizational designs, business process change, adoption and success factors, digital divide, and security. Country-focused studies are frequent and usually take the form of case study of a country as a whole or of individual companies in particular nation-state environments.

Cultural issues are a popular choice. Among these, the topic of trust looms throughout every national context (Kamel, 2006; Cronin, 2000). For example, the authors of research in China (Efendioglu & Yip, 2005) specifically propose that a virtual storefront has to be supported by a local distribution center, which would cater to Chinese culture and overcome a lack of "transactional trust." The problem of trust in on line merchants is also evident in Southern Korea and Latin America (Lee, 1999; Plant, 2000; Travica, 2002). For instance, Costa Rican customers prefer to shop directly from known merchants and thus reduce uncertainty regarding quality of products. Differing kinds and levels of trust are accompanied by particular cultural norms that have come into the relationship with e-commerce. For example, Costa Rica nurtures cultural norms that are responsible for turning a blind eye on violations of satellite regulations by businesses (Travica, 2002) ibid. On the other side of the globe, Russia and Ukraine, the strongest economies in the former Soviet Union, share a host of cultural traits that may constrain e-commerce, including personal networking with the business community, a preference of cash payments, underdeveloped records management (receipts not issued, limited accounting practices), lack of English language skills, a looser approach to time management, and a rigid hierarchal management hostile to information sharing and employee empowerment (Jennex & Amoroso, 2006).

Research on the diffusion of e-commerce in the region interesting to our study is in its initial stage. An early study of 11 countries including Bulgaria, Hungary, Romania, and Slovenia found that the Web sites in English were mostly informational rather than advertising or transaction oriented (Travica & Olson, 1998). Also, ambiguous relationships between sites and the background businesses were detected in Romania, while instances of mixing political expressions with business information were found in Hungary and Slovenia. Furthermore, an important study of Papazafeiropoulou (2004) contains conditions for e-commerce diffusion in some countries in southeast Europe (SEE). The author found government intervention to be a factor for a successful diffusion. This intervention is premised on expected social benefits from greater use of IT, improvements of employees' skills, and increased competition in the telecommunications market that could stimulate new investments and innovative products and services. Country-wise, the study has found that Bulgaria has qualified technical personnel, while it lacks public subsidy needed for commerce entrepreneurs. The Former Yugoslav Republic of Macedonia has many portals and content providers, while suffering from a bad telecommunication infrastructure. In Romania, the IT and telecommunications industries are strong and competitive, while there exist a low penetration of the telephone network and delays in rural development. Albania exhibits a paradox of high annual rates of **Internet** growth countered by limited Internet access by companies and individuals (Papazafeiropoulou, 2004) ibid.

Vidas-Bubanja and colleagues (2002) have provided a study of e-commerce in Serbia, in which they found that about 2,000 firms used the Web sites only for informational purposes. They also reported on interesting examples of e-commerce enterprises in Serbia, including a large portal, a virtual mall, and a content provider specialized in metallurgy. The authors noted the government's efforts in supporting e-commerce, such as establishing strategic partnerships with foreign IT vendors. Maruzzelli (2004) also investigated similar issues in a study sponsored by a private sector arm of the World Bank Group. The study found that, in 2003, Serbia was in an early phase of Internet adoption, with high growth rates. The infrastructure for distributing Internet access was under development, and methods for e-payment were in infancy, and dialup access was dominant as a profitable operation of the government-owned ISP. Maruzzelli also described major players in the telecommunications and e-commerce sectors, and cites the monopolistic role of Telekom Serbia as a limiting factor. Two important researches come from Travica and colleagues in 2006 and 2007, based on the same **model** that is used in this research, and they are expanded and refreshed by the same group of authors.

The research problem of our study concerned the possibilities for developing EC in Serbia. The study is aimed at answering on this research question: What are the conditions for diffusion of EC in Serbia? The term "conditions" refers to the dimensions in our research model discussed below. The term "diffusion" refers to the indications of movement toward EC, which could be understood as initiation, action, change, processes, and institutionalization rather than in the narrow technical sense of diffusion of innovation. The term "EC" implied the B2B and B2C segments. The study was driven by a research **model** of necessary conditions ("layers") for diffusion of

Figure 1. Research model

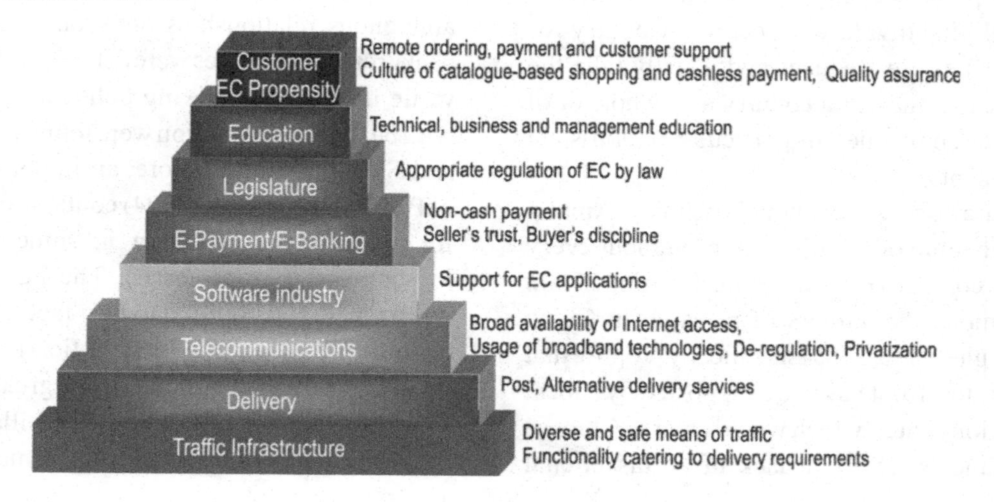

EC, shown in Figure 1. To the original model described by Travica in 2002, two more layers are added: legislature (to reflect the fact that the European EC context is increasingly regulated) and education (to account for the growing importance of education for EC and management). Also, the original e-payment layer is broadened by e-banking, and the bottom layer is renamed into "traffic infrastructure."

Our investigation was designed as an interpretive case study (Baskerville & Myers, 2004). We used interviewing, surveying, observation, document analysis, main national statistical researches, and Web site analysis for collecting data. Most of this data was content analyzed. When our attempts to collect data from intended samples failed, we drew inferences from limited samples, while relying on the individual expertise that each of us has in respective areas.

TRANSPORT INFRASTRUCTURE

The most basic layer in our pyramidal model of EC refers to traffic infrastructure—roads, air traffic facilities, railroads, and waterway (Travica, 2002) ibid, which provide support for delivery services required both in B2C and B2B EC.

The land traffic infrastructure in Serbia is well-developed intercity road network that is comparable in terms of density and pavement type to that of the most advanced Central and East European countries. The total length of roads is 42,692 km, where 24,860 km are paved roads. Roads are provided for the main transportation route in Serbia. Since ancient times, the Morava river valley is the crossroads between the North and South, and East and West. The major road in Serbia is the cross-Europe highway E-75 that connects Norway with Greece and it is well-known as Corridor 10 (ECMT, 2005). Thru the same valley passes another important road: the international highway E-70 that starts in Spain and, via Romania, ends in Turkey. Also an important road connects Niš with Sofia, the capital of Bulgaria. This is a branch of Corridor 10 that links to Corridor 4 and it is important because, in a way, Corridor 4 competes with Corridor 10 as it bypasses Serbia (originates in Germany, and runs through Hungary, Romania, and Bulgaria to Greece and Turkey). Yet, another important road is E-763, the B-category route that links Serbia with Montenegro, which is now in reconstruction process.

The layout of the roads and their inclusion in European Union's strategic corridors create favorable conditions for the commercial traffic in Serbia. Some economic experts contend that the country can become a transportation hub. In addition, the degree of the development of intercity network creates a potential for increasing the reach of delivery that e-commerce may require. However, the scenario of economic development capitalizing on transportation opportunities is far from being uncontested. One difficulty refers to a poor condition of the road network. The funding of road maintenance has decreased dramatically in the 1990s. Unsustainable tariff and financial policies and mismanagement of available funds have resulted in a significant de-capitalization of the transportation sector and in lagging behind the neighboring countries. Serbia spends only $570 per kilometer of road maintenance, which is 26 times less than what is spent in developed European countries.

The railroad traffic infrastructure in Serbia involves over 3,808.5 kilometers of rails (one third being electrified). Backbone lines support the hub position: 40% or railroads are included in Corridor 10 and they fully connect Serbia with the neighbors and with three seas. A railroad also connects Belgrade with the largest seaport Bar in Montenegro. A 500 kilometer-long segment of a high-speed railway is in very slow under way.

Serbia's waterways also have an international character—four of its five longest rivers flow over the country's borders. In contrast to the state of air traffic infrastructure, Serbia's waterways may be exhibiting stronger signs of vitality. There area several significant waterways that support both domestic and international traffic. Here belong the rivers Danube, Sava, Morava, Tisa, and Tamiš. All but the Morava flow over Serbia's borders. The Danube River is crucial since it flows through ten European countries over 2,850 km and it presents a significant economic potential (World Bank, 2005). It runs through ten European countries, making a transportation corridor in itself. This Corridor 7 connects west and east Europe, and the North Sea with the Black Sea. A realization of the traffic scenario, however, is challenged by a poorer condition of the road network and losses in the road and railroad traffic due to mismanagement and destruction in the 1990s. The stretch of the Danube through Serbia amounts for about 20% of its length. Three bigger ports are in Serbia: Novi Sad, Belgrade, and Smederevo. Port Novi Sad is important as the entry point for the pan-European traffic. The Belgrade port is significant not only as a Danube port but also as a crossroads, for that is where the Danube and the Sava meet, and Corridor 7 (the Danube) and Corridor's 10 intersect (indeed, two parts of this corridor—the main trunk and north wing; see Figure 2). Some observers posit that the Danube can present a particular economic advantage for the country. Serbian economy also uses the seaports in Montenegro, Bulgaria and Romania.

Another challenge refers to the state of the air traffic infrastructure. For example, the Belgrade Airport lost its international prominence it enjoyed before the 1990s, and the ensuing drop in income downgraded the maintenance and asset renewal capabilities of this and other airports. NATO's bombing raids in 1999 additionally deteriorated the situation. The air traffic infrastructure in Serbia contains 36 airports (paved or unpaved) and a few heliports. Main airports are in Belgrade (now Nikola Tesla Airport) and Niš (both international). The resent investments in Nikola Tesla Airport promoted this airport as a future hub for Southeast Europe. Another important fact is that this airport is chosen to be the gateway for all flights which are connecting Europe and Cuba.

DELIVERY CHALLENGES

The term delivery can be defined as moving the goods from the seller to the buyer. It includes the services of transportation, warehousing, freight forwarding, logistics (planning the shipment routes and timing, shipment tracking), and other steps in the order fulfillment process. It includes the transportation infrastructure for physical movement of the goods as well as on telecommunications for order placing and shipment management. Fulfilling an order is the final step in a supply chain for a particular commodity. The delivery layer is necessary for shifting commerce into the electronic context.

E-commerce is not just about putting up a Webs storefront or establishing EDI or extranet links between institutional sellers and buyers. If a seller participating in e-commerce markets does not provide delivery on its own, such a seller needs to have stable relationships with providers of delivery services. These relationships could be realized via long-term contracts between sellers and delivery firms. Alternatively, short-term deals suit the purpose, provided that delivery firms operate in the geographical regions in which sellers and buyers reside. The price of jumping into e-commerce without including delivery services into business models can be high.

In Serbia, the main provider of land delivery services is Serbian Post (Public Enterprise of PTT Communications "Srbija;" "PTT" stands for "Post, Telegraph, and Telephone") (PTT Serbia, 2007). This is a government-owned monopoly with major stakes in a number of subsidiary companies, covering landline and mobile telephony, banking, and **Internet** services (see the sections on telecommunications and software industry). Serbian Post provides door-to-door delivery of semi-finished goods between manufacturers and from manufactures to retailers, warehousing, handling of returned shipments, and international delivery in cooperation with DHL. In a process of diversifying its portfolio, Serbian Post has partnered with Neckermann, a German retail firm with a long tradition of catalog sale. Serbian Post delivers products ordered through the catalog, and supports the manual payment procedures.

Railroad traffic adds to the delivery capability of the country. The national railroad company plays part in cargo delivery that is at a modest level. The sole domestic player in this industry is the government owned enterprise Serbian Railways, which owns 158 of active stock and 4800 cargo wagons. In 2000, about 4,000 rail lines were operated, which marked a moderate level of railroad traffic in comparison to the neighbor countries. However, the actual cargo traffic was not at par with these countries, placed Serbia in 2001 next to the lowest ranked Bosnia and Herzegovina.

Other players have more limited capabilities. For example, some whole sellers and retailers offer transportation and warehousing services, and smaller private firms and independent truckers offer transportation. FedEx and UPS are present, expanding the global delivery offerings. There are other players in the delivery industry, although their capabilities are limited. Specifically, some whole sellers and retailers offer their own transportation and warehousing services. In addition, about 20 smaller firms offer some delivery services, and there are dozens of independent truckers. Serbia is behind the neighboring countries in terms of the number of trucks, and nearly 40% of these vehicles have recently been unable to meet the technical standards of European Union (UNECE 2003; USAID, 2007). An overall poorer state of vehicles in Serbia combines with the unsatisfactory road conditions to create a significant risk factor.

Waterways delivery of goods is environmentally safer and can be more cost efficient than delivery via other routes. Since it is also capable of carrying larger shipments, delivery via water yields significant economies of scale. Delivery via waterways in Serbia has a great potential that is still not materialized in right manner.

The most significant river is the Danube, which flows through ten European countries and provides good conditions for sailing in its south/east portion, Serbia including. Conditions for intensifying the international traffic on Serbia's portion of the Danube have recently been surfacing. One of the landmarks in this process was reached in October 2005 with the opening of a new bridge in Novi Sad, a key Danube port in Serbia. The new bridge replaced a pontoon bridge that blocked the international traffic for six and a half years, serving as a substitute for a six-lane bridge destroyed by NATO's missiles. Since the city of Novi Sad sits on a branch of Corridor 10 (a highway and railroad), the enabling of sailing through Novi Sad implies that the second connection between Corridor 10 and Corridor 7 (the Danube itself) is achieved (the first connection is in Belgrade).

The Danube port Smederevo is poised to support the traffic needed for a gigantic complex of metallurgy factories recently acquired by U.S Steel. Their steel products are shipped downstream the Danube to the Black Sea ports in Romania and Bulgaria. As opposed to the growing traffic on the Danube, the process of reviving what used to be high frequency traffic on the river Sava has been slower. Countries that descended from the former Yugoslavia labor on upgrading the status of this river into an international waterway. Serbian economy also uses the seaport Bar, which lies on the Adriatic Sea in Montenegro. This port is operated under special regulations that allow for a free movement of capital, goods and labor, and duty and tax exemptions.

Delivery of goods via air routes is carried by the national airline Jat Airways (formerly JAT—Yugoslav Air Transport). This company is also the main carrier of passenger traffic. A high ranking airline company in Europe in the 1980s, Jat Airways suffered significant resource and market losses due to the breakup of the former Yugoslavia in 1991 and international trade sanctions imposed on Serbia soon after. The company was grounded abroad and it lost the financial capability to regularly maintain its fleet. The airline is attempting to bounce back, while operating an aging fleet of about 20 mid-range passenger planes.

The airline transportation also features several operators of passenger traffic (the charter company Aviogenex, which owns four mid-range planes) and a few independent operators of small passenger planes. Still, true competition comes to JAT Airways only from international airlines that have taken control of key international routes. In this situation, however, JAT Airways preserves an ownership structure that does not oppose inertia; the same applies to Serbian airports. Also, JAT Airways refrains from participating in international alliances of airline companies, and continues to be focused on passenger traffic. These facts are in a stark contrast to changing characteristics of air transportation industry in the world. For example, Bulgaria allowed split-offs from the main national air company, then privatized part of it, and provided conditions for private carriers to enter the business.

TELECOMMUNICATIONS FACILITIES

By January 2007, 433 million hosts were connected to the **Internet**—almost three hundred times the number of ten years ago (ISC, 2007). The number of Internet hosts has been adopted as a measure of the Internet penetration of a country and the degree of national connectivity and it is defined by ITU as the number of computers directly connected to Internet. This number is assigned to country code, so the data shown in Figure 3 is related to Serbia and Montenegro (country code YU), because there is no data available yet for a new country code (RS). Also note that if there is no country code identification in case of generic TLDs (org, com, etc.), such hosts are assigned to US.

Serbia has joined the Internet galaxy. Since 1996, the number of Internet hosts multiplied 75 times. Although this appears to be an impressive achievement, Serbia has just 20% of the population using the Internet and 94.000 Internet hosts. This places it sixth (see Figure 2) and fourth (see Figure 3) from the bottom up in the distribution of the countries in South Eastern Europe (SEE). A technological and institutional inertia in the telecommunications industry may be partly responsible for this comparatively slower pace of Internet adoption.

The Internet backbone in Serbia is Serbian Multiservice Internet Network (SMIN), owned by Telekom Serbia. SMIN is modem accessible from all over Serbia. Primarily intended for Internet services, SMIN is also used for the transfer of voice and data as well as for building Virtual Private Networks (VPNs). SMIN has four Points of Presence (Belgrade, Novi Sad, Niš, and Kragujevac), which are mutually connected by 155 Mbps lines (see Figure4). Two 155 Mbps lines connect SMIN to the global Internet.

Although currently sufficient, SMIN's speed may cause congestion with the expected growth of the customer base. Access opportunities are skewed toward larger urban centers while rural areas are disadvantaged. In contrast NREN of Serbia (AMRES) demonstrates better design (backup connections are provided) (Jovanović, et al, 04) and much better international connections (RCUB NETIS, 07). In addition to two international GEANT (Gigabit European Academic Network) connections (via HUNGARNET and GRNET), AMRES appears as a key node for connecting academic networks of Bosnia and Herzegovina (BIHARNET) and Montenegro (MNNET) to GEANT.

SMIN's basic offering is switched access via public telephone network (the 56Kbps-modem access; $30 buy 200 connect hours monthly) or via Integrated Service Digital Network (ISDN).

Figure 2. The number of Internet users across SEE countries (by 2006)

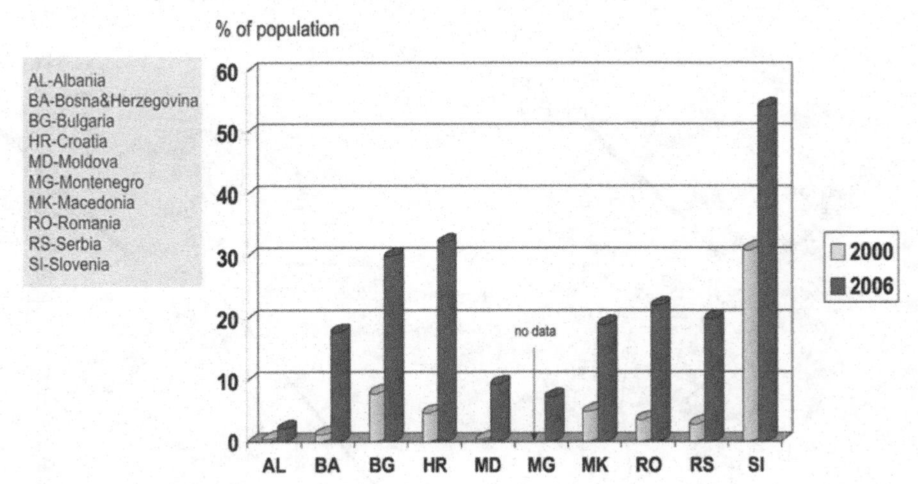

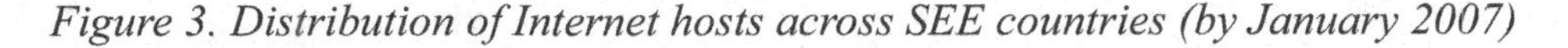

Figure 3. Distribution of Internet hosts across SEE countries (by January 2007)

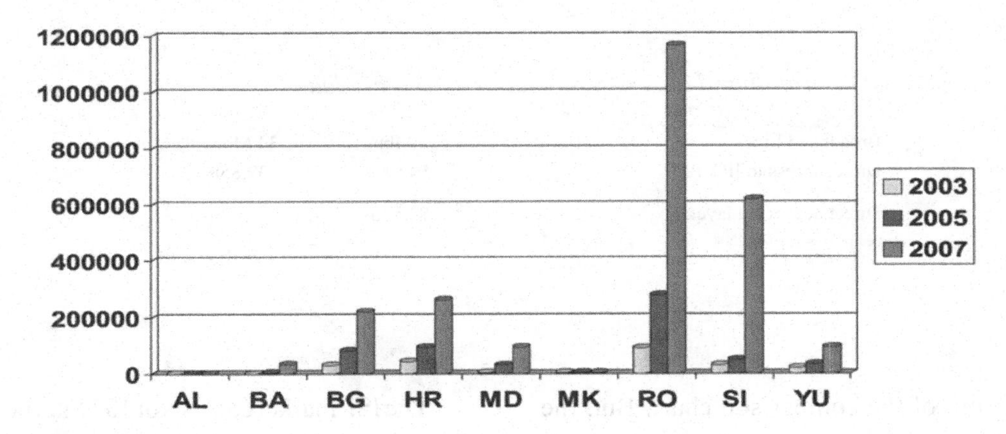

ISDN access has the maximum speed of 128 Kbps and is priced between $200-1,100/year, plus cost of connection time (¢0.37 per minute for local calls). Broadband offerings comprise two types of lines shown in Table 2.

More recently, the Asynchronous Digital Subscribe Line (ADSL) was introduced. The broadband lines are typically unaffordable for small and medium size enterprises and ISDN access is a more feasible solution for this user group (about 80,000 as of October 2005). Although currently sufficient, SMIN's speed may cause congestion with the expected growth of the customer base. Access opportunities are skewed toward larger urban centers while rural areas are disadvantaged.

Broadband is increasingly available worldwide. It was used by 38% of all Internet subscribers in 2004. The figures of broadband access in SEE countries are far away as shown in Figure 5. With only 0.02% of subscribers using broadband technologies by the year 2005, Serbia is placed

Figure 4. SMIN topology (left) vs. AMRES (right) as per July 2007

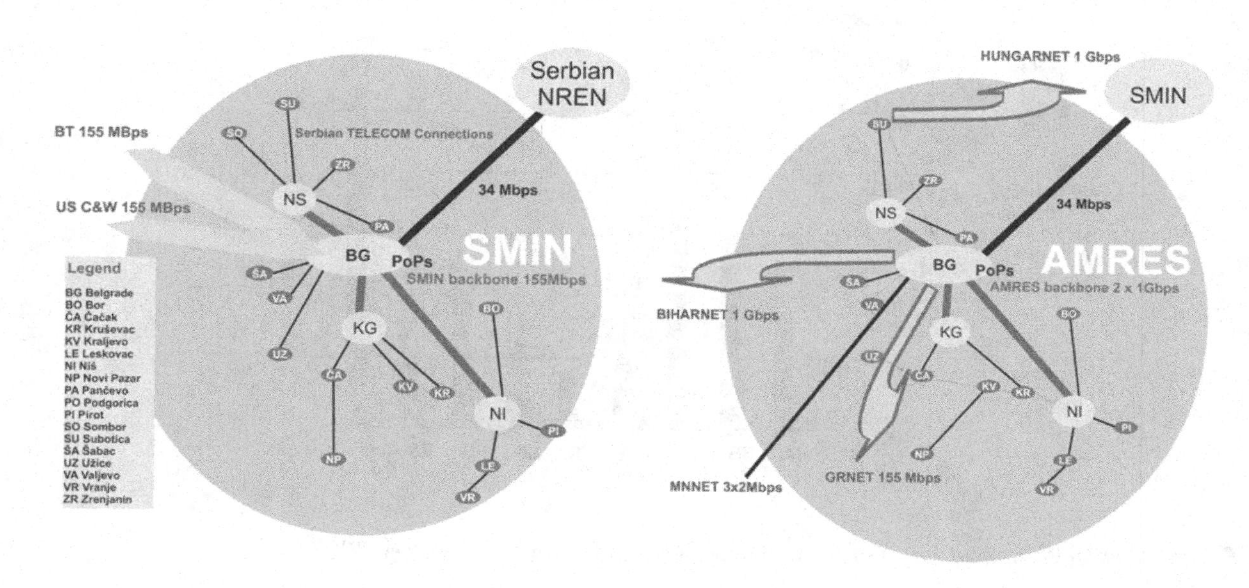

Table 2. Annual cost of broadband access (connection fees included)

Broadband Line	2 Mbps	34 Mbps
Direct access to IP VPN	$4,015	$37,858
Direct access via layer 2	$3,476	$34,826

at the bottom of the comparison chart. But, the other SEE countries on the chart are not much better. However it should be noted that ADSL technology has been widely offered in Serbia since the end of 2006. The bandwidths available vary from 256Kbps/64 Kbps to 768Kbps/192Kbps (download/upload), with the prices for the fastest connections, ca 450 US$ per year for individual subscribers and 650 US$ per year for companies. Data that cover prices for leased ADSL lines are not publicly available. Prices for companies are reasonable, but for individuals, with the average salary of 4800 USD per year, prices are quite high. Emerging broadband technologies such are ADSL2, VDSL, FTTx, WiMax, etc. are not in notable use.

The ISP market consists of 107 Internet Service Providers (ISPs) (Serbian Yellow Pages, 2005). Many ISPs are resellers of Internet access that is controlled by larger ISPs and ultimately by Telekom Serbia, the owner of the national wired network. The major private ISPs are Eunet, Beotel, Verat, and YUBC (Maruzzelli, 2004) ibid. Also noteworthy are SezamPro, Neobee in Novi Sad, and Medianis in Niš. International connectivity is provided mainly by Telekom Serbia and private companies YUBC and Verat (connects to Deutche Telekom's network).

Mobile telephony is on the rise in Serbia. In principle, wireless communications may be conducive to mobile commerce (Varshney &

Vetter, 2002). For example, short messaging service (SMS) enables mass trading that one can easily observe in Serbia. Supported by several TV stations, people advertise, sell and buy. Some companies use this model as an additional sales channel. There are 3 GSM operators in Serbia—Telekom Serbia, Telenor and VIP. It is important to say that VIP is working from the first day July, 2007, so there is not any information about this GSM operator.

In addition to technological limitations, the telecommunications industry is under tight government control. Instead of deliberating over crucial issues of de-monopolization, privatization and deregulation of telecommunications, the government has moved in a zigzag manner, sending confusing signals. For example, a 49% share in the national telephone company had been sold to foreign firms, and then 29% was purchased back. Mobile telephony has followed a similar trajectory. The success story of AMRES development has started in the year 2003, when Telekom finally decided to leave academic network development to the University of Belgrade. Before that, the only international connection between AMRES and GEANT was 2 Mbps!

SOFTWARE INDUSTRY

A viable software industry is necessary for developing EC's front-end (Web sites), back-end (databases systems), and links between buyers and sellers and among trading partners (computer networks). In the 2000s, the software industry in Serbia has been achieving almost three times bigger annual growth than the rest of economy (IDC, 2003). The list of software vendors contained 1,100 companies with over 5,000 employees at the end of 2004 (Medaković, 2005). The company profiles are indicative of new times. Before the 1990s, software development was mainly carried out by internal IS functions of large government-controlled enterprises. Today, smaller private companies and large foreign vendors dominate the industry. The average size of domestic software

Figure 5. Broadband penetration in SEE by technology as per 2005

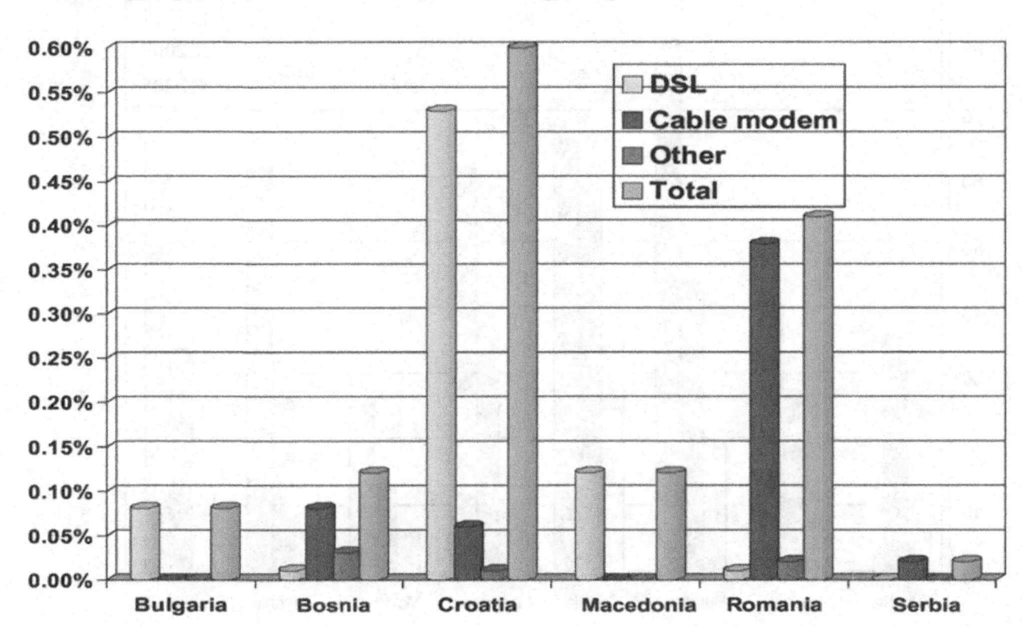

companies is five employees. Software vendors tend to cluster in urban communities, and more than a half of them are in Belgrade. A good level of software supply exists in other four large cities (Maruzelli, 2004) ibid.

A number of vendors offer Web development services, both in the B2B and B2C segment. Examples of the former include PAKOM and Comtrade Group. In the B2C arena, the list of notable vendors includes private companies Yunix Software (powers the on line bookstore Knjizara.com) and Saga. Saga has partnered with Cepp, the e-business department of Serbian Post. The partnership made Cepp the sole enabler of e-business solutions in the Serbian market with a strategy of moving the "trust that customers have in the Post's correctness and efficiency" into virtual space (Maruzelli, 2004) ibid. The software industry outside of Belgrade promoted some successful competitors.

In order to obtain a more comprehensive picture of the industry, we used Serbian Yellow Pages to sample 47 companies offering Internet services and 75 companies offering more general information systems services. We found a wide-variety of applications on the market, from simple applications to complex business information systems. Most of the software vendors use e-mail for business communications and have Web sites. About 28% of the companies offer Web design services, and near 19% are declared builders of EC applications. The education support for software development is quite good. Most of the high schools and faculties which teach software offer crucial courses for electronic commerce and Web development (computer networks, algorithms, databases, software engineering, Internet technologies, Web programming, etc.). There are also some academic research efforts that are directly related to electronic commerce architectures and related

Figure 6. Mobile phones penetration across SEE countries per 100 inhabitants

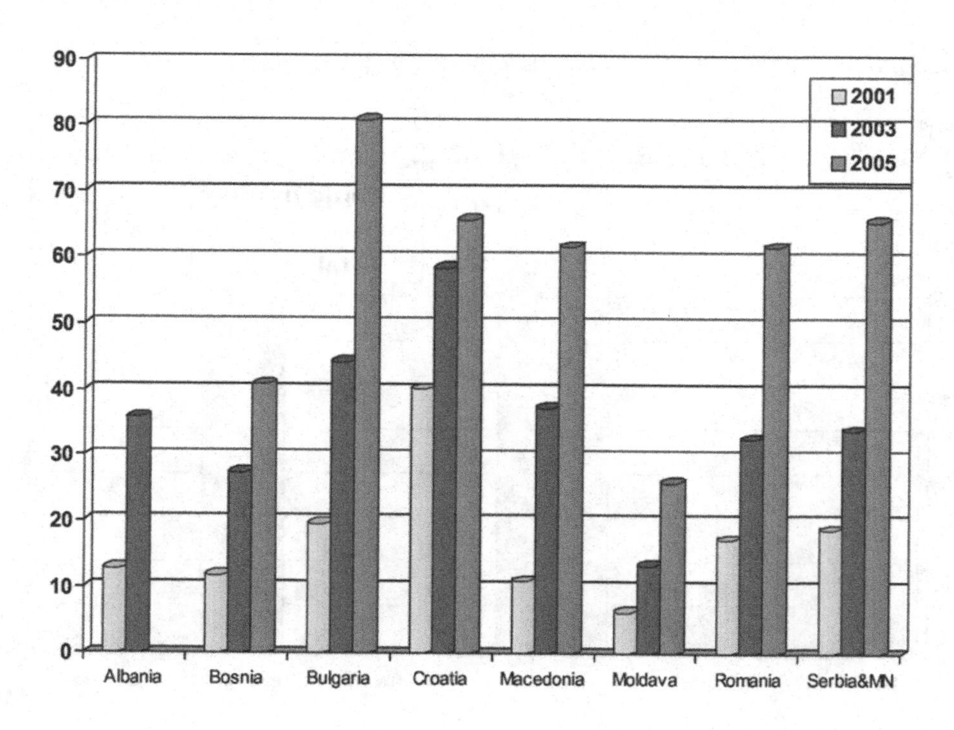

technologies. Some recent research include, but no limited to B2B interoperable frameworks (Kajan & Stoimenov, 05), agent technologies (Badjonski et al., 06), ontology modeling (Djurić et al., 05), etc. These last figures reflect a new trend and can be considered encouraging.

Countering these trends is a mainstream business culture that resists recognizing the economic value of software. The users still wonder "why software is so expensive" and incline to spend money on software only if it is bundled with hardware.

Foreign vendors include AcuCorp, Adobe, Autodesk, Borland, Bull, IBM, Microsoft, SAP, Oracle, Symantec, and TIBCO. Microsoft is especially active. Recently Red Hat has joined, which is big movement in open source software development. The company recently opened a development center in Belgrade and led a campaign for suppressing software piracy. In 2007, the index of software piracy in Serbia is 78%. That is more than double higher of world average (Reporter, 2007), while percentages in the neighboring countries are Slovenia (48%), Croatia (55%), Bosnia and Herzegovina (68%), Macedonia, Romania and Bulgaria (69%), Albania (77%) and Montenegro (82%).

Serbia's software industry is challenged by the state of IT in companies, a lack of IT awareness, and brain drain. Not many companies own IT resources that can be considered appropriate. Examples of successful B2B EC refer to a handful of companies in the chemical, retail, and insurance industry. Although computers are deployed in many companies, typically simpler office automation applications are used, character-based user interfaces are frequent, and file management systems rather than database applications prevail. Furthermore, exposure to the Internet is measured partly by the figure of 22,670 companies owning Web sites in the co.yu domain. There is no data on the extent of using the .com domain.

The brain drain, measured on a seven-point scale, stands at 1.88 (1=high). In contrast, this rate is 2.06 for Romania, 2.10 for Bulgaria, 2.71 for Croatia, 2.71 for Greece, and 4.15 for Slovenia (EU, 2005). A cause to the brain drain could be in internationally non-competitive salaries, although these actually are up to 10 times bigger that the average salary. Finally, in spite of the limited domestic market, the software industry does not show export ambition yet as opposed to its neighbors—Bulgaria, Romania, and Hungary (Karmel, 2003).

E-BANKING AND E-PAYMENT SYSTEMS

In the course of the last five years, a number of reforms were carried out in economic and financial sectors in Serbia, in the process of which, a reform of the payment system was a precondition for further development. Through several systemic projects, a radical reform of this field was carried out in accord with global tendencies of implementing new instruments, procedures, and infrastructure in payment systems under the influence of market competition and technological advancement. Today, Serbia has a modern and efficient payment system which is entirely based on international standards and the best practice of the EU countries (Vuksanović, 2002). The achieved results were given full credits by the relevant international institutions (IMF, IBRD, and ECB). In March 2006, the mission of the FSAP (Financial Sector Assessment Program) gave top marks to all relevant criteria.

A significant progress of the existing elements and the introduction of new elements into e-banking into the Serbian banking system is due to the changes in the macroeconomic environment made in 2003 when the new Law on Payment Operations was passed. The goals of these changes were twofold - to replace the existing monopolistic payment system with a market system, and to establish institutional conditions for the electronic banking development. The current situation in the Serbia's economic system has favorable effects on the further improvement of e-banking and the development of payment-card market. In this connection, the following elements have an enormous impact:

- low inflation,
- a stable foreign exchange rate, and
- new opportunities that will be given to Serbia after the negotiations with the EU have been continued.

The effect of the new Law on Payment Operations enacted on January 1, 2003 on the e-banking development results from direct effects on the very payment system as well as from establishing the preconditions for a radical transformation of the very models of bank operations and their customers. At first, it was the introduction of a payment-card system that was of a primary importance, and later on, it was the implementation of hybrid sorts of mobile telephony.

After the Law on Payment Operations was passed, the banks successfully included in the new systems of inter-bank dealings: the RTGS (Real Time Gross Settlement System) for priority payments and high-value payments, and the net system for low-value payments. Those systems are pursuant to the world principles, organized overtaking of gyro accounts of enterprises and performing payment transactions, simultaneously offering a higher level and quality of services adhering to the slogan "Accommodate demands of customers". The existing basic information systems ("core- banking") were upgraded by a new layer of applications intended for the support of electronic wholesale and retail banking.

The wide range of e-banking supply has been expanding drastically in a very short period. By a PC or mobile phone, banks enable their customers to: get an insight into the balance of the account, review transactions, examine the statements of account changes, receive and send personal messages, pay duties by payment orders dated on the current or later date. Practically, all banks issue several types of international and domestic payment cards. Out of all international payment cards, VISA is the most frequent payment card which, after a ten-year absence from Serbia, reached the one-million figure of cards issued just in a three-year period (in comparison with other countries, only China experienced a faster growth). According to the importance of other payment cards, VISA is followed by MasterCard, Diners, and much less by American Express. The system of DinaCard has increasingly been expanding on the domestic payment card market (Španović, 2005). Lately, hybrid sorts of mobile telephony have more commonly been used.

Since 2003, due to new economic and financial environment, an intensive development of payment card market has commenced. This market has been developing faster than any market in the region, owing to, on the one hand, the previous knowledge and experience acquired in the former Yugoslavia, and on the other hand, to a very strong support of the Government's programs relating to payment cards. The experience from the former Yugoslavia, dates back to the 1980s (VISA was the first card to be issued in 1980, then in 1981, three ATMs (Automated Teller Machines) were installed, and finally, in 1984 the banks started issuing and using payment cards massively, but that successful period lasted only to 1992-93 when the sanctions were imposed).

The Government had a direct interest in giving its full support, because each of these transactions represented a legal cash flow verified by a receipt and meant that taxes had been paid, which was one of the most important factors in fighting the grey economy. The state support became prominent in the course of the national DinaCard system development. Such a situation proves that there is a possibility that a ten-year regression - in this previously developed area - will be made up in a relatively short period of time.

Not only banks, but the related state institutions also back up the activities being carried out, that is promotion of cards as a means of payment. A severe competition between banks has lead to the weakening of the criteria to be met for obtaining payment cards, especially debit ones. These cards (debit) can be obtained free (of charges of issuing and membership fees) provided that a customer has a current account with the bank in question. Some banks provide special stimuli through deal packages (so Delta Bank combines a payment card issuing with particular life policies – Delta Life, or with international insurance cards – Europe Assistance).

Credit card issuing is more complex and it includes membership dues, costs of account maintenance, as well as interest rate on extended credits (which are in most cases the revolving credit options, although all known options are available). But in the banking circles, there is a dilemma about the actual credit worthiness of the major part of population due to its capacity to use the cards massively, taking into account that the monthly interest rate varies from 1,9 to 2.20 percent. To solve problems relating to credit worthiness and to introduce financial discipline, the Credit Bureau (as part of the Association of Banks) was formed. The Bureau keeps records of the total individual indebtedness of each credit beneficiary.

The results of the development of payment card transactions in Serbia can be estimated on the basis of the number of the payment cards issued, the number of POSTs (Point of Sale Transfers) and ATMs, and their application. In 2007, the number of the issued payment cards has reached the figure of 5.6 million, while a rise of 1.2 million was recorded in 2006. The number of the POSTs installed in 2007 has exceeded 50,000, and the number of the ATMs ha reached around 18,000. During the last twelve months, 70 million transactions were made, out of which 6.5 million in May 2007. According to the pace of payment card issuing, Serbia is, on this very day, assigned to be the leader of the region (VISA proclaimed publicly this market to be the leader, due to the fact that in three years only, from 2003 to 2006, three million VISA payment cards came into circulation. As stated by some official research carried out by foreign agencies, Serbia was put on top of the list of the ATMs increase in 2005. Despite some indices that Serbia is the leader in the region, it still lags behind some countries of the EU by the number of transactions.

The reasons for this condition, on the one hand, arise from the population's ignorance of the use of this kind of services, and, on the other hand, from the acquired habit to use checks as a means of deferred payment. Only when the deferred payment by checks - that is, the opportunity that partially compensated needs of the payment card usage - was abolished were payment cards used to a large extent. As the use of checks for deferred payment had been an unofficial "social valve" in the course of prior years, this check function had to be phased out and the deadline for such a practice was extended several times. The government bodies insisted that checks should regain their function of a payment instrument and that the credit function should be transferred to credit cards. The intention of the bodies was to suppress gray economy and legalize all money flows including all beneficial economic effects which payment cards were to take. This problem was solved officially on January 1, 2006, when the institutions gave a strong incentive for credit cards to become a means that would officially replace the previous unofficial use of checks.

Today, there are a number of systems of international, national, company (loyalty) and co-branded cards on the Serbian market. However, the fact that two thirds of customers of banks have and use mobile telephones affords them new opportunities to get used to paying goods and services by their mobile phones and other hybrid technologies. The survey carried out at the beginning of 2005 (comprised the population of 1000 respondents - beneficiaries of banking services) showed that over 61 percent of respondents uses the mobile phone. According to the results, one fourth of the respondents possessing a mobile telephone are interested in these services, so that a more intensive development of m-banking and m- payment can be expected in the forthcoming period.

The national DinaCard Program comprises a wide range of debit and credit cards: "DinaCard Klasik", "DinaCard 3", "DinaCard 6", and "DinaCard 12". "DinaCard Klasik" is a debit card, which is automatically conditioned by a possession of a current account and requires no charges. It is accompanied by special family and pension packages, which are created so as to include larger circles of beneficiaries. The Pension plus package entails beneficiaries of different types of payment cards which can be obtained without any membership dues and card issuance or the maintenance of the account (only a monthly charge for the package maintenance has to be paid). The national programs "DinaCard 3", "DinaCard 6", and "DinaCard 12" relate to credit cards of a revolving type which differ one from the other in the amount of the loan to be repaid.

Pricing and other benefits made possible the DinaCard quick **diffusion**, so that this card has been the most often used card with the largest acceptance net in 2007. Out of the total number of all the cards issued in the country, almost one half of them are DinaCards (around 2.8 million). In the early 2007, the number of the installed POSTs of this system has amounted to around 48,000, while the ATMs figure has reached around 1,450. Out of the above figures, in 2006, 19,000 POSTs and about 400 ATMs were installed. Despite this fact, it is believed that, in 2006, the greatest achievement of this system was that the issued cards were activated and the turnover was increased to nearly RSD 48 billion.

Ways of further development of this system are directed to improvement of the existing services and introduction of new kinds of services (m-payment and the Internet payments). As early as 2006, the DinaCard beneficiaries were given the opportunity to make prepaid calls by mobile phones by sending a text message (SMS). It was planned that this attractive system should be diversified in 2007, at first by introducing a service for SMS payments for postpaid mobile-phone bills, after that for standard (fixed) telephone bills, and finally for utilities payments (electricity, various public services, wireless internet etc.)

SMS payment system is being used in a variety of systems for a parking-bay payment in the open-space parking lot (while in the closed-space parking lot, electronic parking-lot gates are installed). So, for example - when coming onto the parking area, the car owner sends an SMS with the registration number of his car to one of the defined short numbers, depending on the zone of the parking lot. These numbers are unique for both active providers of mobile telephony (Telenor and Telekom) regardless of the mobile network to which the beneficiary is connected. After a very short time, the user receives an answer whether he has made a successful one-hour parking-lot payment as well as the exact time when the payment is made. Five minutes before the paid time expires, the car owner receives an SMS informing him about the expiry of the paid parking time, so that he can send a new SMS and make a payment for an additional hour. The payments made in this way are controlled by the PDA (Personal Digital Assistant) which is in possession of each controller. The control is very simple – the registration number, in the form of a question, is entered into the data base.

Some large trading companies begin to incorporate cashless payment systems. Delta M, the largest retailer, which can be considered to be an indicator of the market conditions, is implementing its own net for the card payment acceptance. In order to eliminate particular defects of the current banking offers (slow and unreliable dial-up connections, not sufficiently integrated systems, more than one EPOS terminal on one cash register, dependence on the bank which provides EPOS terminals, an inflexible process of creating of new functions, an unsatisfactory control, and a lack of reports) Delta M returns the existing

POSTs to banks and introduces its own system. The new system (SecuriLink) uses internal links within Delta, as well as the advantages of its own system of maintenance. The key element of the improvement is a complete integration of the POST and the cash register. Technically, the system is designed so that it can accept all payment cards through one POST. On the basis of this system, Delta is developing a special Delta loyalty concept which offers an opportunity for a holder of several different payment cards to use each one as loyalty in Delta.

In order to get people used to using payment cards, some important activities are being carried out: introduction and co-branding of special international cards for young people (EURO<26) and for students (ISIC). EURO<26 (a European youth card) was given a reword for the most successful developing project in Europe. At the moment, this card is being distributed by 30 distributive centers, and it is being used by 30,000 beneficiaries. Since 2005, the nongovernmental organization IUVIA has had the right to develop the only internationally authorized pupils and students identification card, the ISIC. It is issued by 30 distributive centers and used by 5,000 beneficiaries. Two hundred services - such as travel and purchase in specific fashion houses - are available to beneficiaries of these cards at discount prices. Within the GAUDEAMUS project, a new official student identity card - EURO<26/ISIC was created on the basis of co-branding of the EURO<26 and the ISIC pursuant to international licenses. Currently, these cards decrease students' expenses for food and accommodation, improve their standards of living, and develop a platform for new services to be rendered. Very soon, these cards will be used in public transportation. It is also expected that they will be integrated into banking payment systems.

As Serbia has been experiencing a transition process, it has become attractive for electronic crime, so that it should be expected that it will face with a serious problem of payment card abuse in the forthcoming period. Since the payment card structure is being dominated by debit cards whose owners have a low ability to pay – Serbia has not yet been put on the list of international groups which abuse cards by taking the necessary data and identification number off the every card, so that mostly the stolen cards are being abused. Last year, Belgrade banks suffered a 10-million-dollar damage incurred by falsified cards. Fortunately, due to the efficient fraud monitoring system Euro Planet, this chain of abuse was terminated in March 2007.

LEGISLATURE SUPPORT

The national legislature of Serbia started to regulate this area in 2004 when the Law on digital signature was passed. (On the one hand, Serbia was among the last European countries to pass the mentioned law after the European Directive on digital signature had been passed. On the other hand, this Law comprises all experience and recommendations stated in the European directive. Banks and their partners applied the European directive recommendations on digital signatures as a base for certificates and qualified digital signatures to be formed by developing their own systems (PKI). The Criminal Law of the Republic of Serbia (became effective as at 1 January 2006) comprises the issues of payment card regulating, falsifying and abusing (Article 225), production, obtaining from and giving to other persons the means for falsifying (Article 227), check issuing and usage of uncovered payment cards (Article 228). High technology crime is regulated by the Law on organization and powers of the state bodies in charge of the fight against high-technology crime. A special department for high-technology crime was formed as part of the Belgrade District Prosecutor's Office.

The problems arising in the domain of legal protection in practice relate to the following: deficient collecting and processing of documentation of some participants (banks, the Ministry of Internal Affairs, prosecution authorities) in the course of processing, lack of video surveillance as a means of evidence to support payment card abuse (which may be a potential advantage of the accused), lengthy judicial processes, a high level of uncertainty over the outcome of the dispute, that is, whether the loss sufferer would be compensated for his financial loss resulting from the abuse of his payment card. Due to incompetent court estimations, an expert evaluation is carried out by experts on bookkeeping and finance.

The achieved level of card payment raises a very important issue of payment system costs and, the so called, commercial commission (interchange). Taking into account that the card issuer's commission – guaranteed by international card systems – is disproportionately higher then in the EU, and the fact that there is a possibility that this difference increases after the new rates of the EU have been set up in January 2008, the National Bank of Serbia will have to deal with relations between banks and trade. In order to establish an optimal value of interchange for the usage of payment cards issued in Serbia, the NBS is to make a detailed analysis.

The NBS is going to invite banks to make an inter-agreement and make a decision on the interchange value in the course of the forthcoming months. In this way, banks would solve this problem by self-regulations, so that the NBS would not have to pass its regulations concerning the interchange issue. On September 1, 2007, instead of fixed commercial commissions, a new system is going to be established within the national DinaCard system, in which acceptance banks and traders will be able to regulate these relations among themselves. (It will be 0.7 percent for the largest number of trades, and 0.25 percent of the value of purchased gasoline). The NBS has recently – through the centre for payment cards – become a member of the Berlin Group which is a result of the SEPA initiative on national card systems in Europe.

For conducting e-commerce legal infrastructure is very important precondition. There is significant lack of adequate legislation that would legally regulate framework for conducting the electronic commerce.

An important concern of many countries is that existing legal framework may not adequately accommodate e-commerce, and that existing laws centering on paper-based system may prove a barrier to increase global e-trade. Ideally, national legislation should be passed that gives digital signatures and electronic documents the same legal status as written signatures and paper documents. The use of ICT to conduct trade transactions poses a number of legal challenges concerning, for example, the validity of documents produced and exchanged electronically, security of transactions and trust, copyright and ownership issues in trade using a Website (Vidas-Bubanja, 2001).

The legal infrastructure for e-commerce in Serbia is likely to be shaped by the corresponding EU legislature, international standards, its legal tradition, and certain regional initiatives which Serbia has endorsed. The body of work realized in the European Union, notably the European Directives related to e-commerce and e-signatures, would most likely have a strong influence on the creation for Serbian e-commerce legal framework. Equally important is Model Law on Electronic Commerce elaborated by UNCITRAL in 1996, which offers a set of internationally accepted rules intended to help states remove legal obstacles to the implementation of e-business, and reduces disparities that may exist between national legislations on this matter. The UNCITRAL model legislation can be a logical starting point but wider issues must also be addressed when building the legal basis for e-business (UN/ECE, 2003).

The current legal framework is not fully specified and implemented. The following overview provides more details on the existing regulations and the level of their compliance with the EU legal environment (UNDP and Gov. of Serbia, 2006).

The Law on Telecommunications, adopted in April 2003 (Official Gazette No. 44/03) is partly adjusted to the First European Telecommunications Framework and is the first law that regulates the Internet service as a public telecommunications service materialized by applying the Internet technology. Convergent technologies, such as VoIP are not regulated by this Law. This Law prescribes one license per one telecommunication service provider.

This implies that Telekom Srbija will probably be split into at least three companies. The Law on telecommunications has defined a regulatory framework for the introduction of a universal service. Under the law, Telekom Serbia is obliged to provide for the universal service until its exclusive rights expire, but it is not entitled to the recovery of costs from the universal service reimbursement fund. This clearly calls for new regulations to facilitate the development of the universal service. The Telecommunications Agency and the Broadcasting Agency should ensure, each within its competence, separate funds for the universal and public broadcasting service.

A poor situation in the area of satellite systems is the consequence of unregulated development in the 1990s and war destructions. The main satellite centre in Ivanjica and another satellite post in Krnjača were devastated. The Ivanjica facilities were rebuilt, but the center has not been reopened since. A number of institutions, including Telekom, have been properly licensed, but many work based on inadequate licenses. In order for the satellite communications market to be liberalized, it is necessary to pass a number of by-laws to simplify the licensing procedure. Accordingly, specific regulations are required to define minimum technical requirements to be met by the satellite communications systems and equipment, in line with the rules of the International Telecommunications Union (ITU) and the European Union. Due to deficient legal regulations in the field of cable distribution systems, there are no accurate statistics on the number of Cable Distributive Systems (KDS) operators and subscribers.

Criminal Code has been amended in order to support better e-commerce (Official Gazette 39/03 and 67/03). The amended Criminal Code regulates criminal offences threatening the safety of computer data. It covers seven new criminal acts against the security of computer networks, systems and data—unauthorized use of computers and computer networks, computer sabotage, creation and spreading of computer viruses, computer fraud, disruption of electronic data processing and transmission, unauthorized access to a protected computer or computer network, and protection against unauthorized limits to the access of public computer networks. The Criminal Code also covers criminal offences related to software piracy. The amendments to the

Table 3. Status of relevant legislation for e-commerce and Information Society

Legislation	
Digital Signature Law	Adopted in 2004 and ratified in 2005
E-Commerce Law	Under development process
Law on Telecommunication	Signed and ratified in 2003
Intellectual Property Protection	Trademark Law, Copyright and Related Rights Law, Legal Protection of Design Law, Patent Lawsigned and ratified
Protection of personal data	Signed and ratified in 1998, not in compliance to EU law
Protection of consumers	Signed and ratified in 2002
Public Access to Information	Adopted and ratified in 2004
Amended Criminal Code / Convention on Cyber crime	The Convention on Cyber-crime was signed in 2005, but not ratified; Criminal code was amended in 2003 to include special provisions for computer crimes 11

Criminal Code are in accordance with the basic recommendations but are not in full compliance with the Council of Europe.

Regulating copyright is important for protecting proprietary software used in e-commerce. In this are, the situation in Serbia is also changing. There is Law on Copyrights and Related Rights, which is based on the former Constitution (Constitutional Charter). It regulates the privacy of Personal Data in automated data processing. This law is not fully compliant with the European Directives on data protection (i.e. does not predict the existence of data protection commissioner/ ombudsman). The new Copyright Law that has been recently passed meets the modern standards and is in line with the EU recommendations and WTO TRIPS.

The right to the protection of personal information is guaranteed by the Constitution of the Republic of Serbia (Official Gazette of the Republic of Serbia No. 6/03) and the Charter of Human and Minority Rights and Civil Liberties (Official Gazette of Serbia and Montenegro No. 1/90). Under the two documents, lawmakers have an obligation to govern the protection of personal data by a special law. The existing Law on the Protection of Personal Data (Official Gazette of the Federal Republic of Yugoslavia No. 24/98 and 26/98) is rather defective, ambiguous and far from the EU standards. To make matters worse, the existing piece of legislation has never been applied at all.

The area of intellectual property is covered by the Law on the Protection of Intellectual Property and the Criminal Code. Neither is in full compliance with international regulations, but at least the basic provisions are in place. This Law covers protection of software products as well. The implementation of intellectual property rules has been governed by the Customs Act (Official Gazette of the Republic of Serbia No 73/03) and the Criminal Code (Official Gazette of the Republic of Serbia 39/03 and 67/03) . The Customs Act stipulates in detail a number of measures to protect intellectual property at the border. Criminal Code, as mentioned above, has for the first time defined as criminal offences the unauthorized use of copyrights and related rights and crimes against the security of computer data.

A draft criminal code of the Republic of Serbia has defined criminal offenses against intellectual property rights as a special group of criminal offenses. In this way, the protection of intellectual property has been expanded, because apart from copyrights and related rights, the new legislation has also covered other intellectual property rights (seals, patents, designs, geographic origin, and the like).

Digital signature is regulated by a law adopted in late 2004. This law is in line with common practices and regulations in the EU and the United States, and various players are preparing themselves for the implementation phase (Certification Authorities). This is one of several acts that constitute a legal framework for e-commerce. However, there is no specific regulation or law to cover electronic commerce, and the Law on Digital Signature is believed to be the first step in this direction. Unfortunately up to 2007 the Digital signature Law was not in practical use due to the fact that state certification body was not still founded, although there a some strong candidates for that function. In this respect this present great impediment in legal e-commerce implementation in the Republic of Serbia.

No systemic approach has been taken towards local e-payments as yet. Business players rely on the National Bank of Serbia Ordinance on Electronic Payments and the Law on Payment Operations (Official Gazette of the Federal Republic of Yugoslavia No. 3/02). While issuing payment cards, local banks rely on the Law on Banks and Other Financial Organizations, international standards, and experiences. In order to govern properly the e-payment area under the Harmonization Programme, it is necessary to take into account the European Commission Recommendation No. 87/598 on a European code of conduct related to e-payments and the European Commission Recommendation No. 88/590 defining the relationship between cardholders and card issuers.

The Law on Access to Information is drafted, and it is compliant with international standards. There are some reservations regarding Government's capacity to effectively implement the provisions of this Law. In addition, there is The Law on Advertising that regulates spreading of advertisements via traditional media (press, radio, TV), billboards, voice phone and fax. However, it does not provide protection against unsolicited electronic messages (internet, e-mail, SMS, MMS and other multimedia).

EDUCATION SYSTEM

The ICT business guru Peter Keen (2004) pointed out a tight dependence of digital society on the engineering, English speaking, and the education in IT. Technical studies were always very popular in Serbia, and there is common opinion that Serbs are much better engineers than managers. Technical schools have maintained the capability of educating high quality engineers, especially in the area of electronics. Although these experts may get top salaries in Serbia, opportunities that are more lucrative abroad lure many of them to leave the country (Maruzzelli, 2004) ibid. Brain drain takes its toll.

As for foreign languages, English has become mandatory from the first grade in the elementary school. Previously, English was the first choice in city schools, competing with Russian (preferable in rural areas), and German. At the university level, all departments offer a mandatory introduction into computer skills (Microsoft Office is the training package of choice). Post-secondary business schools have begun educating students for Internet and EC, and the Internet increasingly plays a role in the entire education process, including e-learning. Unfortunately, the level of IT knowledge among the teachers in basic and secondary schools is not satisfactory and they are still learning about "bits and bytes" (less how to use computer as a tool) although every basic and secondary school has computer laboratories. The problem is that a lot of teachers are not properly trained for their work, because a lot of them were teaching technical education in the past period. New, younger IT teachers are improving that picture continuously.

The first impression about educational system in Serbia is: it is one of the few systems that are working continuously in last 15 years, still with acceptable results. Serbia used to have a quality system of public education at all levels, no illiteracy, and a large number of university-educated people. Suffering a lack of funds in the 1990s, public education remained virtually intact throughout this period. Educational system is the follower of the system which existed in former Yugoslavia and it was very similar with those in Croatia, Slovenia, Bosnia and Herzegovina and Macedonia. Main difference is, according to the information from Ministry of Education in Serbia, significant number of private universities and faculties in Serbia: 7 universities with 32 faculties. This situation brought a big problem to the surface, because those private educational institutions, in most cases, are not offering real education, but the fast road to the diploma. In summer 2005, new legislation was introduced in order to meet major aspects of the Bologna Declaration for Higher Education enacted in 1999, and thereby to bring Serbia closer to the EU model. The first steps of evaluation in existing institutions are bringing down the number of those private institutions to the much more acceptable number. One more important fact: distance learning is a part of the new legislation and there are strong efforts to implement it quickly in the practice.

The Internet is taking important role in education process in Serbia. This new legislation defines mandatory contents for Web sites in all higher level institutions. A lot of useful information for students like calendar and results of exams, schedules, teacher's CVs, and other interesting information can be found on these Web sites. It is possible to make consultations with professors with the e-mail and to download papers or PowerPoint presentations from the sites.

Some higher level institutions recognized the importance of education experts for e-business. Courses with e-business are taking part in studies in the significant number of institutions. Studies specialized in e-business are also taking place in Serbia's education space. Business schools first introduced such profiles of experts. There are also master studies and doctor dissertations in that direction. In the results of our investigation we found that the most of those courses are dedicated to the studies for software engineers, where they learn main information about e-commerce, information and communication technologies and the techniques of building Web sites and their integration with information system. Business schools also teach e-marketing techniques. Business models and strategies for the development of e-commerce still don't have an important place in the education process.

CUSTOMER READINESS

The highest level in e-commerce pyramidal model concerns the propensity of customers to engage in e-commerce transactions. This is a compound dimension. It captures a number of traits of economic culture, by taking the perspective of customers. We focused on the issues of trust in merchants, banks and international brands as well on some salient cultural values.

According to the Republic Bureau for Statistics in Serbia, 11.6% of the Internet users ordered some commodities electronically. On the other hand, 97.3% ob business companies are using computers in their work, remote connections are available for 28.4% companies, and access to the Internet exists in 90.2% of them. If we take a look on the functionality of the companies on the Internet, we can see that 65.8% are using financial services, 61% are using the Internet for information from the market, and 15.3% are receiving digital products or services. Web sites are registered in 52.9% of Serbian business companies, but only 8.3% of them received digital orders through the Internet.

The B2B segment of e-commerce in Serbia is still in a rudimentary stage. We have already provided pieces of evidence on B2B e-commerce in the sections on software industry. This evidence indicates success as well as difficulties of growing domestic B2B brands. Another problem is that the growth of commerce in general is impeded by a lack of money in circulation. Due to anti-inflation measures of international lending institutions, the volume of money is strictly controlled, which either slows down trading or pushes it onto the tracks of barter or delayed payment.

The typical Serbian consumer appears to maintain seriously undermined trust, in addition to being disillusioned and impoverished (Vidas-Bubanja et al., 2002) ibid. After the bankrupt of the retail chains during the 1990s, black market and makeshift street shops were the main ways of shopping in Serbia, ruining modern trading methods, quality assurance, product return policies, and product servicing (Dinkić, 1995) ibid. The result of these processes was that the trust in merchants disappeared. Even the worse process happened in the banking system, which trapped hard currency savings and engaged in scheming before the eyes of the government in a social system that had slid into anomaly. More than 10% of population lives under the poverty line. On the other hand, according to the information from National bank of Serbia, people in Serbia changed about DEM 8.000,000,000 for more than 4.000.000.000 Euros, taking all that money to their homes and not trusting to the banks. The situation is changing since the political and economic changes that commenced in 2000, but the restore of trust is not an easy process.

Most of the population is traditionally oriented and prefers stability, even if this implies stagnation (Vujić, 2004). But, international brands could make a difference with younger customer groups. In spite of a significantly limited purchasing power, the young consumer appears to equate fashionable foreign brands with a satisfactory value proposition regardless of price/value ratios (Maričić, 2002). In contrast, the segment of older consumers prefers national brands. Part of the traditionalistic culture is a strong focus on the past time dimension and a longer time horizon (Trompenaars & Hampden-Turner, 1998). On a list of 42 countries based on the perceived length of time horizon (the average of the perceived extension of the past, present, and future taken together), Serbia ranked about the top of the list. For comparison, the US is at the opposite side, while Germany is in the middle of the continuum. Cultures focused on the past tend to recreate a golden age and refuse to change unless their heritage is safe. The past time focus might moderate adoption of new ways of shopping in Serbia.

Shopping in physical market places is still considered an important social event in Serbia. Green markets are still very popular: this is where one can meet a friend, personally pick out the produce, and enjoy bargaining with sellers. Mega-markets, drawing on the Wal-Mart concept, are a new type of shop that quickly gains in popularity. Some of them are offering their catalogues on Internet.

Catalogue-based selling is another innovation that is related to buying on the Internet. The German retail giant Neckermann, in collaboration with Serbian Post, has recently introduced catalogue sales. Delivery times and unfulfilled orders appear to be difficulties with distracting effects that mark the early stage of this sales channel. A counter example is the sales service called "Order Now," which combines TV and the Web for the purpose of display and ordering products. It uses cash-on-delivery payment, and increases customer's value by supporting a product return policy.

REGIONAL COOPERATION

In order to address the challenges of e-commerce implementation and Information Society development, to tap all the potentials offered by modern IT and to increase the possibilities of integration in the current world market, Serbia and other South Eastern European countries are active on the regional level in initaitive dealing with IT introduction and development, that is within eSEE (Electronic South Easten Europe) Initiative of the Stability Pact for SEE.

The aim of the eSEE Europe Initiative is to better integrate SEE countries into the global, knowledge-based economy by supporting the countries of the region in the development of the Information Society, including benchmarking, best practices and the transfer of knowledge. The Initiative is to promote the creation of a proper institutional environment for building the Information Society for all, in line with EU policies (CEC, 2000). It also aims at the co-ordination and facilitation of the introduction of ICT projects in various fields among others business, governance and education.

On October 29, 2002, at the Telecommunications for Development Conference in Belgrade, SEE countries (Albania, Bosnia and Herzegovina, Croatia, FYR Macedonia, Moldova, Montenegro and Serbia) signed and accepted the international agreement, "eSEEurope Agenda for the Development of the Information Society" (eSEE Agenda), as a basic document for IT development activities in their region. This agreement is in line with eEurope 2002 and 2005 Action Plans and eEurope+ plan of candidate countries (CEC, 2001; CEC, 2002) and represents the confirmation of SEE countries` commitment to develop information societies in their economies in accordance with European models and standards, and to associate them with European IT development process. This document was also endorsed by member countries at the March 2003 South East Europe Cooperation Process (SEECP) Summit.

As is defined in the eSEE Agenda, countries from southeast Europe will take concrete actions within the constraints of their specific environments in the fields of (Stability Pact, 2002):

- Adoption of policy and strategy for the Information Society;
- Adoption and implementation of Legal Infrastructure for the Information Society accordingly to Acquis Communitaire settled within European Union countries;
- Establishment of **regional cooperation** and national implementation mechanisms; and
- Promotion of the Information Society for development.

The expected result for SEE countries of the eSEE Agenda for the Development of the Information Society is to get stronger political support first in their own countries, than in the EU and the rest of the world for ICT development actions in order to ensure their realization in practice (CEC, 2002).

On the Regional Ministerial Conference on the Information Society, held in Thessaloniki, Greece between 30th June and 1st July 2005 Southeast European countries took stock and reviewed the progress achieved so far under auspices of the Stability Pact eSEE Initiative and discussed continuation of the eSEE Agenda as a joint action plan for development of the Information Society in this region, and also as a prerequisite for more profound integration of SEE region in European technological and developmental currents.

By recognising the need to align the eSEE Agenda with the new targets set out by the i2010 Initiative and the WSIS documents, and by taking into account regional and national circumstances and priorities, SEE countries also agreed that the eSEE Initiative Working Group shall prepare a proposal of the eSEE Agenda+ to be adopted at the next South Eastern Europe Ministerial Conference on the Information Society in November 2007.

In eSEE Agenda+ the i2010 European defined priorities for Information Society development policies are rephrased into our region specific priorities (Stability Pact, 2007):

- Further development of a Single SEE Information Space which promotes an open and competitive internal market for Information Society and media, moving it toward a common European Information Space in terms of interoperability;
- Strengthening Innovation and Investment in ICT Research and Education while working with the private sector to promote growth and more and better jobs;
- Achieving an Inclusive Information Society that promotes growth and jobs in a manner that is consistent with sustainable development and that prioritizes better public services and quality of life.

The Ministerial Conference held in Greece was also an opportunity for SEE countries, as well as Greece and Romania, to sign the Memorandum of Understanding on the Broadband for Southeast Europe (bSEE) Initiative. The main ideas behind this bSEE Initiative are the following (Stability Pact, 2006): 1) the need to promote integral links in the Electronic Communications sector between the countries of the SE European region with a view to leverage capabilities and opportunities on both sides, 2) common interest in advancing the growth of investments, joint ventures, joint initiatives, technology development and markets in the Electronic Communications sector. The main aim of this new Initiative is to develop a unified broadband market fully interconnected to the European and global networks and to implement a technology and industry co-operation program aimed at fostering business partnerships between countries of the South East Europe region.

The scope of co-operation between countries participating in the bSEE Initiative shall include the following areas relating to broadband:

- Setting statutory and regulatory objectives and frameworks with respect to European Union Directives and global standards;
- Aggregating demand leading to broadband development;
- Evaluating broadband technologies and international best practices;
- Developing skills through exchange programs and through joint sponsorship of conferences, training programs and seminars in the field of broadband technologies and services;
- Prompting planned activities regarding broadband investment that would result in building awareness, increasing level of public interest, and empowering SMEs to participate in such initiatives;
- Addressing market failures that are beyond the reach of policy tools;
- Providing incentives to the private sector for broadband development, especially in rural and remote areas;
- Monitoring progress and producing timely reports; and
- Formulation of agreed regional projects, which could be financed from European Union Funds or other available sources.

Beside eSEE Agenda + and organization of the second Ministerial Conference in Sarajevo by November 2007 other priorities for eSEE Initiative for 2007 are:

- A private sector ICT Forum led by the Stability Pact's Business Advisory Council- an association of leading business persons from the region and from major investor countries, which aims to create closer links between the region's governments and the private sector on ICT;
- And, an "e Government Center" which is public-private sector effort to create an effective platform for supporting the development and implementation of national (and regional) e Government programs in South East Europe and to allow the transfer of the experience and the best practices of more advanced EU member states to the region.

Achieved results under SP eSEEurope Initiative support the fact that **regional cooperation** is an important approach for the IS development. SEE countries share common problems in this area such us: capital shortage, hardware + software shortage, underdeveloped telecommunication infrastructures and telecommunication market monopolies, low public awareness, need for improvement in digital literacy and skills by businesses, organizations and consumers, necessity for organizational transformation and national economy reconstruction, need to follow social and cultural implications of new economy. Through regional cooperation in IS development SEE countries can realize advantages in recognizing common problems and barriers to quicker infrastructure development, in undertaking common actions and cooperation in IS development as a cheaper and quicker way to solutions, in creating regional project proposal which are easier accepted and better valued by international donors and financial institutions, in getting synergies of regional knowledge and in sharing regional best practice experiences. These experiences are easy to be accepted and adopted to local circumstances due to regional similarities by all SEE countries.

Implementation of eSEE Agenda, renewed eSEE Agenda+ and further activities under eSEE and bSEE Initiatives will bring the following results for SEE countries:

- Strengthen promotion and co-ordination of mutual interests in IS development
- Combine and synchronize activities and scarce resources for IT development
- Stimulate innovation and exploit the technology potentials of e-commerce and e-business

- Promote and establishment of Business networking of the IT companies in SEE region
- Create an integral central database of IT resources on national and regional level
- Develop partnership with the public sector and universities for the realization of projects of interest of each state and region as the whole
- Promote and provide the investment in IT modernization regardless of industry/sector
- Organize and introduce services such as e-commerce, e-banking, e-tourism, e-agribusiness etc
- Start initiatives for human resources development
- Jointly to face strong competition in the western countries markets
- Marketing jointly efforts to facilitate SEE companies to find business partners in Western Europe etc.

E-COMMERCE SUCCESS STORIES IN SERBIA

According to the Republic Bureau for Statistics in Serbia from 2006, there are 28% of households with personal computer and 18.5% with the Internet connection. The same research shows that 89.2% of students and 97.3% of Serbian companies are using computers in their work, and 90.2% companies have the Internet connection. Those information shows significant penetration of ICT and a new opportunity for e-commerce implementation.

The survey of Web sites in Serbia resulted with a variety of business models implemented in both the B2C and B2B domains of e-commerce. Thus we found more than 300 Web storefronts with different business models which operate in Serbian Internet market. Web storefronts can take orders on their Web sites using different techniques, but they still do not support e-payment because not a single Internet Payment Gateway exist in Serbia, leaving the customer to pay by cash-on-delivery or he can use some classical method of pre-payment. Table 2 shows some interesting examples of B2C models that can be considered as the most successful Serbian stories in their industries.

On the list of 10 the most popular sites in Serbia there are 4 search engines, 3 sites of daily newspaper publishers and 3 sites that are intended to our Diaspora. Among the oldest and the most popular types of Web sites are Web portals. Among numerous entering points to the virtual world there are 2 most prominent: Krstarica and B92.

Krstarica.com (the cruiser, in English), the largest Balkan Web portal, is located in Belgrade. The site is established in 1999 on the concepts of knowledge and information, by a group of students of electrical engineering. This hybrid business model registers 21,300,000 visited pages monthly (Cruiser, 2007). It provides the only research engine in Serbian language, catalogue of sites, forum, magazine, and some commercial services as well: selling merchandise, advertisements, ISP services, etc.

Very popular model in e-commerce in Serbia is content provider. The highest rank among content providers has B92, a very popular news medium, with the Web site which has 100,000 visitors and 900,000 visited pages a day (B92.net, 2007). It is important entry point to the Internet in Serbia, whose blogs are prestige place in Serbian intellectual environment, especially among younger generations. This private organization also owns one of the most popular TV stations in Serbia, and also a very popular radio station. In the chaotic 1990s B92 played very important role in fighting with the oppressive government in Serbia and it survived as an information media which investigates inheritance from the recant past. As it is a business organization, it has added a Web storefront to its business which sells books, music CDs, computers, and digital accessories.

Web storefronts in Serbia don't have full transactional capability that would include e-payment and typically present data on products and services. Well-known example is Knjizara.com, the on line bookstore, the largest in the region, in the style which follows the Amazon.com. Statements of the company's representatives are giving deeper picture about this pure dot-company: there are between 8,700 and 13,700 visitors daily, which can browse a catalog featuring offerings with about 30,000 titles from 850 publishers and 10,000 secondhand titles. About 85% of their selling is in the domestic market, in the other countries of former Yugoslavia (where people speak the same or similar language) Knjizara is selling mostly scientific or expert books, but there are a significant number of orders from Western Europe, USA, Canada and Australia. The stuff with 10 employers sends between 30 and 70 parcels daily. Another important storefront, worth to be mentioned, is Mobilnisvet.com, which is selling mobile phones (we believe that it is important to say that there are about 5,200,000 registered users of mobile phones, still waiting for the third operator).

Among the first implemented business models in Serbian virtual world are malls, banks, content providers, and tourist, real estate, advertisement, and job agencies.

The oldest mall in Serbia is Yu Internet Bazaar, found in 2000, which offers the list with 95 links in 18 categories of business on the site Prodavnice.com. MyShop.co.yu is selling products in almost all categories. This relatively new shopping center is open for all sellers and it makes a profit on cost-per-click model. Among the others, relatively new SrbijaTrguje.com, with the concept to bring small and medium-sized enterprises to the Internet market, is winning the expert prices.

Strong penetration of the international capital made real revolution in Serbian banking market and e-payment and e-banking systems will be analyzed in the special chapter. Among about 5,000,000 electronic card users new technologies like Verified from VISA and MasterCard SecureCode are on the way to find respective place.

The most important content provider is B92, which still does not sell contents. The subscription business model is the most popular among the media which are selling contents and in that group are newspaper and magazine publishing companies, like NIN and Nedeljni telegraf, but the most of them are still offering their contents for free.

As the most Europeans, people in Serbia like to spend their holidays somewhere far enough from their homes and jobs. Tourism is taking an important place in the Serbian information society. Business model implemented in tourist agencies is the similar with the agencies in western world, but in the most of them it is still not possible to make a reservation through the Internet, and the same state is in the most of Serbian hotels. In this group we find the new model, the agency of agencies, which is collecting arrangements and offering the opportunity to make on line reservation with a discount or some other benefit. The most prominent in that group are putovanja.info & pakujse.com. Another interesting group makes the Web sites which are trying to bring tourists to Serbia. In this group is the first on line reservation system called visitserbia.org and the interesting catalogue of rural tourism selo.co.yu.

In the real estate world in Serbia we are finding a substantial growth. The virtual real estate world is also growing and we can find a lot of Web sites which are offering them. The largest in that group is Nekretnine.net, which is offering 2,223 flats, 2,432 houses and 2,337 real estates of other types. This model is offering the first information and it is a kind of guide to the brick-and-mortar agency, where real job will be done.

As Serbia has very high unemployment rate, Web sites with advertisements and jobs are making very large groups with the high rates of visits. We will just mention two with the highest rates: Halooglasi.co.yu is the most important place for advertisements and Poslovi.net is interesting place for job seekers.

Table 4. Business models in B2C e-commerce in Serbia

B2C Business Models	Example	URL
Portal	Krstarica	http://www.krstarica.com/
Content Provider	NIN	http://nin.co.yu/
Mall	Yu Internet Bazaar	http://www.prodavnice.com
Web Storefront	Knjizara.com	http://www.knjizara.co.yu/
Jobs Agency	Poslovi	http://www.poslovi.net/
Classified Ads	Halo oglasi	http://www.haloglasi.co.yu/
Real Estate	Berza nekretnina	http://www.nekretnine.net/
Tourist agency	Putovanja	http://www.putovanja.info/
Hybrid	B92	http://www.b92.net

It is interesting to say that some of the key B2C e-commerce Web sites, which are intended to the Serbian population, are located outside the boarders of Serbia. For example, Balkanmedia is the Web-based music store with the shopping cart capability and credit card payment. The main, winning idea of this company, which operates from Germany since 1995, is to connect nostalgic Serbian Diaspora (people who live out of their native country) with the music from their origins. Another example of the impact from abroad is Serbian Café (also selling music) and YuSerach.com that are operating out of Canada since the middle of 1990s. Beograd.com operates from the United States through different business models: content provider, air tickets reseller, etc.

The B2B e-commerce is still very limited in Serbia by a small number of electronic marketplaces and vertical portals. We will mention only two excellent implementations: IDEA and Key-to-Steel.

The wholesaler IDEA has a private electronic marketplace which is supporting its sales operations. The concept is organized on the model of pre-authorized partners which are sending their electronic orders to IDEA. The main partners are small and medium-size retailers and the software is fully developed, maintained and distributed to the retailers by IDEA. Information system called "IDEA on line buyer" is accessible through the Internet, and it processed over 3,000,000 transactions last year.

The concept of vertical portal which sells industry-related information is implemented in Key-to-Steel and Key-to-Metals solutions. An interesting example is the Key-to-Steel portal serving with information the steel industry. This portal has very interesting history. As it was founded in Serbia, the firm was unable in the first year of existence to attract a single customer, because e-marketplaces crucially depend on trust (Hafez, 2006; Humphrey et al., 2003; Pucihar & Podlogar, 2006). After moving the site to Switzerland, the business made a huge success, measured by tens of thousands of subscribers in almost 150 countries, including the world largest companies like Lloyds, Alcatel, GE, Ford, Honda, Black & Decker, Thyssen-Krupp, Shell, Siemens, Chevron, and Total (Jošanov & Perić, 2005).

PRECONDITIONS FOR E-COMMERCE DEVELOPMENT IN SERBIA

Serbia must generate and exploit new economic opportunities through the adoption of e-commerce practices in order to reach the following goals (UNDP and Gov. of Serbia, 2006) ibid:

- To promote economic growth and social development,
- To enhance business efficiency and productivity,
- To decrease the cost of doing business,
- To enable domestic companies easier re-integration to European and world market.

Application of e-commerce in various sectors of national economy increases the linkages and interdependence among computerized networks of private and public organizations involved in internal and international economic activities. In this way, the national economy is moving from interaction of atomistic actors to an integrated system of information flow management and gets the characteristics of e-economy- information based society. In modern global era of world society development, e-commerce is the world's growth engine. Not to move with e-commerce is to limit your nation's growth.

Advantages of e-commerce applications can be defined as following: efficiency improve in terms of lower costs, improve effectiveness in terms of widening market potentials and better meeting of customers` need, enhanced product and service innovation through customer-supplier interaction, raising competitiveness and employment possibilities.

The framework for e-commerce cannot emerge by itself. National authorities of Serbia should be involved in its creation, taking into account the evolving circumstances in the increasingly global economy. Firstly, as the strategic choice of Serbia is integration with the European Union, its policy should be aligned with the spirit and recommendations of the eEurope programme and EU legislation in this area.

One of the preconditions for national authority to deal with e-commerce framework is creation of complete national strategy for Information Society Development that will define among others, activities in e-commerce area development as well. Second important step is to have institution in charge to deal with strategy implementation and e-commerce framework creation. In October 2006 Serbia adopted its National strategy for information society development and within the latest government a Ministry for telecommunication and information society was formed as the institution in charge.

After creating strategy and institution in charge for IS and e-commerce development it is important to define concept and responsibilities of public and private sector in e-commerce development process.

The development of e-commerce in a country is a multisector and collaborative undertaking as the process cuts across a broad range of technical, legal, economic and institutional issues. In e-commerce development both the private and the public sector should take an active part. As a rule, the private sector takes the lead in technological developments and practical e-commerce applications, and Governments in (a) creating an enabling environment, (b) facilitating the coordination of private/public sector e-commerce initiatives, and (c) supporting the establishment of an Information Society, including the preparation of the general public, SMEs and the public sector for the opportunities offered by new information technologies (UN/ECE, 2003) ibid. Given the multisector nature of e-commerce and the need to associate both the private and the public sector to the process of its implementation, it is important that individual and potentially scattered efforts be streamlined, coordinated and promoted jointly by all relevant players in a country. It would be useful to create guidelines and mechanisms for public-private partnership (PPP) in e-business development aiming to initiate and enable coordination and cooperation between specific industrial sectors and the government how to optimally use ICT in order to increase their performance and competitiveness.

The strategy for the creation of an e-commerce enabling framework should consider the following issues (UN/ECE, 2003) ibid: business process analysis and re-engineering; adapting the national telecommunication networks and educational systems to the development needs of business; creating the legal basis for e-commerce, in compliance with the acquis communautaire; and harmonizing document and data requirements with international standards and requirements.

Also, one of the key responsibilities of the public sector is to create a trustful and secure environment for e-commerce. This would include: a reliable legal framework for doing business electronically, where actors would trust electronic transactions the way they trust traditional ones; intellectual property protection of ICT innovations and digital products; and action to protect companies and users of the network against spam and viruses.

The implementation process of e-commerce in Serbia is very complex and should be realized through the following steps:

Creation of Telecommunication Infrastructure and Affordable Access to Internet Services

Telekom operator/ISPs have monopolistic behavior and considerably high price of services. Services have long delivery time and relatively low quality. Huge, state owned Telekom often favors own ISPs. Such behavior slows down the spread of secondary ISPs network. It means that Internet penetration is significantly reduced, and that is the major obstacle for business to spread in cyber space.

One of the priority tasks is to continue the liberalization of network infrastructure and promotion of broadband competition. It is important to encourage the expanding use of affordable broadband networks, to which a critical mass of SMEs and consumers can be linked. Where needs exist, and without pre-empting private initiative, complement private investment with public financial assistance should be realised, especially with a view to cover under-served groups and remote areas. Interested potential subscribers should be involved in financing broadband infrastructure.

It is necessary to move beyond the provision of basic connectivity and ICT readiness, and facilitate a more integrated approach to the participation of public and private entities in e-commerce. Special programmes should target areas where market failures can be clearly identified, e.g. R&D incentives, implementing standards and best practices, skill formation, dissemination of information on recent developments and benefits of the use of ICT, taking into account commercial considerations of the private sector as a driving force for implementing innovative technologies.

Application of Business Process Reengineering

For individual enterprises, the private sector as a whole, public administration and the way the public and private sectors interact, introduction of e-commerce offered an opportunity to re-engineer their practices and procedures, and to switch in an integrated way from traditional paper-based processes to electronic means in the exchange of data. This would result in savings of cost and time for both companies and whole countries.

The first step in the analysis and re-engineering of business processes should be to look at the needs of both business and the regulatory authorities, and at the requirements of the international supply chains. The re-engineering of the business processes should start from addressing these needs. The next phase only would include identifying and implementing IT solutions that can fit these requirements.

Through the business process reengineering the concepts of the firm and other economic operators change. They shift from the organizational structure to the way work is organized, the business process, the demand of the market, and the potential of new technology. Economic activity is reorganized around the idea of reunifying the tasks of various agents into coherent business processes. The "new economy" transforms the way business transactions take place. Limiting the reselling of goods and services through direct B2C and B2B transactions saves resources; e-business gives birth to "community business" and a "networked economy".

Facilitation of Business Processes and Acceptance of Internationally Harmonized Standards

Facilitation of commerce processes in terms of simpler procedures and internationally and internally harmonized standards has to take place prior to any meaningful attempt at doing commerce electronically.

The most important step in the process of creating the foundations of e-commerce in Serbia is the harmonization of documentary and data requirements for international trade as a prerequisite to doing e-commerce.

Harmonizing documentary and data requirements would be a step in the development and implementation of such important elements of e-commerce as: (1) national electronic documents aligned with international standards and (2) systems for single, electronic submission of trade and transport data for both nationals and foreigners.

Ultimately, this harmonization should be focused on standards and requirements, accepted by the European Union, the World Customs Organization, the United Nations, ISO and other international organizations. For example, the alignment of customs declarations to the EU Single Administrative Document (SAD), itself based on the United Nations Layout Key (UNLK), would help create compatible electronic documents, for example in the eXtensible Markup Language (XML), which can easily be exchanged in advance of the actual movement of goods, thus facilitating risk analysis, single submission of data and a faster movement of goods. In perspective, this would provide the basis for linking national economies to the European computerized systems for binding tariff and trade information, VAT regime, etc (UN/ECE, 2003) ibid.

Appropriate Management of Human Resources

Business process re-engineering and related systems applications should be integrated through appropriate management of human resources and, especially, by the provision of training in both the public and private sectors.

In order to create conditions for e-commerce, it is important to build, over time, ICT skills, respecting gender equality principle, through the national education system and programmes targeting SMEs.

Both public and private sector should encourage higher-level ICT and e-business skill formation, which should include marketing, organizational, security, trust and management skills, in conjunction with educational institutions, business and individuals (UNDP and Gov. of Serbia, 2006) ibid.

CONCLUSION

Our findings on the conditions for diffusing e-commerce in Serbia corroborate previous research (Maruzzelli, 2004; Vidas-Bubonja et al., 2002) ibid, enriching the picture of opportunities and constraints pertaining to **diffusion** of e-commerce in Serbia. This investigation of diffusion of e-commerce in Serbia, driven by a multidimensional model, provided interesting and useful results which suggests two implications. First, the case of Serbia teaches about consequences of being late in catching the wave of the ongoing information revolution, and second, the case demonstrates possible means of catching up with the wave. The first implication makes it clear that an economic marginalization is the destiny of the countries that fail to espouse the revolution engendered by computer networks, modern telecommunications, and new generations of computer-based information systems. Serbia was at least five years late in adopting the Internet, and this precipitated a slower rate of e-commerce diffusion. The telecommunications poses a serious roadblock to diffusing e-commerce. Both introduction of new technologies and improvements in the speed of data transfer have been slower that in other SEE countries. Broadband lines are expensive, and rural areas are nearly cut off from the Internet, just like in the other countries in the region (Papazafeiropoulou, 2004) ibid. The government monopoly on the Internet's infrastructure is likely to be responsible for expensive lines that limit the range of business uses of the Internet. The software industry, another pillar to e-commerce, faces several key challenges: an obsolete IT base in organizations, lower IT readiness, and high brain drain. Furthermore, the inauguration of the legal infrastructure for e-commerce has also started later than in comparable countries, and the school system has just recently begun to transform. Finally, Serbian customers show a lack of trust in merchants, banks, and foreign brands (older consumers). Certain cultural traits could mediate the diffusion of e-commerce, such as a past time orientation, longer time horizon, cultural valuing of the traditional shopping in physical stores, lack of tradition of catalog-based shopping, and mixed experiences from early uses of this channel.

The second implication of our study concerns the possible means of catching up with the wave of the information revolution that Serbia missed in the 1990s. Experiences from the other developing countries show that the later challenge can be difficult enough (Pavlou, 2003). Serbia's convenient geographical location translates into land and water connections with three seas and the inclusion in two important European corridors. Delivery services are enhanced by operations of global providers of these services. Also, the software industry in Serbia shows signs of vitality. It grows faster than the rest of the economy caters to B2C and B2B e-commerce, nurtures private initiative, and has strategic support of the Serbian government. The area of e-payment and e-banking is another scene of encouraging developments. The government and commercial banks work on enabling cashless payment and once retired credit cards system (domestic and foreign). Rapid moves have also been recently made in laying down building blocks of a legal foundation for e-commerce (IS security, digital signature, intellectual property, and protection of personal information). Education is not in the same category of performance yet, but it may start catching up soon. Finally, the customer propensity for adopting e-commerce might be bolstered by regulatory changes and actions of financial institutions, while younger consumers may be the candidate for increasing the country's involvement in international flows of goods.

Serbia could benefit from a more ambitious strategy that draws on transforming obsolete economic institutions, capitalizing on Serbia's geographical location, and leaping into the electronic space (USAID, 2007). The first point refers to abandoning government monopolies in telecommunications and delivery. The last two points have to do with seeking development opportunities through participation in international B2B trading cycles. In so doing, Serbia can draw on its potential of a geographical hub. For example, it could find a lucrative placement for its software industry since flows of goods via land need to be accompanied by information services taking part in order fulfillment. To this end, becoming an off-shore location for foreign software vendors is an option to consider. The ongoing changes in e-banking/e-payment and legislature are supportive of such a B2B strategy, and are the new business conditions that have made Serbia the leading reformer in 2005. As opposed to a Serb traditionalist that inclines to explaining national historical misfortunes by an "unfortunate" crossroads-based position of Serbia, we concur with today's experts that praise this location as a great developmental opportunity. We extend this proposition by suggesting that flows of electrons, i.e. inclusion in the global electronic economy, are the way of capitalizing on Serbia's crossroads location.

The practical contribution of our study is in the detailed look at e-commerce in the country that could become attractive for business. Theoretically, our study contributes to understanding e-commerce in developing countries and particularly in the region of SEE. In addition, the research model we deployed proved to be useful and it lends itself to future uses.

REFERENCES

B92.net. (2007). Available: http://www.b92.net. Accessed: November 12, 2007.

Badjonski, M., Gašević, D., & Budimac, Z. (2006). AJA-Tool for Programming Adaptive Agents. In *Applied Intelligent Applications and Innovations*. Springer, pp. 516–523.

Baskerville, R., & Myers, M. (Eds.). (2004). Special issue on action research in information systems: making IS research relevant to practice (foreword). *MIS Quarterly, 28*(3), pp. 329–335.

Castells, M. (2000). Information technology and global capitalism. In Hutton, W., and Giddens, A. (Eds.), *Global capitalism* (pp. 52–74). New York: The New Press.

Commission of the European Communities, (2001) *eEurope+ 2003*, Action Plan, June.

Commission of the European Communities, (2002) *eEurope 2005*, June 21/22 .

Council of the European Union, Commission of the European Communities, (2000). *eEurope 2002, An Information Society for All, Action Plan*, Brussels, June.

Cronin, M. (2000). *Unchained value: The new logic of digital business*. Boston, MA: Harvard Business Press.

Cruiser. (2007). Available: http://www.krstarica.com/eng/catalog/Business_and_Economy/Companies/Transportation. Accessed: November 24, 2007.

Dinkić, M. (1995). An *economy of destruction: the great robbery of the people*. Belgrade, Serbia: VIN.

Dragutinović, G. (2007). *EURO <26 & ISIC International & Student Cards* (in Serbian), Paying Cards – Actual Trends, Chamber of Commerce in Serbia, Belgrade.

Djurić, D, Gašević, D., & Devedžić, V. (2005). Ontology Modeling and MDA, *Journal of Object Technology*, 4(1), pp. 109–128.

Djordjević B. (2007). Strategic Options in the Development on Mobile Banking Services (in Serbian), Bankarstvo, no. 3–4, pp. 38–50.

ECMT—European Conference of Ministers of Transport. (2005). Pan-European transport corridors. Available: http://www.cemt.org/topics/paneurop/corridors.htm. Accessed: November 17, 2007.

Efendioglu, A., & Yip, V. (2005). E-commerce in developing countries: issues and influences." Proceedings of the IBEC Annual Conference, Honolulu, Hawaii, January 6-9, 2005, pp. 10–15.

EU – European Union. (2005). Broadband access in EU: situation at January 1, 2005. Available: http://europa.eu.int/rapid/pressReleasesAction.do?reference=MEMO/05/format=HTML&aged=0&language=EN&guiLanguage=en. Accessed: November 10, 2005.

Hafez, M. (2006). Role of culture in electronic business in developing countries. In Sherif, K. (Ed.), *Electronic business in developing countries: Opportunities and challenges* (pp. 34–44). Hershey, PA: Idea.

Humphrey, J., Mansell, R., Paré, R., & Schmitz, H. (2003). *The reality of e-commerce with developing countries.* IDS. Brighton, UK: Institute of Development Studies.

ISC – Internet Systems Consortium. (2007). Internet domain host count. Retrieved July, 15, 2007, from http://www.isc.org.

ITU – International Telecommunication Union. (2003). Retrieved July, 15, 2007, from http://www.itu.int/ITU-D/statistics/WTI_2003.pdf.

ITU – International Telecommunication Union. (2006). *World Telecommunications Development Report 2006: Measuring ICT for Social and Economic Development.*

Jennex, M., & Amoroso, D. (2006). An e-commerce longitudinal case study from Ukraine. In Kamel, S. (Ed.), *Electronic business in developing countries: opportunities and challenges* (pp. 376–391). Hershey, PA: Idea Group.

Jošanov B., & Jošanov, I. (2006). "Serbia: on the Road for Determination of e-Readiness Index", *Proceedings from Mipro 06: International Conference on Digital Economy*, Opatia: pp. 79–86.

Jošanov B., & Perić, D. (Eds.) (2005). *Electronic business: Serbian perspective* (in Serbian). Belgrade, Serbia: Electro- technical College Press.

Jovanović, Z., Gajin, S., Bukvić, M., Vuletić, P., & Vulović ,Dj. (2004). The optical NREN of Serbia and Montenegro – new solutions in infrastructure and monitoring, TNC 2004. Retrieved July, 15, 2007, from http://www.terena.nl/conferences/tnc2004/programme/people/show.php?person_id=167

Kajan E., & Stoimenov, D. (2005). Toward an Ontology-Driven Architectural Framework for B2B. *Communications of the ACM*, 48(12), pp. 60–66.

Kamel, K. (2006). Preface. In Sherif, K. (Ed.), Electronic *business in developing countries: Opportunities and challenges* (pp. vi-xiv). Hershey, PA: Idea.

Karmel, E. (2003). Taxonomy of new software exporting nations. *Electronic Journal of Information Systems in Developing Countries*, 13(2), pp. 1-6.

Keen, P. (2004). Bled e-commerce manifesto. Keynote speech at the 17th Bled eCommerce Conference, Bled, Slovenia, June 21-23, 2004.

Klein, H., & Myers, M. (1999). A set of principles for conducting and evaluating interpretive fields studies in information systems. *MIS Quarterly, 23*(1), pp. 67–94.

Lee, O. (1999). An action research report of an e-commerce firm in South Korea. In Sudweeks, F., & Rom, C. (Eds.), *Doing Business on the Internet: Opportunities on the Internet* (pp. 246–258). London: Springer.

Maričić, B. (2002). *Consumer behavior* (in Serbian). Belgrade, Serbia: Savremena Administracija.

Maruzzelli, G. (2004). *Republic of Serbia: investing in Serbia's Internet and IT sector: challenges and opportunities.* Retrieved July, 15, 2007, from http://www.b92.net/download/Internet_in_Serbia_public_report_15_july_2004.doc.

McMaster, J., & Nowak, J. (2006). The evolution of trade portals and the Pacific islands countries e-trade facilitation and promotion. *Electronic Journal on Information Systems in Developing Countries, 26*(3), 1–27.

Medaković, R. (2005). *ICT in Serbia.* Elitex: New Delhi.

Palvia, P., S. Palvia, E. Roche. (Eds.). (2002). *Global information technology and electronic commerce.* Marietta, GA: Ivy League Publishing.

Palvia, P., Palvia, S., & Whitworth, E. (2002). Global information technology environment: Representative world issues. In Palvia, P., Palvia, S., & Roche,

E. (Eds.). (2002), *Global information technology and electronic commerce* (pp. 2–27). Marietta, GA: Ivy League Publishing.

Papazafeiropoulou, A. (2004). Inter-country analysis electronic commerce adoption in South Eastern Europe: policy recommendations fore the region. *Journal of Global Information Technology Management, 7*(2), pp. 35–45.

Pavlou, P. (2003). Consumer acceptance of electronic commerce: Integrating trust and risk with the technology acceptance model. *International Journal of Electronic Commerce, 7*(3), 101–34.

Plant, R. (2000). *E-commerce: Formulation of strategy.* Upper Saddle River, NJ: Prentice-Hall.

Ponder, J. (2006). Developing Next Generation Access Networks: Challenges in the SEE Region, In *The first SEE Broadband Conference*, Belgrade, April, 2006.

PTT Serbia. (2007). Available: http://www.posta.co.yu/english/onama/GodisnjiIzvestaj.asp. Accessed: October 25, 2007.

Pucihar, A., & Podlogar, M. (2006). E-marketplace adoption success factors: Challenges and opportunities for a small developing country. In Sherif, K. (Ed.), *Electronic business in developing countries: Opportunities and challenges* (pp. 89–117). Hershey, PA: Idea.

RCUB NETIS (2007), Retrieved July, July, 6, 2007, from http://netiis.rcub.bg.ac.yu/netiis/NetIIS?service=main&action=show&ID=group.13952,

Reporter (2007). Retrieved July, 6, 2007, from http://www.reporter.gr/default.asp?pid=16&la=2&art_aid=73175.

Serbian Yellow Pages (2005). Available: http://www.yuyellowpages.net/search.php?delatnost=173. Accessed: October, 20 2005.

Sridhar, V., & Sridhar, K. (2006). E-commerce infrastructure and economic impacts in countries: Case of India. In Sherif, K. (Ed.), *Electronic business in developing countries: Opportunities and challenges* (pp. 63–87). Hershey, PA: Idea.

Stability Pact, eSEE Initiative, (2007) eSEE Agenda+, October, 2007, Sarajevo.

Stability Pact, bSEE Initiative, (2006) bSEE Action Plan, October.

Stability Pact, eSEE Initiative. (2002). *Agenda for the development of the information society.* June, 4, 2002.

Španović, M. (2005). Credit card as an alternative to checks (in Serbian). In *Pay cards: development and prevention of abuse* (in Serbian). Belgrade: The Chamber of Commerce of Serbia.

The World Factbook. (2007). Available: http://www.cia.gov/cia/publications/factbook/geos/yi.html#Econ. Accessed: November 21, 2007.

Trompenaars, S., & Hampden-Turner, C. (1998). Riding the waves of culture: understanding cultural diversity in global business. New York: McGraw Hill

Travica, B., Kajan, E., Jošanov, B., Vidas-Bubanja, M., & Vuksanović, E. (2007). E-Commerce in Serbia: Where Roads Cross Electrons Will Flow, *Journal of Global Information Technology Management (JGITM),* 10(2), 34–56.

Travica B., Kajan, E., Jošanov, B., Vidas-Bubanja, M., & Vuksanović, E. (2006). „E-Commerece in a developing Country: Casa Study of Serbia", *Proceedings from IADIS International Conference e-Commerce 2006*, Barcelona: pp. 19–26.

Travica, B. (2002). Diffusion of electronic commerce in developing countries: the case of Costa Rica. *Journal of Global Information Technology Management, 5*(1), 4–24.

Travica, B., & Olson, R. (1998). Electronic commerce in east and central Europe. *Proceedings of the ASIS 1998 Annual Conference*, October 24-29, 1998, Pittsburgh, PA, pp. 40–55.

Trompenaars, A., & Hampden-Turner, C. (1998). *Riding the waves of culture: understanding cultural diversity in global business*. New York: McGraw Hill.

UNCTAD (2006). *Information Technology Report 2006: The Development Perspective*. Retrieved July, 10, 2007, from http://www.unctad.org/sdateecb2006ch1-en.pdf.

UNDP and Government of Republic of Serbia, (2006) *National Strategy for Information Society of Republic of Serbia*, Belgrade.

UN/ECE (2003) *Guidelines for Creation of National Strategy*, Geneva.

USAID. (2007). Available: http://www.usaid.org.yu/left/facts_about_serbia.php. Accessed: October 25, 2007.

Varshney, U., & Vetter, R. (2002). "Mobile commerce: framework, applications and networking support". *Mobile Networks and Applications*, 7, 185–198.

Vidas-Bubanja, M, (2001). The importance of information technology for national economic development (in Serbian). *Ekonomski anali*, April, 2001.

Vidas-Bubanja, M, Jošanov, B., & Vuksanović, E. (2002). Role of e-business in transition of Yugoslav Economy. *Proceedings of the 15th Bled Electronic Commerce Conference*. Bled, Slovenia, June 17–19, 2002, pp. 19–35.

Vujić D. (2004). *Motivation for quality* (in Serbian). Belgrade, Serbia-Montenegro: Center for Applied Psychology Press.

Vuksanović, E. (2002). The role of bankcard industry in transition of Yugoslav Economy. *Proceedings of The International Conference "ICES 2002"*. Sarajevo, Bosnia-Herzegovina, October 17-18, 2002, pp. 767–775.

Vuksanović E. (2005). A Selection of e-Business Cases in Financial System of Serbia, *Proceedings from the International Scientific Session: Internationalization and Globalization*, Pitesti.

Whiteley, D. (1999). Internet commerce – hot cakes and dead ducks. In Sudweeks, F., and Celia R. (Eds.), *Doing business on the internet: Opportunities on the Internet* (pp. 9–20). London: Springer.

Wolcott, P., Press, L., McHenry, W., Goodman, S. E., & Foster, W., (2001). "A framework for assessing the global diffusion of the Internet." *Journal of the Association for Information Systems, 2*(6).

World Bank. (2005). Serbia ranked number one business reformer. Available: http://www.worldbank.org.yu. Accessed: July 12, 2007.

Compilation of References

Aaker, D. A., & Joachimsthaler, E. (2000). The brand relationship spectrum: The key to the brand architecture challenge. *California Management Review*, 42, 8-23.

Abd.Mukti, N. (2000). Barriers to Putting Business on the Internet in Malaysia. *Electronic Journal on Information Systems in Developing Countries, 2*(6), 1-6.

Abernathy, W. J. & Clark, K. B. (1978). Patterns of Industrial Innovation. *Technology Review, 80*(7), 40-47.

Abeyesekera, A., Criscuolo, C., Barreto, E. and Gallagher P. (1999) Partners speak out: Views on e-commerce, *International Trade Forum*, (2), 23-25.

Abhilash, C. M. (2002). E-Commerce Law in Developing Countries: An Indian Perspective. *Information and Communication Technology Law, 11*(3), 269-281.

Accessibility on the Web (2004), International Center for Disability Resources on the Internet [online], Available: www.icdri.org [accessed: December 2004].

Agarwal, R. (2000). Individual Acceptance of Information Technologies. *Framing the Domains of IT Management: Projecting the Future through the Past.* Edited by Zmund, R., & Price, M. Pinnaflex Educational Resources, Inc. Cincinnati, OH., 85-104.

Agarwal, R., & Prasad, J. (1997). The Role of Innovation Characteristics and Perceived Voluntariness in the Acceptance of Information Technologies. *Decision Sciences*, 28(3), 557-582.

Agarwal, R., & Prasad, J. (1999). Are Individual Differences Germane to the Acceptance of New Information Technologies? *Decision Sciences*, 30(2), 361-391.

Agboola, A.A.A. (2006). Electronic Payment Systems and Tele-banking Services in Nigeria, *Journal of Internet Banking and Commerce, 11*(3).

Aggestam, L. & Söderström, E. (2006). Managing Critical Success Factors in a B2B Setting. *IADIS International Journal on WWW/Internet, Vol.4, No.1,* 96-110.

Aggestam, L. (2004). A Framework for supporting the preparation of ISD. *Proceedings of the Doctoral Consortium, held in conjunction with the Conference on Advanced Information Systems Engineering* (CAiSE'04).

Aguolu, I. (1997). Accessibility of information: a myth for developing countries? *New Library World, Vol.98, No.1132,* 25-29.

Ah-Wong, J., Gandhi, P., Patel, H., Shah, U (2001) E-commerce Progress: Enablers, Inhibitors and the Short-term Future, *European Business Journal*, vol. 13, No. 2, pp. 98-107, 2001.

Ainin, S., Lim, C. H. & Wee, A. (2005). Prospects and Challenges of E-banking in Malaysia. *Electronic Journal on Information Systems in Developing Countries, 22*(1), 1-11.

Ajzen, I. & Fishbein, M. (1980). *Understanding attitudes and predicting social behavior.* Englewood Cliffs, NJ: Prentice Hall.

Ajzen, I. (1991). The Theory of Planned Behavior. *Organizational Behavior and Human Decision Processes,* 50, 179-211.

Ajzen, I. (2001). Nature and operation of attitudes. *Annual Review of Psychology,* 52, 27–58.

Copyright © 2009, IGI Global, distributing in print or electronic forms without written permission of IGI Global is prohibited.

Ajzen, I., & Fishbein, M. (1980). *Understanding attitudes and predicting social behavio*r, Englewood Cliffs, NJ: Prentice Hall.

Ajzen, I., & Fishbein, M. (2005). The influence of attitudes on behavior. In D. Albarracín, B. T. Johnson, & M. P. Zanna (Eds.), *The handbook of attitudes*. (pp. 173-221). Mahwah, NJ: Lawrence Erlbaum

Akel, M. & Phillips, R. (2001). The Internet Advantage: A Process For Integrating Electronic Commerce Into Economic Development Strategy. *Economic Development Review, 17*(3), 13-19.

Akkeren, J. & Cavaye, A. (1999). *Factors Affecting the Adoption of E-commerce Technologies by Small Business in Australia – An Empirical Study*, Australian Computer Society. Retrieved November 30, 2005, from http://www.acs.org.au/act/events/io1999/akkern.html.

Al Sukkar, A. & Hasan, H. (2005). Toward a Model for the Acceptance of Internet Banking in Developing Countries. *Information Technology for Development, 11*(4), 381-398.

Aladwani, A. M. (2003). Key Internet Characteristics and E-commerce Issues in Arab Countries. *Information Technology and People, 16*(1), 9-20.

Al-Gahtani, S. S., Hubona, G. S. and Wang, J. (2007). Information technology (IT) in Saudi Arabia: Culture and the acceptance and use of IT. *Information & Management*. 44(8), 681-691

Aljifri, H. A., Pons, A. & Collins, D. (2003). Global E-commerce: A Framework for Understanding and Overcoming the Trust Barrier. *Information Management and Computer Security, 11*(2/3), 130-1358.

Alm & Melnik (2005) "Sales and tax decision to purchase online", Public Finance Review, 33 (2), 184 (29)

Al-Sabbagh, I. & Molla, A. (2004). Adoption and Use of Internet Banking in the Sultanate of Oman: An Exploratory Study. *Journal of Internet Banking and Commerce, 9*(2).

American Chamber of Commerce in Egypt (2002) Information Technology in Egypt, Business Studies and Analysis Center, April

Andaleeb, S. S. (1996). An experimental investigation of satisfaction and commitment in marketing channels: The role of trust and dependence. *Journal of Retailing, 96*(1), 77-93.

Anderson, B., Fell, J. M. (US Government Export Portal) (2003), Taming the Red Dragon: Getting in and Succeeding in China, Available: www.export.gov/comm_svc/pdf/RedDragon.pdf [accessed: 2004].

Andrieu, O., & Lafont D. (1996): *Internet et l'Entreprise*, Paris: Editions Eyrolles.

Ang, C., Tahar, R. M. & Murat, R. (2003). An Empirical Study on Electronic Commerce Diffusion in Malaysian Shipping Industry. *Electronic Journal on Information Systems in Developing Countries, 14*(1), 1-9.

Angeles R (2006) Business-to-business E-Procurement Corporate Initiative: A Descriptive Empirical Study, ICEC Conference, Fredericton, NB, Canada, pp. 391-402

Anigan, G (1999). *Views on electronic commerce*. International Trade Forum, 2, 23–27.

Annual reports of the National Office of Posts, Tunis: ONP Publication

Anthopoulos, L., & Tsoukalas, I. (2005). A Cross Border Collaboration Environment, as a Means for Offering Online Public Services and for Evaluating the Performance of Public Executives. *Proceedings of the 2005 IEEE International Conference on e-Technology, e-Commerce and e-Service (EEE'05) on e-Technology, e-Commerce and e-Service*. pp.: 622-627. ISBN: 0-7695-2274-2.

Ardissono, L., Goy, A., Petrone, G., Segnan, M. (2002), "Personalization in B2C interaction", Communications of the ACM, Vol. 45, Issue 5 (May 2002).

Argyris, C., Putnam, R., & McLain Smith, D. (1990). *Action Science: Concepts, Methods, and Skills for Research and Intervention*. San Francisco: Jossey-Bass.

Arunachalam, S. (1999). Information and Knowledge in the Age of Electronic Communication: A Developing Country Perspective. *Journal of Information Science, 25*(6), 465-476.

Asuncion, R. M. (1997). Potentials of Electronic Markets in the Philippines. *Electronic Markets, 7*(2), 34-37.

Atkins, M. H. (1998). The role of appropriability in sustaining competitive advantage - an electronic auction system case study. *Journal of Strategic Information Systems, 7*(2), 131-152.

Au, K. F. & Ho, D. C. K. (2002). Electronic Commerce and Supply Management: Value Adding Service for Clothing Manufacturing. *Integrated Manufacturing Systems, 13*(4), 247-254.

Austin, J. (1990). MANAGING IN DEVELOPING COUNTRIES - STRATEGIC ANALYSIS AND OPERATING TECHNIQUES. Free Press. ISBN 0029011027.

Avery S (2005) Intel Goes Global with Indirect Buying Strategy, Purchasing Magazine, April

Ayadi, A. (2006). Technological and organizational preconditions to Internet Banking implementation: Case of a Tunisian bank, *Journal of Internet Banking and Commerce, 11*(1).

Ayo, C.K. & Babajide, D.O. (2006). Designing a Reliable E-payment System: Nigeria a Case Study, *Journal of Internet Banking and Commerce, 11*(2).

Ayo, C.K. (2006). The Prospects of E-Commerce Implementation in Nigeria. *Journal of Internet Banking and Commerce, 11*(3).

Azjen, I. & Fishbein, M. (1980). *Understanding Attitudes and Predicting Social Behavior.* Englewood Cliffs, NJ: Prentice Hall.

Azjen, I. (1991). The Theory of Planned Behavior. *Organizational Behavior, and Human Decision Processes, 50*(2), 179-211.

B92.net. (2007). Available: http://www.b92.net. Accessed: November 12, 2007.

Badjonski, M., Gašević, D., & Budimac, Z. (2006). AJA-Tool for Programming Adaptive Agents. In *Applied Intelligent Applications and Innovations.* Springer, pp. 516–523.

Bagchi. K., Cerveny. R., Hart. P. & Peterson. M. (2003). *The Influence of national culture in Information Technology product adoption*, In Proceedings of the 9th Americas Conference on Information Systems (AMCIS), AIS, 112- 131

Bajaj, A. & Leonard, L. N. K. (2004). The CPT Framework: Understanding the Roles of Culture, Policy and Technology in Promoting E-commerce Readiness. *Problems and Perspectives in Management,* 3, pp. 242-252.

Bakos, J. Y. (Winter 2001). The emerging landscape for retail e-commerce. *The Journal of Economic Perspectives,* 15 (1), 69-80.

Bakos, J.Y. (1991). A Strategic Analysis of Electronic Marketplaces, *MIS Quarterly, 15*(3), 295–310.

Bakos, J.Y., & Kemerer, C.F. (September 1992). Recent applications of economic theory in information technology research. *Decision Support Systems,* 8 (5), 365-386.

Bakos, Y. (1998). The emerging role of electronic marketplaces on the Internet. *Communications of the ACM, 41*(8): 35-42.

Bandura, A. (1986). *Social foundations of thought and action: A social cognitive theory.* Englewood Cliffs. Prentice-Hall.

Bandyopadhyay, K., & Fraccastoro, A. F. (2007). The effect of culture on user acceptance on Information Technology. *Communications of the Association for Information Systems.* 19(23), 522-543.

Barnett, R. C., & Marshall, N. L. (1991). The relationship between women's work and family roles and their subjective wellbeing and psychological distress, in (eds) *Women, Work and Health: Stress and Opportunities*, M. Frankenhaeuser, V. Lundber, and M.A.Chesney. (pp. 111-136). Plenum, New York.

Barney, J. (1991). Firm Resources and Sustained Competitive Advantage. *Journal of Management, 17*(1), 99-120.

Barney, J. B. (1997). *Gaining and Sustaining Competitive Advantage*, Reading, MA: Addison-Wesley.

Barnickel, N., Matthias, M. & Schmidt, K. (2006). Interoperability in eGovernment Through Cross-Ontology Semantic Web Service Composition, *Workshop on Semantic Web for eGovernment of ESWC 2006*, 11-14 June 2006, Budva, Montenegro. pp 37-47.

Baron, S., Patterson, A. & Harris, K. (2006). Beyond technology acceptance: understanding consumer practice. *International Journal of Service Industry Management*, 17(2), 111-136.

Barrientos, S. (1998). How To Do Literature Study. In A., Thomas, J. Chatway and M., Wuyts (Eds.) *Finding Out Fast.* London: Sage.

Baskerville, R. (1999). Investigating Information Systems with Action Research. *Communications of the Association of Information Systems*, 2(19).

Baskerville, R., & Myers, M. (Eds.). (2004). Special issue on action research in information systems: making IS research relevant to practice (foreword). *MIS Quarterly, 28*(3), pp. 329–335.

Bastöe, P. Ö. & Dahl, K (1996). *Organisationsutveckling i offentlig verksamhet.* Utbildningshuset Studentlitteratur.

Bauer, C. & Glasson, B. (1999) A Classification Framework for Electronic Commerce Research. In A. Bytheway (Ed.), *Proceedings of BitWorld 99 Conference*, June 30th-July 2nd, Cape Town, South Africa [CD-ROM].

Beatty R.C., Shim J.P & Jone M.C(2001). Factors influencing corporate web site adoption: a time based assessment, *Information & Management* (38), 337–354.

Becker, K. (2007), The impact of e-commerce and information technology in developing countries, In Krishnamurthy and Isaias (eds.), Proceedings of the IADIS International Conference e-Commerce, December 7-9, Algarve, Portugal, pp.230-235

Bekele, D. (2000). EthioGift: A Unique Experience in Electronic Commerce in Ethiopia. *Electronic Markets, 10* (2), 146.

Belanger, France Carter, Lemuria D. Schaupp, & L. Christian (2005). U-government: a framework for the evolution of e-government. *Electronic Government, an International Journal*, Volume 2, Number 4, pp. 426-445(20).

Belkhamza, Z., & Syed Azizi Wafa, S. K. W. (2006). Evaluation of the effect of perceived system risk on the intention to use e-commerce: An empirical study on tourism organization. In Proceedings of *Le 3ième Ecole Informatique de Printemps – EIP'06. Sécurité Informatique: Tendances et Applications.* (pp.189-198). INI. Algiers.

Bellens, Jan, Chris Ip, and Anna Yip (2007). Developing a new rural payments system in China. McKinsey Quarterly (Web Exclusive), May 2007. http://www.mckinseyquarterly.com/article_print.aspx?L2=22&L3=77&ar=2002 Accessed on 5/2/2007.

Benbasat, I., Dexter, A.S., Drury, D.H. & Goldstein, R.C. (1984). A critique of the stage hypothesis: Theory and empirical evidence. *Communications of the ACM,* 27(5), 476-485.

Benbasat, I., Ives, B., Piccoli, G., & Weber, R. (2000) E-commerce Top Questions. ISWorld. Retrieved November 20 2007 from http://www.isworld.org/isworldarchives/research.asp#.

Benjamin, R. & Wigand, R. (1995). Electronic Markets and Virtual Value Chains on the Information Superhighway. *Sloan Management Review 36*(2), 62-72.

Benjamin, R., Gladman, B., Randel, B. (1998), "Protecting IT systems from cyber crime", The Computer Journal Vol. 41, Number 7, pp. 429-443 Available: www.cs.ncl.ac.uk/research/pubs/trs/papers/631.ps [accessed: December 2004].

Bernstein,T., Bhimani, A.B., Schultz, E., & Siegel, C. (1997): *Sécurité Internet pour l'Entreprise*, Paris: International Thomson Publishing.

Berril, A, Goode S. & Hart D. (2004). Managerial Expectations of Internet Commerce Adoption after the "Tech Wreck. *Journal of Global Information Technology Management, 7*(3), 45-63.

Berryman, E. (1999). *Getting on with the Business of E-business*. PriceWaterhouseCoopers, USA.

Bertolotti, D. S. (1984). *Culture and Technology*. Bowling Green, OH: Bowling Green State University Popular Press.

Bettman, J. R., Luce, M. F. & Payne, J. W. (1998). Constructive Consumer Choice Processes. *Journal of Consumer Research, 25*(3), 187-217.

Beyer, H. & Holtzblatt, K. (1998). *Contextual Design Defining Customer-Centered Systems*. Morgan Kaufman, Publishers Inc.

Bhabuta, L. (1988). *Sustaining Productivity and Competitiveness by Marshalling IT. In Information Technology Management for Productivity and Strategic Advantage*, Proceedings of the IFIP TC8 Open Conference, Singapore.

Bharadwaj, A., Sambamurthy, V., Zmud, M. (1999). IT Capabilities: Theoretical Perspectives and Empirical Operationalization. *ICIS Proceedings*.

Bharadwaj, A.S. (2000) A Resource-Based Perspective On Information Technology Capability and Firm Performance: An Empirical Investigation, *MIS Quarterly, 24*(1), 169-196.

Bharati, P. & Tarasewich, P. (2002). Global Perceptions of Journals Publishing E-Commerce Research. *Communications of the ACM, 45*(5), 21-26.

Bhatnagar, P. (1999a). Telecom Reforms in Developing Countries and the Outlook for Electronic Commerce. *Journal of World Trade, 33*(4), 143-155.

Bhatnagar, P. (1999b). Telecom Reforms in Developing Countries and the Outlook for Electronic Commerce. *Journal of International Economic Law, 2* (4), 695-712.

Bhatnagar, S. (2001) Social Implications of Information and Communication Technology in Developing Countries: Lessons from Asian Success Stories, *The Electronic Journal on Information Systems in Developing Countries*, vol. 1, No. 4, pp. 1-10

Bhatnagar, S. (1997). Electronic Commerce in India - The Untapped Potential. *Electronic Markets, 7*(2), 22-24.

Bichler, M., Field, S., & Werthner, H. (2001). Introduction: theory and application of electronic market design. *Electronic Commerce Research*, 1 (3), 215-220(6).

Bin, Q., Chen, S. & Sun, S. Q. (2003). Cultural differences in E-commerce: A Comparison Between the U.S and China. *Journal of Global Information Management, 11*(2), 48-55.

Bingi, P., Mir A., & Khamalah J. (2000). The challenges facing global e-eommerce, *Information systems Management* 17(4), 26–35.

Bitwayiki, C., & de Jager, A. (2004). *Building Capacity for Embedding: The DistrictNet Uganda Programme*. IICD / capacity.org. Retrieved from http://www.capacity.org and http://www.iicd.org.

Boateng, R. & Molla, A. (2006). Developing E-banking Capabilities in a Ghanaian Bank: Preliminary Lessons. *Journal of Internet Banking and Commerce, 11*(2).

Bochicchio, M., & Fiore, N. (2005). Supporting the Conceptual Modeling of Web Applications: The MODE Project. *Proceedings of the 19th International Conference on Advanced Information Networking and Applications*. Volume 1. pp.: 495-500. ISBN ~ ISSN:1550-445X, 0-7695-2249-1.

Bode, S & Burn, J.M.,(2002). Strategies for consultancy engagement for e-business development -a case analysis of Australian SMEs, S. Burgess (ed.), *Managing Information Technology in Small Business:challenges and solutions*, Idea Group, Melbourne, Australia, 227-245.

Bohman, P. (2003), Using Opera to check for accessibility, Available: www.webaim.org/techniques/articles/opera [accessed: 2004].

Bolin, S. (2004). The Nature and Future of ICT Standardization. Retrieved June 21, 2004, from: http://www.sun.com/software/standards/natureandfuture_ICT.pdf

Bolman, L.G. & Deal, T.E. (1997). *Nya perspektiv på organisation och ledarskap.* Andra upplagan, Lund, Studentlitteratur.

Bolongkikit, J., Obit, J.H., Asing, J.G. & Geoffrey, H. (2006). An Exploratory Research of the Usage Level of E-Commerce among SMEs in the West Coast of Sabah, Malaysia, *Journal of Internet Banking and Commerce, 11*(2).

Bond, M. H. (1986). The Psychology of the Chinese People, Hong Kong: Oxford University Press.

Bonnet Ph., Bressan S., Leth L., & Thomsen B. (1996). Towards ECLiPSe Agents on the Internet, Proceedings of the 1st *Workshop on Logic Programming Tools for Internet Applications*, Bonn, Germany, 1996 – pp 1-9.

Bordage, S. (2001): *Conduite de Projet Web*, Paris: Editions Eyrolles.

Bouwman, H. (2002). The Sense and Nonsense of Business Models. *International workshop on business models*, Lausanne.

Brandman, J. (2000) Bridging the emerging markets Internet divide, *Global Finance*, 14 (4), 34.

Brezis, Elise S. & Daniel Tsiddon (1998).Economic Growth, Leadership and Capital Flows: The Leapfrogging Effect. *Journal of International Trade & Economic Development*, 7 (September), 261-277.

Brislin, R. (1993). *Understanding culture's influence on behavior.* Harcurt Brace College, Publishers. Orlanda Florida.

Brousseau, E. (2002). The governance of transactions by commercial intermediaries: an analysis of the re-engineering of intermediation by electronic commerce. *International Journal of the Economics of Business*, 9 (3), 353-374.

Brown, I. & Molla, A. (2005). Determinants of Internet and Cell Phone Banking Adoption in South Africa. *Journal of Internet Banking and Commerce, 10*(1).

Brown, I., Hope, R., Mugera, P., Newman, P. & Stander, A. (2004). The Impact of National Environment on the Adoption of Internet Banking: Comparing Singapore and South Africa. *Journal of Global Information Management, 12*(2), 1-26.

Browne, G. J. & Ramesh, V. (2002). Improving information requirements determination: a cognitive perspective. *Information and Management,* 1-21.

Bubenko jr, J.A. (1993). Extending the Scope of Information Modelling. *4:th International Workshop on the Deductive Approach of Inforamtion Systems and Databases, Lloret, Costa Brava,(Catalonia), Sept 20-22 1993.* Departmentd de Llenguatges i Sistemes Informaticsn Universitat Politecnica de Catalunya, Report de Recerca LSI/93-25, Barcelona (http://www.dsv.su.se/~janis/jbpaper/library/bib.htm)

Bui, T., Le, T., & Jones, W. (2006). An exploratory case study of hotel e-marketing in Ho Chi Minh City. *Thunderbird International Business Review, 48*(3), 369-388.

Bundesagentur fuer Aussenwirtschaft (2007). Retrieved July 31, 2007, from http://www.bfai.de/DE/Navigation/Datenbank-Recherche/datenbank-recherche-node.html.

Burgess, L. & Cooper, J. (1999). A model for classification of business adoption of Internet commerce solutions, Global Networked Organizations: 12th International Bled Electronic Commerce Conference, Bled, Slovenia, June 7–9, pp. 46–58.

Burgess, L. & Cooper, J. (2000). *Extending the Viability of Model of Internet Commerce Adoption (MICA) as a Metric for Explaining the Process of Business Adoption of Internet Commerce.* Paper presented at 3rd International Conference on Telecommunications and Electronic Commerce, Dallas, TX.

Burn, J. M. (1995). The new cultural revolution: The impact of EDI on Asia. *Journal of Global Information Management.* 3(4),16-23.

Burns, Enid (2005). U.S. Tops Broadband Usage, For Now. ClickZ Stats, November 14, 2005. http://www.clickz.com/showPage.html?page=3563966 Accessed on 7/2/2007.

Burns, Enid (2007). Internet Audience up 10 Percent Worldwide. March 6, 2007. http://www.clickz.com/showPage.html?page=36251683, accessed on /6/2007.

Burns, Enid (2007a). Kids Chores Turn Wired. May 14, 2007. http://www.clickz.com/showPage.html?page=3625858 Accessed on 7/10/2007.

California State University, Sacramento (2002), Web Design Principles, Available: www.csus.edu/uccs/training/online/design/d_principles.htm.

Cao, J. X. (2007). Logistics service in e-commerce in China. *Management Exploration,* 3, 17-18.

Carayannis E G and Popescu D (2005) Profiling a Methodology for Economic Growth and Convergence: Learning from the EU eProcurement Experience for Central and Eastern European Countries. Technovation, Volume 25, Number 1, January, pp. 1-14

Carr A S and Pearson J N (1999) Strategically Managed Buyer-Supplier Relationships and Performance Outcomes. Journal of Operations Management, Volume 17, Number 5, August, pp. 497-519

Carr, N. G. (2000). Hypermediation: Commerce as clickstream. *Harvard Business Review,* January-February, 46-47.

Castells, M. (2000). Information technology and global capitalism. In Hutton, W., and Giddens, A. (Eds.), *Global capitalism* (pp. 52–74). New York: The New Press.

Cattani, C.F., (2000) Electronic finance: A cornerstone to trade and compete internationally, *International Trade Forum,* (3), 13-14.

Champy, J. A. (1997) Preparing for OC In Hesselbein, F., Goldsmith, M. & Beckhard, R. (1997). *The Organiszation of the Future.* Jossey-Bass, Publisher San Francisco,

Chan, C. & Swatman, P. M. C., (2004). *B2B E-Commerce Stages of Growth: The Strategic Imperatives.* Proceedings of the 37th Hawaii International Conference on System Sciences,

Chan, S. & Lu, M. (2004). Understanding Internet Banking Adoption and Use Behavior: A Hong Kong Perspective. *Journal of Global Information Management, 12*(3), 21-43.

Chao, P., Samiee, S. & Yip, L. S. (2003). International Marketing and the Asia-Pacific Region – Developments, Opportunities and Research Issues. *International Marketing Review, 20*(5), 480-492.

Chau, P. Y. K. & Hu, P J. (2001). Information Technology Acceptance by Professionals: A Model Comparison Approach. *Decision Sciences,* 32(4), 699-719.

Chau, P. Y. K. (1996). An Empirical Assessment of a Modified Technology Acceptance Model. *Journal of Management Information Systems, 13*(2), 185-204.

Chau, P. Y. K. (2001). Inhibitors to EDI Adoption in Small Business. *Journal of Electronic Commerce Research, 2*(2), 78-88.

Chau, S.B. & Turner, P. (2001). *A four phase model of EC business transformation amongst small to medium sized enterprises,* Proceedings of the 12th Australasian Conference on Information Systems. Coffs Harbour: Australia.

Chau,P.Y.K and Jim,C.C.F.(2002). Adoption of Electronic Data Interchange in Small and Medium Sized Enterprises, *Journal of Global Information management*,44,4, 332–351

Chen, C., Wu, C., Wu, C.R. (2006) e-Service enhancement priority matrix: The case of an IC foundry company, *Information & Management, 43*(5)572-586.

Chen, J. C. H. & Ching, R. K. H. (2004). An Empirical Study of the Relationship of IT Intensity and Organizational Absorptive Capacity on CRM Performance. *Journal of Global Information Management, 12*(1), 1-17.

Chen, J. C., Lin, H., B., Li, L. & Chen, P. S. (2004). Logistics Management in China: A Case Study of Haier. *Human Systems Management, 23* 15-27.

Chen, J.-J. (2007). The difficulties and strategies in e-commerce development in China. *Technology & Management*, 2, 14-16.

Chen, L.-D., Gillenson, M. L., & Sherrell, D. L. (2002). Enticing online consumers: An extended technology acceptance perspective. *Information & Management, 39*(8), 705-719.

Chen, Min (1993). Understanding Chinese and Japanese Negotiation Styles. International Executive 35: 147-159.

Chen, S. & Ning, J. (2002). Constraints on E-commerce in Less Developed Countries: The Case of China. *Electronic Commerce Research, 2*(1-2), 31-42.

Chen, Shu-Ching Jean (2007). China Is No. 2 Online. Forbes.com, January 12, 2007. http://www.forbes.com/2007/01/12/china-internet-stats-biz-cx_jc_0112china_print.html accessed on 6/9/2007.

Chen, Y.N., Chen, H.M., Huang, W., & Ching, R.K. (2006). E-Government Strategies in Developed and Developing Countries: An Implementation Framework and Case Study, *Journal of Global Information* Management, *14*(1), 23-46.

Cheng et.al, (2006) "Consumer acceptance of the Internet as a channel of distribution in Taiwan- a channel function perspective", Technovation, 26 (7), 356 (9)

Cheng, H., Fang, M., Guan, L. & Hong, Z. (2004). Design and Implementation of an E-Commerce Platform-SIMEC. *Journal of Electronic Commerce in Organizations, 2*(2), 44-54.

Chernaouti, H.S. (2000): *Sécurité Internet, Stratégies et Technologies*, Paris: Editions Dunod.

Cherry, C. & Macredie, R.D. (1999). The Importance of Context in Information System Design: An assessment of Participatory Design. *Requirements Engineering, 4* 103-114.

Chiemeke, S. C., Evwiekpaefe, A. E., & Chete, F. O. (2006). The Adoption of Internet Banking in Nigeria: An Empirical Investigation. *Journal of Internet Banking and Commerce, 11*(3).

Chin, W., & Marcolin, B. (2001). The Future of Diffusion Research. *The Data Base for Advances in Information Systems,* 32(3), 8–12.

China Internet Network Information Center (2007). Retrieved July 31, 2007, from http://www.cnnic.net.cn/en/index/0O/index.htm.

China Internet Network Information Center (CNNIC). (2006). The18th statistical survey report on Internet development in China. Retrieved June 14, 2007, from http://www.cnnic.net.cn/uploadfiles/doc/2006/7/19/103601.doc

China Internet Network Information Center, 2002. Semiannual Survey Report on the Development of China's Internet (1997-2002), Retrieved 11th September 2002 from the World Wide Web http://www.cnnic.net.ch/develst/2002-7e/5.shtml

China Internet Network Information Center, 2003. Semiannual Survey Report on the Development of China's Internet (1997-2003), Retrieved 20th September 2003 from the World Wide Web http://www.cnnic.net.cn/develst/2003-1e/444.shtml

China Internet Network Information Center. (2007) Statistical Survey Report on the Internet Development in China. http://www.cnnic.net.cn/uploadfiles/pdf/2007/2/14/200607.pdf

China Internet Network Information Centre (CNNIC) (2007). The 19th statistical survey report on the Internet development in China. Retrieved June 18, 2007, from http://www.cnnic.cn/download/2007/cnnic19threport.pdf

China Internet Network Information Centre (CNNIC) (2007). The 20th statistical survey report on the Internet development in China. Retrieved July 13, 2007, from http://www.cnnic.cn/uploadfiles/pdf/2007/7/18/113918.pdf

China Market Information Center. (2007) 2006-2007 Annual report on China's E-Commerce Market. http://china-market.ccidnet.com/pub/enreport/show_18116.html

China Market Information Centre (CCID). (2006). B2B market will continue develop in China. Retrieved June 14, 2007, from http://news.ccidnet.com/art/1032/20060214/428239_1.html

ChinaCSR.com (2006). China Releases E-commerce Credibility Regulations. May 16, 2006. http://www.chinacsr.com/2006/03/16/362-china-releases-e-commercecredibility-regulation/ Accessed on 6/9/2007.

Chircu, A. M. & Kauffman, R.J. (1999). Strategies for Internet Middlemen in the Intermediation/Disintermediation/Reintermediation Cycle, *Electronic Markets, 9*(1-2), 109-117.

Chiu, Y., Lin, C. & Tang, L. (2005). Gender Differs: Assessing A Model of Online Purchase Intentions in E-tail Service. *International Journal of Service Industry Management, 16*(5), 416-435.

Choi, J. & Geistfeld, L.V. (2004). A cross-cultural investigation of consumer e-shopping adoption. *Journal of Economic Psychology*, 25 (6), 821-83

Chong S. & Pervan G.,(2007). Factors Influencing the Extent of Deployment Electronic Commerce for Small- and Medium-Sized Enterprises, *Journal of Electronic Commerce in Organizations,* 5(1), 1-29,

Chong Sandy (2006). An empirical study of factors that influence the extent of deployment of electronic commerce for small- and medium-sized enterprises in Australia. *Journal of Theoretical and Applied Electronic Commerce Research* 1(2), ISSN:0718-1876

Chung, I. K., & Adams, C. R. (1997). A Study on the characteristics of group decision making behavior: Cultural difference perspective of Korea Vs US. *Journal of Global Information Management*, 5(3), 18-29

Chwelos, P., Benbasat, I. & Dexter, A. (2001) Research Report: Empirical Test of an EDI Adoption Model, *Information Systems Research, 12*(3), 304-321.

Chwelos, P., Benbasat, I. & Dexter, A. (2001). Research Report: Empirical Test Of An EDI Adoption Model. *Information Systems Research, 12*(3), 304-321.

Clavadetcher, C. (1998). *User involvement: key to success.* IEEE SoftWare March/April.

Cloete, E., Courtney, S. & Fintz, J. (2002). Small Businesses Acceptance and Adoption of E-commerce in the Western Province of South Africa. *Electronic Journal on Information Systems in Developing Countries, 10*(4), 1-13.

Coase, R. H. (1937). The Nature of the Firm. *Economica, 4*, pp. 386-405.

Coleman, S. (2005). *African e-Governance: Opportunities and Challenges.* Commission for Africa. Retrieved from http://www.commissionforafrica.org.

Commission of the European Communities, (2001) *eEurope+ 2003*, Action Plan, June.

Commission of the European Communities, (2002) *eEurope 2005*, June 21/22 .

Communicate in your customers' language (2000), WorldLingo Press Releases [online], Available: www.worldlingo.com/company_information/pr20000625_01.html [accessed: November 2004].

Compeau, D. & Higgins, C. (1995). Computer self-efficacy: Development of a measure and initial test (in Theory and Research). *MIS Quarterly*. 19(2) 189-211.

Corbitt, B., G. Behrendorf, & J. Brown-Parker. (1997). *Small and medium-sized enterprises and electronic commerce,* The Australian Institute of Management 14, 204–222.

Cordell, V. V. (1994). Information exchange and the diffusion of computer based information technologies in U.S. and Japanese distribution channels. *Journal of Euromarketing, 3*(3, 4), 161-175.

Council of the European Union, Commission of the European Communities, (2000). *eEurope 2002, An Information Society for All, Action Plan*, Brussels, June.

Crick, F. & Koch, C. (2003). A framework for conscious. *Nature neuroscience, Vol6, no 2,* 19-126.

Cronin, M. (2000). *Unchained value: The new logic of digital business.* Boston, MA: Harvard Business Press.

Croom S Johnston R (2003) E-service: Enhancing Internal Customer Service through eProcurement, International Journal of Service Industry Management, Volume 14, Number 5, pp. 539-555

Cruiser. (2007). Available: http://www.krstarica.com/eng/catalog/Business_and_Economy/Companies/Transportation. Accessed: November 24, 2007.

Cui, L, Zhang, C., Zhang, C. & Huang, L. (2006). Exploring E-Government Impact on Shanghai Firms' Informatization Process. *Electronic Markets, 16*(4), 312 – 328.

Cummings, M. L. & Guynes, J. L. (1994). Information system activities in transnational corporations: A comparison of U.S. and Non-U.S. subsidiaries. *Journal of Global Information Management*, 2(1), 12-27.

Dada, D. (2006a) The failure of e-government in developing countries: A literature review, *Electronic Journal on Information Systems in Developing Countries, 26*(7), 1-10.

Dada, D. (2006b) E-readiness in developing countries: Moving focus from the environment to the users, *Electronic Journal on Information Systems in Developing Countries, 27*(6), 1-14.

Damanpour, F. (1991) Organizational Innovation: A Meta-Analysis of Effects of Determinants and Moderators. *Academy of Management Journal, 34*(3), 555–591.

Damsgaard, J. & Farhoomand, A. (1999). Electronic Commerce in Hong Kong A Special Administrative Region of the People's of Republic of China. *Electronic Markets, 9*(1/2), 73-80.

Damsgaard, J. (1998). Electronic Markets in Hong Kong's Air Cargo Community: Thanks, But No Thanks. *Electronic Markets, 8*(3), 46-49.

Danda, M. (2001): *La Sécurité sur leWeb*, Paris: Microsoft Press.

Darley, W. (2001). The Internet and Emerging E-commerce: Challenges and Implications for Management in Sub-Saharan Africa. *Journal of Global Information Technology Management, 4*(4), 4-18.

Darley, W. (2003). Public Policy Challenges and Implications of the Internet and the Emerging E-commerce for Sub-Saharan Africa: A Business Perspective. *Information Technology for Development, 10*(1), 1-12.

Darley, W. K. (2001). The Internet and emerging e-commerce: Challenges and implications for management in Sub-Saharan Africa. *Journal of Global Information Technology Management, 4*(4), 4-18.

Darrell, M. (2005). *Global E-Government Report.*

Dasgupta, P. & Sengupta, K. (2002). E-Commerce in the Indian Insurance Industry: Prospects and Future. *Electronic Commerce Research, 2*(1-2), 43-60.

Davenport, T. H. & Markus, L. M. (1999). Rigor vs. Relevance Revisited: Response to Benbasat and Zmud. *MIS Quarterly, 23*(1), 19-24.

Davies, H. and Lsung, H. (1995). The Benefits of Guanxi: The Value of Relationships. Industrial Marketing Management 24: 207-213.

Davila A, Gupta M and Palmer R (2003) Moving Procurement Systems to the Internet: The Adoption and Use of e-Procurement Technology Models, European Management Journal, Volume 21, Number 1, February, pp. 11-23

Davis, C. H. (1999). The Rapid Emergence Of Electronic Commerce In A Developing Region: The Case Of Spanish-Speaking Latin America. *Journal of Global Information Technology Management, 2*(3).

Davis, F. (1986). *Technology acceptance model for empirically testing new end-user information systems:*

theory and results, unpublished doctoral dissertation, MIT.

Davis, F. D. (1985). *A Technology Acceptance Model for Empirically Testing New End-User Information Systems: Theory and Results*. Doctoral Dissertation. Cambridge, MA: MIT Sloan School of Management.

Davis, F. D. (1989). Perceived usefulness, perceived ease of use and user acceptance of information technology. *MIS Quarterly,* (13) 3, 319-340.

Davis, F. D. (1993). User acceptance of information technology: system characteristics, user perceptions and behavioral impacts. *International Journal of Man-Machine Studies,* 38, 475-487.

Davis, F. D., Bagozzi, R. P., & Warshaw, P. R. (1989). User Acceptance of Computer Technology: A Comparison of Two Theoretical Models. *Management Science,* 35, 982-1003.

Davis, F. D., Bagozzi, R. P., & Warshaw, P. R. (1992). Extrinsic and intrinsic motivation to use computers in the workplace. *Journal of Applied Social Psychology,* 22, 1111-1132.

Davis, F.D. (1986). Technology Acceptance Model for Empirically Testing New End-User Information Systems: Theory and Results. *Unpublished doctoral dissertation, Massachusetts Institute of Technology.*

Davis, F.D. (1989). Perceived Usefulness, Perceived Ease of Use and User Acceptance of Information Technology. *MIS Quarterly,* 13(3), 319-340.

Davis, F.D. (1993). User Acceptance of Information Technology: System Characteristics, User Perceptions and Behavioral Impacts. *International Journal of Man-Machine Studies,* 38(3), 475-487.

Davis, F.D., Bagozzi, R.P. & Warshaw, P.R. (1989). User acceptance of computer technology: a comparison of two theoretical models. *Management Science, 35*(8), 982-1003.

Davison, R. M., Vogel, D. R. & Harris, R. W. (2005). The E-Transformation of Western China. *Communications of the ACM, 48*(4), 62-67.

Davison, R., Vogel, D., Harris, R., and Jones, N. (2000) Technology Leapfrogging in Developing Countries - An Inevitable Luxury?, *The Electronic Journal on Information Systems in Developing Countries,* vol. 1, No. 5, pp. 1-10, 2000.

Debreceny, R. Putterill, M., Tung, L., & Gilbert, A.L. (2002). New tools for the determination of e-commerce inhibitors, *Decision Support Systems, 34*(2), 177-195.

Decker, R., Hermelbracht, A., & Kroll, F. (2005). The Importance of E-Commerce in China and Russia – An Empirical Comparison. In D. Baier, R. Decker, & L. Schmidt-Thieme (Eds.), *Data Analysis and Decision Support* (pp. 212-221), Springer, Berlin.

Dedrick, J. & K.L. Kraemer (2001). China IT Report. *Electronic Journal on Information Systems in Developing Countries* 6(2), 1–10.

Dedrick, J. and Kraemer, K.L. (2001) China IT report, *The Electronic Journal on Information Systems in Developing Countries,* vol. 6, Issue 2, pp. 1-10, 2001.

DeGouvea, R. & Kassicieh, S. K. (2002). Brazil.com. *Thunderbird International Business Review, 44*(1), 105-115.

Dempsey, J. X. (2004). Creating the Legal Framework for Information and Communications Technology Development: The Example of E-Signature Legislation in Emerging Market Economies. *Information Technologies and International Development, 1*(2), 39-52.

Dennis, A., & Haley Wixom, B. (2000). *Systems Analysis and Design: An applied approach.* New York: Wiley.

Devaraj, S, Fan, M., Kohli,R. (2002). Antecedents of b2C channel satisfaction and preference: Validation e-Commerce metrics. *Information Systems Research,* 13(3), 316-333.

Dewan, S., & Kraemer, K. (2000). Information technology and productivity: evidence from country-level data. *Management Science,* 46(4), 548-562

Dinkić, M. (1995). An *economy of destruction: the great robbery of the people.* Belgrade, Serbia: VIN.

Djordjević B. (2007). Strategic Options in the Development on Mobile Banking Services (in Serbian), Bankarstvo, no. 3–4, pp. 38–50.

Djurić, D, Gašević, D., & Devedžić, V. (2005). Ontology Modeling and MDA, *Journal of Object Technology*, 4(1), pp. 109–128.

D-Lib Magazine (2003), Trends in the Evolution of the Public Web, Available: www.dlib.org/dlib/april03/lavoie/04lavoie.html [accessed: 2004].

Doern, D.R. & Fey, C.F. (2006). E-commerce developments and strategies for value creation: The case of Russia. *Journal of World Business, 41*(4), 315-327.

Doern, R., & Fey, C. F. (2006). E-Commerce Developments and Strategies for Value Creation: The Case of Russia. *Journal of World Business*, *41*, 315-327.

Domeisen, N., (1999) Exporters and importers in developing countries: Investing in the Internet, *International Trade Forum*, (1), 12-13.

Doney, P.M.., Cannon, J.P., and Mullen, M.R. (1998). Understanding the influence of national culture on the development of trust. Academy of Management Review 23: 601-620.

Dragutinović, G. (2007). *EURO<26 & ISIC International & Student Cards* (in Serbian), Paying Cards – Actual Trends, Chamber of Commerce in Serbia, Belgrade.

Du, J. (2006). E-commerce development in the world in 2005. Retrieved June 12, 2007, from http://www.istis.sh.cn/list/list.asp?id=2853

Duncombe, R., & Molla, A. (2006). E-commerce development in developing countries: profiling change-agents for SMEs. *International Journal of Entrepreneurship and Innovation, 7*(3), 185.

Dutta, A. (1997) The physical infrastructure for electronic commerce in developing nations: Historical trends and the impact of privatization. *International Journal of Electronic Commerce, 2*(1), 61-83.

Dutta, A. (1997). The Physical Infrastructure for Electronic Commerce in Developing Nations: Historical Trends and the Impact of Privatization. *International Journal of Electronic Commerce, 2*(1), 61.

EBPG (2002). *Europe go digital: Benchmarking national and regional e-business policies for SMEs*. Final report of the EBusiness Policy Group, 28 June 2002.

ECMT—European Conference of Ministers of Transport. (2005). Pan-European transport corridors. Available: http://www.cemt.org/topics/paneurop/corridors.htm. Accessed: November 17, 2007.

E-commerce and Development Report (2001) prepared by UNCTAD Secretariat

E-commerce and Development Report (2002) prepared by UNCTAD Secretariat

E-commerce and Development Report (2003) prepared by UNCTAD Secretariat

E-Commerce News (2006). Is China the next eCommerce superpower? E-Commerce News, September 15, 2006. http://www.ecommercenews.org/e-commerce-news-009/0243-091406-ecommerce-news.html accessed on 6/9/2007.

Efendioglu et.al, (2005)"E-commerce in developing countries: Issues and Influences", 2005 IBEC Annual Conference, Honolulu, Hawaii,P.6-9

Efendioglu, A., & Yip, V. (2005). E-commerce in developing countries: issues and influences." Proceedings of the IBEC Annual Conference, Honolulu, Hawaii, January 6-9, 2005, pp. 10–15.

Efendioglu, A.M. & Yip, V. F (2004). Chinese culture and e-commerce: an exploratory study. *Interacting with Computers, 16*(1), 45-62.

Efendioglu, Alev M. and Vincent F. Yip (2004). Chinese Culture & E-Commerce: An Explatory Study. Interacting with Computers, Vol. 16/1, pp. 45-62, 2004.

Ein-Dor, P., & Orgad, M. (1993). The effect of national culture on IS: implications for international information systems. *Global Journal of Information Management*, 1(1), 33-44.

E-Japan (2001). http://www.kantei.go.jp/foreign/it/network/0122full_e.html. Last visted: Nov 6 2007.

El-Nawawy, M.A. & M.M. Ismail. (1999). *Overcoming deterrents and impediments to electronic commerce in light of globalisation: the case of Egypt,* Proceedings of the 9th Annual Conference of the Internet Society, INET 99, San Jose, USA.

Enns H.G. & Huff S.L.,(1999). Information technology implementation in developing countries: advent of the Internet in Mongolia, *Journal of Global Information Technology Management* 2(3), pp. 5–24.

Erez, M., & Earley, P. C. (1987). Comparative analysis of goal-setting strategies across cultures. *Journal of Applied Psychology,* 72, 658-665.

Ersala, N., Yen, D. & Rajkumar, T. (2002). Enterprise Application Integration in the electronic commerce world. *Computer Standards & Interfaces,* 2189, 1-14.

EU – European Union. (2005). Broadband access in EU: situation at January 1, 2005. Available: http://europa.eu.int/rapid/pressReleasesAction.do?reference=MEMO/05/format=HTML&aged=0&language=EN&guiLanguage=en. Accessed: November 10, 2005.

Evaluating Web Pages: Techniques to apply and questions to ask (2004), UC Berkeley – Teaching Library Internet Workshop [online], Available: www.lib.berkeley.edu/TeachingLib/Guides/Internet/Evaluate.html [accessed: December 2004].

Ewusi-Mensah, K & Przasnyski, Z.H. (1994). Factors contributing to the a bondonment of information systems development projects. *Journal of Information Technology, 9,* 185-201.

Ewusi-Mensah, K & Przasnyski, Z.H. (1995). Learning from abandoned information systems development projects. *Journal of Information Technology, 10,* 3-14.

Ezehoha, A. E. (2005). Regulating Internet Banking In Nigeria: Problems and Challenges – Part 1. *Journal of Internet Banking and Commerce, 10*(3).

Ezehoha, A. E. (2006).Regulating Internet Banking In Nigeria: Some Success Prescriptions – Part 2. *Journal of Internet Banking and Commerce, 11*(1).

Faster Growth Heightens Web Class Divide (2002), TRN (Technology Research News) [online], Available: www.trnmag.com [accessed: December 2004].

Fay, B. (1987). Critical Social Science: Liberation and its Limits. Ithaca, NY: Cornell University Press.

Fazio, R. H., & Olson, M. A. (2003). Implicit measures in social cognition: Their meaning and use. *Annual Review of Psychology,* 54, 297-327.

Ferran, C., & Salim, R.(2006). Electronic business in developing countries: the digitalization of bad practices? In Sherif, K. (Ed.), *Electronic business in developing countries: opportunities and challenges* (pp. 1-33). IDEA Group Publishing.

Fey, C. F., & Doern, R. (2002). *The Role of External and Internal Factors in Creating Value Using eCommerce: The Case of Russia* (Tech. Rep. No. 02-102). St. Petersburg, Russia: Stockholm School of Economics Russia.

Fishbein, M., & Ajzen, I. (1975). *Belief, Attitude, Intention and Behavior: An Introduction to Theory and Research.* Reading, MA: Addison-Wesley.

Fishman, S. *Software Development: A legal guide,* Nolo Press, Berkeley, 1994, First Edition.

Fjermestad, J., Passerini, K., Patten, K., Bartolacci, M. & Ullman, D. (2006). Moving Towards Mobile Third Generation Telecommunications Standards: The Good, and the Bad of the 'Anytime/Anywhere Solutions'. *Communications of AIS, 17*(3), 2-33.

Flamholtz, E. (1995). Managing Organisational Transitions: Implications for Corporate and Human Resource Management. *European Management Journal vol.13, No1,* 39-51.

Ford, D. P., Connelly, C. E., & Meister, D. B. (2003). Information systems research and Hofstede's Culture's Consequences: An uneasy and incomplete partnership.

IEEE Transactions on Engineering Management, 50(1), 8-26

Fraser, S. & Wresch, W. (2005). National Competitive Advantage in E-Commerce Efforts: A Report from Five Caribbean Nations. *Perspectives on Global Development and Technology, 4*(1), 27-44.

Frempong, G. and Stark, C. (2005). Ghana. In A. Gillwald, (Ed.), *Towards an African e-Index: Household and individual ICT Access and Usage across 10 African Countries.* Research ICT Africa, Retrieved March 22 2007 from http://www.researchictafrica.net/modules.php?op=modload&name=News&file=article&sid=504.

Friedman, B., Kahn, P. H. J., & Howe, D. C. (2000). Trust Online. *Communications of the ACM, 43*(12), 34-40.

Galliers, R.D. and Sutherland, A.R. (1994). Information Systems Management and Strategy Formulation: Applying and Extending the 'Stages of Growth' Concept. *In Strategic Information Management:Challenges and Strategies in Managing Information Systems*, R.D. Galliers and B. S. H. Baker (eds.),Butterworth-Heinemann Ltd., Oxford, 91-117.

Gallivan, MJ (1997). *Value in triangulation: a comparison of two approaches for*

Ganesh, J., Madanmohan, T. R., Jose, P. D. & Seshadri, S. (2004). Adaptive Strategies of Firms in High-Velocity Environments: The Case of B2B Electronic Marketplaces. *Journal of Global Information Management, 12*(1), 41-59.

Garau, C. (2005). ICT Strategies for Development: Implementing Multichannel Banking in Romania. *Information Technology for Development, 11*(4), 343-362.

Garcia-Murillo Martha (2004). Institutions and the Adoption of Electronic Commerce in Mexico. *Electronic Commerce Research*, 4, 201-219

Garcia-Murillo, M. (2004). Institutions and the Adoption of Electronic Commerce in Mexico. *Electronic Commerce Research, 4*(3), 201-219.

García-Murillo, M. (2004). Institutions and the Adoption of Electronic Commerce in Mexico. *Electronic Commerce Research, 4,* 201-219.

Garicano, L. and Kaplan, S. (2001). *The Effects of Business-to-Business E-commerce on Transaction Costs,* Social Science Research Network (SSRN Resources). Retrieved May 01 2007, from http://ssrn.com/abstract=252210.

Gartner Dataquest (May 2007).

Gefen D., & Straub, D. W. (2000). The relative importance of perceived ease of use in IS adoption: A study of e-commerce adoption. *Journal of the Association for Information Systems,* 1(8), 1-30

Gefen et.al, (2006) "On the Need to Include National Culture as a Central Issue in e-commerce Trust Beliefs", Journal of Global Information Management, 14(4), P. 1-30

Gefen, (2000) "E-commerce: The role of familiarity and trust", Omega 2000; 28(6), P. 725-737

Gefen, D., & Straub, D. W. (1997). Gender differences in the perception and use of e-Mail: an extension to the technology acceptance model. *MIS Quarterly*, 21(4), 389-400.

Gefen, D., & Straub, D.W. (1997). Gender Differences in the Perception and Use of E-Mail: An Extension to the Technology Acceptance Model. *MIS Quarterly, 21(4),* 389-400.

Gefen, D., & Straub, D.W. (2000). The Relative Importance of Perceived Ease-of-Use in IS Adoption: A Study of E-Commerce Adoption. *Journal of the Association for Information Systems,* 1(8), 1-27.

Gefen, D., Straub, D. W., & Boudreau, N. C, (2000). Structural equation modeling and regression: guideline for research practice. *Communications of the Association of Information Systems,* 4(7), 1-79.

Generation X: Definitions. (2002). http://www.coloradocollege.edu/Dept/EC/generationx96 /genx/genx10.html.

Genis-Gruber & Onur, (2006) "The Effect of Cultural Perception on e-commerce", Proceedings of IADIS International Conference e-commerce 2006, Barcelona, P.346-350

Genus, A. & Nor, M. A. M. (2005). Socializing the Digital Divide: Implications for ICTs and E-Business Development. *Journal of Electronic Commerce in Organizations, 3*(2), 82-94.

Gesteland, (2002) "Cross Cultural Business Behavior", Copenhagen Business School Pr; 3rd edition

Ghiladi, V. (2003). The Importance of International Standards for Globally Operating Businesses. *International Journal of IT Standards & Standardization Research, Vol.1, No.1, Idea Group Publishing,* 54-56.

Ghiya K and Powers M (2005) eProcurement – Strengthening the Indirect Supply Chain through Technology Globalization

Gibbs, J. & Kraemer, K. (2004). A Cross Country Investigation of the Determinants of Scope of E-commerce Use: An Institutional Approach. *Electronic Markets, 14*(2), 124-137.

Ginige A., Murugesan S. & Kazanis P.(2001). A Roadmap for Successfully Transforming SMEs in to E-Businesses, *Cutter IT Journal*,May 2001,Vol 14

Goi, C.L. (2006). Factors Influence Development of E-Banking in Malaysia. *Journal of Internet Banking and Commerce, 11*(2).

Goldstein et.al, (2001) "Navigating between Scylla and Charybdis: Will e-commerce help solve problems that are dogged developing countries for decades, or will a widening digital divide entrench them still further in a vicious circle of poverty?", OECD Observer, 72 (3)

Goldstein, A. and D. O'Connor (2000). *E-Commerce for Development: Prospects and Policy Issues*, Technical Paper No. 164, Paris: OECD Development Centre.

Gong, W. (2004). A Conceptual Solution to E-business Models in Developing Countries: Post-Crisis Domestic Procurement Network to Facilitate Humanitarian Assistance. *Electronic Journal on Information Systems in Developing Countries, 18*(4), 1-8.

Goodman, S. (1991). Computing in a Less-Developed Country. *Communications of the ACM, vol.34, no.12,* 25-29.

Goodman, S. (1994). Computing in South Africa: An end to 'apartness'? *Communications of the ACM, 37*(2), 19–24.

Grabner-Kraeuter, (2002) "The role of customer's trust in online shopping", Journal of Business Ethics 39, P.43-50

Grabner-Kraeuter, S. (2002). The role of consumers' trust in online shopping. Journal of Business Ethics 39: 43-50.

Grace-Farfaglia, P., Dekkers, A., Sundararajan, B., Peters, L. & Park, S. (2006). Multinational web uses and gratifications: Measuring the social impact of online community participation across national boundaries. *Electronic Commerce Research, 6*(1), 75-101.

Grandon, E. & Mykytyn, P. P. (2004). Theory-based Instrumentation to Measure the Intention to Use Electronic Commerce in Small and Medium Sized Businesses. *The Journal of Computer Information Systems, 44*(3), 44-57.

Grandon, E. & Pearson, J. M. (2003). Strategic Value and Adoption of Electronic Commerce: An Empirical Study of Chilean Small and Medium Businesses. *Journal of Global Information Technology Management, 6*(3), 22-43.

Grandon, E. & Pearson, J. M. (2004). E-commerce Adoption: Perception of Managers/Owners of Small and Medium Sized Firms in Chile. *Communications of the Association for Information Systems, 13* 81-102.

Grant, R. M. (1991). The Resource-Based Theory of Competitive Advantage: Implications for Strategy Formulation. *California Management, Review, 33*(1), 114-135.

Grant, S. (1999). *E-commerce for small businesses*, in Proceedings of the 2nd International Conference IeC '99, Manchester, England, November 1–3, pp 65–72.

Gray, H. & Sanzogni, L. (2004). Technology Leapfrogging in Thailand: Issues for the Support of E-commerce Infrastructure. *Electronic Journal on Information Systems in Developing Countries, 16*(3), 1-26.

Greenspan, Robyn (2002). China Pulls Ahead of Japan. E-Commerce Guide, April 22, 2002. http://www.clickz.com/showPage.html?page=clickz_print&id=1013841 Accessed on 6/29/2007.

Grönlund, Å. (2005). *What's In a Field – Exploring the eGoverment Domain*. Örebro University. Sweden. 0-7695-2268-8/05 IEEE.

Grover, V., & Ramanlal, P. (1999). Six myths of information and markets: Information technology networks, electronic commerce, and the battle for consumer surplus. *MIS Quarterly, 23*(4), 465-495.

Grover, V., & Yeng, J. T. C. (2001). E-commerce and the information market. *Communications of the ACM, 44*(4), 79-86.

Grover, V., Golsar, M.D. & Segars, A. (1995). Adopters of telecommunications initiatives: a profile of progres-sive US corporations. *International Journal of Infor-mation Management*, 15(1), 33-46.

Gunasekaran, A. & Ngai, E.W.T (2005). E-commerce in Hong Kong: An Empirical Perspective And Analysis, *Internet Research, 15*(2), 141-159

Gupta, O., Priyadarshini, K., Massoud, S. & Agrawal, S. K. (2004). Enterprise Resource Planning: A Case of a Blood Bank. *Industrial Management and Data Systems, 104*(7), 589-603.

Guru, B. K., Shanmugam, B., Alam, N. & Perera, C. J. (2003). An Evaluation of Internet Banking Sites in Islamic Countries. *Journal of Internet Banking and Commerce, 8*(2).

Gustafsson, A., Roos, I. & Edvardsson, B. (2004). Customer clubs in a relationship perspective: A telecom case. *Managing Service Quality, 14* (2/3), 157-168.

Hafez, M. (2006). Role of culture in electronic business in developing countries. In Sherif, K. (Ed.), *Electronic business in developing countries: Opportunities and challenges* (pp. 34–44). Hershey, PA: Idea.

Hair, J. F. Jr, Anderson, R. E., Tatham, R. L., & Black, W. C. (1998). *Multivariate Data Analysis* (5th ed.). Englewood Cliffs, NJ: Prentice Hall.

Hair, J. F., Jr., Anderson, R.E, Tatham, R. L, & Black, W.C. (1998). *Multivariate data analysis with readings*. 5th Edition. Englewood Cliffs, NJ: Prentice Hall.

Haley, G. T. (2002). E-commerce in China changing business as we know it. *Industrial Marketing Management*, 31, 119-224.

Hall, (1990) "Understanding Cultural Differences", Intercultural Press

Hammer, M., & Champy J. (1993). *Reengineering the Corporation: A manifesto for business revolution.* New York: HarperCollins.

Hanrahan, M., Kwok, Wei-Tai (2001), A New Connectivity - How Technology is Changing the Marketing World. Available: iaa2001.atalink.co.uk/html/p026.htm [accessed: 2004].

Harbhajan, K., & Varinder, P. S. (2005). *Digital economy, impacts, influences and challenges.* IDEA Group Publishing.

Harris, P., Rettie, R. & Kwan, C. C. (2005). Adoption and Usage of M-Commerce: A Cross-Cultural Comparison. Journal of Electronic Commerce Research, 6 (3), 210-224.

Hasan, H. and Ditsa, G. (1999). The Impact of Culture on the Adaptations of IT: An Interpretive Study. Journal of Global Information Management 7-1: 5.

Hasselbring, W. (2000a). Information System Integration. *Communications of the ACM, June, vol.43, no.6,* 33-38.

Hatch, M. J. (1997). *Organisation Theory Modern, Symbolic, and Postmodern Perspectives.* Oxford University, Press.

Hawk, S. (2002). The Development of Russian E-commerce: The Case Ozon. *Management Decision, 40*(7), 702-709.

Hawk, S. (2004). A Comparison of B2C E-Commerce in Developing Countries. *Electronic Commerce Research, 4*(3), 181-199.

Hawk, S. (2004). A Comparison of B2C E-Commerce in Developing Countries. *Electronic Commerce Research, 4*, 181-199.

Hawk, S. (2004). A comparison of B2C e-commerce in developing countries. *Electronic Commerce Research, 4*,181-199.

Hawking P, Stein A, Wyld C D and Foster S (2004) E-Procurement: Is the Ugly Duckling Actually a Swan Down Under. Asia Pacific Journal of Marketing and Logistics, Volume 16, Number 1, pp. 3-26

Haythornthwaite, C., & Wellman, B. (1998). Work, friendship and media use for information exchange in a networked organization. *Journal of the American Society for Information Science*, 49(12), 1101–1114.

He, Q., Duan, Y., Fu, Z. & Li, D. (2006). An Innovation Adoption Study of Online E-Payment in Chinese Companies. *Journal of Electronic Commerce in Organizations, 4*(1), 48-69.

Heeks, R. & Wilson, G. (2000). *Technology, Poverty and Development: into the 21st Century*, In T. Allen & A. Thomas (2000) Poverty and Development into the 21st Century, 2nd Edition, pp. 23-48. Oxford: Open University, Oxford University Press.

Heeks, R. (1999). *Information and Communication Technologies, Poverty and Development.* Development Informatics Working Papers Series No. 5. Manchester: IDPM, University of Manchester.

Heeks, R. (2000). Analyzing E-Commerce for Development, Information Technology in Developing Countries, *Information Processing (IFIP) Working Group 9.4*, 10(3).

Heeks, R. (2001a). Understanding e-Governance for Development. *I-Government Working Papers No. 11.* Manchester, United Kingdom: University of Manchester, Institute for Development Policy and Management. Retrieved May 2007, from http://www.man.ac.uk/idpm.

Heeks, R. (2001b). Building e-Governance for Development: A Framework for National and Donor Action. *I-Government Working Papers No. 12.* Institute for Development Policy and Management, University of Manchester. Retrieved May 2007, from http://www.man.ac.uk/idpm)

Heeks, R. (2002) i-Development not e-development: Understanding and implementing ICTs and development, *Journal of International Development, 14*(1).

Heeks, R. (2002). E-Government in Africa: Promise and Practice. iGovernment Working Paper Series. Institute for Development Policy and Management.

Heijden Van Der, H. (2003). Factors influencing the usage of websites: the case of a generic portal in The Netherlands. *Information & Management,* 40(6), 541–549.

Heijden Van Der, H. (2004). User acceptance of hedonic information systems. *MIS Quarterly*, 4, 695-704.

Helm, J. C. (2001), Web based Application Quality Assurance, Available: sce.cl.uh.edu/helm/Helm_html/papers/QW2001_PaperJune0101.pdf [accessed: 2004].

Hinson R. (2006). The Internet for Academics: Towards A Holistic Adoption Model. *Online Information Review, 30*(5).

Hirsh, L. (2002, February 25), Online Shopping and the Human Touch, E-Commerce Times: The E-Business and Technology Supersite [online], Available: www.ecommercetimes.com/.../16483.html [accessed: December 2004].

Ho, C., & Chen, J. (1999). The prospects of B2B e-commerce in China's Internet industry. *Business Forum, 24*(3, 4), 62-69.

Ho, C., Chi, Y. & Tai, Y. (2005). A Structural Approach to Measuring Uncertainty in Supply Chains. *International Journal of Electronic Commerce, 9*(3), 91-114.

Ho, S., Kauffman, R. and Liang, T-P. (2005), A growth theory perspective on the international diffusion of e-commerce, In Proceedings of the International Conference on E-Commerce (ICEC'05), August 15-17, Xi'an, China, pp.57-65

Ho, T. H., Raman, K. S., & Watson, R.T. (1989). Group decision support systems: the cultural factor. *Proceedings of the Tenth Annual International Conference on Information Systems*. Boston. pp.119-129.

Hoff, Robert D. (2004). EachNet: Bringing E-Commerce to China. Business Week (Asian Cover Story), March 15, 2004. http://www.businessweek.com/print/magazine/content/04_11/b3874020.htm?chan=mz accessed on 7/4/2007.

Hoffman, L.W. (1972). Early childhood experiences and women's achievement motives. *Journal of Social Issues*, 28(8), 129-155.

Hofstede, (2005) "Culture and Organizations: Software of Mind", McGraw Hill, USA

Hofstede, (2007) Website of Geert Hofstede

Hofstede, G, (1985). The interaction between national and organizational value systems. *Journal of Management Studies, 22*(4), 347–357.

Hofstede, G. (1980) *Culture's consequences: International differences in work-related values*. Beverly Hills: Sage.

Hofstede, G. (1980). *Culture's Consequences: International Differences in Work-related Values*. Newbury Park, CA: Sage.

Hofstede, G. (1980). *Culture's Consequences: international differences in work-related values*. CA: Newbury Park, Sage.

Hofstede, G. (1991). *Cultures and organizations: software of the mind*, McGraw-Hill, London.

Hofstede, G. (1991). *Cultures and Organizations*. Berkshire: McGraw-Hill Book Company Europe.

Hofstede, G. (2001). *Culture's Consequences*, 2nd Ed., Sage, Thousand Oaks, CA.

Hofstede, G., & Bond, M. H. (1988). The Confucius connection: from cultural roots to economic growth. *Organizational Dynamics*, 16(4), 4-21.

Hofstede, G.H. (1980). Culture's Consequences, Sage: Beverly Hills, CA.

Hofstede, G.H. (1991). Cultures and Organizations: Software of the Mind, McGraw-Hill: London.

Hollensen, S. (2007). *Global Marketing – A Decision-Oriented Approach*. Harlow, Prentice Hall.

Hong, S. & Tam, K.Y. (2006). Understanding the Adoption of Multipurpose Information Appliances: The Case of Mobile Data Services, *Information Systems Research, 17*(2), 162-179.

Hong, W., Thong, J.Y.L., Wong, W., & Tam, K.Y. (2002). Determinants of User Acceptance of Digital Libraries: An Empirical Examination of Individual Differences and System Characteristics. *Journal of Management Information Systems*, 18(3), 2002.

Housley, S. (2004), Web site Globalization, Available: www.onevision.co.uk/xq/ASP/id.1072 [accessed: 2004].

Hsu C., Lu H., and Hsu H., (2007) Adoption of the mobile Internet: An empirical study of multimedia message service (MMS). *Omega* 35(6), 715-726.

http://www.mba.org.cn, April 17, 2000.

Hu, Q., Wu, X. & Wang, C. K. (2004). Lessons From Alibaba.com: Government's Role in Electronic Contracting. *INFO, 6* (5), 298-307.

Huang, J. H., Zhao, C. J. & Huang, H. (2004). An E-readiness Assessment Framework And Two Field Studies. *Communications of the Association for Information Systems, 14*(19), 364-386.

Huang, J., Zhao, C., & Li, J. (2007). An Empirical Study on Critical Success Factors for Electronic Commerce in the Chinese Publishing Industry. *Frontiers of Business Research in China, 1*(1), 50-66.

Huang, L. (2006). Building up a B2B e-commerce strategic alliance model under an uncertain environment for

Taiwan's travel agencies. *Tourism Management, 27*(6), 1308–1320.

Huang, M.-H. (2000). Information load: Its relationship to online exploratory and shopping behavior. *International Journal of Information Management*, 20, 337-347.

Huang, Z. & Palvia, P. (2001). ERP Implementation Issues in Advanced and Developing Countries. *Business Process Management Journal, 7*(3), 276-284.

Huff, S. & P. Yoong. (2000). *SMEs and e-commerce: current issues and concerns. A preliminary report.* In Proceedings of the International Conference on E-commerce, Kuala Lumpur, Malaysia, 21 November 2000, pp. 1–5.

Humphrey, J., Mansell, R., Paré, R., & Schmitz, H. (2003). *The reality of e-commerce with developing countries.* IDS. Brighton, UK: Institute of Development Studies.

Hung, S., Ku, C. & Chang, C. (2003). Critical Factors of WAP Services Adoption: An Empirical Study. *Electronic Commerce Research and Applications, 2*(1), 42-60.

Huy Le Van & Filiatrault, P. (2006). *The Adoption of E-Commerce in SMEs in Vietnam: A Study of Users and Prospectors*, The 10th Pacific Asia Conference on Information Systems.

Hwang, W., Jung, H.-S. & Salvendy, G. (2006). Internationalization of e-commerce: a comparison of online shopping preferences among Korean, Turkish and US populations. *Behavior and Information Technology, 25*(1) 3-18.

Iacovou, A., Benbasat L., I. & Dexter, A. (1995).Electronic Data Interchange And Small Organizations: Adoption And Impact Of Technology. *MIS Quarterly, 19*(4), 465-48.

Iacovou, C.L., Benbasat, I. & Dexter, A.A. (1995). Electronic data interchange and small organizations: adoption and impact of technology, *MIS Quarterly*, 19, 4, 465-485.

Igbaria, M., Zinatelli, N., Cragg, P., & Cavaye, A.L.M. (1997) "Personal Computing Acceptance Factors in Small Firms: A Structural Equation Model," *MIS Quarterly* 21(3), 279-305.

IICD. (2004). *The ICT Roundtable Process: Lessons Learned from facilitating ICT-Enabled Development.* The Hague: International Institute for Communication and Development.

Instat (2007), SMS in the Middle East and Asia. Retrieved May 9, 2007 from http://www.instat.com/

Intel (2003). Collaborative RosettaNet Implementation: Intel and Fujitsu streamline e-Business automation across the supply chain. *Intel Information Technology White Paper, October.*

Interface Design (2002), Web Style Guide 2nd Edition [online], Available: www.webstyleguide.com/interface/user-centered.hmtl [accessed: December 2004].

International Telecommunications Union (ITU) (2006). *ICT Statistics. World Telecommunications Indicators Database 9th Edition.* International Telecommunication Union (ITU). Retrieved March 12, 2006, from http://www.itu.int/ITU-D/ict/statistics/ict/index.html.

International Trade Centre (ITC) (2001). Are Developing Countries Ready? Three ITC Surveys, Close Up, *International Trade Forum*, 1, p.19.

Internet Guide (2002), Canada Government [online], Available: www.cio-dpi.gc.ca/ig-gi/m/wsm-msw/wsm-msw_e.asp [accessed: December 2004].

Internet World Stats, March 19, 2007. http://www.internetworldstats.com/stats.htm

Iowa University (1999), Designing accessible web sites booklet, Available: www.uiowa.edu/infotech/WebAccess.htm [accessed: 2004].

IResearch. China B2B e-commerce research report. Retrieved June 14, 2007, from http://www.iresearch.com.cn/html/B2B/detail_free_id_45218.html

ISC – Internet Systems Consortium. (2007). Internet domain host count. Retrieved July, 15, 2007, from http://www.isc.org.

Ismail, M. M. & El-Nawawy, M. A. (2000). The Imminent Challenge of Click and Mortar Commerce in Egypt, Africa and Middle East. *Electronic Markets, 10*(2), 73-79.

ITU – International Telecommunication Union. (2003). Retrieved July, 15, 2007, from http://www.itu.int/ITU-D/statistics/WTI_2003.pdf.

ITU – International Telecommunication Union. (2006). *World Telecommunications Development Report 2006: Measuring ICT for Social and Economic Development.*

ITU Report (2002) Telecommunications Indicators, Geneva: International Telecommunication Union. http://www.itu.org

Jackson, C.M., Chow, S., & Leitch, R.A. (1997). Towards an Understanding of the Behavioral Intention to Use an Information System. *Decision Sciences.* 28(2), 357-389.

Jakobs, K., Procter, R. & Williams, R. (2001). The Making of Standards: Looking Inside the Work Groups. *IEEE Communications Magazine,*.2-7.

Janejira, S. (2006). E-Commerce Adoption: Perceptions of Managers/Owners of Small- and Medium-Sized Enterprises (SMEs) in Thailand. *Journal of Internet Commerce, 5*(3), 53-82

Jantan, M., Ndubisi, N. O. & Yean, O. B. (2003). Viability of E-commerce As An Alternative Distribution Channel. *Logistics Information Management, 16*(6), 427-439.

Jaruwachirathanakul, B. & Fink, D. (2005). Internet Banking Adoption Strategies for a Developing Country: The Case of Thailand. *Internet Research, 15*(3), 295-311.

Jarvenpaa, S. L. & Leidner, D. E. (1998). An Information Company In Mexico: Extending The Resource-Based View Of The Firm To A Developing Country Context. *Information Systems Research, 9*(4), 342-361.

Jarvenpaa, S.L., Tractinsky, N., Saarinen, L. and Vitale, M. (1999). Consumer trust in an Internet store: a cross-cultural validation. Journal of Computer-Mediated Communication 5(2): 1-29.

Javalgi, R. G., Martin, C. L. & Todd, P. R. (2004). The Export of E-services in the Age of Technology Transformation: Challenges and Implications for International Service Providers. *Journal of Services Marketing, 18*(7), 560-573.

Javalgi, R., Wickramasinghe, N., Scherer, R. F. & Sharma, S. (2005). An Assessment and Strategic Guidelines for Developing E-Commerce in the Asia-Pacific Region. *International Journal of Management, 22*(4), 523-531.

Jaw, Y.L. & Chen, C.L. (2006). The influence of the Internet in the internationalization of SMEs in Taiwan. *Human Systems Management, 25*(3), 167–183.

Jeffcoate, J., Chapell, C. & Feindt, S. (2000). Attitudes Towards Process Improvement Among SMEs Involved in E-commerce. *Knowledge and Process Management, 7*(3), 187-195.

Jennex, M. E. & Amoroso, D. (2002). E-business and Technology Issues for Developing Economies: A Ukraine Case Study. *Electronic Journal on Information Systems in Developing Countries, 10*(5), 1-14.

Jennex, M. E., Amoroso, D. & Adelakun, O. (2004). E-Commerce Infrastructure Success Factors for Small Companies in Developing Economies. *Electronic Commerce Research, 4*(3), 263-286.

Jennex, M., & Amoroso, D. (2006). An e-commerce longitudinal case study from Ukraine. In Kamel, S. (Ed.), *Electronic business in developing countries: opportunities and challenges* (pp. 376–391). Hershey, PA: Idea Group.

Jennex, M., Amoroso, D. & Adelakun, O. (2004). E-commerce infrastructure success factors for small companies in developing economies. *Electronic Commerce Research, 4,* 263-286.

Jenny Y.Y. Wong, Dickson K.W. Chiu, & Kai Pan Mark. (2007). Effective e-Government Process Monitoring and Interoperation- A Case Study on the Removal of Unauthorized Building Works in Hong Kong, *Proceedings of the 40th Hawaii International Conference on System Sciences.* 1530-1605/07, IEEE.

Jeon B.N., Han K.S. & Lee M.J (2006). Determining factors for the adoption of e-business: the case of SMEs in Korea, *Applied Economics*, 38, 1905-1916.

Jiang, J., Hsu, M.K., Klein, G., Lin, B. (2000). E-Commerce User Behavior Model: An Empirical Study. *Human Systems Management,* 19(4), 265-277.

Jih, W. K., Helms, M. M. & Mayo, D. T. (2005). Effects of Knowledge Management on Electronic Commerce: An Exploratory Study in Taiwan. *Journal of Global Information Management, 13*(4), 1-24.

Joachimsthaler, E., & Aaker, D. A. (1997). Building brands without mass media. *Harvard Business Review,* January-February, 39-50.

Johnson, Tim (2007). E-commerce soaring in China. McClatchy Newspapers, May 30, 2007.http://www.realcities.com/mld/krwashington/news/world/17300776.htm?source=rss&channel=krwashington_world accessed on 6/9/2007.

Joia, L. A. & Sanz, P. S. (2006). The Financial Potential of Sporadic Customers in E-Retailing: Evidence from the Brazilian Home Appliance Sector. *Journal of Electronic Commerce in Organizations, 4*(1), 18-32.

Joia, L. A. & Zamot, F. (2002). Internet-Based Reverse Auctions by Brazilian Government. *Electronic Journal on Information Systems in Developing Countries, 9*(6), 1-12.

Joia, L.A. & Sanz, P.S.(2006). The Financial Potential of Sporadic Customers in E-Retailing: Evidence from the Brazilian Home Appliance Sector. *Journal of Electronic Commerce in Organizations, 4*(1), 18-32.

Jones, M. C., Ku, Y. & Berry, R. L. (2000). Electronic Data Interchange: A Cross-Cultural Comparison Of Key Usage Aspects Between U.S. And Taiwanese Firms. *Journal of Global Information Technology Management, 3* (4).

Jones, R. & Basu, S. (2002). Taxation of Electronic Commerce: A Developing Problem. *International Review of Law, Computers and Technology, 16*(1), 35-52.

Jones, S., Wilikens, M., Morris, P., & Masera, M. (2000). Trust requirements in e-business. *Communications of the ACM, 43*(12), 81-87.

Jordan, E. (1994). *National and organisational culture: their use in information systems design* (Report). Hong Kong: City Polytechnic of Hong Kong. Faculty of Business.

JORT: Official Journal of the Republic of Tunisia: Various Articles; notably: Law n° 2000-57 (June, 13, 2000), JORT n° 48 p.1456; and Law n° 2000-83 (August, 9, 2000), JORT n° 64 p. 1887.

Jošanov B., & Jošanov, I. (2006). "Serbia: on the Road for Determination of e-Readiness Index", *Proceedings from Mipro 06: International Conference on Digital Economy*, Opatia: pp. 79–86.

Jošanov B., & Perić, D. (Eds.) (2005). *Electronic business: Serbian perspective* (in Serbian). Belgrade, Serbia: Electro- technical College Press.

Joseph, G. T. J. (2004). Electronic Commerce and the United Nations Double Taxation Convention. *International Tax Review, 32*(8/9), 387-401.

Jovanović, Z., Gajin, S., Bukvić, M., Vuletić, P., & Vulović ,Dj. (2004). The optical NREN of Serbia and Montenegro – new solutions in infrastructure and monitoring, TNC 2004. Retrieved July, 15, 2007, from http://www.terena.nl/conferences/tnc2004/programme/people/show.php?person_id=167

Juhua, C., Yong, H. & Wei, W. (2004). E-commerce Education in China. *Journal of Electronic Commerce in Organizations, 2*(2), 65-77.

Julien, P.A. & Raymond, L. (1994). Factors of New Technology Adoption in the Retail Sector. *Entrepreneurship: Theory and Practice*,18, 5, 79-90.

Jun,M. & Cai,S. (2003). Key Obstacles to EDI Success from the US Small Manufacturing Companies' Perspective, *Industrial Management and Data Systems,* 103, 3, 152-165

Juniper Research (2007). *M-Commerce Hot Spots*, Part 1: Beyond Ringtones and Wallpaper. Retrieved May 9, 2007, from http://www.ecommercetimes.com/story/ebiz/57109.html

Kafka Report (2006). Available at http://www.kafka.be. Last visited March 1, 2007.

Kajan E., & Stoimenov, D. (2005). Toward an Ontology-Driven Architectural Framework for B2B. *Communications of the ACM,* 48(12), pp. 60–66.

Kamel S (2000a) Egypt Goes Online, Newsletter of IFIP Working Group 9.4 and Commonwealth Network for Information Technology, Volume 10, Number 3, December

Kamel S (2000b) Electronic Commerce in Egypt in M. Khosrowpour (ed.), Managing Web-Enabled Technologies in Organizations: A Global Perspective, Hershey: Idea Group Publishing, pp. 210-232

Kamel, K. (2006). Preface. In Sherif, K. (Ed.), Electronic *business in developing countries: Opportunities and challenges* (pp. vi-xiv). Hershey, PA: Idea.

Kamel, N. M. (2006). International e-commerce: language, cultural, legal, and infrastructure issues, challenges, and solutions. In Sherif, K. (Ed.), *Electronic business in developing countries: opportunities and challenges* (pp. 45-62). IDEA Group Publishing.

Kamel, S. & Hassan, A. (2003). Assessing the introduction of electronic banking in Egypt using the technology acceptance model. In M. Khosrow-Pour (Ed.) *Annals of Cases on information Technology* (1-25). Hershey PA: IGI Publishing.

Kamel, S. & Hussein, M. (2001). The Development of E-commerce: The Emerging Virtual Context within Egypt. *Logistics Information Management, 14*(1/2), 119.

Kamel, S. & Hussein, M. (2002). The Emergence of E-commerce in a Developing Nation. *Benchmarking, 9*(2), 146-153.

Kamel, S. & Hussein, M. (2004). King Hotel Goes Online: The Case of a Medium Enterprise in Using E-commerce. *Journal of Electronic Commerce in Organizations, 2*(4), 101-115.

Kamel, S., & Assem, A. (2003). Assessing the Introduction of Electronic Banking in Egypt Using the Technology Acceptance Model. *Annals of Cases On Information Technology*, 1-25.

Kannabiran, G. & Narayan, P. C. (2005). Deploying Internet Banking and e-Commerce—Case Study of a Private-Sector Bank in India. *Information Technology for Development, 11*(4), 363-379.

Kao, D. & Decou, J. (2003). A Strategy-Based Model for E-Commerce Planning. *Industrial Management and Data Systems, 103*(4), 238-252.

Kaplan, D. (2000): *Guide du Commerce Electronique* , Paris: Editions Servidit.

Karanasios, S. & Burgess, S. (2006). Exploring the Internet use of small tourism enterprises: evidence from a developing country, *Electronic Journal on Information Systems in Developing Countries, 27*(3), 1-21.

Kardaras, D. & Karakostas, B. (2001). An empirical investigation of the management practices and the development of electronic commerce in Mauritius. *International Journal of Information Management, 21*(6), 441-455.

Karlsen, M. E., Helgemo, I., & Gripsrud, M. (2001). *Useful, cheap and fun: A survey of teenagers demands for mobile telephony.* Norway: Telenor R&D.

Karmel, E. (2003). Taxonomy of new software exporting nations. *Electronic Journal of Information Systems in Developing Countries*, 13(2), pp. 1-6.

Kasesniemi E. E. L. & Rautiainen P. (2002). Mobile culture of children and teenagers in Finland. In J.E. Katz and M. Aarkhus (Editors), *Perpetual Contact* (pp. 170-193). Cambridge: CUP.

Katerattanakul, P., Siau, K. (1999), "Measuring Information Quality of Web sites", Proceedings of the 20th International Conference of Information Systems [online], Charlotte, North Carolina, United States, Available: portal.acm.org [accessed: December 2004].

Kauffman, J. R., & Walden, A. E. (Summer 2001). Economics and electronic commerce: survey and directions for research. *International Journal of Electronic Commerce*, 5 (4), 5-116.

Kaynak, F., Tatoglu, E. & Kula, V. (2005). An Analysis of the Factors Affecting the Adoption of Electronic Commerce by SMEs. *International Marketing Review, 22*(6), 623-640.

Kearns, G.S. & Leder, A.L. (2000). The effect of strategic alignment on the use of IS-based resources for competitive advantage. *Journal of Strategic Information Systems 9,* 265-293.

Keen, P. (2004). Bled e-commerce manifesto. Keynote speech at the 17th Bled eCommerce Conference, Bled, Slovenia, June 21-23, 2004.

Keil, M., Tan, B.C.Y., Wei, K.K. and Saarinen, T. (2000). A cross-cultural study on escalation of commitment behavior in software projects. MIS Quarterly 24(2): 299-324.

Kennedy, G. (2000a). China rushes to catch up with the Internet. *International Financial Law Review*, 19, 36-42.

Kennedy, G. (2000b). E-commerce: The taming of the Internet in China. *The China Business Review*, July-August, 34-39.

Kenny, (2002) "The Internet and economic growth in LDCs: A case of managing expectations?" UNU WIDER Paper No. 2002/75

Kettinger, W. J. (1997). The use of computer-mediated communication in an intraorganizational context. *Decision Sciences*, 28(3), 513-555.

Khalfan, A. M. & Alshawaf, A. (2004). Adoption and Implementation Problems of E-Banking: A Study of the Managerial Perspective of the Banking Industry in Oman. *Journal of Global Information Technology Management, 7*(1), 47-64.

Kibati, M., & Krairit, D. (1999) The wireless local loop in developing regions. *Communications of the ACM, 42*(6), 60-66.

Kimbrough, S. O., & Lee, R. M. (1997) Formal aspects of electronic commerce: Research issues and challenges. *International Journal of Electronic Commerce, 1*(4), 11-30.

King, W. R. & He J. (2006). A meta-analysis of the technology acceptance model. *Information & Managemen,t* 43, 740–755.

Kini, R.B. & Thanarithiporn, S. (2004). Mobile commerce and electronic commerce in Thailand: a value space analysis, *International Journal of Mobile Communications, 2*(1), 22-37.

Kintu, M.J.R., & Mbeine, E. (2004). *Output to Purpose Review DistrictNet Uganda.* FIT Uganda. Retrieved from http://www.iicd.org.

Kirby, D. & Turner, M. (1993). IT and the Small Retail Business, *International Journal of Retail and Distribution Management*, 21, 7, 20-27.

Kirkman, G. & Sachs, J. (2001). Subtract the Divide. *World Link, 14*(1), 60-63.

Klein, H. K. & Myers, M. D. (1999). A Set of Principles for Conducting and Evaluating Interpretive Field in Information Systems. *MIS Quarterly, 23*(1), 67-93.

Klein, H., & Myers, M. (1999). A set of principles for conducting and evaluating interpretive fields studies in information systems. *MIS Quarterly, 23*(1), pp. 67–94.

Klepperer, S, & Graddy, E. (1990). The evolution of new industries and the determinant of market structure. *Journal of Economics, 21*(1), 27-44.

Kling, R. (1999). Can the "Next-Generation Internet" Effectively Support "Ordinary Citizens", *The Information Society 15*(1), 57-63.

Knezevic, Boris R. and Vidas-Bubanja, Marijana, (2006) "Analysis of Electronic Commerce Adoption in Serbia, Available at SSRN: http://ssrn.com/abstract=941390

Knol, W.H.C. & Stroeken, J.H.M. (2001). The diffusion and adoption of information technology in small- and medium -sized enterprises through IT Scenarios, *Technology Analysis & Strategic Management,* 13(2),227-246.

Knowledge@Wharton, 2007. How To Tap Chinese Consumers? Market Online. http://www.forbes.com/2007/04/10/pepsico-dell-samsung-ent-sales-cx_kw_0410whartonchina_print.html accessed on 6/9/2007.

Komp Leonard L N (1999) Validating the Electronic Commerce Success Model through the Supply Chain Management Model. Doctoral Dissertation, University of Arkansas

Kosanke, K. & Nell, J. (1999). Standardisation in ISO for enterprise engineering and integration. *Computers in Industry, 40,* 311-319.

Kotonya, G & Sommerville, I. (1998). *Requirements Engineering.* ISBN 0-471-97208, WILEY.

KPMG (1997). *Electronic Commerce Research Report.* London, UK: KPMG.

Kraut, R., Steinfield, C., Chan, A. P., Butler, B. & Hoag, A. (1999). Coordination and Virtualization: The Role of Electronic Networks and Personal, Relationships, *Organization Science, 10*(6), 722-740.

Kroeber, A., & Kluckhohn. C. (1952). *Culture: a critical review of concepts and definitions*, Peabody Papers, 27(1).

Kshetri, N. (2007), Barriers to e-commerce and competitive business models in developing countries: A case study, *Electronic Commerce Research and Applications*, 6 (2007), pp.443-452

Kuan, K. K. Y. & Chau, P. Y. K. (2001). A Perception-based Model for EDI Adoption in Small Businesses Using A Technology-Organization-Environment Framework. *Information and Management, 38*(8), 507-521.

Kumar, R. & Best, M. L. (2006). Impact and Sustainability of E-Government Services in Developing Countries: Lessons Learned from Tamil Nadu, India. *Information Society, 22*(1), 1-12.

Kumar, S. Nicol, D. M., & Rude, D. E. (1993). *The State of cross-cultural decision making research: A critique and foundations for future research* (Working paper). University of Houston. Department of Management.

Lai, M. K., Humphreys, P. K. & Sculli, D. (2001). The Implications of Western Electronic Commerce for Chinese Business Networks. *Industrial Management and Data Systems, 101*(6), 281-289.

Lane, M. S., Van Der Vyer, G., Delpachitra, S. & Howard, S. (2004). An Electronic Commerce Initiative in Regional Sri Lanka: The Vision for the Central Province Electronic Commerce Portal. *Electronic Journal on Information Systems in Developing Countries, 16*(1), 1-18.

Langlois, M., & Gasch, S. (2001): *Le Commerce Electronique B to B de l' EDI à l'Internet*, Paris: Editions Dunod.

Laosethakul , K., Boulton,W.,(2007). Critical Success Factors for E-commerce in Thailand: Cultural and Infrastructural Influences, *The Electronic Journal on Information Systems in Developing Countries* (http://www.ejisdc.org), 30, 2, 1-22.

Lau, A., Yen, J. & Chau, P. Y. K. (2001). Adoption of Online Trading in the Hong Kong Financial Market. *Journal of Electronic Commerce Research, 2*(2), 58-62.

Laudon, K., & Laudon, J. (2006). *Management Information Systems.* 9th Edition.

Lawson, R., Alcock, C., Cooper, J., & L. Burgress. (2003). Factors affecting adoption of electronic commerce technologies by SMEs: an Australian study. *Journal of Small Business and Enterprise Development, 10(3)*, 265-276.

Layne, K., & Lee, J. (2001). Developing fully functional E-government: A four stage model. *Government Information Quarterly.* VOL 18; NUMBER 2, pages 122-136.

Le, T. (2002). Pathways to Leadership for Business-to-Business Electronic Marketplaces, *Electronic Markets, 12*(2), 12–119.

Le, T. T. & Koh, A. C. (2002). A Managerial Perspective on Electronic Commerce Development in Malaysia. *Electronic Commerce Research, 2*(1-2), 7-29.

LeClaire, Jennifer (2004). China Cracking Down on Internet Cafes. E-Commerce Times, 11/01/04. http://www.ecommercetimes.com/story/37752.html Accessed on 6/9/2007.

Lederer, A., Maupin, D., Sena, & M. Zhuang, Y. (2000). The Technology Acceptance Model and the World Wide Web. *Decision Support Systems,* 29(3), 269-282.

Lee, A. S. (2001). Editor's comments: Research in Information Systems: What We haven't Learned. *MIS Quarterly, 25*(4), V-XV.

Lee, M., & Turban, E. (2001). A trust model for consumers Internet shopping. International Journal of Electronic Commerce 6: 75-91.

Lee, O. (1999). An action research report of an e-commerce firm in South Korea. In Sudweeks, F., & Rom, C. (Eds.), *Doing Business on the Internet: Opportunities on the Internet* (pp. 246–258). London: Springer.

Lee, T., Chun, J., Shim, J. & Lee, S. (2006). An Ontology-Based Product Recommender System for B2B Marketplaces. *International Journal of Electronic Commerce, 11*(2), 125-155.

Leer, A. (2000). *Welcome to the Wired World: Tune in to the Digital Future.* Pearson, Harlow/London.

Lefebvre. L.A. & Lefebvre, E. (2002). E-commerce and virtual enterprises: issues and challenges for transition economies, *Technovation*, *22*(5), 313-323.

Leffingwell, D. & Widrig, D. (2000). *Managing Software Requirements A unified Approach* .Addison, Weasley.

Legris P., Ingham J., Collerette P. (2003). Why do people use information technology? A critical review of the technology acceptance model. *Information & Management* 40, 191–204

Lemon, Sumner (2006). China's Internet industry potential is great, but most of its affluent population has yet to get online. IDG News Service, February 28, 2006. http://www.infoworld.com/archives/emailPrint.jsp?R=printThis&A=/article/06/02/28/75933_HNecommercechina_1.html accessed on 6/9/2007.

Leonard-Barton, D. (1992). Core capabilities and core rigidities: A paradox in managing new product development. *Strategic Management Journal, 13*, pp. 111-125.

Lertwongsatien, C. & Wongpinunwatana, N. (2003). E-commerce Adoption in Thailand: An Empirical Study of Small and Medium Enterprises. *Journal of Global Information Technology Management, 6*(3), 67-83.

Leung, L. (2007). Unwillingness-to-communicate and college students' motives in SMS mobile messaging. *Telematics and Informatics,* 24(2), 115-129.

Levy, D., Bergen, M., Dutta, S., & Venable, R. (August 1997). The magnitude of menu costs: direct evidence from large U.S. supermarket chains. *Quarterly Journal of Economics,*112, 791-824.

Lewis, C. (2005). Negotiating the Net: The Internet in South Africa (1990–2003). *Information Technologies and International Development, 2*(3), 1-28.

Li, H., & Suomi, R. (2006). E-Commerce Development in China: Opportunities and Challenges. *IADIS International Conference on e-Commerce*, December 9-11, Barcelona, Spain, 413-417

Li, L. & Buhalis, D. (2006). E-Commerce in China: The case of travel. *International Journal of Information Management, 26*(2), 153-166.

Li, P. P. & Chang, S. T. (2004). A Holistic Framework of E-Business Strategy: The Case of Haier in China. *Journal of Global Information Management, 12*(2), 44-62.

Liao, C., To, P. & Shih, M. (2006) Website practices: A comparison between the top 1000 companies in the US and Taiwan. *International Journal of Information Management, 26*(3), 196-211.

Liebowitz, J. S. (2002). *Re-thinking the network economy: the true forces that drive the digital marketplace.* AMACOM: A Division of American Management Association.

Lim, K.H., Sia, C.L., Lee, M.K.O. & Benbasat, I. (2006). Do I Trust You Online, and If So, Will I Buy? An Empirical Study of Two Trust-Building Strategies. *Journal of Management Information Systems, 23*(2), 233-266.

Lima, M. I. & Alcoforado, I. (1999). Electronic Commerce: Aspects of the Brazilian Experience. *Electronic Markets 9*(1/2), 132-135.

Limaye, M., & Victor, D. (1991). Cross-cultural business communication research: State of the art and hypotheses for the 1990's. *Journal of Business Communication*, 28(3), 277-299.

Limaye, M., Hirt, S. G. & Chin, W.W. (2001). Intention does not always matter: the contingent role of habit on IT usage behavior, *In Proceedings of The 9th European Conference on Information Systems, Bled, Slovenia*, 27-29 June, pp. 27-9.

Lin B and Hsieh C T (2000) Online Procurement: Implementation and Managerial Implications, Human System Management, Volume 19, Number 2, pp. 105-110

Lin, H., & Wang, Y. (2006). An examination of the determinants of customer loyalty in mobile commerce contexts. *Information & Management, 43*(3), 271-282.

Ling, C.Y. (2001). *Model of factors influence on electronic commerce adoption and diffusion in small and medium enterprises,* ECIS Doctoral Consortium, AIS region 2 (Europe, Africa, Middle-East), 24-26 June.

Liu, C., Marchewka, J. T. & Ku, C. (2004). American and Taiwanese Perceptions Concerning Privacy, Trust, and Behavioral Intentions in Electronic Commerce. *Journal of Global Information Management, 12*(1), 18-40.

Lo, W. C. W., & Everett, A. M. (2001). Thriving in the regulatory environment of e-commerce: A guanxi strategy. *SAM Advanced Management Journal*, Summer, 17-24.

Loch, K. D., Straub, D. W., & Kamel, S. (2003). Diffusing the Internet in the Arab World: The Role of Social Norms and Technological Culturation. *IEEE Transactions on Engineering Management,* 50(1), 45-63.

Lohse, G. L. & Wu, D. J. (2001). Eye Movements Patterns on Chinese Yellow Pages Advertising. *Electronic Markets, 11*(2), 87-96.

Looi, H.C. (2005). E-Commerce Adoption in Brunei Darussalam: A Quantitative Analysis of Factors Influencing Its Adoption. *Communications of the Association for Information Systems, 15*(1), 61-81.

Love, P. & Irani, Z. (2004). An exploratory study of information technology evaluation and benefits management practices of SMEs in the construction industry, *Information & Management, In press.*

Lowry, P. B., Romans, D. & Curtis, A. (2004). Global Journal Prestige and Supporting Disciplines: A Scientometric Study of Information Systems Journals. *Journal of Association of Information Systems, 5*(2), 29-77.

Lu, J. & Lu, Z. (2004). Development, Distribution and Evaluation of Online Tourism Services in China. *Electronic Commerce Research, 4*(3), 221-239.

Lu, M., & Lu, D. H. (1995). Cultural impact on information systems: a framework for research. Waiman Cheung ed. *Selected Essays on Decision Sciences*, The Chinese University of Hong Kong. pp.20-30.

Lu, Y., Deng, Z., & Wang, B. (2007). Tourism and Travel Electronic Commerce in China, *Electronic Markets, 17*(2), 101-112.

Lund, M. F. & McGuire, S. (2005). Institutions and Development: Electronic Commerce and Economic Growth. *Organization Studies, 26*(12), 1743-1763.

Lynch & Beck, (2001) " Profiles of Internet buyers in 20 countries: Evidence for region-specific strategies", Journal of International Business Studies, Vol.32, No.4, P. 725-748

Lynch, G. (2001) The world vs. America, *America's Network,* 105 (1), 34-38.

Macdonnel, J., & Perkins, D. W. (1996): *L'avantage Internet pour l'Entreprise*, Paris: Editions Dunod.

Macromedia – Accessibility (2004), Macromedia [online], Available: www.macromedia.com/macromedia/accessibility [accessed: December 2004].

Madon, S. (2000). The Internet and Socio-Economic Development: Exploring the Interaction. *Information Technology and People, 13*(2), 85-101.

Maeurer, T. (2006). *The Language of the Net (in German). Asia Bridge, 10*, 36-37.

Mahajan, V., Siriniwasan, R.& Wind, J. (2002). The dot.com Retail Failures of 2000: Were there any Winners? *Academy of Marketing Science Journal*, 16(3), 335-340.

Mahmood, M. A., Bagchi, K. & Ford, T. C. (2004). On-line Shopping Behavior: Cross-Country Empirical Research. *International Journal of Electronic Commerce, 9*(1), 9-30.

Mahone, J. T. & Pandian, J. R. (1992). The Resource-Based View Within The Conversation Of Strategic Management. *Strategic Management Journal, 13*(5), 363-380.

Makadok, R. (2001). Toward a Synthesis of the Resource-Based and Dynamic-Capability Views of Rent Creation. *Strategic Management Journal, 22*(5), 387-401.

Making your Web sites Accessible with Microsoft FrontPage (2002), Microsoft Corporation [online], Available: www.microsoft.com [accessed: December 2004].

Malhotra, N. K., & McCort, J. D. (2001). A cross-cultural comparison of behavioral intentions models: theoretical considerations and an empirical investigation. *International Marketing Review*, 18(3), 235-269

Malone, T.W., Yates, J. & Benjamin, R. (1987). Electronic markets and electronic hierarchies, *Communications of the ACM, 30* (6), 484-497.

Mann, C.L. (2000) Electronic Commerce in Developing Countries: Issues For Domestic Policy And WTO Negotiations, Institute For International Economics, March 2000

Mann, C.L. (2000). Electronic Commerce In Developing Countries: Issues For Domestic Policy And WTO Negotiations (Working Paper 00-3). Washington, DC: Institute for International Economics.

Mann, L. C., Eckert, E. S., & Knight, C. S. (July 2000). *Global electronic commerce: a policy primer.* Washington, DC: Institute for International Economics.

Mansell, R. (2001). Digital Opportunities and The Missing Link for Developing Countries. *Oxford Review of Economic Policy, 17*(2), 282-295.

Mansell, R. (2001). Digital opportunities and the missing link for developing countries. *Oxford Review of Economic Policy*, Vol. 17, No. 2, 282-295.

Marchand, R., Agnoux, H., & Chiaramonti, C. (1999): *Applications EDI sur l'Internet, Commerce Electronique B to B* , Paris: Editions Eyrolles.

Maričić, B. (2002). *Consumer behavior* (in Serbian). Belgrade, Serbia: Savremena Administracija.

Markus, L., & Soh, C. (2002). Structural Influence on Global E-Commerce Activity. *Journal of Global Information Management,* 10(1), 5-12.

Markus, L., & Soh, C. (2003). Structural influence on global e-commerce activity. *Journal of Global Information Management, 10*(1), 5-12.

Marshall, P., Sor, R. & McKay, J. (2000). An industry case study of the impacts of electronic commerce on car dealerships in Western Australia. *Journal of Electronic Commerce Research*, 1(1).

Martinsons, M. G. (2002). Electronic Commerce in China: Emerging Success Stories. *Information and Management, 39*(7), 571-579.

Martinsons, M.G. (2002). Electronic Commerce in China: Emerging Success Stories. *Information & Management*, 39(7), 571-579.

Maruzzelli, G. (2004). *Republic of Serbia: investing in Serbia's Internet and IT sector: challenges and opportunities.* Retrieved July, 15, 2007, from http://www.b92.net/download/Internet_in_Serbia_public_report_15_july_2004.doc.

Mathieson, K, Peacock, E., & Chinn, W.C. (2001). Extending the Technology Acceptance Model: The Influence of Perceived User Resources. *The Data Base for Advances in Information Systems,* 32 (3), 86-112.

Mathieson, K. (1991). Predicting user intention: comparing the technology acceptance model with the theory planned behavior. *Information systems research,* 2(3), 173-1991.

Matta, K. F., & Boutros, N., (1989). Barriers to electronic mail systems in developing countries. *Computer & Society*, 19 (1), 1-6

Maugis, V., Choucri, N., Madnick, S. T., Siegel, M. D., Gillett, S. E., Haghseta, F., Zhu, H. & Best, M. L. (2005). Global e-Readiness—for What? Readiness for e-Banking. *Information Technology for Development, 11*(4), 313-342.

Mbarika, V. A. & Okoli, C. (2003). A Framework for Assessing E-commerce in Sub-Saharan Africa. *Journal of Global Information Technology Management, 6*(3), 44-66.

Mbarika, V. W. A., Byrd, T. A., Raymond, J., & McMullen, P. (2001) Investments in telecommunications infrastructure are not the panacea for least developed countries leapfrogging growth of tele-density, *International Journal on Media Management, 2*(1), 133-142.

Mbarika, V., Musa, P., Byrd, T.A., and McMullen, P. (2002) Tele-density Growth Constraints and Strategies for Africa's LDCs: 'Viagra' Prescriptions or Sustainable Development Strategy?, *Journal of Global Information Technology Management*, vol. 5, No.1, pp.25-42.

McConnell, S. (2000). A Champion in Our Midst: Lessons Learned from the Impacts of NGOs' Use of the Internet. *Electronic Journal on Information Systems in Developing Countries, 2*(5), 1-15.

McCormick, D. & Kinkajou, M.N. (2002). *E-Commerce In The Garment Industry In Kenya, Usage, Obstacles and Policies.* Sussex: Institute For Development Studies. Retrieved November 24, 2004, from http://www.gapresearch.org/production/B2BKenyagarmentsfinal.pdf.

McCubbrey, D. J. & Gricar, J. (1995). The EDI Project in Slovenia: A Case Study and Model for Developing Countries, *Information Technology and People, 8*(2), 6-16.

McGrath, R. G., Tsai, M. H., Venkataraman, S. & MacMillan, I. C. (1996). Innovation, competitive advantage, and rent: A model and test. *Management Science, 42*(3), 389-403.

McHenry, W. & Borisov, A. (2006a). Measuring e-government: a case study using Russia. *Communications of AIS, 17*(42), 905-940.

McHenry, W. & Borisov, A. (2006b). E-Government and Democracy in Russia. *Communications of AIS, 17*(48), 1064-1123.

McKay, J., Marshall, P., and Prananto, A. (2000). *Stages of maturity for e-business: The SOG-e model.* Conference Proceedings of the 4th Pacific Asia Conference on Information Systems, Hong Kong University of Science and Technology, Hong Kong.

McKnight, D., & Chervany, N. (2001). What trust means in e-commerce customer relationships: An interdisciplinary conceptual typology. International Journal of Electronic Commerce 6: 35-59.

McKnight, D., & Cummings, L., & Chervany, N. (1998). Initial trust formation in new organizational relationships. Academy of Management Review 23: 473-490.

McKnight, W. L., & Bailey, P. J. (November/December 1997). Internet economics: when constituencies collide in cyberspace. *Internet Computing IEEE*, 1 (6), 30-37.

McManis, B. L., Ryker, R., Cox, K. C. (2001), "An Examination of Web Usage in a global context", Industrial Management and Data Systems, 101/9, pp. 470-476.

McMaster, J., & Nowak, J. (2006). The evolution of trade portals and the Pacific islands countries e-trade facilitation and promotion. *Electronic Journal on Information Systems in Developing Countries, 26*(3), 1–27.

Medaković, R. (2005). *ICT in Serbia.* Elitex: New Delhi.

Mehrtens, J., Cragg, P.B. & Mills, A.M. (2001). A model of Internet adoption by SMEs. *Information and Management*, 39.165-176.

Melone, N. P. (1990). A Theoretical Assessment of the User-Satisfaction Construct in Information Systems Research. *Management Science*, 36 (1), 76-91.

Menda, A., *Computerising Local Government in Tanzania: The Kinondoni Experience.* iConnect Online, 2005. (www.iconnect-online.org)

Meskaran, F. & Ghazali, M. (2007), B2C in Iran: A case study to improve trust in developing countries, In Krishnamurthy and Isaias (eds.), Proceedings of the IADIS International Conference e-Commerce, December 7-9, Algarve, Portugal, pp.129-136

Mhlanga, B. (2006). Information and communication technologies (ICTs) Policy for change and the mask for development: A critical analysis of Zimbabwe e-readiness survey report. *Electronic Journal of Information Systems in Developing Countries, 28*(1), 1-16.

Milgrom, P. & Roberts, J. (1992). *Economics, Organization, and Management*, Englewood, NJ: Prentice Hall.

Milis, K. & Mercken, R. (2002). Success factors regarding the implementation of ICT investments projects. *(Article in Press) Elsevier Science BV.*

Mingers, J. (2000). 'The contribution of critical realism as an underpinning philosophy for OR/MS and systems', *Journal of the Operational Research Society*, 51(11), pp. 1256-70.

Ministry of Information Industry (MII). The report of telecommunication industry in China in 2006. Retrieved June 14, 2007, from http://www.cnii.com.cn/20070108/ca398639.htm

Minton, H. L., & Schneider, F. W. (1980). *Differential Psychology.* Waveland Press, Prospect Heights, IL.

Mitchell, A. D. (2001). Towards Compatibility: The Future of Electronic Commerce within the Global Trading System. *Journal of International Economic Law, 4*(4), 683-723.

Miyazaki, K. (1995). *Building Competences in the Firm: Lessons from Japanese and European Optoelectronics.* New York: St. Martin's Press.

Moeti, N., Mburu, P. & Kealisitse, B. (2006). Smart Card Perception Gaps: Encumbrance on E-Tailing in Botswana. *Problems and Perspectives in Management, 4*(4), 95-104.

Molla, A. & Licker, P. S. (2001). E-commerce Systems Success: An Attempt to Extend and Respecify the Delone and Maclean Model of IS Success. *Journal of Electronic Commerce Research, 2*(4), 131-141.

Molla, A. & Licker, P. S. (2004). Maturation Stage of eCommerce in Developing Countries: A Survey of South African Companies. *Information Technologies and International Development, 2*(1), 89-98.

Molla, A. & Licker, P. S. (2005a). E-commerce Adoption in Developing Countries: A Model and Instrument. *Information and Management, 42*(6), 877-899.

Molla, A. & Licker, P. S. (2005b). Perceived E-Readiness Factors in E-Commerce Adoption: An Empirical Investigation in a Developing Country. *International Journal of Electronic Commerce, 10*(1), 83-110.

Molla, A. (2001) The Impact of eReadiness on eCommerce Success in Developing Countries: Firm Based Evidence. *Development Informatics Working Papers No. 18.* Manchester, United Kingdom: University of Manchester. Institute for Development Policy and Management. Retrieved from http://www.man.ac.uk/idpm.

Molla, A. (2006). E-readiness and successful e-commerce diffusion in developing countries: results from a cluster analysis. In Sherif, K. (Ed.), *Electronic business in developing countries: opportunities and challenges* (pp. 214-233). IDEA Group Publishing.

Molla, A., Taylor, R. & Licker, P.S. (2006). E-commerce Diffusion in Small Island Countries: The Influence of Institutions in Barbados, *Electronic Journal on Information Systems in Developing Countries, 28*(2), 1-15.

Montagna, J.M. (2005). A framework for the assessment and analysis of electronic government proposals. *Electronic Commerce Research and Applications, 4*(2), 204-219.

Montealegre, R. & Keil, M. (2000). De-escalating Information Technology Projects: Lessons from the Denver International Airport. *MIS Quarterly, 24*(3), 417-447.

Montealegre, R. (1996) Implications of electronic commerce for managers in less-developed countries, *Information Technology for Development, 7*(3), 145-152.

Montealegre, R. (1996). Implications of Electronic Commerce for Managers in Less-Developed Countries. *Information Technology for Development, 7*(3), 145-152.

Montealegre, R. (1998) Managing information technology in modernizing "against the odds": Lessons from an organization in a less-developed country, *Information & Management, 34*, 103-116.

Montealegre, R. (1999). A Case For More Case Study Research In The Implementation Of IT, *Information Technology For Development, 8*(4), 199-207.

Montealegre, R. (2001) Four visions of e-commerce in Latin America in the year 2010, *Thunderbird International Business Review, 43*(6), 717-735.

Montealegre, R. (2001). Four Visions of E-Commerce in Latin America in the Year 2010. *Thunderbird International Business Review, 43*(6), 717-735.

Montealegre, R. (2002). A Process Model of Capability Development: Lessons from the Electronic Commerce. *Organization Science, 13*(5), 514-531.

Monteiro da Rocha, P., & Boutain, F. (2000): *Net Entreprises réussir on line,* Paris: Compus Press.

Moodley, S. & Morris, M. (2004). Does E-commerce Fulfill its Promise for Developing Country (South African) Garment Export Producers? *Oxford Development Studies, 32*(2), 155-178.

Moodley, S. (2002a). *E-Commerce & the Export Market Connectivity of South African Garment Producers: Disentangling Myth from Reality.* Cape Town, South Africa: Human Sciences Research Council, Knowledge Management Programme. Mimeo. Retrieved November 20, 2004, from http://www.irfd.org/events/wf2003/vc/papers/papers_africa/R34.pdf.

Moodley, S. (2002b). Global Market Access in the Internet Era: South Africa's Wood Furniture Industry. *Internet Research, 12*(1), 31-42.

Moodley, S. (2003). Whither Business-to-business Electronic Commerce in Developing Economies? The Case of the South African Manufacturing Sector. *Information Technology for Development, 10*(1), 25-40.

Moon, J., & Young-Gul, K. (2001). Extending the TAM for a World-Wide-Web Context. *Information and Management,* 38, 217 – 230.

Moore, C. (1967). The Chinese Mind: Essentials of Chinese Philosophy and Culture, Honolulu: University of Hawaii Press.

Moore, G.C., & Benbasat, I. (1991). Development of an Instrument to Measure the Perceptions of Adopting an Information Technology Innovation. *Information Systems Research,* 2(1), 192-222.

Morris, M.G. & Dillon, A. (1997). How User Perceptions Influence Software Use. *IEEE Software, 14*(4), 58-65.

Morris, M.G., & Dillon, A. (1997). How User Perceptions Influence Software Use. *IEEE Software.* 14 (4), 58-65.

Motwani, J., Youssef, M., Kathawala, Y. & Futch, E. (1999). Supplier selection in developing countries: a model development. *Integrated Manufacturing Systems, vol.10, no.3,* 154-161.

Mugellini, E., Khaled, O.A., Pettenati, M.C., & Kuonen, P. (2005). eGovSM metadata model: towards a flexible, interoperable and eGovernment service marketplace. e-Technology, e-Commerce and e-Service, 2005. EEE apos;05. *Proceedings. The 2005 IEEE International Conference on.* Volume, Issue , 29. pp.: 618-621. Digital Object Identifier 10.1109/EEE.2005.67.

Mukti N.A.,(2000). Barriers to putting businesses on the Internet in Malaysia, *Electronic Journal of Information Systems in Developing Countries* 2(6), 1–6.

Mukti, N. (2000) Barriers to Putting Business on the Internet in Malaysia. *Electronic Journal on Information Systems in Developing Countries, 2*(6), 1-6.

Muthitacharoen, A. & Palvia, P. (2002). B2C Internet Commerce: A Tale of Two Nations. *Journal of Electronic Commerce Research, 3*(4), 201-212.

Mutula, S. M. (2002). Current Developments in the Internet Industry in Botswana. *The Electronic Library, 20*(6), 504-511.

Mwangi, W. (2006). The Social Relations of e-Government Diffusion in Developing Countries: The Case of Rwanda. *Proceedings of the 2006 international conference on Digital government research, ACM International Conference Proceeding Series, vol.151, San Diego, USA,* 199-208.

Myers, M. D. & Avison, D. (2002). An Introduction to Qualitative Research in Information Systems In M. D., Myers & D., Avison (Eds.) *Qualitative Research in Information Systems,* A Reader. London: Sage Publications.

Mykytyn, P.P. & Harrison, D.A. (1993) The Application of Theory of Reasoned Action to Senior Management and Strategic Information Systems. *Information Resources Management Journal, 6*(**2**), **15-26.**

Nair, K.G.K. and Prasad, P.N. (2002) Development through Information Technology in Developing Countries: Experiences from an Indian State, *The Electronic Journal on Information Systems in Developing Countries,* vol. 8, Issue 2, pp. 1-13.

National Bureau of Statistics of China (2007). Retrieved July, 31, 2007, from http://www.stats.gov.cn/english.

Ndou, V. (2004). E – GOVERNMENT FOR DEVELOPING COUNTRIES: OPPORTUNITIES AND CHALLENGES. The Electronic Journal on Information Systems in Developing Countries.

Ndubisi, N. O., & Jantan, M. (2003). Evaluating IS usage in Malaysian small and medium-sized firms using the technology acceptance model. *Logistics Information Management*, 16(6), 440-450.

Neilson G L, Pasternack B A and Visco A J (2000) Up (E)Organization! A seven Dimensional Model for the Center Less Enterprise, Strategy and Business, Number 18, January, pp. 52-57

Netease. (12.08.2006). The pain after the happiness of pay with credit cards. Retrieved June 16, 2007, from http://finance.163.com/06/0812/12/2OAT80T800251SBB.html

Ngai, E. W. T. & Gunasekaran, A. (2004). Implementation of EDI in Hong Kong: An Empirical Analysis. *Industrial Management and Data Systems, 104*(1), 88-100.

Ngai, E. W. T. & Wat, F. K. T. (2002). A Literature Review and Classification of Electronic Commerce Research. *Information and Management, 39*(5), 415-429.

Ngai, E. W. T. (2004). Teaching and Learning of E-Commerce at the Hong Kong Polytechnic University: From A Business Education Perspective. *Journal of Electronic Commerce in Organizations, 2*(2), 17-27.

Ngai, E. W. T., & Wat, F. K. T. (2002) A literature review and classification of electronic commerce research, *Information & Management, 39*(5), 415-429.

Ngudup, P., Chen, J. C. H. & Lin, B. (2005). E-commerce in Nepal: A Case Study of An

Nielsen, J. (1999), "User interface directions for the web", Communications of the ACM, 42(1):65-72.

Nolan, R. L. (1973). Managing the Computer Resource: A Stage Hypothesis. *Communications of The ACM, 16*(7), 399-405.

Nolan, R.L. (1973). Managing the Computer Resource: A Stage Hypothesis. *Communications of the ACM,* 16(7), 399-406.

Nord, J. H. & Nord, G. D. (1995). MIS Research: Journal Status and Analysis. *Information and Management, 29*(1), 29-42.

Novell (2004), "Securing your Web site", Novel [online], Available: www.novell.com/documentation/nw6p/index.html [accessed: December 2004].

NStat 2007, ICT in the middle east, acced 25th August 2007

Nysveen, H., Pedersen P. E. & Thorbornsen, H. (2005). Intention to use mobile services: Antecedents and cross-service comparison, *Journal of the Academy of Marketing Science,* 33(3), 330-346.

O'Connor, J. & Galvin, E. (1998). Creating Value through E-commerce. *Financial Times*, PitmanPublishing, London.

O'Kane, G., (2000) World Bank to boost Internet in Africa, *African Business*, (252), 30.

O'Neil, J. M. (1982). Gender-role conflict and strain in Men's lives: implications for psychiatrists, psychologists, and other human-service providers. *Men in Transition: Theory and Therapy*. K. Solomon and N. B. Levy (eds.), Plenum, New York. pp.5-44.

Odedra, M., Lawrie, M., Bennet, M., & Goodman, S. E. (1993) Sub-Saharan Africa: A technological desert, *Communications of the ACM, 36*(2), 25-29.

Odedra, M., Lawrie, M., Bennett, M., Goodman, S. & (2003). *Information Technology in Sub-Saharan Africa, International Perspective.* Pennsylvania: CACM, University Of Pennsylvania - African Studies Center. Retrieved on November 20, 2005, from: http://www.africa.upenn.edu/Comp_Articles/Information_Technology_117.html.

OECD (1998). *SMEs and electronic commerce*, Ministerial Conference on Electronic Commerce, Ottawa, Canada.

Ohlin, B. (1983). *Interregional and international trade.* Cambridge, Mass: Harvard University Press.

Okazaki, S., & Taylor C. R. (2008). What is SMS advertising and why do multinationals adopt it? Answers from an empirical study in European markets. *Journal of Business Research*, 61(1), 4-12.

Olin, J., (2001) Reducing international e-commerce taxes, *World Trade*; Troy, 14 (3), 64-67.

Oliver, C. (1997). Sustainable competitive advantage: Combining institutional and resource-based views. *Strategic Management Journal, 18*(9), 697-713.

Olson, J. S., & Olson, G. M. (2000). i2i Trust in e-commerce. *Communications of the ACM, 43*(12), 41-44.

Orlikowski, W. J. & Baroudi, J. J. (1991). Studying Information Technology in Organizations: Research Approaches And Assumptions. *Accounting, Management And Information Technologies, 1*(1), 9-42.

Osterwalder, A., & Pigneur, Y. (2002). An E-Business Model Ontology for Modelling E Business. *15th Bled Electronic Commerce Conference*, Bled.

Oyserman, D., Coon, H.M. and Kemmelmeir, M. (2002). Rethinking individualism and collectivism: evaluation of theoretical assumptions and meta-analyses. Psychological Bulletin 128: 3-72.

Palmer, J. J. (2000). Internet Access in Bahrain: Business Patterns and Problems. *Technovation, 20*(8), 451-458.

Palvia, P., Palvia, S., & Whitworth, E. (2002). Global information technology environment: Representative world issues. In Palvia, P., Palvia, S., & Roche, E. (Eds.). (2002), *Global information technology and electronic commerce* (pp. 2–27). Marietta, GA: Ivy League Publishing.

Palvia, P., S. Palvia, E. Roche. (Eds.). (2002). *Global information technology and electronic commerce.* Marietta, GA: Ivy League Publishing.

Panagariya, A. (2000). E-commerce, WTO and developing countries. *The World Economy*, 23 (8), 959-978.

Panagariya, A. (2000). E-Commerce, WTO, and Developing Countries, *World Economy* 23(8), 959–979.

Panagariya, A., (2000) E-commerce, WTO and developing countries, *The World Economy*, 23 (8), 959-978.

Pani A K (2007) Perspective from IOIS, EDI and Channel Management: Research Issues in E-Procurement in E-Procurement in Emerging Economies Theory and Cases edited by Ashis K Pani and Amit Agrahari, Hershey: Idea Group Publishing, pp. 1-20

Pani A K and Agrahari A (2007) E-Procurement in E-Procurement in Emerging Economies Theory and Cases (eds), Hershey: Idea Group Publishing, pp. vi-xiii

Pani, A. K. & Agrahari, A. (2004). E-Markets in Emerging Economy: A Case Study from Indian Steel Industry. *Journal of Electronic Commerce in Organizations, 2*(4), 116-126.

Papazafeiropoulou, A. (2004). Inter-country analysis electronic commerce adoption in South Eastern Europe: policy recommendations fore the region. *Journal of Global Information Technology Management, 7*(2), pp. 35–45.

Pare, D. J. (2003). Does This Site Deliver? B2B E-commerce Services for Developing Countries. *The Information Society, 19*(2), 123-134.

Parikh, D. (2006). Profiling Internet Shoppers: A Study of Expected Adoption of Online Shopping in India, *IIMB Management Review, 18*(3), 221-231.

Park, C. & Kim, Y. (2006).The Effect of Information Satisfaction and Relational Benefit on Consumers' Online Shopping Site Commitments. *Journal of Electronic Commerce in Organizations, 4*(1), 70-90.

Park, H. (1993). Cultural impact on life insurance penetration: a cross-national analysis. International Journal of Management 10(3): 342-350.

Parker, E.B. (1992) Developing Third World Telecommunications Markets, *The Information Society*, vol. 8, No. 3, pp. 147-167.

Pavlou, P. (2003). Consumer acceptance of electronic commerce: integrating trust and risk with the technology acceptance model. *International Journal of Electronic Commerce,* 7, 69-103.

Pavlou, P. (2003). Consumer acceptance of electronic commerce: Integrating trust and risk with the technology acceptance model. *International Journal of Electronic Commerce, 7*(3), 101–34.

Pavlou, P. A. & Chai, L. (2002). What Drives Electronic Commerce Across Cultures? A Cross-Cultural Empirical Investigation of the Theory of Planned Behavior. *Journal of Electronic Commerce Research, 3*(4), 240-253.

Payton, F. C., & Brennan, P. F. (1999). How a community health information network is really used. *Communications of the ACM, 42*(12), 85-89.

Peevers G., Douglas G. & Jack M. A. (2008). A usability comparison of three alternative message formats for an SMS banking service. *International Journal of Human-Computer Studies*, 66(2), 113-123.

Peha, J. M. (1999) Lessons from Haiti's Internet development, *Communications of the ACM, 42*(6), 67-72.

Peng, Y., Trappey, C. V. & Liu, N. Y. (2005). Internet and E-commerce Adoption by the Taiwan Semiconductor Industry. *Industrial Management and Data Systems, 105*(4), 476-490.

Petrazzini, B. & Kibati, M. (1999). The Internet in Developing Countries. *Communications of the ACM, 42*(6), 31-36.

Petrazzini, B., & Kibati, M. (1999) The Internet in developing countries, *Communications of the ACM, 42*(6), 31-36.

Philips P and Piotrowicz W (2006) E-Procurement: How Does it Enhance Strategic Performance? Working Paper Series Number 113, Kent Business School, April

Phillips P A (2003) E-Business Strategy: Text and Cases, McGraw-Hill, Maidenhead, England

Pinsonneault, K. Kraemer (1993). Survey research methodology in management information systems: an assessment, *Journal of Management Information Systems* 10(2), 75–105.

Pitsilis, E. V., Woetzel, J. R.., & Wong, J. (2004). Checking China's Vital Signs. McKinsey Quarterly, Special Edition 2004. http://www.mckinseyquarterly.com/article_abstract.aspx?ar=1483&L2=7&L3=8&srid=63&gp=0 accessed on 2/12/2005.

Plant, R. (2000). *E-commerce: Formulation of strategy.* Upper Saddle River, NJ: Prentice-Hall.

Plouffe, C., Hulland, J. & M., V. (2001). Richness Versus Parsimony in Modeling Technology Adoption Decisions - Understanding Merchant Adoption of a Smart card-based Payment System. *Information Systems Research, 12*(2), 208-222.

Podlogar M (2007) E-Procurement Success Factors: Challenges and Opportunities for a Small Developing Country in E-Procurement in Emerging Economies Theory and Cases edited by Ashis K Pani and Amit Agrahari, Hershey: Idea Group Publishing, pp. 42-75

Pohl, K. (1998). Requirements engineering: An overview. *CREWS Report Series CREWS-96-02.*

Poirier C C and Bauer M J (2001) E-Supply Chain: Using the Internet to Revolutionize your Business, San Fransisco: Berrett-Koehler Publishers

Ponder, J. (2006). Developing Next Generation Access Networks: Challenges in the SEE Region, In *The first SEE Broadband Conference*, Belgrade, April, 2006.

Pons, A. (2004). E-Government for Arab Countries. *Journal of Global Information Technology Management, 7*(1), 30-46.

Poon, P. & Wagner, C. (2001). Critical success factors revisited: success and failure cases of information systems for senior executives. *Decision Support Systems 30,* 393-418.

Poon, S. & Chau, P. Y. K. (2001). Octopus: The Growing E-payment System in Hong Kong. *Electronic Markets, 11*(2), 97-106.

Poon, S. & Huang, X. (2002). Success at E-Governing: A Case Study ESDLife in Hong Kong. *Electronic Markets, 12*(4), 270-280.

Poon, S. (1999). *Management's role and internet commerce benefit among online small businesses,* in Proceedings of the 7th Conference on Information Systems, J. Pries-Heje, C. Ciborra, and K. Kautz, Eds. Copenhagen, Denmark: Copenhagen Business School, . 559-571.

Porter, E. M. (1990). *The Competitive advantage of nations.* New York: The Free Press.

Porter, M. (1985) Competitive advantage: Creating and sustaining superior performance, Free Press, USA

Porter, M. E. & Millar, V. E. (1985). How Information Gives You Competitive Advantage. *Harvard Business Review, 63*(4)149-160.

Porter, M. E. (1998). *Competitive advantage: Creating and sustaining superior performance.* New York, the U.S.: Free Press.

Porter, M. E. (1998). *The Competitive Advantage of Nations.* Basingstoke: Macmillan.

Porter, M.E. (1990). *The Competitive Advantage of Nations.* London: Macmillan.

Prahalad, C. K., & Ramaswamy, V. (2000). Co-opting customer competence. *Harvard Business Review,* January-February, 79-86.

Prananto, A., McKay, J., & Marshall, P. (2003). *A study of the progression of e-business maturity in Australian SMEs: Some evidence of the applicability of the stages of growth for e-business model.*7th Pacific Asia Conference on Information Systems (PACIS) 2003, University of South Australia,Adelaide, Australia.

Premkumar, G., Ramamurthy, K. & Nilakanta, S. (1994). Implementation of electronic data Interchange: an innovation diffusion perspective, *Journal of Management Information Systems*, 11, 157–86.

Premkumar, G., Ramamurthy, K. & Nilakanta, S. (1994). Implementation of Electronic Data Interchange: An Innovation Diffusion Perspective. *Journal of Management Information Systems, Fall, Vol.11, No.2,* 157-186.

Presutti W D (2003) Supply Management and e-Procurement: Creating Value Added in the Supply Chain, Industrial Marketing Management, Volume 32, Number 3, April, pp. 219-226

Privacy and Data Sharing. A Performance and Innovation Report (2002), Cabinet Office (UK Government – Department of Constitutional Affairs) [online], Available: www.foi.gov.uk/sharing/pubs.htm [accessed: December 2004].

Procaccino, D.J., Verner, J.M., Overnyer, S. P. & Darter M. E. (2002). Case study: factors for early prediction of software development success. *Information and Software technology 44 (2002),* 53-62

PTT Serbia. (2007). Available: http://www.posta.co.yu/english/onama/GodisnjiIzvestaj.asp. Accessed: October 25, 2007.

Pucihar, A., & Podlogar, M. (2006). E-marketplace adoption success factors: Challenges and opportunities for a small developing country. In Sherif, K. (Ed.), *Electronic business in developing countries: Opportunities and challenges* (pp. 89–117). Hershey, PA: Idea.

Pun, K-F. (2001). Cultural influences on total quality management adoption in Chinese enterprise: An empirical study. *Total Quality Management, Vol.12 Issue 3,* 323, 20p.

Purcell, F. & Toland, J. (2004) Electronic Commerce for the South Pacific: A Review of E-Readiness. *Electronic Commerce Research, 4*(3), 241-262.

Purcell, F. & Toland, J. (2004). Electronic Commerce for the South Pacific: A Review of E-Readiness. Electronic *Commerce Research, 4,* 241-262.

Pyatt, E. J., Pennsylvania State University (2004), Creating Accessible Web Sites, [accessed: Dec. 2004].

Rabaiah, A., Vandijck, E. & Musa, F. (2006). Abstraction of e-Government. *Proceedings of the IADIS International Conference E-Commerce*, Barcelona, Spain, pp. 27-34. ISBN: 972-8924-23-2.

Radovilsky Z and Hegde G V (2004) Factors Influencing e-Commerce Implementation: Analysis of Survey Results, Journal of Academy of Business and Economics, Volume 4, Number 1, March, pp. 29-37

Ramayah, T., Taib, F. & Ling, K.P. (2006). Classifying Users and Non-Users of Internet Banking in Northern Malaysia. *Journal of Internet Banking and Commerce, 11*(2).

Ramsey, J. (1998). Developing an IT Strategy. *Computer Bits, 8 (8).* Retrieved August, 1998 from http://www.computerbits.com.

Rao, M. (1998). AD Convention: Indian Advertising Agencies Urged to Harness Internet Technologies. *Electronic Markets, 8*(1), 48-49.

Rao, S. S. (2003). Electronic Commerce Development in Small and Medium Sized Enterprises: A Stage Model and Its Implications. *Business Process Management Journal*, 9(1), 11-32.

Rao, S. S. (2000). E-commerce: The Medium is the Mart. *New Library World, 101*(1154), 53-59.

Rashid M.A., & Al_Qirim,(2001). N.A. E-commerce technology adoption framework by New Zealand small to medium size enterprises, *Research Letters in the Information and Mathematical Sciences, Institute of Information and Mathematical Sciences*, 2, pp 63-70.

Rau, P. P., Gao, Q., & Wu, L. (2008). Using mobile communication technology in high school education: Motivation, pressure, and learning performance, *Computers & Education* 50(1), 1-22.

Rauch, J.E. (2001). Business and Social Networks in International Trade, *Journal of Economic Literature, 39*, pp.1177-1203.

Rayport, J.F., & Jaworski, B. J.(2003). *Commerce electronique*, Cheneliere / McGraw–Hill, Montreal (quebec), Canada, 652 pages

Rayurn, J. M. & Conrad, C. (2004). China's Internet structure: Problems and control measures. *International Journal of Management, 21*(4), 471-480.

RCUB NETIS (2007), Retrieved July, July, 6, 2007, from http://netiis.rcub.bg.ac.yu/netiis/NetIIS?service=main&action=show&ID=group.13952,

Reboul, P. (1999): *Le guide du Commerce Electronique*, Paris: Publi-U-Editions.

Reboul, P., & Xardel ,D. (1997): *Commerce Electronique*, Paris: Editions Eyrolles.

Reid, F. J. M. & Reid D. J. (2004). Text appeal: the psychology of SMS texting and its implications for the design of mobile phone interfaces. *Campus-Wide Information Systems,* 21(5), 196-200.

Reimers, K., Li, M. & Chen, G. (2004). A Multi-Level Approach for Devising Effective B2B E-Commerce Development Strategies with an Application to the Case of China. *Electronic Commerce Research, 4*(3), 287-305.

Rein, S. (2007) Yearning for E-Commerce in China. *e-commerce News.* February 10. http://www.e-commercetimes.com/story/55680.html

Rein, Shaun (2006). China's Booming Online Sales. Posted on Sep 12th, 2006. http://china.seekingalpha.com/article/16768 accessed on 6/9/2007.

Rein, Shaun (2007a). Chinese Cozy Up to E-Commerce. Business Week, February 8, 2007. http://www.businessweek.com/print/globalbiz/content/feb2007/gb20070208_810426.htm accessed on 6/9/2007.

Rein, Shaun (2007b). China's Virtual, e-Commerce Currency. Posted on Jan 16th, 2007. http://china.seekingalpha.com/article/24227 accessed on 6/9/2007.

Ren, R. (2007). The constraints and developing strategies in e-commerce in China. *Market Modernization, 491*(1), 134-135.

Reporter (2007). Retrieved July, 6, 2007, from http://www.reporter.gr/default.asp?pid=16&la=2&art_aid=73175.

Ricardo, D. (1963). *The Principles of political economy and taxation.* Homewood, Ill: Irwin.

Richard Freeman (2005). *Human Resource Leapfrogging.* The Globalist. Available at: www.theglobalist.com/StoryId.aspx?StoryId=4759. Last visited: June 24, 2007.

Riquelme, H. (2002). Commercial Internet adoption in China: comparing the experience of small, medium and large businesses. *Internet Research: Electronic Networking Applications and Policy, 12*(3), 276-286.

Robey, D., & Rodriguez-Diaz, A. (1989). The organizational and cultural context of systems implementation: Case experience from Latin America. *Information & Management*, 17, 229-239

Robichaux, B. P., & Cooper R. B. (1998). GSS participation: a cultural examination. *Information & Management*, 33, 287-300.

Roche, E. and Blaine, M.J. (1997) Research Note: The MIPS Gap, *Information Technology in Developing Countries*, vol. 7, No. 4, pp.12-13, 1997.

Rodriguez, F. & Wilson, I. E. J. (2000). *Are Poor Countries Losing the Information Revolution?* InfoDEV Working Paper Series. Washington, DC: The World Bank.

Rodriguez, G. R. (2005). Information and Communication Technology and Non-Governmental Organizations: Lessons Learnt From Networking in Mexico. *Electronic Journal on Information Systems in Developing Countries, 25*(3), 1-29.

Rogers, E. M. (1983). *Diffusions of Innovation.* New York: Free Press.

Rogers, E.M. (1983). *Diffusion of Innovations.* New York, NY: Free Press.

Rogers, E.M. (1995). *The Diffusion of Innovations, 4th ed.*, New York: Free Press.

Rogers, E.M. (1995). *Diffusions of Innovation, 4th Edition.* New York: Free Press.

Rohm, A., Kashyap, V., Thomas, G. B. & Milne, G. R. (2004). The Use of Online Marketplaces for Competitive Advantage: A Latin American Perspective. *Journal of Business and Industrial Marketing, 19*(6), 372-385.

Rombel, A., (2000) The global digital divide, *Global Finance,* 14 (12), 47.

Rose, E. (2000). Balancing Internet marketing needs with consumer concerns: A property rights framework. *Computers and Society*, June, 20-24.

Rose, G., & Straub, D. (1998). Predicting general IT use: applying TAM to the Arabic World, *Journal of Global Information Management,* 6(3), 39-46

Rosen, D. H. (1999). Hype Versus Hope for e-commerce in China. *The China Business Review,* July/August, 38-41.

Rosen, D. H. (1999). Hype versus hope for eCommerce in China. *The China Business Review,* July-August, 38-41.

Rosenbaum, H. (2000) The Information Environment of Electronic Commerce: Information Imperatives for the Firm," *Journal of Information Science*, vol. 26, No. 3, pp. 161-171, 2000.

RosettaNet (2001). Case Study: Arrow and UTEC replace EDI-based purchase order process with RosettaNet standards. *Case study report.* Retrived 20 February, 2004 from http://www.rosettanet.org/RosettaNet/Doc/0/D074294MUC4KJD8GF7HQL8RE67/Arrow_case_study.pdf.

Rotchanakitumnuai, S. & Speece, M. (2003). Barriers to Internet Banking Adoption: A Qualitative Study Among Customers in Thailand. *International Journal of Bank Marketing, 21*(6/7), 312-323.

Rotchanakitumnuai, S. & Speece, M. (2004). Corporate Customer Perspectives on Business Value of Thai Internet Banking. *Journal of Electronic Commerce Research, 5*(4), 270-286.

Rouibah, K. (2008). Social Usage of Instant Messaging by Employees outside the workplace in Kuwait: A structural Equation Model. *IT and People* (Forthcoming)

Rouibah, K., & Abbas, H. (2006). Modified Technology Acceptance Model for Camera Mobile Phone Adoption: Development and validation. *17th Australian Conference on Information System*, 6-8 December 2006, Adelaide, Australia. NOT SURE

Rouibah, K., & Hamdy, H. (2006). Does instant messaging usage impact students' performance in Kuwait? *In Proceedings of the IASTED International Conference Networks and Communication Systems*, 29-31 March, Chiang Mai Thailand

Rouibah, K., (2007). Does mobile payment technology Mnet attract potential consumers: A Kuwaiti Study. In M. Toleman, A. Cater-Steel, and D. Roberts (Editors), *18th Australian Conference on Information System*. 199-211, Queensland, Australia, 4-5 December 2007. NOT SURE

Rousseau, D.M., Sitkin, S.B., Burt, R.S. and Camerer, C. (1998). Not so different after all: a cross-discipline view of trust. The Academy of Management Review, 23(3): 393-404.

Roy, M. Christine, Dewit, O., Aubert, B. A. (2001), "The impact of interface usability on trust in Web retailers", Internet Research: Electronic Networking Applications and Policy, Vol. 11 No. 5, pp. 388-398.

Roy, S. & Biswas, S. (2007). Collaborative ICT for Indian Business Clusters. *Proceedings of the WWW 2007 Conference, May 8-12, Banff, Alberta, Canada,* 1115-1116.

Rutherford, E. (2002), How to Avoid Global Website Disasters, Available: www.cio.com/research/.../111400_disaster.html [accessed:2004].

Sadowsky, G. (1993). Network connectivity for developing countries. *Communications of the ACM, vol.36, no.8,* 42-47.

Sadowsky, G. (1993). Networking Connectivity for Developing Countries. *Communications of the ACM, 36*(8), 42-47.

Saiedian, H. & Dale, R. (2000). Requirements engineering: making the connection between the software developer and customer. *Information and Software Technology 42),* 419-428.

Salleh, N.A.M., Rhode, F. & Green, P. (2006). The Effect of Enacted Capabilities on Adoption of a Government Electronic Procurement System by Malaysian SMEs, *Electronic Markets, 16*(4), 292–311.

Salman, A. (2004). Elusive Challenges of E-change Management in Developing Countries. *Business Process Management Journal, 10*(2), 140-156.

Salman, A. (2004). Elusive challenges of e-change management in developing countries. *Business Process Management Journal, vol.10, no.2,* 140-157.

Sanchez, R., Heene, A. & Thomas, H. (1996). *Introduction: Towards the Theory and Practice of Competence-Based Competition*, Oxford: Pergamon Press.

Sang M. Lee, Xin Tan, & Silvana Trimi (2006). M-government, from rhetoric to reality: learning from leading countries. *Electronic Government, an International Journal.* Issue: Volume 3, Number 2/2006. pp.:113-126.

Sarantakos, S. (1998). *Social Research, Second Edition.* Basingstoke, Hampshire: Palgrave.

Schech, S. (2002) Wired for change: The links between ICTs and development discourses, *Journal of International Development, 14*(1), 13-23.

Schein, E. H. (1985). *Organizational Culture and Leadership.* Jossey-Bass, San Francisco. CA.

Schein, E.H. (2004). *Organisational culture and Leadership (3rd edition).* John Wiley & Sons, Inc. ISBN: 0-7879-6845-5.

Schendel, D. (1994). Introduction to Competitive Organizational Behavior: Toward An Organizationally Based Theory Of Competitive Advantage, *Strategic Management Journal, 15*, pp. 1-4.

Schmid, B., K. Stanoevska-Slabeva, & V. Tschammer. (2001). *Towards the E-Society*: E-Commerce, E-Business, E-Government, Zurich, Switzerland, 13 October.

Schneider, (2007) "Electronic commerce", Thompson Canada, P.5 &P. 33

Schoder, D., & Yin, P.-L. (2000). Building firm trust online. *Communications of the ACM, 43*(12), 73-79.

Scholl, H. (2005). *Interoperability in e-Government*: More Than Just Smart Middleware. IEEE Computer Society, USA.

Scott, N., Batchelor, S., Ridley, & J., Jorgensen, B. (2004). *The Impact of Mobile Phones in Africa. Commission for Africa.* Retrieved from http://www.commissionforafrica.org.

Sekaran. U. (2000). *Research Methods for Business – A Skill Building Approach*, 3rdEdition, John Wiley & Sons, Inc.

Serbian Yellow Pages (2005). Available: http://www.yuyellowpages.net/search.php?delatnost=173. Accessed: October, 20 2005.

Seyal, A., Awais, M. M., Shamail, S. & Abbas, A. (2004). Determinants of Electronic Commerce in Pakistan: Preliminary Evidence from Small and Medium Enterprises. *Electronic Markets, 14*(2), 372-387.

Seyal, A.H. & Rahim, M. (2006). A preliminary investigation of electronic data interchange adoption in Bruneian small business organizations. *Electronic Journal on Information Systems in Developing Countries, 24*(4), 1-21.

Shang, R., Chen, Y. & Shen, L. (2005). Extrinsic Versus Intrinsic Motivations for Consumers to Shop On-line. *Information and Management, 42*(3), 401-413.

Shapiro, C., & Varian, H. R. (1999). *Information rules: a strategic guide to the network economy.* Boston, Massachusetts: Harvard Business School Press.

Sharma, S. & Gupta, J. N. D. (2003). Socio-economic Influences of E-commerce Adoption. *Journal of Global Information Technology Management, 6*(3), 3-21.

Shelly, G., Cashman, T.J, & Rosenblatt, H.J. (2001). *Systems Analysis and Design.* Boston: Course Technology/Thomson.

Sherif, K. (Ed.), (2006). *Electronic business in developing countries: opportunities and challenges.* IDEA Group Publishing.

Sheth, N. & Sharma, A. (2005). International E-marketing: Opportunities and Issues. *International Marketing Review, 22*(6), 611-622.

Shih, H. (2004). Extended Technology Acceptance Model of Internet Utilization Behavior. *Information and Management, 41*(6), 719-729.

Shih, H. P, (2004). Extended technology acceptance model of internet utilization behavior. *Information & Management,* 41(6), 719-729

Shih, Y., & Fang K. (2006). Effects of network quality attributes on customer adoption intentions of Internet Banking. *Total Quality Management & Business Excellence*, 17(1), 61-77.

Shih, Y., and Fang, K., (2004). The use of a decomposed theory of planned behavior to study Internet banking in Taiwan, *Internet Research* (14)3, 213-223.

Sia, C., Lee, M. K. O., Teo, H. & Wei, K. (2001). Information Instruments for Creating Awareness in IT Innovations: An Exploratory Study of Organizational Adoption Intentions of ValuNet. *Electronic Markets, 11*(3), 206-215.

Simms, C., (2000) The third-world Web world, *LIMRA's marketFacts*, 19 (4), 54-55.

Simon, S. J. (2004). Critical Success Factors for Electronic Services: Challenges for Developing Countries. *Journal of Global Information Technology Management, 7*(2), 31-53.

Simpson, J. (2002). The impact of the Internet in banking: observations and evidence from developed and emerging markets, *Telematics and Informatics, 19*(4), 315-330.

Singh, B. & Malhotra, P. (2004). Adoption of Internet Banking: An Empirical Investigation of Indian Banking Sector. *Journal of Internet Banking and Commerce, 9*(2).

Singh, J. & Gilchrist, S. (2002). Three layers of the electronic commerce network: challenges for the developed and developing worlds. *Info, vol.4, no.2,* 31-41.

Singh, J. P. & Gilchrist, S. M. (2002). Three Layers of the Electronic Commerce Network: Challenges for Developed and Developing Worlds. *INFO, 4*(2), 31-41.

Singh, N., Xhao, H. & Hu, X. (2003). Cultural Adaptation on the Web: A Study of American Companies Domestic and Chinese Websites. *Journal of Global Information Management, 11*(3), 63-80.

Siyal, M.Y., Chowdhry, B.S. & Rajput, A.Q. (2006) Socio-economic factors and their influence on the adoption of e-commerce by consumers in Singapore, *International Journal of Information Technology & Decision Making, 5*(2), 317–329.

SLBDC, (2002). *Survey on E-Commerce Implementation in the SME Sector of Sri Lanka* Conducted by the SLBDC

Slywotzky, A. (1996). *Value Migration*, Harvard business school press.

Slywotzky, A. J. (2000). The age of the Choiceboard. *Harvard Business Review,* January-February, 40-41.

Smith, A. (1937). *The wealth on nations.* New York: The Modern Library.

SMS Research and Statistics (2005). Chinese send 750 million SMS daily. Retrieved December 31, 2007 from http://smschronicle.com/?q=taxonomy/term/12

Söderström, E. & Pettersson, A.H. (2003). The Use of B2B Process Standards. *Proceedings of the 15th International Conference on Advanced Information Systems Engineering Forum* (CAiSE Forum 2003), 121-124.

Söderström, E. (2004). *B2B Standards Implementation: Issues and Solutions.* PhD Thesis, Department of Computer and Systems Sciences, Stockholm University, Akademitryck, ISBN 91-7265-942-4.

Soh, C., and Markus, M.L. (1995). How IT Creates Business Value: A Process Theory Synthesis. In G. Ariav, et al. (Eds.), *Proceedings of the Sixteenth International Conference on Information Systems,* December 10-13. (29-41). Amsterdam, The Netherlands.

Somasundaram R (2007) Challenges in Implementation of E-Procurement in the Indian Government in E-Procurement in Emerging Economies Theory and Cases edited by Ashis K Pani and Amit Agrahari, Hershey: Idea Group Publishing, pp. 76-100

Sorensen, O. J. & Buatsi, S. (2002). Internet and Exporting: The Case of Ghana. *Journal of Business and Industrial Marketing, 17*(6), 481-500.

Spahni, D. (2004). Managing Access to Distributed Resources. *IEEE Computer Society*, USA.

Španović, M. (2005). Credit card as an alternative to checks (in Serbian). In *Pay cards: development and prevention of abuse* (in Serbian). Belgrade: The Chamber of Commerce of Serbia.

Sparks, R., Desai, N., Thirumurthy, P. & Kistenberg, C. (2007), An analysis of e-commerce adoption between developed and developing countries: A holistic model, In Krishnamurthy and Isaias (eds.), Proceedings of the IADIS International Conference e-Commerce, December 7-9, Algarve, Portugal, pp.11-18

Speedsend.com Company Reports (2007) www.speedsend.com (website) last accessed 25 July

Sprano, E. & Zakak, A. (2000). E-commerce Capable: Competitive Advantage For Countries in the New World Economy. *Competitive Review, 10*(2), 114-122.

Sprano, E. (2000) E-commerce capable: Competitive advantage for countries in the new world e-conomy, *Competitiveness Review, 10*(2), 114.

Sprano, E. and Zakak, A., (2000) E-commerce capable: Competitive advantage for countries in the new world e-conomy , *Competitiveness Review*, 10 (2), 114-131.

Sridhar, V. (1998) Analysis of Telecommunications Infrastructure in Developing Countries. *Proceedings of the Association for Information Systems 1998 Americas Conference*, Baltimore, August 14-16, 1998.

Sridhar, V. (2006) Modeling the growth of Mobile telephony services in India, *VISION - The Journal of Business Perspective, 10*(3).

Sridhar, V., & Sridhar, K. (2006). E-commerce infrastructure and economic impacts in countries: Case of India. In Sherif, K. (Ed.), *Electronic business in developing countries: Opportunities and challenges* (pp. 63–87). Hershey, PA: Idea.

Srite, M. D. (2000). *The influence of national culture on the acceptance and use of information technologies: an empirical study.* Doctoral Dissertation. The Florida State University.

Srivastava, A., & Thomson, S. B. (2007). E-Business law in China: Strengths and Weaknesses, *Electronic Markets, 17*(2), 126 – 131.

Stability Pact, bSEE Initiative, (2006) bSEE Action Plan, October.

Stability Pact, eSEE Initiative, (2007) eSEE Agenda+, October, 2007, Sarajevo.

Stability Pact, eSEE Initiative. (2002). *Agenda for the development of the information society.* June, 4, 2002.

Stafford, T.F., Turan, A.H. & Khasawneh, A.M. (2006). MIDDLE-EAST.COM: Diffusion of the Internet and Online Shopping in Jordan and Turkey. *Journal of Global Information Technology Management, 9*(3), 43-61.

Stauss, B., Chojnacki, K., Decker, A., & Hoffmann, F. (2001). Retention effects of a customer club. *International Journal of Service Industry Management, 12*(1), 7-19.

Steinert-Threlkeld, T. (2000). China holds Internet dragon by tail. *Inter@ctive Week, 7*(19), 86-91.

Steinfield, C., Kraut, R. & Plummer, A. (1995). The Impact of Interorganizational Networks on Buyer-Seller Relationships, *Journal of Computer Mediated Communication, 1*(3).

Steinfield, C., Kraut, R., & Chan, A. (2000). Computer Mediated Markets:An Introduction and Preliminary Test of Market Structure Impacts, *Journal of Computer Mediated Communication, 5*(3).

Stickiness in an eTailing environment (2000), Northwestern University [online], Available: www.medill.northwestern.edu/imc/studentwork/projects/Sticky/index.htm [accessed: November 2004].

Stout, Kristie Lu (2005). China gears up for e-commerce boom. CNN, November 1, 2005. http://edition.cnn.com/2005/TECH/11/01/spark.china.payment/index.html accessed on 6/9/2007.

Straub, D. (1994). The effect of culture on IT diffusion: e-mail and fax in Japan and the U.S. *Information Systems Research*, 5(1), 23-47.

Straub, D. W., Loch, K. D., Evaristo, R., Karahanna, E., & Srite, M. (2002) Toward a Theory Based Definition of Culture, *Journal of Global Information Management, 10*(1), 13-23.

Straub, D., Keil, M., & Brenner, W. (1997). Testing the technology acceptance model across cultures: a three country study. *Information & Management*, 33(1), 1-11.

Straub, D., Loch, K., Evaristo, J. R., Karahanna, E., & Srite, M. (2002). Toward a theory-based measurement of culture. *Journal of Global Information Management*, 10(1), 13-23.

Stroud, D. (1998). *Internet Strategies: A Corporate Guide to Exploiting the Internet.* London: Macmillan Press Ltd.

Stylianou, A. C., Robbins, S. & Jackson, P. (2003). Perceptions and Attitudes About E-Commerce Development in China: An Exploratory Study. *Journal of Global Information Management, 11*(2), 31-47.

Stylianou, A. C., Robbins, S. S., & Jackson, P. (2003). Perceptions and attitudes about eCommerce development in China: An exploratory study. *Journal of Global Information Management, 11*(2), 31-47.

Subramaniam C and Shaw M J (2002) A Study of the Value and Impact of B2B E-Commerce: The Case of Web-Based Procurement. International Journal of Electronic Commerce, Volume 6, Number 4, Summer, pp. 1940

Suganthi, B. & Balachandran (2001). Internet Banking Patronage: An Empirical Investigation of Malaysia. *Journal of Internet Banking and Commerce, 6*(1).

Suh, B. & Han, I. (2002). Effects of trust on customer acceptance of Internet banking, *Electronic Commerce Research and Applications*, 1(3/4), 247-63.

Sulaiman, A., Jaafar, N. I. & Kiat, T. C. (2005). Internet Activities among Malaysian Insurance Companies. *Journal of Internet Banking and Commerce, 10*(1).

Sullivan, N. (2004), Why design accessible websites, PostDiluvian Org. [online], Available: postdiluvian.org/~nicole/work/why.php [accessed: December 2004].

Summary of the United Nations Conference on the Least Developed Countries (2001). *The Digital Economy: Integrating the LDCs into the Digital Economy.* A/CONF.191/L.15. Brussls, Belgium, 14-20 may 2001.

Sutcliffe, A. (2002), "Heuristic Evaluation of Website Attractiveness and Usability", Proceedings of the 35th Hawaii International Conference on System Sciences [online], Available: csdl2.computer.org/comp/proceedings/hicss/2002/1435/05/14350137.pdf [accessed: December 2004].

Sutcliffe, A.G., Economou, A. & Markis, P. (1999). Tracing requirements problems in the requirements engineering process Requirements. *Engineering, 4,* 134-151.

Svet, B., State University of New York, Buffalo (2003), Personalization and Customization in eCommerce, Available: www.cse.buffalo.edu/~sbraynov/seninar2003/presenttations/lecture.pdf [accessed: 2004].

Talh, M. & Salim, A. S. A. (2005). Incorporating Electronic Business Initiatives in Health Services and Health Tourism: A Case Study of Malaysia. *Journal of Internet Banking and Commerce, 10*(1).

Tan J, Tyler, K., & Manica A. (2007). Business-to-business adoption of eCommerce in China, *Journal of Information & Management* 44, 332–351

Tan J., Tyler K. & Manica A. (2007). Business-to-business adoption of eCommerce in China, *Journal of Global Information management*,10,4,61-85

Tan, B. C. Y., Wei, K., Watson, R. T., Watson, R. T., & Walczuch, R. M. (1998). Reducing status effects with computer-mediated communication: evidence from two distinct national cultures. *Journal of Management Information Systems*, 15(1), 119-141.

Tan, J., Tyler, K. & Manica, A. (2007). Business-to-business adoption of eCommerce in China. *Information & Management, 44,* 332-351.

Tan, M., & Teo, T.S.H.(2000). Factors influencing the adoption of internet banking, *Journal of the Association of Information Systems* (1,5), pp.14

Tan, Z. & Ouyang, W. (2004). Diffusion and Impacts of the Internet and E-commerce in China. *Electronic Markets, 14*(1), 25-35.

Tan, Z., & Ouyang, W. (2004). Diffusion and impacts of the Internet and e-commerce in China. *Electronic Markets, 14*(1), 25-35.

Tan, Z., & Wu, O. (2004). Diffusion and Impacts of the Internet and E-Commerce in China. *Electronic Markets, 14*(1), 25-35.

Tan, Z., & Wu, O. (2006). China: Overcoming Institutional Barriers to E-Commerce. In K. L. Kraemer, J. Dedrick, N. P. Melville, & K. Zhu (Eds.), *Global e-Commerce* (pp. 209-246). Cambridge, MA: Cambridge University Press.

Tang, F-F., & Lu, D. (2001). Pricing patterns in the online CD markets: an empirical study. *Electronic Markets*, 11 (3) 171-185(15)

Tapscott, D. (1996). *The digital economy, promise and peril in the age of networked intelligence.* McGraw-Hill.

Tarafdar, M. & Vaidya, S. D. (2004). Adoption of Electronic Commerce by Organizations in India: Strategic and Environmental Imperatives. *Electronic Journal on Information Systems in Developing Countries, 17*(2), 1-25.

Task Force for Small & Medium Enterprise Sector Development Program (2002), *National Strategy for Small and Medium Enterprise Sector Development in Sri Lanka,*White Paper, Colombo

Taylor, M. C., & Hall, J. A. (1982). Psychological androgyny: theories, methods, and conclusion. *Psychological Bulletin*, 92, 347-366.

Taylor, S. & Todd, P. (1995). Decomposition and Crossover Effects in the Theory of Planned Behavior: A Study of Consumer Adoption Intentions. *International Journal of Research in Marketing, 12*(2), 137-156.

Taylor, S., & Todd, P. A. (1995). Understanding information technology usage: a test of competing models. *Information System Research,* 6(2), 144-174.

Teece, D. J., Pisano, G. & Shuen, A. (1997). Dynamic Capabilities and Strategic Management. *Strategic Management Journal, 18*(7), 509-533.

Teltscher, S. (2002). Electronic Commerce and Development: Fiscal Implications of Digitized Goods Trading. *World Development, 30* (7), 1137-1158.

Teng, J. T. C., Fiedler, K. D., & Grover, V. (2000). A cross cultural study on the organizational context of process redesign initiatives: U.S. vs. Taiwan. *Journal of Global Information Management*, 3(3), 7-28.

Teo & Liu, (2005) "Consumer trust in e-commerce in the U.S., Singapore and China", The International Journal of Management Science, P.22-38

Thatcher, S. M. B., Foster, W. & Zhu, L. (2006). B2B E-commerce Adoption Decisions in Taiwan: The Interaction of Cultural and Other Institutional Factors. *Electronic Commerce Research and Applications, 5*(2), 92-104.

The 2004 e-readiness rankings, Economist Intelligence Unit, 2004. Retrieved 20th April 2004 from World Wide Web http://graphics.eiu.com/files/ad_pdfs/ERR2004.pdf

The Public Opinion Foundation (2007). Project "The Internet in Russia/Russia on the Internet" - 19th Release. Retrieved July 31, 2007, from http://bd.english.fom.ru/report/map/projects/ocherk/eint0702.

The World Factbook (2007). Retrieved July 31, 2007, from https://www.cia.gov/library/publications/the-world-factbook/index.html.

The World Factbook. (2007). Available: http://www.cia.gov/cia/publications/factbook/geos/yi.html#Econ. Accessed: November 21, 2007.

Thelwall, M. (2000), "Commercial Web sites: lost in cyberspace?", Internet Research Vol. 10 Issue 2, pp. 150-159.

Themistocleous, M., & Irani, Z. (2005). Developing E-Government Integrated Infrastructures: A Case Study. *IEEE Computer Society*, USA.

Thompson, T. & Ranganathan, C. (2004). Adopters and non-adopters of business-to-business electronic commerce in Singapore. *Information & Management, Vol.42,* .89-102.

Thong, J. Y. L. (1999). An integrate model of information systems adoption in small business, *Journal of Management Information Systems*, 15, 187–214.

Tigre, P. B. & Dedrick, J. (2004). E-commerce in Brazil: Local Adaptation of a Global Technology. *Electronic Markets, 14*(1), 36-47.

TMC Net. (2008). 2006 Will Be the Year of Mobile Advertising Experimentation,, *TMC net news* (2006), March 16. Retrieved December 3, 2008, from http://www.tmcnet.com/usubmit/2006/03/16/1465460.htm

Todaro, M. & Smith, S. C. (2003). *Economic Development, 8th edition.* Essex, UK: Pearson Education Ltd.

Tongeren, v. M. Lussanet. de, Favier J. & Jennings R. (2004). Mobile campaigns that don't annoy: how should marketers create successful SMS campaigns? *Trends. Forrester research* March 8, Web http://www.forrester.com

Tornatzky, L. G. & Fleischer, M. (1990). *The Process of Technological Innovation*, Lexington Books, Lexington, MA.

Tornatzky, L. G. & Fleischer, M. (1990). *The Processes of Technological Innovation.* Lexington, MA: Lexington Books.

Trappey, C. V., & Trappey, A. J. C. (2001). Electronic Commerce in Great China. *Industrial Management & Data Systems, 101*(5), 201-209.

Traunmüller, R., & Wimmer, M. (2002). Web Semantics in e-Government: A Tour d'Horizon on Essential Features. Institute of Applied Computer Science, University of Linz. *IEEE Computer Society*, USA.

Travica B. (2002). Diffusion of electronic commerce in developing countries: the case of Costa Rica, *Journal of Global Information Technology Management* 5(1)

Travica B., Kajan, E., Jošanov, B., Vidas-Bubanja, M., & Vuksanović, E. (2006). „E-Commerece in a developing Country: Casa Study of Serbia", *Proceedings from IADIS International Conference e-Commerce 2006*, Barcelona: pp. 19–26.

Travica, B. (2002). Diffusion of Electronic Commerce in Developing Countries: The Case of Costa Rica. *Journal of Global Information Technology Management, 5*(1), 4-24.

Travica, B. (2002). Diffusion of electronic commerce in developing countries: The case of Costa Rica. *Journal of Global Information Technology Management, 5*(1), 4-24.

Travica, B. (2002). Diffusion of electronic commerce in developing countries: The case of Costa Rica. Journal of Global Information Technology Management, 5(1), 4-24.

Travica, B. (2002). Diffusion of electronic commerce in developing countries: the case of Costa Rica. *Journal of Global Information Technology Management, 5*(1), 4–24.

Travica, B., & Olson, R. (1998). Electronic commerce in east and central Europe. *Proceedings of the ASIS 1998 Annual Conference*, October 24-29, 1998, Pittsburgh, PA, pp. 40–55.

Travica, B., Kajan, E., Jošanov, B., Vidas-Bubanja, M., & Vuksanović, E. (2007). E-Commerce in Serbia: Where Roads Cross Electrons Will Flow, *Journal of Global Information Technology Management (JGITM),* 10(2), 34–56.

Trends in the Evolution of the Public Web (2003), D-Lib Magazine [online], Available: www.dlib.org/dlib/april03/lavoie/04lavoie.html [accessed: November 2004].

Tricker, R. I. (1988). Information resource management: a cross cultural perspective. *Information & Management*, 15, 37-46.

Trompenaars, (2003) "Business across cultures", Capstone

Trompenaars, A., & Hampden-Turner, C. (1998). *Riding the waves of culture: understanding cultural diversity in global business.* New York: McGraw Hill.

Trompenaars, S., & Hampden-Turner, C. (1998). Riding the waves of culture: understanding cultural diversity in global business. New York: McGraw Hill

Tsai, Y. (2006). Effect of Social Capital and Absorptive Capability on Innovation in Internet Marketing. *International Journal of Management, 23*(1), 157-166.

Tsang, M. M., Ho, S. & Liang, T. (2004). Consumer Attitudes Toward Mobile Advertising: An Empirical Study. *International Journal of Electronic Commerce, 8*(3), 65-78.

Turban E, King D, Viehland D and Lee J, Electronic Commerce: A Managerial Perspective, Pearson-Prentice Hall, Upper Saddle River, NJ

Turel, O., Serenko A., & Bontis N., (2007). User acceptance of wireless short messaging services: deconstructing perceived value. *Information & Management, 44*(1), 63-73.

Turel, O., Serenko, A., Detlor, B., Collan, M., Nam, I. & Puhakainen, J. (2006). Investigating the Determinants of Satisfaction and Usage of Mobile IT Services in Four Countries. *Journal of Global Information Technology Management, 9*(4), 6-27.

Tusubira, F.F., Kaggwa I., & Ongora J. (2005). In: A. Gillwald (Ed.), *Towards an African e-Index: Household and Individual ICT Access and Usage across 10 African Countries.* The LINK Centre, Wits University School of Public and Development Management.

UN/ECE (2003) *Guidelines for Creation of National Strategy*, Geneva.

UNCTAD (2000). *Building confidence: electronic commerce and development.*

UNCTAD (2001- 2004). *E-commerce and development report.*

UNCTAD (2001). *E-Commerce And Development Report, Internet Edition, Trends and Executive Summary*, United Nations Conference On Trade And Development, United Nations, New York. Retrieved **22 May 2004, from http://www.unctad.org/en/docs/ecdr01ove.en.pdf.**

UNCTAD (2002) *Building Confidence. Electronic Commerce and Development.* United Nations publication, sales no. E.00.II.D.16, New York and Geneva.

UNCTAD (2002) *E-Commerce And Development Report 2002.* United Nations Conference on Trade and Development, New York. Retrieved July 9, 2001, from http://r0.unctad.org/ecommerce/ecommerce_en/edr02_en.htm.

UNCTAD (2006). *Information Technology Report 2006: The Development Perspective.* Retrieved July, 10, 2007, from http://www.unctad.org/sdateecb2006ch1-en.pdf.

UNCTAD (2006). *UNCTAD ICT and E-business Branch Publications and Documents. E-commerce and Development Report 2001-2004.* United Nations Conference on Trade and Development. Retrieved March 12, 2006, from http://r0.unctad.org/ecommerce/ecommerce_en/docs_en.htm

Underdeveloped Country. *International Journal of Management and Enterprise Development, 2*(3/4), 1-1.

UNDP and Government of Republic of Serbia, (2006) *National Strategy for Information Society of Republic of Serbia*, Belgrade.

UNDP, Human Development Report (2004), retrieved July 2007 from http://hdr.undp.org/reports/global/2004

United Nations. (2003). *World Public Sector Report 2003: E-Governance at the Crossroads.* New York: United Nations, Department of Economic and Social Affairs.

Universal Web Site Accessibility Policy for State Web Sites – Version 4.0, (2004), State of Connecticut Web site Accessibility Committee [online], Available: www.cmac.state.ct.us/access/policies/accesspolicy40.html [accessed: December 2004].

Urban, G., & Sultan, F., & Qualls, W. (2000). Placing trust at the center of your Internet strategy. Sloan Management Review 42: 1-13.

Ure, J. (2002). Modeling Critical Mass for E-Commerce: the Case of Hong Kong. *Electronic Commerce Research, 2*(1-2), 87-111.

USAID. (2007). Available: http://www.usaid.org.yu/left/facts_about_serbia.php. Accessed: October 25, 2007.

Uzoka, F.-M. & Seleka, G. (2006). B2C E-Commerce Development in Africa: Case Study of Botswana. *Proceedings of the Electronic Commerce conference (EC) Ann Arbor, Michigan, USA,* 290-295.

Vadapalli, A., and Ramamurthy, K. (1998). Business Use Of The Internet: An Analytical Framework And Exploratory Case Study. *International Journal of Electronic Commerce, 2*(9) 2, 71-94.

Van Gigch, J.P. (1991). *System Design Modeling and Metamodeling.* New York, Plenum Press.

Van Rooyen, J. & Willem, R. (2004). The Future Effect of E-business on Treasury and Risk Management Systems and Treasury Management in South Africa. *Development Southern Africa, 21*(2), 399-414.

Van Slyke, C., Belanger, F. & Sridhar, V. (2005). A Comparison of American and Indian Consumers Perceptions of Electronic Commerce. *Information Resources Management Journal, 18*(2), 24-40.

VanHoose, D. (2003). *E-commerce economics*. South-Western, a Division of Thomson Learning.

Varshney, U., & Vetter, R. (2002). "Mobile commerce: framework, applications and networking support". *Mobile Networks and Applications*, 7, 185–198.

Venkatesh, V. & Davis, F. D. (2000). A theoretical extension of the technology acceptance model: Four longitudinal studies. *Management Science*, 46(2), 186-204.

Venkatesh, V. (1999). Creation of Favorable User Perceptions: Exploring the Role of Intrinsic Motivation. *MIS Quarterly,* 23(2), 239-260.

Venkatesh, V., & Davis, F. D. (2000). A theoretical extension of the technology acceptance model: Four longitudinal field studies. *Management Science*, 46(2), 186-204.

Venkatesh, V., & Davis, F.D. (2000). A Theoretical Extension of the Technology Acceptance Model: Four Longitudinal Studies. *Management Science*, 46(2), 186-204.

Venkatesh, V., & Morris, M. G. (2000). Why don't men ever stop to ask for directions? gender, social influence, and their role in technology acceptance and usage behavior. *MIS Quarterly*, 24(1), 115-140.

Venkatesh, V., Morris, M. G., Davis, G. B., & Davis, F. D. (2003). User acceptance of information technology: toward a unified view. *MIS Quarterly*, 27(3), 425-478.

Verisign (2002), "Guide to securing your Web site for business", Verisign [online], Available: www.verisign.com/resources/gd/secureBusiness/secureBusiness.html [accessed: December 2004].

Vidas-Bubanja, M, (2001). The importance of information technology for national economic development (in Serbian). *Ekonomski anali*, April, 2001.

Vidas-Bubanja, M, Jošanov, B., & Vuksanović, E. (2002). Role of e-business in transition of Yugoslav Economy. *Proceedings of the 15th Bled Electronic Commerce Conference.* Bled, Slovenia, June 17–19, 2002, pp. 19–35.

Vijayan, P. & Shanmugam, B. (2003). Service Quality Evaluation Of Internet Banking In Malaysia. *Journal of Internet Banking and Commerce, 8*(1).

Viswanathan, N. K. & Pick, J. B. (2005). Comparison of E-commerce in India and Mexico: An Example of Technology Diffusion in Developing Nations. *International Journal of Technology Management, 31*(1/2), 2-19.

Vivekanandan, K. & Rajendran, R. (2006). Export marketing and the World Wide Web: perceptions of export barriers among Tirupur knitwear apparel exporters - an empirical analysis. *Journal of Electronic Commerce Research, 7*(1), 27-40.

Vujić D. (2004). *Motivation for quality* (in Serbian). Belgrade, Serbia-Montenegro: Center for Applied Psychology Press.

Vuksanović E. (2005). A Selection of e-Business Cases in Financial System of Serbia, *Proceedings from the International Scientific Session: Internationalization and Globalization*, Pitesti.

Vuksanović, E. (2002). The role of bankcard industry in transition of Yugoslav Economy. *Proceedings of The International Conference "ICES 2002"*. Sarajevo, Bosnia-Herzegovina, October 17-18, 2002, pp. 767–775.

Wade, M. & Hulland, J. (2004). Review: The Resource-Based View and Information Systems Research: Review, Extension and Suggestions For Future Research, *MIS Quarterly, 28*(1), 107-142.

Wagner, B.A., Fillis, I., & Johansson, U.(2003). E-business and e-supply strategy in small and medium sized businesses (SMEs), *Supply Chain Management*, 8(4), 343 – 354.

Wagner, C., Cheung, K., Lee, F., & Ip, R. (2003). Enhancing E-Government in Developing Countries: Managing Knowledge through Virtual Communities. The Electronic Journal on Systems in Developing Countries. 14, 4, 1-20.

Wang, J.-Y. (2001). The Internet and e-commerce in China: Regulations, judicial views, and government policy. *Computer and Internet Law,* 18, 12-30.

Wang, S. & Cheung, W. (2004). E-Business Adoption by Travel Agencies: Prime Candidates for Mobile e-Business. *International Journal of Electronic Commerce, 8*(3), 43-63.

Wang, X., Yen, D. C., & Fang, X. (2004). E-commerce development in China and its implication for business. *Asia Pacific Journal of Marketing and Logistics, 16*(3), 68-83.

Wang, Y. C. W., Chang, C. & Heng, M. S. H. (2004). The Levels of Information Technology Adoption, Business, Network, and A Strategic Position Model For Evaluating Supply Chain Integration. *Journal of Electronic Commerce Research, 5*(2), 85-98.

Wang, Y., Tang, T. & Tang, J. E. (2001). An Instrument for Measuring Customer Satisfaction toward Websites that Market Digital Products and Services. *Journal of Electronic Commerce Research, 2*(3), 89-102.

Watson, R., Ho, T. H., & Raman, K. S. (1994). Culture: a fourth dimension of group support systems. *Communications of the A CM,* 37(10), 45-55.

webMethods (2003). GEAR 6 RosettaNet Implementation Guide: Project Planning Guide, *Whitepaper.*

Webster, J. & Waston, R. T. (2002). Analyzing The Past To Prepare For The Future: Writing A Literature Review. *MIS Quarterly, 26*(2), 13-23.

Weddi, D. (2005). *Transforming Local Government: E-Governance in Uganda.* iConnect Online, Retrieved from http://www.iconnect-online.org.

Weiss, A. M., & Kurland, N. (1997). Holding distribution channel relationships together: The role of transaction-specific assets and length of prior relationship. *Organization Science, 8*(6), 612-623.

Westland, C. & Ming, S. S. (1997). Automation of China's Securities Markets. *Electronic Markets, 7*(2), 25-29.

Westland, C., Kwok, M., Shu, J., Kwok, T. & Ho, H. (1997). Electronic Cash in Hong Kong. *Electronic Markets, 7*(2), 3-6.

Westland, C., Kwok, M., Shu, J., Kwok, T. & Ho, H. (1998). Customer and Merchant Acceptance of Electronic Cash: Evidence from Mondex in Hong Kong. *International Journal of Electronic Commerce, 2*(4), 5.

Whinston, B. A., Dale, O.S., & Choi, S-Y (1997). *The economics of electronic commerce.* Macmillan Technical Publishing.

Whiteley, D. (1999). Internet commerce – hot cakes and dead ducks. In Sudweeks, F., and Celia R. (Eds.), *Doing business on the internet: Opportunities on the Internet* (pp. 9–20). London: Springer.

Wigand R.T. (1995) Electronic Commerce And Reduced Transaction Costs: Firms' Migration Into Highly Interconnected Electronic Markets, *Electronic Markets, 16/17,* 1-5.

Wigand, R. Picot, A. & Reichwald, R. (1997). *Information, Organization and Management: Expanding Markets and Corporate Boundaries.* Chester, England: John Wiley and Sons.

Wigand, R. T. (1997). Electronic Commerce: Definition, Theory, And Context. *The Information Society, 13*(1), 1-16.

William E., & Lewis, D. (1992). *Higher Education and Economic Growth.* Kluwer Academic Publishers. ISBN: 978-0792392354.

Williamson, O E. (1985). *The Economic Institutions of Capitalism: Firms, Markets, Relational Contracting.* New York: Free Press.

Williamson, O. (1981). The Economics of Organization: The Transaction Cost Approach, *American Journal of Sociology, 87*(3), 548-577.

Williamson, O. E., & Masten S. E. (1995). *Transaction cost economics. theory and concepts,* Edward Elgar, Aldershot.

Wilson, E. (2000). Wiring the African Economy. *Electronic Markets, 10*(2), 80-86.

Winter, S.G. (2003). Understanding Dynamic Capabilities, *Strategic Management Journal, 24*(10), 991-995.

Wolcott, P., & Press, L., & McHenry, W., & Goodman, S. E., & Foster, W. (2001). A framework for assessing the global diffusion of the Internet. Journal of the Association for Information Systems, 2(6), 1-53.

Wolcott, P., Press, L., McHenry, W., Goodman, S. E., & Foster, W. (2001) A framework for assessing the global diffusion of the Internet, *Journal of the Association for Information Systems, 2*(6)

Wolcott, P., Press, L., McHenry, W., Goodman, S. E., & Foster, W., (2001). "A framework for assessing the global diffusion of the Internet." *Journal of the Association for Information Systems, 2*(6).

Wolcott, P., Press, L., McHenry, W., Goodman, S.E. & Foster, W. (2001) A Framework for Assessing the Global Diffusion of the Internet. *Journal of the Association for Information Systems, 2*(6), 1-50.

Wong, X., Yen, D. C., & Fang, X. (2004). E-Commerce Development in China and its Implication for Business. *Asia Pacific Journal of Marketing and Logistics, 16*(3), 68-83.

Wong, Y.H. & Tam, J. L.M. (2000). Mapping relationships in China: Guanxi dynamic approach. Journal of Business and Industrial Marketing, 15(1): 57–70.

Wood, C. (2004): Marketing and e-commerce as tools of development in the Asia-Pacific region: a dual path. *International Marketing Review, vol.21, no.3,* 301-320.

Wood, C. M. (2004). Marketing and E-commerce as Tools of Development in the Asia-Pacific Region: A Dual Path. *International Marketing Review, 21*(3), 301-320.

Woodall, P., 2000. Survey: The new economy: Falling through the net?, *The Economist*, 356 (8189), S34-S39.

Wood-Harper, T., Ithnin, N., & Ibrahim, O. (2004). *Effective Collaborative Partnership for Malaysian Electronic Government Service Delivery.* Proceedings of the 6th international conference on Electronic commerce. Delft, The Netherlands. ISBN:1-58113-930-6.

World Bank (2001) *Global Economic Prospects and Developing Countries 2001*, The World Bank, Washington DC. Retrieved May 09 2004, from http://www.worldbank.org/prospects/gep2001/full.htm.

World Bank Report (2002) *World development indicators*, Washington, D.C.: World Bank.

World Bank. (2005). Serbia ranked number one business reformer. Available: http://www.worldbank.org.yu. Accessed: July 12, 2007.

World development Indicators (2007). Retrieved June 23, 2007, from Internet database. Web: http://devdata.worldbank.org/

World Economic Forum (2007). The Global Information Technology Report 2006-2007. Retrieved July 31, 2007, from http://www.weforum.org/pdf/gitr/rankings2007.pdf.

World Trade Organization (WTO) (1998) *Electronic Commerce and the Role of the WTO*, World Trade Organization, Geneva.

Wresch, W. (2003). Initial E-commerce Efforts in Nine Least Developed Countries. *Journal of Global Information Management, 11*(2), 67-78.

WTO (1998) *Electronic Commerce and the Role of the WTO.* Geneva.

WTO (1998). *Electronic commerce and the role of the WTO.*

Wu &Chang, (2006) "The effect of transaction trust on e-commerce relationships between travel agencies", Tourism Management 27 (2006), P.1253-1261

Wu, C., Cheng, F. & Lin, H. (2004). Web site Usability Evaluation of Internet Banking in Taiwan. *Journal of Internet Banking and Commerce, 9*(1).

Wu, J. & Wang, S. (2005). What Drives Mobile Commerce? An Empirical Evaluation of the Revised Technology Acceptance Model. *Information and Management, 42*(5) 719-729.

Wynne, C., Bethon, P., Pitt, L., Ewing, M. & Napoli, J. (2001). The Impact of the Internet on the Distribution Value Chain. *International Marketing Review, 18*(4), 420-431.

Xanthidis, D., Nicholas D. (2004), "Evaluating internet usage and ecommerce growth in Greece", Aslib Proceedings, Vol. 56 No. 6, pp. 356-366.

Xanthidis, D., Nicholas, D. (2007), "A pilot qualitative study of eCommerce practices and attitudes of medium-large companies' executives in Greece", WSEAS Transactions on Information Science and Applications, Vol. 4, Issue 2, pp. 354-361.

Xiang, J. Y., & Kim, J. K. (2007). A Comparative Analysis of International, Korean and Chinese E-Commerce Research, *International Journal of Electronic Business, 5*(1), 65-106.

Xu, S., Zhu, K. & Gibbs, J. (2004). Global Technology, Local Adoption: A Cross Country Investigation of Internet Adoption by Companies in the United States and China. *Electronic Markets, 14*(1), 13-24.

Yamamoto G T and Karaman F (2007) Barriers to E-Procurement Adoption: The Turkish Case in E-Procurement in Emerging Economies Theory and Cases edited by Ashis K Pani and Amit Agrahari, Hershey: Idea Group Publishing, pp. 101-125

Yan, W. (2005). The Electronic Signatures Law: China's First National E-Commerce Legislation. *Intellectual Property & Technology Law Journal*, 17(6), 6.

Yan, W. (2005). The electronic signatures law: China's first national e-commerce legislation. *Intellectual Property & Technology Law Journal, 17*(6), 6-10.

Yan, X., Gong M., & Thong J. Y. L. (2006). Two tales of one service: user acceptance of short message service (SMS) in Hong Kong and China. *Info*, 8 (1), 16-28.

Yang, Z., Shaohan, C., Zhou, Z. & Zhou, N. (2005). Development and validation of an instrument to measure user perceived service quality of information presenting Web portals. *Information and Management, 42*(4), 575-589.

Yap, A., Das, J., Burbridge, J., & Cort, K. (2006). A Composite-Model for E-Commerce Diffusion: Integrating Cultural and Socio-Economic Dimensions to the Dynamics of Diffusion. *Journal of Global Information Management, 14*(3), 17-34,38.

Yavwa, Y. and Kritzinger, P.S. (2001) Enabling Communication In Developing Regions," *The Electronic Journal on Information Systems in Developing Countries,* vol. 6, No.1, pp. 1-15, 2001

Yen, B. P. C. & Su, C. J. (1997). Information Technology Infrastructure for Textile and Apparel Industry in Hong Kong. *Electronic Markets, 7*(2), 9-12.

Yi, M. Y., Jackson J. D., Park J. S., & Probst J. C. (2006). Understanding information technology acceptance by individual professionals: toward an integrative view, *Information & Managemen,t* 43, 350-363.

Yin, RK (1994), *Case study research: Design and methods*, 2nd edn, Sage Publications Ltd, Thousand Oaks.

Yu, C. (2006). Influences on Taiwanese SME E-Marketplace Adoption Decisions. *Journal of Global Information Technology Management, 9*(2), 5-21

Yu, J. (2006). B2C Barriers and Strategies: A Case Study of Top B2C Companies in China. *Journal of Internet Commerce, 5*(3), 27-51.

Yu, J. (2006). B2C Barriers and Strategies: A Case Study of Top B2C Companies in China, *Journal of Internet Commerce, 5*(3), 27-51.

Zhang, Q. B. & Chau, P. Y. K. (2002). Creating E-commerce Courses with Regional Intent. *Communications of the ACM, 45*(2), 35-37.

Zhang, X., Keeling, B. K., Pavur, J. R. (2000), "Information Quality of commercial Web sites Home Pages: An explorative analysis", ACM [online], Available: portal.acm.org [accessed: November 2004].

Zhang, X., Li, Q. & Lin, Z. (2005). E-Commerce Education in China: Driving Forces, Status, and Strategies. *Journal of Electronic Commerce in Organizations, 3*(3), 1-17.

Zhang, X.-F., Li, Q., & Lin, Z.-X. (2005). E-commerce education in China: Driving forces, status and strategies. *Journal of Electronic Commerce in Organizations*, July-September, 1-17.

Zhao, Li Qin (2004). Author's personal interview with Mr. Zhao on his perceptions and use of Internet based commerce. The interview was conducted in Guangdong Province of China.

Zhu, K. & Kraemer, K. (2005). Post-Adoption Variations in Usage and Value of E-Business by Organizations: Cross-Country Evidence from the Retail Industry. *Information Systems Research, 16*(1), 61-84.

Zhu, K., Kraemer, K., Xu, S. & Dedrick, J. (2004). Information Technology Payoff in E-Business Environments: An International Perspective on Value Creation of E-Business in the Financial Services Industry. *Journal of Management Information Systems, 21*(1), 17-54.

Zhu, K., Kraemer, K.L. & Xu, S. (2003) E-business Adoption by European Firms: A Cross-country Assessment of the Facilitators and Inhibitors, *European Journal of Information Systems, 12*(4), 251-268.

Zhu, K., Kraemer, K.L., & Xu, S. (2006) The Process of Innovation Assimilation by Firms in Different Countries: A Technology Diffusion Perspective on E-Business, *Management Science, 52*(10), 1557-1576.

Zhu, K., Xu, S., & Dedrick, J. (2003). Assessing Drivers of E-business Value: Results of a Cross-country Study, In: *Proceedings of the 24th International Conference on Information Systems* (pp. 181-193). Seattle: Washington State University.

Ziadi, J. (2005): Vers une approche originale de la pratique e-manageriale pour les entreprises Tunisiennes. *International Journal of Management and Technologies, 1*, 137-158.

Zukauskas, P., & Kasteckiene, A. (2002). THE ROLE OF E-GOVERNMENT IN THE DEVELOPMENT OF THE NEW ECONOMY IN LITHUANIA.

Zwass, V. (1996). Electronic Commerce: Structure And Issues. *International Journal of Electronic Commerce, 1*(1), 3-23.

Zwass, V. (1996). Electronic commerce: Structure and issues. *International Journal of Electronic Commerce, 1*(1), 3-23.

Zwass, V. (1996). Electronic commerce: Structure and issues. International Journal of Electronic Commerce, 1(1), 3-23.

Zwass, V. (1998). Structure And Micro-Level Impacts Of Electronic Commerce: From Technological Infrastructure To Electronic Market Places. In E. K. Kenneth (Ed.), *Emerging Information Technologies*. (pp. 1-32) Thousand Oaks, CA: Sage Publications.

Zwass, V. (Fall 1996). Electronic commerce: structures and issues. *International Journal of Electronic Commerce*, 1 (1), 3-23.

About the Contributors

Kamel Rouibah is an Associate Professor of information systems, College of Business Administration (CBA) at Kuwait University. He hold a PhD in Information Systems from Ecole Polytechnique of Grenoble, France. Before joining CBA, he worked at Faculty of Technology Management at Eindhoven (Netherlands) and Institut National de la Recherche Scientifique (France). His research interests include design of information systems, management information systems, engineering data management, workflow management, information system and information technology acceptance. He was involved in several European projects. His publications appeared in several leading journals: *Journal of Strategic Information System, IT & People, Computers in Industry; International Journal of Computer Integrated Manufacturing; Robotics & Computer Integrated Manufacturing Journal; Journal of Decision System; Journal of Engineering Design*. Has taught many information systems courses in France, Netherlands, and Kuwait.

Omar Khalil is currently a Professor of Information Systems, Quantitative Methods & Information Systems (QMIS) Department, College of Business Administration, Kuwait University. He has a PhD in Information Systems from the University of North Texas. His publications have appeared in journals such as the *Journal of Global Information Management, Journal of Organizational and End-User Computing, Information Resources management Journal, International Journal of Production and Economics, International Journal of Man-Machine Studies, Journal of Business Ethics, Journal of informing Science, and International journal of Enterprise Information Systems*. His research interest includes information systems effectiveness, global information systems, information quality, and knowledge management. He has taught many graduate and undergraduate information systems courses in a number of universities in Egypt, USA, and Kuwait. He has served as the program committee member of various international conferences and reviewer for various international journals.

Aboul Ella Hassanien received his BSc with honours in 1986 and MSc degree in 1993, both from Ain Shams University, Faculty of Science, Pure Mathematics and Computer Science Department, Cairo, Egypt. On September 1998, he received his doctoral degree from the Department of Computer Science, Graduate School of Science & Engineering, Tokyo Institute of Technology, Japan. He is an associated Professor at Cairo University, Faculty of Computer and Information, IT Department. Currently, he is a visiting professor at Kuwait University, College of Business Administration, Quantitative and Information System Department. He has authored/coauthored over 80 research publications in peer-reviewed reputed journals and conference proceedings. He has served as the program committee member of various international conferences and reviewer for various international journals. Since

Copyright © 2009, IGI Global, distributing in print or electronic forms without written permission of IGI Global is prohibited.

2004, he is actively involved as technical committee in the International Association of Science and Technology for Development (IASTED) for Image Processing and Signal Processing. He has received the excellence younger researcher award from Kuwait University for the academic year 2003/2004. He has guest edited many special issues for international scientific journals. He has directed many funded research projects. Dr. Abo was a member of the Interim Advisory Board committee of the International Rough Set Society. He is the editor and co-editor for more than six books in the area of rough computing, computational intelligence, and E-commerce.His research interests include, rough set theory, wavelet theory, X-ray Mammogram analysis, medical image analysis, fuzzy image processing and multimedia data mining.

* * *

Lena Aggestam is a lecturer at the University of Skövde (Sweden). She holds a Licentaite degree in Computer and System Science from the University of Stockholm/Royal Institute of Technology. Her research focus is Knowledge Management in which area she also has most of her publications.. Lena Aggestam teaches at both a BSc and MSc level. She has also a black belt in Six sigma.

Paris Argyrides is currently working as an IT and Networks Administrator in Trust International Insurance Company (Cyprus division). His duties include administering the company's client Database as well as the company's Servers and Network infrastructure. He also provides IT and HCI support to the company's employees. Paris holds an MSc Computer Science degree from University College London. His BSc. in Management Information Systems was obtained at New York College, Thessaloniki in collaboration with the State University of New York and Southern Illinois University, Carbondale USA.

Zakariya Belkhamza holds BA in Economics, Master of Science in Business from the School of Business and Economics, Universiti Malaysia Sabah (UMS). He is a lecturer of Information Systems subjects. He is the president of the Postgraduate Association at the Centre for Postgraduate Studies, Universiti Malaysia Sabah. He is also a member of the Association for Information Systems (AIS). His current research interests include e-commerce, IT/IS adoption, IS success and IT organizational performance. His work has been appeared in several conferences proceedings locally and internationally.

Richard Boateng is an ICT Researcher, doing his PhD on E-commerce in developing countries at the Institute for Development Policy and Management, University of Manchester, United Kingdom. He holds an MSc in Management and Information Systems. Mr Boateng's research interests include Internet marketing strategy, knowledge management, and e-commerce and ICT and socio-economic development. Mr. Boateng's professional career has been in the ICT and banking sector in Ghana. His research has been published in *Journal of Internet Banking and Commerce, Information Development and the Electronic Journal of Information Systems in Developing Countries.*

Reinhold Decker is Professor of Marketing at the Department of Business Administration and Economics at Bielefeld University, Germany. His research has been published in such journals as *Forest Products Journal, International Journal of Business and Economics, International Journal of Business Intelligence and Data Mining, International Review of Retail, Distribution and Consumer Research, Journal of Academic Librarianship, Journal of Data Science, Journal of Targeting, Measurement and*

Analysis for Marketing, Library Hi Tech, and *Marketing Intelligence & Planning.* His current research focuses on quantitative methods in marketing research, consumer behavior modeling, and data mining in marketing.

Arjan de Jager, after he studied Physics and Mathematics in Utrecht, the Netherlands, he worked as a lecturer in Computing Science in the Netherlands and in Zimbabwe. From 1996, he was an Intranet consultant for the Polytechnic of Amsterdam and Greenpeace International, both in Amsterdam. Arjan is currently Country Programme Manager for Uganda at the International Institute for Communication and Development (IICD) (www.iicd.org) in the Netherlands. IICD was founded in 1996 as a not-for-profit, international non-governmental organisation by the Netherlands Ministry for Development Cooperation to help developing countries exploit the potential of information and communication technologies (ICTs) to alleviate poverty and promote national development. IICD currently supports Country Programmes in nine developing countries: Ghana, Burkina Faso, Mali, Zambia, Uganda, Tanzania, Jamaica, Ecuador and Bolivia. Through these Country Programmes, IICD empowers local organisations from both the private and public sector to develop and implement their own ICT projects in five sectors: education, health, the environment, good governance, and livelihood opportunities.

Alev M. Efendioglu earned his PhD in Management from LSU-Baton Rouge and he teaches Competitive Strategy at MBA and undergraduate levels. His primary research interests are in Strategy and Competitive Advantage and Use of Technology in global environments. His research has focused on organizational implications of technology (e-commerce), distance education and training (e-education and e-training), globalization and outsourcing, and industry evolution. His current research interest also includes the Small/Family Business issues. He is the author of two books, chapters in eight other books (*Small Business Clustering Technologies: Applications in Marketing, Management, IT and Economics; Outsourcing & Offshoring in the 21st Century – A socio economic perspective; Chinese Economic Transition and Its Impact on Marketing Strategy; Encyclopedia of E-Commerce, E-Government and Mobile Commerce; Digital Economy: Impacts, Influences and Challenges; Online Distance Learning: Concepts, Methodologies, Tools, and Applications; The Design and Management of Effective Distance Learning Programs;* and *Encyclopedia of Online Learning*), and articles in numerous professional publications, including *Business Horizons, China International Review, Journal of Asia-Pacific Business, Journal of Small Business Strategy, SAM Advanced Management Journal*, and *Interacting with Computers*. He is a recipient of a number of School of Business and Management (SOBAM) outstanding research and service awards, and his research has been recognized by other researchers in the field. For the first eight months of its publication in 2004, his research paper titled "Chinese Culture & E-Commerce: An Exploratory Study" was listed on the 25 most requested journal articles list as number 1 and has constantly been listed in the TOP TEN of this list since then. It is currently (on 9/24/2007) listed as number 6. His research "Acceptance and Use of Information Technology among Small Retail and Service Businesses," was awarded the "best paper in the Small Business/Entrepreneurship Track" award at the Western Decision Sciences Institute, Twenty-Sixth Annual Meeting in 1997. For his recent research presentation at The Global Business & Economics Research Conference in August 2007, he was awarded the "Best Presenter Award". He has served at various times as chair of SOBAM's many faculty committees (including Peer Review and Academic Standards Committees), Coordinator of the Management Teaching Area, and the Coordinator of USF-EMBA Program for Guangdong Enterprises in China (Hong Kong, Shenzhen, and Guangzhou). He holds leadership positions in a number of domestic and international professional organizations, including Academy of Management, and has held leadership positions in Decision Sciences Institute. Dr. Efendioglu also serves as on the Editorial Board of the Journal of Industrial Relations and Human Resources and is Internet Editor for both *Journal of Asia Business Studies* and *Journal of Asia-Pacific Business.* He has extensive consulting experience and is currently a member of the Board of Trustees for Ameristock Mutual Fund and for Ameristock ETF Trust, and the Chair of the Audit Committee of the Ameristock ETF Trust.

Omar A. El Sawy is Professor of Information Systems at the Marshall School of Business, University of Southern California (USC) since 1983. From 2001 through 2007, he was also the Director of Research, Center for Telecom Management at USC. He holds a PhD from Stanford Business School, an MBA from the American University in Cairo, and a BSEE from Cairo University. He has served as Fulbright Scholar in Finland, and a UNDP information systems advisor in Egypt. Prior to joining USC, he worked as an engineer and manager, first at NCR Corporation in the Middle East, and then as a manager of computer services at Stanford University. His interests include redesigning and managing IT-based value chains and capabilities for dynamic environments, business models for digital platforms, and designing vigilant information systems for fast-response and turbulent environments. El Sawy is the author of over 80 papers and his writings have appeared in both information systems and management journals. He serves on several journal editorial boards, and is a six-time winner of the Society for Information Management's Paper Awards Competition. He is the winner of the Association of Information Systems' 2007 Publication of the Year Award, as well as the 2007 Best Published Paper Award in the INFORMS journal *Information Systems Research.*

Ahu Genis-Gruber got her Bachelors Degree from Ankara University, Political Science Faculty, Labor Economics and Industrial Relations Department. She got her MA and PhD degree from Johannes Kepler University, Linz-Austria, International Management Department. Genis-Gruber is currently working as assistant professor at TOBB University of Economics and Technology at Business Administration Department. Her research areas are international management, joint ventures, cross cultural management, theory of organization, e-commerce.

Jatinder Gupta is currently Eminent Scholar of Management of Technology, Professor of Management Information Systems, Industrial and Systems Engineering and Engineering Management at the University of Alabama in Huntsville, Huntsville, Alabama. Most recently, he was Professor of Management, Information and Communication Sciences, and Industry and Technology at Ball State University, Muncie, Indiana. He holds a PhD in Industrial Engineering (with specialization in Production Management and Information Systems) from Texas Tech University. Co-author of a textbook in Operations Research, Dr. Gupta serves on the editorial boards of several national and international journals. Recipient of the Outstanding Faculty and Outstanding Researcher awards from Ball State University, he has published numerous papers in such journals as *Journal of Management Information Systems, International Journal of Information Management, Operations Research, INFORMS Journal of Computing, Annals of Operations Research*, and *Mathematics of Operations Research.* He co-edited books that included *Decision Making Support Systems: Achievements and Challenges for the New Decade* and *Creating Knowledge-based Healthcare Organizations* published by Idea Group Publishing. He is also the coeditor of the book: *Managing E-Business* published by Heidelberg Press, Heidelberg, Australia and the book: *Intelligent Decision-making Support Systems*, published by Springer. His current research interests include information security, e-commerce, supply chain management, information and decision technologies, scheduling, planning and control, organizational learning and effectiveness, systems education, knowledge management, and enterprise integration. Dr. Gupta has held elected and appointed positions in several academic and professional societies including the Association for Information Systems, Production and Operations Management Society (POMS), the Decision Sciences Institute (DSI), and the Information Resources Management Association (IRMA).

Richard Heeks is Professor and chair of Development Informatics at the Institute for Development Policy and Management, University of Manchester, United Kingdom. His research interests include e-governance, information systems success and failure, information systems in developing countries, and IT sector development. His research has been published in the *European Journal of Information Systems, IEEE Software, Communications of the ACM, and The Information Society.* He has authored a number of books including *Implementing and Managing eGovernment: An International Text*; and *Reinventing Government in the Information Age.*

Pam Jackson is assistant dean for Assessment, Retention, and Advisement at the School of Business and Economics at Fayetteville State University. She received her PhD in Information Technology program at the University of North Carolina at Charlotte. Her research interests are in the areas of technology acceptance and adoption.

Borislav Jošanov teaches at the Higher School of Professional Business Studies, Novi Sad, in Serbia. Dr. Jošanov's research focuses on the use of information and communication technologies in e-business and development of business information systems. He authored over sixty papers, a research book on electronic data interchange, and several textbooks. In the past, he was manager of a software development department in a computer factory.

Mahesha Kapurubandara, a lecturer in Information Systems at the University of Western Sydney, Department of Computing and Mathematics, Australia, is currently reading for her PhD there. Her Master's Degree is from the Asian Institute of Technology, Thailand. Among her main research interests are e-commerce and e-transformation of SMEs in developing countries with particular reference to IT adoption and implementation, use and impact of the Internet in the South Asia region. She takes credit for publishing over 15 research papers at various national and international conferences in the areas of electronic commerce and information systems. She has 12 years industry experience where she was involved in software development projects.

Ejub Kajan teaches at the High school of applied studies of Vranje and is research fellow at the Faculty of Electronic Engineering in Niš in Serbia. Mr. Kajan's research focuses on e-commerce architectures, semantic interoperability, computer networks, and open systems. He authored over fifty papers, four research books, and two textbooks. In the past, he worked as software engineer and general manager in the computer industry.

Sherif H. Kamel is associate professor of MIS in the Department of Management and Director of the Management Center in the School of Business, Economics and Communication at The American University in Cairo. From 1992 to 2001, he was the Director of the Regional IT Institute and from 1987 to 1992; he co-established and managed the training department of the Cabinet of Egypt Information and Decision Support Centre (Egypt). Dr. Kamel designs and delivers executive development programs in IT management. In 1996, he was one of the founding members of the Internet Society of Egypt. He has publishes in ICT transfer to developing countries, electronic commerce, human resources development, and decision support applications. He serves on the editorial and a review board of a number of IS journals and is the associate editor of the *Journal of Cases on Information Technology, Journal of IT for Development and the Electronic Journal of IS in Developing Countries.* He is a member of the board of trustees of the Information Technology Institute and the Sadat Academy for Management Sciences (Egypt). During the period 2000-2007, he was a member of the Executive Council of the Information Resources Management Association (US) and its director of communications. He was awarded the Eisenhower Fellowship in 2005. He is a graduate of London School of Economics and Political Science (UK) and The American University in Cairo (Egypt).

Frank Kroll (MBA) is Lecturer at the Department of Business Administration and Economics at Bielefeld University, Germany. His research interests include data mining, e-commerce as well as quantitative sales force management. He has published in reviewed conference proceedings and edited volumes.

Robyn Lawson is a senior lecturer with the School of Computing and Mathematics at the University of Western Sydney. She is also Associate Director of the Advanced Enterprise Information Management Systems (AeIMS) Research Group, which focuses on research into e-business solutions for small and medium enterprises (SMEs). Robyn's PhD investigated electronic commerce adoption in manufacturing. In addition, Robyn has published papers in the areas of e-business and e-collaboration, and is also on the Review Board for the *Journal of Information Systems and Small Business.*

Hongxiu Li is a graduate student in Information Systems Institute of Turku School of Economics, Finland. Her academic interests focus on e-commerce and e-services. She has together more than 10 publications published in international conference proceedings and academic journals in China.

Alemayehu Molla is a Senior Lecturer in Information Systems at the School of Business Information Technology, RMIT University, Australia. Dr. Molla's research interests include B2B e-business, information systems outsourcing and success, ERP and culture, diffusion, use and impact of the Internet, and ICT and socio-economic development. His research has been published in the *European Journal of Information Systems, International Journal of Electronic Commerce, Information & Management, Electronic Commerce Research, The Information Society, Journal of Information Technology Cases and Application Research, Journal of Information Technology Management, International Journal of Entrepreneurship and Innovation, Journal of Internet Banking and Commerce, Information Technologies and International Development, Journal of IT for Development, and Electronic Journal of Information Systems in Developing Countries* and in book chapters and more than 25 conference proceedings.

David Nicholas is Professor and Director of the School of Library, Archive and Information Studies (SLAIS) at UCL. He is also the Director of the UCL Centre for Publishing and Director of CIBER (Centre for Information Behaviour and the Evaluation of Research). He has undertaken more than 30 research projects and published 500+ peer reviewed articles. Research interests largely concern the

Digital health consumer, digital shopper and the virtual scholar and currently engaged in investigations of e-journals and e-books.

Samia Ould-Ali is assistant Professor at the College of Business Administration. Her doctoral research at the Univesity of Joseph Fourrier (University of Grenoble 1, France) dealt with multicriteria decision analysis. Her current research interests include computer support decision making, motivational determinants of information technology adoption, and performance impact of IT. She has published several papers that appeared well known journals: *International Journal of Computer Integrated Manufacturing, Robotics & Computer Integrated Manufacturing Journal, Journal of Strategic Information System, Journal of Decision System, Arab Journal of Administrative Sciences.*

Abdelbaset Rabaiah is a senior researcher at the Vrije Universiteit Brussel, Belgium. He is doing extensive research in e-government. He is also working with FEDICT which is the unit responsible for implementing e-government in Belgium. He had published relevant topics in different conference proceedings and Journals.

Stephanie S. Robbins is Professor of MIS/OM at The University of North Carolina at Charlotte and earned her PhD degree from Louisiana State University. Dr. Robbins does research in the areas of management information systems, international information systems and marketing management. Her publications have appeared in journals such as: *Information & Management, The Journal of Computer Information Systems, Journal of Systems Management, Behavioral Science, and The Journal of the Academy of Marketing Science.* She has also presented numerous papers at international, national and regional professional meetings. Dr. Robbins has been very active in the Decision Sciences Institute and has held a number of officer positions within the organization.

Abderrazzak Ben Salah is an assistant professor at the Higher Institute of Computer Science- University of Tunis-El Manar, Tunisia. He obtained his PhD from the University of Warsaw, Poland and he is a consultant in electronic commerce for many national and international enterprises.

Sushil K. Sharma is an Associate Professor of Information Systems and Operations Management at Ball State University, Muncie, Indiana, USA. Co-author of two textbooks and co-editor of four books, Dr. Sharma has authored over 100 refereed research papers in many peer-reviewed national and international MIS and management journals, conferences proceedings and books. His primary teaching and research interests are in e-commerce, computer-mediated communications, community informatics, information systems security, e-government, ERP systems, database management systems, cluster computing, Web services and knowledge management. He has a wide consulting experience in information systems and e-commerce and has served as an advisor and consultant to several government and private organizations including projects funded by the World Bank.

Eva Söderström holds a PhD in Computer and System Science from the University of Stockholm/Royal Institute of Technology (Sweden). Her research focus is on standardization, primarily for in electronic business as well as for interoperability purposes. Other relevant areas are IT strategy management in small and medium-sized businesses. She is currently employed as an assistant professor at the University of Skövde, and also manages the Centre for Teaching and Learning in Higher Education.

Dr Söderström has over 60 publications. She teaches at both a BSc and MSc level, and is a member of several industry-focused projects, both in Sweden and in Europe.

Antonis C. Stylianou has over 20 years of experience in computer information systems. Currently, he is Professor of management information systems and a member of the graduate faculty at the University of North Carolina at Charlotte. His industry experience includes an appointment in the information management department at Duke Energy. Dr. Stylianou has published numerous research articles in the *Communications of the ACM, Management Science, Decision Sciences, Information & Management,* and other journals. He is a frequent presenter on the management of information systems, and serves as a consultant to organizations. He is currently on the Editorial Board of the *Database for Advances in Information Systems* journal.

Reima Suomi is a professor of Information Systems Science at Turku School of Economics, Finland since 1994. He is a docent for the universities of Turku and Oulu, Finland. Years 1992-1993 he spent as a "Vollamtlicher Dozent" in the University of St. Gallen, Switzerland, where he led a research project on business process re-engineering. Currently he concentrates on topics around management of telecommunications, including issues such as management of networks, electronic and mobile commerce, virtual organizations, telework and competitive advantage through telecommunication-based information systems. Different governance structures applied to the management of IS and are enabled by IS belong too to his research agenda, as well as application of information systems in health care. Reima Suomi has together over 400 publications, and has published in journals such as *Information & Management, Information Services & Use, Technology Analysis & Strategic Management, The Journal of Strategic Information Systems, Behaviour & Information Technology, Journal of Management History and Information Resources Management Journal.* For the academic year 2001-2002 he was a senior researcher "varttunut tutkija" for the Academy of Finland. With Paul Jackson he has published the book *Virtual Organization and workplace development* with Routhledge, London.

Bedri Kamil Onur Tas got his BS degree in Management from Bilkent University. He got his MA and PhD in Economics from Boston College. Bedri Kamil Onur Tas is currently working at TOBB University of Economics and Technology at Department of Economics. His research areas are applied macroeconomics, financial econometrics, asset pricing and monetary economics.

Bob Travica teaches at University of Manitoba in Canada. Dr. Travica's research focuses on information view of organization, new organizational designs, and international aspects of information systems with a particular focus on e-commerce in East Europe and in Americas. He published in various outlets, including *JGITM, The Database, IJIM, JASIS,* and *Informing Science Journal.* In the past, he taught at Indiana University and University of Texas, and worked as journalist and software entrepreneur.

Eddy Vandijck is full time professor teaching Information Systems, Databases and ICT-auditing at the Vrije Universiteit Brussel, Belgium.

Victor van Reijswoud is Professor of Information Systems at Université Lumière in Bujumbura, Burundi, visiting professor at Uganda Martyrs University on Nkozi, Uganda, and a researcher for the World Dialogue on Regulation (www.regulateonline.org). He has lectured in Europe, the USA, and

Africa, authored over 60 publications, and worked as an ICT4D consultant on projects in Uganda, Burundi, Tanzania, Malawi, and Ghana. He has extensive experience of industry having served as Director of Innovation and Research at Devote/Ordina in the Netherlands. As a leading ICT4D and Free/Open Source Software (F/OSS) academic and consultant in Africa, Dr van Reijswoud was the initiator and coordinator of the largest F/OSS migration on the African continent (total migration to F/OSS (servers and desktops) of Uganda Martyrs University), co-founder of the East African Center for Open Source Software (EACOSS), and adviser to several other migration projects. He is currently researching appropriate ICT for developing economies and the role of F/OSS for development.

Marijana Vidas–Bubanja teaches at Belgrade Business School and BK University in Serbia. Dr. Vidas–Bubanja's research focuses on international economy, e-economy, information society, and economic impacts of e-business practices. She authored three books and over a hundred articles. She has also been Chair of the Electronic South East Europe (SEE) Initiative within the SEE Stability Pact. In the past, she worked as senior research fellow at Belgrade's Institute of Economic Sciences.

Emilija Vuksanović teaches bank management at University of Kragujevac and electronic banking at Belgrade Banking Academy in Serbia. Dr. Vuksanović's research focuses on the use of information and communication technologies in e-payment and e-banking. She authored over 70 papers, a book on electronic banking, and several textbooks. In the past, she served on the Board of Directors of The Belgrade Stock Exchange, and on the Board of Directors of The Bank of Niš.

Syed Azizi Wafa is a Professor at the School of International Business and Finance, and the Director of Labuan International Campus, Universiti Malaysia Sabah (UMS), Malaysia. Dr Syed holds BBA from Ohio University, MBA from San Diego State University and DBA from the US International University. He is the founding member and the President of the Asian Academy of Applied Business (AAAB). He is actively involved in consultancy and Executive Development Programs of many Malaysian and Multinational companies. His current research interests are in managerial styles of Malaysian managers, cross-cultural managerial issues, corporate strategy, corporate culture, corporate ethics, regional business issues and small business management.

Dimitrios Xanthidis is a Senior Lecturer at DEI College Thessaloniki in collaboration with the University of Central Lancashire (UK) and a Lecturer at NYC Thessaloniki affiliated with the State University of New York, Empire State College. He is a candidate for the PhD in Electronic Information Sciences at the School of Library, Archive and Information Sciences of the University College of London and holds a BSc and an MSIS degrees from the Hawaii Pacific University at Honolulu, Hawaii (U.S.). His has published about a dozen papers all related to electronic commerce. Research interests concern computer programming, systems analysis and design, databases and electronic commerce and Web technologies and programming.

Ayoub Yousefi earned the PhD degree in Economics from the University of Tennessee, Knoxville, USA in 1992. During his graduate study, he was awarded with Ronald H. Wolf Excellence in Economics Scholarship for three consecutive years. During this time, he served as a research assistant at the Center for Business and Economic Research, UTK. Currently, Ayoub is an associate professor of economics at the department of Economics, Business and Mathematics at King's University College, at University of Western Ontario, London, Ontario, Canada. He joined King's University College in 2001, after six years of dedicated teaching at the University of Waterloo, Ontario, Canada. Ayoub has developed interest in teaching corporate finance, derivative securities markets, and econometrics. His current courses include international trade, comparative international business, and macroeconomics. He has 15 years of teaching experience at the undergraduate and graduate levels. Ayoub specializes in international finance, monetary macroeconomics, and applied econometrics. His research interests are in the areas of exchange rate and balance of payments, exchange rate pass-through, and sticky prices. He has published papers in such journals as *Health Economics, OPEC Review, Journal of Energy Economics, New Horizon, and Survey of Business.* Ayoub is a member of Canadian Economic Association. Outside the classroom, he volunteers with the local communities and enjoys nature and outdoor activities.

Jameleddine Ziadi is a lecturer in management at the Juridical, Economic Sciences and Management-Jendouba University, Tunisia. He taught during several years different courses in management sciences at Tunisian and French universities. He is a member of the international association of management and the international association of strategic management. He is also an international consultant for many international organizations and various national and international enterprises. Among his duties, he is a counselor in information technologies to the Republic of Congo (through the United Nations) and the President of the world e-management consortium.

Index

Copyright © 2009, IGI Global, distributing in print or electronic forms without written permission of IGI Global is prohibited.

T

U